IMAGES
*of America*

# SUDBURY

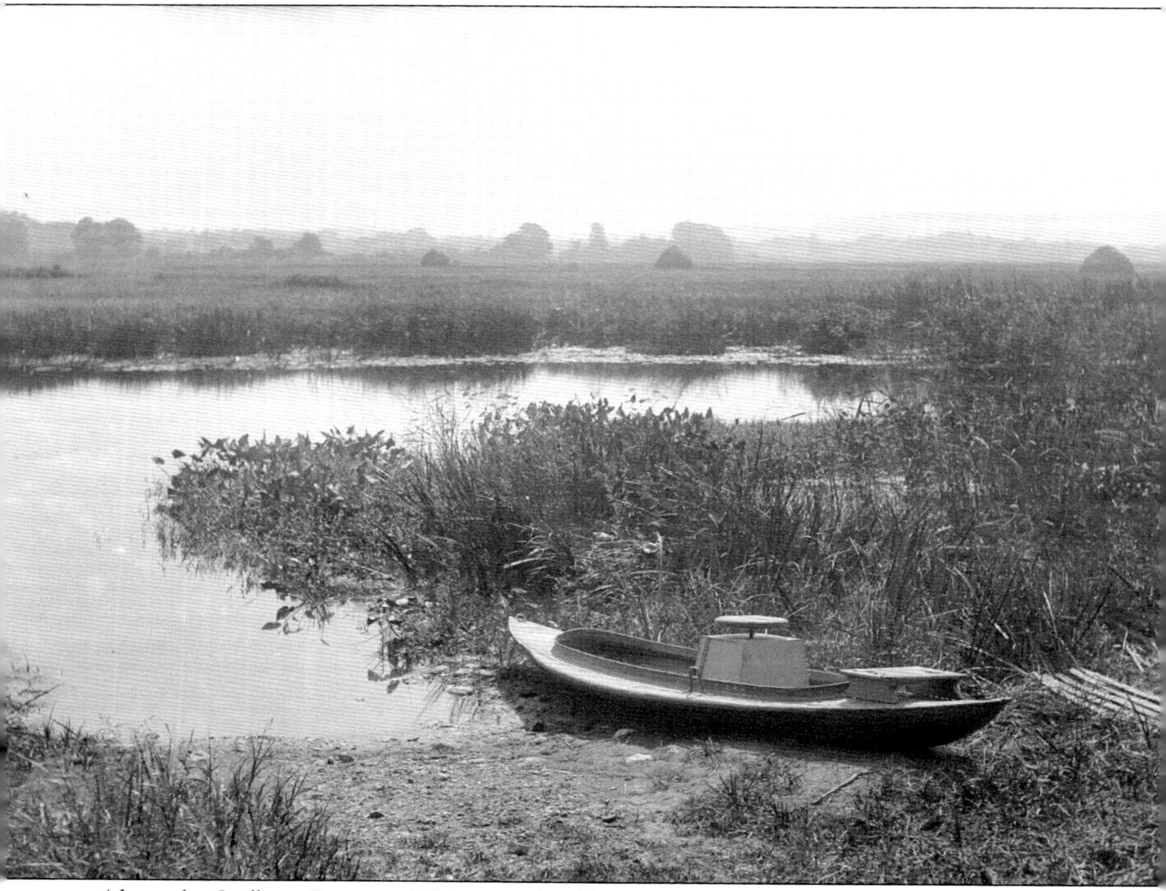

Along the Sudbury River in 1906, mounds of hay, known as haycocks, are seen in the distance. The mounds were gathered by farmers on wood stakes to dry. The hay was what attracted the original settlers and led to the publication of William Wood's *New England Prospect* in 1633, which states, "These marshes be rich ground and bring plenty of hay." Farmers sought this rich reed grass and reed canary grass (now almost extinct) to fatten their cattle. The gun punt boat in the foreground was used for hunting. (Photograph by Hattie Goodnow.)

**On the Cover:** Dominion Day in Sudbury, Massachusetts, was the idea of George J. Raymond, the owner of Raymond's Department Stores. On every July 1 from 1905 until 1915, Raymond brought all of his 1,000 employees on a train to South Sudbury, where they walked a mile through his extensive estate dressed in whites and reds with brass bands leading them to a grand banquet and games. Raymond became a millionaire with the success of his stores, which were famous for the slogan, "Where you bot the hat?" Raymond, who was Canadian and employed many Canadians, advertised "Quality goods at the lowest possible price for cash." (Courtesy of the Sudbury Historical Society, Inc.)

IMAGES
*of America*

# SUDBURY

Sudbury Historical Society, Inc.

ARCADIA
PUBLISHING

ISBN 978-0-7385-9754-6

Published by Arcadia Publishing
Charleston, South Carolina

Printed in the United States of America

Library of Congress Control Number: 2012937098

For all general information, please contact Arcadia Publishing:
Telephone 843-853-2070
Fax 843-853-0044
E-mail sales@arcadiapublishing.com
For customer service and orders:
Toll-Free 1-888-313-2665

Visit us on the Internet at www.arcadiapublishing.com

*This book is dedicated to our late volunteer, Virginia A. "Ginny" Maenpaa, and to Taka Morita, a former intern from Japan and a loyal contributor since 2000.*

# Contents

# ACKNOWLEDGMENTS

The completion of such a large project is generally beyond the scope of one or two people. We would like to thank the people of Sudbury for all of their donations, which have resulted in the collections now preserved at the Sudbury Historical Society, Inc. (SHS). Their pictures, objects, books, and art have helped make up the history of the town.

We would also like to thank the Sudbury Foundation for its financial support, Town Manager Maureen G. Valente, and Town Clerk Rosemary Harvell for permission to use images under their responsibility.

The society would like to thank the book committee members and staff: Mary Collins Vivaldi, SHS president and committee member; Ursula Lyons, SHS vice president, committee member, Arcadia publishing liaison, and editor; Chuck Zimmer, who created a relational database, completed high-quality scanning and picture restoration, and whose skills this book would not have been possible without; Lee Swanson, the curator/archivist for the Sudbury Historical Society, Inc., who provided the inspiration to start this project, was a continuous source of information about people, places, and events, and was recently named town historian; Nancy Somers, a society trustee and committee member who provided unique military pictures; Joan Meenan, a society trustee and committee member whose weekly commitment to the committee chair was invaluable; and Beth Gray-Nix, a society trustee and committee chair who spearheaded and organized the project through its completion.

Unless otherwise noted, all images are courtesy of the Sudbury Historical Society, Inc.

# INTRODUCTION

In 1638, Sudbury attracted its first settlers because of its slow moving river, its rich reed grass and reed canary grass used to fatten cattle, and its good land to grow what was needed. On September 4, 1639, the settlement in Sudbury became incorporated, as shelters were built on the east side of the river in what was the original Sudbury but is now Wayland. A primitive wooden bridge was built across the river to the west side, which was also settled, starting in the 1650s. This west settlement is now known as the town of Sudbury.

Sudbury remained an agricultural town but was aided in its connection to larger cities, like Boston, by the arrival of railroad lines and the King's Highway, later called the Boston Post Road, which became a route going west. Weary travelers often stopped for food, drink, and lodging at the inns along the way. The oldest inn is now called Longfellow's Wayside Inn and has been a popular inn and restaurant in almost continuous existence since 1716.

The 19th century did not change Sudbury much, as people still lived simply and frugally. As they had in the Revolutionary War, Sudbury sent its men to serve in the Civil War, World Wars I and II, and the Korean War. Sudbury remained a sheltered community until World War II, when the population began to grow from less than 2,000 to today's 18,000 in six decades.

Flower growing in greenhouses became very popular, and a few large companies, like Raytheon and Sperry Rand, moved into Sudbury. In the last 30 years, Sudbury has improved its schools and town services and built larger, more affluent homes. It continues to have a strong sense of community and a desirable quality of life, which make it one of the most attractive towns west of Boston.

The Sudbury Historical Society, Inc., has sampled its archives to provide fleeting windows through which readers can glimpse the town's history. We know that many important people and places are not included, as we could only choose from what was generously given to us over the years. We chose the chapters in the hope that everyone who has ever had a connection with Sudbury will find something that awakens a warm memory of the town.

# *One*
# Agriculture

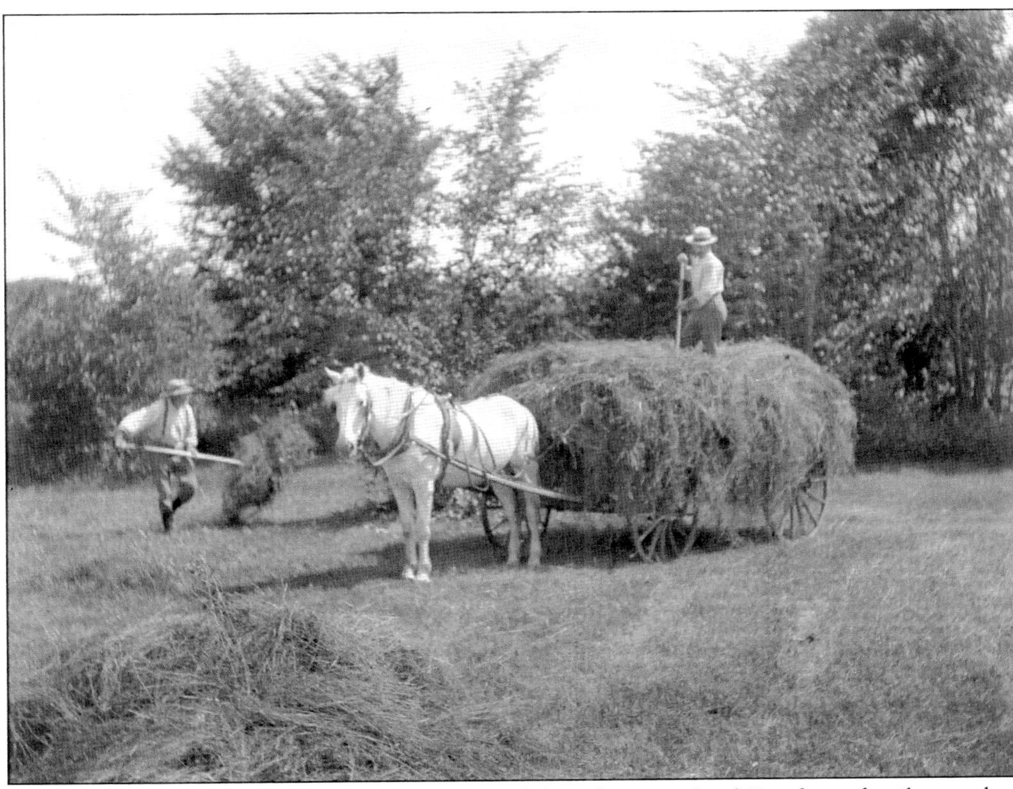

In 1905, Hattie J. Goodnow won a top prize with her photograph of Goodnow family members haying in their fields on Green Hill in South Sudbury. Haying was a dry, hot job that had to be done on sunny days, as rain would ruin the hay or cause spontaneous combustion in a barn. A stoneware jug of "Haymaker's Switchel" kept in the shade would quench their thirst.

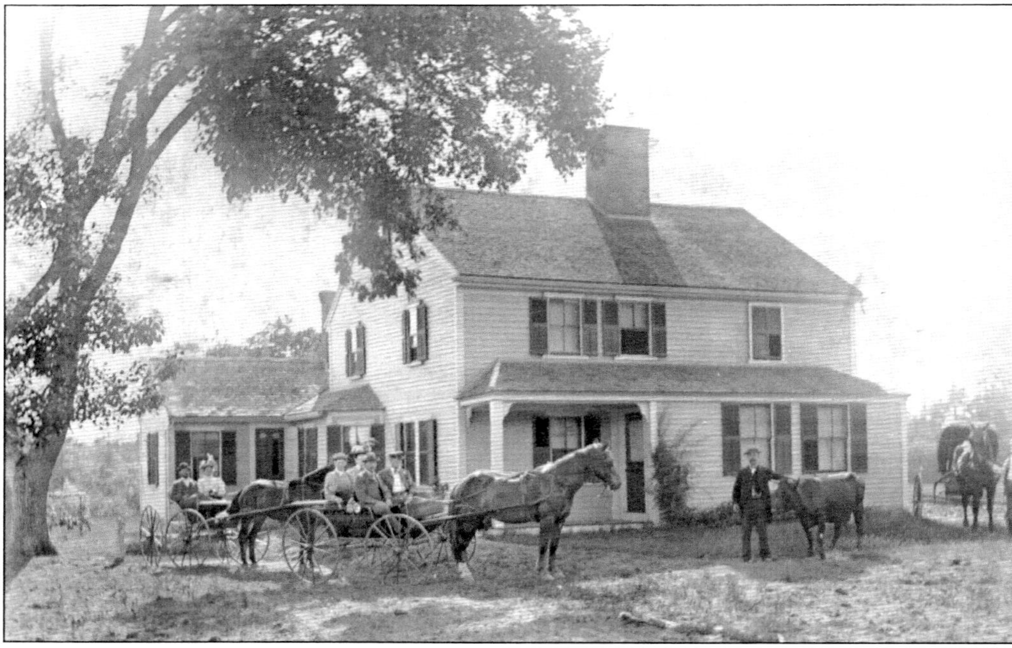

The Willis Place at 333 Maynard Road was built in 1704 by Roger Willis and his son Samuel and stayed in the Willis family until 1881. Its unique features include the present living room, which was the original kitchen, and a walk-in fireplace with a beehive oven. The porch was removed long ago, and the front door was moved to the side of the house. Here, the Willis family poses proudly in front of the house in 1879.

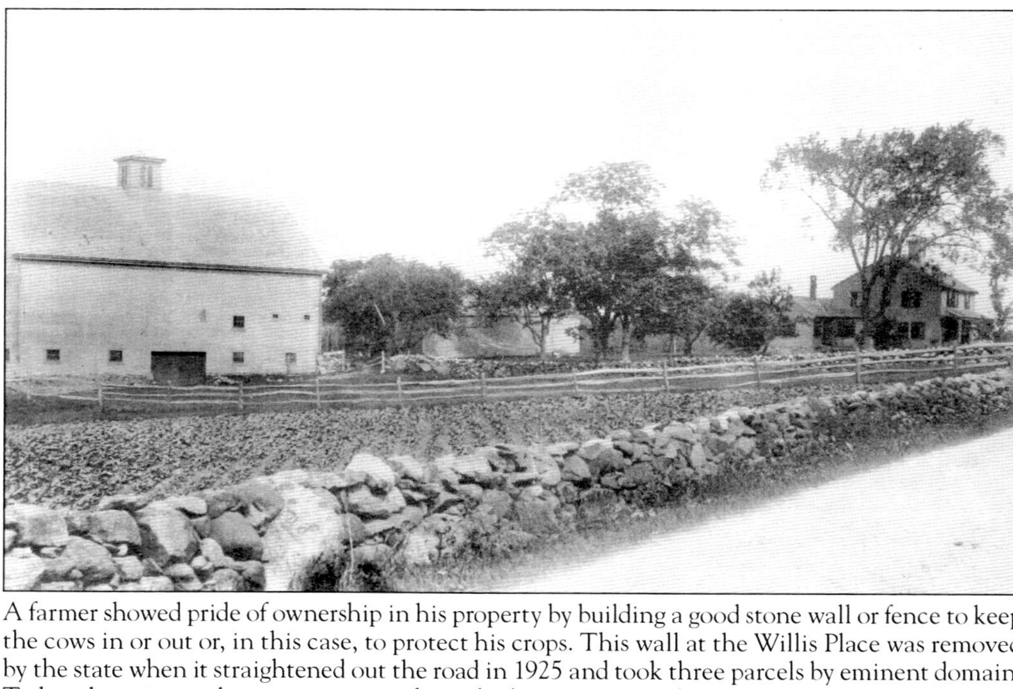

A farmer showed pride of ownership in his property by building a good stone wall or fence to keep the cows in or out or, in this case, to protect his crops. This wall at the Willis Place was removed by the state when it straightened out the road in 1925 and took three parcels by eminent domain. Today, there is a replacement garage where the barn once stood.

Thomas H. Ashe lived as a renter in a private house on King Philip Road in 1916 and did odd jobs in the neighborhood. He was dependable but did take his time, especially if one had not heard a funny story he had just heard. He left his mark in a unique way, signing and dating the back of a cedar clapboard on an outbuilding he had built for a resident of King Philip Road.

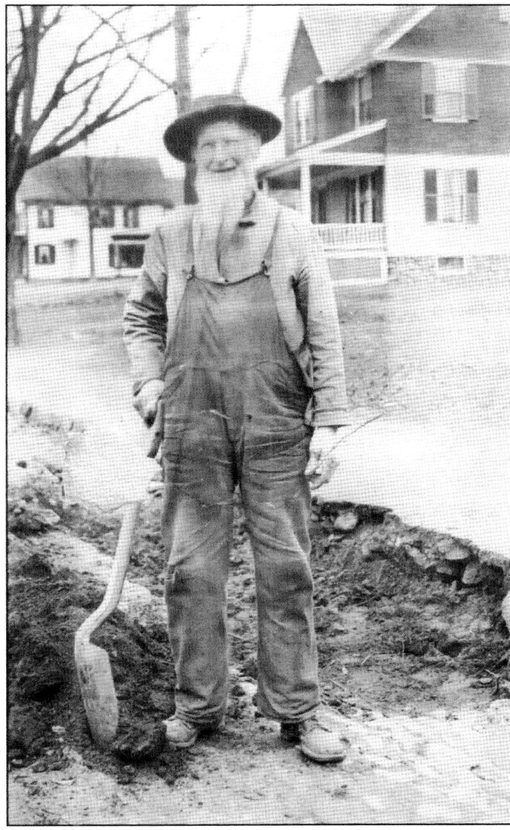

Hattie Goodnow, who took the photograph below in 1905 with her wooden box camera, followed the admonition of the magazine *Photo Era*, learning how to compose photographs and to record different themes the magazine suggested like cows, clouds, snow scenes, portraits, haying, and street scenes. She succeeded with a heavy camera, a wooden tripod, and glass-plate negatives. The historical society has more than 250 photographs she produced until the 1930s. She lived at 293 Concord Road.

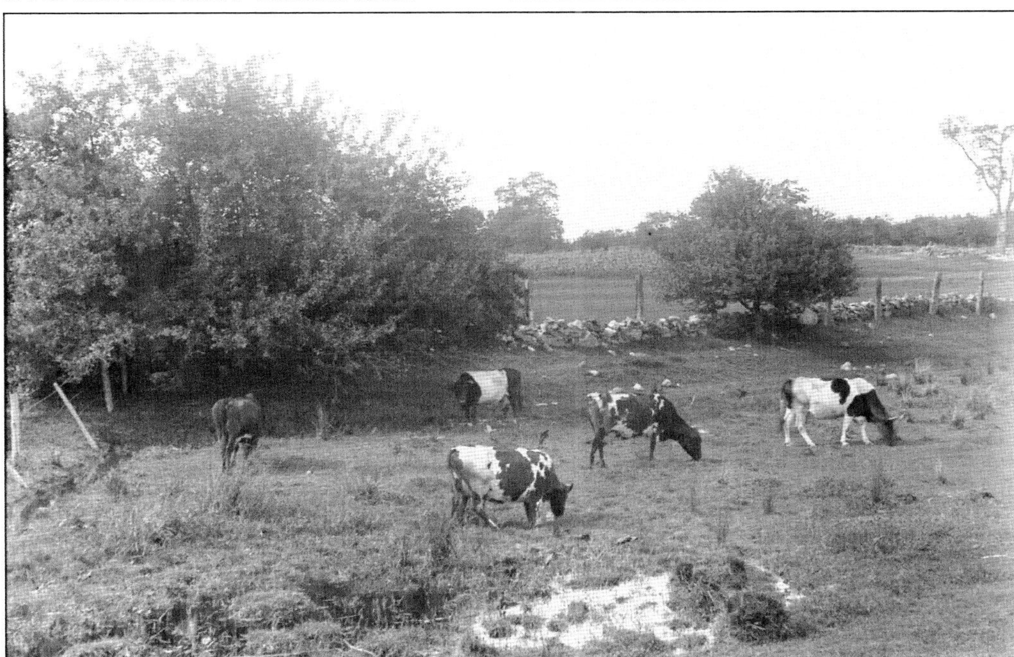

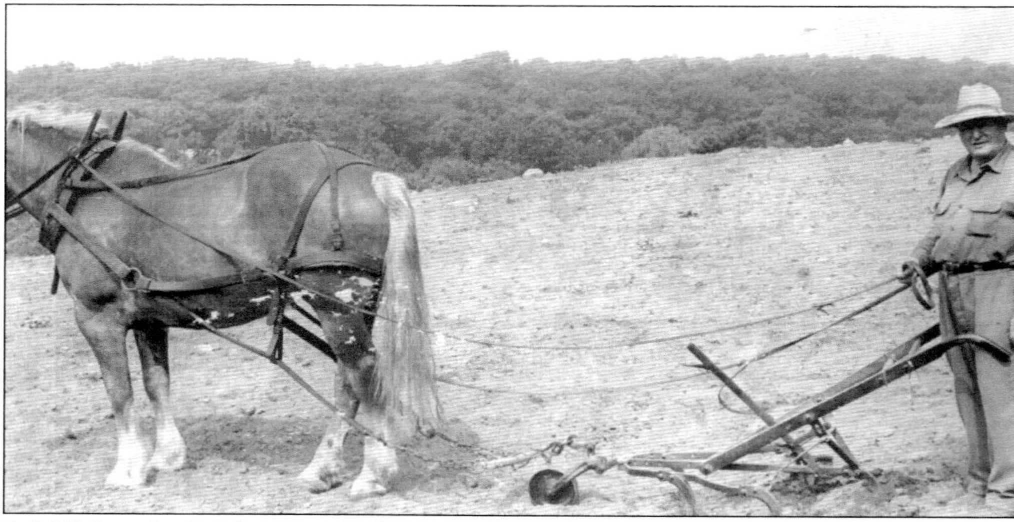

Bob Walker, the last farmer in Sudbury to plow with a horse, is seen here at his farm at 55–62 Goodman's Hill Road. He had more than 50 acres under cultivation until his death in 1983. The house that once occupied this site was called the Bogle-Walker House. In 1806, Bogle family members built it from white-oak timbers and other wood they brought down from New Hampshire, where they owned land. It had been in the National Register of Historic Places but was torn down on its 200th anniversary.

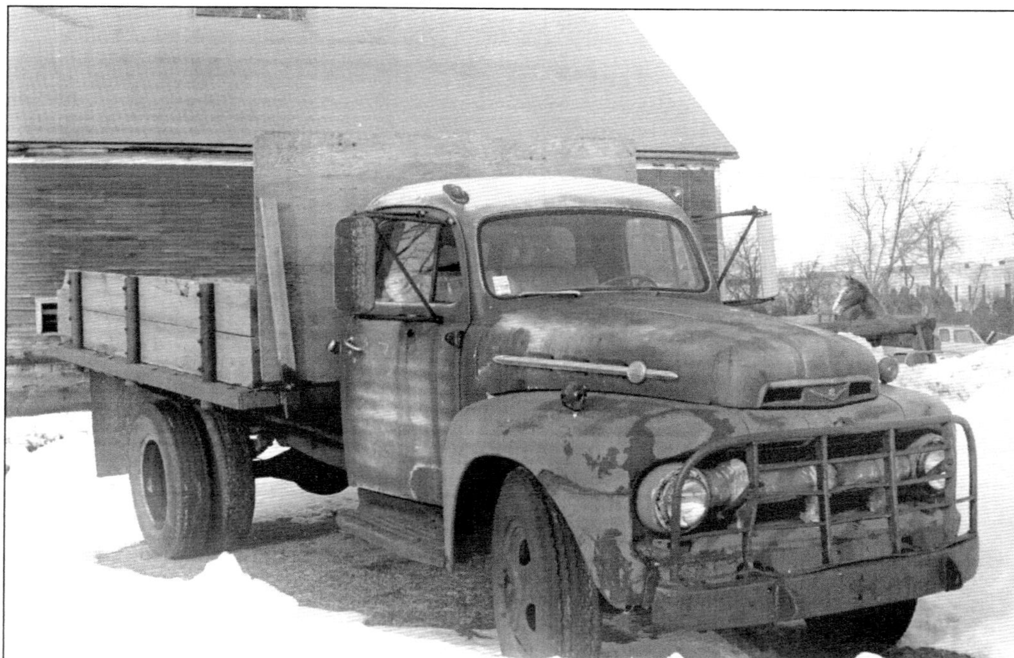

Bob Walker's truck and barn are seen here. The Walkers' original house was built in 1722 across the street from where the Bogle-Walker House once stood. After Walker died in 1983, the barn was purchased, dismantled, and rebuilt in New Hampshire. Recently, the land has grown houses instead of crops.

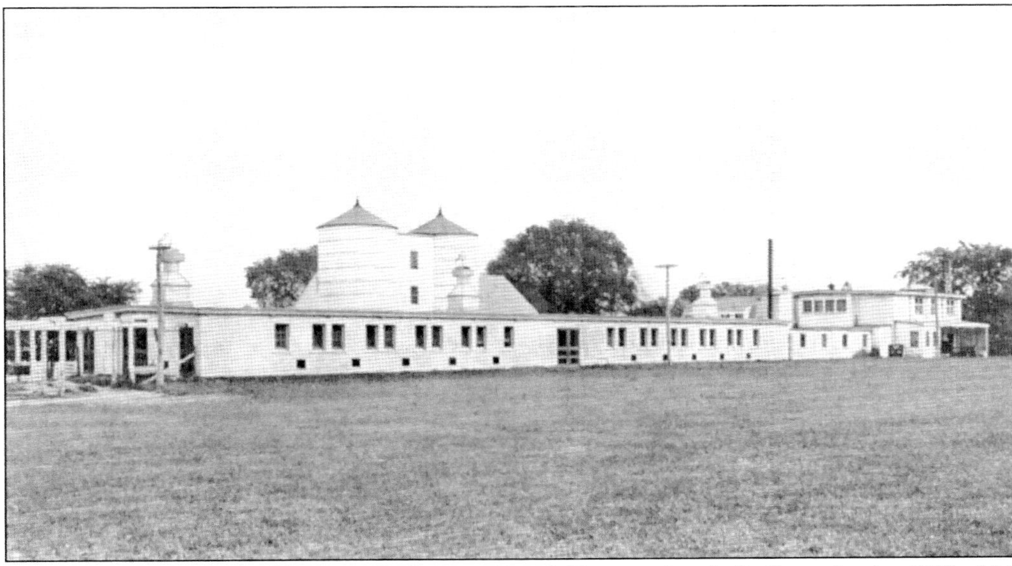

These were the dairy buildings at the Bonnie Brook Farm in South Sudbury. In the 1920s, H.P. Hood and Sons bought the farm from Aubrey Borden and made it into a model farm to educate the public about where milk and milk products came from. It is interesting that even in the 1920s, the public was losing touch with the sources of what they ate and drank. Presently, the Raytheon Company is located on this site at 528 Boston Post Road.

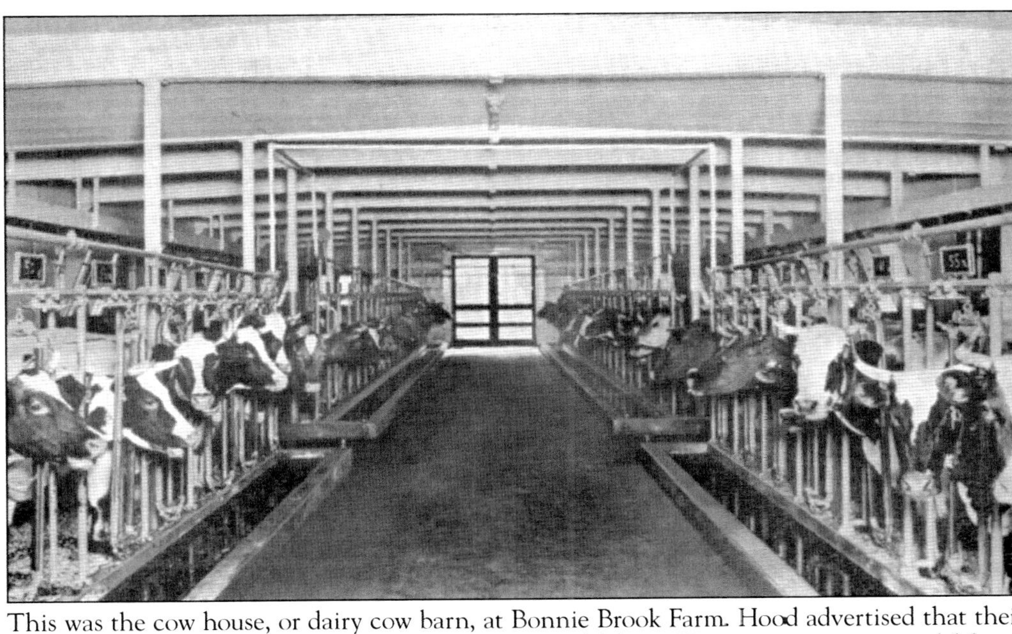

This was the cow house, or dairy cow barn, at Bonnie Brook Farm. Hood advertised that their cows lived in a clean, light, airy cow house on the model farm. However, many non-model farms were not well maintained. H.P. Hood and Sons was organized in 1846.

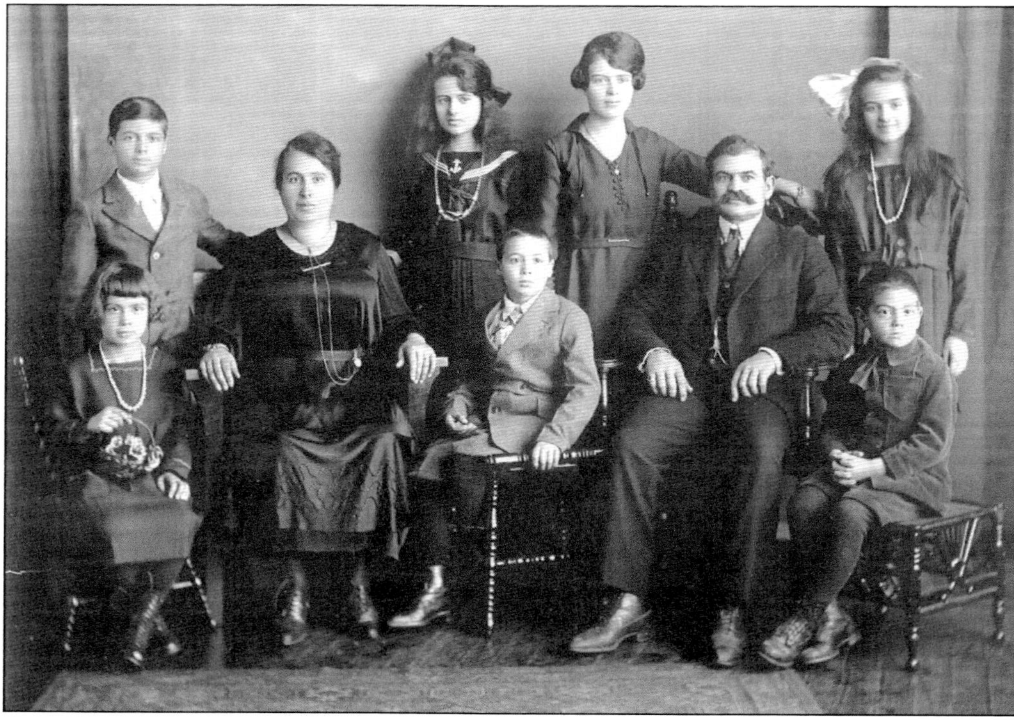

In 1910, the Cavicchio family emigrated from Italy to Sudbury. They started with 56 acres of land, where they developed an orchard and had field-grown vegetables that were delivered and sold in the Boston markets. This portrait was taken about 1923 and shows the Cavicchio family, from left to right, (first row) Virginia; Civita, the mother; James; Giuseppe, the father; and Gaetano "Emmy"; (second row) Paul, Catherine, Anna, and Mary.

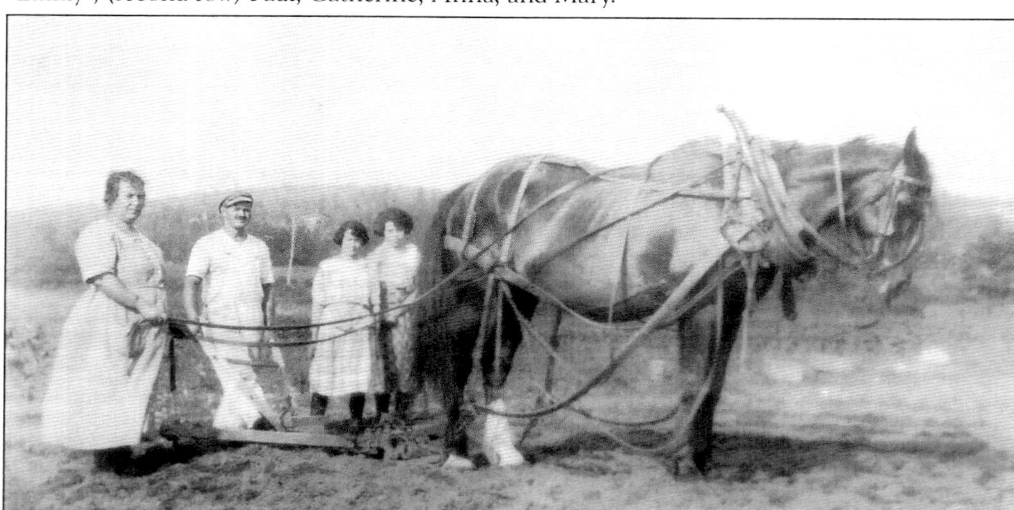

Civita and Giuseppe Cavicchio and their two oldest daughters, Anna and Catherine, are working on their farm at 110 Codjer Lane. Over the years, the family has expanded its operation and has become a major grower of quality horticultural products in New England while preserving 200 acres of agricultural land.

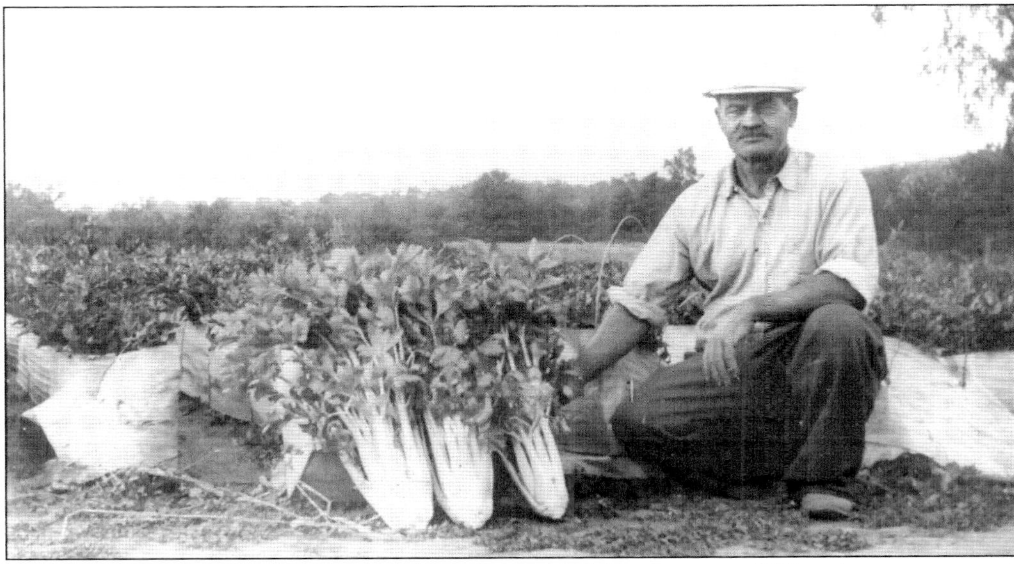

Giuseppe Cavicchio shows his pride in his celery in 1925. Beginning in 1928 and continuing until 1938, Henry Ford's agents made continuous offers for the Cavicchio farm, first for all of it and then just 1.5 acres for placement of a dam that would be a part of Ford's Wash Brook Project. The dam would provide waterpower to the Mill Village for an auto parts factory manufacturing Bakelite parts. Cavicchio refused to sell it at the price offered and is often credited with saving Sudbury.

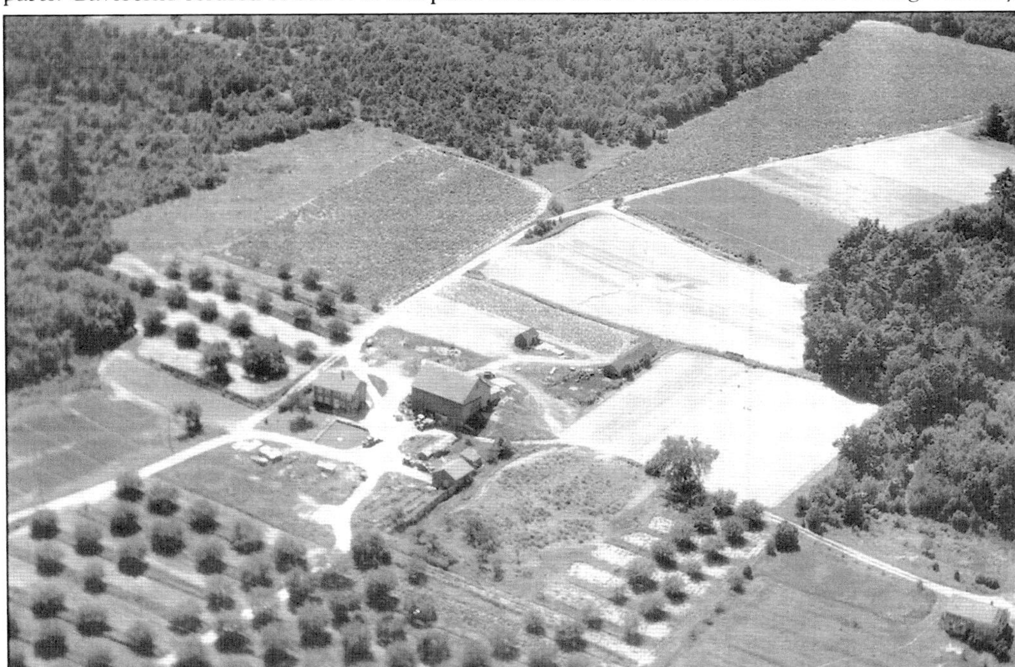

This aerial view shows the Cavicchio farm before the 1938 hurricane that destroyed most of their apple orchard with 120-mile-per-hour winds and gusts up to 186 miles per hour. They were forced to expand into new crops, such as winter squash, zucchini, peppers, greens, carrots, celery, and corn, which were all cultivated and tended by the family and then driven daily to Boston's Quincy Market.

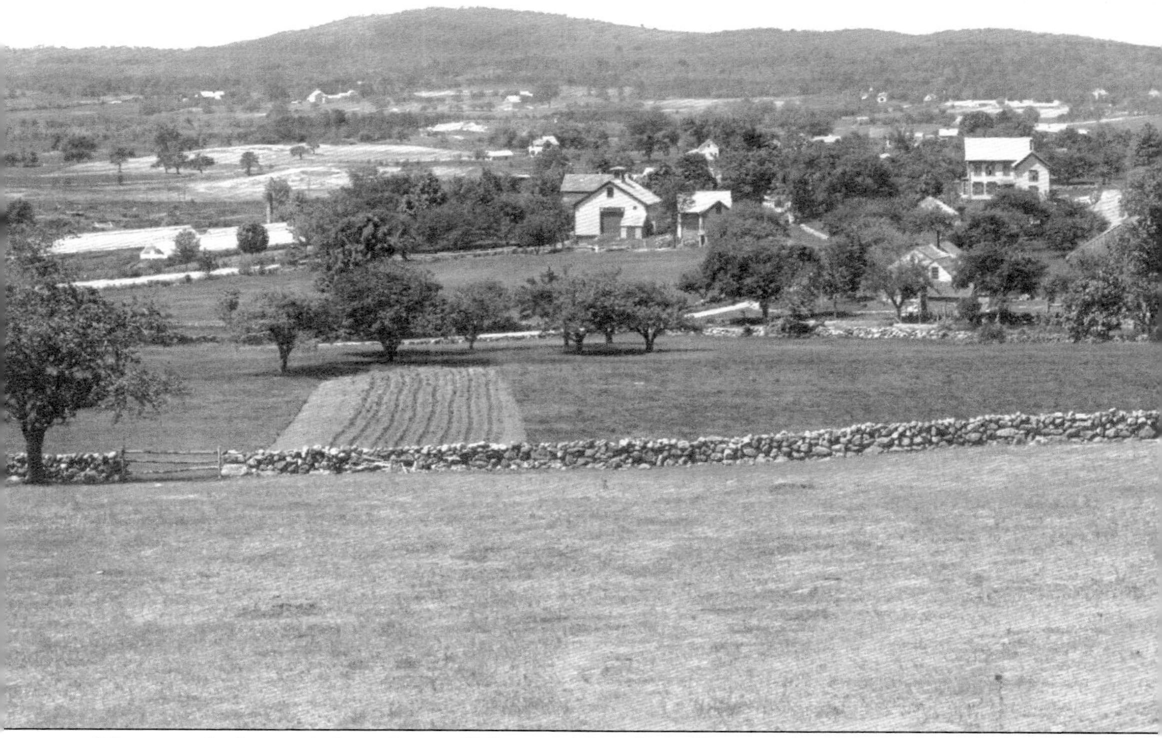

This view looks south from Green Hill toward South Sudbury in about 1905. By this time, almost all of the land had been cleared for farming, orchards, and dirt roads all the way to Mount Nobscot. This image shows an almost-idealized landscape of beautifully maintained farms and buildings. But that is the way it was, due to pride in ownership and the importance of good relations with one's

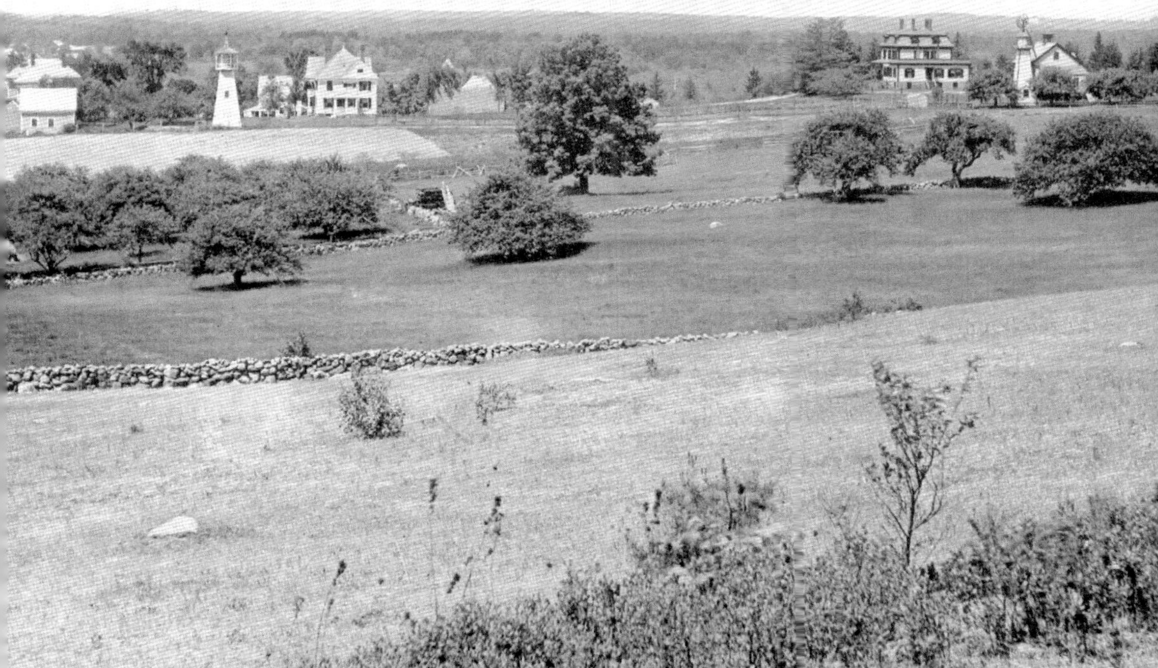

neighbors. King Philip Road is to the left, the Boston Post Road is in the middle, and Concord Road is to the right. The preponderance of windmills looks strange today, but they were labor saving and added a sound to the landscape, which is rarely heard today.

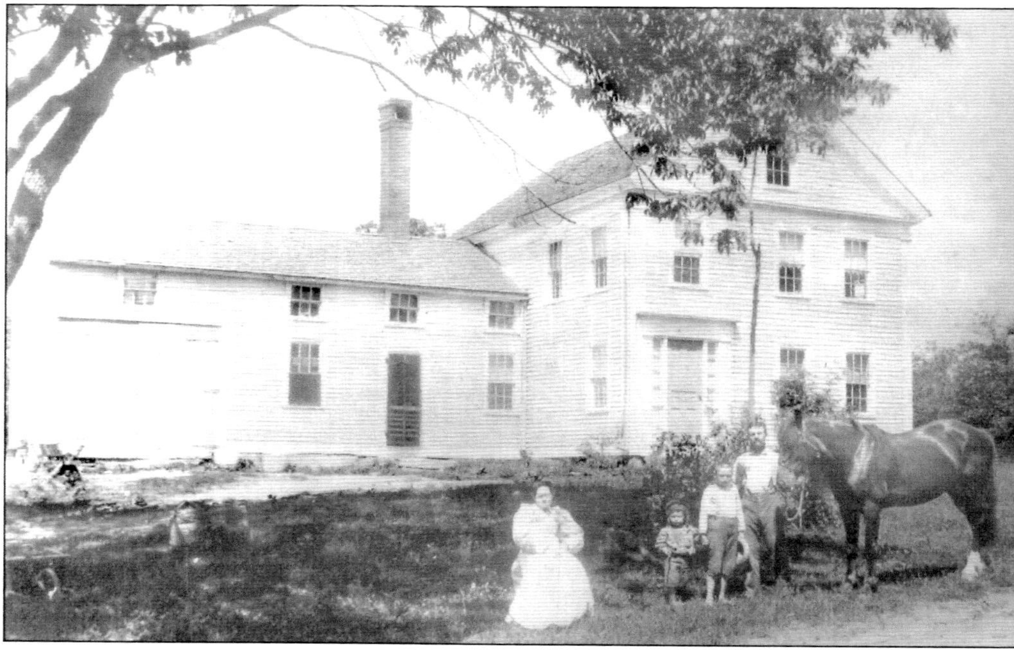

Capt. Israel Haynes had the house above built in 1840 as a wedding gift for his son Leander Haynes and his wife, Mary Gleason. The house, at 113 Haynes Road, was passed down to Clarence Austin (right) and his wife, Angelina Haynes. The younger child is Herman Austin, who died in 1969. The Haynes family is one of the founding families of Sudbury.

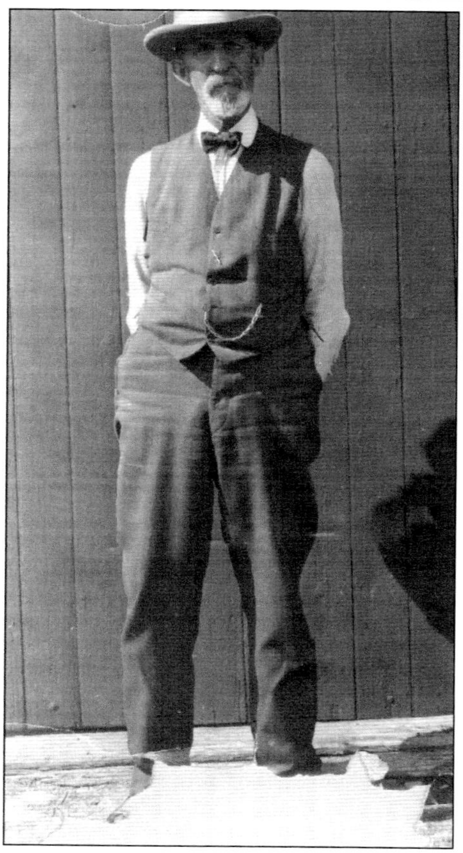

Hubbard Brown (1839–1922) was a farmer and a horticulturist. He originated the practice of growing under glass in Sudbury in 1879 and gained some renown for raising greenhouse cucumbers, which he sold in the winter in Boston for the princely sum of 10¢ a piece. His greenhouse was located at 79 Nobscot Road. After he retired, Brown lived at 16 Concord Road and worked as a real estate agent.

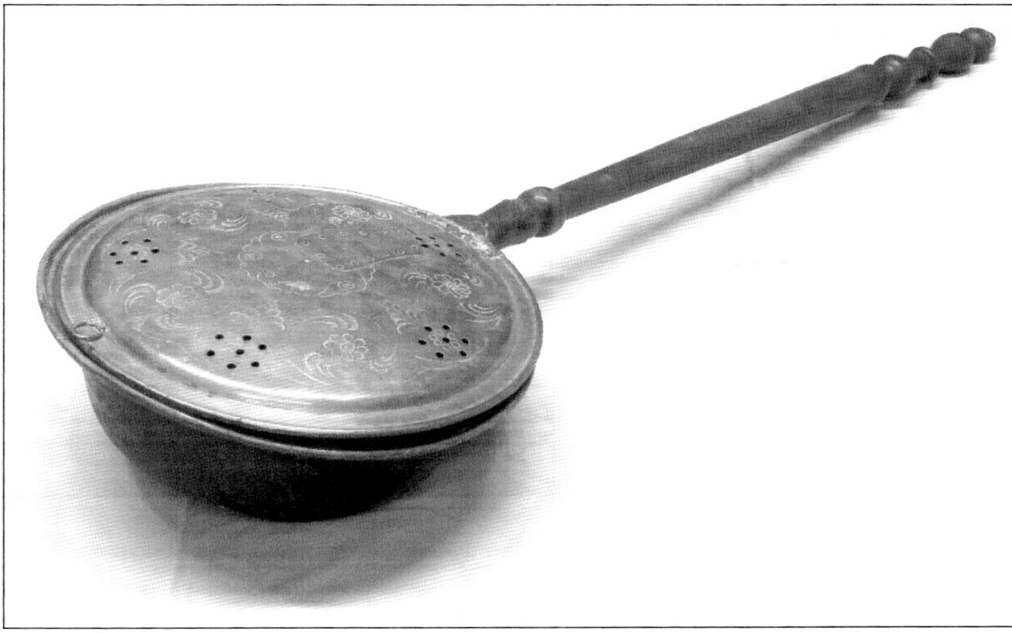

This warming pan is from the home of Deacon William Brown at 79 Nobscot Road. It is made out of brass with a turned walnut handle. The top of the pan lifts up, and coals were put inside. Before central heating existed, one would move it between the sheets and the down comforter to warm up the bed before going to sleep. (Photograph by Chuck Zimmer.)

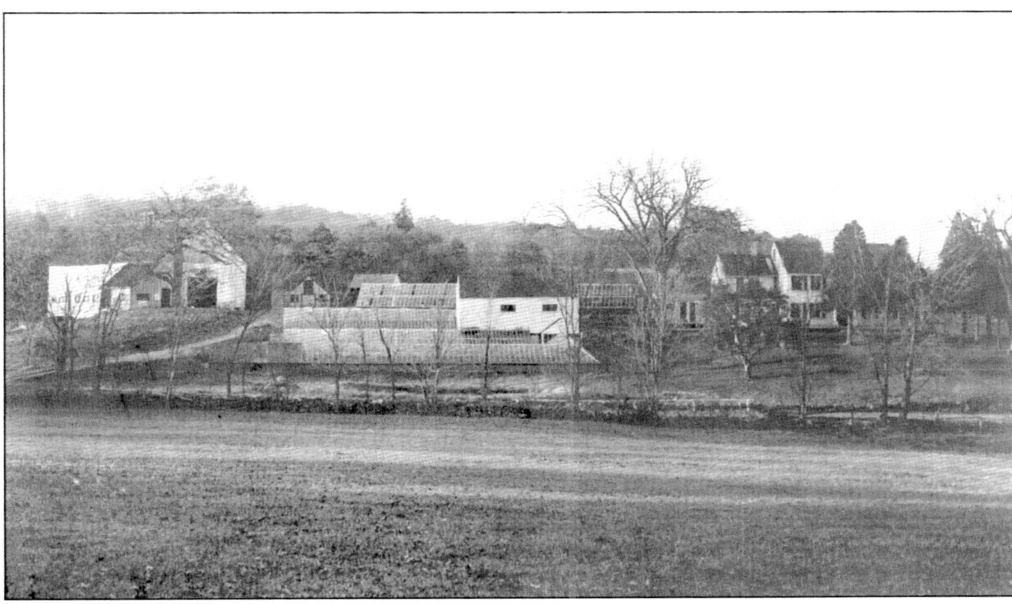

Hubbard Brown's house and the greenhouses he built are seen here in the 1890s. The house was built in 1780 and was originally situated higher up on the hill. Along with his 10¢ cucumbers, Brown grew tomatoes and celery in the winter, which he took to the Boston market until 1907.

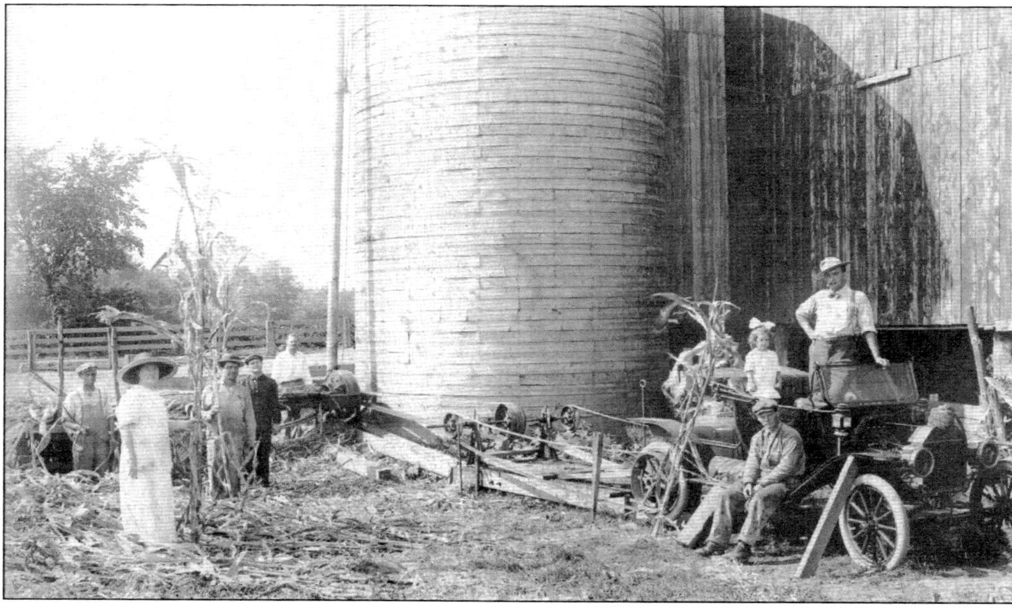

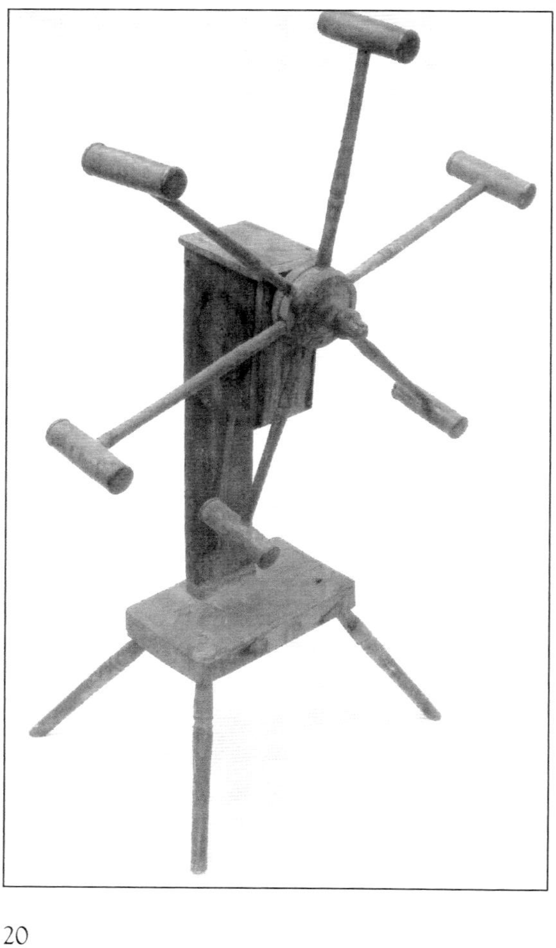

The Aubrey Borden farm was located at 68 Old County Road and stretched over toward Goodman's Hill. Here, the family uses a Model T car engine to power a gadget that chopped corn stalks and then carried them up to the top of the silo. The resulting silage, or green fodder, was then used to feed the cows—a great demonstration of Yankee ingenuity. The 1938 hurricane collapsed the barn, killing 50 cows.

A Yarn Counter does exactly what its name implies. The tops of the mallets were one foot apart, and in a full rotation, there was a length of six feet. The internal mechanism hidden from view was able to automatically count the distance. Part of the machine is called the weasel, and it "pops" at 72 feet, which may be where the nursery rhyme "Pop, goes the weasel" originated in the 1850s. (Gift of John Borden; photograph by Chuck Zimmer.)

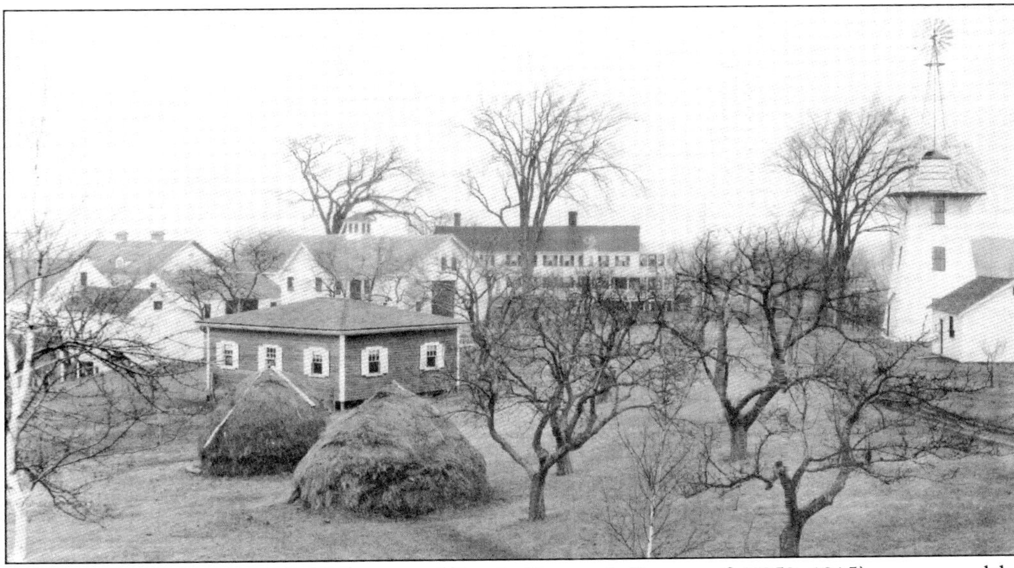

The Raymond Farm was at 80 Raymond Road. George J. Raymond (1852–1915) was a wealthy businessman who owned Raymond's Department Stores in the Boston area. Home of Uncle Eph and "Where you bot the hat?" fame, it was in existence from 1879 until 1973. The home was built in 1750 by the Hunt family, but Raymond added a water tower, barns, and many outbuildings, including a mausoleum, on the 500 acres. Stained-glass windows from a steamboat were installed in the house.

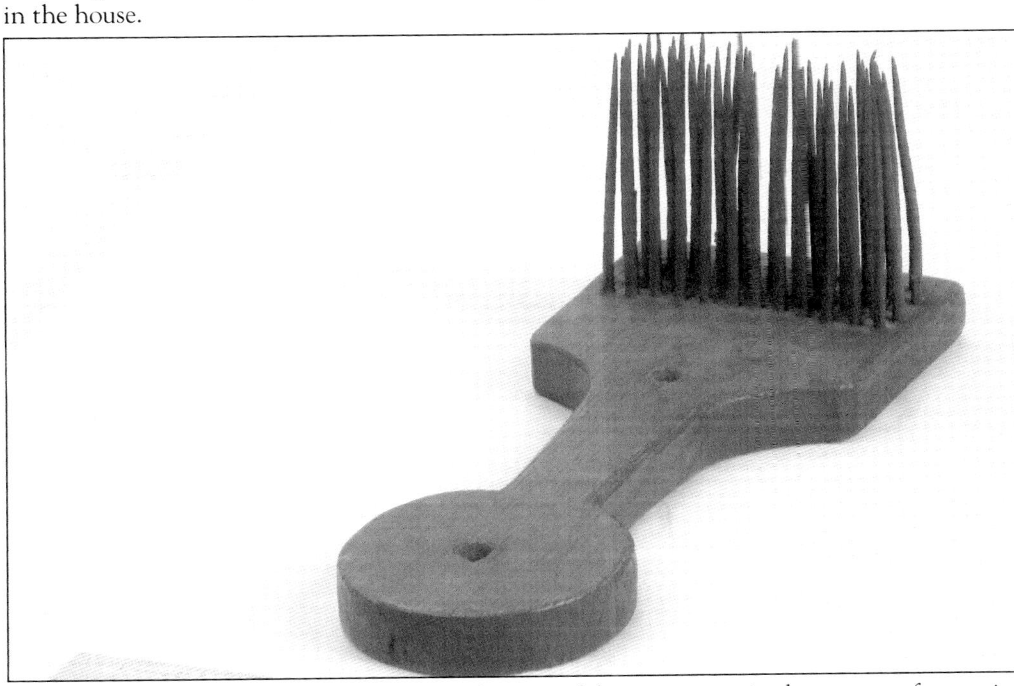

This flax hetchel dates from 1690. It was used in one of the many steps in the process of preparing flax so that it could be spun into linen. Flax is an annual herb plant whose fibers are separated by pulling handfuls through the tines of different comb-like devices to separate them after breaking or scutching the fiber. (Gift of Loren Hayden; photograph by Chuck Zimmer.)

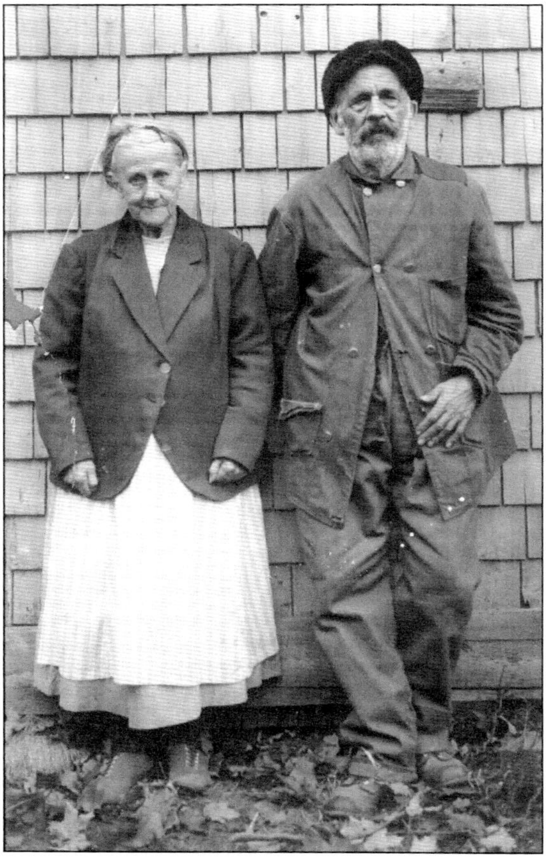

John Murray and his wife, Mary, were farmers in South Sudbury. As of 1890, they owned a good amount of farmable land, including the land surrounding the Wadsworth Cemetery. They had six cows, one yearling, one horse, a carriage, two houses, and barn and yet could not "make a go of it." By the time this picture was taken in 1914, they were living hand-to-mouth. There was no Social Security at that time, but the town took care of its own.

The Davis Turkey Farm in South Sudbury was located where the Wayside Carriage House Inn is today at 738 Boston Post Road. The farm operated in the 1930s and the 1940s. At that time, there were a lot of turkey farms in the area to provide freshly killed poultry to the locals and to sell it at Quincy Market in Boston.

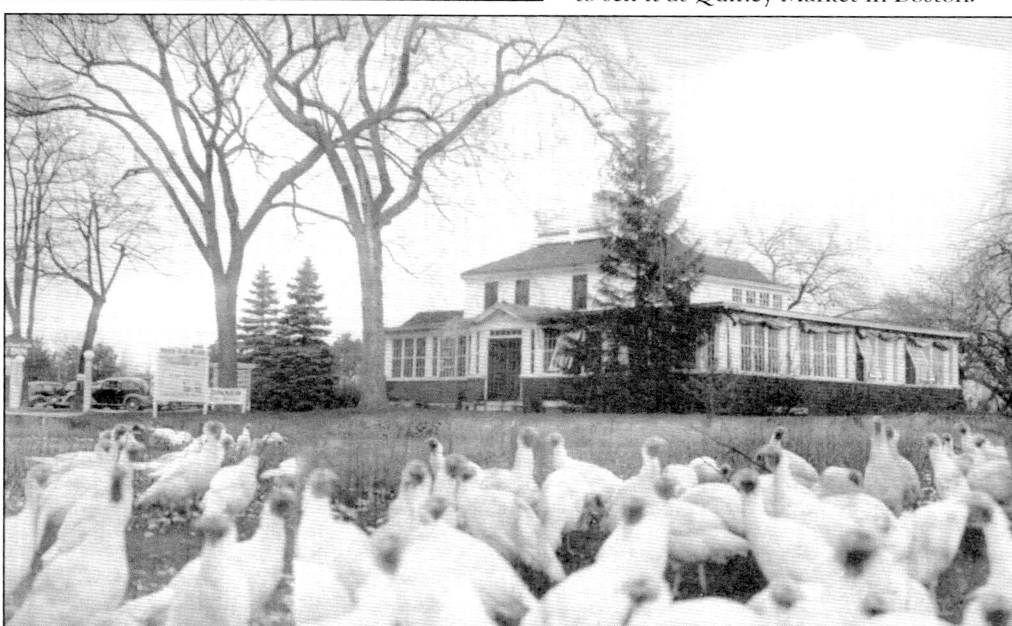

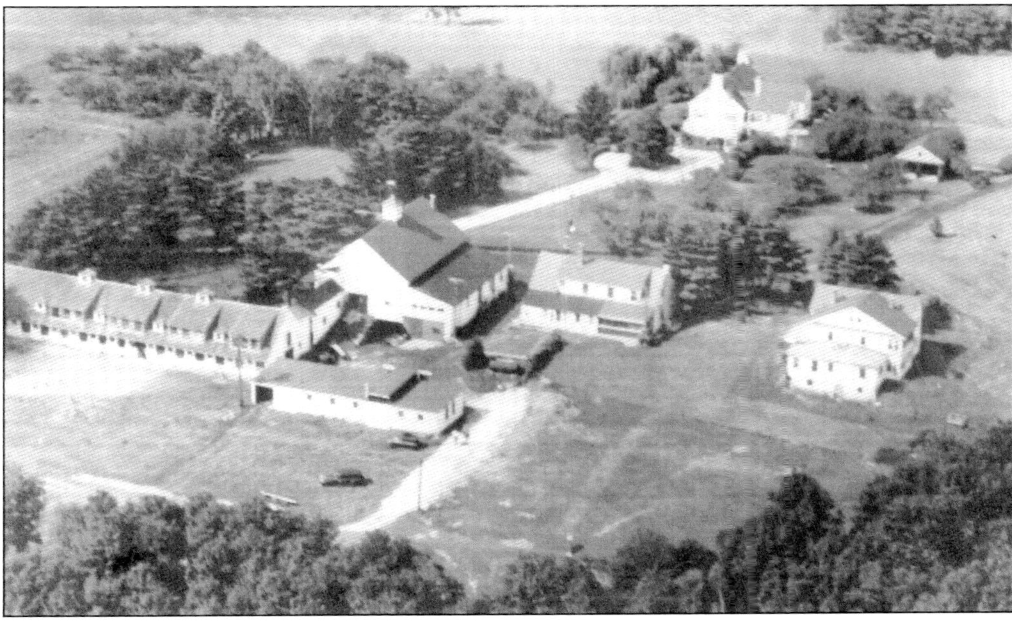

This aerial view of the Briardale-Frost Farm was taken in the late 1940s. It was a successful dairy farm in its day, operated by the Frost family in the area of 148 Great Road. Sperry Rand later developed this land. The main house still exists, partially surrounded by the Frost Farm complex of elderly housing.

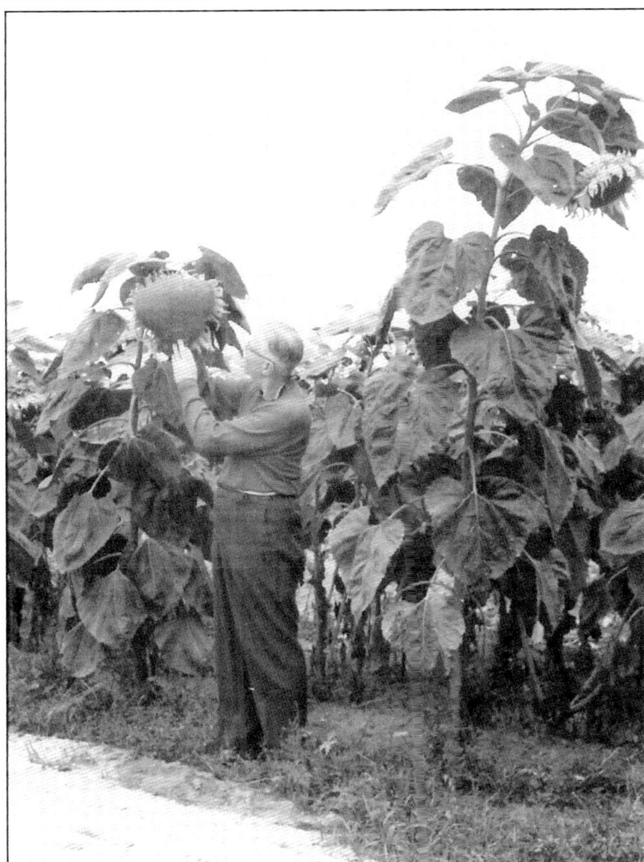

Gurnseyl Frost examines his sunflower crop on Briardale-Frost Farm at 148 Great Road around 1948. Sunflowers—usually Russian sunflowers—became very popular to grow in this time period, as the demand was growing for bird food due to the public's awareness of and love of bird watching. The area now houses the Frost Farm condominium complex.

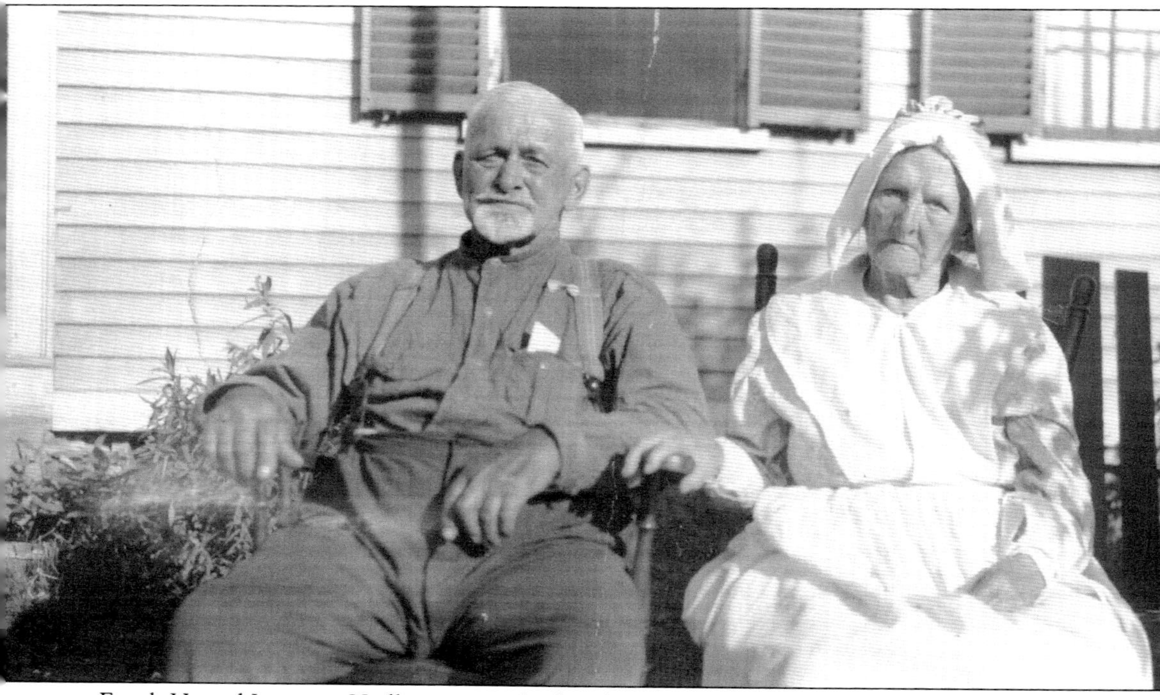

Frank H. and Lauretta Hadley sit outside their house at 308 Concord Road in Sudbury Center. Frank H. Hadley was a retired railroad man. Lauretta is dressed in a costume for the town's 300th anniversary in 1939.

# *Two*

# PEOPLE A TO Z

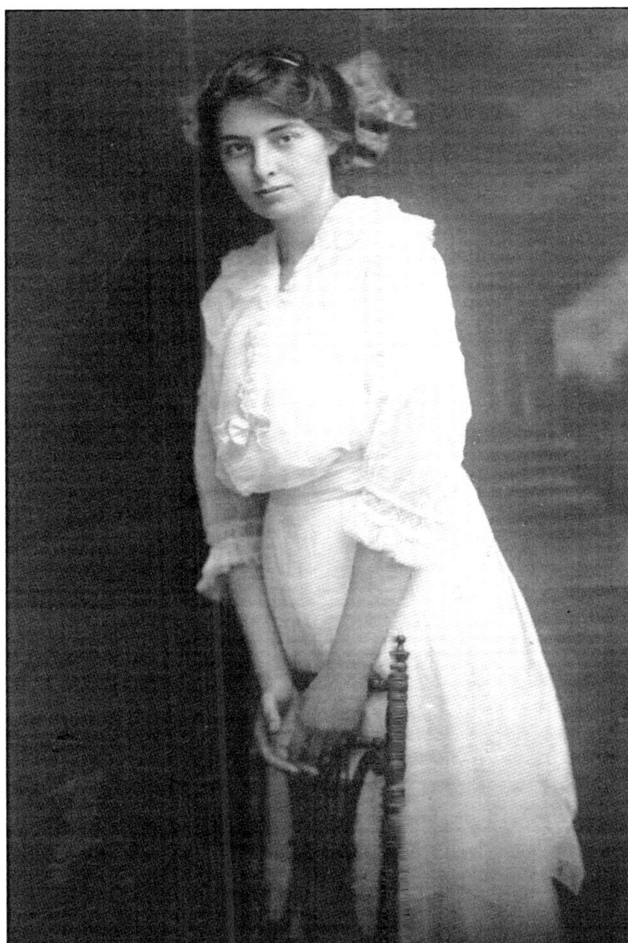

This is a lovely portrait of Ruth Ames. She was born in 1899, never married, and was the last owner of the Ames Farm, originally consisting of 150 acres at 37 Landham Road. She was famous for her pies and she funded the Ames Hall at the Memorial Congregational Church.

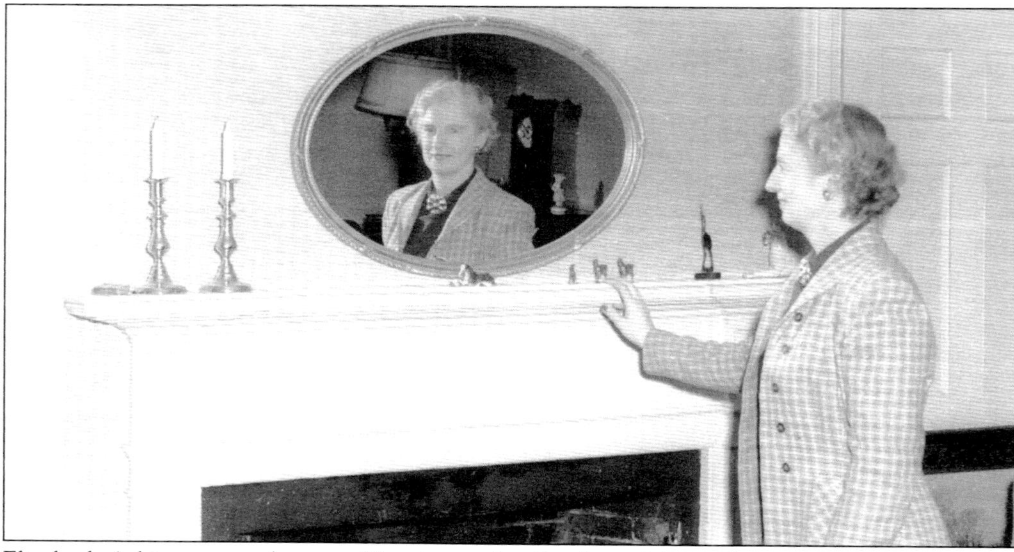

Elizabeth Atkinson was the town librarian at the Goodnow Library from 1937 to 1970. She lived with her sister at 85 Raymond Road in a house built in 1826 by Jonas Hunt for his son Sewell Hunt. Atkinson was highly regarded and loved by townspeople, especially by their children, as she paid special attention to the shy children who needed assistance in learning how to enjoy reading. The society has a collection of artistic photographs taken of her in her house with her Great Dane.

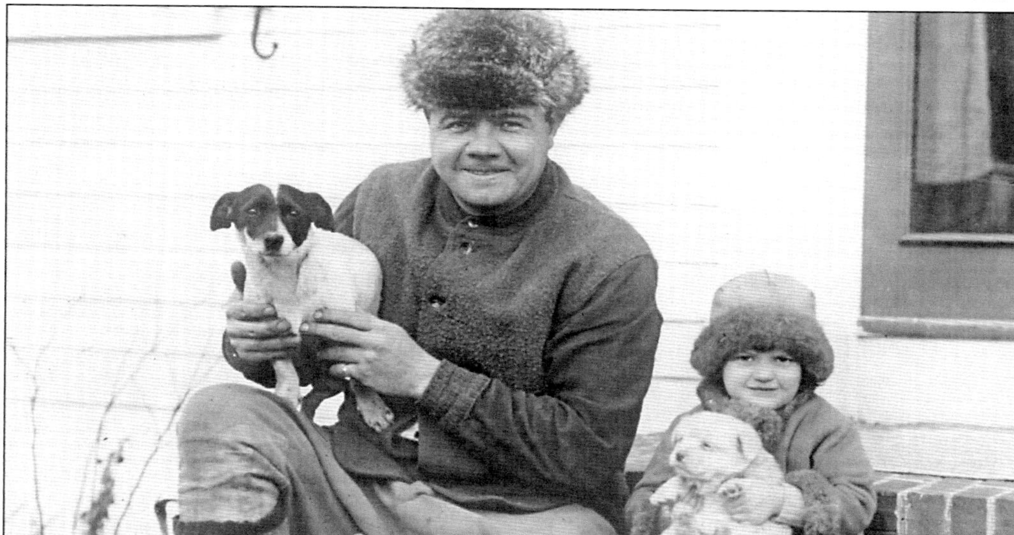

Baseball legend Babe Ruth, his daughter Dorothy, and their dogs pose in front of their home in Sudbury. In 1923, he bought the Obadiah Perry farm at 558 Dutton Road, built in 1800, and renamed it Home Plate. In 1927, it was sold to Herbert and Esther Atkinson, who started a company in the barn called Sudbury Labs, making everything from soil-testing kits to invisible boats. The Atkinsons also created the Sudbury Foundation, a local charity that has done much for Sudbury and the surrounding area.

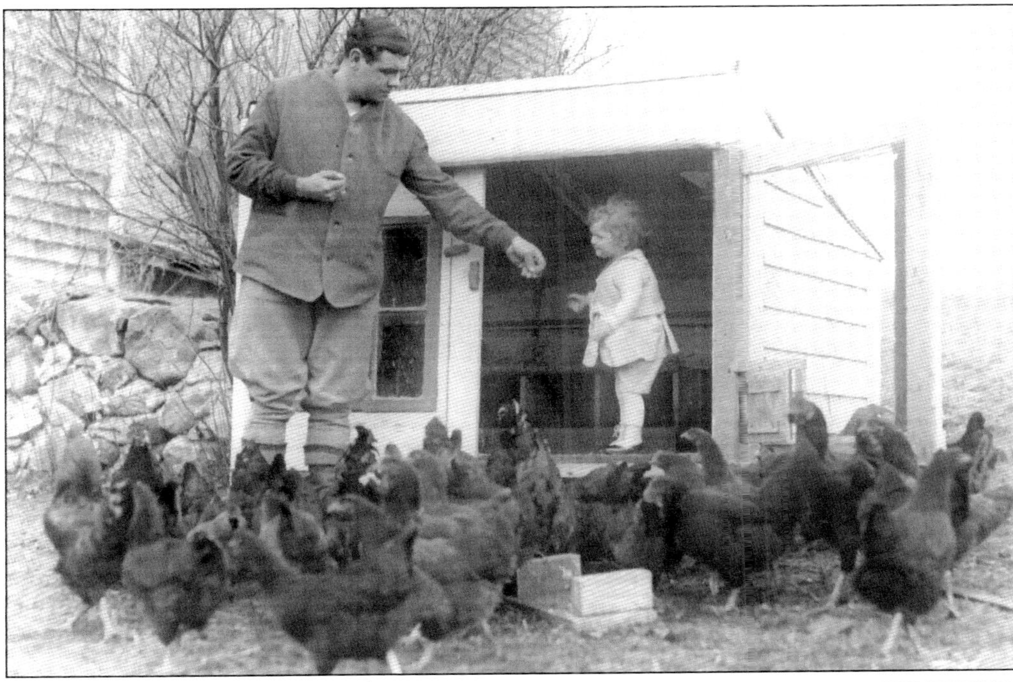

Babe Ruth (above) became a gentleman farmer in Sudbury, and for a few years, it was his place to relax, especially in the winter. Here, he helps his daughter Dorothy feed the chickens in a planned photograph opportunity for the visiting press, who made many demands on him. The son of the home's current owners claims to have broken the Red Sox "Curse of the Bambino" when he was hit by a fly ball in 2004 at Fenway Park. Later that year, the Red Sox won the World Series for the first time since Ruth was infamously traded to the Yankees.

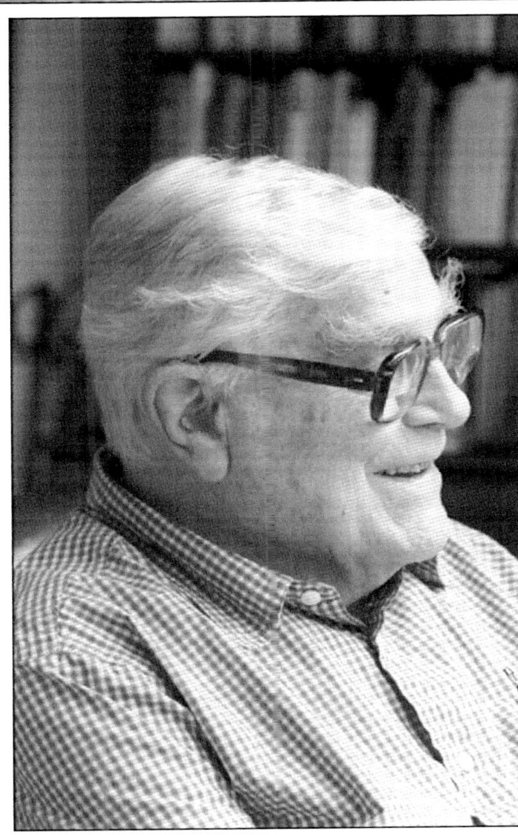

Loring Coleman, shown at right, is a well-known artist in New England. Born in 1918 in Chicago, he is a descendant of Rev. Jacob Bigelow, an early minister in Sudbury. He spent summers at his grandmother's house in Concord, where he filled his sketchbooks with drawings. Boarding school brought him back to Massachusetts, where painting became his passion as he moved from oils to watercolors. Coleman has taught at Vesper George School in Boston and Middlesex School in Concord and was the supervisor of art programs for Sudbury schools. (Photograph by Hugh Portmiller.)

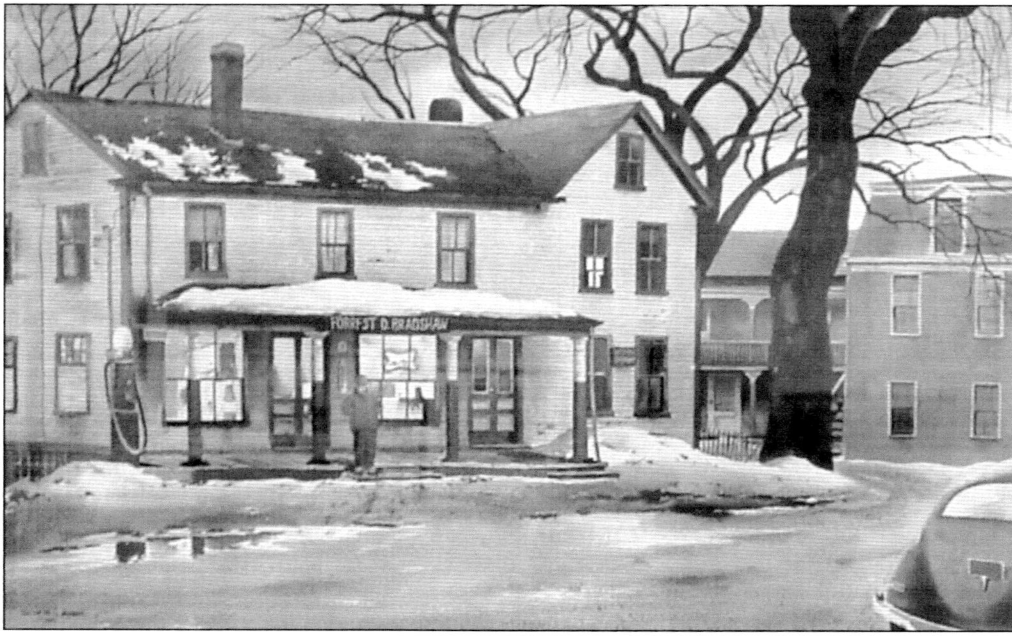


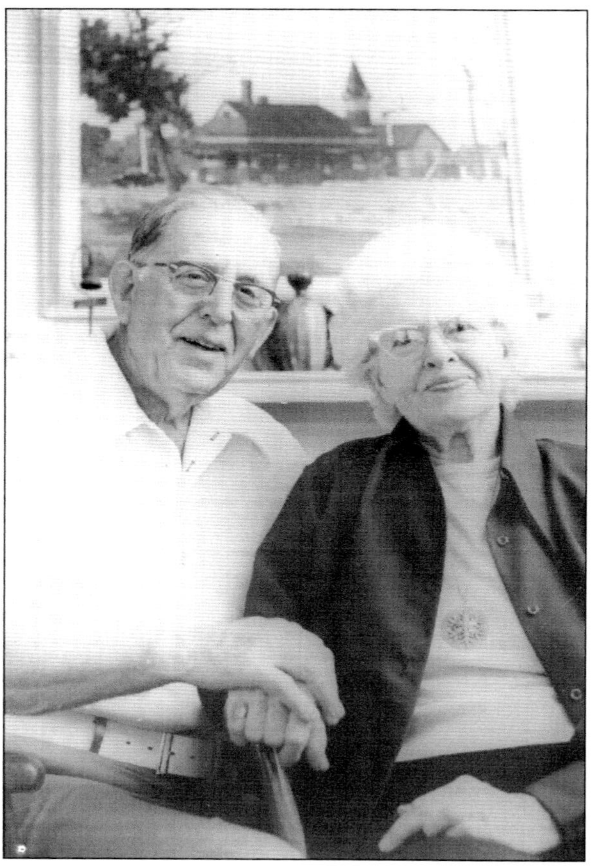

The watercolor above shows the Forrest D. Bradshaw store, which once occupied 361 Boston Post Road opposite Concord Road, next to where Mill Village is now. The Bradshaws bought the store in 1921. The original owner, Enoch Kidder, built it in 1820 and made shoes and boots. The second floor was the meeting place for local abolitionists and the location of the founding of the Sudbury Republican party. The watercolor is by Sudbury artist Loring Coleman. (Reprinted with permission by the owner, Dr. Donald Oasis.)

Forrest D. and Katherine Rogers Bradshaw pose under a painting of the South Sudbury railroad station, which now hangs in the Goodnow Library. Forrest was a World War I veteran who served in the Balloon Observation Corps. In addition to running his general store, he loved town history and was the town historian and a founder of the Sudbury Historical Society, Inc. He also found time to be a town selectman while he was also the Sudbury postmaster.

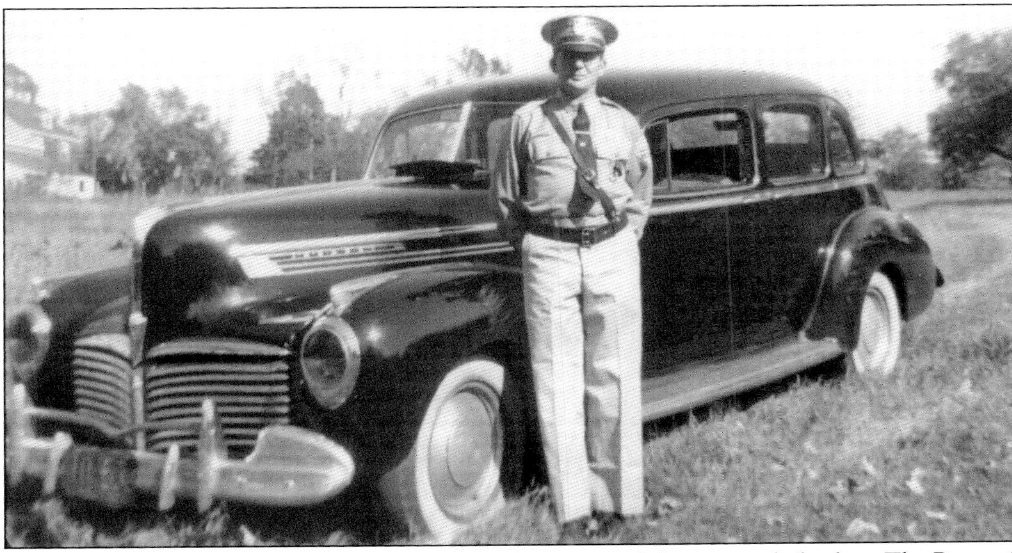

Auxiliary officer Lloyd Bancroft and his 1943 Hudson automobile were ready for duty. The Bancroft family lived at 277 Old Sudbury Road in what was known as the Harrington Place. Bancroft was a full-time baker of bread and rolls in his own bakeshop on the property. The baked goods were delivered to local restaurants and clients. The family won fifth place in a contest as the "Most Typical American Family in Massachusetts" in 1939.

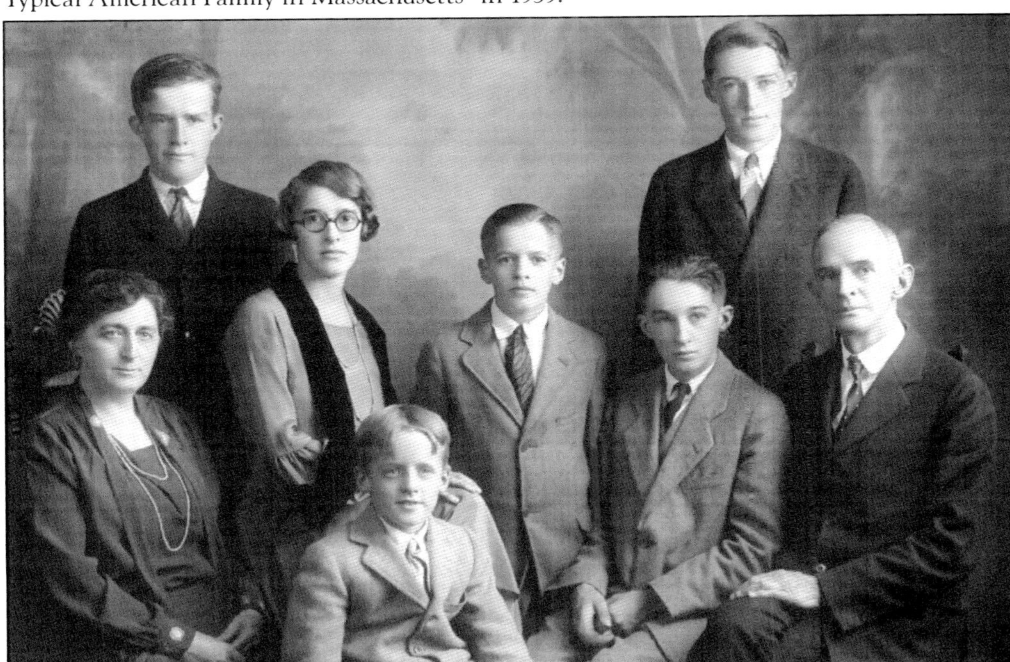

This formal portrait of the Cutler family in the mid-1930s includes, from left to right, Mary Edith Goodnow Cutler, Richard Thompson Cutler, Isadora Goodnow Cutler, Philip Loring Cutler, Edward Roland Cutler, Joseph Stone Cutler, Roland Rogers Cutler Jr., and Roland Rogers Cutler Sr. Their middle names reveal connections to other longtime residents of the community, such as Goodnow, Loring, Rogers, and Stone. The Cutlers live on Landham Road.

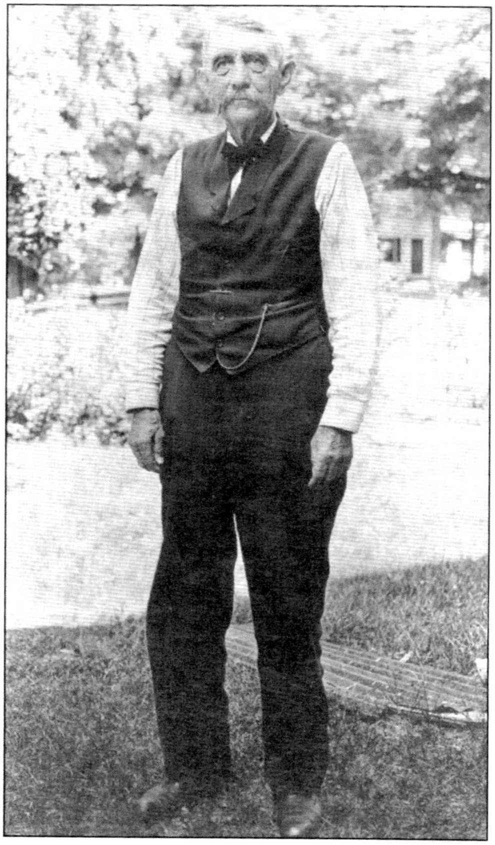

John H. Eaton was born on November 17, 1838, in Sudbury. He lived here his whole life and worked as a carpenter, never marrying. In 1910, he was living with his sister Sarah Butterfield and was also the brother of Edward and Newell Eaton. The Eaton family still lives in Sudbury today.

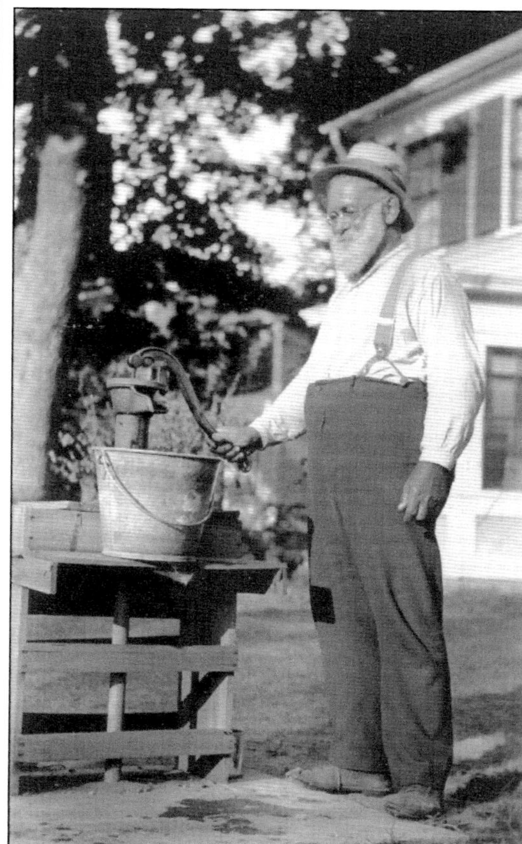

Frank H. Hadley fills up his pail at his pump in the town center around 1920. Hadley used to offer passing residents a cool drink from his well. The pump was renovated by the current owner. The superbly restored and maintained house is located at 308 Concord Road in the Sudbury Center Historic District.

Herbert Frost, dressed in his good straw hat and vest, carries his watering can on April 27, 1915, at his home at 47 Concord Road, which is known as the Richard Rush Horr House. The monument in the background was perhaps in the nearby Wadsworth Cemetery, where he could have been watering flowers.

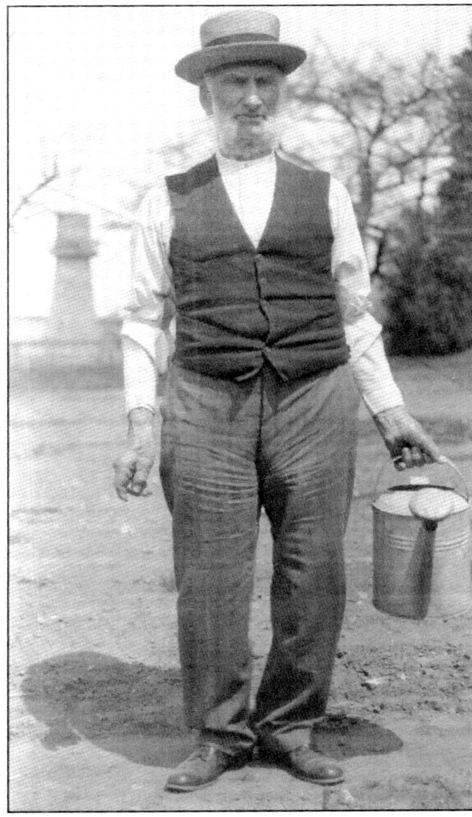

The Goodnow family proudly poses in front of their farm at 163 Landham Road, which was built from 1884 to 1886. The photograph was taken in 1888, showing the barn, which was constructed before the house, and the house, when it was a simpler Queen Anne style. Windmills were a common sight in that day. They used the wind to pump up water from a well to a holding tank in the attic of the house or barn, sometimes both, after which gravity would deliver it to indoor plumbing or to watering troughs for the animals.

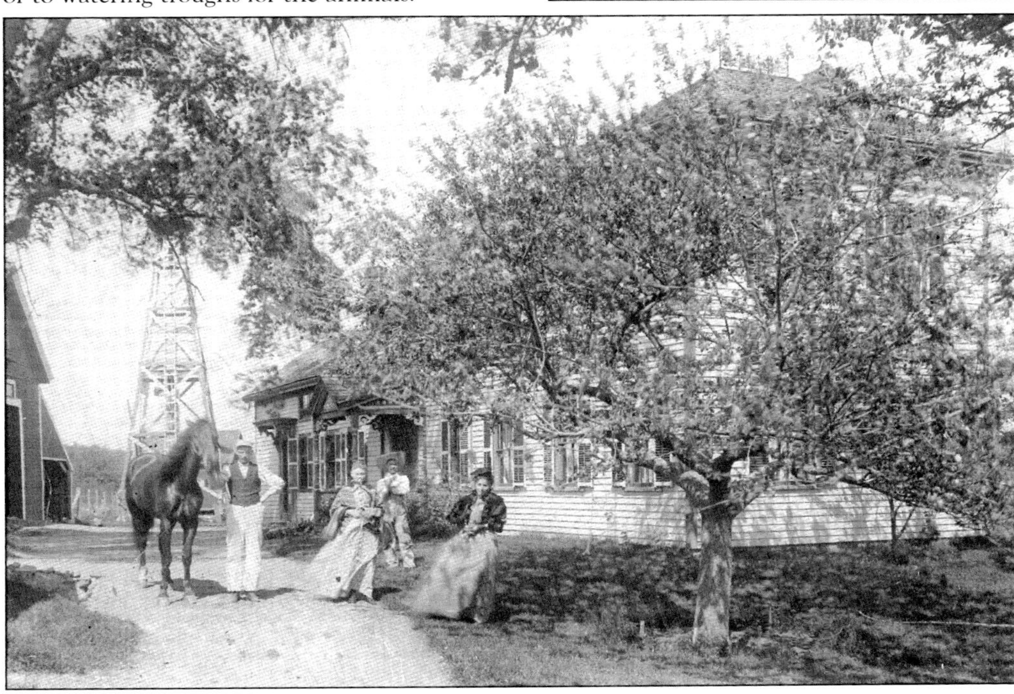

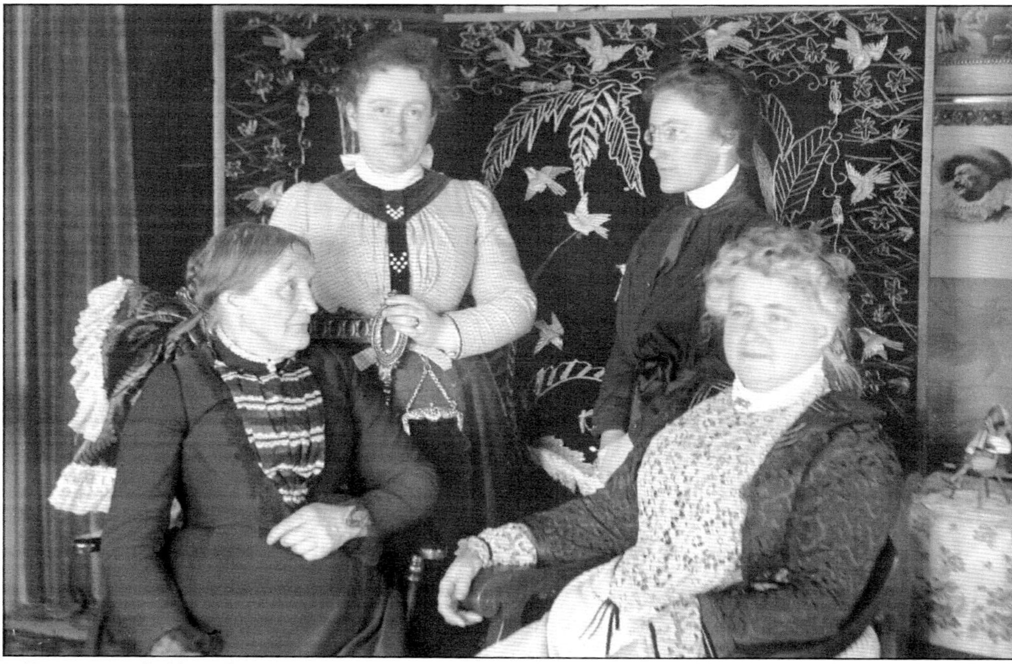

Lillian Hunt (left) and Hattie Goodnow (third from the left) pose above with two other unidentified Hunt relatives. Goodnow was a photographer who took many photographs of her family and the Sudbury area in all kinds of weather. When the Griswolds purchased her house at 293 Concord Road, they gave the historical society Goodnow's camera and glass-plate negative slides.

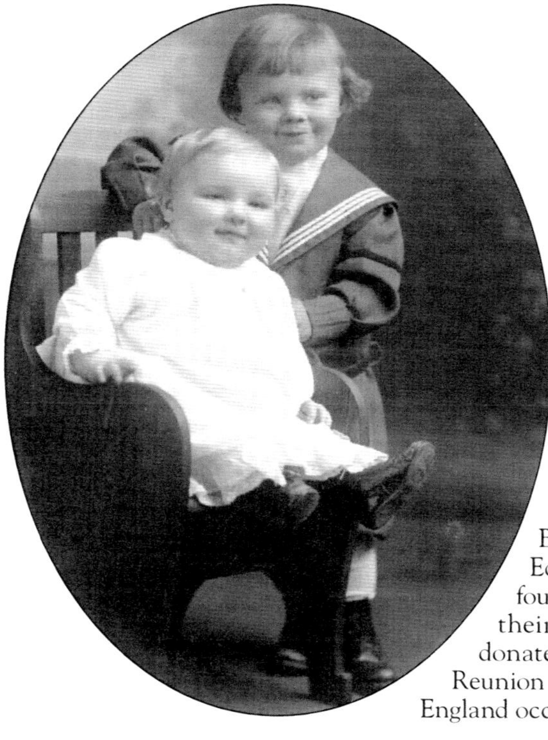

Baby Edgar Goodnow and three-year-old Edward Cookson smile for the camera. Another founding family of Sudbury, the Goodnows left their mark on Sudbury when John Goodnow donated a public library in 1863. The Goodnow Reunion Group is very active and even goes back to England occasionally on tours.

Edgar W. Goodnow was dressed for a formal occasion, complete with a waxed handlebar moustache. His son Edgar W. Goodnow Jr. lived at 10 Hudson Road in the 1802 Joel Moore House until he passed away recently.

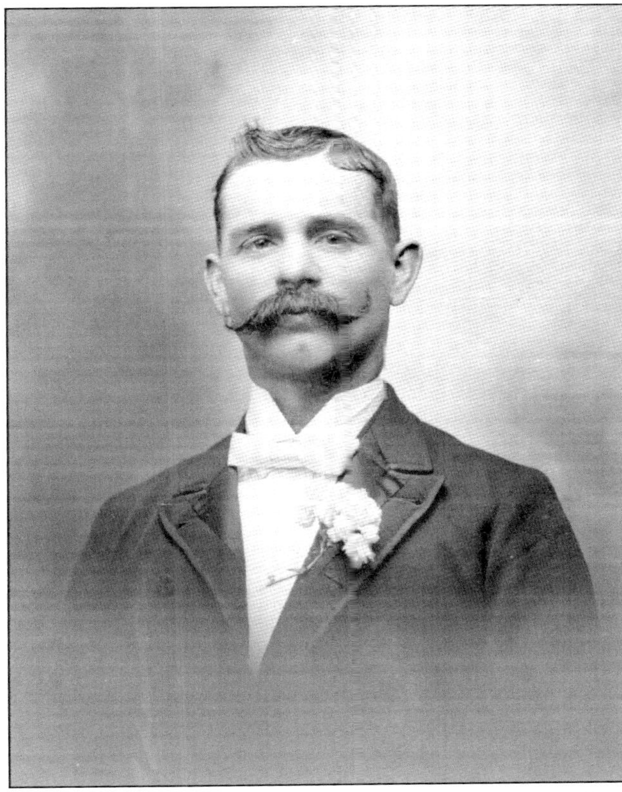

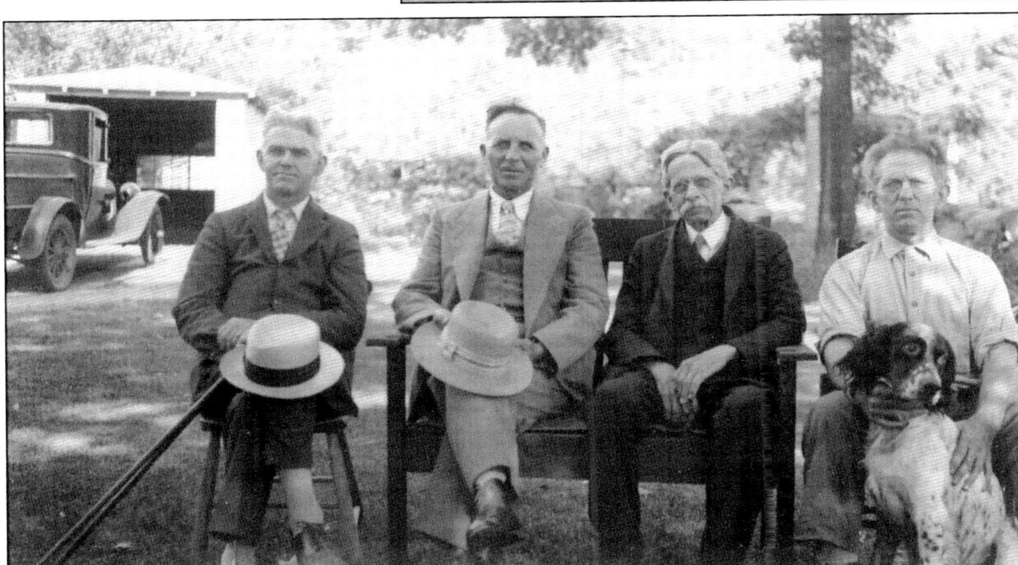

On a hot summer day, Ruth Goulding took this photograph of, from left to right, her brother-in-law Bill Goulding, Frank Taylor, George W. Hunt, and Leonard Goulding, with his Springer Spaniel. The Gouldings ran a very successful antique business at 88 Concord Road, and Henry Ford was a good customer. Leonard Goulding used to strip the antique finish off his pieces in the yard behind the house, which explains why nothing grows there.

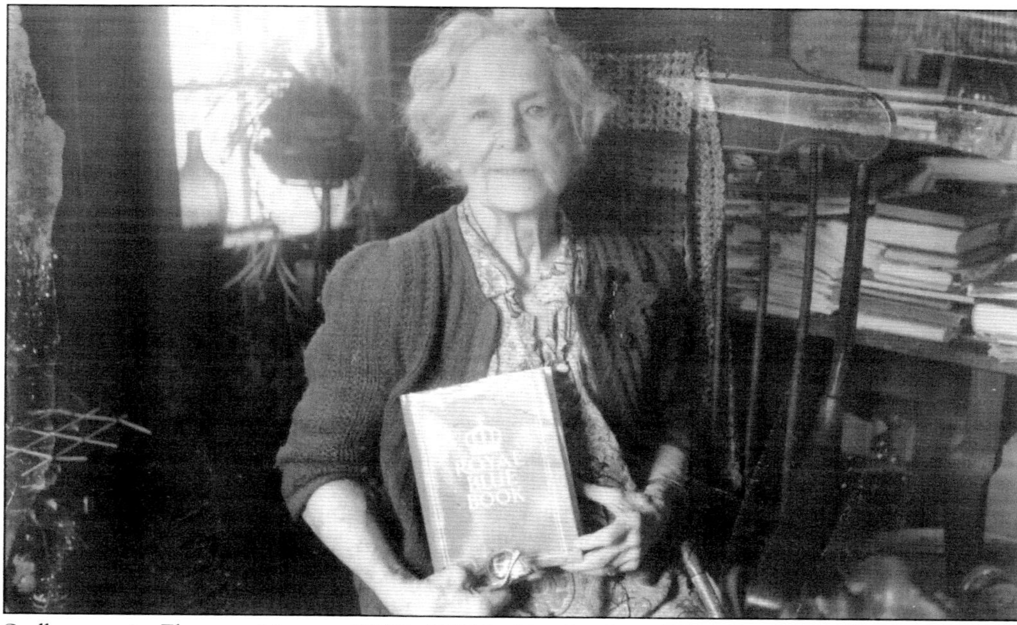

Sudbury artist Florence Hosmer (1880–1978) holds a book with her family listed in it. She was a professional portrait artist of prominent people and painted over 500 known works. She studied at Massachusetts Normal Art School and the Boston Museum School as well as with other notable painters. She exhibited at the Copley Society of Art and the Boston Art Club. A recent book, *My Dear Girl*, was written about her life and her art by Sudbury author Helen Marie Casey.

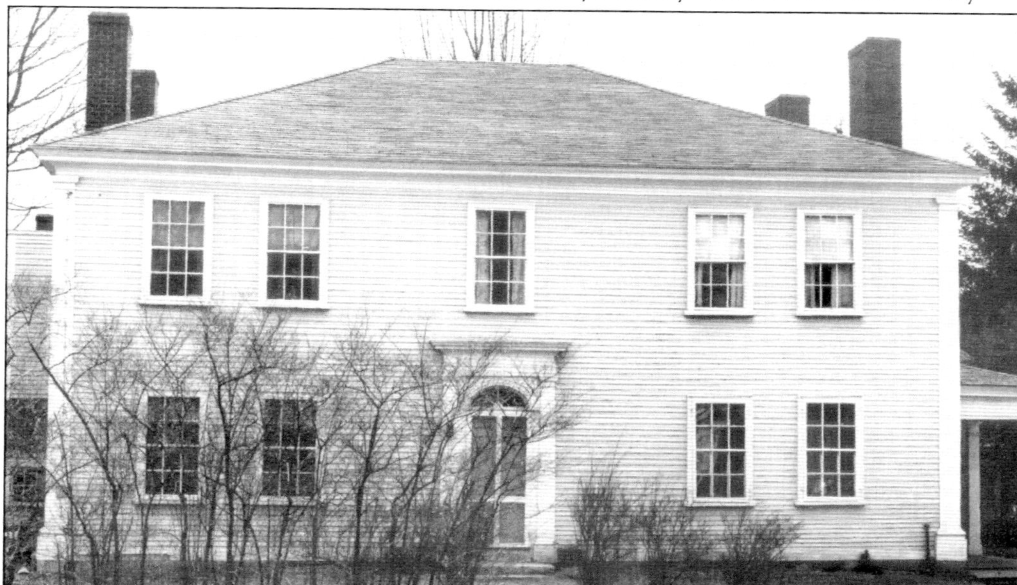

Hosmer House is located at 299 Old Sudbury Road at the corner of Concord Road. It was originally built in 1793 by Elisha Wheeler and was bought in 1897 by Edwin Hosmer. Hosmer's daughter Florence a noted artist in her time, deeded the house to the town in memory of her father and her brother in 1959, with the provision that she could live there and the town would take care of her until her death.

Sudbury resident William Haynes, seen here on April 25, 1901, worked as an officer at the Charlestown prison. He was later presented with a special song called "Oh Charlestown, Oh Charlestown" by its lyrical composer E.M. Dana and musical composer Leroy J. Pierce. It was sung at a minstrel show on February 24 and 25, 1919.

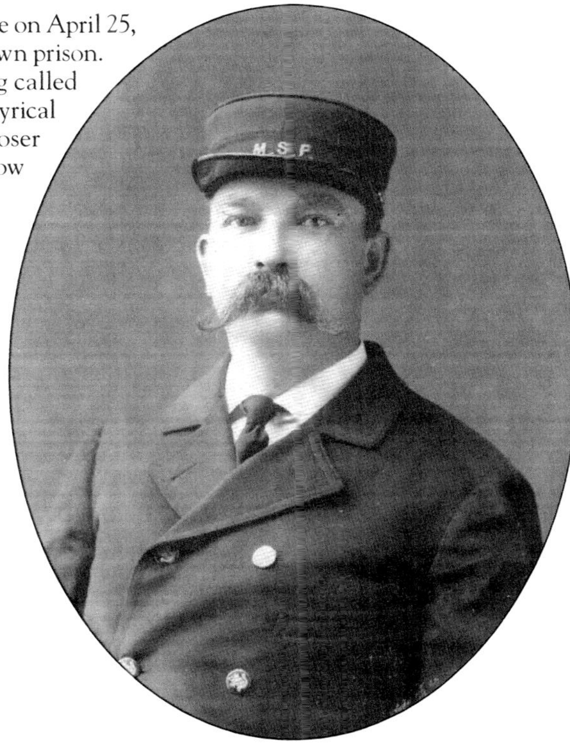


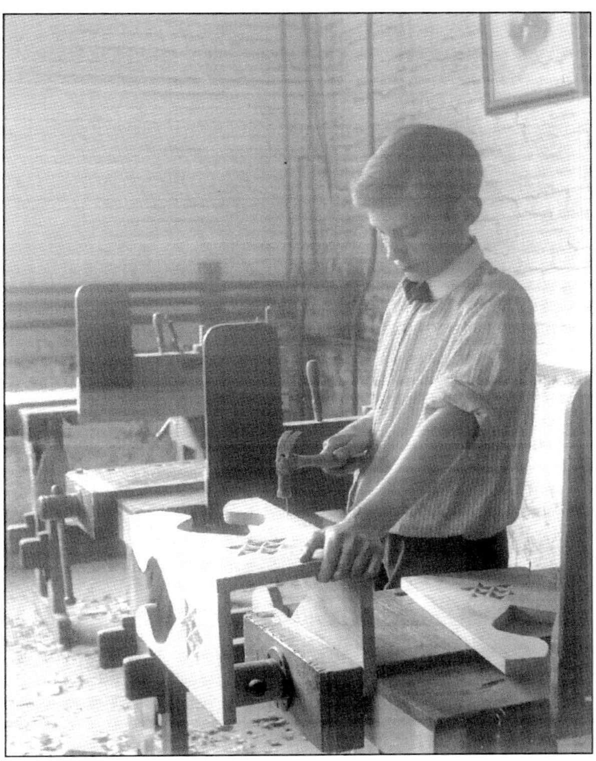

A young Harry Hunt finishes up a woodworking project in the new woodworking shop in the basement of the new high school, which now houses town offices and is called the Flynn or White Building. He was a member of one of Sudbury's early families, and his aunt Hattie Goodnow took this photograph of him.

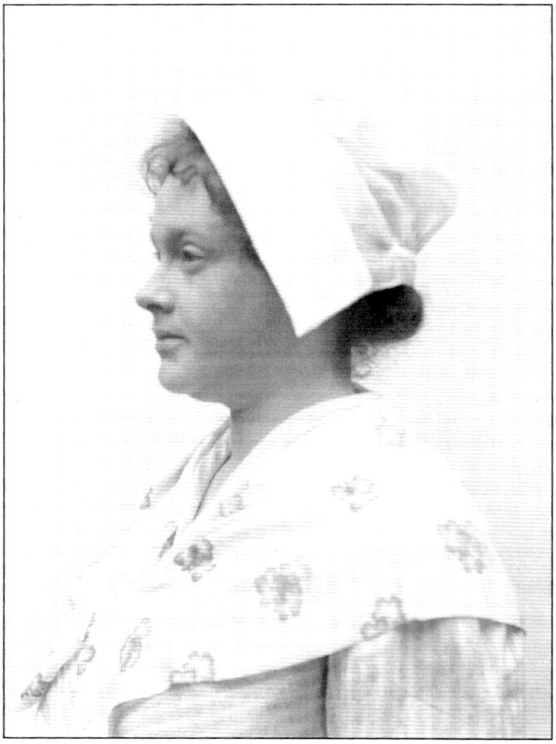

Lillian Goodnow Hunt, the mother of Harry Hunt, posed in costume to emulate a classic painting for her sister Hattie Goodnow. (Photograph by Hattie Goodnow.)

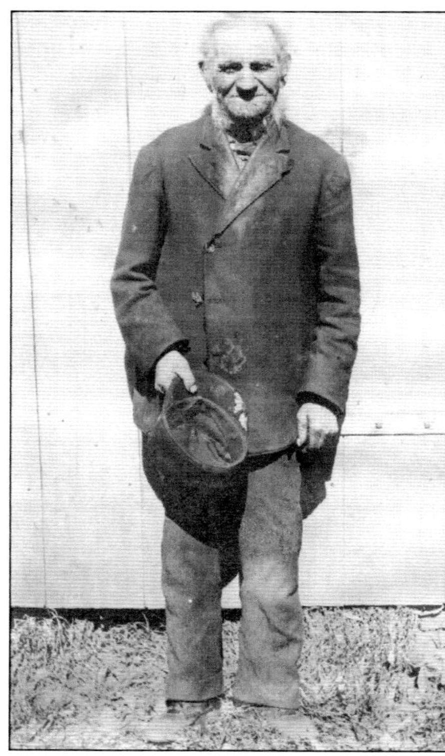

Bill Hanley lived in the King Philip neighborhood in 1917 and did odd jobs. He was willing to work hard, and as these were his normal work clothes, his wife was not shy about asking him to shovel coal or whatever was needed, as he could not get any dirtier. (Photography courtesy of Harriet Richardson.)

Leona Johnson stands by a fireplace in her home at 301 Old Lancaster Road. Note the tags on the two jugs—she marked everything in her house as to where it would go when she passed away. As the town archivist, she not only saved everything but also did so in an orderly way. One could ask her to find anything and off she would go to one of her antique trunks and pull it out. She kept scrapbooks of different pieces of Sudbury history, which are now at the Goodnow Library and at the town clerk's office.

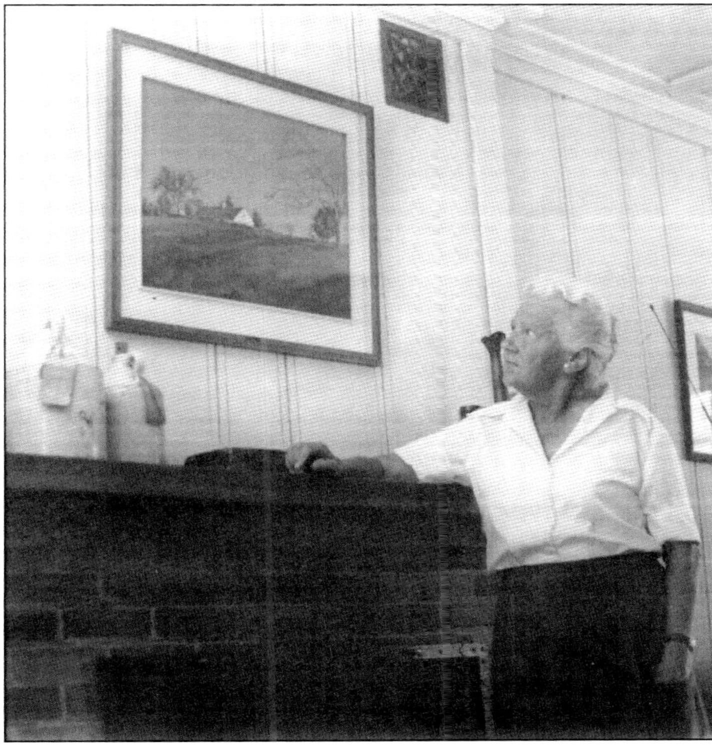

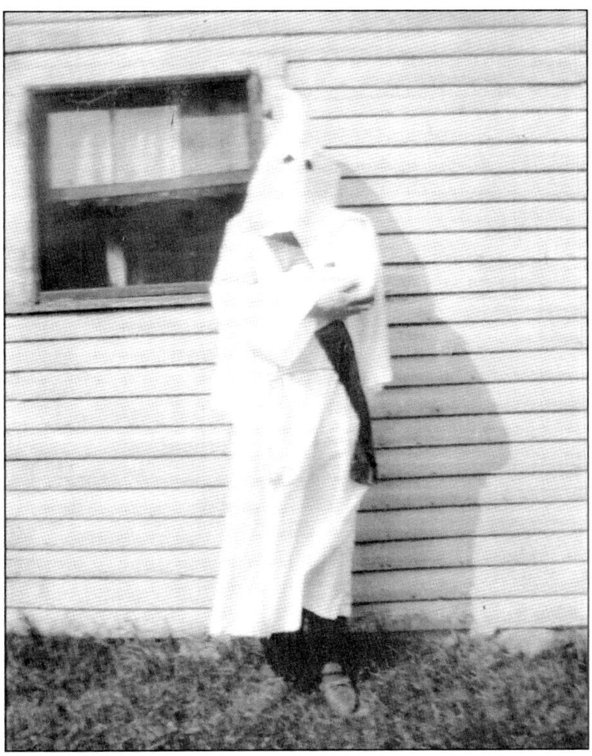

This Klansman is one of the men in the Oliver family, either Reginald, Basil, or grandfather Horace. The photograph was taken at 623 Peakham Road and donated by Linda L. Muri. The KKK had made inroads in Sudbury in the early 1920s due to unrest about the separation of church and state, Prohibition, and the influx of new ethnic groups. It culminated on August 9, 1925, with more than 150 men assembled at the Libbey Farm off Landham Road. After the armed men rioted, the state police had to be called in. In all, 75 men were arrested and 24 were tried. The judge warned them that they had the right to assemble but not to bear arms, and he essentially dropped the case.

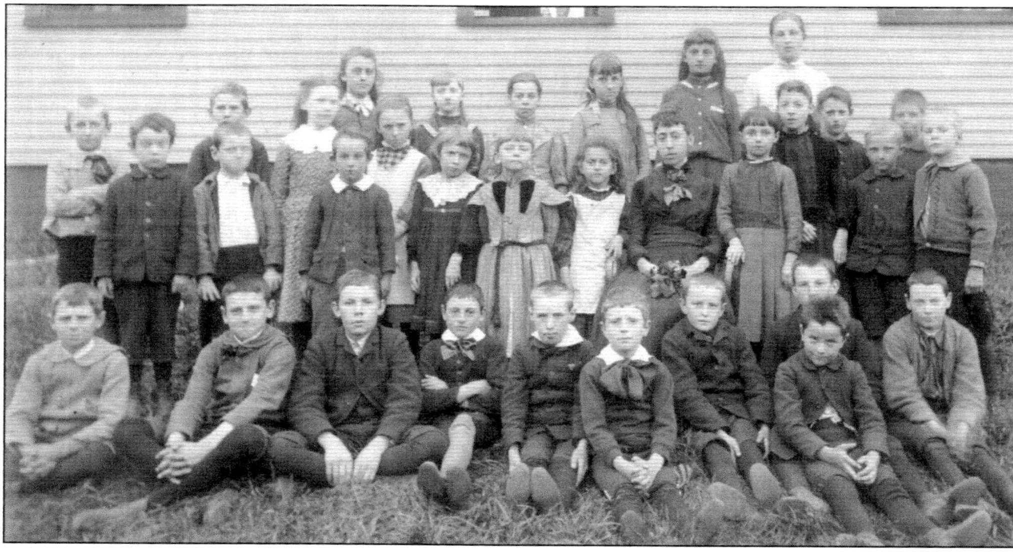

An 1893 Wadsworth School class poses in front of the school, which was on the site of current police station at 415 Boston Post Road. The towns did not hire married schoolteachers until after World War II. These two teachers shown are Marion Eaton (second row, seated) and Jennie Hunt (rear). The teachers' common complaint back then regarded the animal odor of the students in close quarters.

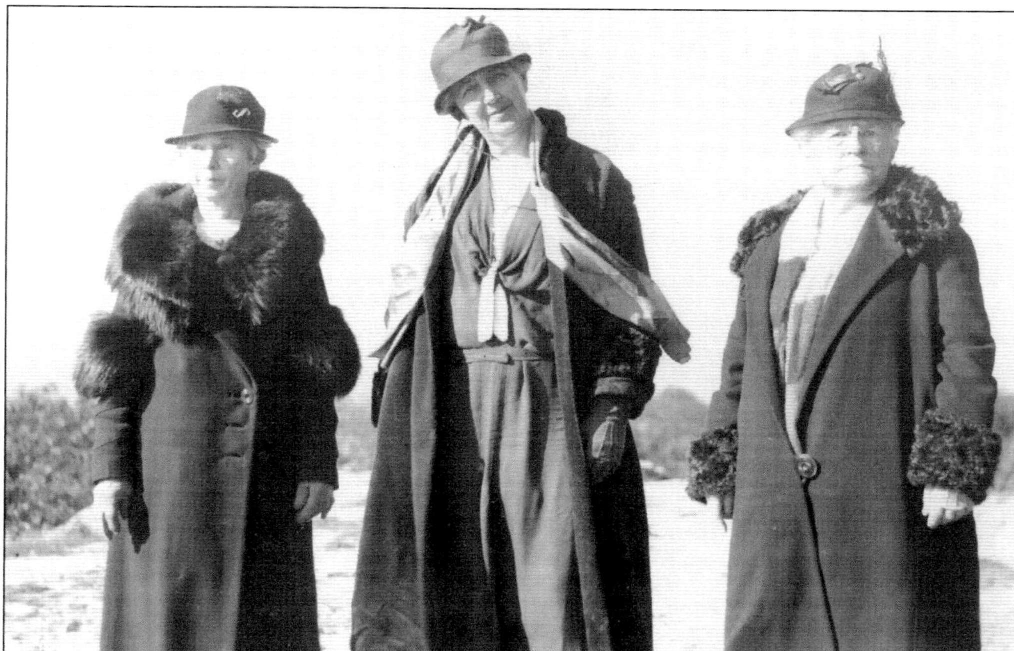

These lovely ladies in their Sunday best in 1919 were, from left to right, Ella Oviatt, Lottie Smith, and Harriet Goodnow after they attended a service at Memorial Congregational Church. Oviatt was married to Dr. George A. Oviatt, and they lived at 394 Boston Post Road. Smith was the aunt of Curt Garfield, who was a published author on birds and horticulture and the town historian and lived at 106 Woodside Road. Harriet Goodnow lived at 4 King Philip Road.

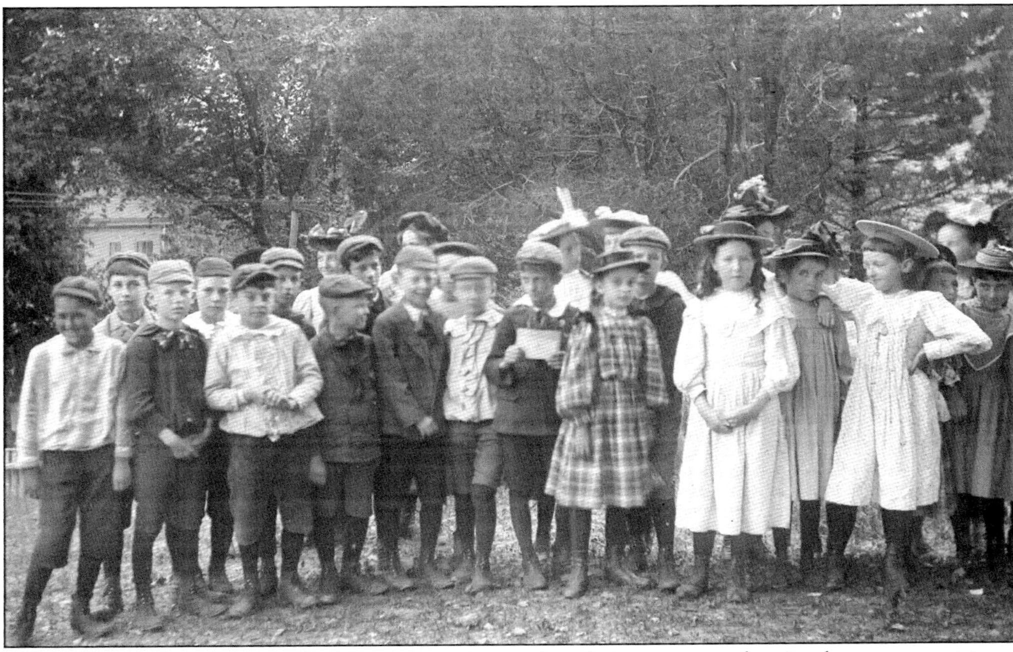

When Hattie Goodnow took this picture, she made a living as a teacher in the communities of Sudbury, Weymouth, and Newton, seen here in 1902. Either this was a special dress-up day or Newton folks dressed their children very well.

Harry Rice stands in the doorway of Broadmeadow Stable, which was once at 130 Water Row near Plympton Road. He is guarding two family muskets. The one on the left was made by H. Sleur. It is called a fowler and was carried to Concord by Ezekiel Rice on April 19, 1775. The second one was made by Thomas Holbrook. Through the generosity of an SHS member, the Rice musket was donated and is on exhibit at the National Heritage Museum in Lexington.

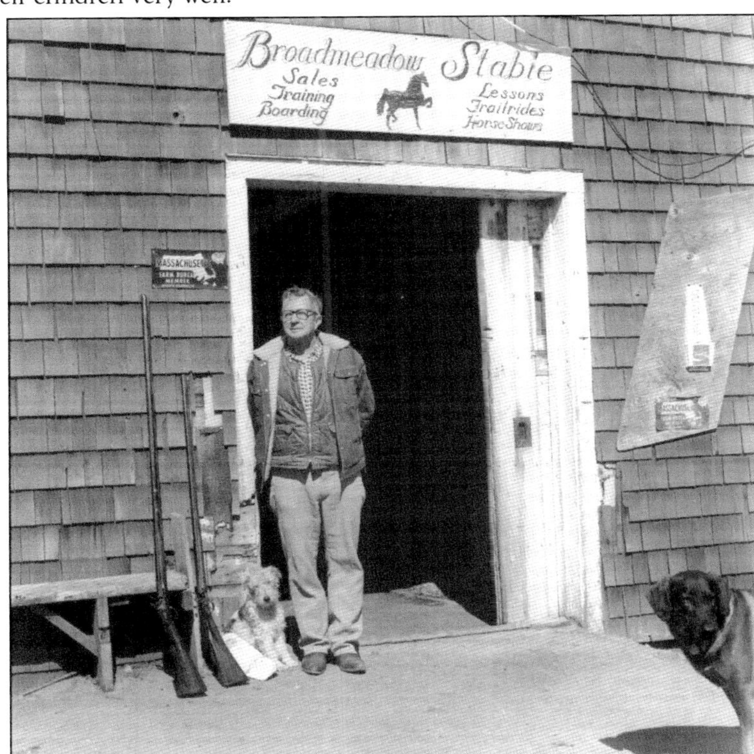

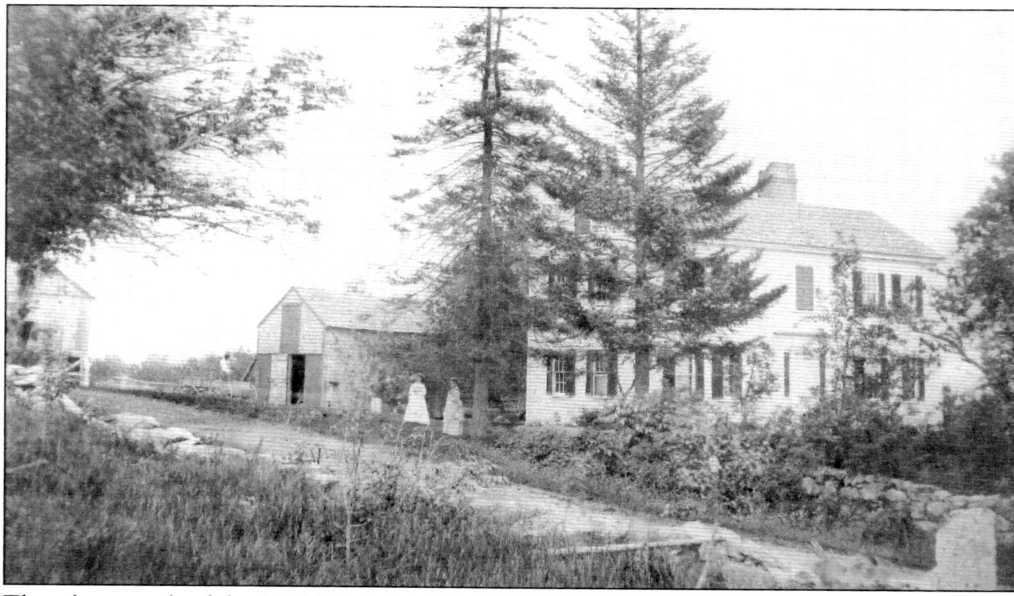

This photograph of the 1787 Rice-Haynes-Smith homestead at 130 Water Row was taken about 1870. The house was carefully torn down in 1981 by Charles and Ann Orr and put in storage until it was lovingly rebuilt at 137 Plympton Road. Standing in the photograph are two members of the Smith family and their farmhand. Around 1810, it was sold to Benjamin Smith, whose daughter married into the Rice family. Three generations later, Harry Rice, the last family member to live there, was born.

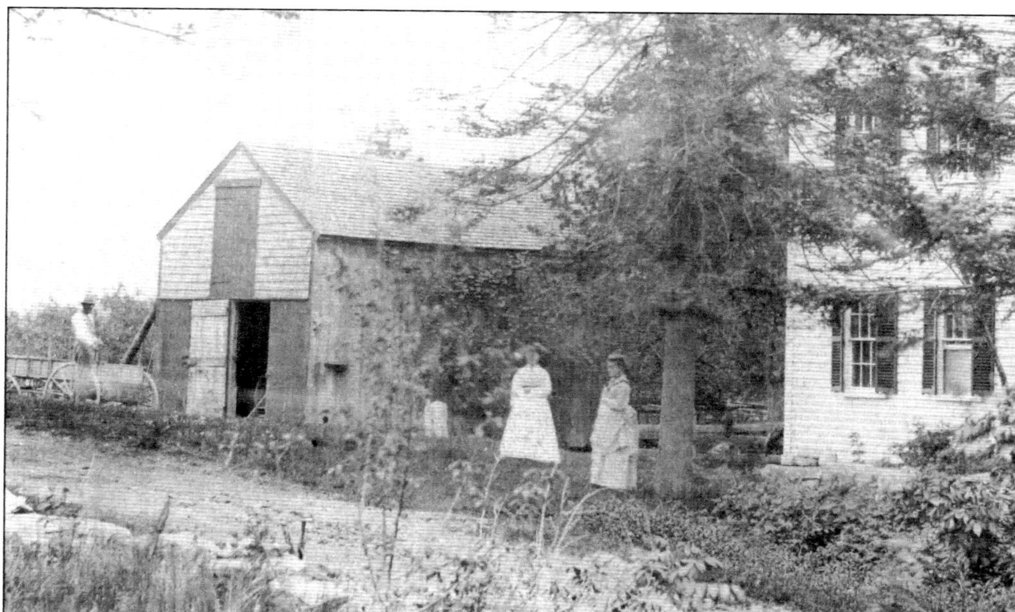

This close-up photograph shows the Rice-Haynes-Smith homestead in the 1870s. The Smith ladies are wearing their Sunday best, complete with hoop skirts and bustles, which were very stylish at the time. The hired hand in the background kept the farm running. The Rice family has been in Sudbury since the 1600s.

Artist and schoolteacher Gertrude "Lizzie" Rice relaxes outdoors. She was related to one of the founding families of Sudbury and lived from 1877 to 1960. She enjoyed sketching wildflowers throughout the area. Between 1915 and 1920, she sketched more than 180 flowers with colored pencils in a notebook, which is in the SHS collection. She lived at 328 Goodman's Hill Road, which was later owned by the famed calligrapher and illuminator E. Helene Sherman.

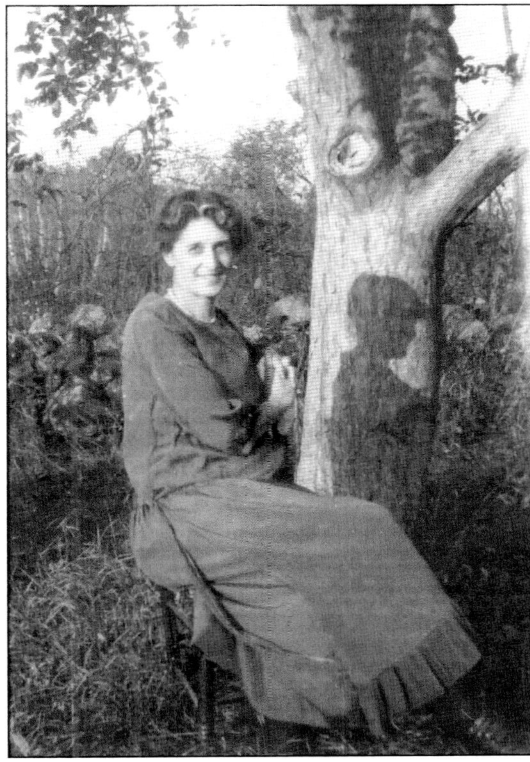

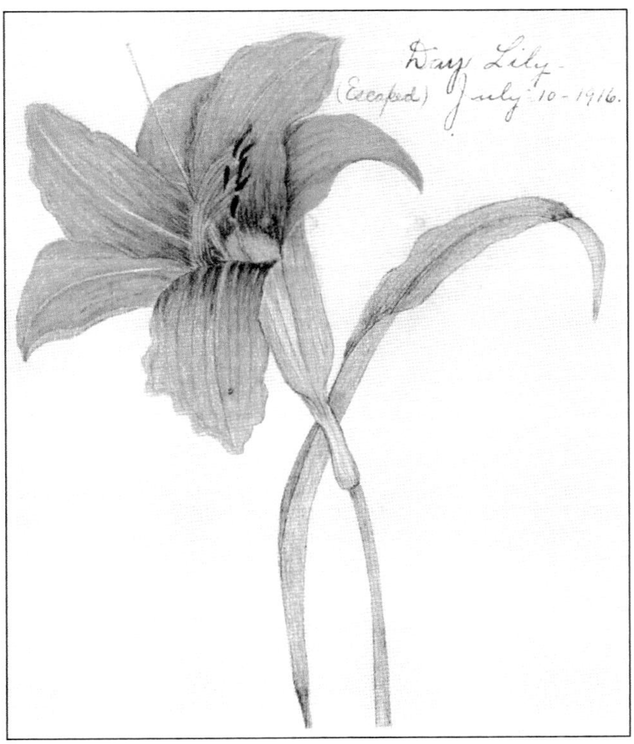


This daylily drawing was done by Gertrude Rice in 1916. Rice enjoyed roaming around Sudbury in her buggy drawn by her faithful horse, Old Guy, or on her bike, to different fields, brooks, woods, and swamps to capture wildflowers with colored pencils. She had no training, but her flowers speak volumes with their careful attention to detail. The Sudbury Historical Society sells full-color note cards of three of her images.

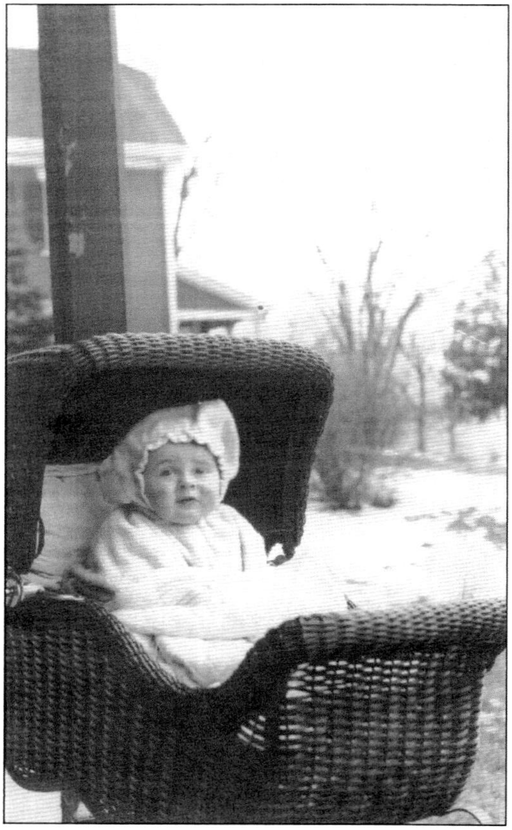

Phil Richardson rides in his wicker baby carriage in 915. A member of another founding Sudbury family, young Phil was doted on and is seen in several period pictures from when he was a baby to when he joined the Coast Guard in World War II. The Richardson homes are in South Sudbury on King Philip Road.

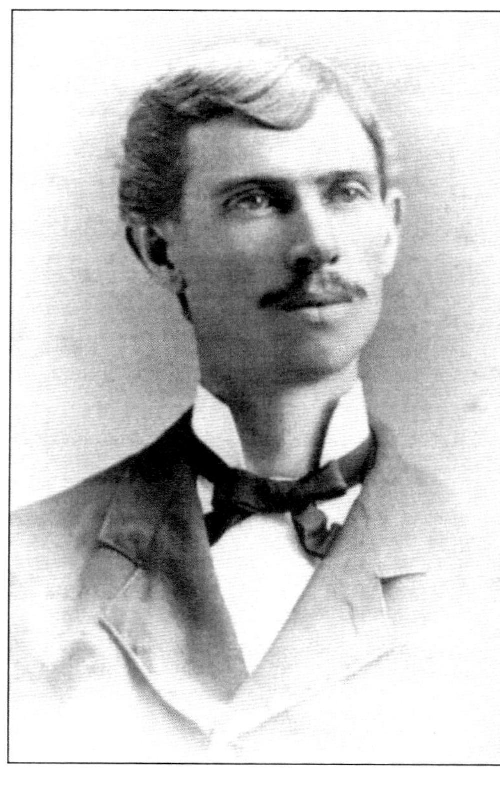

This is a portrait of Henry Smith, a commercial flower grower around 1900 who also packaged seeds. He sold the seeds through his own catalog and was innovative in his growing of popular flowers, collecting the seeds, and packaging them attractively. Henry developed the very popular present-day Cosmos flower from a wild, late-blooming Cosmos. Smith was the grandfather of the former town historian, Curt Garfield, and lived at 106 Woodside Road and 94 Woodside Road.

E. Helene Sherman was a remarkable artist who was born in Wayland in September 1908. Her family had a long artistic background and her first teacher was her maternal grandfather, noted French painter Edmond Prang, the cofounder of the Prang Company, well-known color printmakers around 1900. She learned her lettering in art school and taught herself illumination. She studied at the Pierpont Morgan Library in New York City, at the Boston Public Library,at the Huntington Library in California, in Paris, and in the Archives of the Vatican in Rome. Her illuminated paintings, miniature books, and bas-relief art are exhibited in several locations all over the world, including the National Archives.

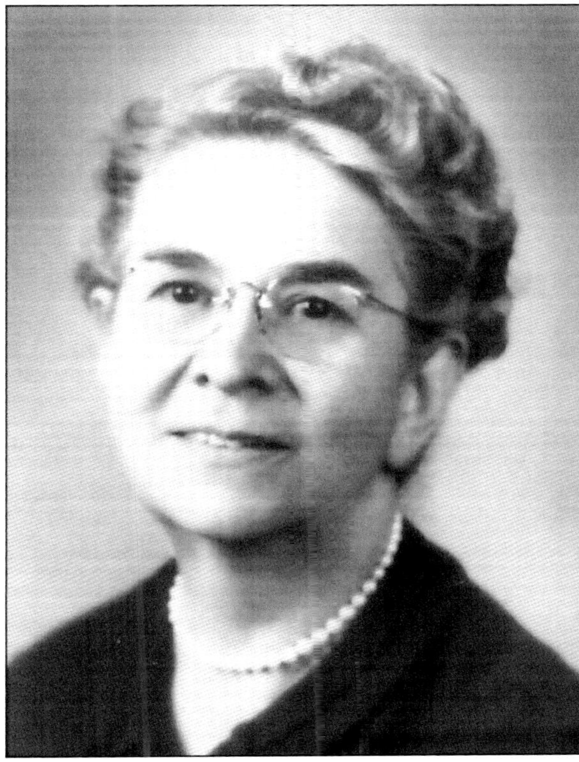

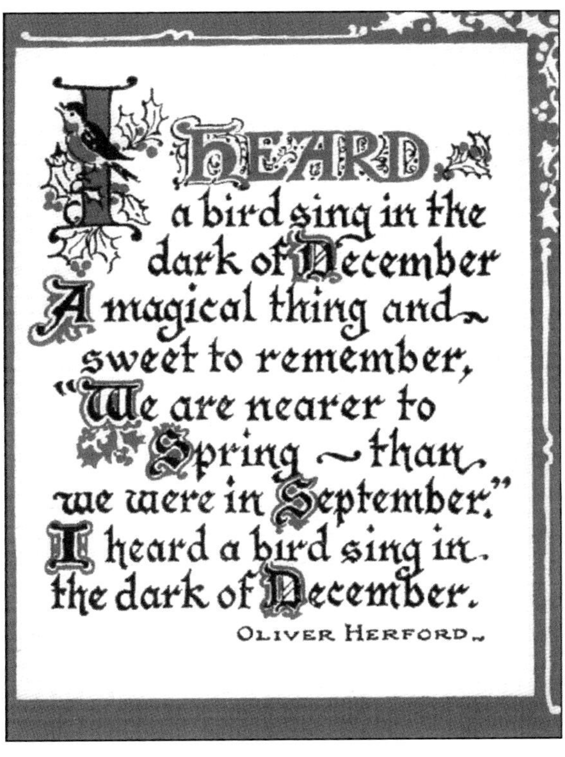


This is an example of illumination by E. Helene Sherman, a nationally known calligrapher and manuscript illuminator as well as watercolorist. Illumination is an ancient profession dating from the first century AD. Most of the completed works were done by cloistered monks on religious texts. Later, in the 12th century, the "first initial" decoration was developed, which included raised and burnished gold and detailed miniatures within the letter itself. The SHS has a collection of her works.

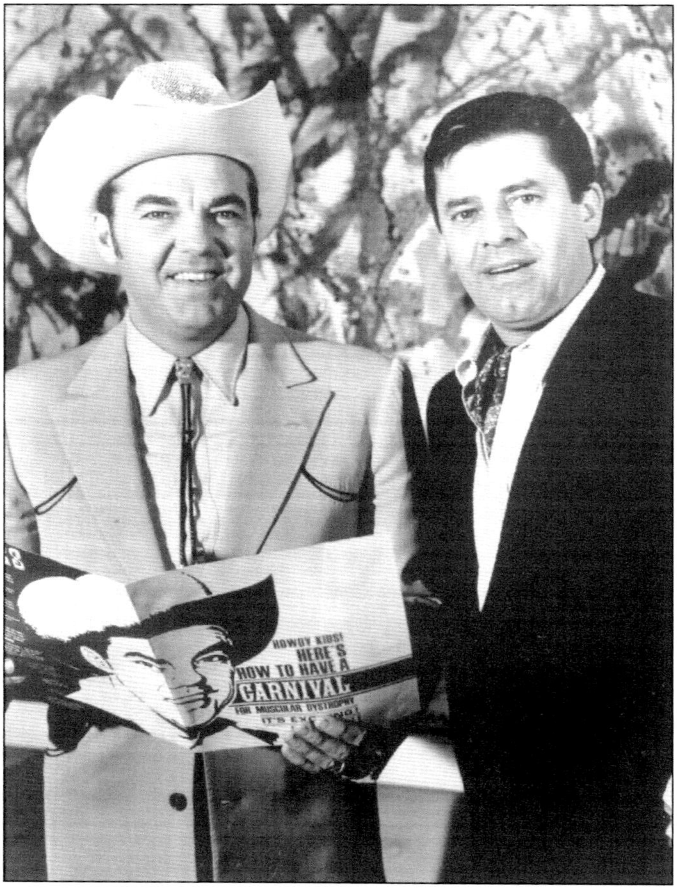


Rex Trailer (left), a Sudbury resident and local celebrity, is seen here with Jerry Lewis raising funds for the Muscular Dystrophy Association. Trailer was a real cowboy and hosted a Boston and Baltimore television show called *Boomtown* from 1956 to 1974. In 2012, as "the cowboy with a conscience," Trailer was named the Official Cowboy of Massachusetts. This photograph was taken for WBZ-TV on May 15, 1969.

Shown below, from left to right, Sam Underwood, Percival "Dad" Jones, and John Goulding sit in front of the Goulding House at 88 Concord Road. The house was originally in Wayland and known as the Moses Brewer House, before it was moved to this spot and reassembled from 1919 to 1925. It was then opened as an antique shop by Leonard Goulding.

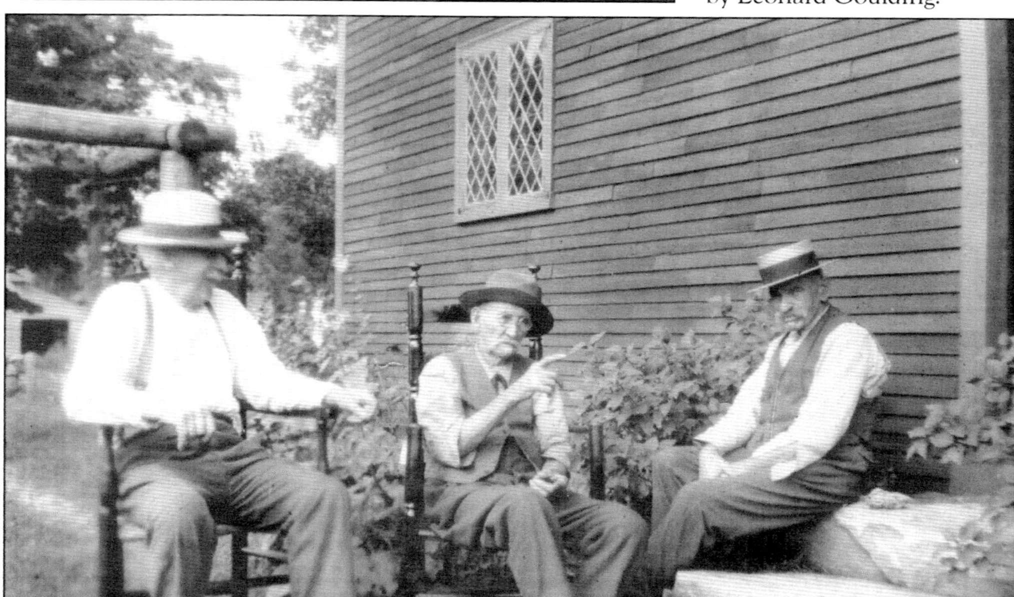

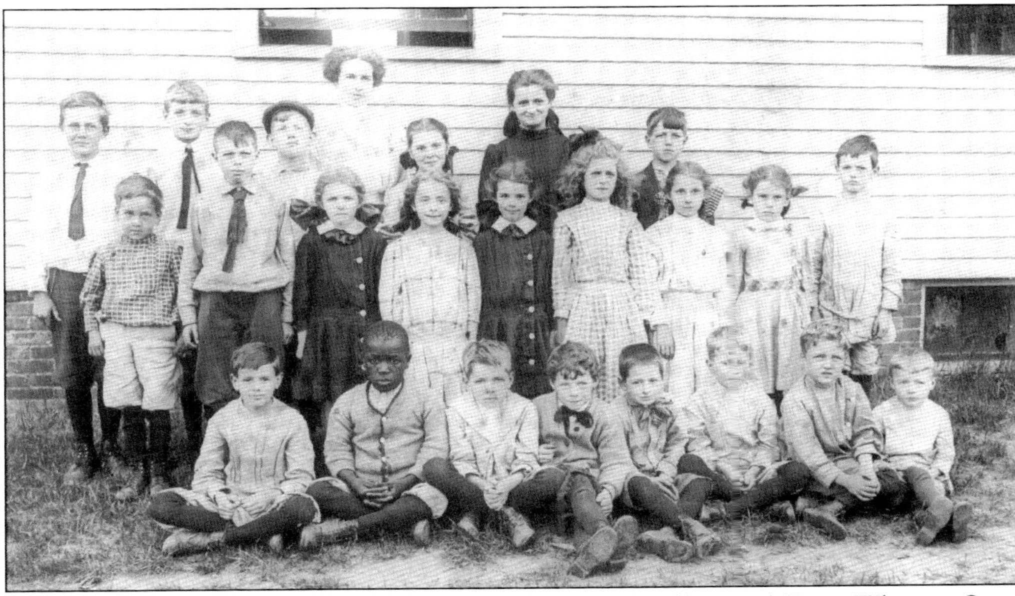

This Wadsworth Academy class included, from left to right, (first row) Dana Whiting, Oscar Morris, Alvin Noyes , Robert Taft, Frankie Adams, Maxwell Eaton, Edmond Garfield, Frank Taft, and Francis Kennedy; (second row) Fred Chamberlain, Ralph Wilson, Laurice Rogers, Margaret Taft, Erskin Rogers, Elizabeth Atkinson, Alberto Stone, Hope Whitney, and Elbridge Whitney; (third row) Fordis Garfield, Robert Atkinson, Clarence Chickering, teacher Loren P. Burke, Marie Fisher, Mary Adams, and Ralph Eaton. The school was located at 26 Concord Road before it burned in 1879. The Memorial Congregational Church occupies that site now.

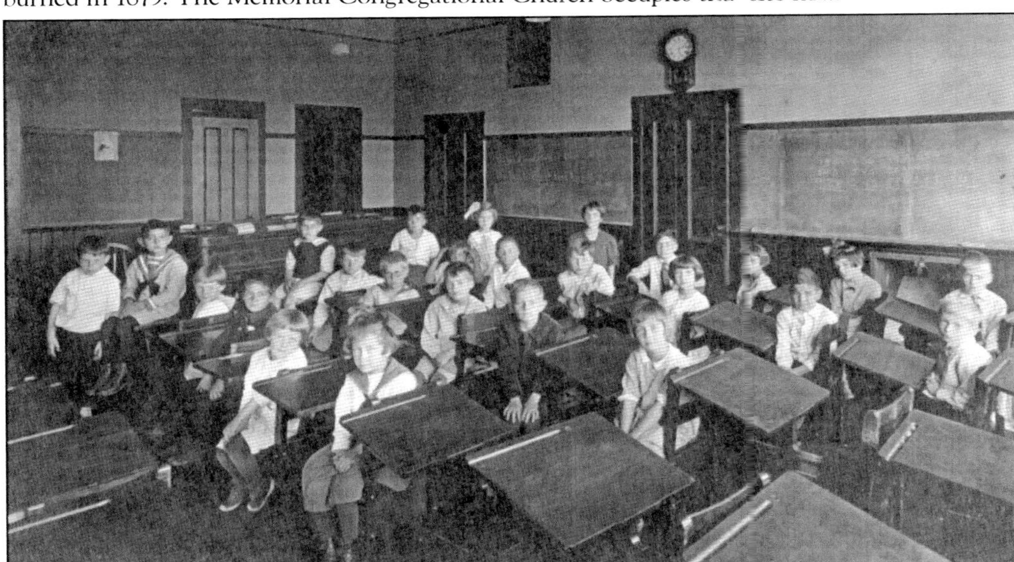

This 1930s classroom was at the South School, found at 29 Massasoit Avenue in South Sudbury. Included in this photograph, in no particular order, are Robert Walker, Phil Richardson, Phil and Annie Cutler, Erica Johnson, Sally Perry, Charlotte Whitworth, Dean Honks, and Earl Hoyle. The group may also have included Ruth Way, Patsy Mercury, George Duane, Ruth Stone, and Paul Carr. The SHS has one desk from this school in its collection.

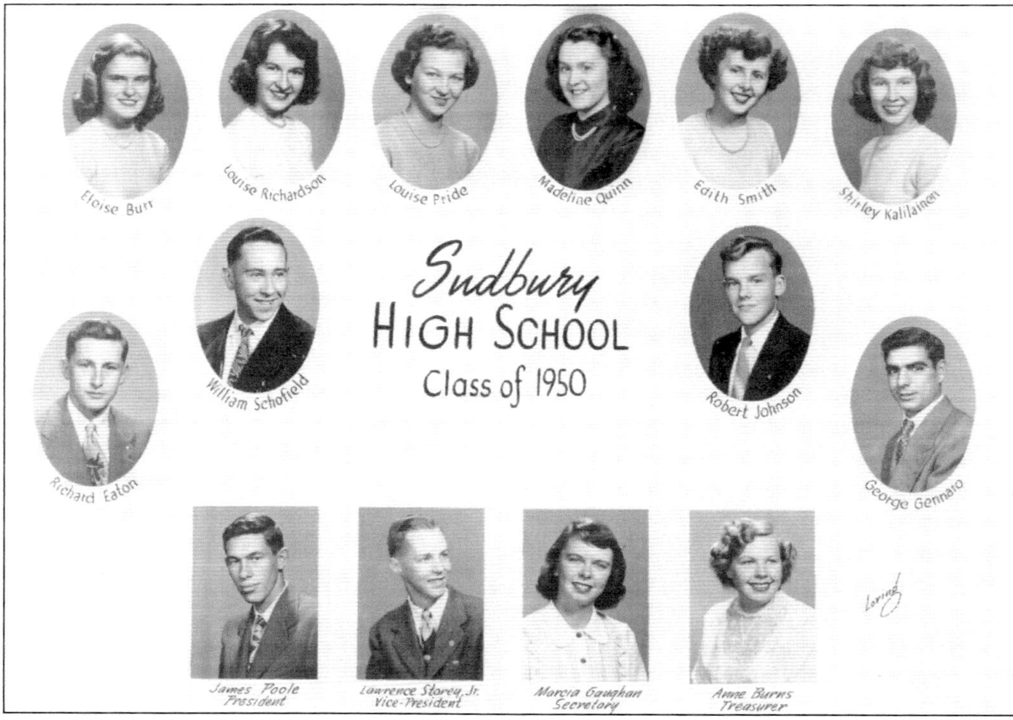


The Sudbury High School class of 1950 went to school in what is now the Flynn or White Building at 278 Old Sudbury Road. Only 14 students graduated that year, six years before the new Lincoln Sudbury Regional High School opened.

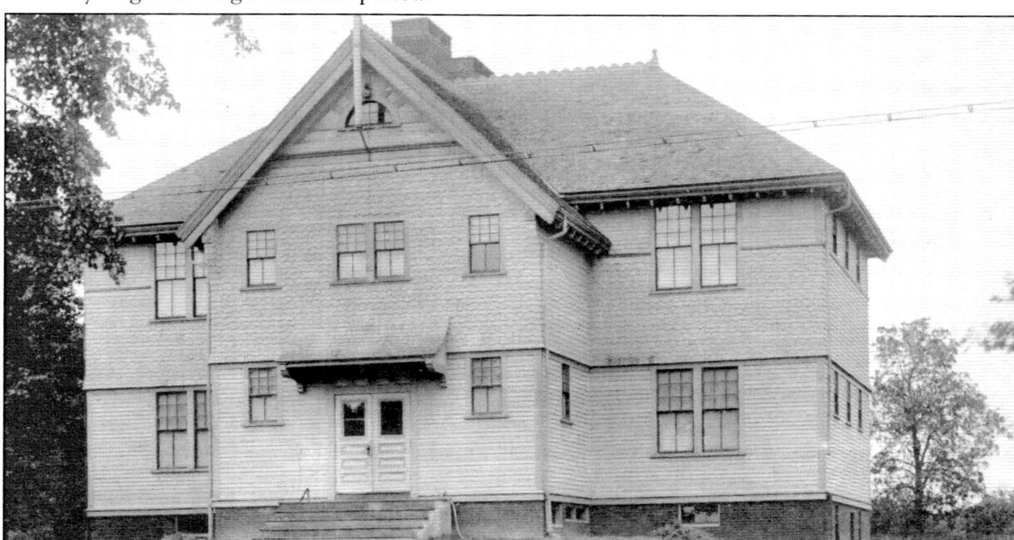

The Center School was built in 1891 as a combined grammar school and the area's first high school. The design was so well thought of that it was entered in a World's Fair competition. It served as the high school through the 1953–1954 school year. Currently housing town offices, it is now known as the Flynn Building, named for Alan Flynn, a beloved principal of the high school, or the White Building.

# *Three*
# CELEBRATIONS

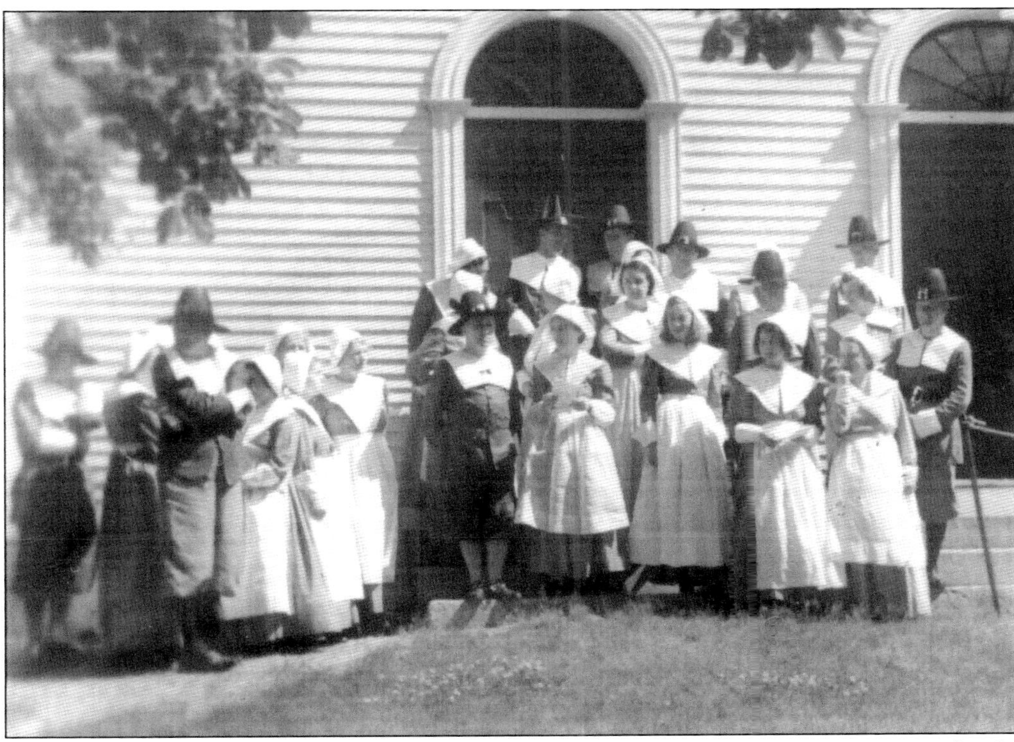

Sudbury residents are seen in front of the First Parish Church dressed up as Puritans for the celebration of the 300th anniversary of the town in 1939. There were recreations of church services, town meetings, singing, and historic speeches. Only 56 individuals and families began the settlement in 1639 on the other side of the Sudbury River in what is now Wayland.

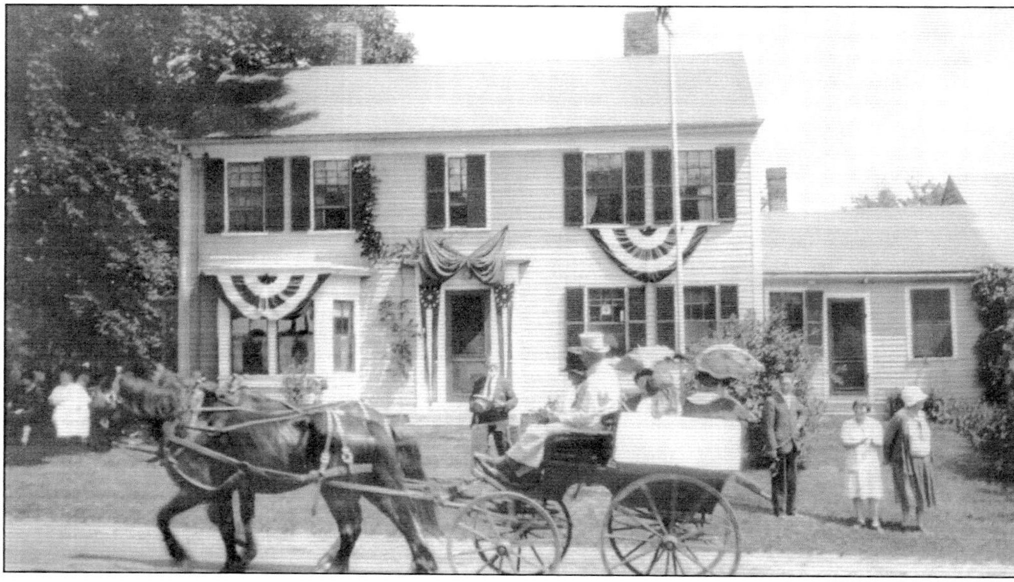

In 1939, Frank H. Hadley stood out in front of his house at 308 Concord Road and personally thanked every participant and vehicle in the 1930 Fourth of July Parade, offering them a drink of his cold, pure well water. Nowadays in the parade, by the time marchers get to this house, Boy Scouts and Girl Scouts have probably offered them bottled water, but it must have tasted great back then.

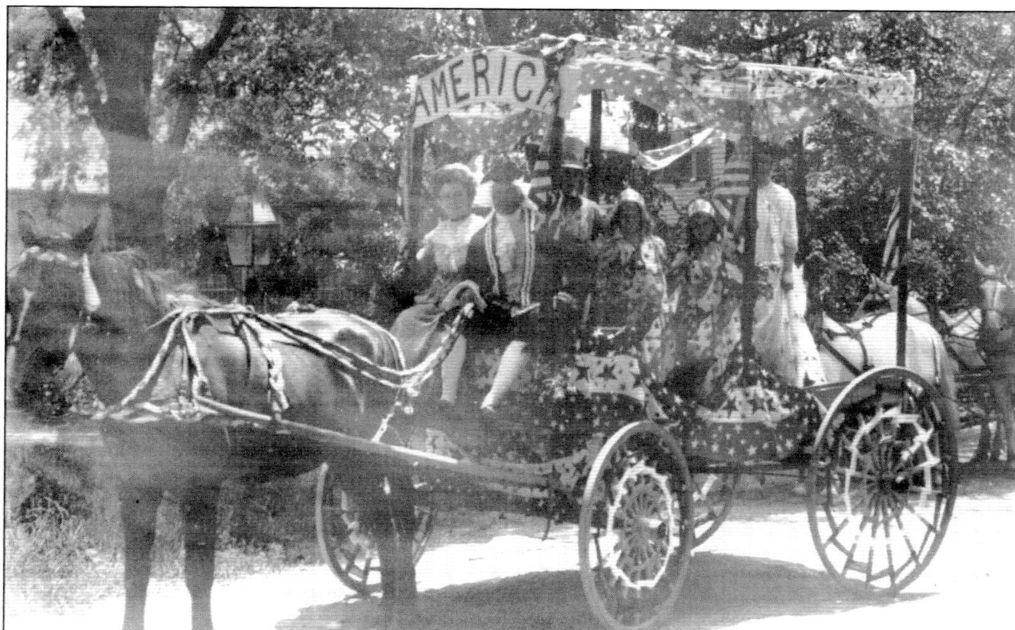


The family of Samuel B. Rogers turned their horse and buggy into a parade float in 1926 to celebrate the country's 150th birthday. Sudbury loves parades, and the Fourth of July Parade continues to be one of the biggest around, supported by the chamber of commerce. Unfortunately, fireworks are no longer set off behind the Flynn Building.

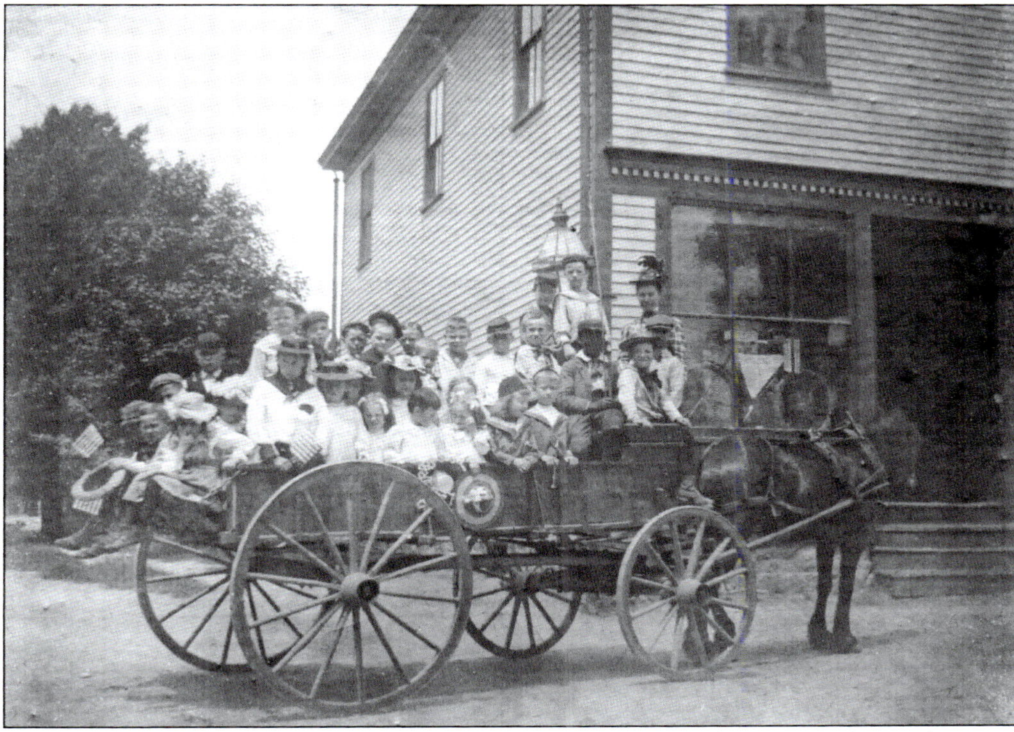

This wagon stops in front of Hunt's Store at 356 Boston Post Road in 1915 and is ready to join the Fourth of July Parade. The children are dressed in their Sunday best, and some of the boys are wearing Civil War caps. Sudbury had several African American families, beginning with the Morris family, who lived at 253 Concord Road. (Photograph by Harriet Richardson.)

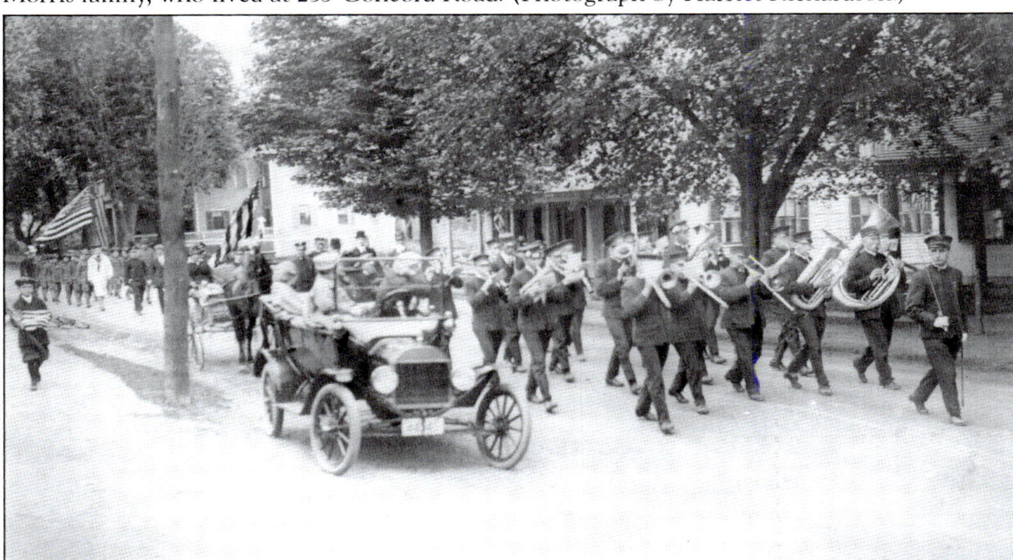

The town of Sudbury enjoys the parade in 1915. A Model T Ford waits to enter the parade, with a horse and buggy behind it. The parade used to start at Massasoit Avenue. Harriet Richardson took this photograph on the Boston Post Road opposite No. 353.

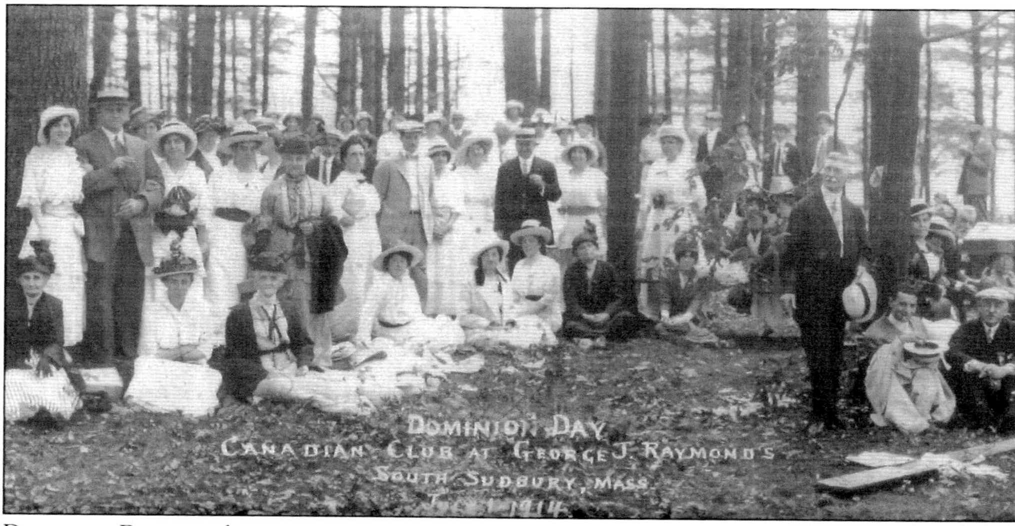

Dominion Day, seen here in 1914, was hosted by Raymond's Department Store owner Canadian-born George J. Raymond and his wife, Lydia, at the Raymonds' Sudbury estate at 80 Raymond Road. Raymond stands to the left with a young lady in white on either side of him. This holiday celebrates the confederation of Canada on July 1 and is now known as Canada Day.

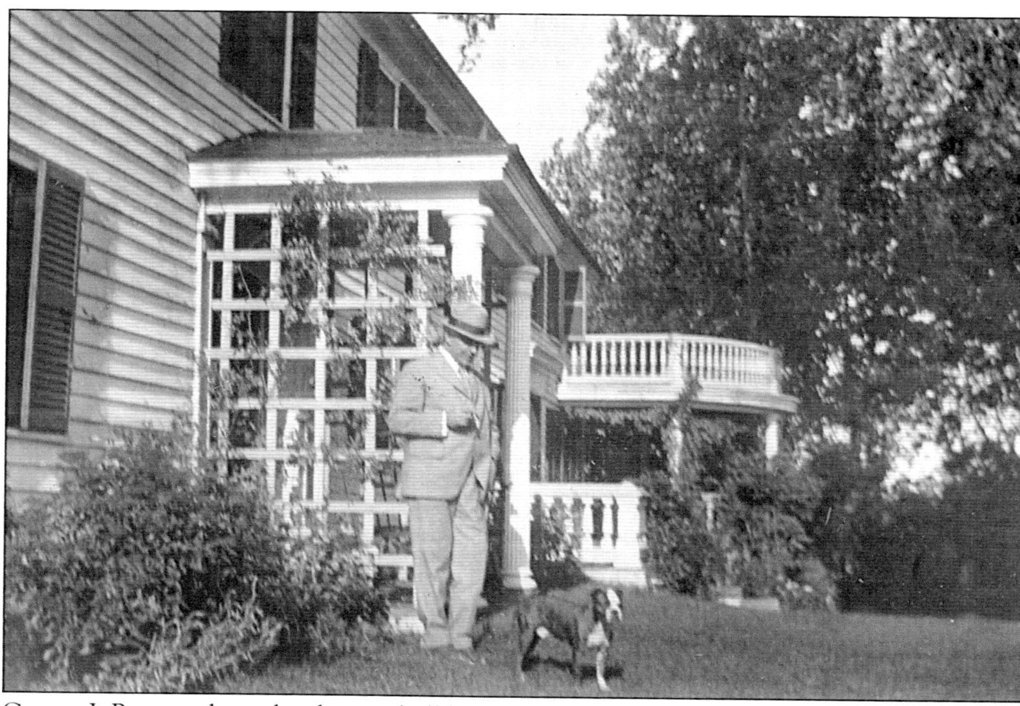
George J. Raymond watches his toy bulldog. The Raymonds moved into their 500-acre estate in 1903, making several additions to the house and adding extensive gardens over several cultivated acres.

Temperance Oakes Guptill poses in the entrance to the gazebo on the Raymond estate, with more than five acres of flowers, bushes, and trees cared for by five full-time gardeners and much part-time help on the 500-acre estate. Guptill was a strikingly handsome woman even into her late years. Participants in the Raymond parties were always encouraged to come in ethnic costumes like hers.

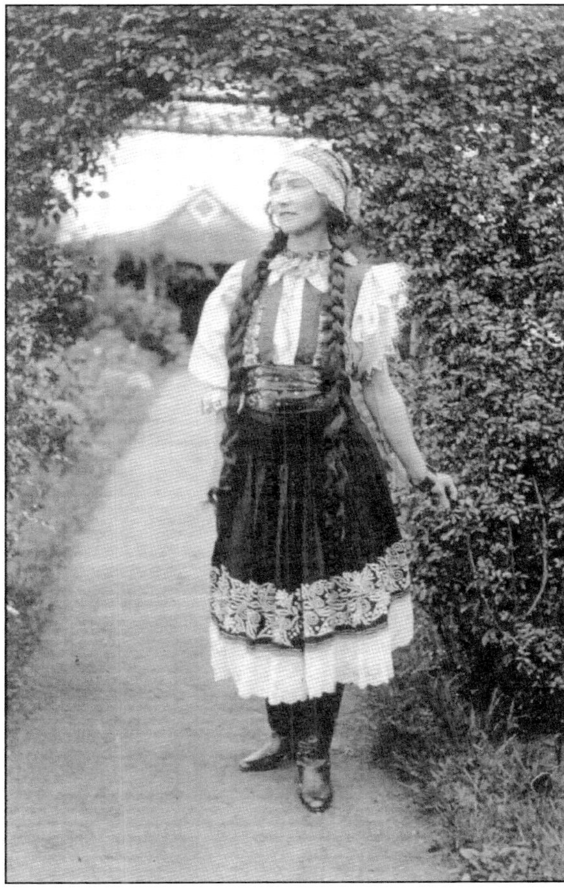

George Raymond was known to be theatrical, and skits were a part of the Dominion Day celebrations. Here, Frank I. Dorr holds the paddle as these rowdy partygoers attempt to row a canoe through the grass. Interestingly, the Algonquin name for the Sudbury River is Musketaquid, meaning "grassy ground." Dorr would later become the president of the Raymond's Department Store syndicate and have even bigger parties at his estate in Framingham.

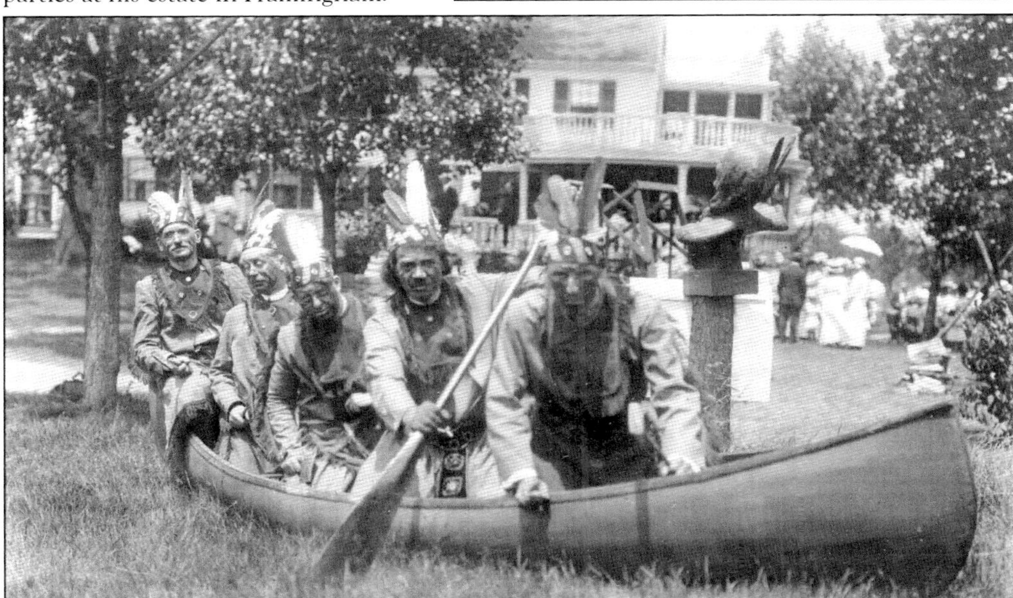

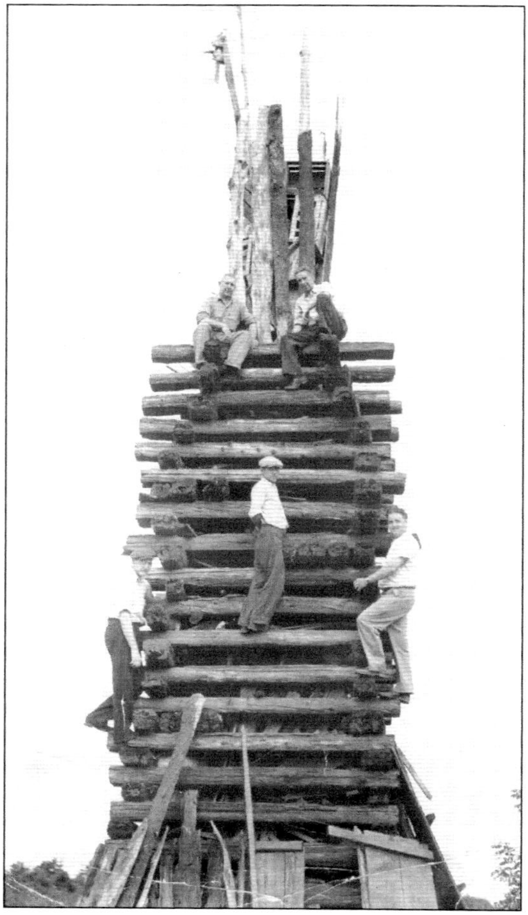

Creating the town bonfire are, from left to right, (halfway up) Lawrence B. Tighe, Ray Phelps, and Myron Siegars; (at top) town firefighter J. Leo Quinn and Leonard Stiles. Looking closely, there is a rag doll monkey at the top. In 1934, the bonfire was built near where the Peter Noyes School is now located. (Photograph by Harriet Ritchie.)

Below, a 1930s Kayopha girls' camp gathered for their summer photograph here in Sudbury as a part of the Congregational Church's outreach program for girls. Kayopha is a Native American word that translates to "where the sky and the peaks touch."

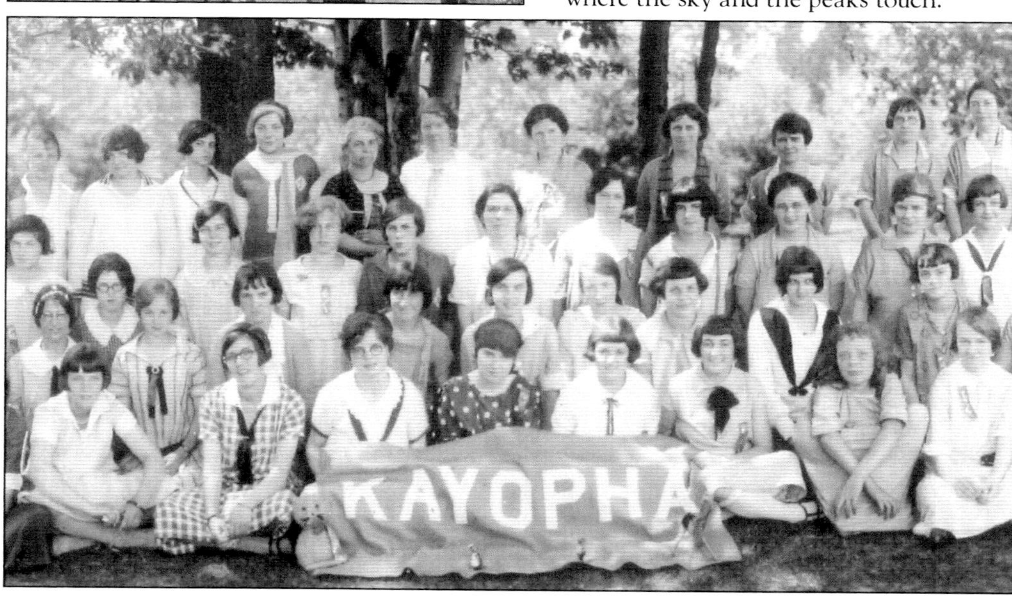

Elizabeth Atkinson (left) and Marion Raymond Lundberg, George J. Raymond's daughter, are dressed as Puritan ladies for Sudbury's 1939 tercentennial. They are standing in front of the milk shed at the Raymond estate. Marion Lundberg served as president of the Sudbury Historical Society in the 1970s.

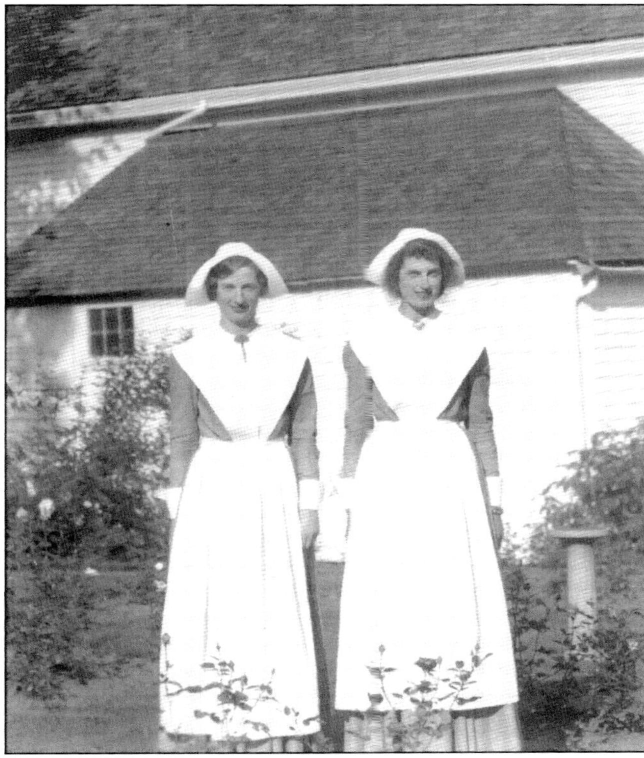

Lloyd and Kay Bancroft and their children, from left to right, Fred, Patty, and Lloyd Jr. pose in front of their house on Concord Road near Plympton Road. They are all dressed up for the 1939 tercentennial. The Bancroft family had deep roots in Sudbury and added to every occasion in which they participated.

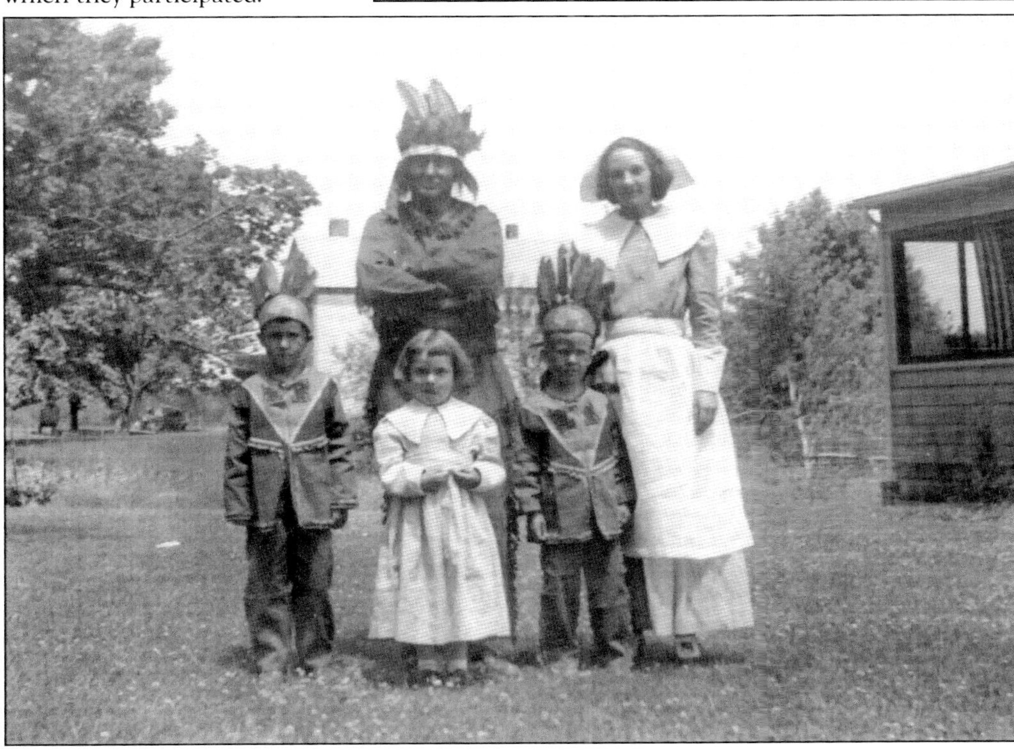

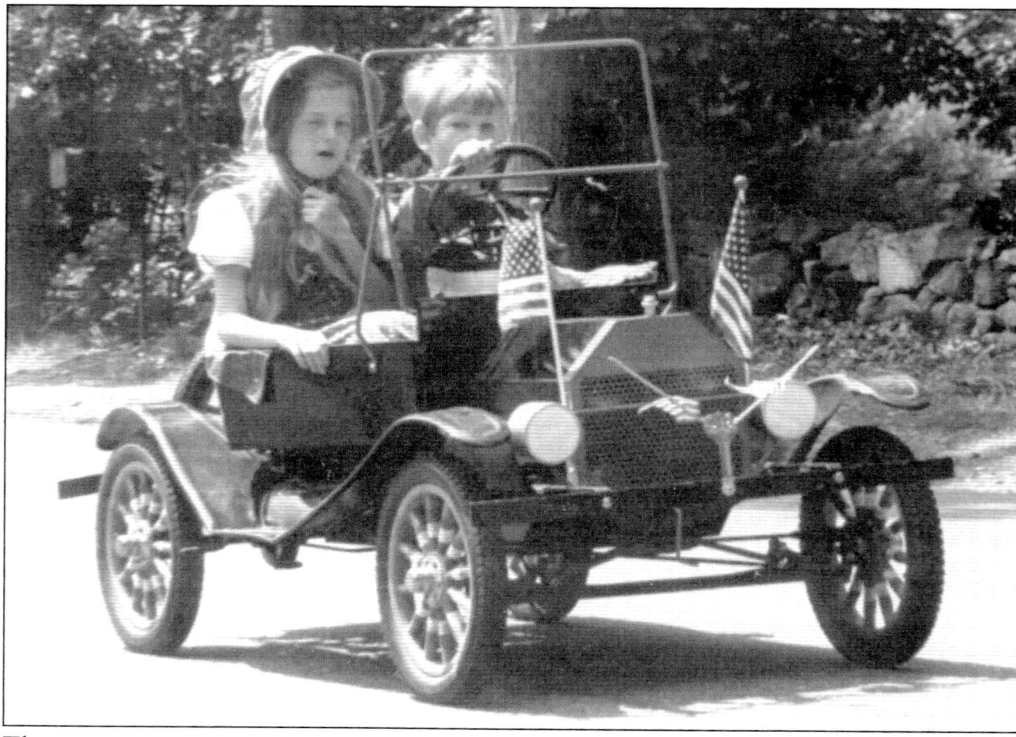

This very young couple is seen driving a sparkling new model car in the 1976 Fourth of July Parade.

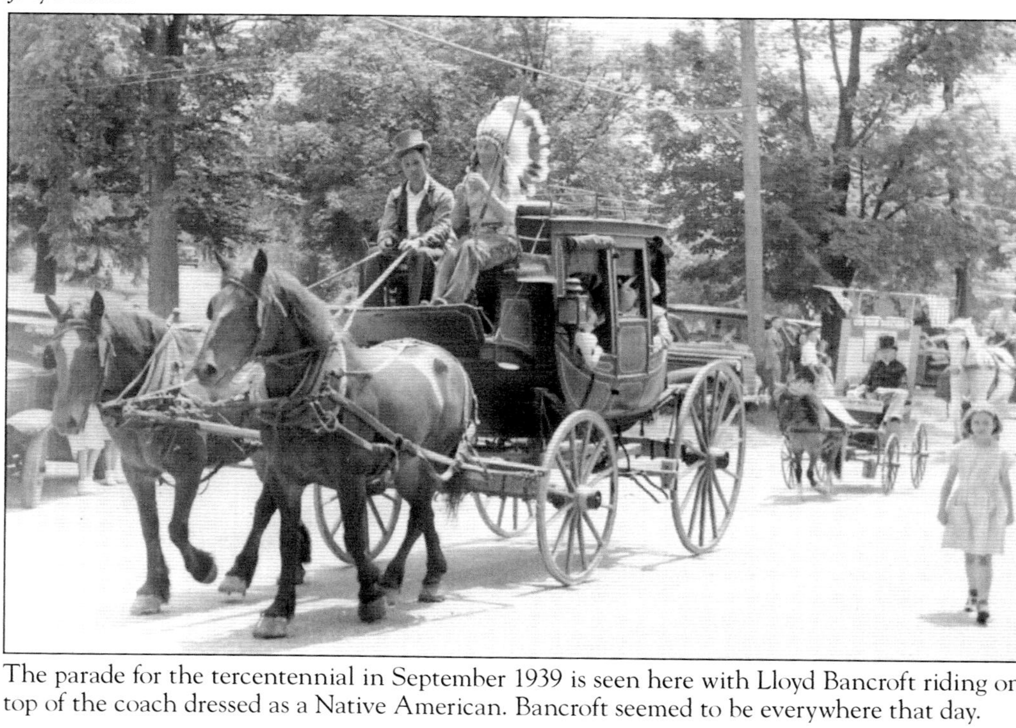

The parade for the tercentennial in September 1939 is seen here with Lloyd Bancroft riding on top of the coach dressed as a Native American. Bancroft seemed to be everywhere that day.

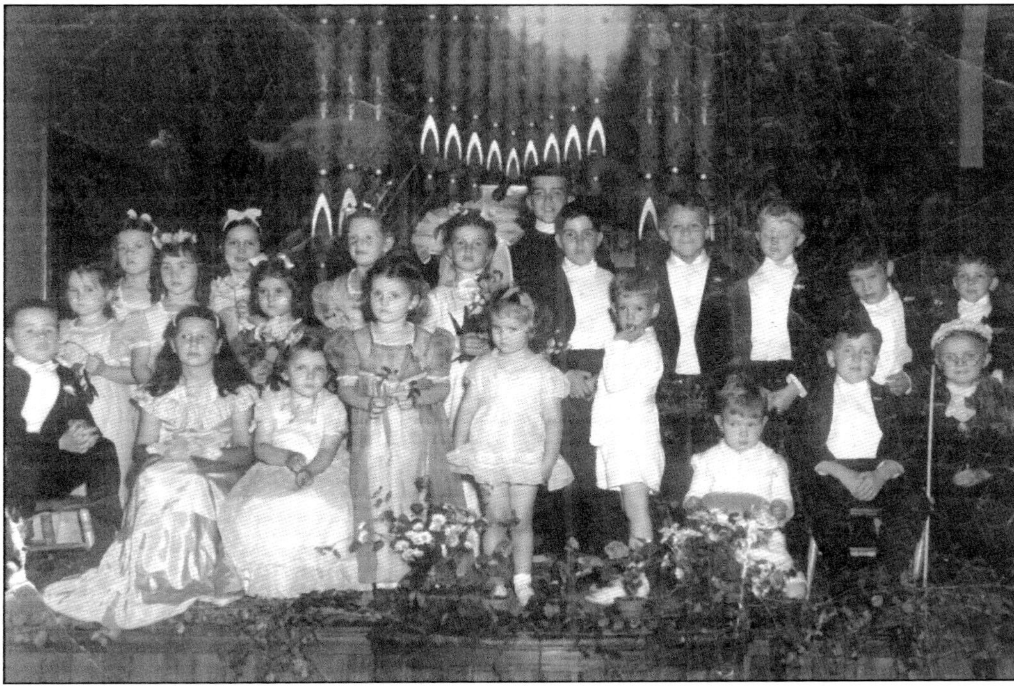

This Tom Thumb wedding at the Memorial Congregational Church in 1946 married Jane Flynn to Lloyd Bancroft Jr. John Hall was the minister, Fred Bancroft (far right) was a groomsman, and Patty Bancroft (back row, far left) was a bridesmaid. Tom Thumb weddings, based on the nuptials of Gen. Tom Thumb, who worked in the circus for P.T. Barnum in 1863, were popular, fashionable, and fun.

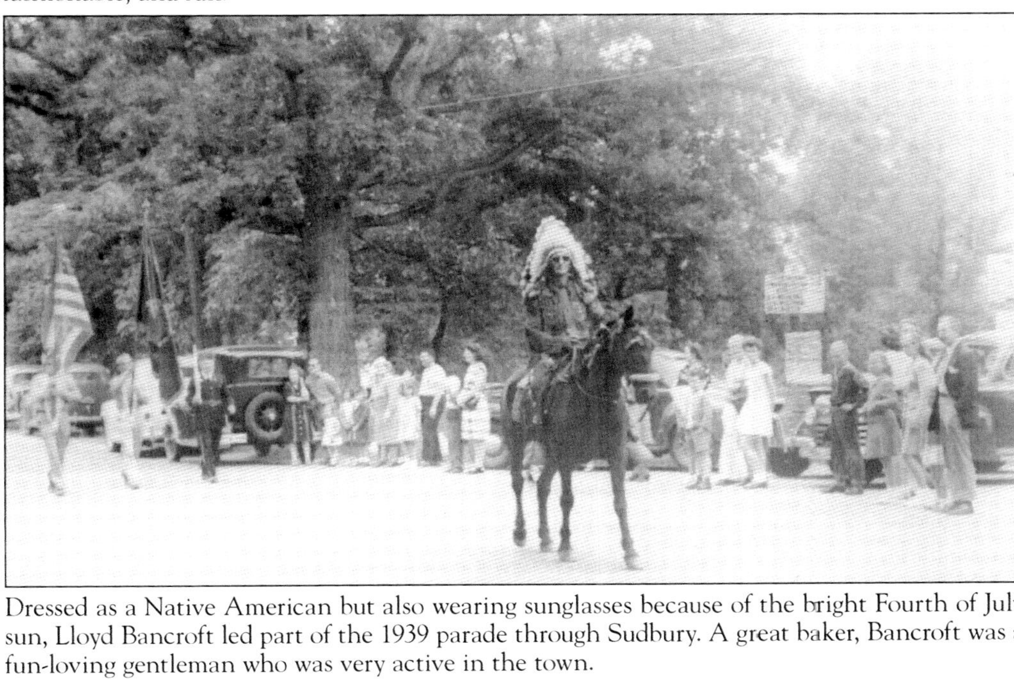

Dressed as a Native American but also wearing sunglasses because of the bright Fourth of July sun, Lloyd Bancroft led part of the 1939 parade through Sudbury. A great baker, Bancroft was a fun-loving gentleman who was very active in the town.

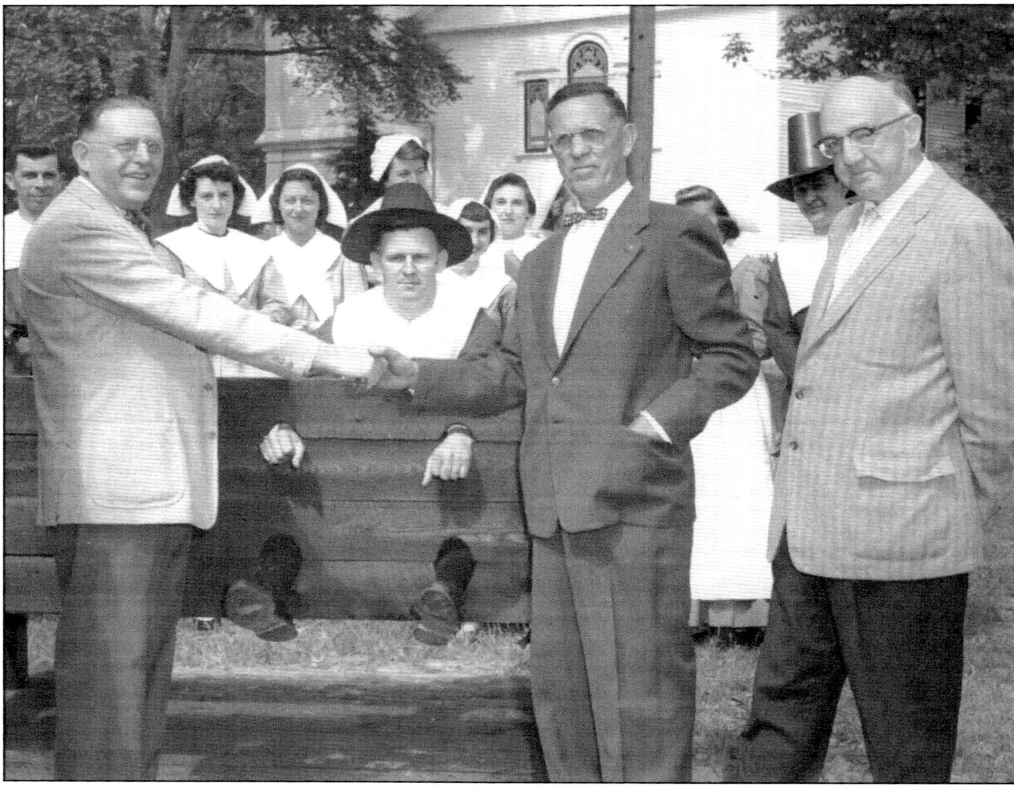

Forrest Bradshaw (left) shakes hands with selectman Harvey Fairbank, with selectman Laurence Tighe on the right. They are accepting the gift of a recreated set of stocks from the Sudbury Historical Society, Inc., which were set on the town common on May 18, 1957. Stocks were a way of punishing a person with public embarrassment and humiliation. These were destroyed by a school bus in 1968. (Photograph by Harriet Ritchie.)

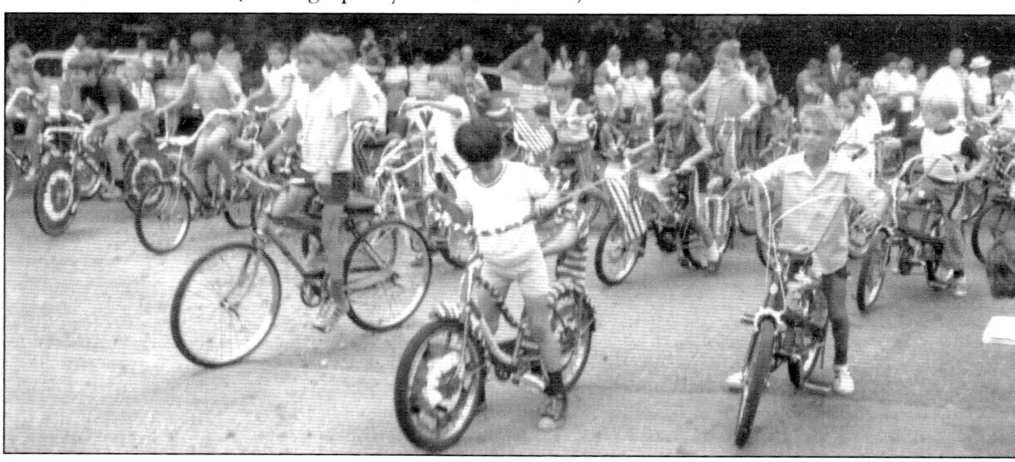

These children have outfitted their bikes for the annual Fourth of July bike-decorating contest. This contest is still run on the Fourth of July, usually by the American Legion Post No. 191. This photograph was taken for the July 19, 1972, *Sudbury Citizen* newspaper by editor Mary Jane Hillery. At the time, there were two Sudbury newspapers, plus *Bentley's Calendar*, a weekly magazine.

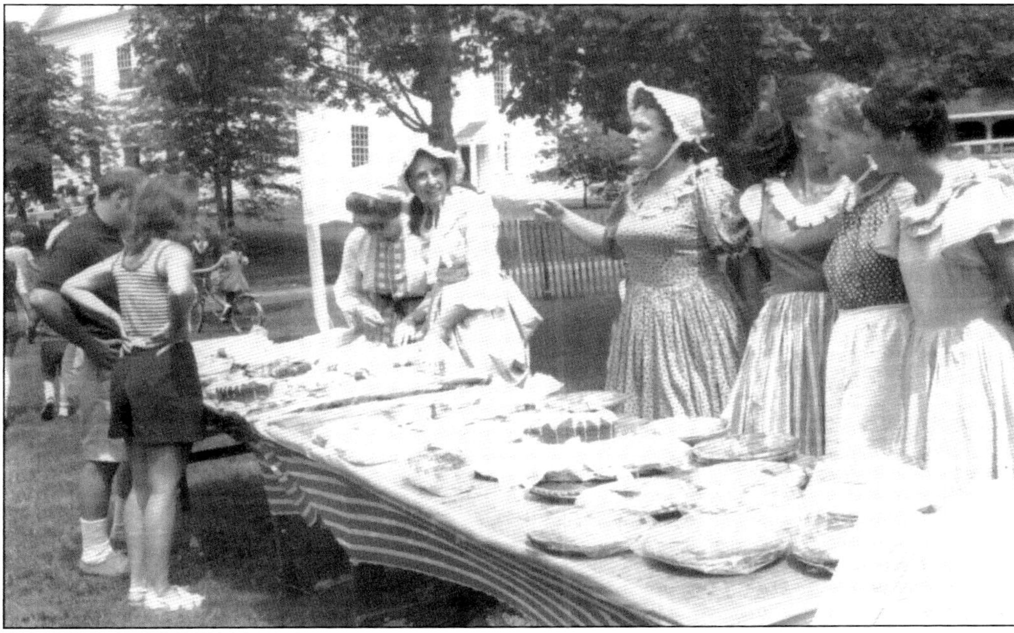

The Sudbury Women's Club had this American pie sale on the town common on the Fourth of July to benefit their scholarship fund. The women participating included, from left to right, Lou Cali, Carol Bowman, Peggy Feistkorn, Lee Hamill, Ann Pettigrew, and Frances Schlichter.

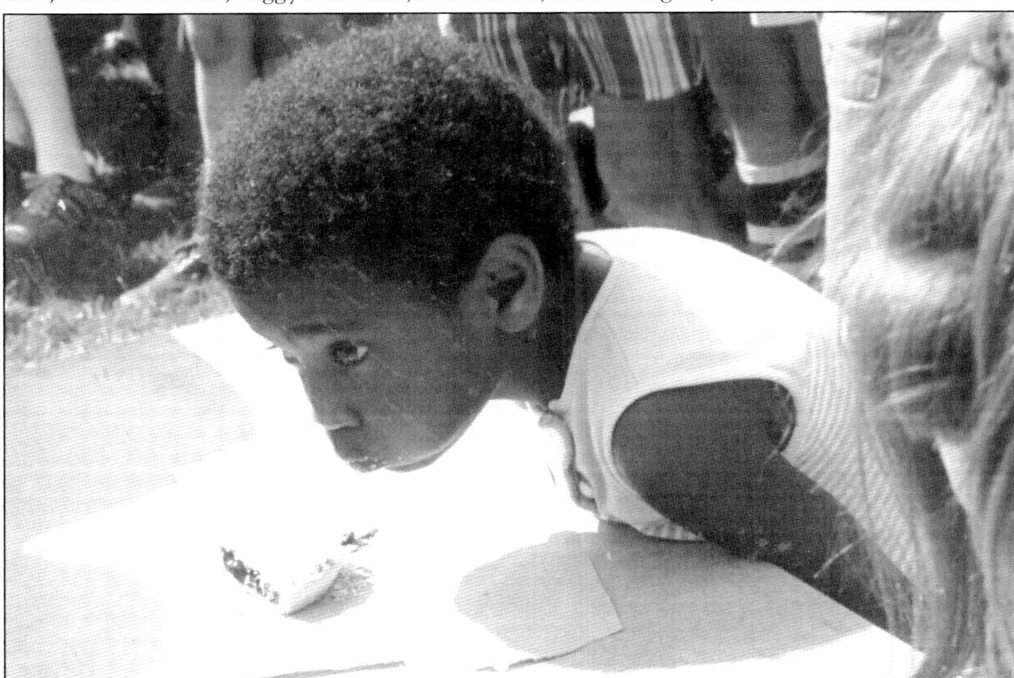

Casey Nolan finds his last bite tough going in the pie-eating contest at the 1972 Fourth of July celebration. This contest was usually held in the Peter Noyes field after the parade. (Photograph by *Sudbury Citizen*.)

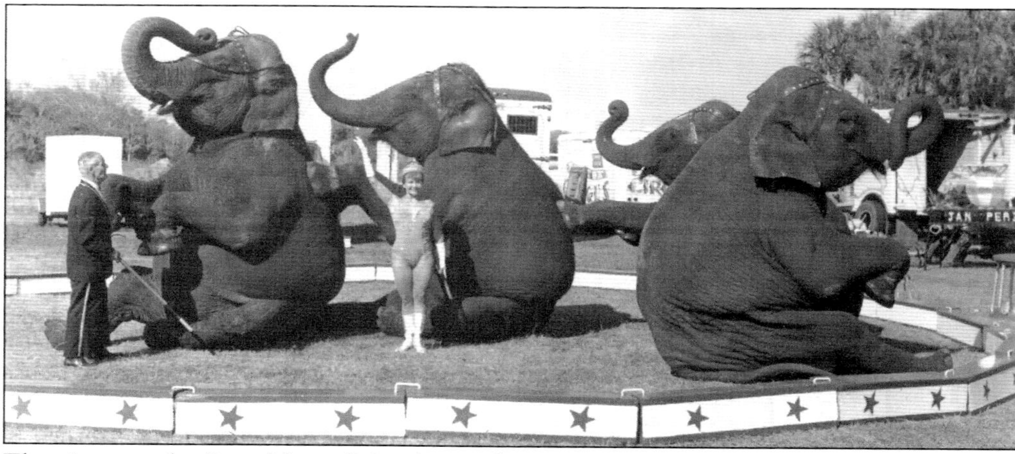

The circus at the Peter Noyes School, seen here on August 13, 1970, was sponsored by the Sudbury police as a fundraiser for charity. At least two carnivals and a circus passed through town every year, aglow at night with strange sounds, sights, smells, and adventures. (Photograph by *Sudbury Citizen*.)

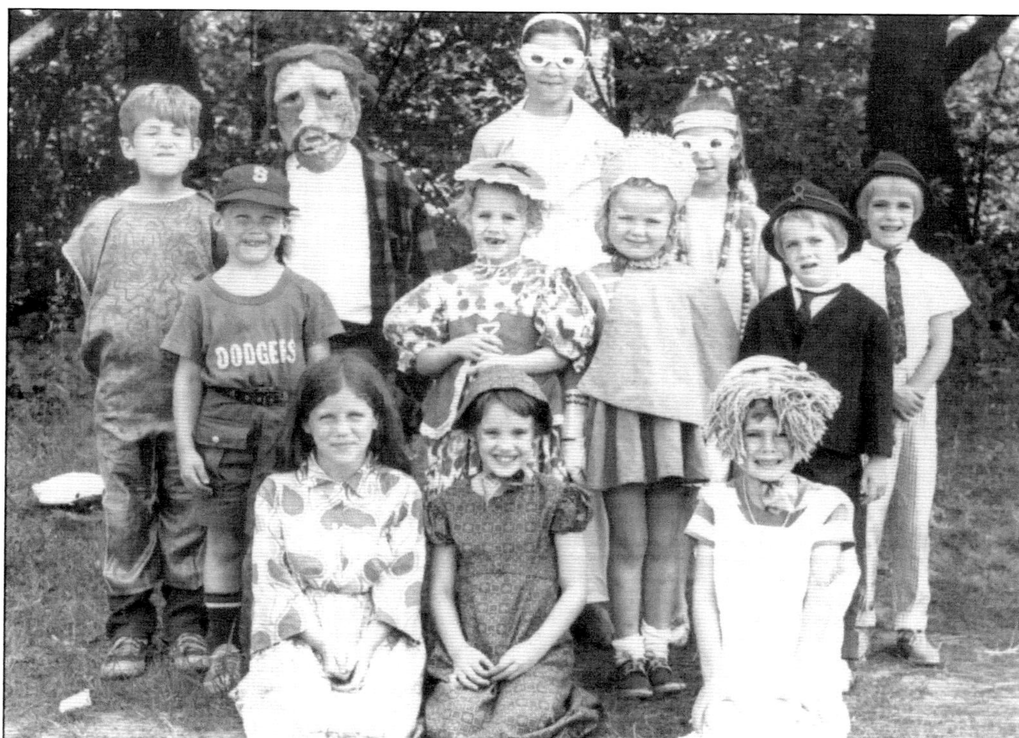


The 1968 Masquerade Parade at the Featherland playground included, from left to right, (first row) Terrie Bierig, Cheryl Slomski, and Clay Booma; (second row) Bobby Bierig, Robin Slomski, Missy Clark, and Alison Booma; (third row) Jason Doyle, Brian Bierig, Donna Roessler, Andrea Roessler, and Gretchen Booma. (Photograph by P. Brown for the *Sudbury Citizen*.)

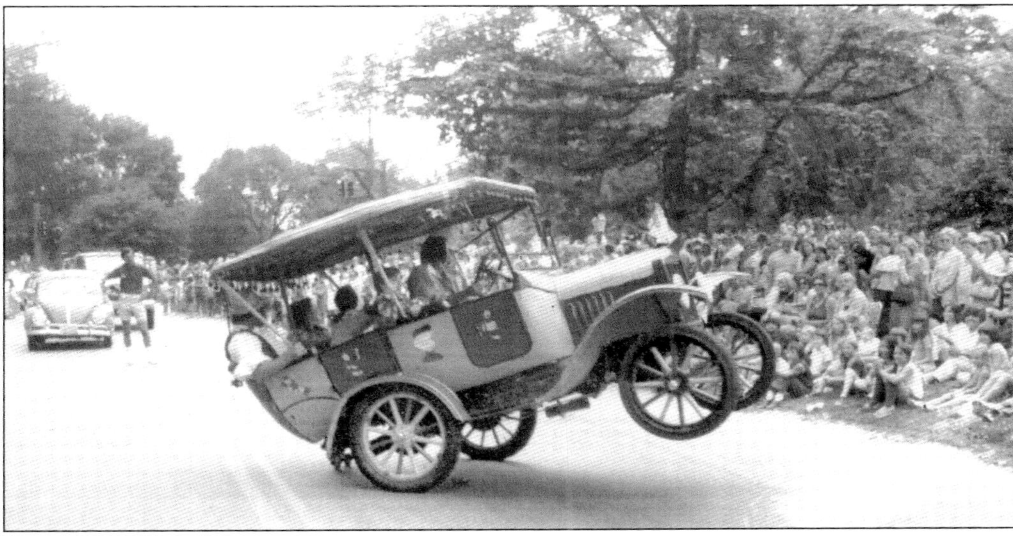

A Leaping Lena clown car performs for the crowd during the 1968 Fourth of July Parade on Concord Road. This was a paid attraction sponsored by a local company as part of the Sudbury Chamber of Commerce parade.

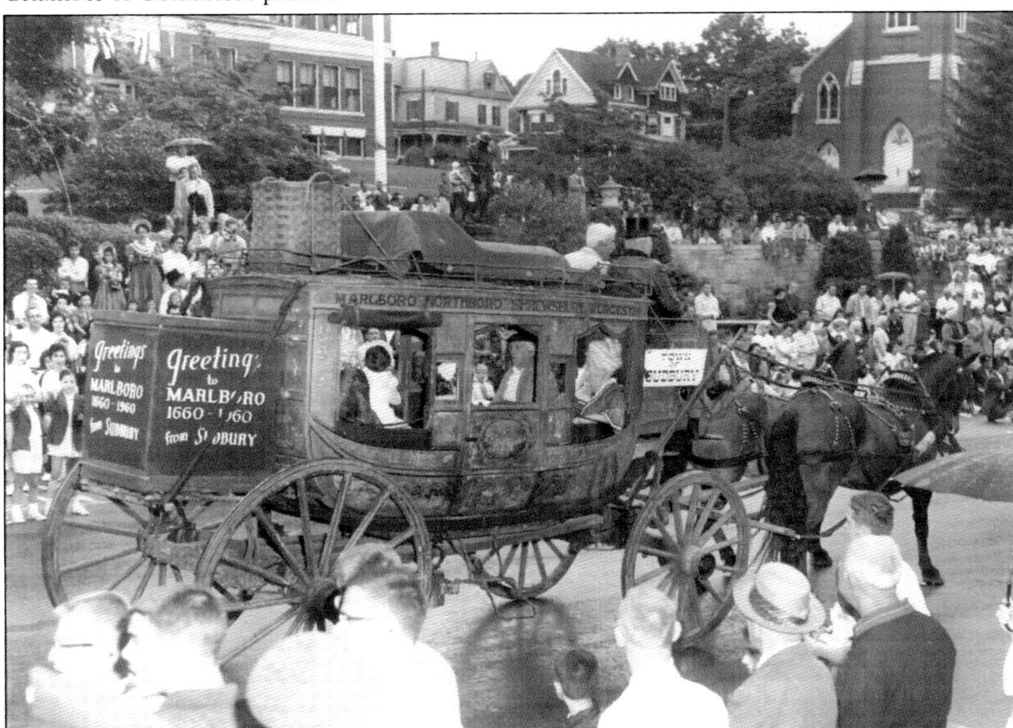


The Wayside Inn stagecoach—before it was restored—drove through the Marlborough tercentennial in June 1960. Stagecoaches ran on the Post Road west from Boston to Marlborough and beyond. The passengers included Forrest and Katherine Bradshaw, Maud Clark, Elizabeth Atkinson, and Linda and Holly Peterson. The Walker Building is on the left, and Immaculate Conception Church is on the right.

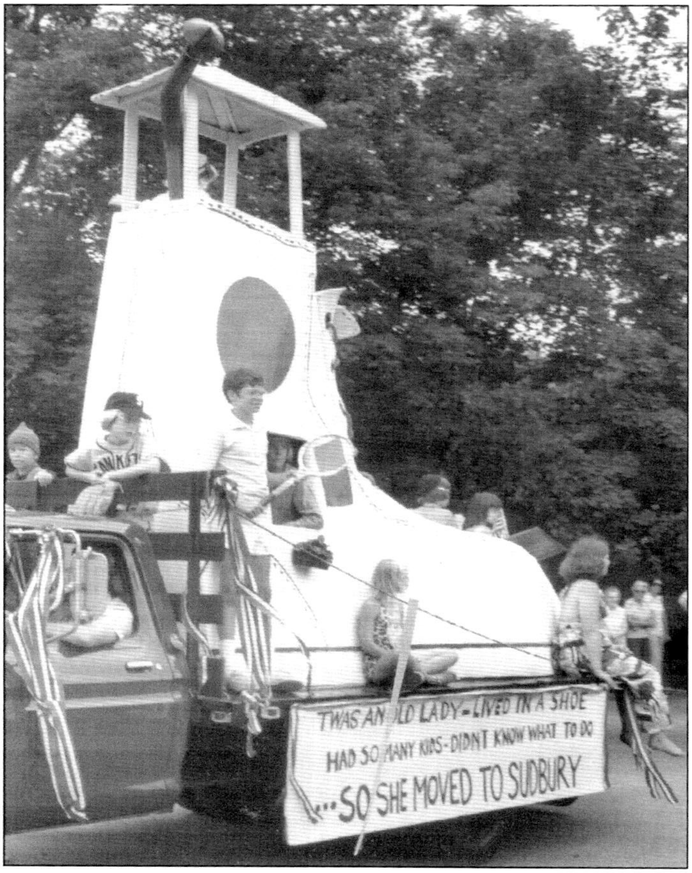


This funny parade float in 1968 included the following joke: "Twas an old woman – lived in a shoe / Had so many kids – didn't know what to do / . . . so she moved to Sudbury." The joke was a commentary on the increased number of families moving to Sudbury at the time.

Below, the restored Wayside Inn stagecoach carried innkeeper Francis Koppeis and others in the 1975 Fourth of July Parade. The Abbot and Downing coach was restored by the fundraising of the Sudbury Companies of Militia and Minute and is now on display in the Collings Museum in Stow. It is still used at the end of the Sudbury Fourth of July parade every year.

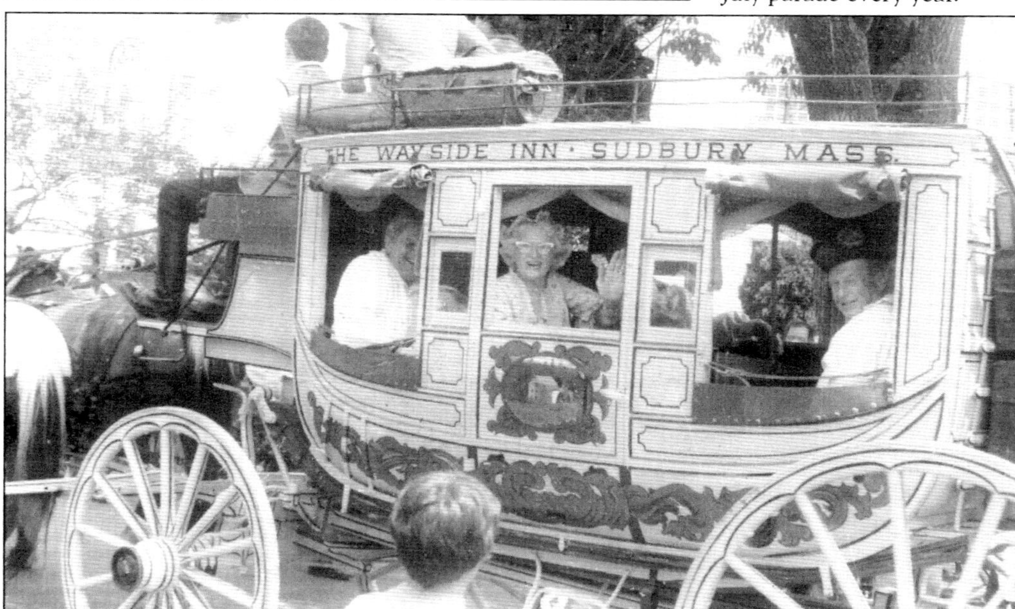

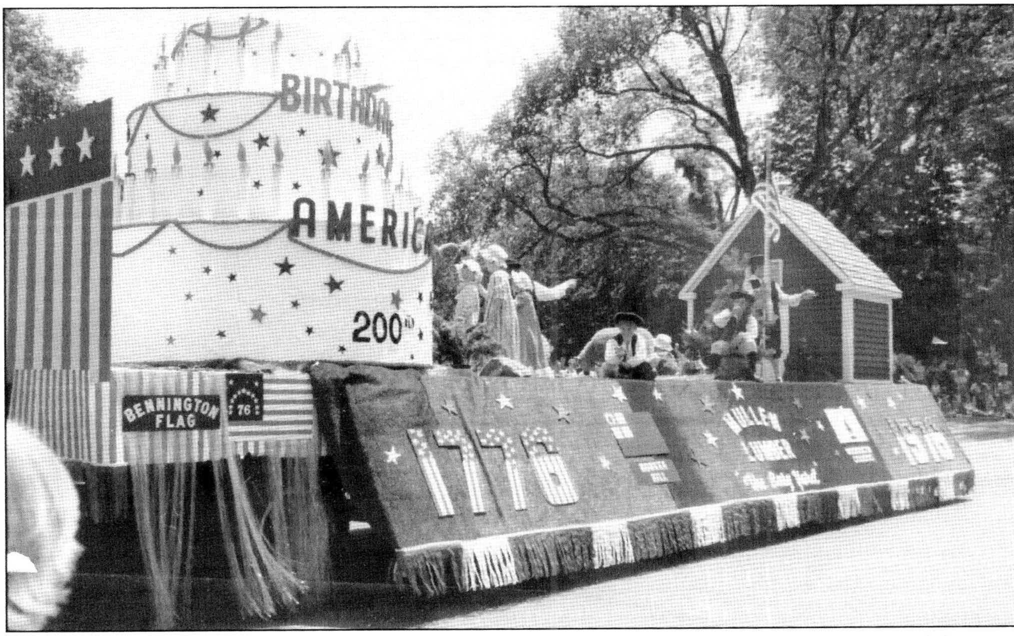


This Fourth of July 1976 Parade float was sponsored by Mullen Lumber Company and featured a replica of the Redstone Schoolhouse with enthusiastic students.

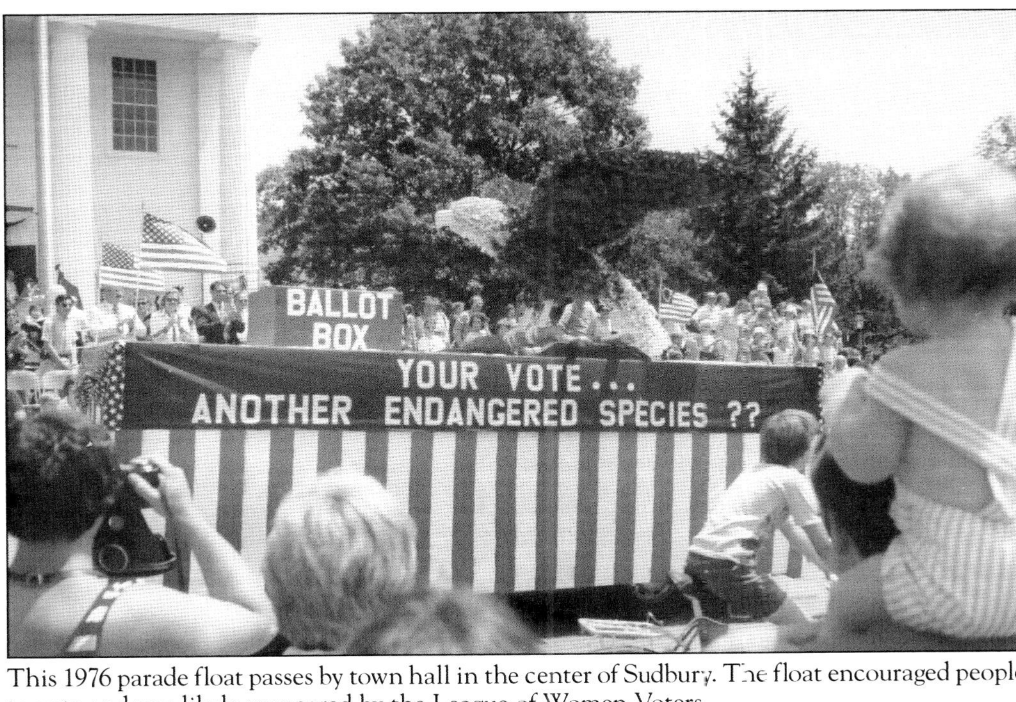


This 1976 parade float passes by town hall in the center of Sudbury. The float encouraged people to vote and was likely sponsored by the League of Women Voters.

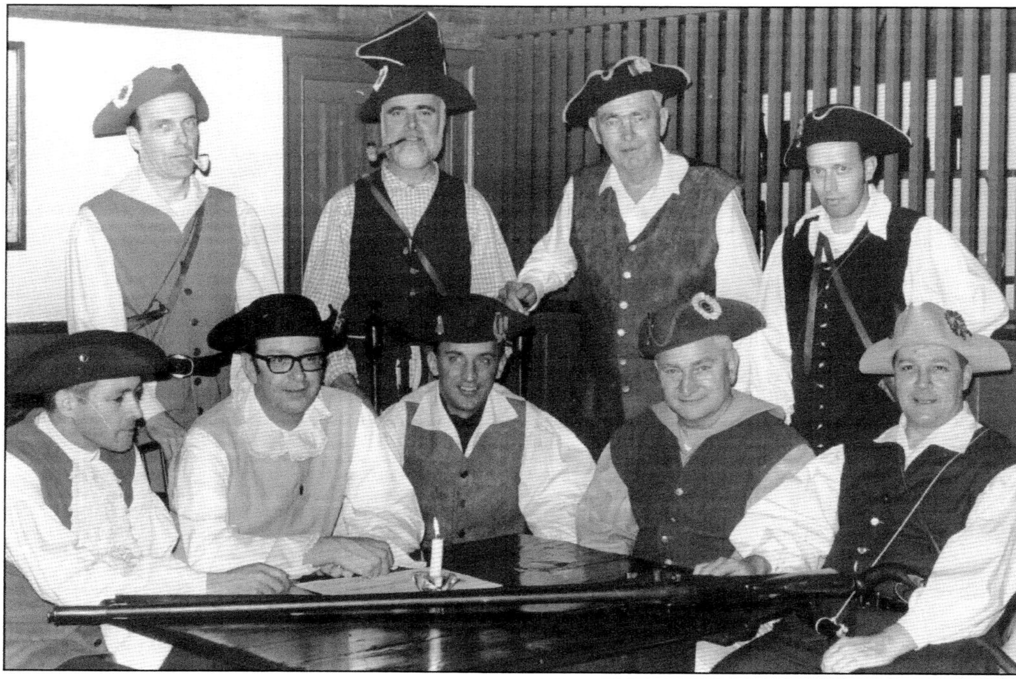

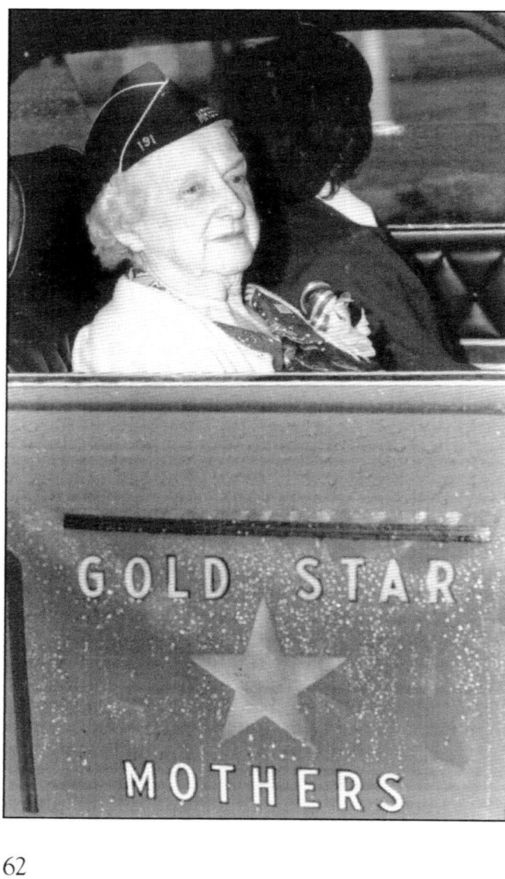


This early meeting of the Sudbury Companies of Militia and Minute took place at the Old Bar in the Wayside Inn in 1965. The late innkeeper, Francis Koppeis, was always a perfect host and helped start the recreated Minute Company and the Fife and Drum Corps. The meeting included, from left to right, (seated) Bob Oram, Roger Bump, John Palutchco, David Bentley, and Paul MacNally; (standing) Russ Kirby, Ira Amesbury, Bob McLean Sr., and an unidentified British spy.

Mrs. Charles (Marion) Spiller (left) was the parade marshal of the 1973 Memorial Day Parade. She is dressed with her American Legion Post No. 191 cap and is pinned with a corsage. Spiller was a Gold Star Mother—someone who lost a son in World War II—for having lost her son Albert. The Memorial Day Committee plans a year in advance how to honor those who fought for their country. (Photograph by Clay Allen for the *Sudbury Citizen*.)

# *Four*
# SACRED SPACES

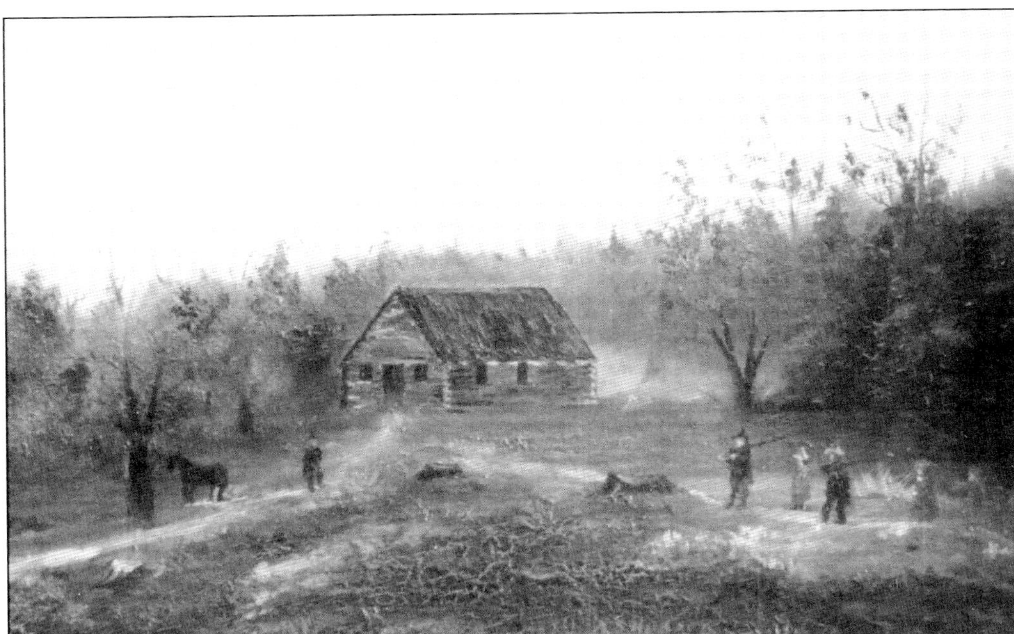

The first meetinghouse and church in Sudbury was built in what is now the North Cemetery in Wayland on Old Sudbury Road, where the honored dead were buried around the church. This location served as the site of three different meetinghouses until the center of Wayland was reestablished at Route 20 and Route 126/27. A.S. Hudson, who wrote *The History of Sudbury*, painted this based on what he was told it looked like.

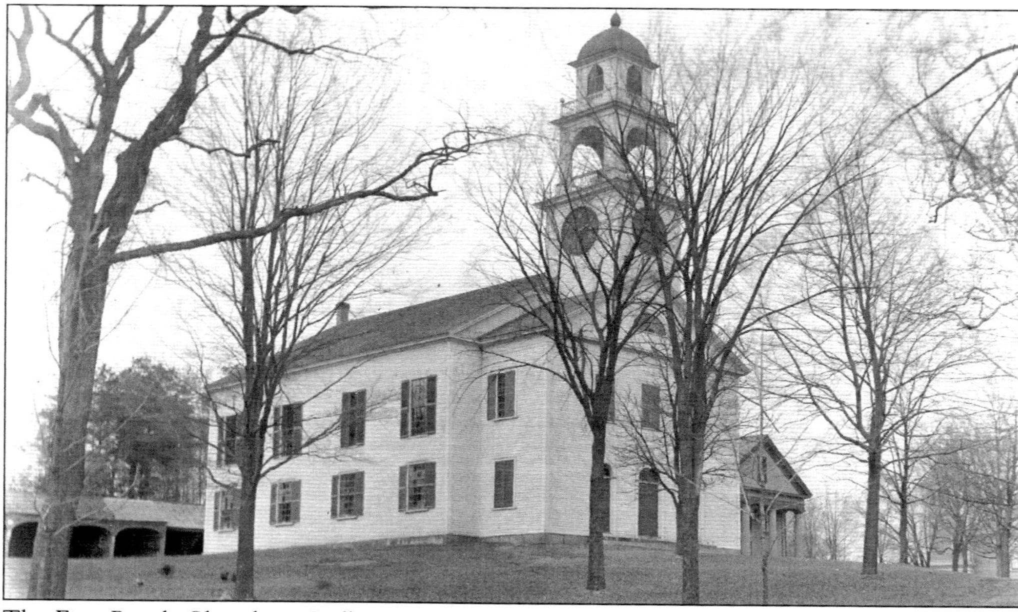

The First Parish Church in Sudbury's town center was originally built by journeymen builders in 1723 on what was known as Rocky Plain. The present structure was built in 1797 and reused some of the material from the original, smaller structure. The building's design was purchased from Benjamin Thompson of Boston and features design elements borrowed from famed English architect Christopher Wren. Town meetings were held here until 1846, when the town house was built and the separation of church and state was recognized.

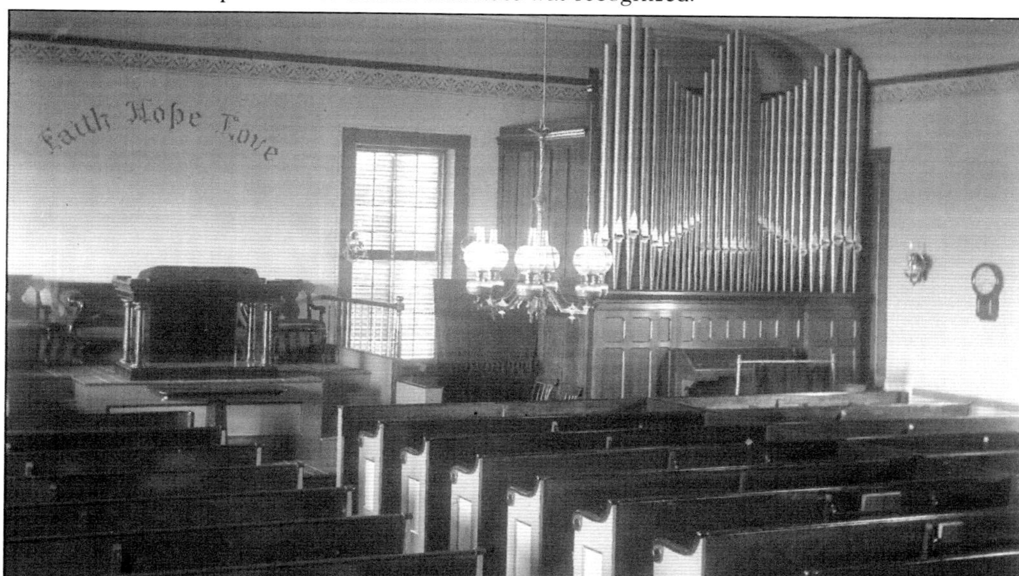


This rare photograph of the interior of the First Parish Church was taken in 1904 by Hattie Goodnow. Originally, church services here were five hours long with a lunch break in the middle. There was no heat in the church, so members went to warm up by the fire in a nearby building called a noon house. To the right is the 1875 pump organ that was originally powered by a young man pumping a lever up and down during the service.

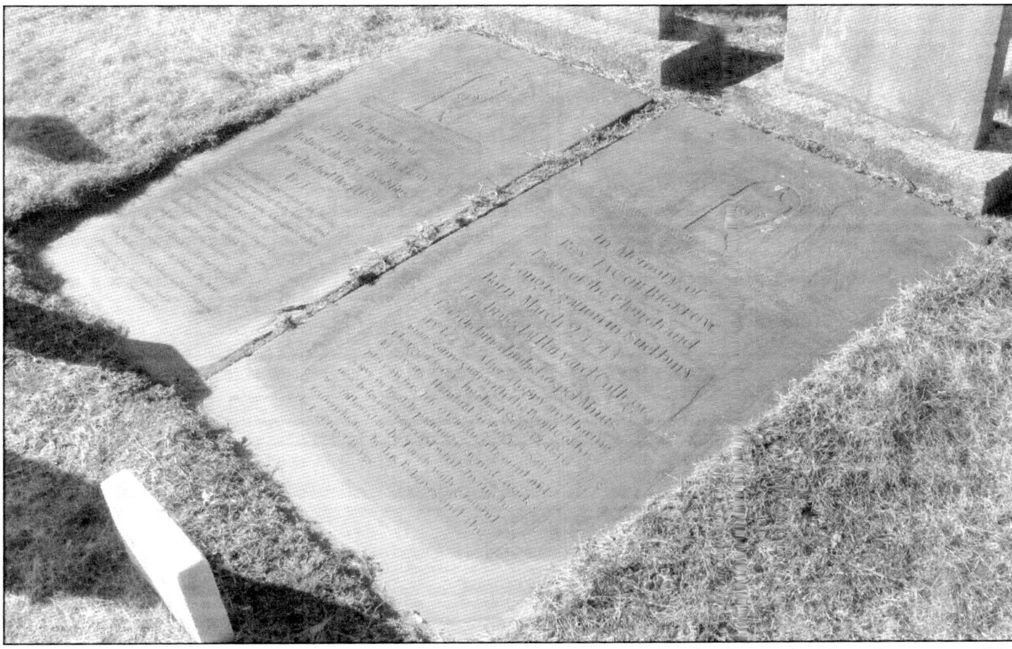

These are the gravestones of Rev. Jacob Bigelow and his wife, Elizabeth in the Revolutionary War Cemetery. The family had the original inscribed-slate stones laid flat and had placed fashionable new vertical marble schist monuments in front of them. Sadly, the schist is greatly affected by acid rain, and the inscription on the slate is almost unreadable. Reverend Bigelow was ordained on November 11, 1772, as the minister at First Parish, succeeding Rev. Israel Loring after his death.

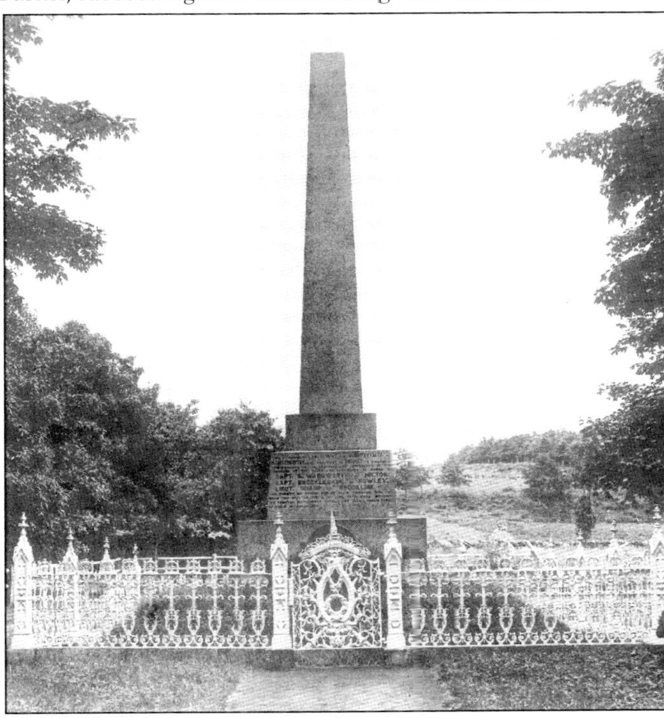

The Wadsworth Memorial Monument in Wadsworth Cemetery is opposite 71 Concord Road. It was named after Capt. Samuel Wadsworth, a militiaman from Milton. Captain Wadsworth and most of his company were attacked and killed while defending the frontier at the Battle of Green Hill. They fought the Native Americans during the King Philip's War on April 21, 1676. The first slate marker to identify the gravesite of the 26 militiamen and three officers who were killed was erected in 1730 by Wadsworth's son. In 1852, the 21.5-foot-tall granite obelisk was erected, and the cemetery was named in honor of Wadsworth.

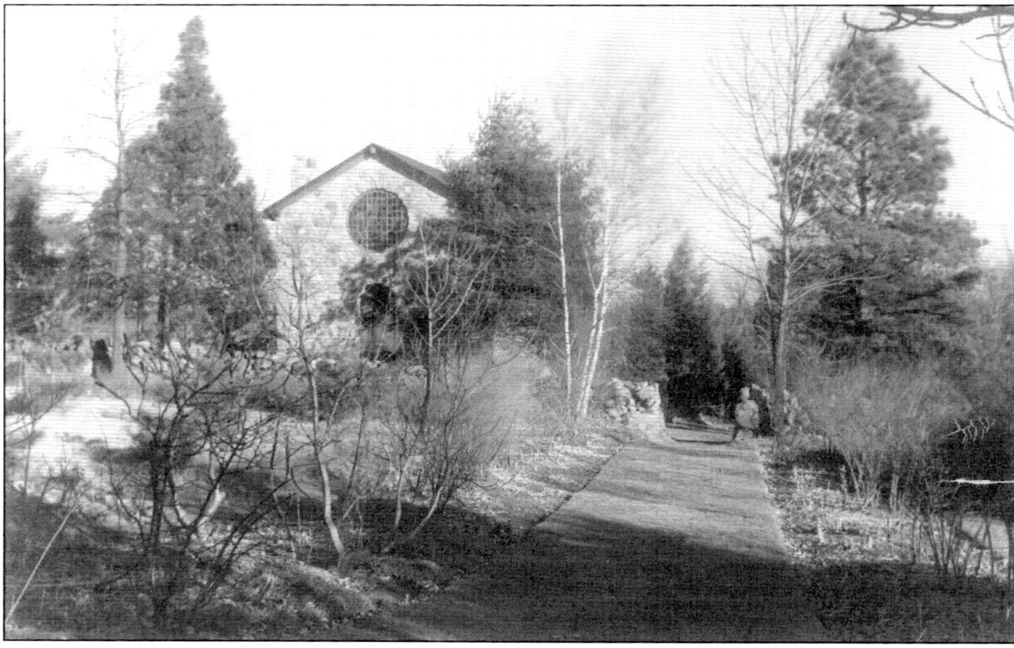

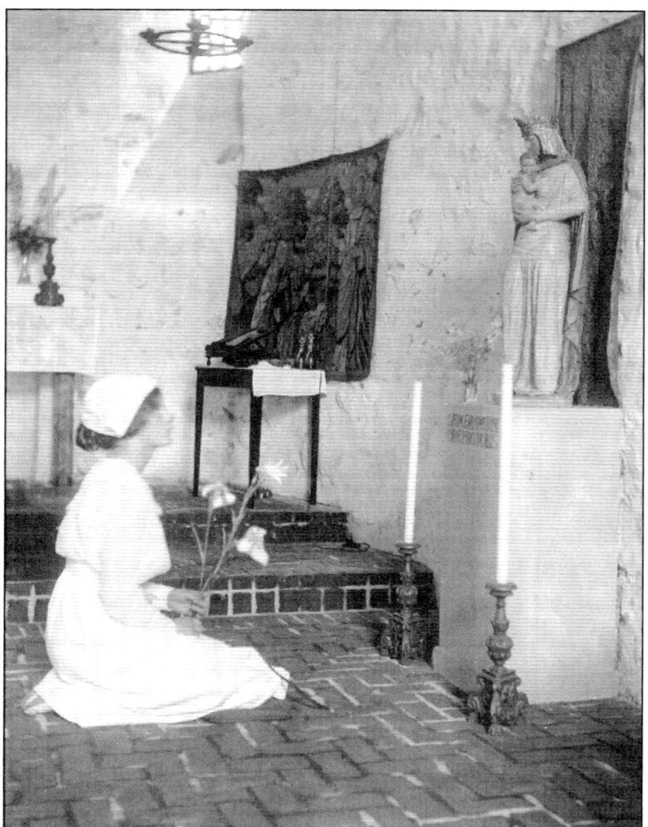

The Cram Chapel is located in front of Ralph Adams Cram's home, Whitehall, at 435 Concord Road. Cram described it as a simple country chapel built for his private use. This Medieval-style building was constructed by hand, largely by local Sudbury craftsmen, including renowned ironworker Samuel Yellen, who built the fine iron strap-work, the lock on the doors, and components of the interior.

At left, Cram's daughter Mary Cram Carrington prays in Cram Chapel in 1902. The chapel was deeded to St. Elizabeth's Episcopal Church and used by the congregation until a much larger church was built nearby. The chapel is still used for summer services.

The Crams, standing at the Cram Chapel entrance, lived on the property, primarily in the summer, from 1900 to 1942. The couple is buried next to the chapel. The Crams owned a house in the city but were not unique in discovering the pleasures of a country town, especially after the arrival of the railroads in the 1870s, after which well-to-do men could live in Sudbury and travel to the city easily.

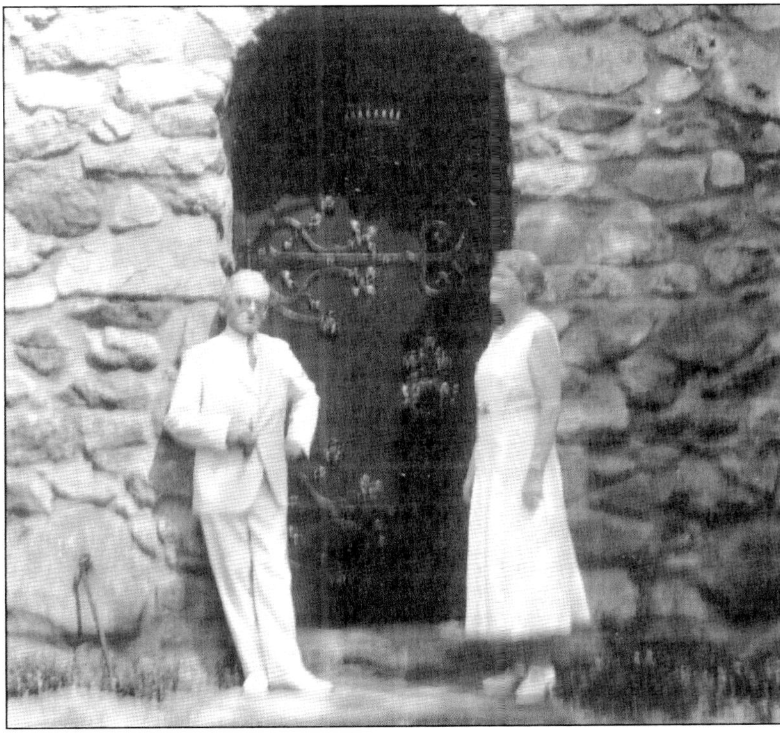

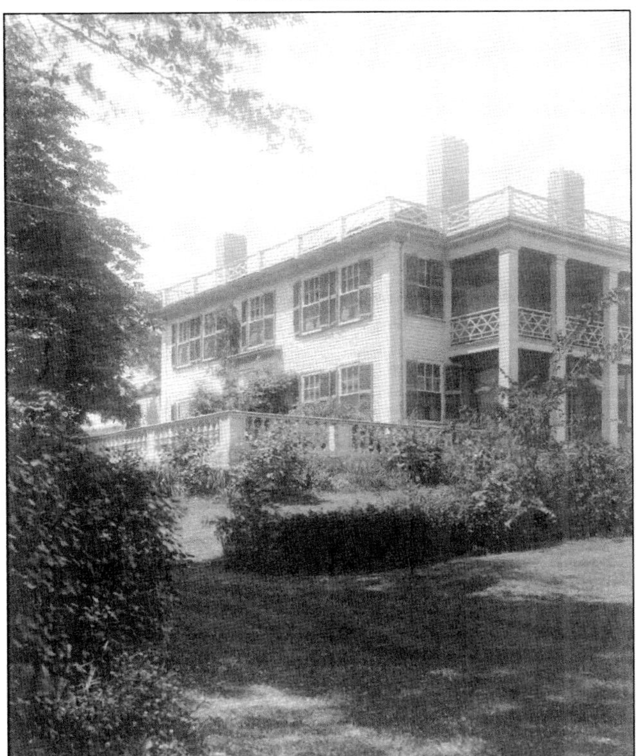

Ralph Adams Cram, who lived here, at Whitehall, was America's foremost ecclesiastical architect. He was internationally famous for his reinterpretation of the Gothic style of architecture and for incorporating it into modern structures. His most famous work was the Cathedral Church of Saint John the Divine in New York City.

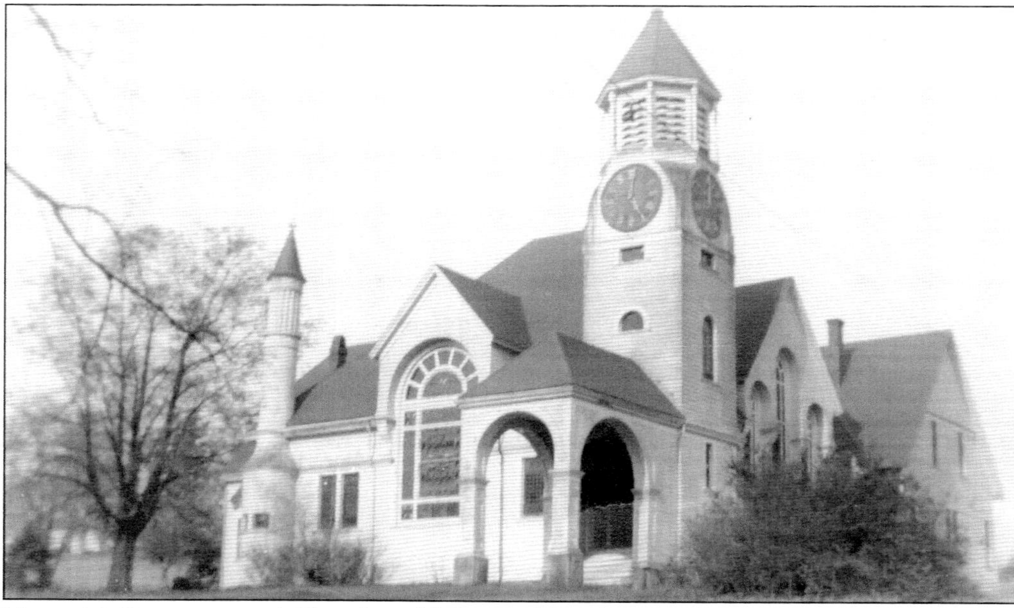

Memorial Congregational Church at 26 Concord Road is seen here in 1944. The church was built in 1889 and dedicated on March 8, 1891. Today, it is well known for its annual Messiah Sing in December, which everyone is invited to participate in. It occupies the previous site of the Wadsworth Academy.

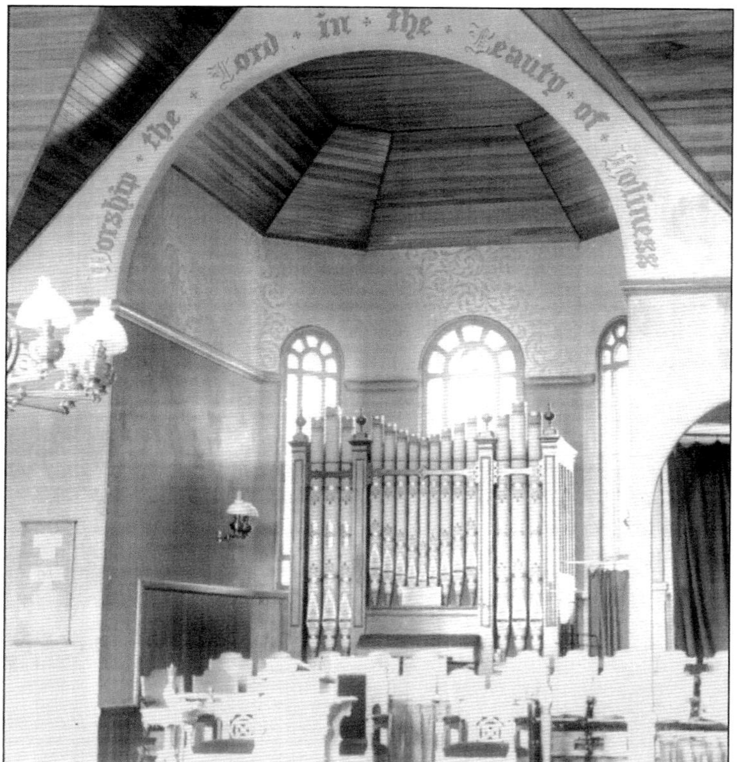


The Memorial Congregational Church received this new organ in 1904. The interior has since been completely remodeled and rearranged. The photograph was taken by Hattie Goodnow, whose work chronicling the town through photographs likely made this book possible.

The Evangelical Union Society was located at 277 Concord Road across from Goodman's Hill Road. It was dedicated on January 1, 1840, by the Evangelical Union Society, when it split from the Unitarians in 1837. The congregation chose to erect a new church in 1889 at 26 Concord Road in South Sudbury. The building has since gone through many uses, first as a music hall and lastly as a home to a basketball league, before it burned in 1925. The present house at this address was moved onto the site from another location.

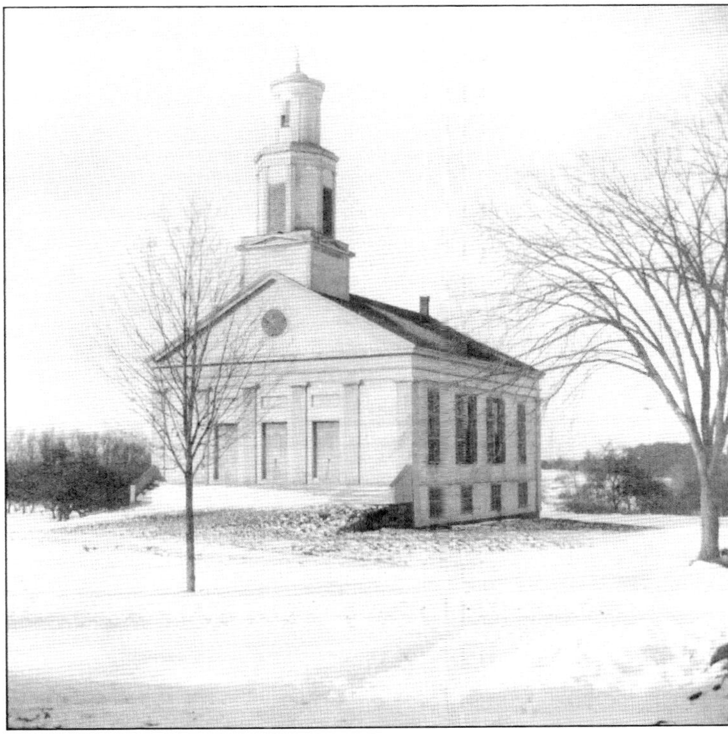

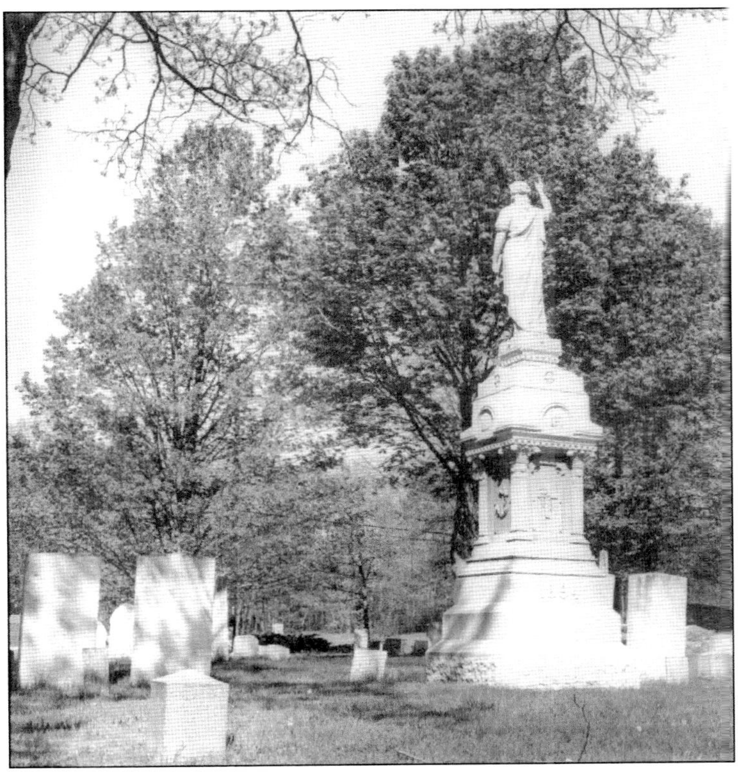

North Cemetery on Pantry Road features the statue shown at left, which is engraved with "Maynard" at its base. It is a very rare hollow zinc statue. In the 1830s, a John Maynard lived in Sudbury and is remembered for saying, "Everyone who called, from minister to tramp, was offered a common drink."

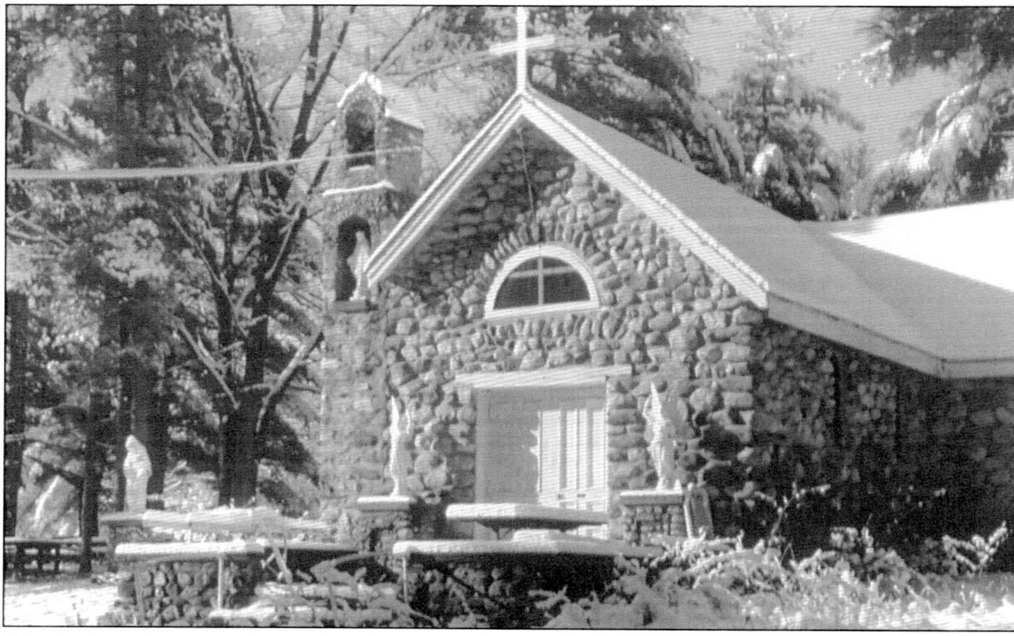

This Italian chapel was located on Mossman Road and built by the Maria SS. Indulgence Society, which was founded in 1914. The chapel itself was built in the 1920s, and society membership was limited to descendants of residents of the town of Sant' Elia Fiuma Rapido near Monte Cassino, Italy. The society functioned as a mutual aide society, providing health and unemployment benefits. However, as time passed, younger generations became disinterested. The chapel was torn down in 1988, and the land was sold for housing.

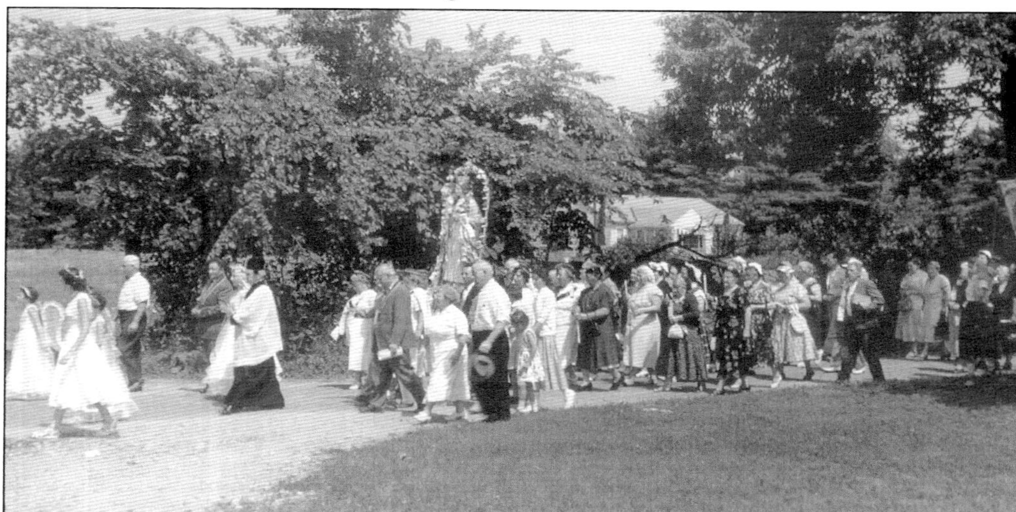

Every year on the third Sunday of July, members of the Maria SS. Indulgence Society carried over the tradition from Italy of the procession to the chapel for adoration of the Madonna. The statue was brought to the Micelli house on Route 117 the Thursday before and decorated with contributions from the devout. Mass was celebrated at the entrance to the stone chapel because the large crowd attending could not fit inside. The afternoon was spent with picnics, dancing, and family gatherings.

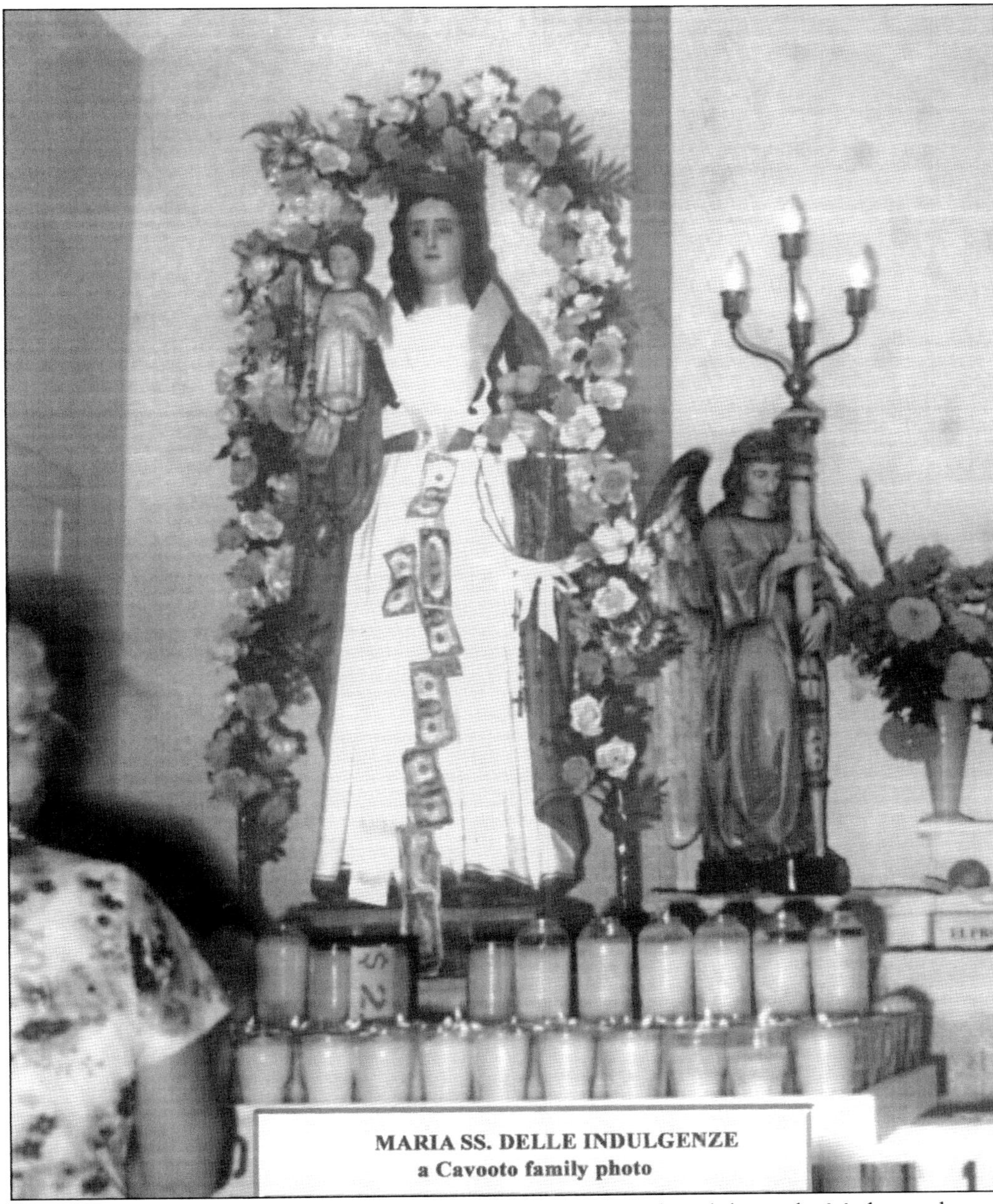


This interior photograph of the Maria SS. Indulgence Society chapel shows the Madonna draped with traditional money offerings. Due to the limited size of the chapel, an outside area was created that was much like an amphitheater, with a roof under which as many as 30,000 people could assemble, including those who were seated, standing, and enjoying picnic lunches under the trees. John F. Kennedy visited the chapel to promote his senatorial campaign.

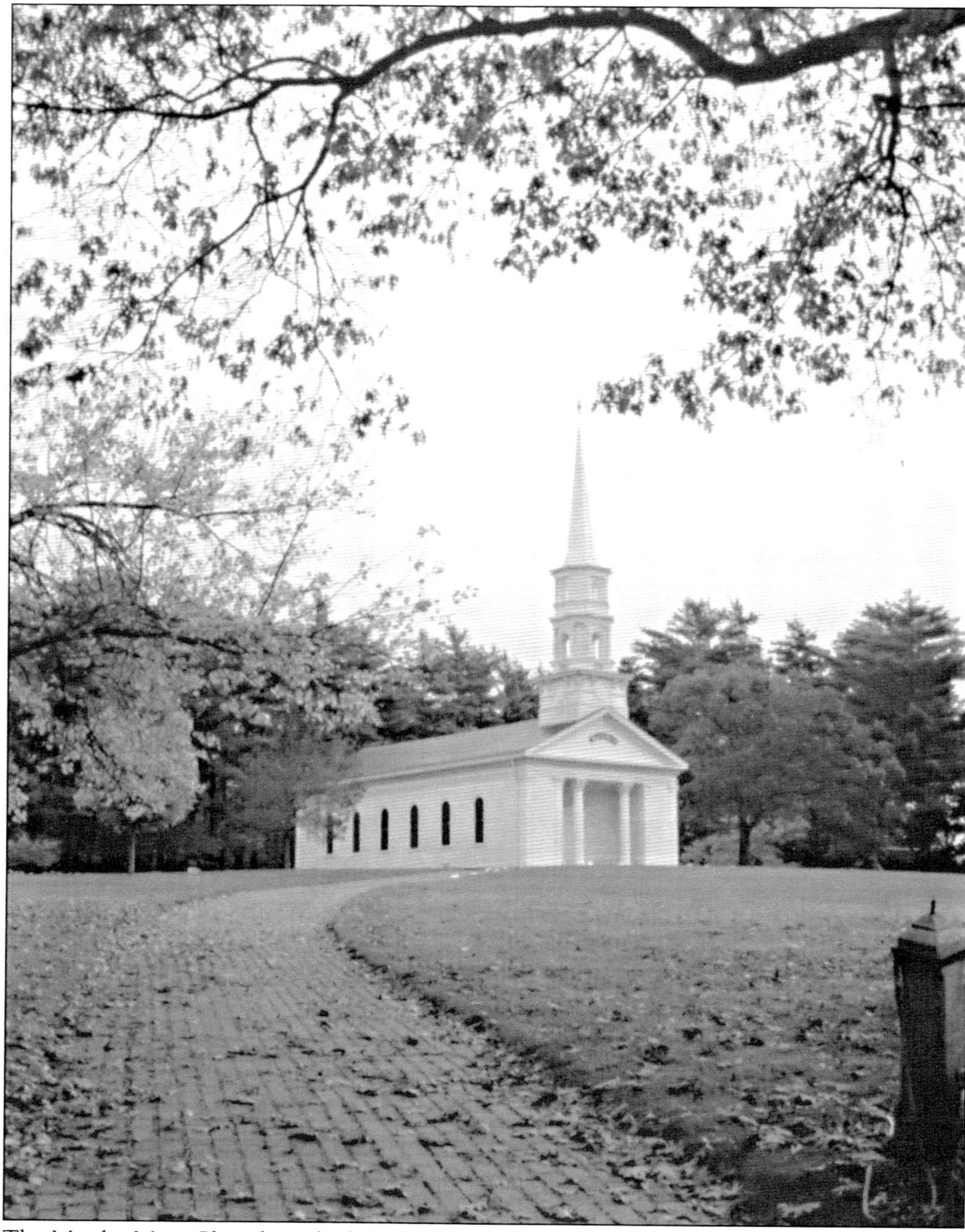

The Martha Mary Chapel was built in 1939 by students from the Wayside Inn Boys School, the Redstone Schoolhouse, and the South West School, assisted by local craftsmen. The craftsmen used the massive white pines that were downed by the 1938 hurricane to build the chapel, which was named after the mothers of Clara and Henry Ford. It is on the grounds of the Wayside Inn in the Wayside Inn Historic District. Since 1940, it has been the chapel of choice for 150 to 200 weddings a year. The chapel is a one-quarter-scale copy of the Bradford, Massachusetts, First Parish Chapel, and Henry Ford had five other similar chapels built wherever he had a school.

*Five*

# MILITARY

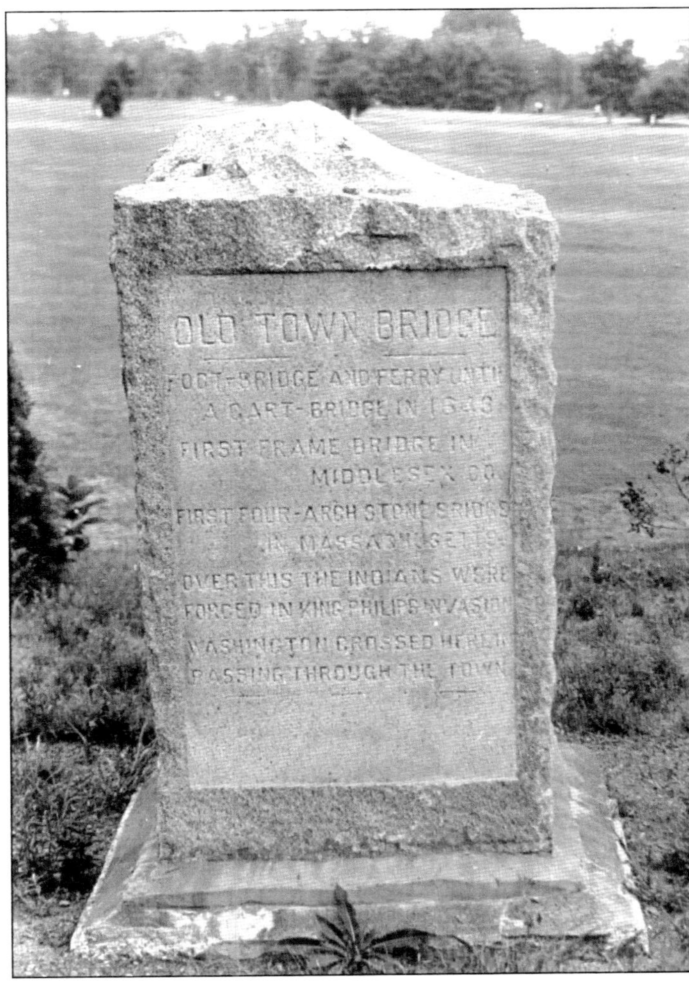


This Old Town Bridge marker is on the original Route 27 beside the Wayland Country Club. It marks the place where eight Concord men died on April 22, 1676, while coming to Sudbury's aid during the King Philip's War. The names of the men, listed on the side, are as follows: James Hosmer, John Barnes, Samuel Potter, Daniel Comy, Joseph Butterick, David Curry, Josiah Wheeler, and William Hayward.

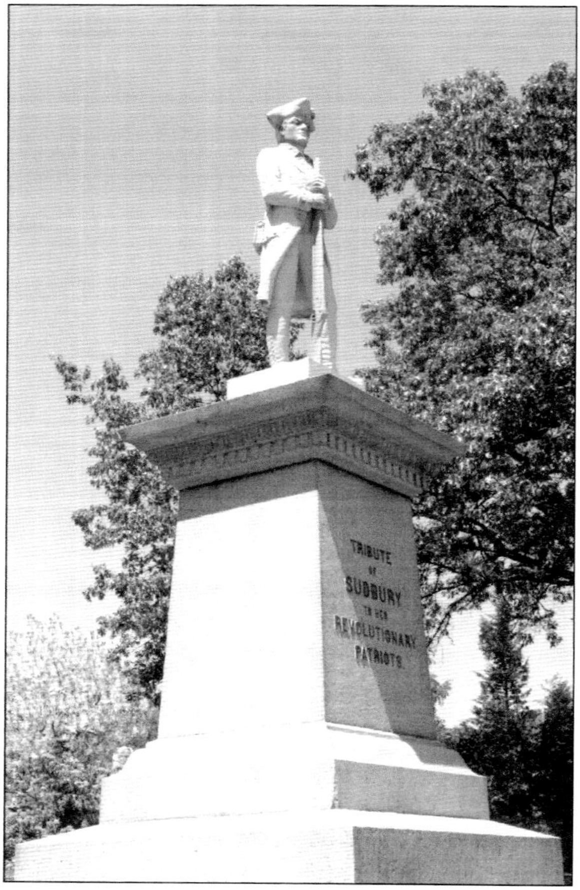


The Revolutionary Patriots Monument was dedicated on June 17, 1896, in honor of the soldiers and sailors of Sudbury who fought at Lexington, Concord, Bunker Hill, and in other battles of the Revolutionary War from 1775 to 1783. William Stone's father, Waldol, posed for the monument. One of the gentlemen who addressed the crowd that day was noted historian A.S. Hudson, who reported that out of the Sudbury population of 2,100, probably 500 were in the Concord and Lexington fights on April 19, 1775.

Below is the Revolutionary War Cemetery in Sudbury's town center. It was originally known as Ye Olde Burying Ground and began in 1716. At the time of the American Revolution, Sudbury was the largest town in Middlesex County.

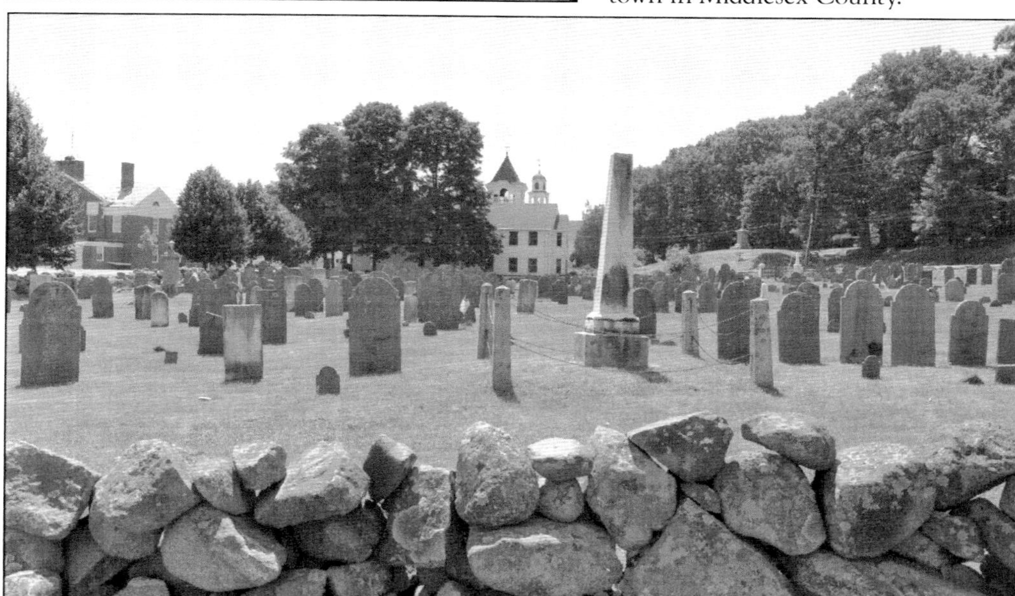

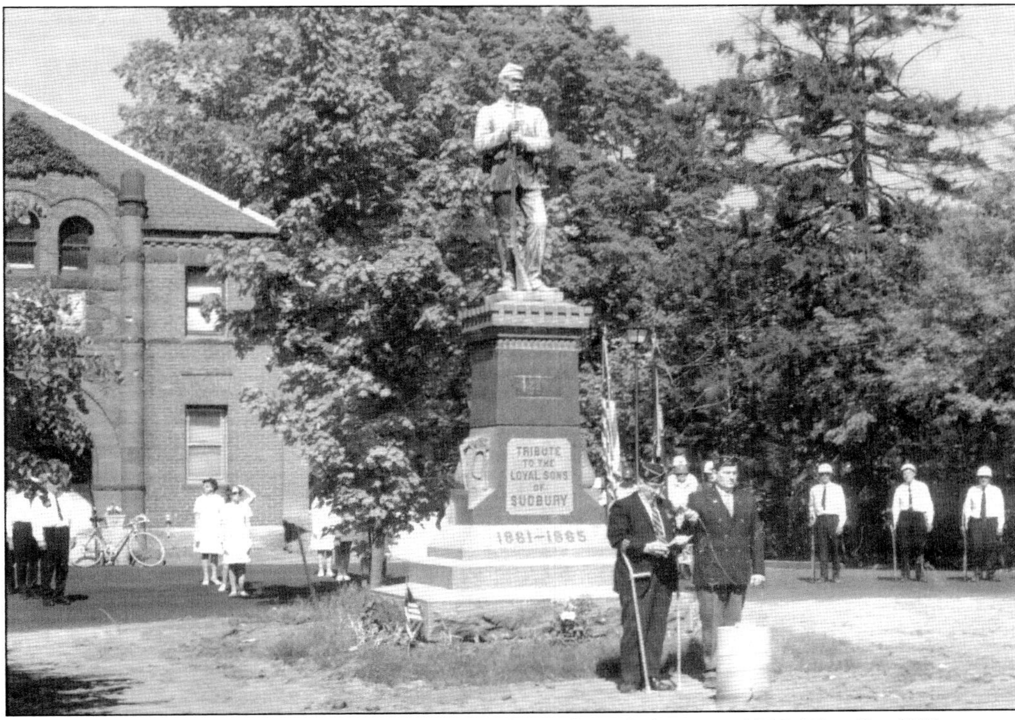


This was a Memorial Day observance in front of Goodnow Library in 1980. The Civil War statue was erected in honor of those who fought from Sudbury. Doug Lewis is shown standing on the right, with Forrest Bradshaw, the town historian at the time, reading from his notes.

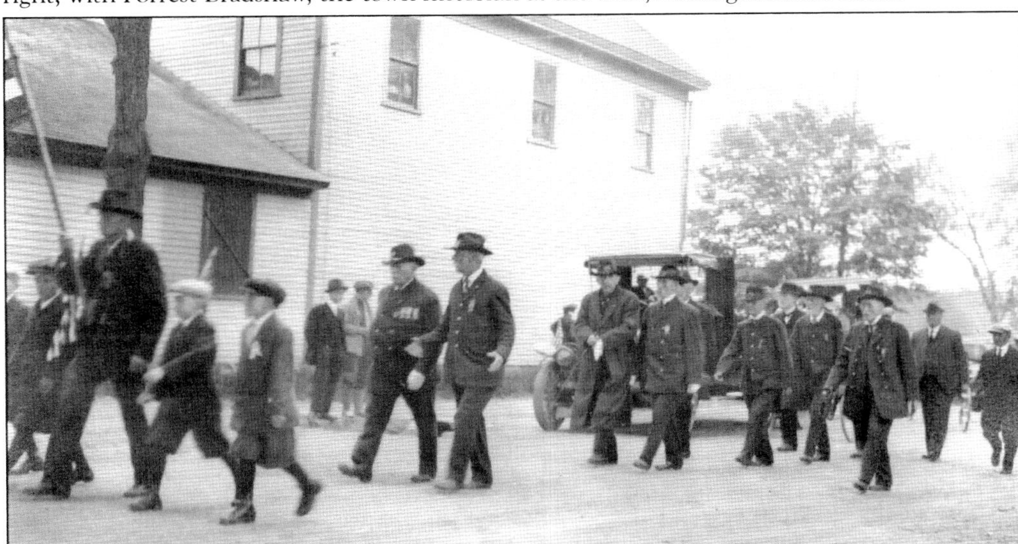

The Grand Army of the Republic (GAR) marches on Memorial Day 1916, turning the corner onto Concord Road. The GAR was a Civil War veterans group that banded together to fight for Veterans' rights. On this day, 10 Sudbury veterans marched or were driven. The SHS's remarkable collection of letters from Pvt. George F. Moor and his family (1862–1865) formed the basis of the SHS's new book, *From Your Loving Son*, in 2012. (Photograph by Harriet Richardson.)

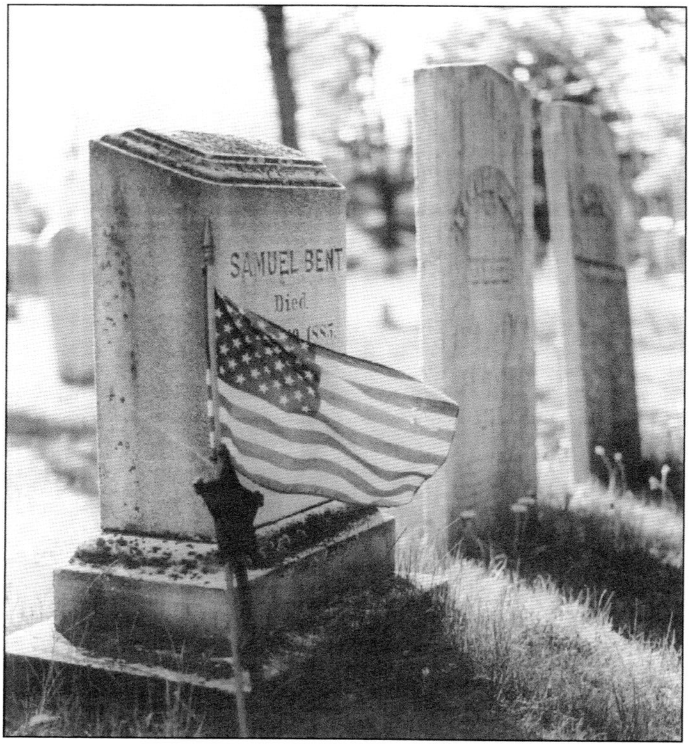


This is the grave of Civil War veteran Samuel Bent Jr., who died on July 18, 1885. Bent, from an old Sudbury family, was a farmer who was conscripted into the Civil War in 1863 at age 30. Every year for Memorial Day, all the graves of veterans are honored with flags placed in specific flag holders in their honor.

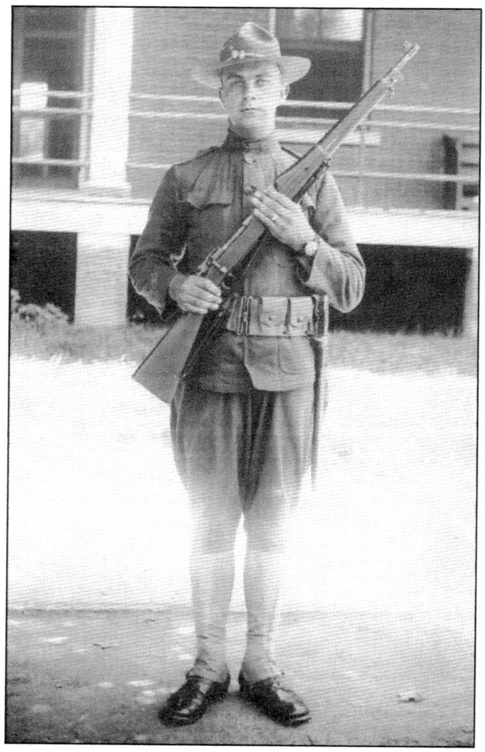

This postcard shows World War I soldier Maurice B. White in full uniform. White, a Sudbury youth, was stationed at Fort Myer, Virginia, in May 1918 attached to the 37th Engineering Corps of Company D. The postcard was sent to the Richardson family on King Philip Road. Luckily, Sudbury did not lose any native sons in World War I.

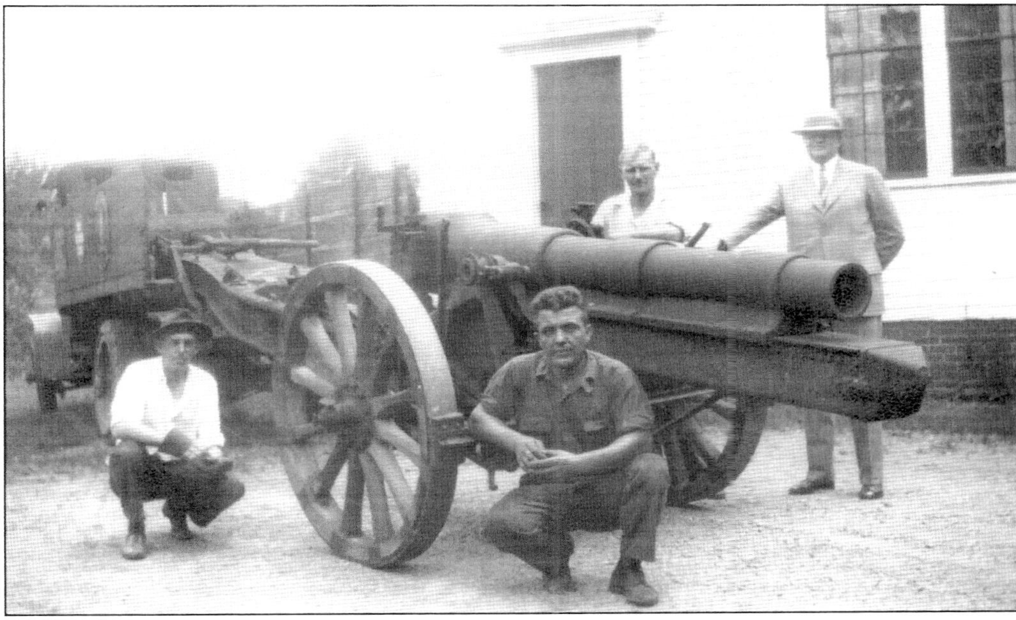

American Legion Post No. 191 used to be located at 415 Boston Post Road, at the previous location of the Wadsworth School, which now houses the police department. Members of the post worked together to obtain the cannon shown above to decorate the front lawn. The World War I Italian field piece was obtained from the Framingham National Guard arsenal in 1926. Posing with the cannon are, from left to right, Forrest Bradshaw, Alfred F. Bonazzoli, Albert Tallant, and Maj. Dr. Albert Owen, who hauled it over with a Bonazzoli coal truck.

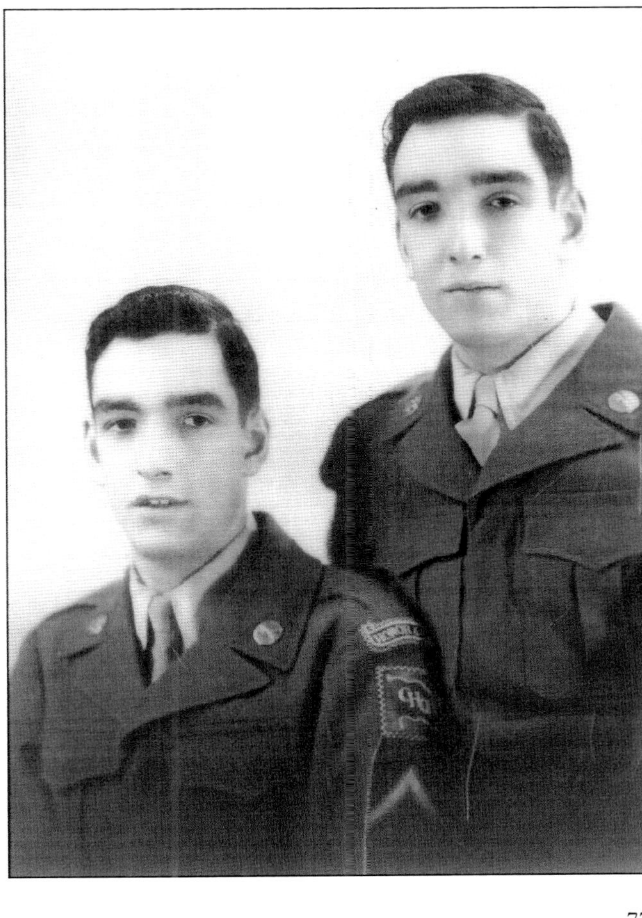

Sudbury twins Russell (left) and Robert Mugford are dressed in their World War II uniforms, which specify that they were in the honor guard at command headquarters in the Pacific Theater of the war. One of their duties was to drive and escort Gen. Douglas MacArthur.

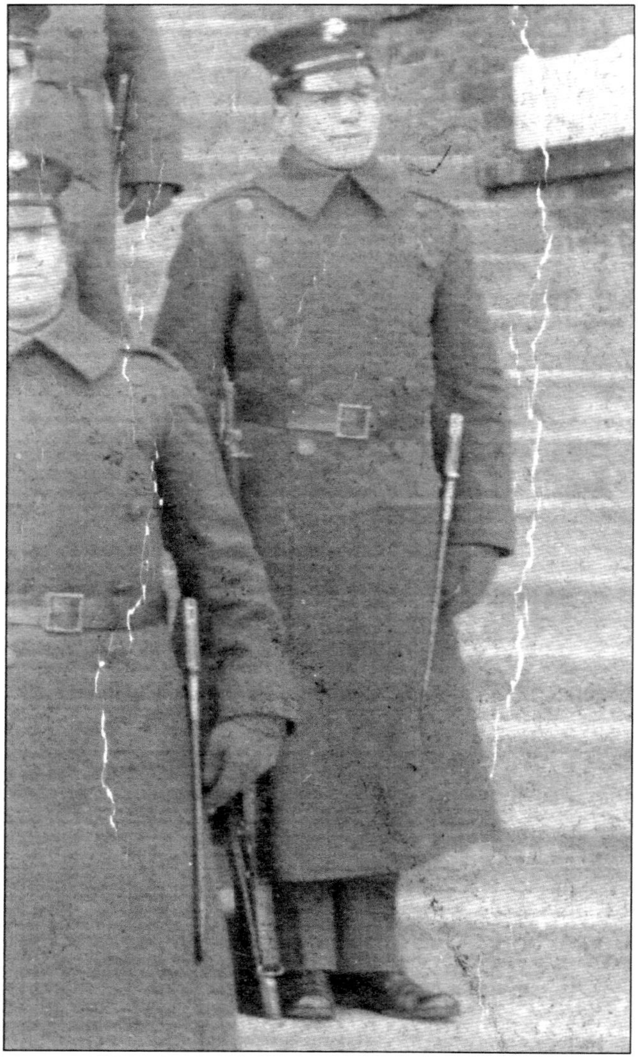

Marine sergeant Leo Spottswood of Sudbury was photographed with his boot camp class at Norfolk, Virginia, on June 16, 1915, the same year he achieved marksman status. Spottswood was the father of local artist Joan Meenan.

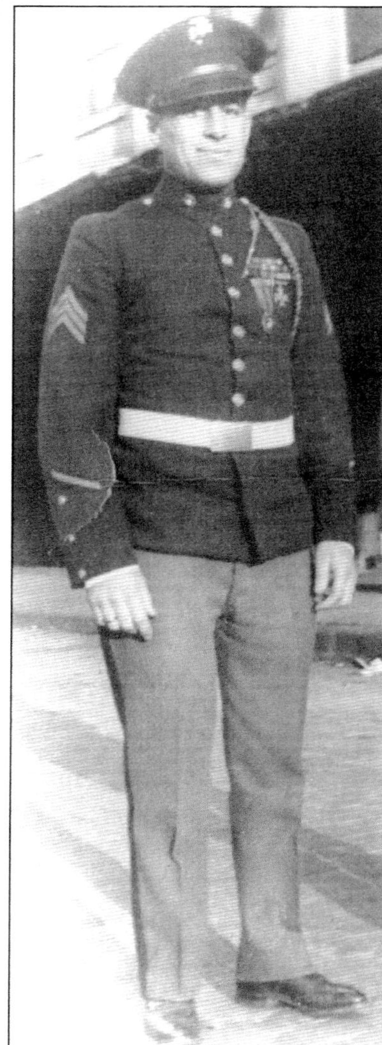

Sergeant Spottswood is seen at right at the end of World War I, after he survived fighting in the trenches in France and was decorated with a Purple Heart and other ribbons. Later, as a civilian, he had the unique opportunity of driving Charles Lindbergh and his new wife, Anne Morrow, on their honeymoon in the United States.

Don Somers of Sudbury climbs into an SNJ fighter plane during basic flight training in the US Navy. Somers fought in the Korean War from 1950 to 1953. His wife, Nancy, is an SHS trustee.

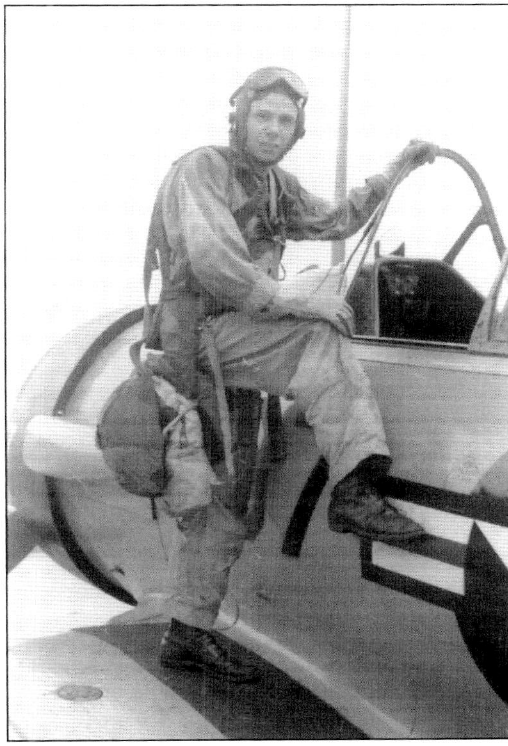

This photograph shows the Raising of the Colors on Memorial Day 1972 at the flagpole in front of the town hall. From left to right are Doug Lewis of American Legion Post No. 191; Al Bonazzoli, formerly of the 26th Yankee Division; and Sgt. Leo Spottswood. Bonazzoli helped start the Sudbury Companies of Militia and Minute in 1962.

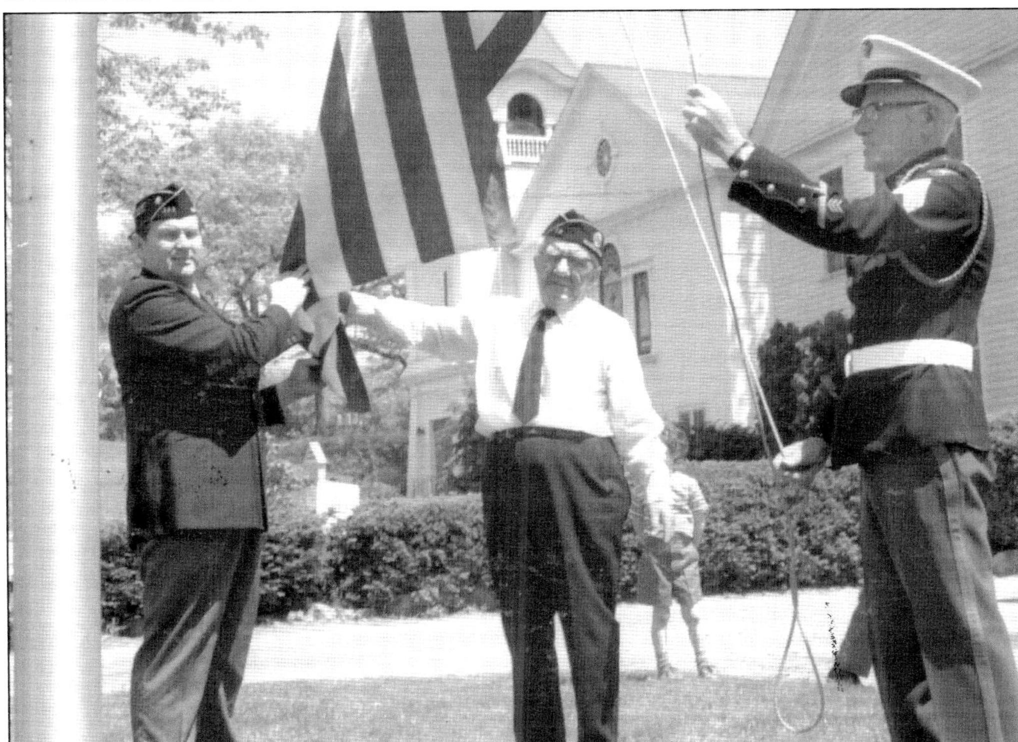

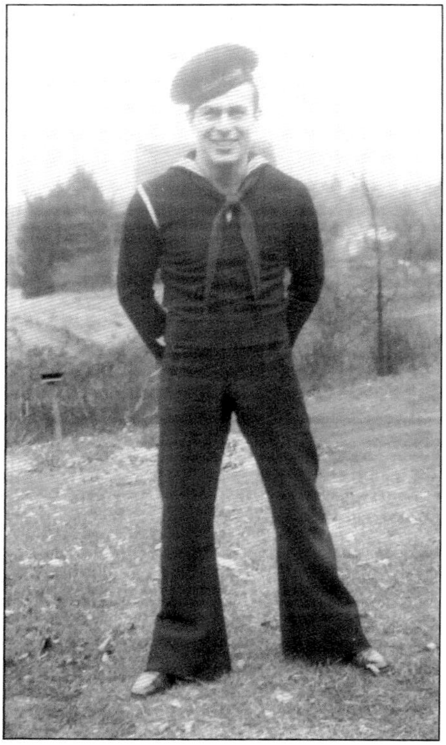

Sudbury local Phillip Richardson looks very happy in his Coast Guard uniform during World War II. As a child, he used to play being a soldier, sailor, or cowboy with his gang on King Philip Road. The SHS has been gifted with his uniforms along with much historical material from the Richardson family.

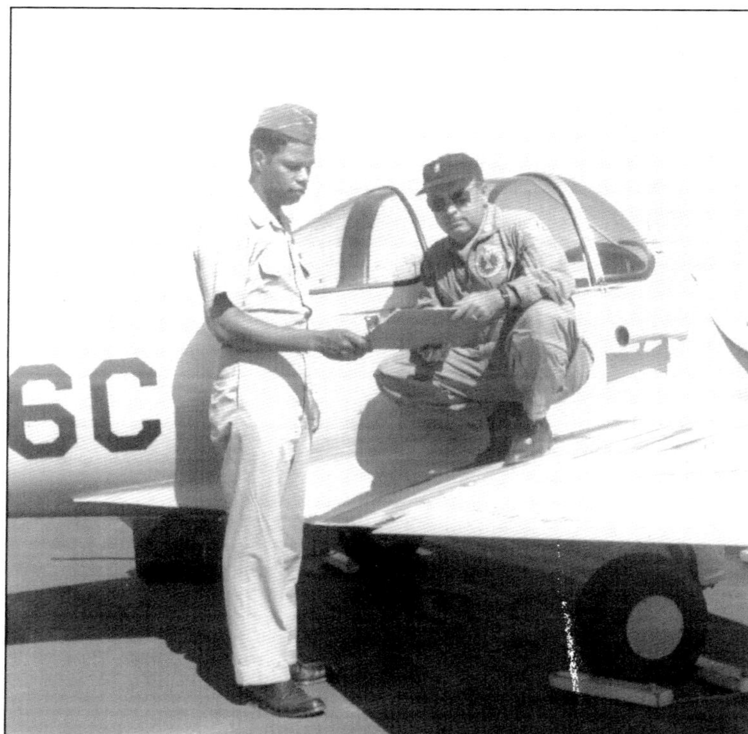


Maj. Herbert Hardy (left), of Normandy Drive in Sudbury, and Maj. Leslie Caufield, of Moore Road in Wayland, are seen with this Civil Air Patrol plane. In the late 1930s, more than 150,000 volunteers with a love for aviation argued for an organization to put their planes and flying skills to use in defense of their country. As a result, the Civil Air Patrol was born one week prior to the Japanese attack on Pearl Harbor.

Charles Pepper, of Sudbury, smiles broadly with his cleaned mess kit in his hand in Okinawa in 1944.

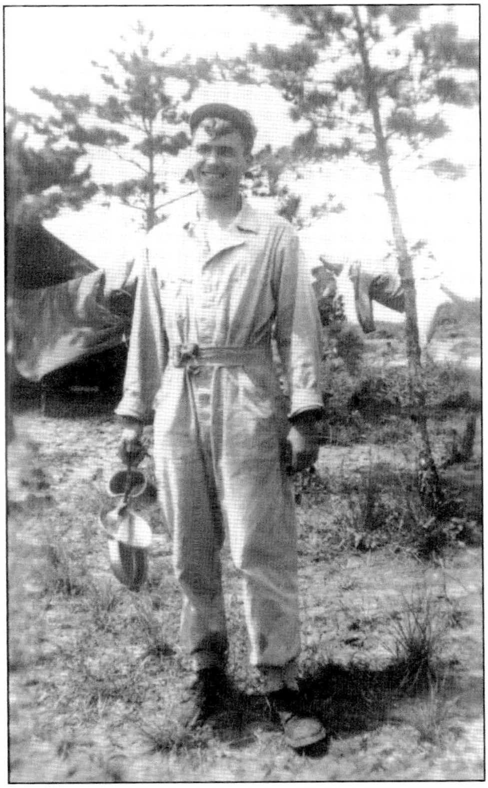

Preparing for a parade on Memorial Day 1998 are Sudbury veterans, from left to right, Don Somers, Charlie Pepper, Don Peirce, Lincoln Sudbury Regional High School student Mark Wyman, and Air Force colonel Clay Allen, who once displayed his medals, citations, and awards, which took up two full tables. Here, Colonel Allen still fits into his original dress uniform and marched in the parades into his 90s.

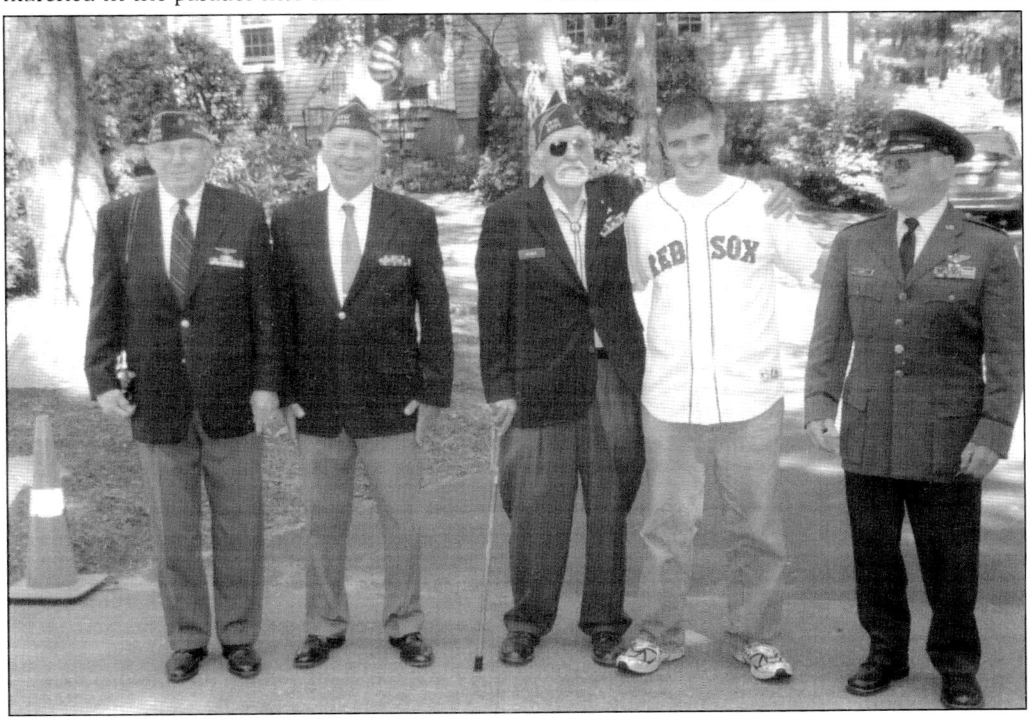

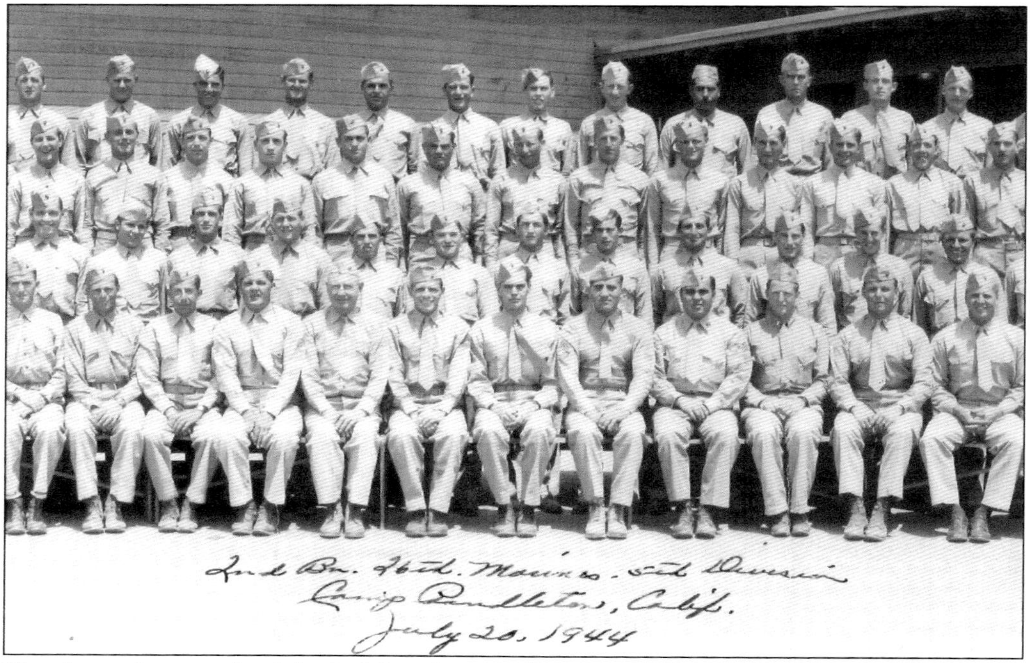


The above photograph of the 2nd Battalion, 26th Marines, 5th Division was taken on July 20, 1944 during training at Camp Pendleton in California. This is the middle portion of a three-foot panoramic picture and is believed to include an unidentified Sudbury boy. (Courtesy of Spencer Goldstein.)

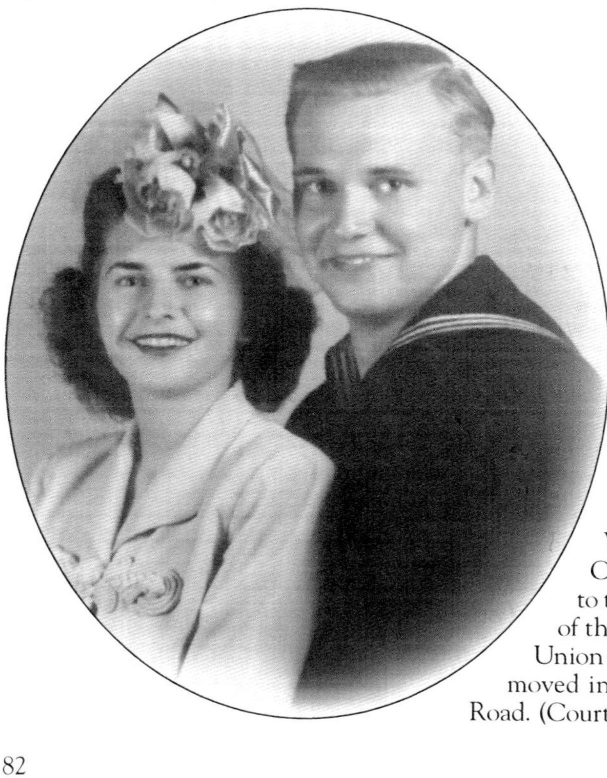

This photograph of a Navy man and his fashionable wife was found in a wooden Commander Beverage case in Wellesley. The Commander Beverage Company operated from around 1900 up to the 1960s, initially on the eastern corner of the intersection of Boston Post Road and Union Avenue in Sudbury. In the 1930s, they moved into a new building at 621 Boston Post Road. (Courtesy of Doreen Kemp.)

# *Six*

# TRANSPORTATION

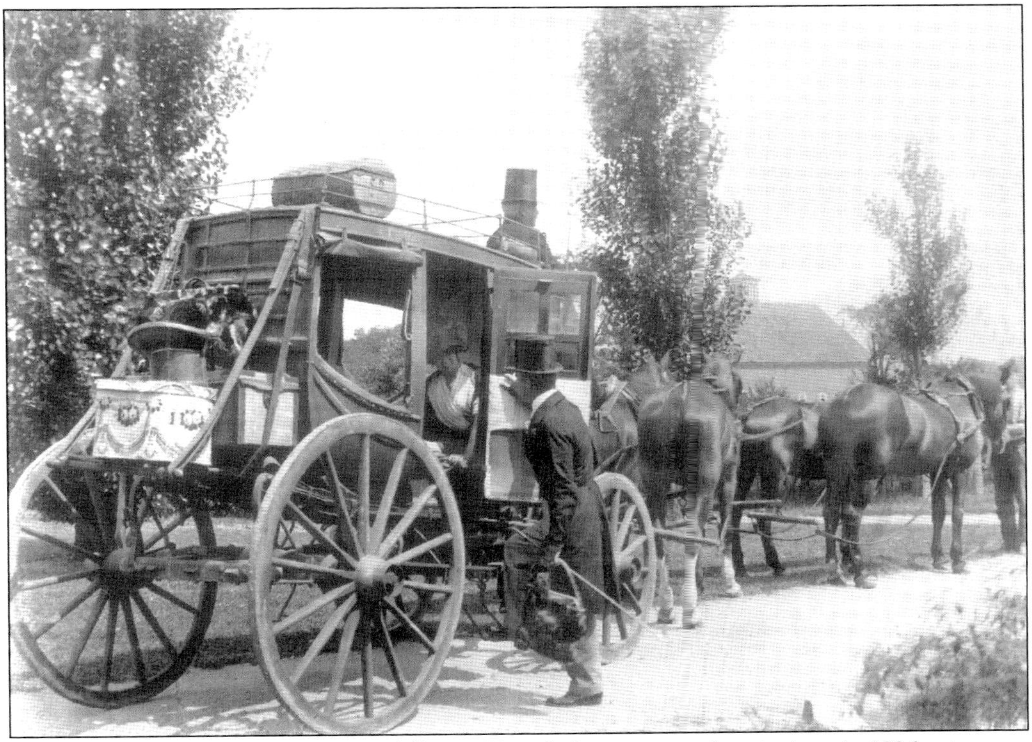

This photograph was posed at Longfellow's Wayside Inn in several variations in 1926 using one of the stagecoaches that late innkeeper Edward R. Lemon had collected. The purpose was to create a historical jigsaw puzzle. It was the start of the national craze for jigsaw puzzles, which continued unabated during and after the Great Depression. At the time, one could buy daily jigsaw puzzles at newsstands.

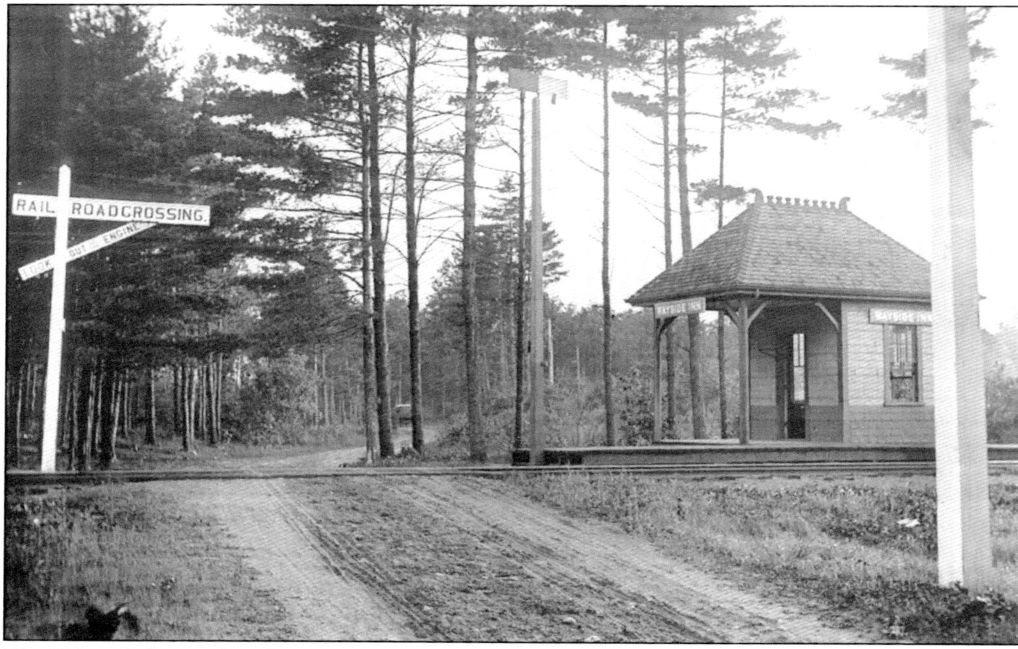


The Wayside Inn railroad waiting room was of a very stylish Japanese design and was built by the Boston & Maine Railroad in 1897. At the time, it was described as a cozy, comfortable depot. It was located on Dutton Road at the railroad track, and those inside had to flag down the trains themselves. Babe Ruth, Henry Ford, and guests of the inn all had to do just that. The building was burned by vandals in the 1940s, and its remains are no longer visible. (Courtesy of Robert Seymour.)

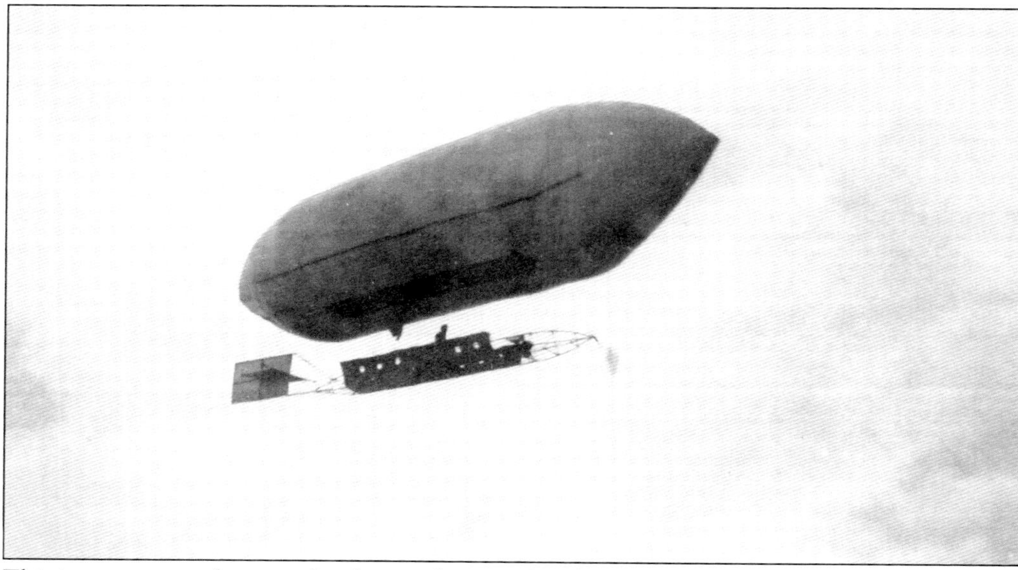

This is a very rare photograph taken at the 1910 Brockton Fair, where the world-famous aviator Alberto Santos-Dumont displayed his powered dirigible for the edification and wonder of the public. A caricature of Santos-Dumont appeared in the British *Vanity Fair* in 1899, showing this very same dirigible, No. 6. This photograph was taken by Harriet Richardson on one of her family's expeditions to other parts of the state.

In this 1913 photograph, a young girl is dressed all in white on the right and a boy rides a bicycle on the left. Behind them, a man works in the field where the village green is today at 29 Hudson Road.

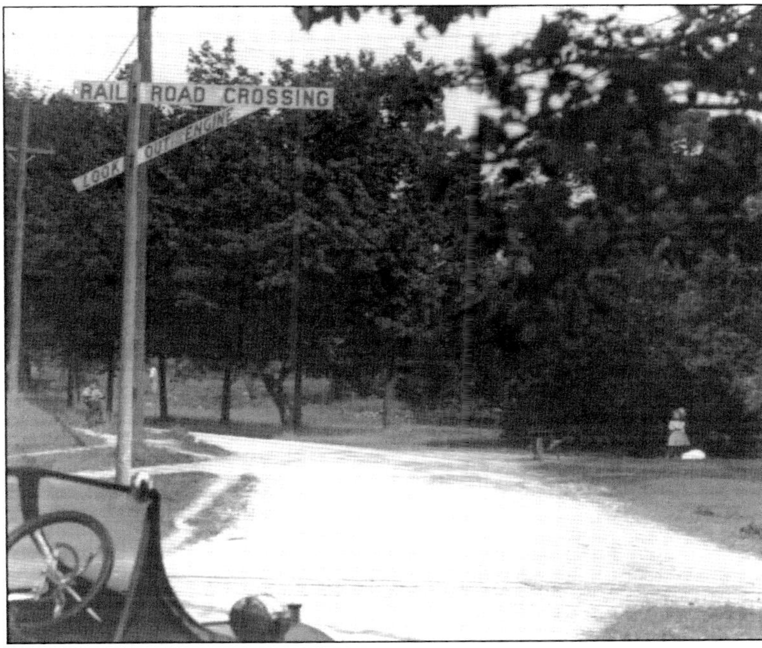


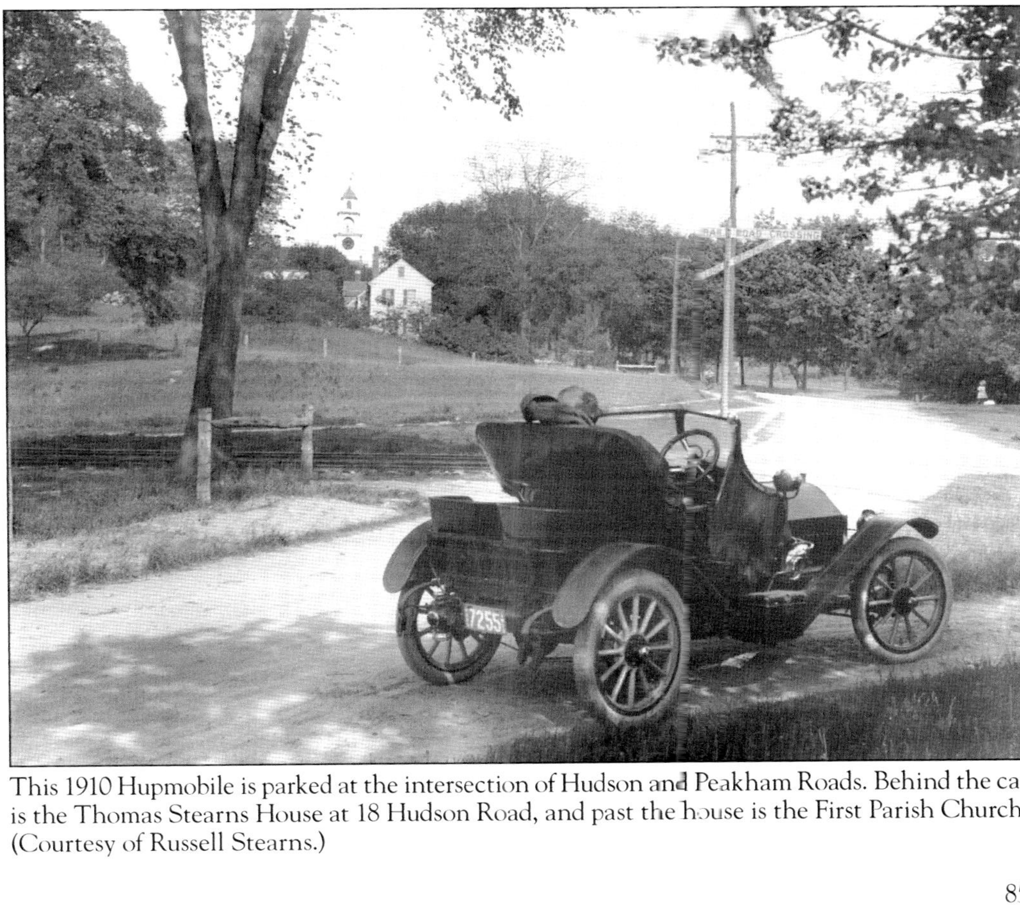

This 1910 Hupmobile is parked at the intersection of Hudson and Peakham Roads. Behind the car is the Thomas Stearns House at 18 Hudson Road, and past the house is the First Parish Church. (Courtesy of Russell Stearns.)

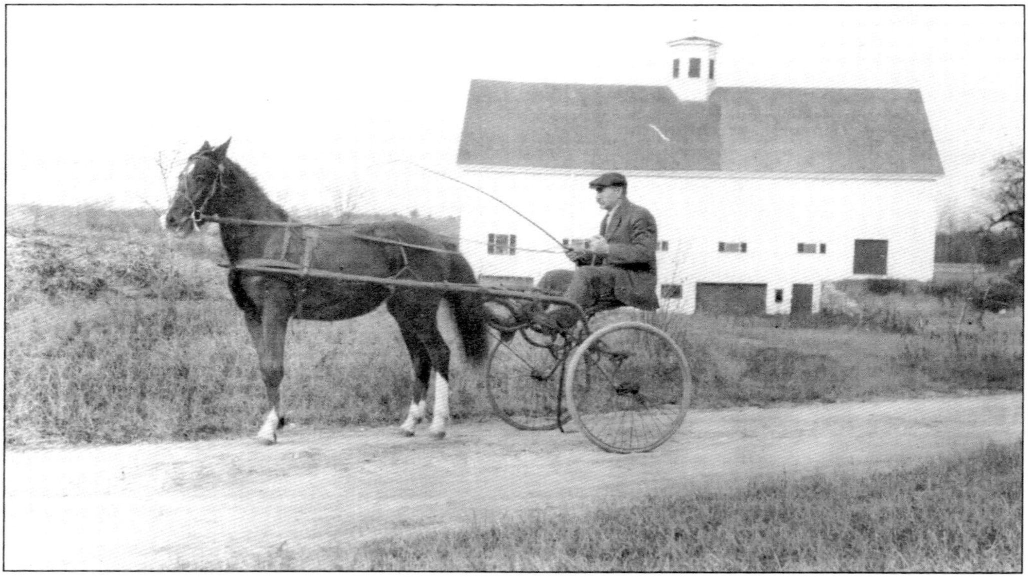

Edward McLaughlin used to live at the end of Garrison House Lane near the Wayside Inn. He eventually sold his house and land to Henry Ford in the 1920s, but his house was still called the McLaughlin House by the boys' school and the inn employees. McLaughlin fancied a high-stepping horse that he would put through its paces on the dirt roads around the inn. This barn became one of Henry Ford's dairy barns.

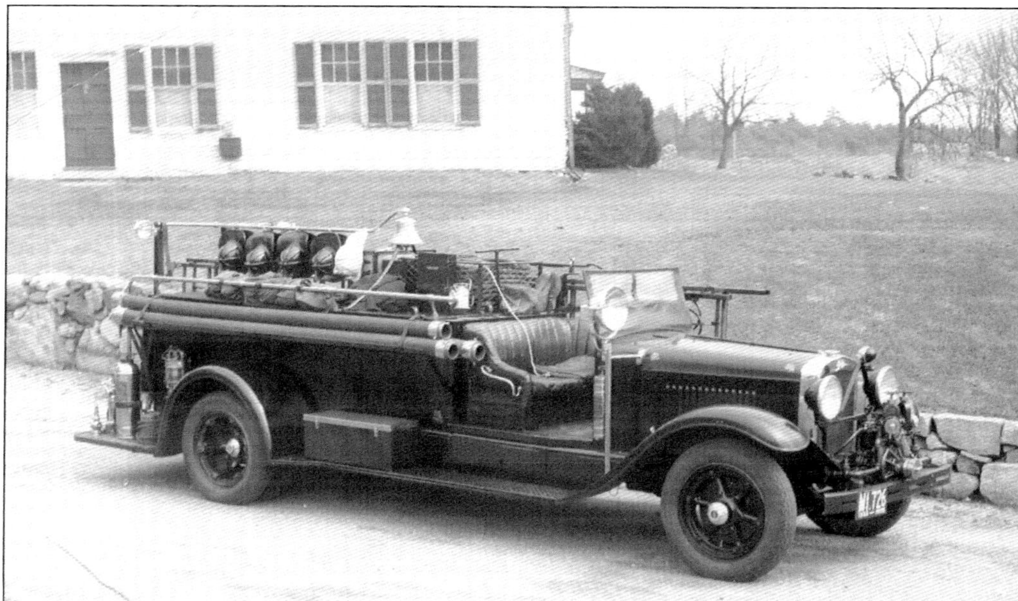

It took the town a long time to purchase this 1930 International fire truck. There were two major fires in 1925, which led the town to appoint a fire committee to make recommendations on new equipment. In 1926, it was recommended that a pumper be purchased, but the idea languished until the town hall burned on February 5, 1930, spurring the town to form the fire department in 1931.

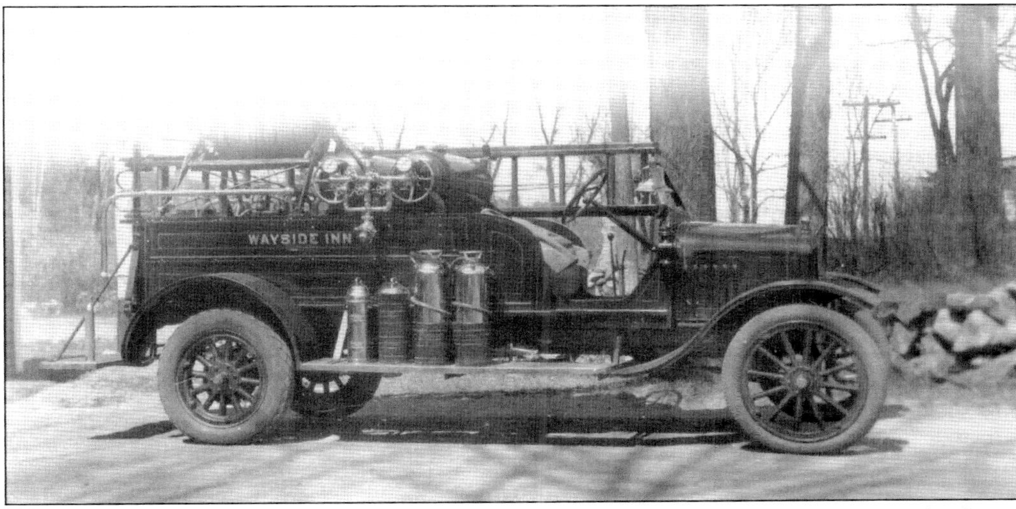


The Wayside Inn fire truck is seen here in 1934. It was a pumper, bringing water to the fire or drawing the water from a nearby well or pond. The inn property included 40 houses, barns, a gristmill, schoolhouses, a lumber mill, and lumberyards on its 2,995 nearly contiguous acres. Although the greatest fear was forest fires, the inn's most damaging fire began in the inn itself in 1955.

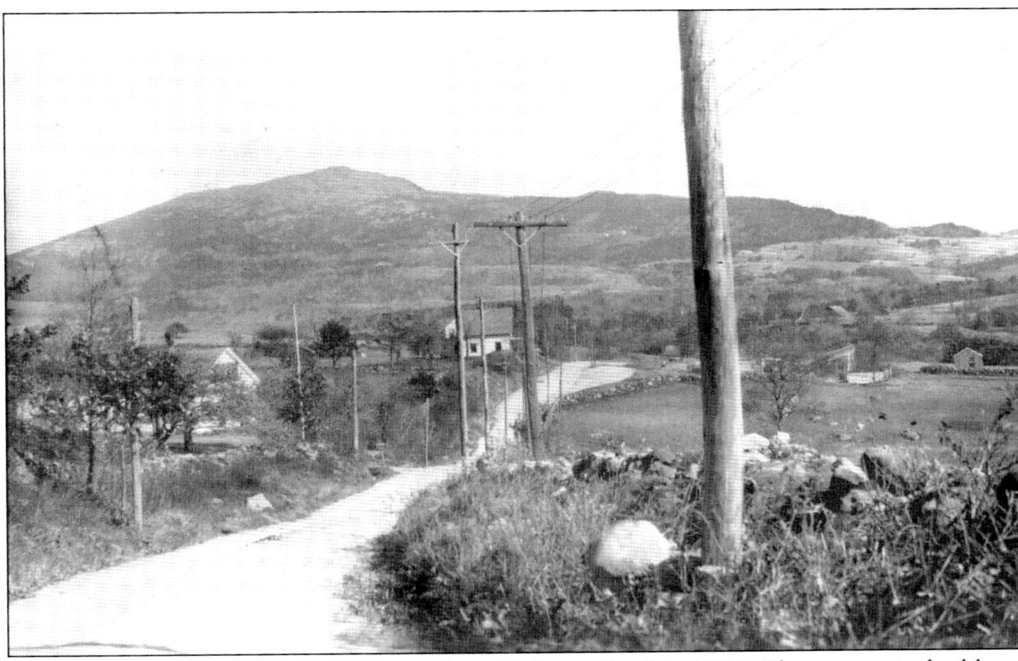

This view of Mount Nobscot looks south on Nobscot Road in 1904. The mountain had been almost entirely clear-cut for firewood and lumber. This is what the countryside all around Sudbury looked like at the time, as citizens raised crops and planted orchards, keeping an odd woodlot of fine chestnut for fence rails and black locust for fence posts or just firewood.

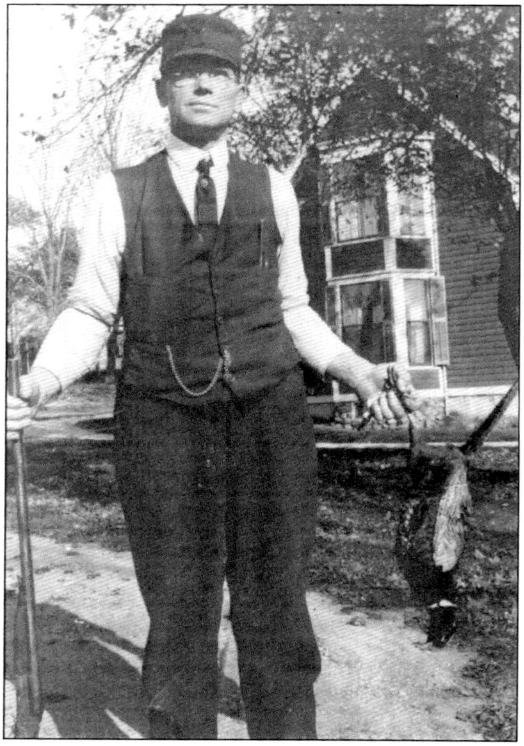

In 1916, Harry Baldwin was the stationmaster at the South Sudbury station across from 28 Union Avenue. He is shown here holding a small-bore rifle with a pheasant in his other hand. Years earlier, John Goulding had reintroduced pheasants into Sudbury. Harry Baldwin was Hope Baldwin's father.

Below, Jack McKinnon (left) and an unidentified merchant pose at an Old Time Value Days promotion in the 1950s. The McKinnons owned a market and then a liquor store in Sudbury for three generations. The store was originally located at 320 Boston Post Road and later moved to 450 Boston Post Road. This photograph was taken at the Wayside Inn, where they had borrowed a carriage for the promotion.

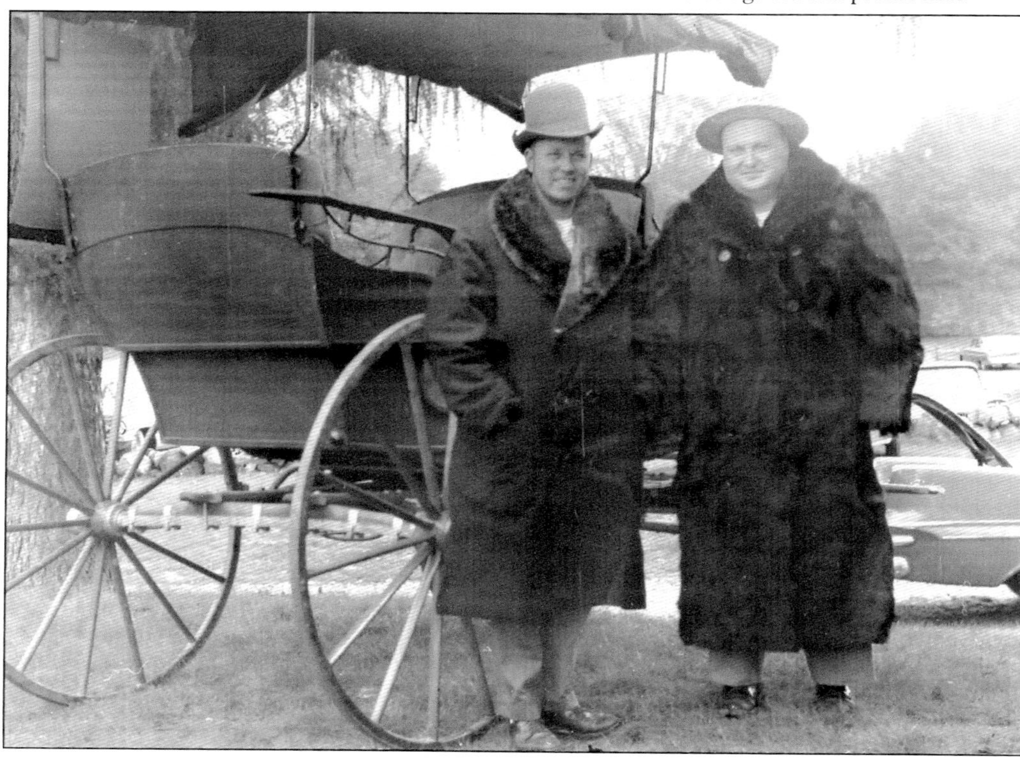

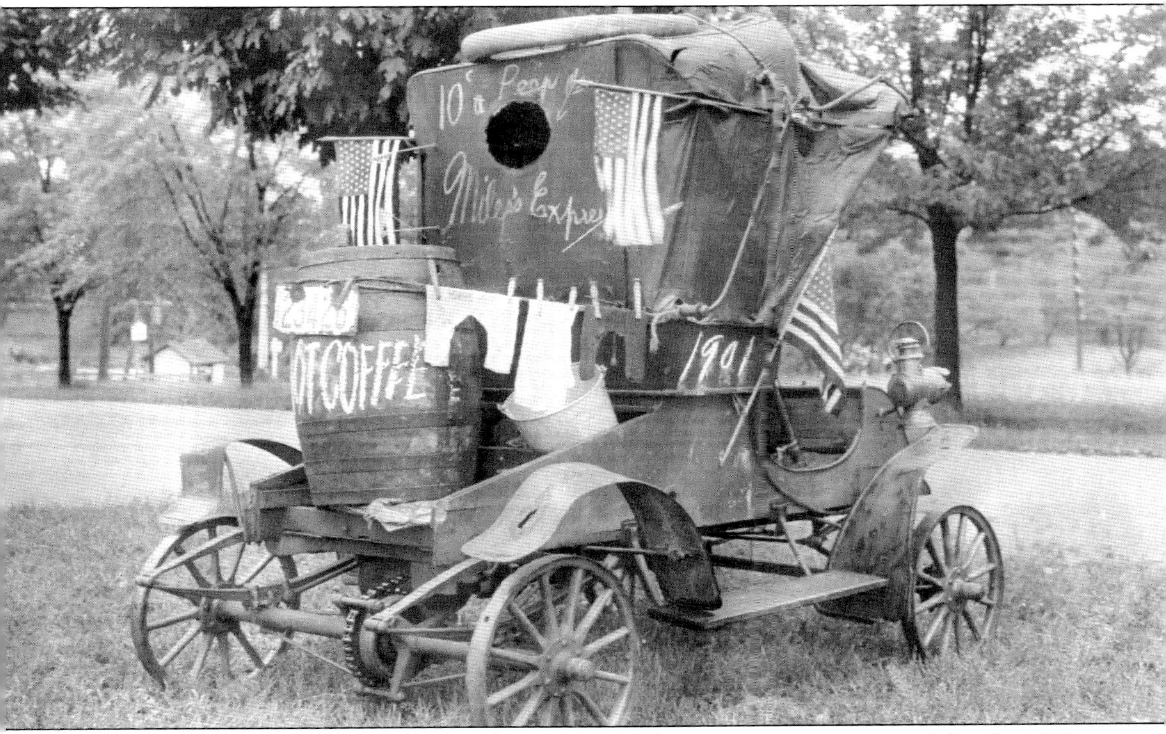


Miles's Express, a 1901 Ford with zany decorations and inscriptions, was created for the 1939 Tercentennial Parade and looks like it actually ran.

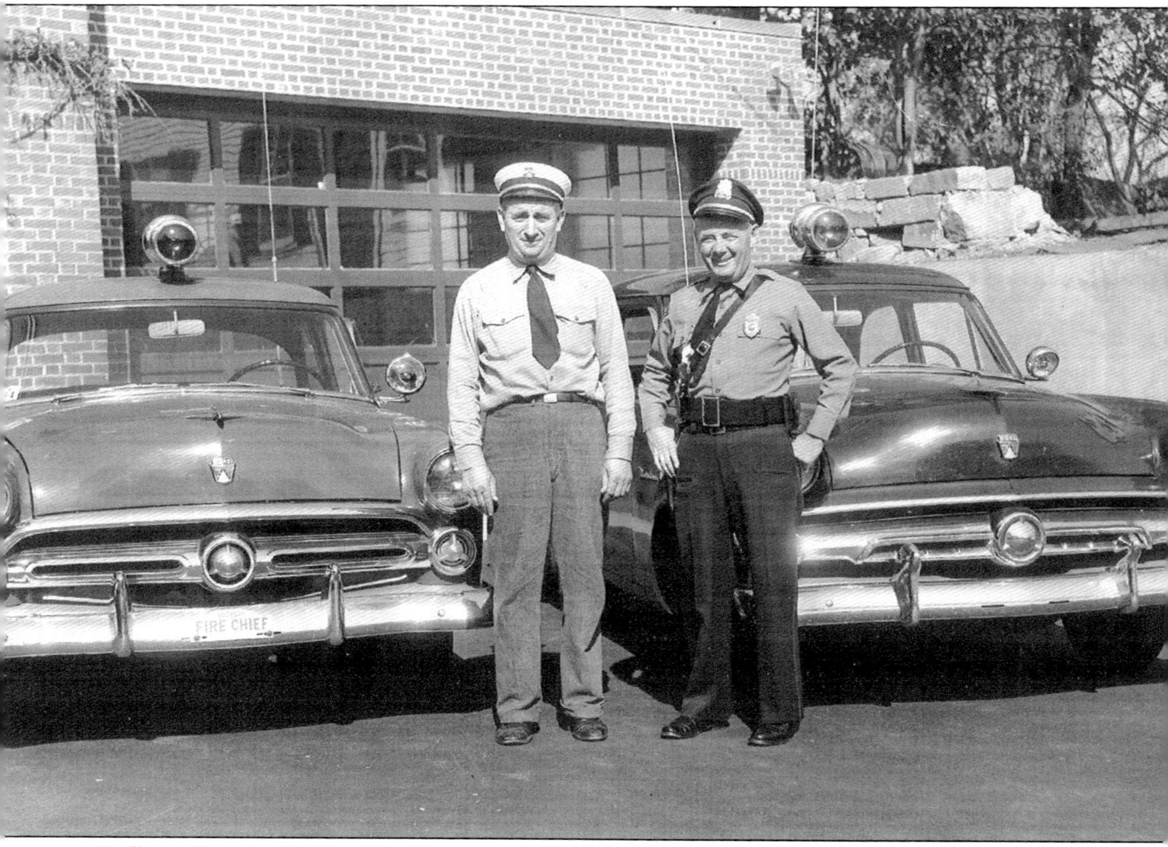


Sudbury fire chief Alfred St. Germain (left) and police chief John Mc Govern stand in front of their vehicles at the lower town hall fire station in 1954. The fire station, the town's first, was built in 1932.

# Seven
# RECREATION

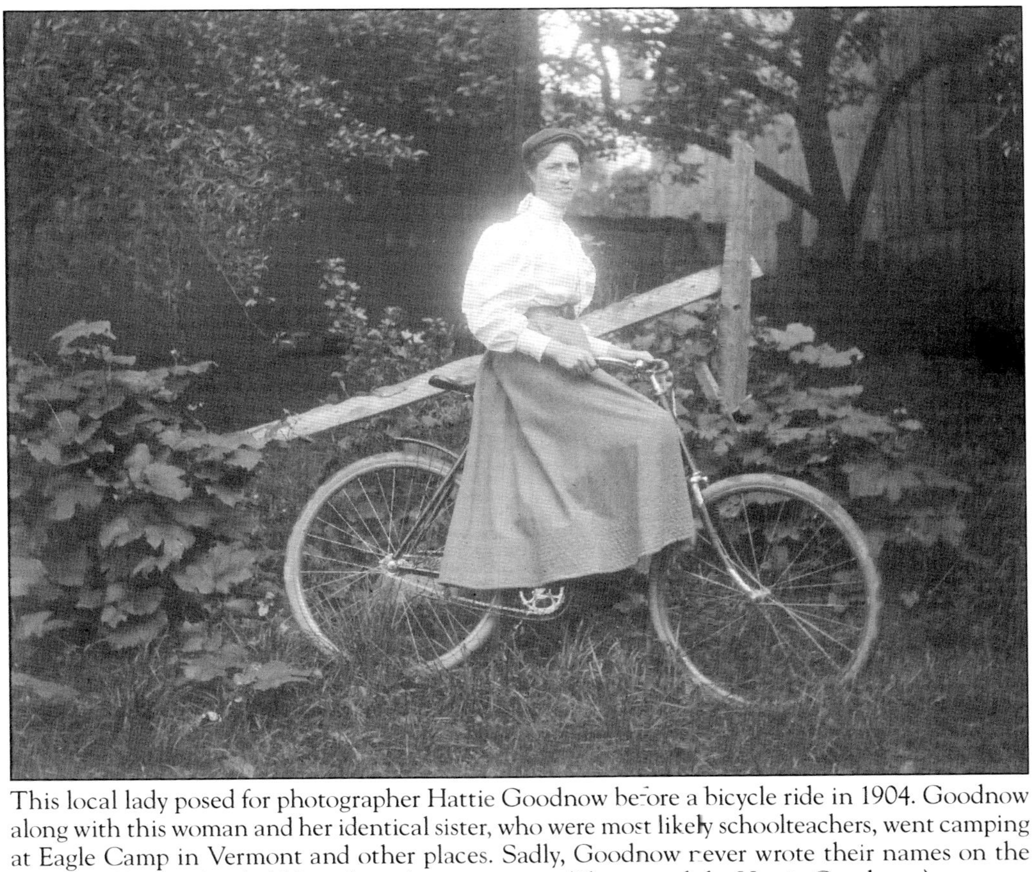

This local lady posed for photographer Hattie Goodnow before a bicycle ride in 1904. Goodnow along with this woman and her identical sister, who were most likely schoolteachers, went camping at Eagle Camp in Vermont and other places. Sadly, Goodnow never wrote their names on the cardboard boxes that held her glass-plate negatives. (Photograph by Hattie Goodnow.)

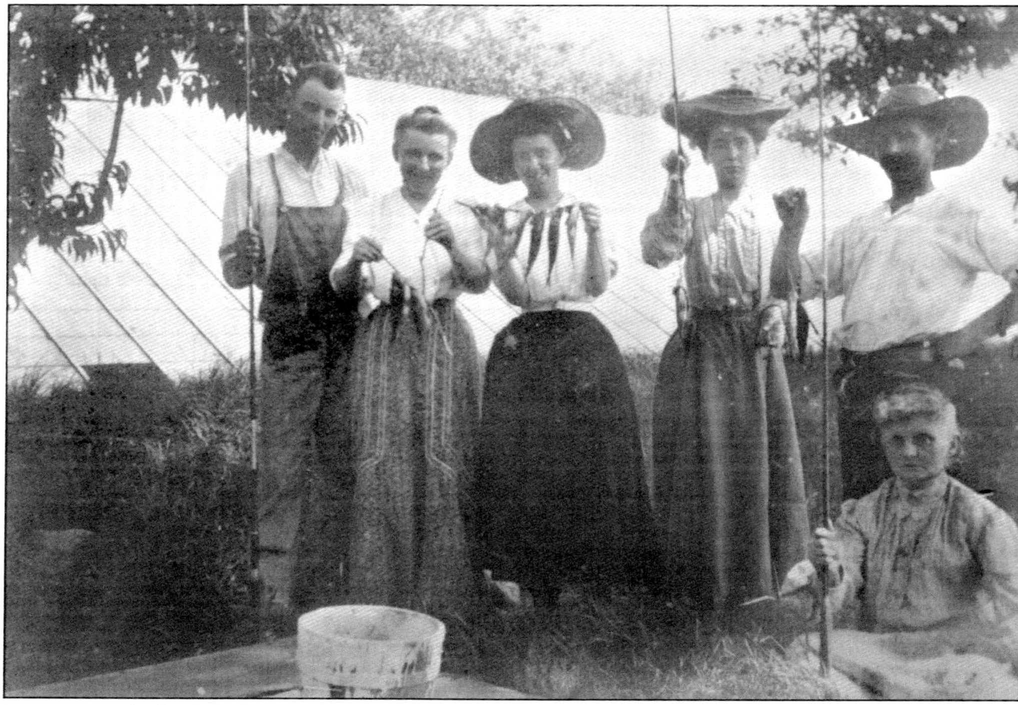

Henry Smith (right) shows off his catch of brook trout with his employees after a summer day spent fishing at the Raymond farm pond, located on what is now near Warren Avenue. Smith lived at 106 Woodside Road and fished in this pond, which was never stocked—the fish were introduced by birds picking up fish eggs on their feet and transferring them. Note the glass of Smith's greenhouse in the background; he was quite the horticulturalist!

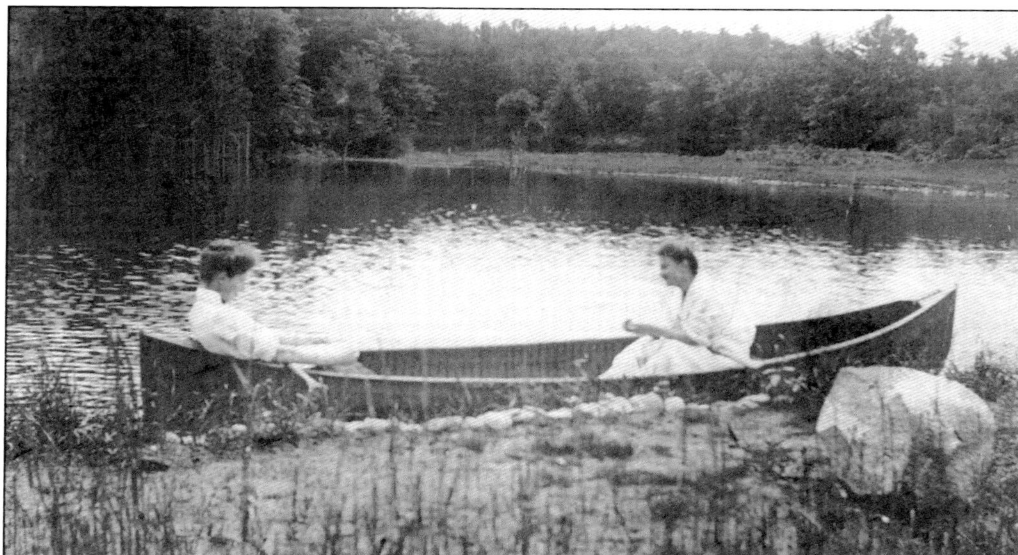

Helen Smith (left) and Lillie Lutz enjoy a summer day in a wooden canoe on the pond at the Raymond farm. They were relatives of Henry Smith who worked for him at the Cosmos Seed Company at 106 Woodside Road in 1910.

This young man, likely a Raymond heir, rides a tricycle in the early 1900s on the grounds of the Raymond estate.

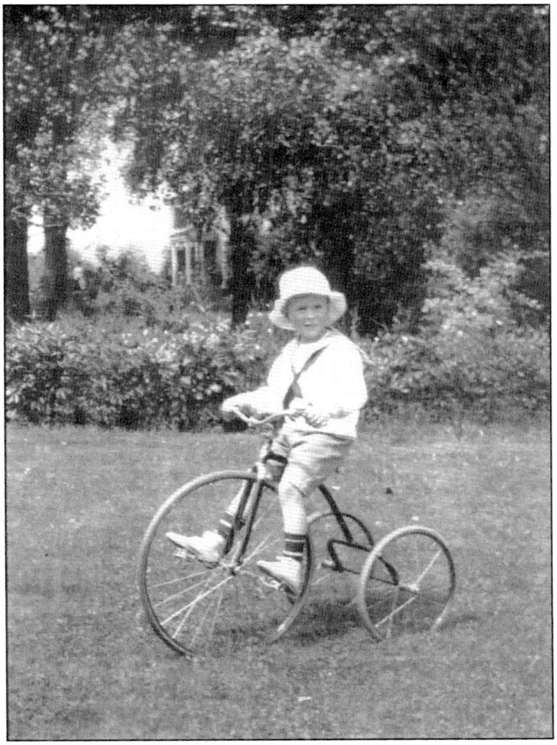

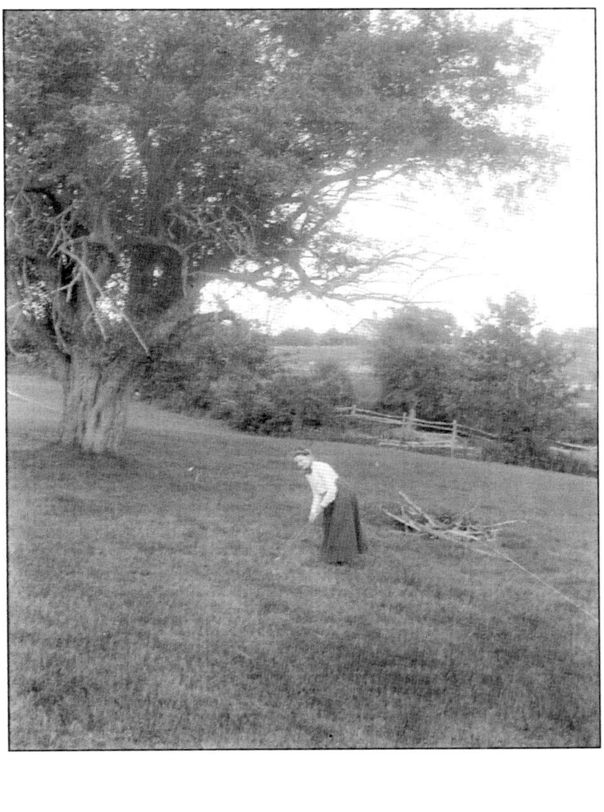

Loretta Hunt plays a rough game of golf in a field that had just been hayed in 1902. The field was on Green Hill in Sudbury and belonged to the Goodnow family. (Photograph by Hattie Goodnow.)

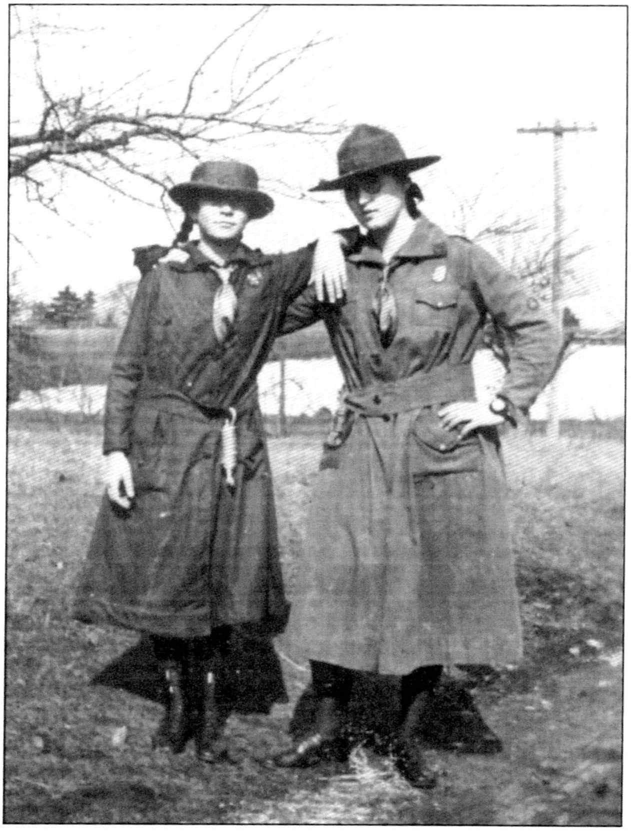

E. Helene Sherman (left) and her sister Anna pose in their Girl Scout uniforms in 1920. Helene, who celebrated 65 years as a Scout in 1985, eked out a living as an artist specializing in illumination and calligraphy and went on to achieve fame with her works. She owned her house at 328 Goodman's Hill Road.

Unlike some baseball teams, the local team below actually had uniforms, which were usually supplied by a local business. The young man in front, James Bartlett, was the batboy. The partial list of names on this photograph includes, from left to right, (first row) Walter Carson, Ross ?, Patsy Mercury, John M., unidentified, and Charlie Whitworth; (second row) ? Whitney, unidentified, Lawrence Deroll, Jack Borden, Jack Giddings, and unidentified.

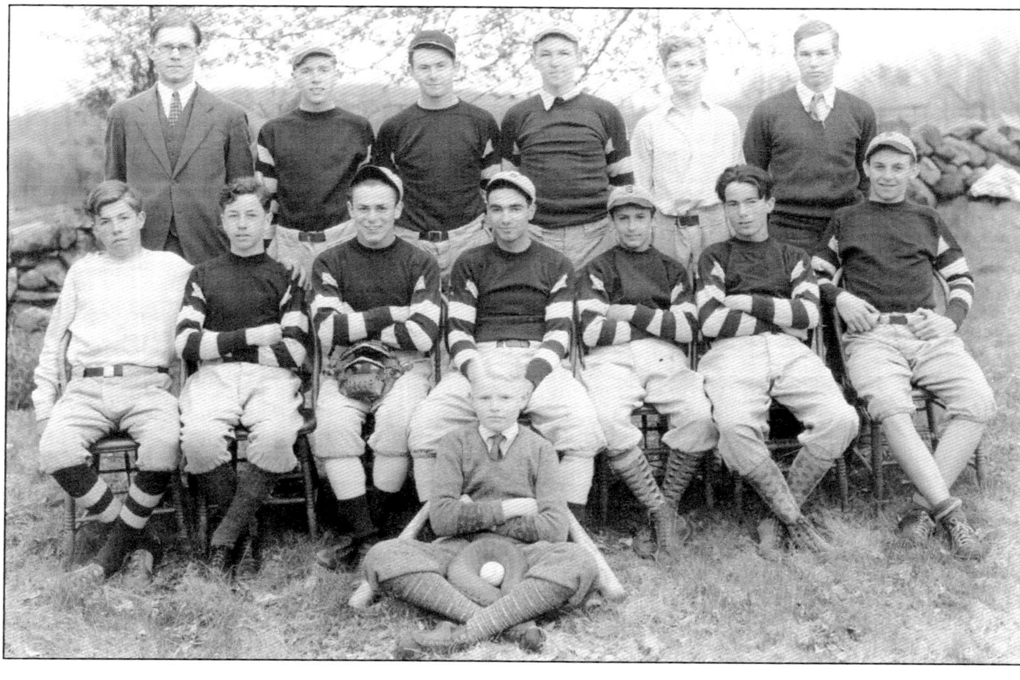

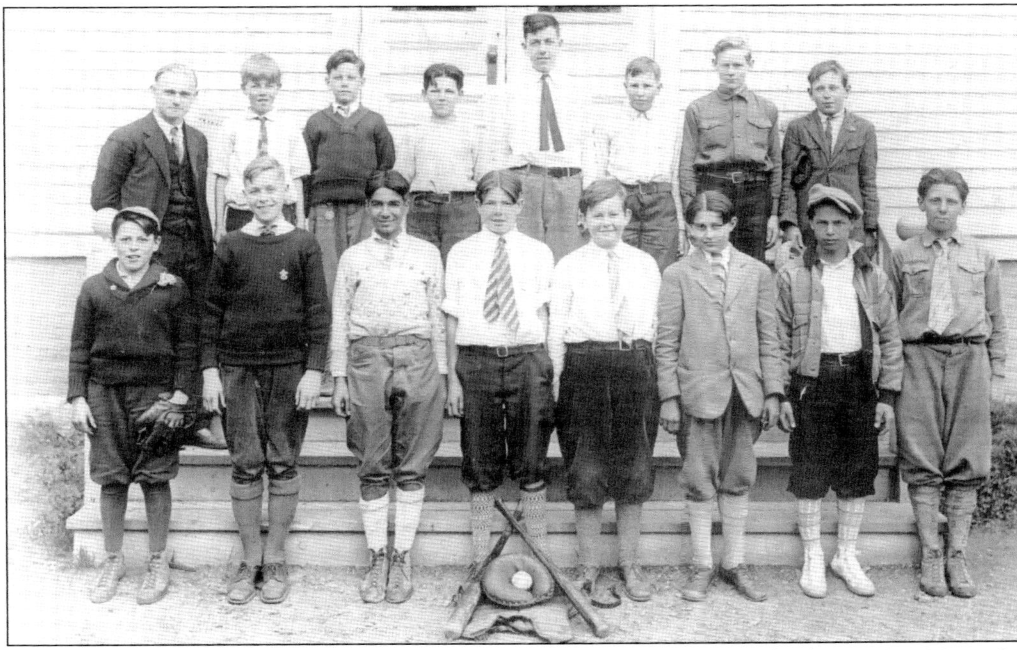

This baseball team and their coach line up for a team photograph in the late 1930s. Note the details of the early baseball glove at the bottom. This image also contains only a partial list of names, including, from left to right, (first row) Reynolds, Carson, two unidentified boys, George Duane, Norman Noyes, Bob Miller, and unidentified; (second row) Phil Richardson, unidentified, Patsy Mercury, Larry Hogan, James Deroll, Walter Stone, unidentified, and Little Joe Gleason.

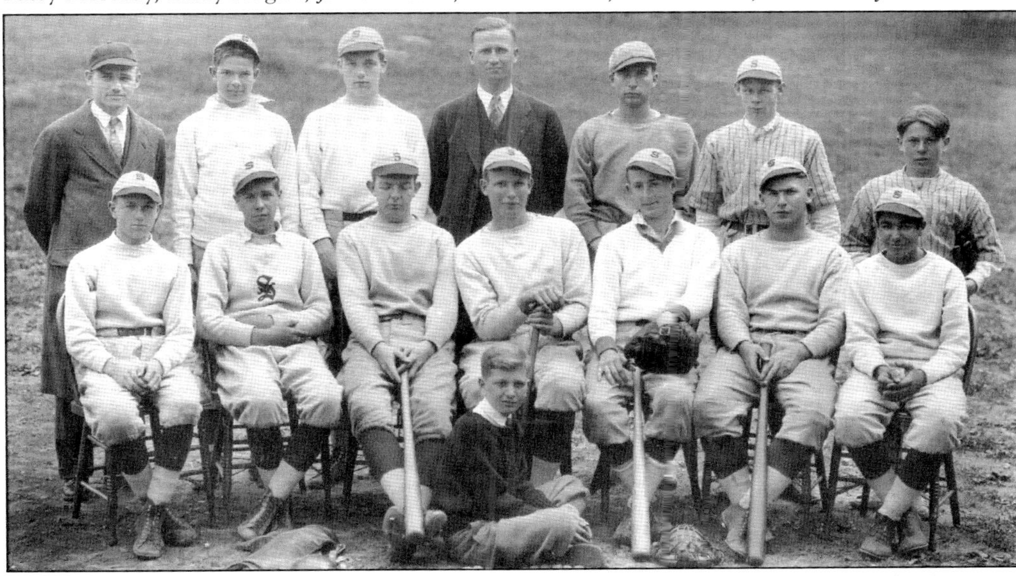

These two coaches are formally dressed for the team photograph in the 1930s, taken for the *Green and White* commencement issue. The team included, from left to right, (seated) Ken Farrell, two unidentified boys, Al Clarke, unidentified, ? Lowell, and Patsy Mercury; (second row) unidentified, Loring Hogan, unidentified, Al Flynn, ? Lowell, Bob Miller, and Phil Richardson. The batboy is unidentified.

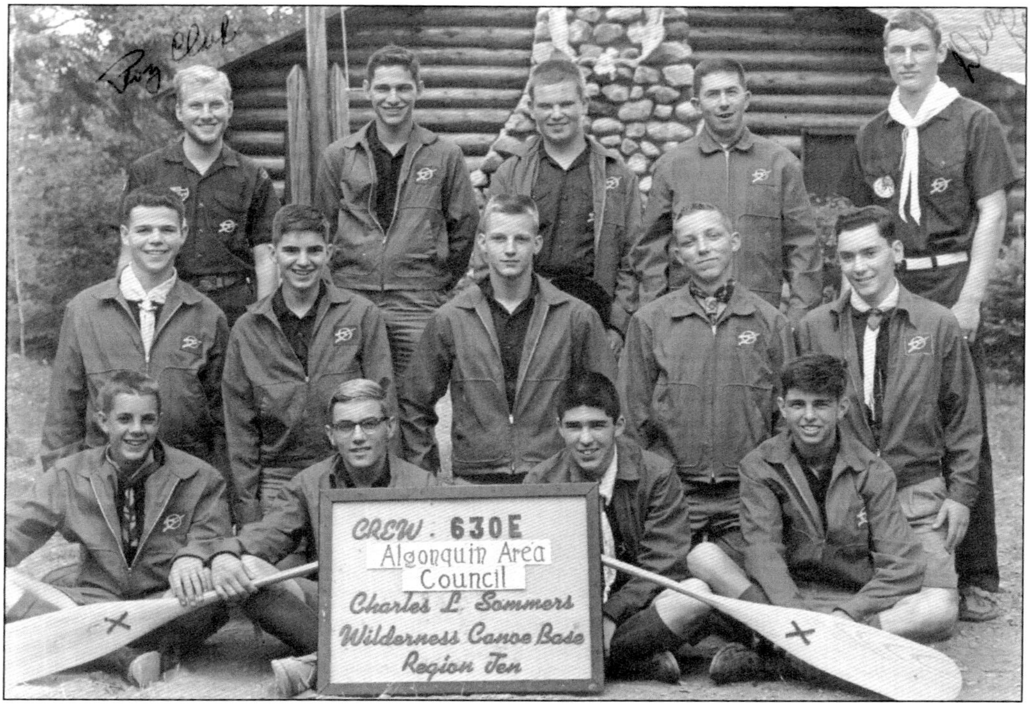


A group of explorers from the Algonquin Area Council went out to Minnesota for a canoe trip at the Wilderness Canoe Base. Only Roy Club (third row, far left), Curt Garfield (third row, second from right), and Dean Ram (third row, far right) were identified. The tradition continues today.

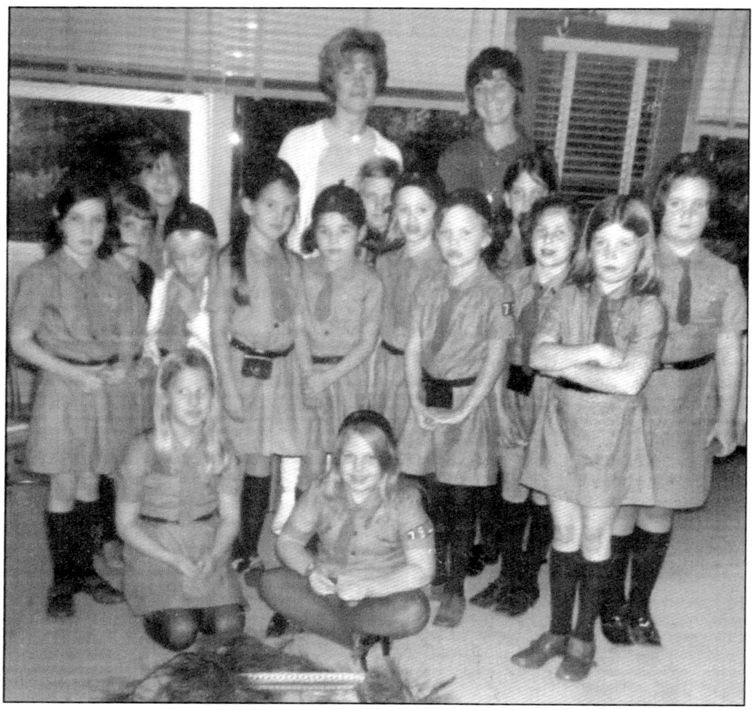

Brownie Troop No. 781 and their leaders pose at a local meeting. The year 2012 marked the 100th anniversary of the national Girl Scout organization.

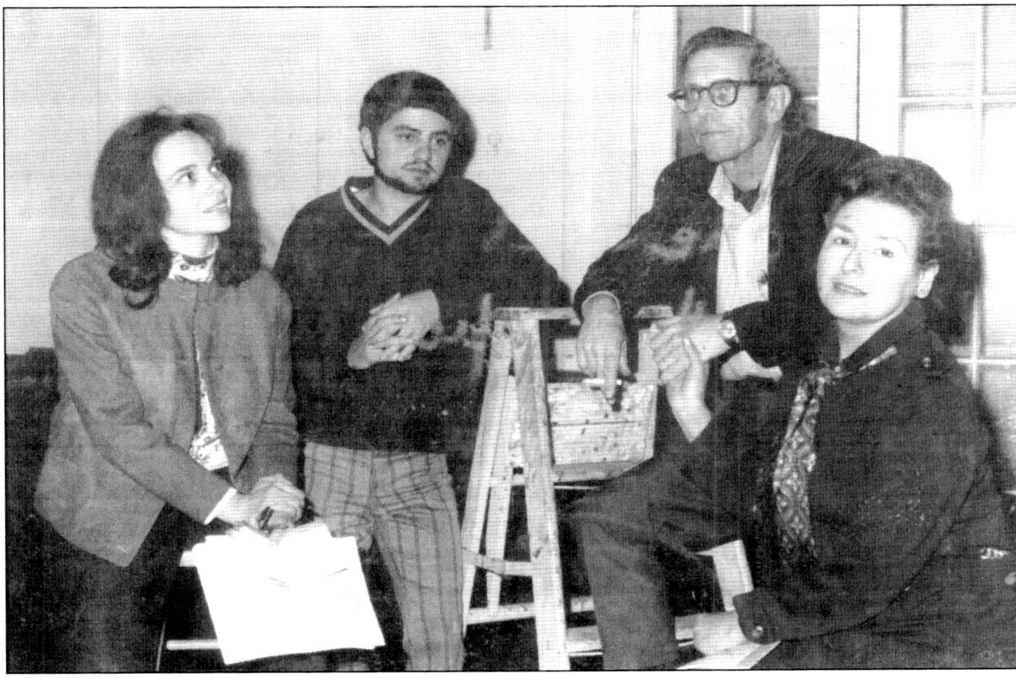

These members of the Sudbury Players, seen here rehearsing *Footsteps of Doves*, are, from left to right, Carol Peskin, Guy Vincent, Ray Fawcett, and Judy Davis. In the 1960s, the group put on *You Know I Can't Hear You When the Water Is Running.*

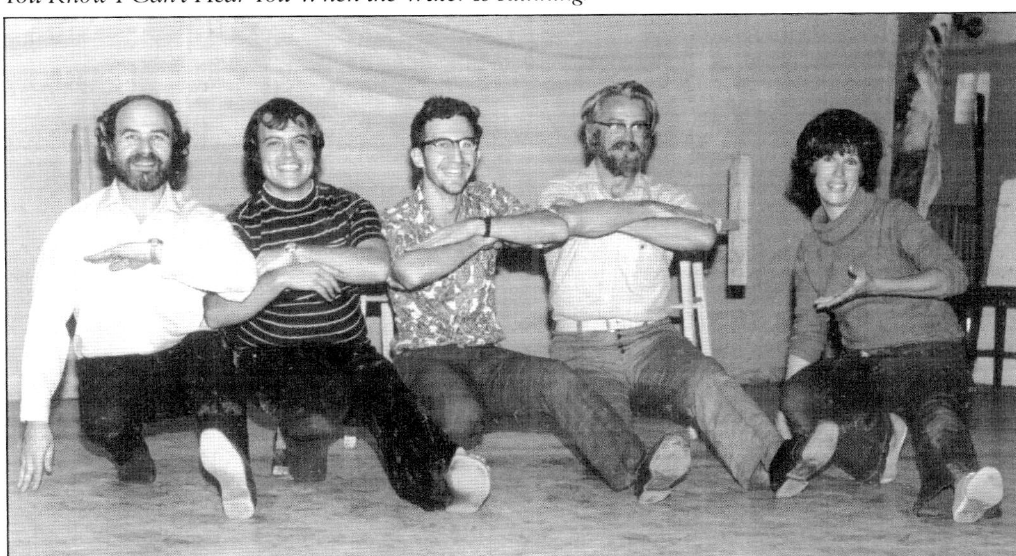

The Sudbury Players were a local theater group who rehearsed and performed their plays on the second floor of the town hall until the Americans with Disabilities Act was passed in 1986. As there was no elevator in the town hall, the Sudbury Players had to look for other venues but could not afford the alternatives. In 1999, the Sudbury Historical Society was given the use of the second floor of town hall as a tenant-at-will. Only four of these players were identified; they are, in no particular order, Marshall Deutsch, Peter Sesen, Jim Moore, and Ginny Manzer.

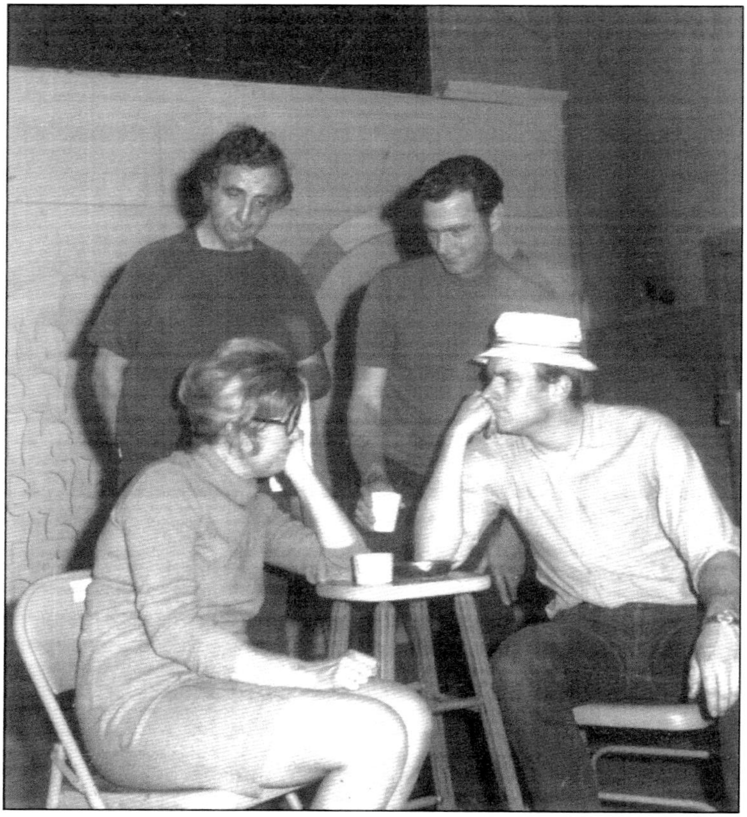

The Sudbury Players are seen here rehearsing *Schubert*. They are, from left to right, (seated) Bette Cloud and Al Berberian; (standing) Ray Curran and Chris Childs.

The United Way campaign below was assisted by the local Boy Scouts and Girl Scouts posing here in front of the Wayside Inn in the 1970s.

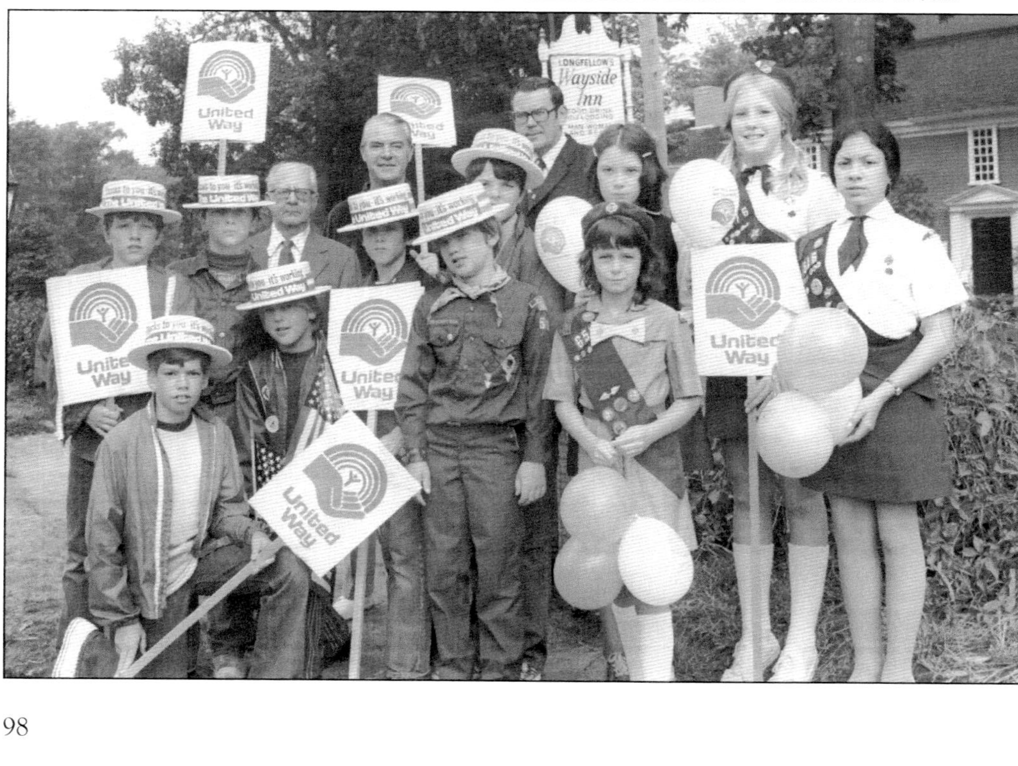

# *Eight*
# AROUND TOWN

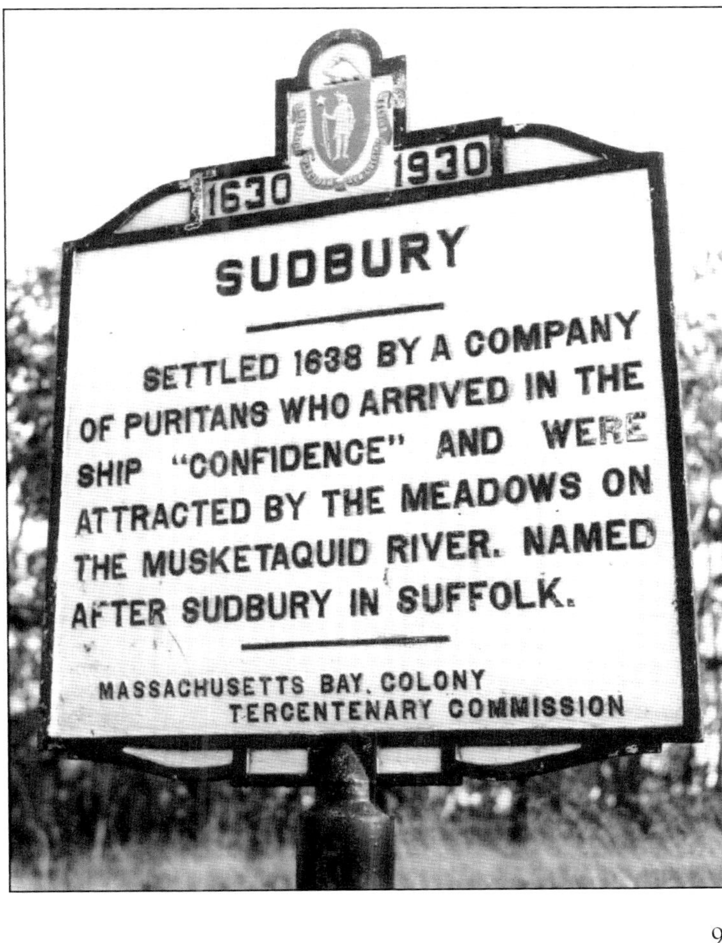


In 1930, the Massachusetts Bay Colony Tercentenary Commission created six markers for the town of Sudbury. The sign from the Marlborough entrance was stolen, while the marker at the Wayland entrance is still in place. The other markers noted historical sites in Sudbury such as the Goodnow Garrison.

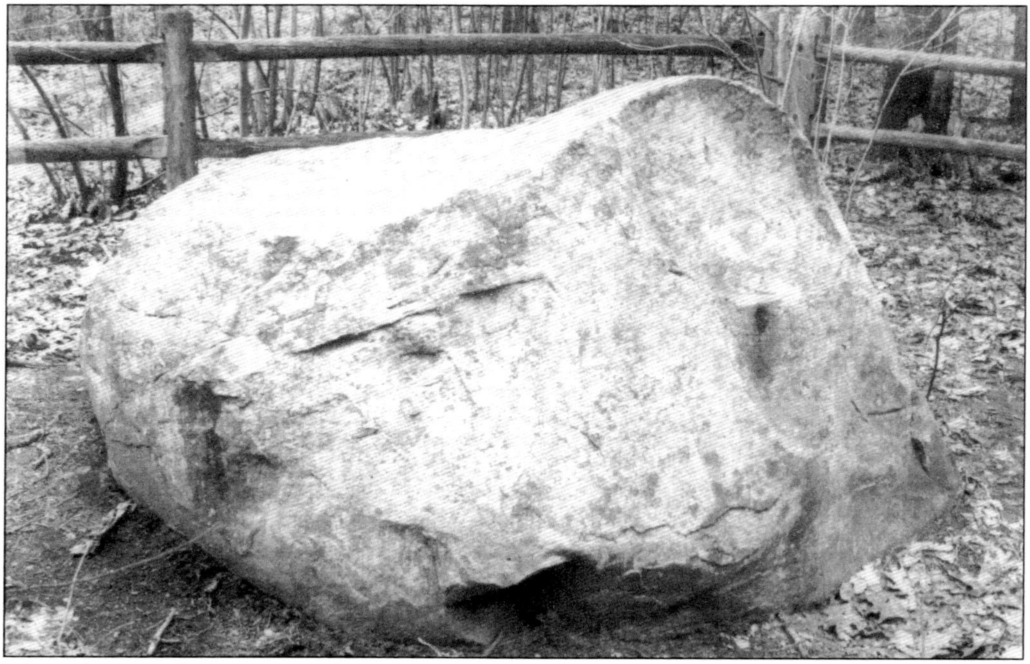

The Indian grinding stone seen here sits on the southeast slope of Green Hill near the intersection of Singletary and Green Hill Roads. The boulder is six feet in diameter. The Nipmuc/Nipnet Native Americans ground corn, grains, and nuts into meal or flour against the indentation in the rock with a round stone. This mortar is unusually large but has a seat, as all of the other mortar stones in Sudbury do.

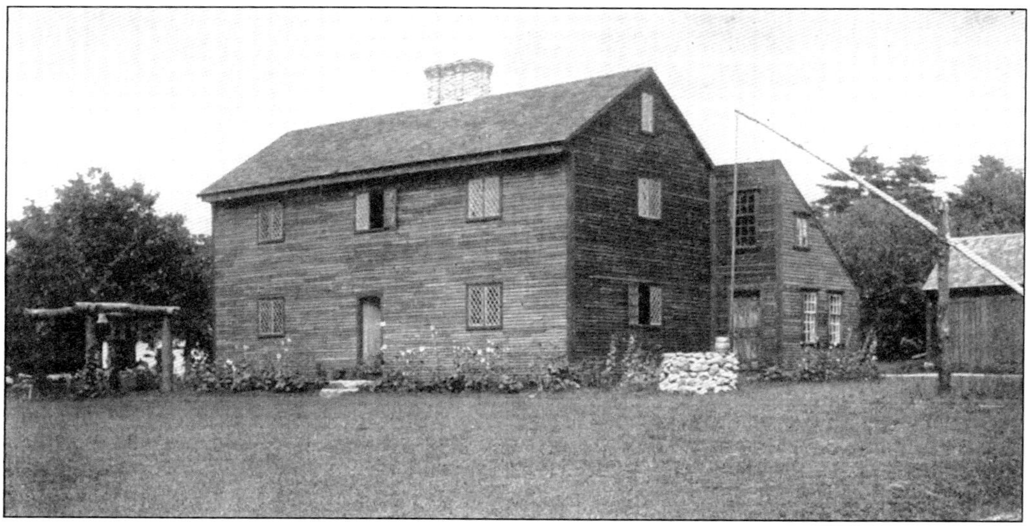

Goulding's Antique Shop, at 88 Concord Road, was originally known as the Moses Brewer House and was built in East Sudbury (now Wayland) on Route 27 around 1720. It was moved to its present location in 1918 by Leonard Goulding and restored to its original Saltbox style. The house has diamond-paned windows and a centered entrance. The contraption to the right side is known as a well sweep, which was used as a fulcrum to get water out of the well. The house is in the National Register of Historic Places.

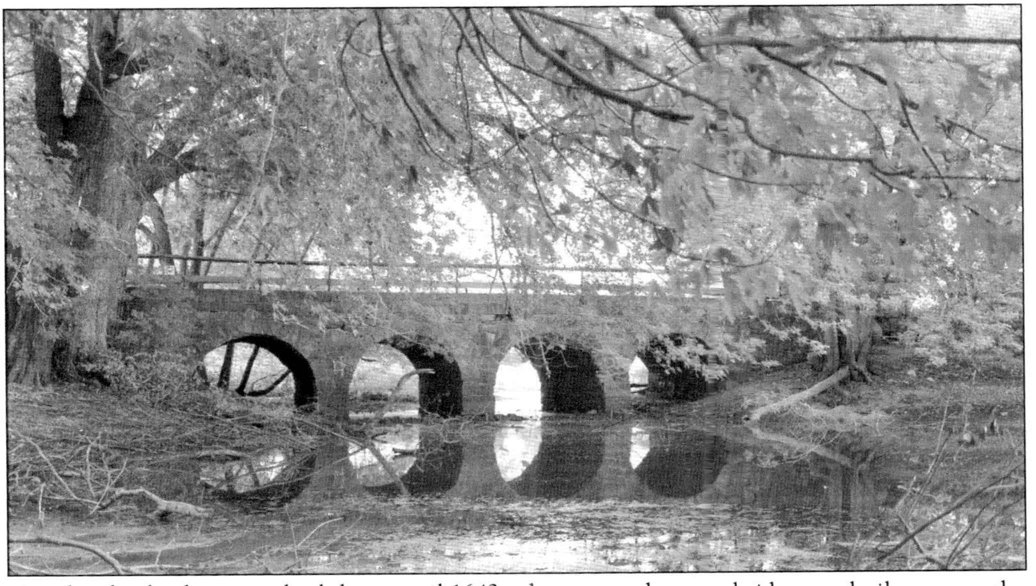

Wooden footbridges were built here until 1643, when a wooden cart bridge was built to cross the Sudbury River. It was the primary connection between the settlements on the east and west sides of the river. Because the bridges washed away in the river so many times, it was continuously rebuilt over the next 143 years until 1866, when this fine stone bridge, which survives to this day, was built near 121 Old Sudbury Road in Wayland.

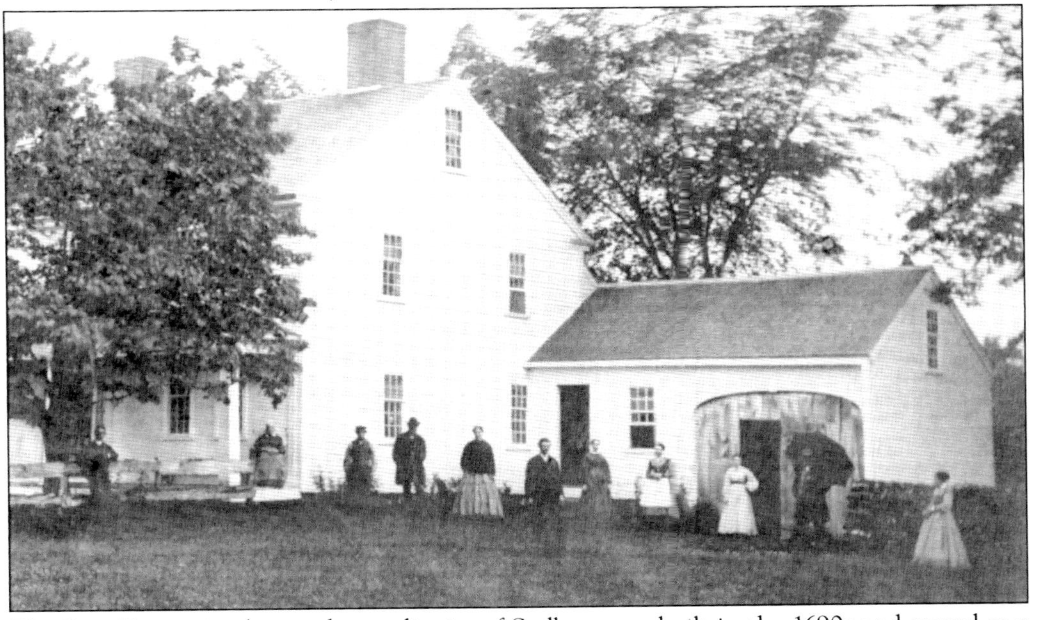

The Rice Tavern in the northwest district of Sudbury was built in the 1690s and served as a meeting place for many important selectmen and town meetings starting in the early 1700s. Many important decisions were made here to oppose the British crown and their taxes. It closed in 1815, but the Vose and Hunt family had a reunion there in 1880 when they owned it. The building's foundation still exists past the FEMA headquarters at the end of Old Marlborough Road off Route 27 in Maynard.

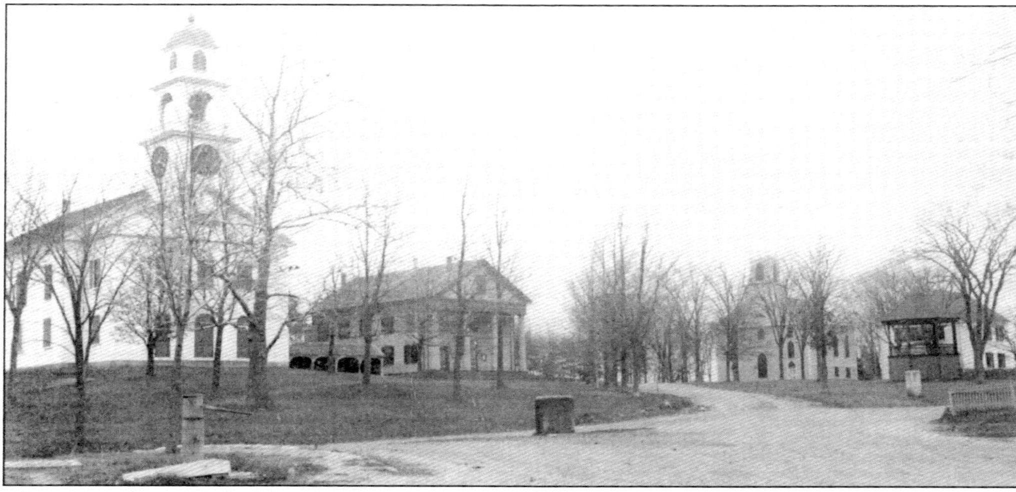

This 1896 photograph of Sudbury's town center is from a rare church calendar published by the Sudbury Methodist Episcopal Church. The church is the second building from the right, which was originally built as a Methodist church in 1836 and is now a Presbyterian church. On the right, the Sudbury Grange is hiding behind the town bandstand on the common. The building in the middle was the original town house, which was built in 1836 and burned in 1930.

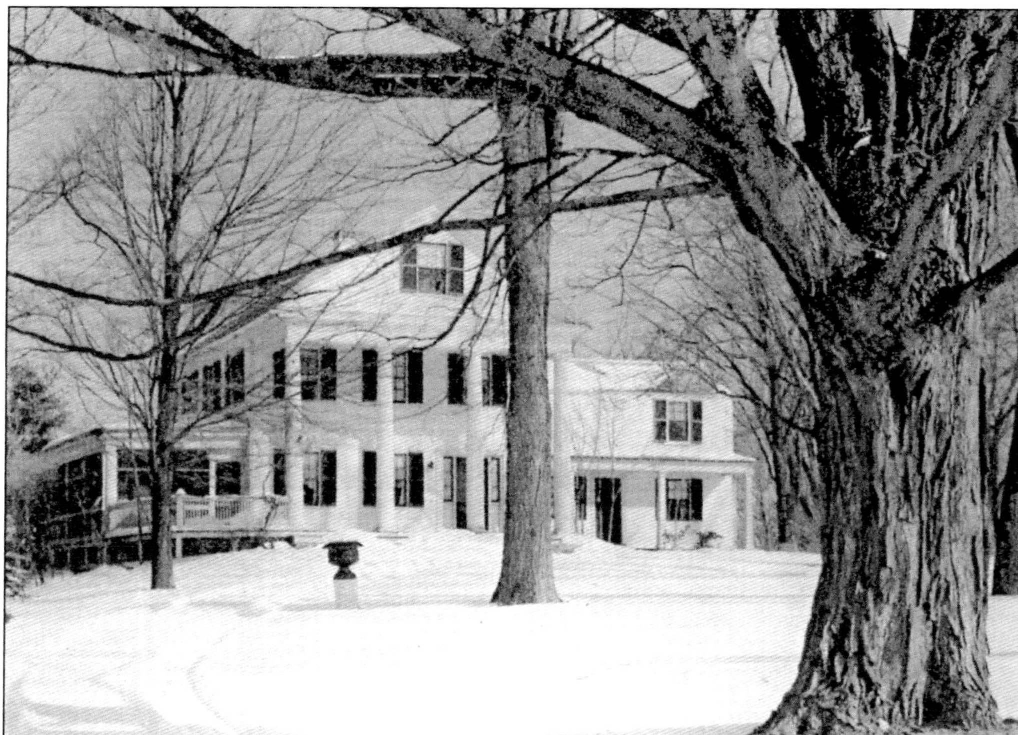

The Adam Howe Jr. House is at the intersection of Wayside Inn Road at 882 Boston Post Road. The house was built by the son of the third innkeeper of the Red Horse Tavern (later known as the Longfellow's Wayside Inn). Built just before 1830 and remodeled between 1900 and 1915 with the addition of the columns and other improvements, the house still stands today.

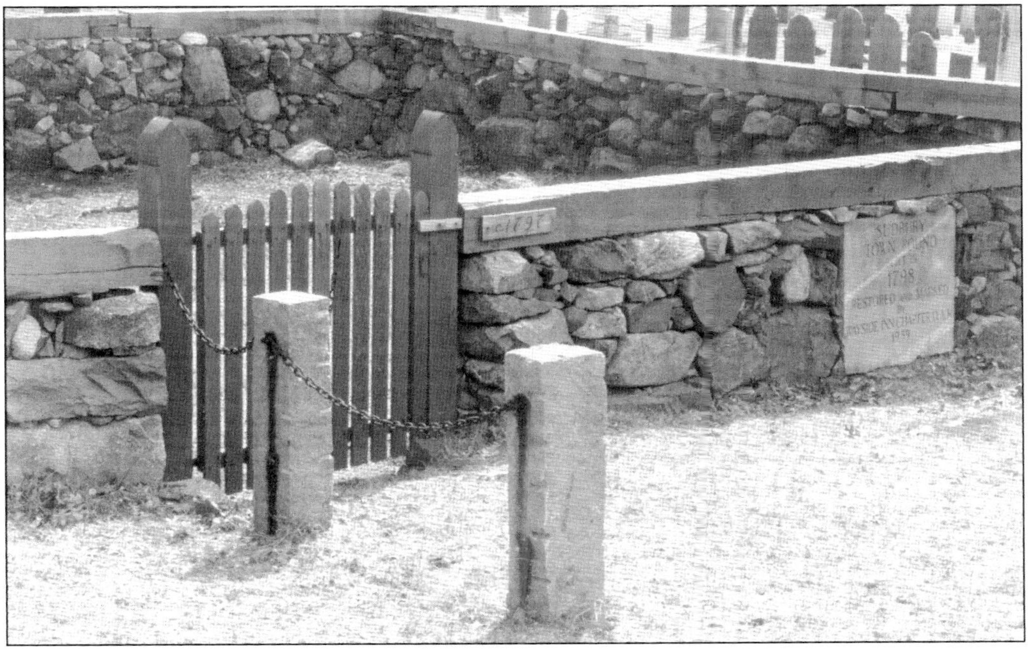

The town pound was located on Concord Road next to the Revolutionary War Cemetery. Stray cattle, horses, sheep, and swine were kept and maintained by an official of the town called the pound keeper. A pound was first built in Sudbury around 1664, and this one was built in 1797 for $20. Another town official, the field driver, found the stray animals and drove them on foot to the pound. The recreated gate was made by the late Sam Reed of SHS in 1975.

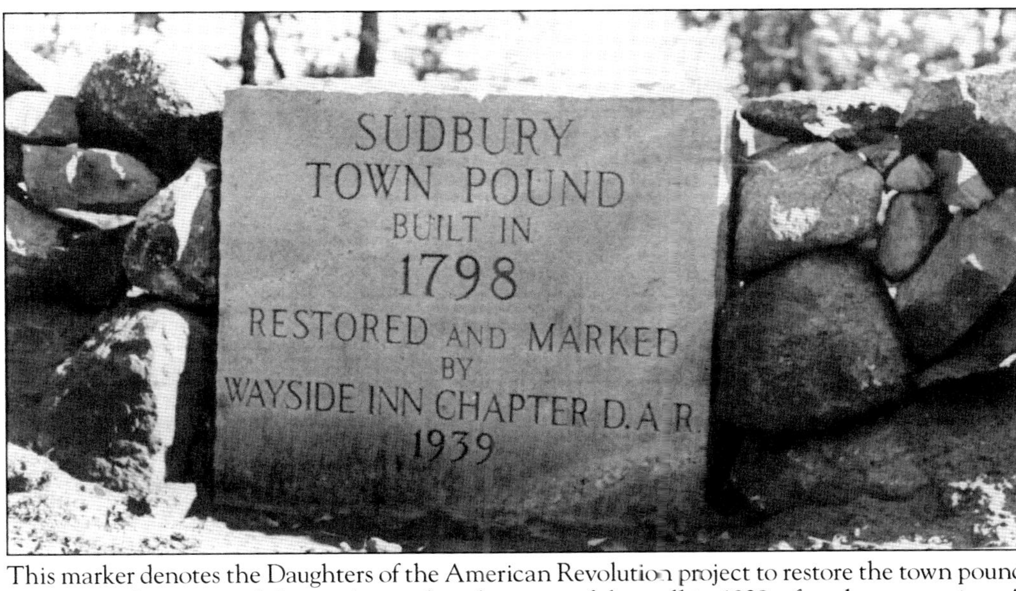


This marker denotes the Daughters of the American Revolution project to restore the town pound structure. They inserted the marker and made it part of the wall in 1939, after the restoration. A person driving by may think it is an unfinished foundation of a house, but it is not; it is one of only three known maintained town pounds in Massachusetts.

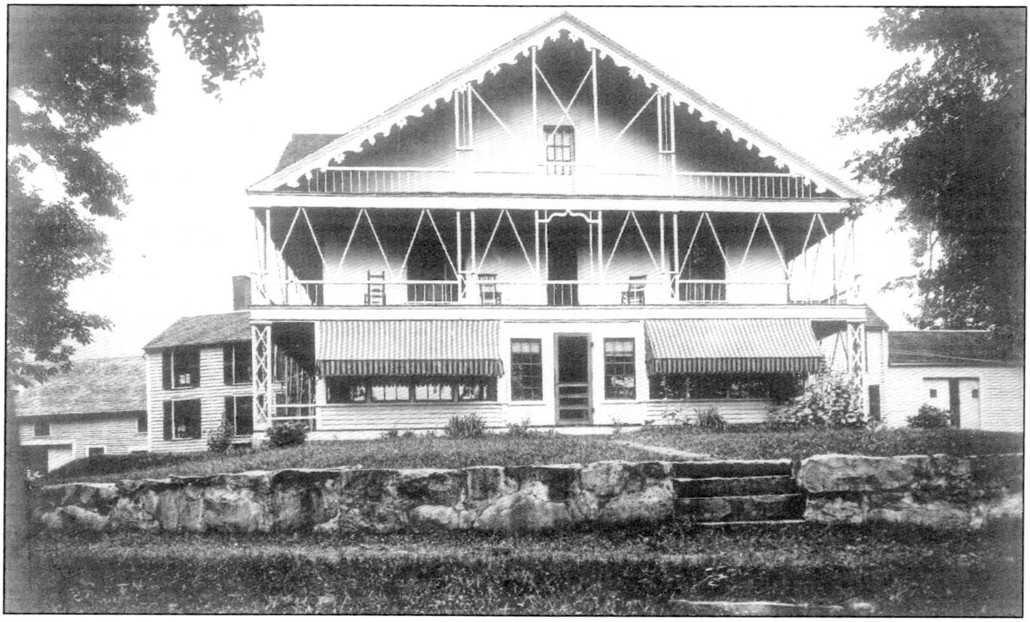

The original occupants of this unusual-looking house were Rev. Jacob Bigelow and his wife, Elizabeth. It was originally built in the Federalist style in 1773 and still stands at 250 Old Sudbury Road. Reverend Bigelow was hired by the town to serve as the minister. He had J. Thompson design and build the house. It was changed to look like this between 1900 and 1920.

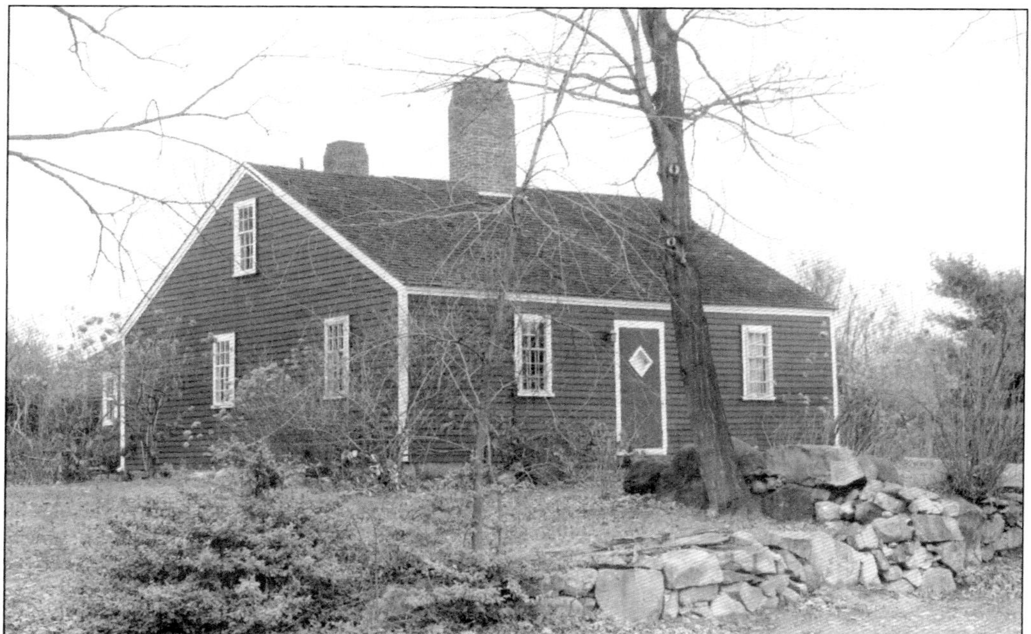

The historic Walker House is located at 95 Peakham Road. Thomas Walker taught school for the town here and in other homes. In 1926, the house was restored by Henry Ford, who owned this and 40 other houses and buildings in the area. Its origins are somewhat of a mystery because none of the records from before Ford owned it still exist.

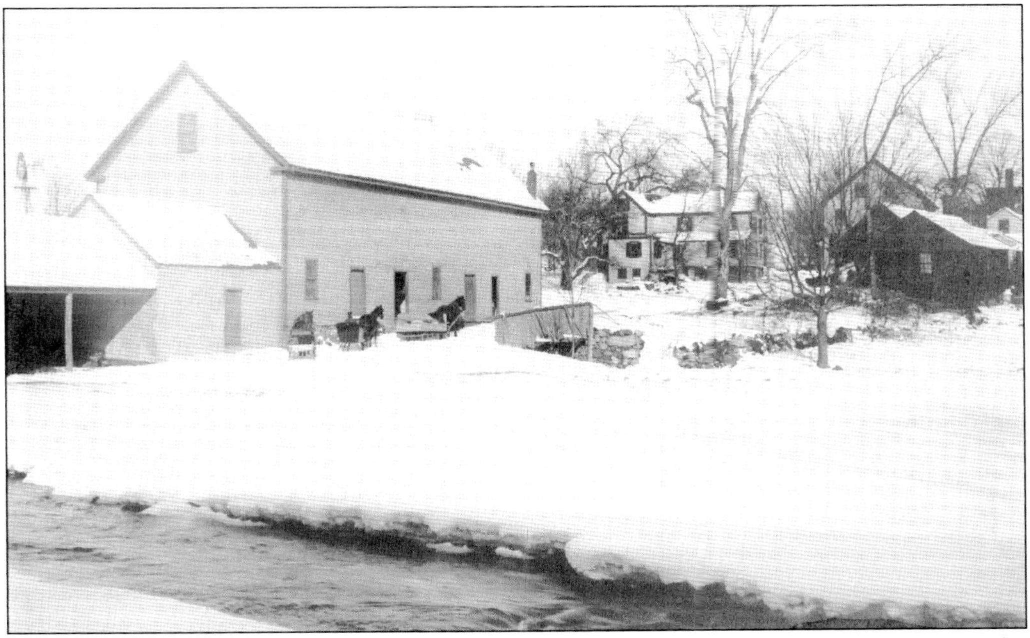

A gristmill and sawmill were located behind what is now the Mill Village shopping center. The Hurlbut and Rogers Machine Shop was also in the area. It has been a commercial center since 1659, when Peter Noyes and Abraham Wood built a gristmill on Hop Brook. By 1889, Mill Village consisted of a general store, a post office, a machine shop, a blacksmith, a schoolhouse, a church, a gristmill, a junction depot, the Goodnow Library, and 50 homes. It was considered quite progressive at the time.

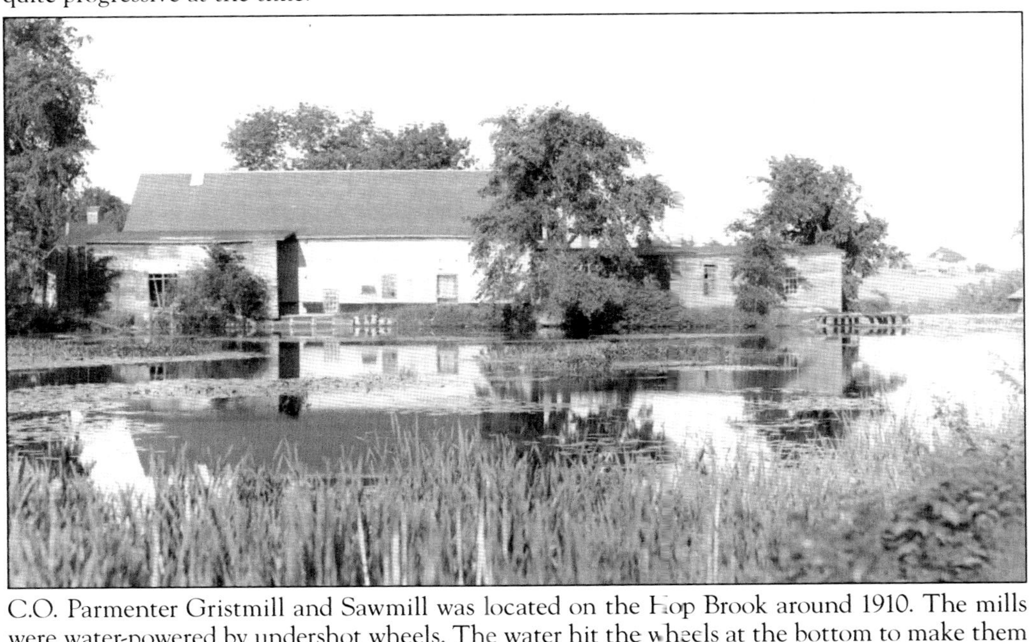

C.O. Parmenter Gristmill and Sawmill was located on the Hop Brook around 1910. The mills were water-powered by undershot wheels. The water hit the wheels at the bottom to make them turn. The buildings have long since been torn down, and the area now serves as a parking lot for Mill Village.

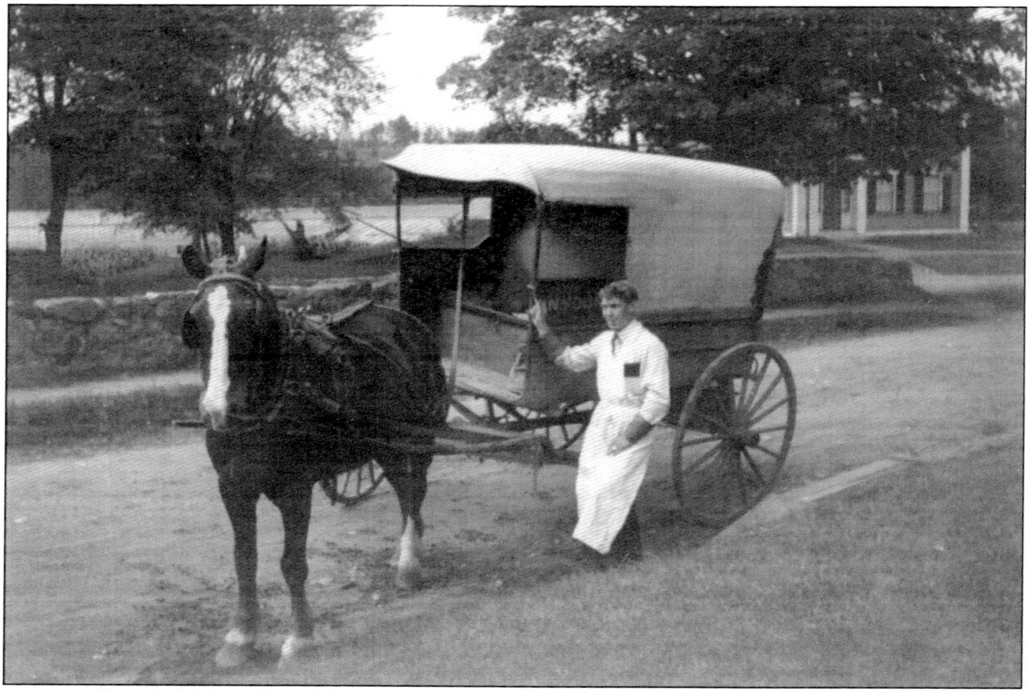

Everett M. Saunders holds up butcher Al Young's delivery wagon. In that time, orders were home delivered—Saunders would visit houses to take orders before going back to the store to pack the orders and deliver them.

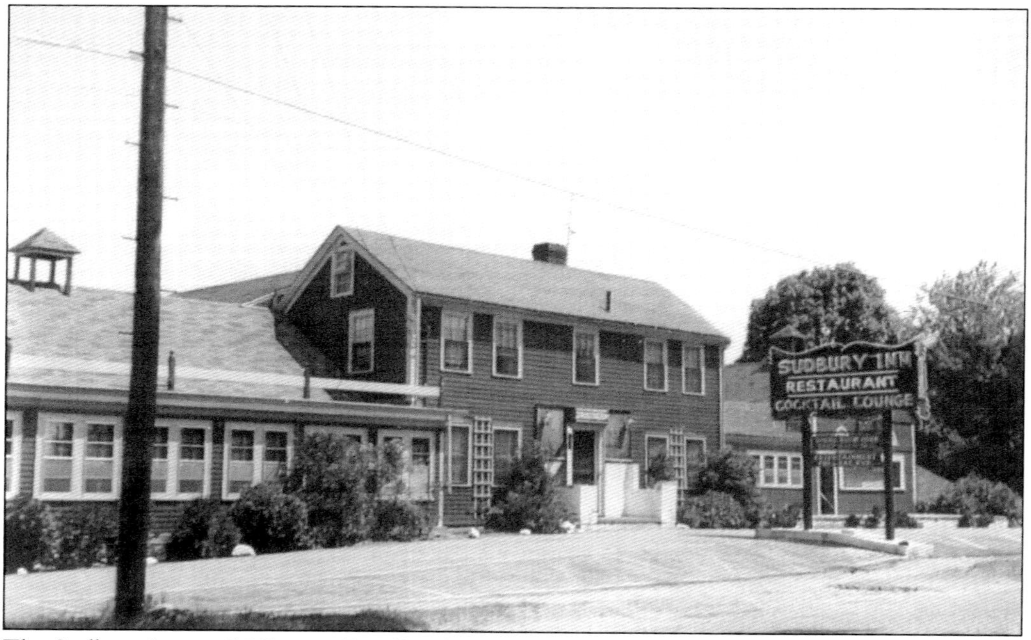


The Sudbury Inn at 410 Boston Post Road was an old building that was not treated well through the years. It was reportedly built in the 1750s and was owned by the Wheeler family in 1830. In the 1920s, it was known as Ye Olde Barbeque Inn.

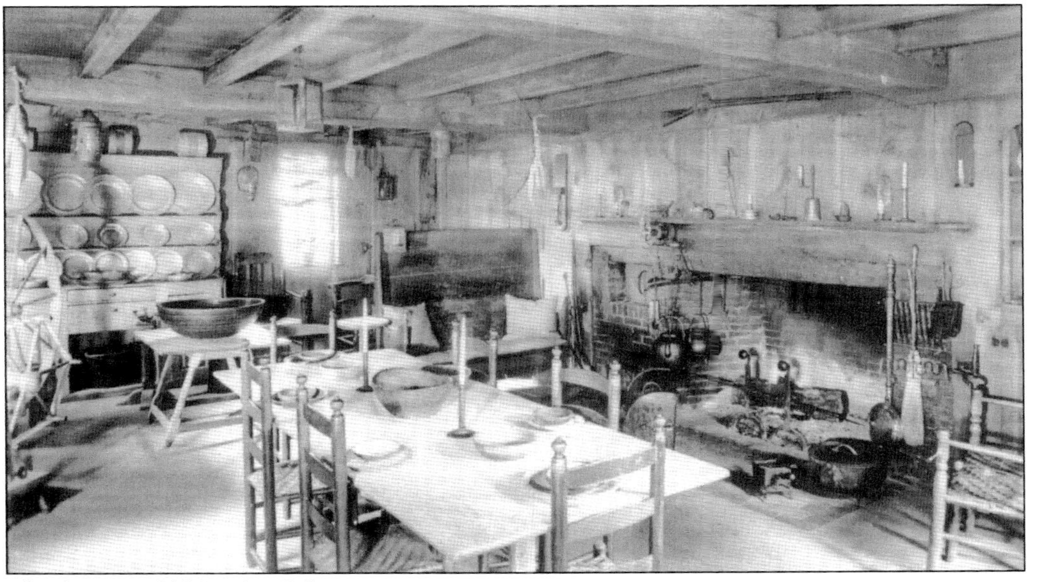

The famous "Old Kitchen" dining room at Longfellow's Wayside Inn is seen above in 1937. At the time, Henry Ford owned the inn and 2,995 acres around it. It was not a public dining area and could only be viewed on a paid tour. In 1945, on Ford's last visit to the inn before he died in 1947, he had 14 prominent industrialists to lunch in this room. Ford was known for his peculiar diet theories, but that particular lunch was especially befuddling to his guests.

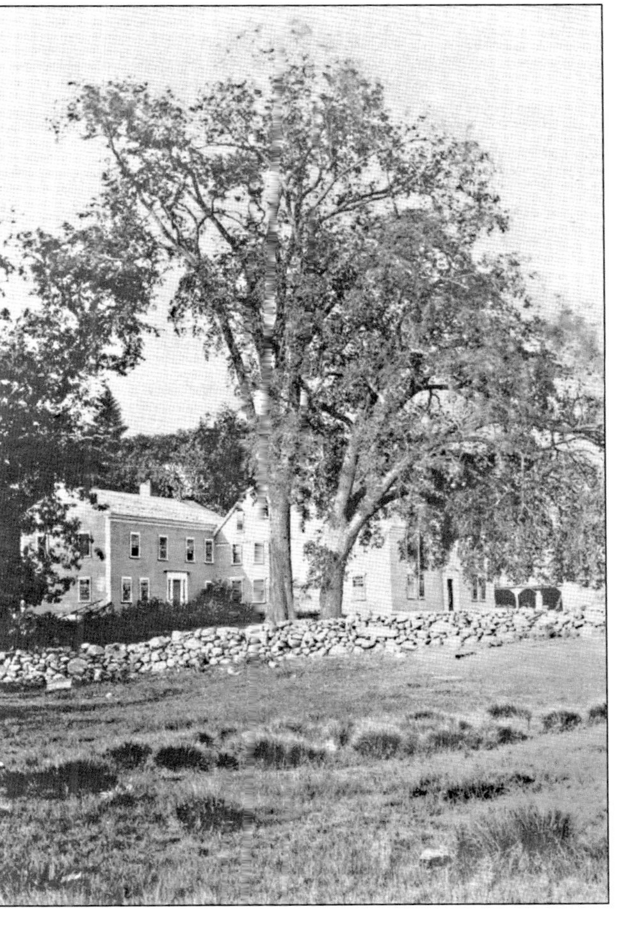

This western view of the Wayside Inn was taken in 1885. The inn was on the Boston Post Road, which was originally called the Bay Path and King's Highway. When first licensed, it was called How's Inn or How's Tavern. The license allowed David How "to keep a house of entertainment for travelers," which meant he could serve alcohol and offer hospitality to strangers. Early laws of the Massachusetts Bay Colony required an innkeeper to provide for a man, his horses, and his cattle.

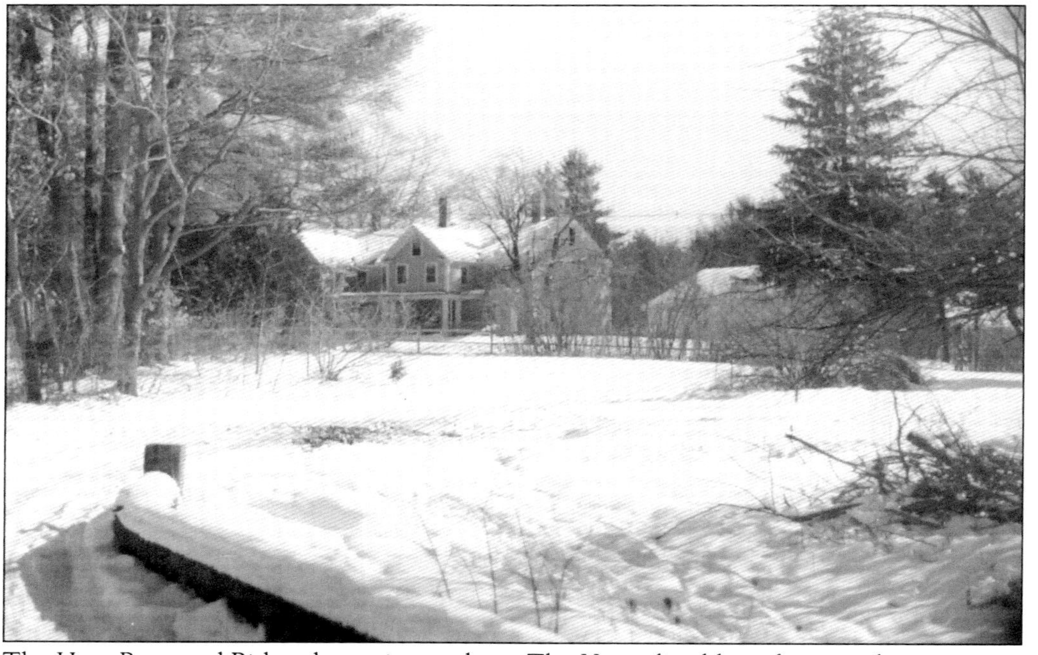

The Hunt-Raymond-Bishop house is seen here. The Hunts lived here for several generations. Brothers Newell and Sewell Hunt sold the house to George J. Raymond in 1903. The owner of Raymond's Department Stores in Boston, Raymond was known for treating his employees fairly. In fact, employee Frank I. Dorr became president after Raymond's death in 1915. (Photograph by Donald D. Bishop.)

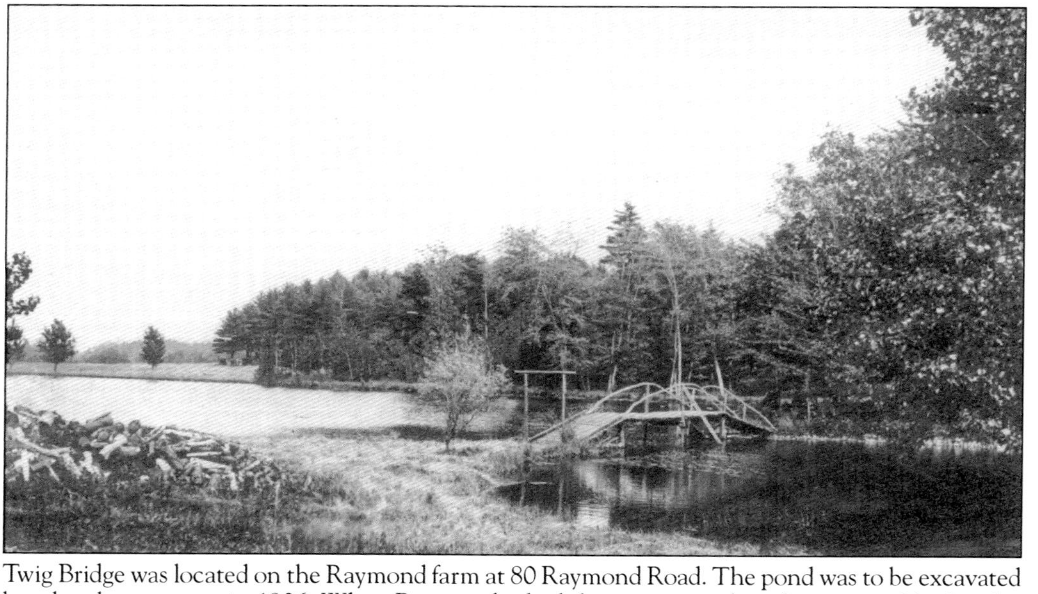

Twig Bridge was located on the Raymond farm at 80 Raymond Road. The pond was to be excavated by a local contractor in 1906. When Raymond asked the contractor how long it would take, the contractor replied that it would take 11 days. Raymond asked how many men he would need. The answer was three. Raymond replied, "Why don't you use 11 men and get it done in three days?" And so it was done.

John P. Bartlett, the son of the founder of Bartlett Greenhouses, poses in one of the family greenhouses, surrounded by geraniums. John was an engineer and developed many ways to increase production of what the Bartlett Greenhouses have become famous for: geraniums in all their resplendent colors and their greenery. The greenhouses are located at 578 Boston Post Road.

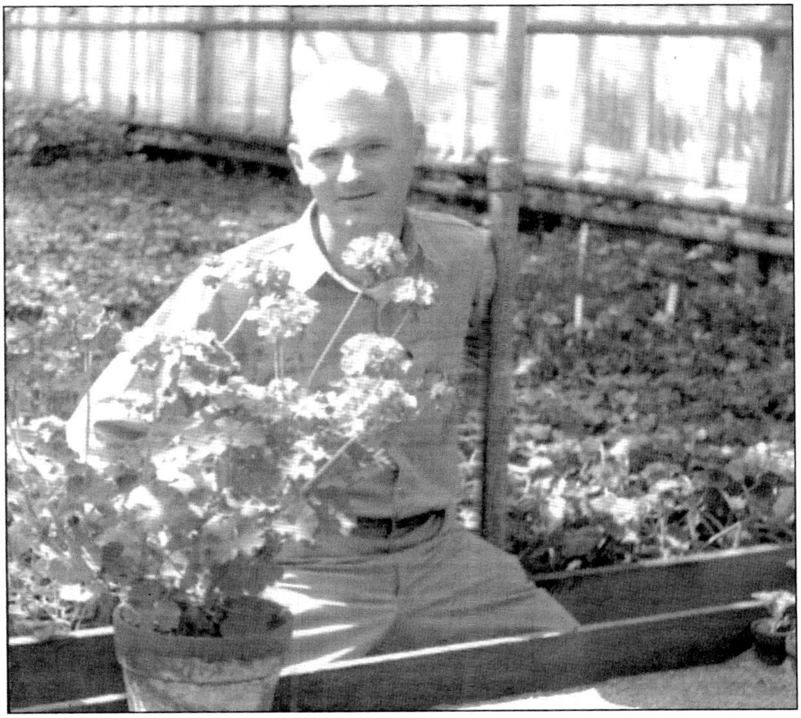

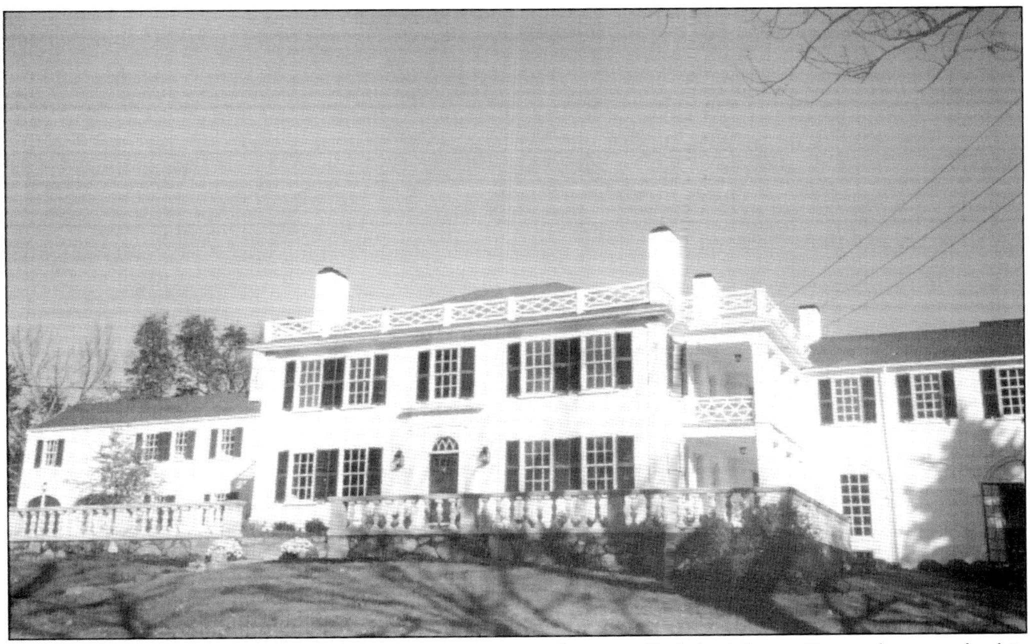

This was the home of one of America's greatest architects, Ralph Adams Cram, known for his American Gothic style. Cram is most famous for his design of St. John the Divine Church in New York City and many chapels in major universities, such as Princeton. He purchased this modest New England tavern/farmhouse in 1900 and turned it into the fine Federal-style home that still stands today at 427 Concord Road. He lived here year-round from 1930 on.

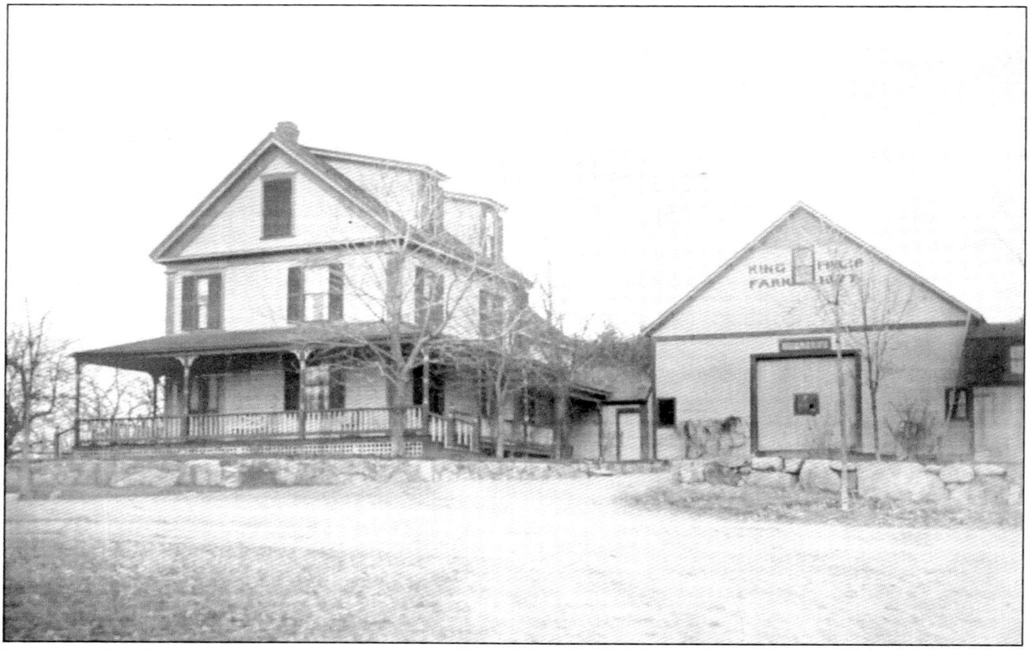

King Philip Farm was at the corner of Old Lancaster and Concord Roads, near 160 Concord Road. It was built in 1877 by the Hunt family. Patriarch Aaron Hunt was very well-to-do and had acquired a large estate before his death in 1877. The SHS has a collection of deeds for this property dating back to 1838. The parish house for Our Lady of Fatima Catholic Church now occupies this space.

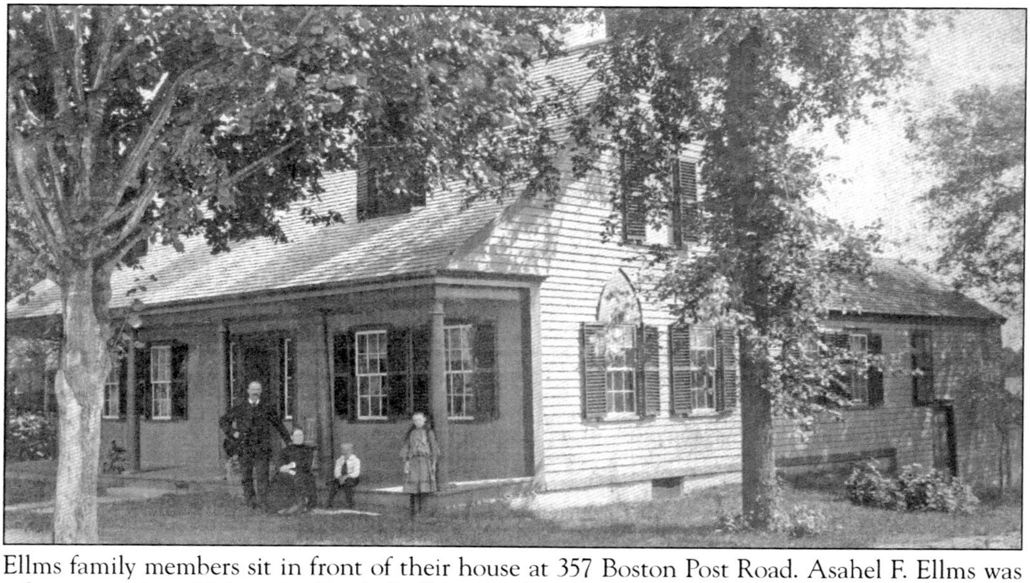

Ellms family members sit in front of their house at 357 Boston Post Road. Asahel F. Ellms was a farmer, raising chickens in South Sudbury for decades. In 1890, he owned the house, the hen house, and the half-acre of land it was set on. This house still retains the Cape Cod style but no longer has a center chimney. It is now used as business offices and has a recessed entrance.

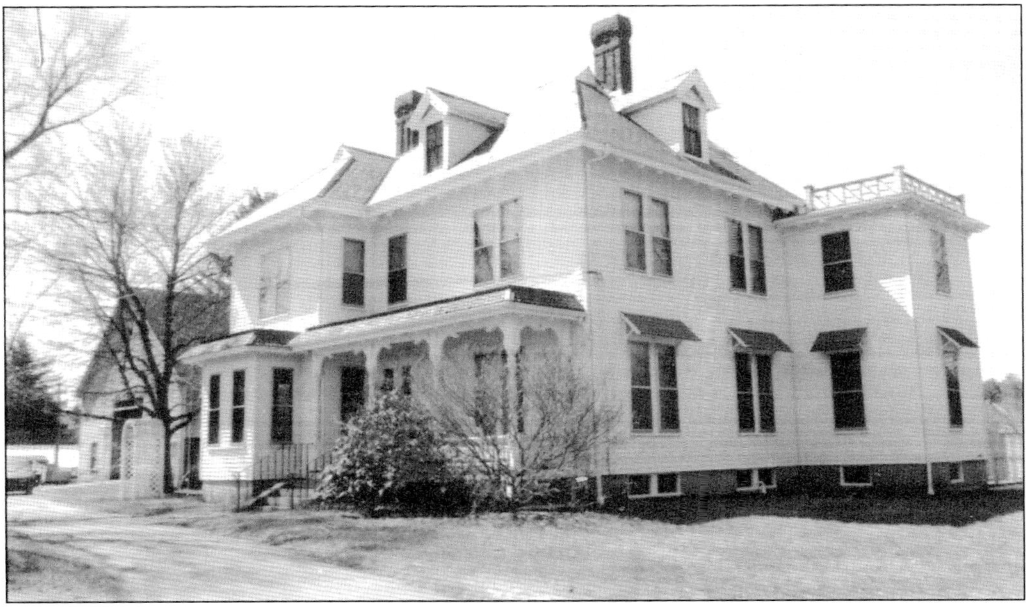

The Nahum Goodnow house is located at 163 Landham Road. It is a Queen Anne–style house built from 1884 to 1886. Nahum was the grandson of John Goodnow, who originally owned the property and whose estate sold it to Nahum after John's death. Nahum Goodnow lived from 1843 to 1897 and was a vegetable farmer. The house is still owned by Goodnow relatives.

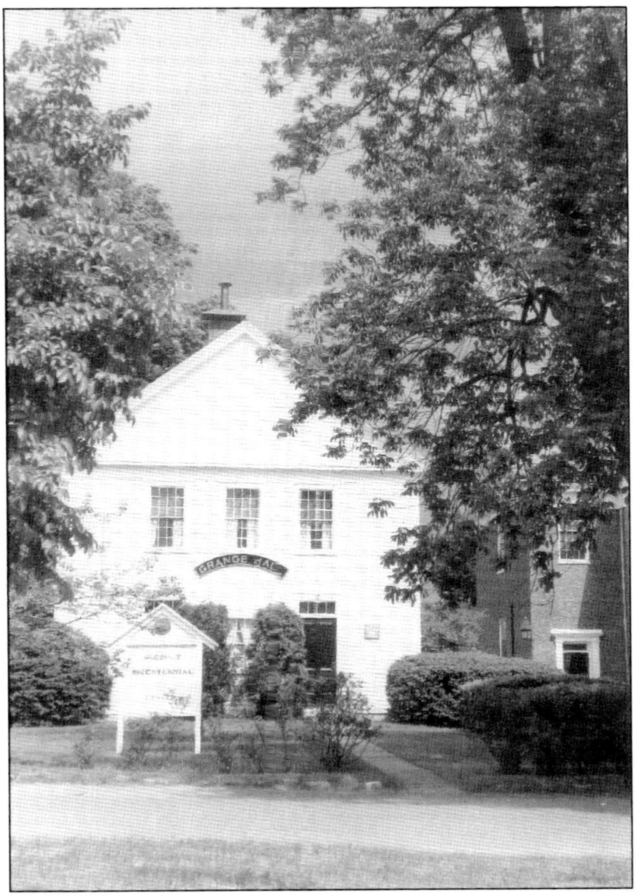


The Grange Hall was formerly the Center Schoolhouse in 1849. Shortly after it was built, the building was lifted up and a first floor was added. It served all eight grades until it was condemned by the state for not having good air. It was sold at auction to the Grange in 1891. The Sudbury Grange is a fraternal order that continues to hold its meetings there today. This photograph was taken by Victor Neumeier during the American bicentennial in 1976, when it was the bicentennial headquarters.

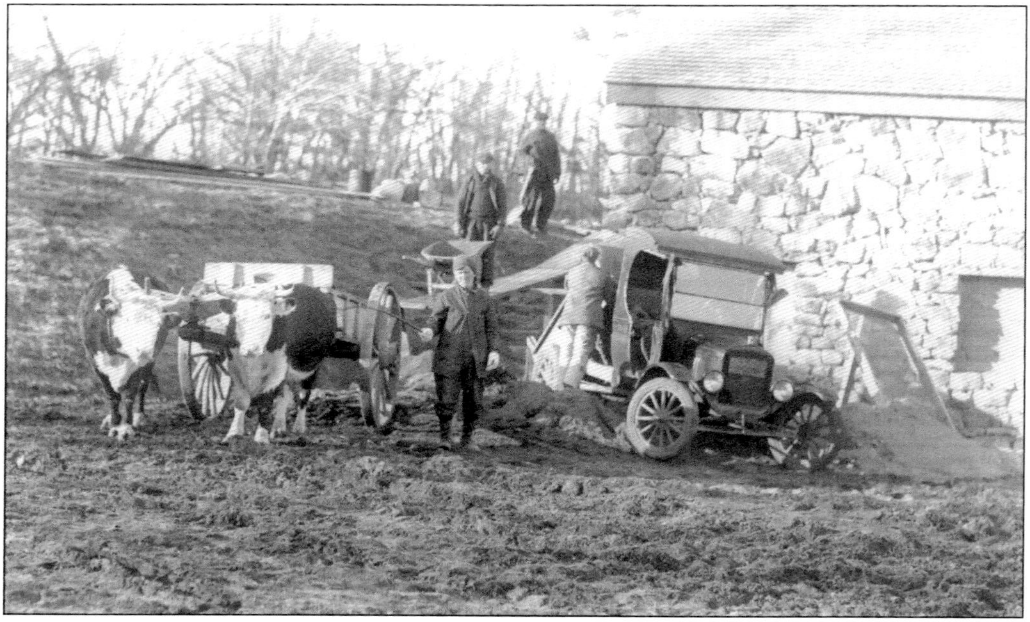

This gristmill is being built for Henry Ford's Wayside Inn village complex. Ford wanted everything to look as picturesque as possible. He used this team of oxen to help move materials to the sites, but around back, the men were using a modern truck for the real work—a Ford, of course.

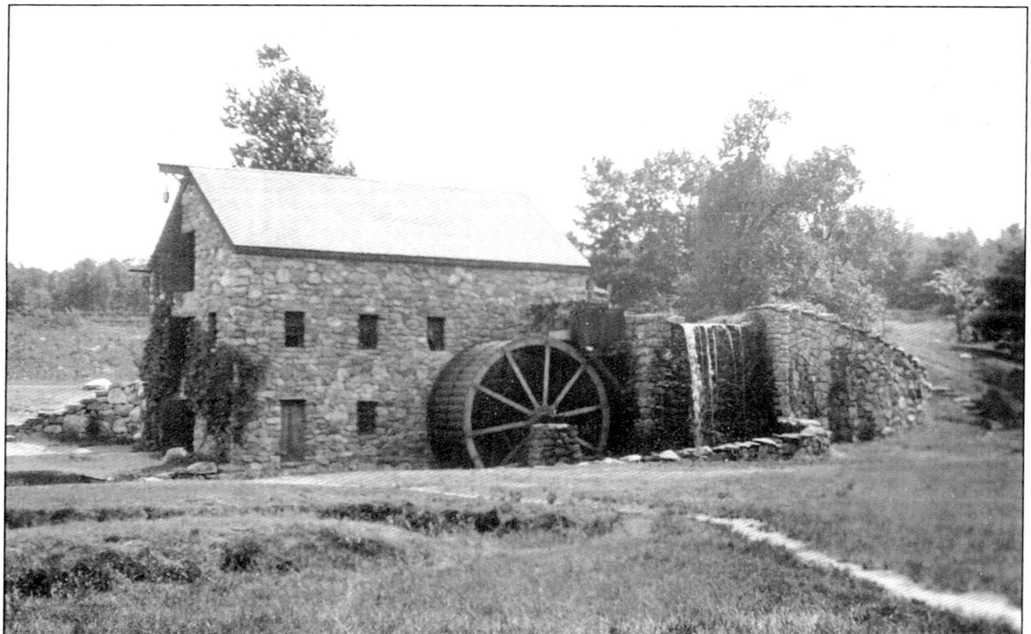

The Wayside Inn Gristmill is located at 131 Wayside Inn Road. Construction of the mill was started in 1927 on the orders of Henry Ford and completed in 1929. Ford wanted it to be built as an example of the use of waterpower and automation. John B. Campbell of Philadelphia designed the mill. The exterior is cut stone from Mount Nobscot and other local Ford land. It is still a working mill, grinding flour and cornmeal for the Wayside Inn.

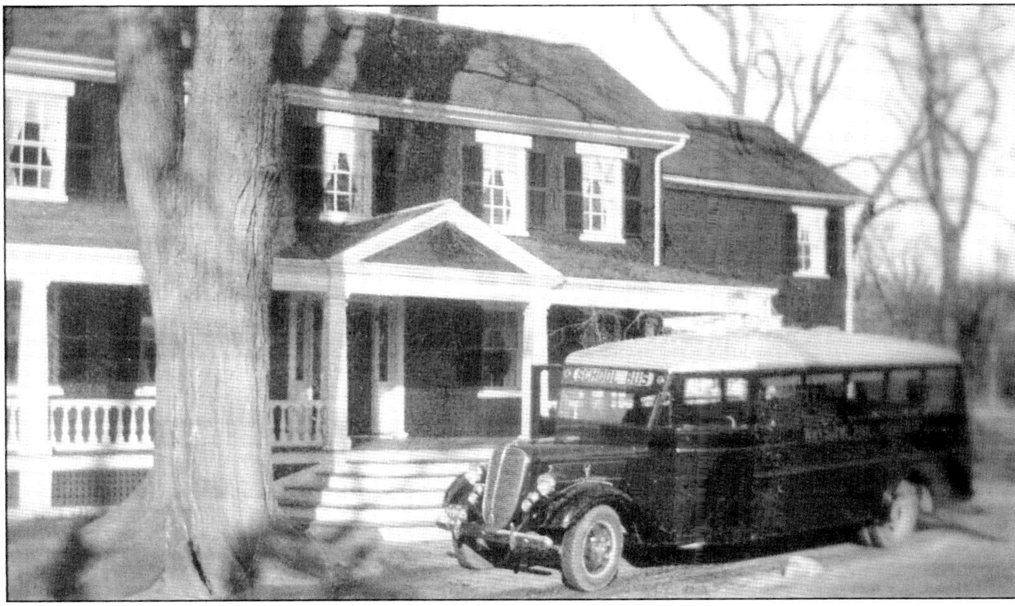


The Wayside Inn Boys' School utilized all of the Wayside Inn Estate. The former Calvin Howe house at 150 Wayside Inn Road, which is now an empty lot, was the main school and a partial dormitory for the 75 students attending in 1943. Henry Ford believed in education and learning trades of a practical nature. The boys helped build the Martha Mary Chapel that is also on the grounds of the inn.

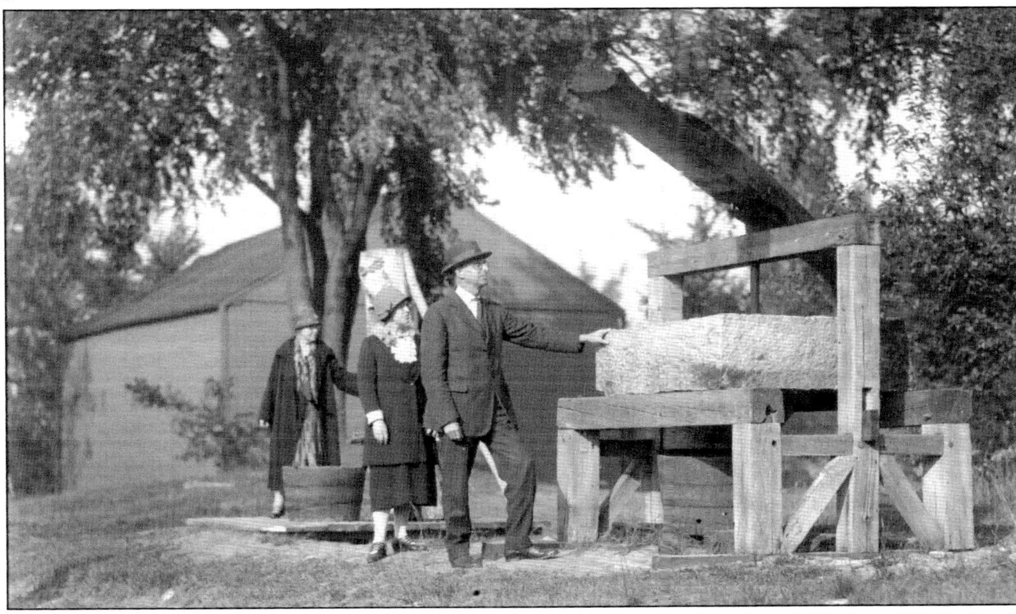

In 1923, when Henry Ford purchased the inn and surrounding land, he hired William W. Taylor to search out objects and buildings in New England that would be used in the New England village he was creating around the inn's 2,995 acres. This cider press is one of thousands of objects that were purchased. The apples were placed between the block, and the tray and the block's heavy weight pressed the juice into the barrel below.

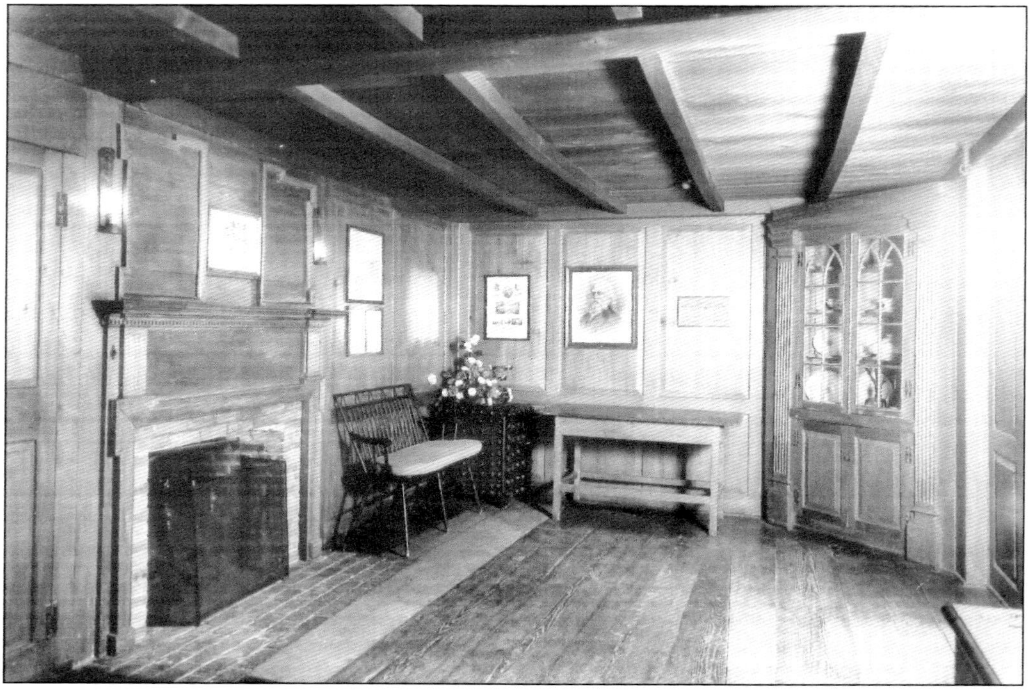

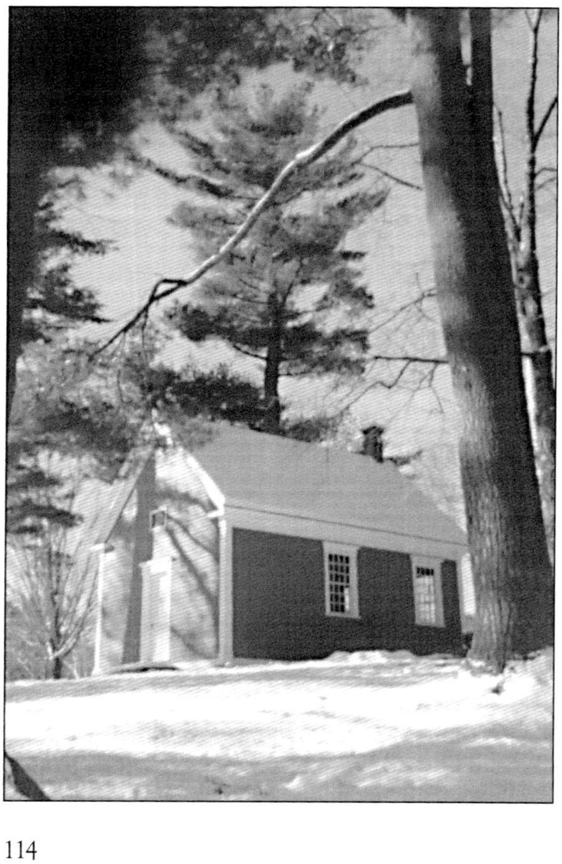

The Wayside Inn has many intimate rooms. This was once the Ford Sitting Room and is now called the Inn Keeper's Room and is used for dining. In 1979, Robert Spaulding made one-inch-to-one-foot models of the inn, the gristmill, the chapel, and the Redstone Schoolhouse, and they were displayed in this room. The models were later given to the SHS. (Photograph by Victor Neumeier.)

The Redstone Schoolhouse—also called the Mary Lamb Schoolhouse—at 9 Dutton Road was originally located on the side of Redstone Hill in Sterling. The school had been torn down but the wood was recycled into a barn/garage. Henry Ford bought the barn, dismantled it, and brought it to Sudbury in 1926, where, after extensive research, it was reassembled as close to the original school as possible.

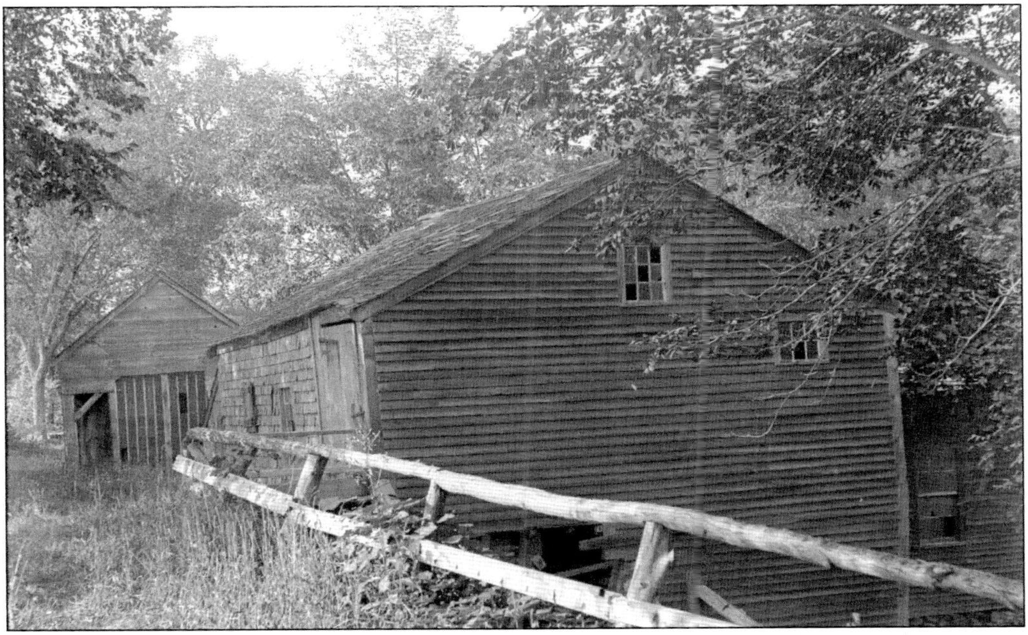

The Knight-Dutton Gristmill was on Dutton Road, where the Hop Brook goes under it at 181 Dutton Road. Joel and Samuel Knight built the mill in 1780 and operated it. A West India goods store was run by them on the nearby Dutton farm. Hattie Goodnow took this rare photograph and one other of the mill in 1899. The mill was powered by an interior turbine, thus it had no exterior wheel that could freeze in the winter. The mill was on the right side of the driveway, and only its foundation stones still exist.

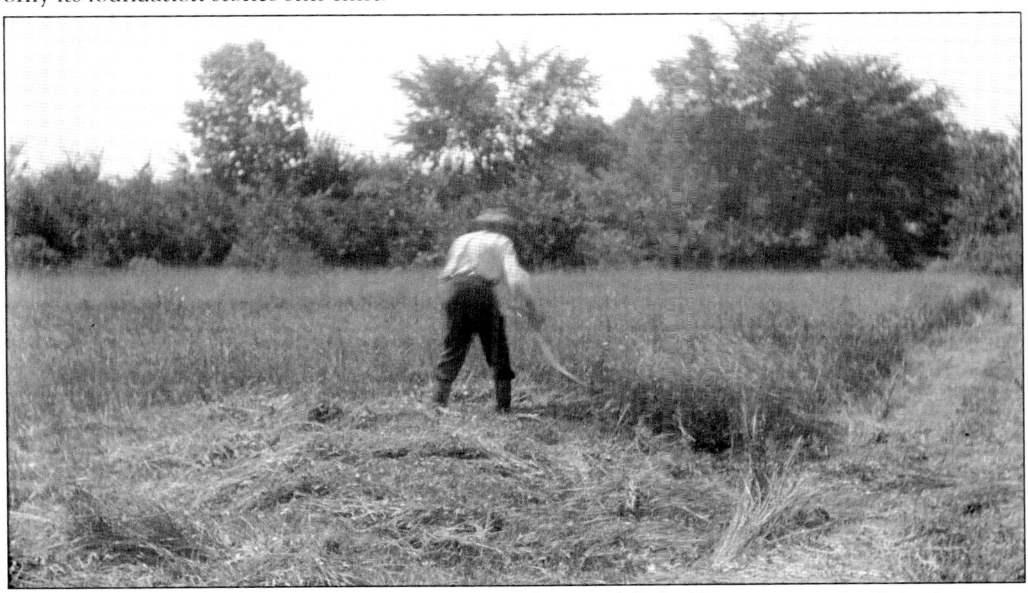

An acre a day of hay could be cut by one man with a good, light European scythe. Mowing grass was a meditative experience—step and swing, swing and step, working one's way down the field, then looking over one's shoulder to view with pride the neat, straight line of mown grass, and breathing the aroma of freshly cut hay. (Photograph by Hattie Goodnow.)

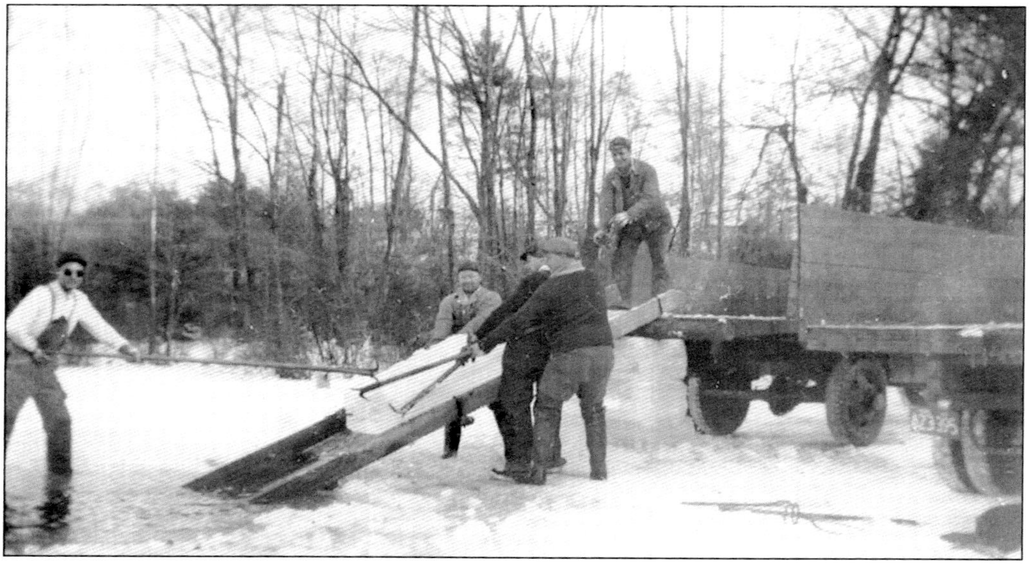

Harvesting ice was a common occupation but it was quite arduous to cut, haul, and store the ice. Sudbury had a few independent ponds with spring-fed water that was not tied into the Hop Brook water system of ponds and streams. This photograph shows Blanchard's Pond on the Cavicchio farm. Their ice was for their own use, and they had an insulated icehouse to carry it through the summer.

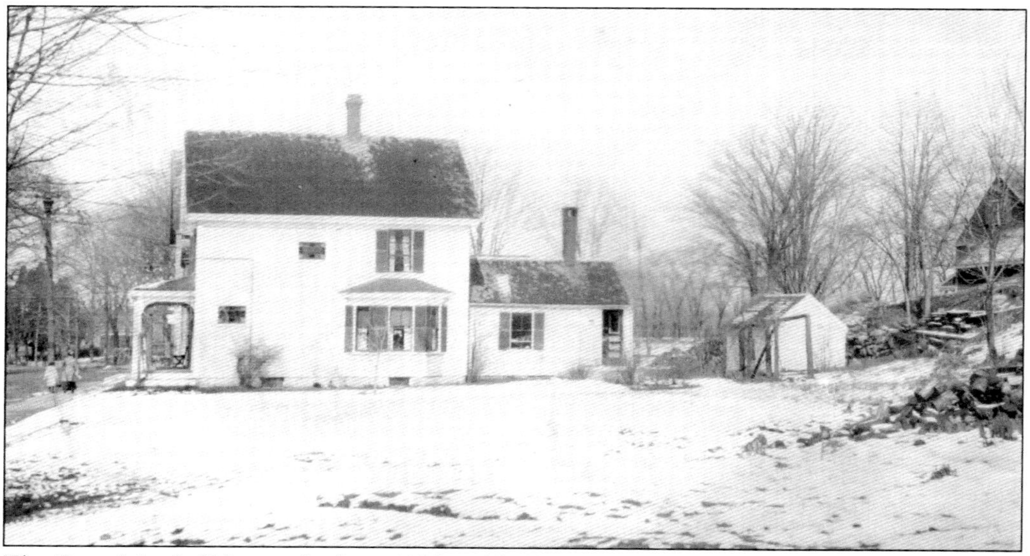

The Dave Marshall house, built in 1900 at 354 Boston Post Road, is now the Sudbury Music Center. Marshall worked at the Hurlbut and Rogers machine shop behind the present Mill Village shopping district.

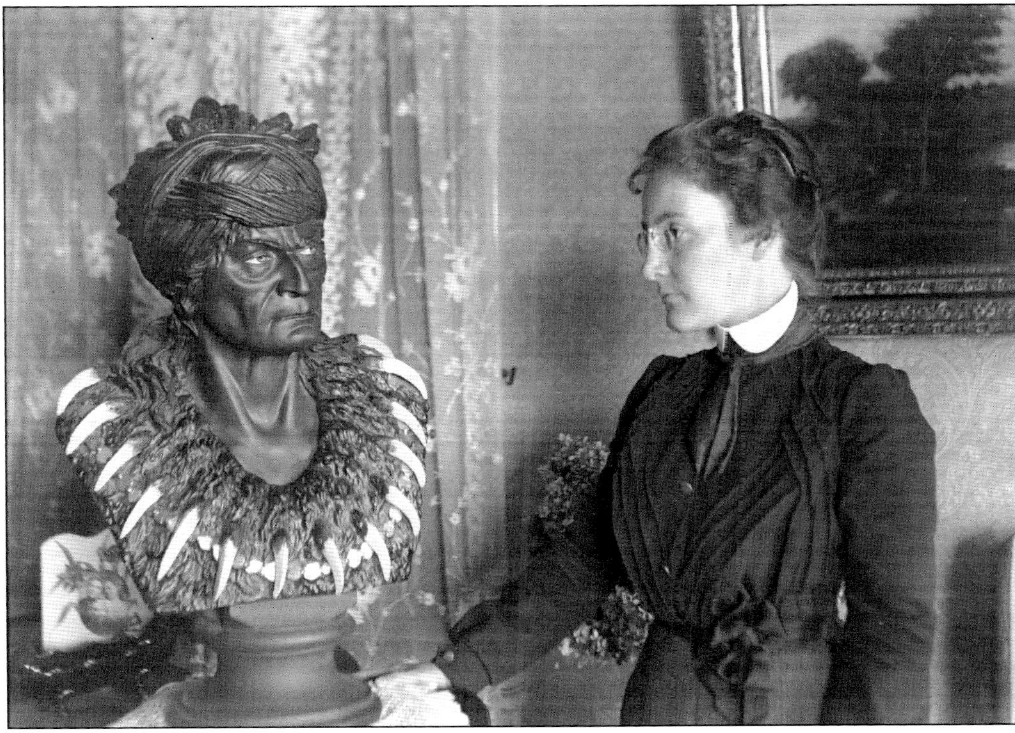

Hattie Goodnow was able to trip her camera lens and take self-portraits. Here, she poses with a bust of an Indian in the house, showing off her ability to compose a photograph well in 1903.

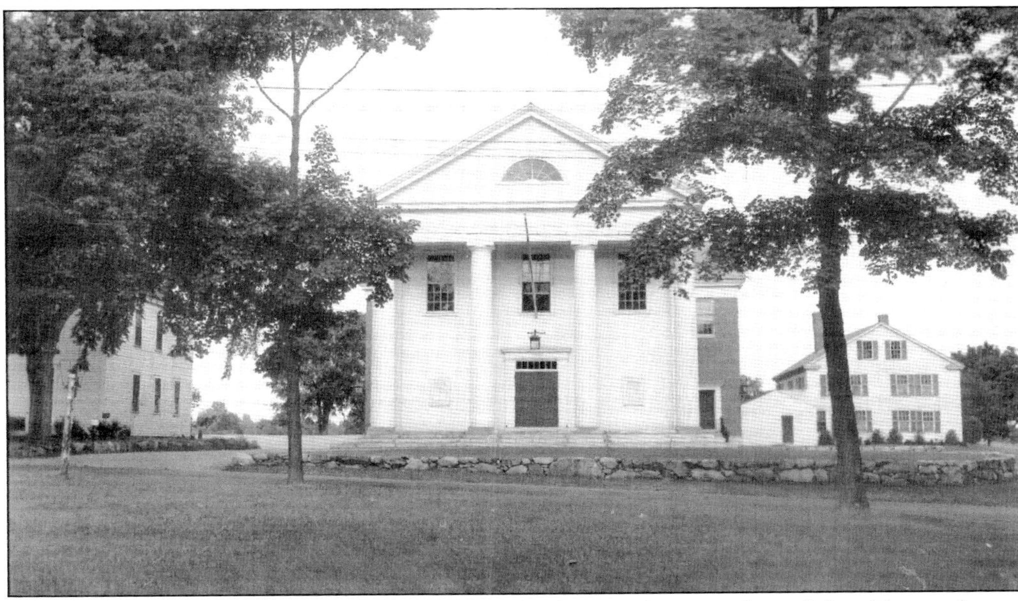

The town hall was dedicated on February 22, 1932. It was a larger replica of the old town house, which burned in 1930. The hall was built to be fireproof. The architect was Charles H. Way of Sudbury. Note the telephone and electric lines overhead that were buried in the center at great but worthwhile expense in the mid-1970s.

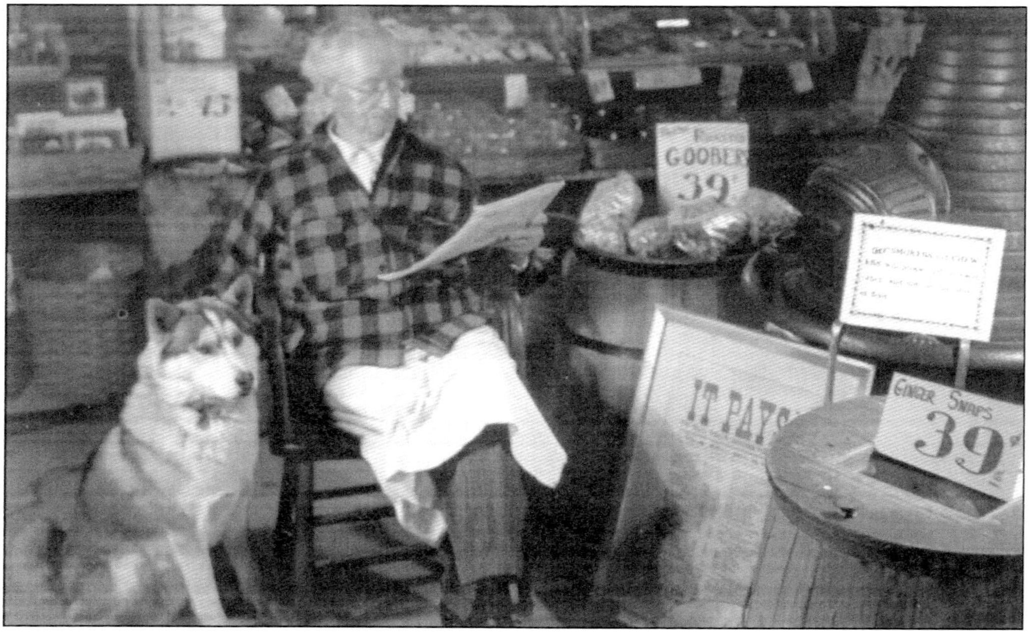


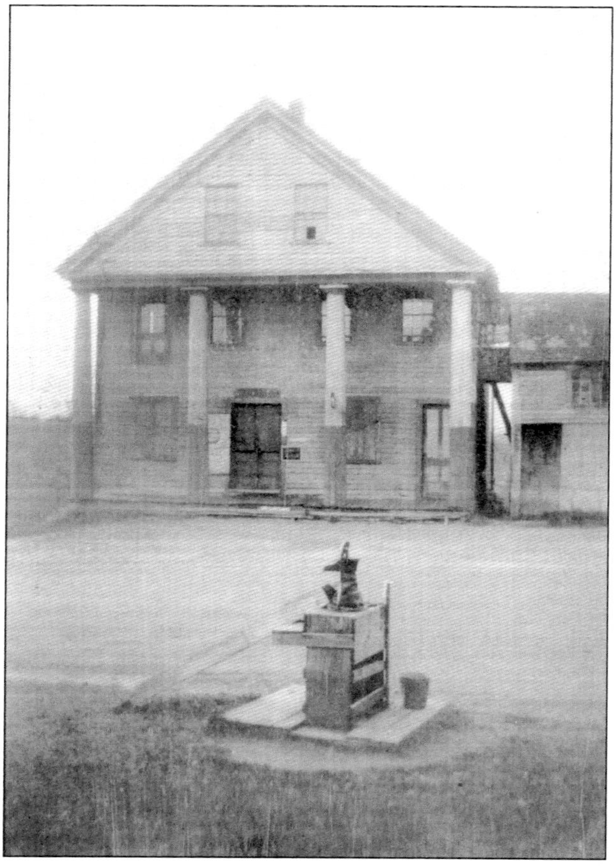

In 1947, Milton and Edna Swanson purchased the general store, which had been closed after running from 1930 to 1938 on the Henry Ford estate, and reopened it as the Wayside Country Store. Milton's father, Fred Swanson, worked in the store and became identified with it. He is seen above in front of the potbelly stove with Attic, the first of the Siberian huskies used to haul goods out of snow-bound warehouses buried in the woods.

The Parmenter-Garfield general store was originally located in the town center at what is now Grinnell Park. Future president James Garfield once taught school on the second floor. In 1929, the store was purchased by Henry Ford and moved to 1015 Boston Post Road in Marlborough by cutting it in half and hauling it with teams of oxen in the winter. It was reopened in 1930 as the general store, and students at the Wayside Inn Boys' School worked there. Christmas celebrations were held out front in December.

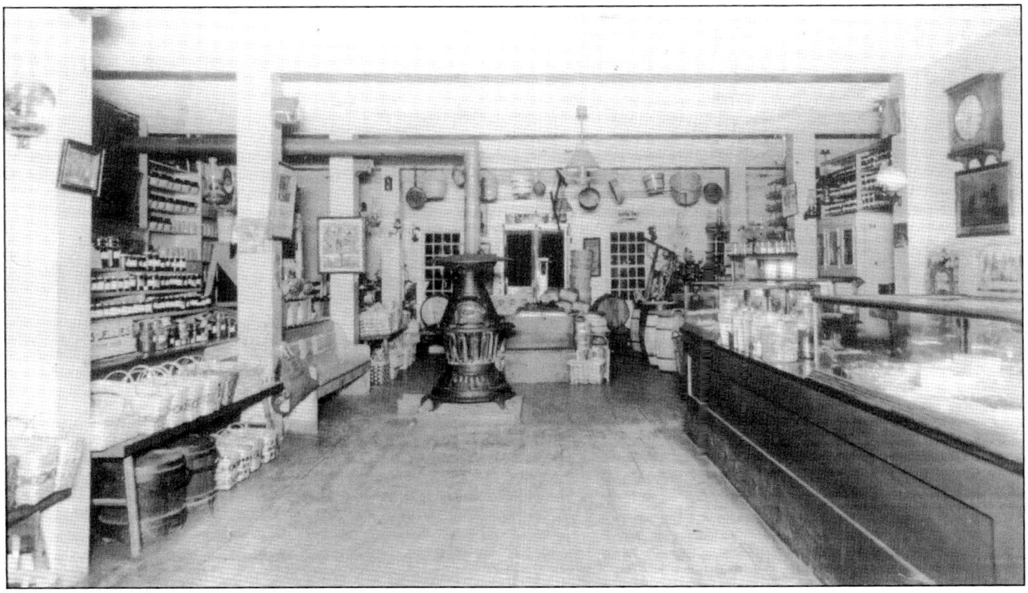

The general store was reopened in 1930 by Henry Ford as the first restored country store in America. One could shop there and buy a wide assortment of goods, as seen in the displays. Ford's wife, Clara, was behind the project. She especially wanted to show farmers how to display and merchandise their own fruits and vegetables in the stand to the left of the building. She also encouraged many colonial crafts on the second floor of the store, including weaving and spinning.

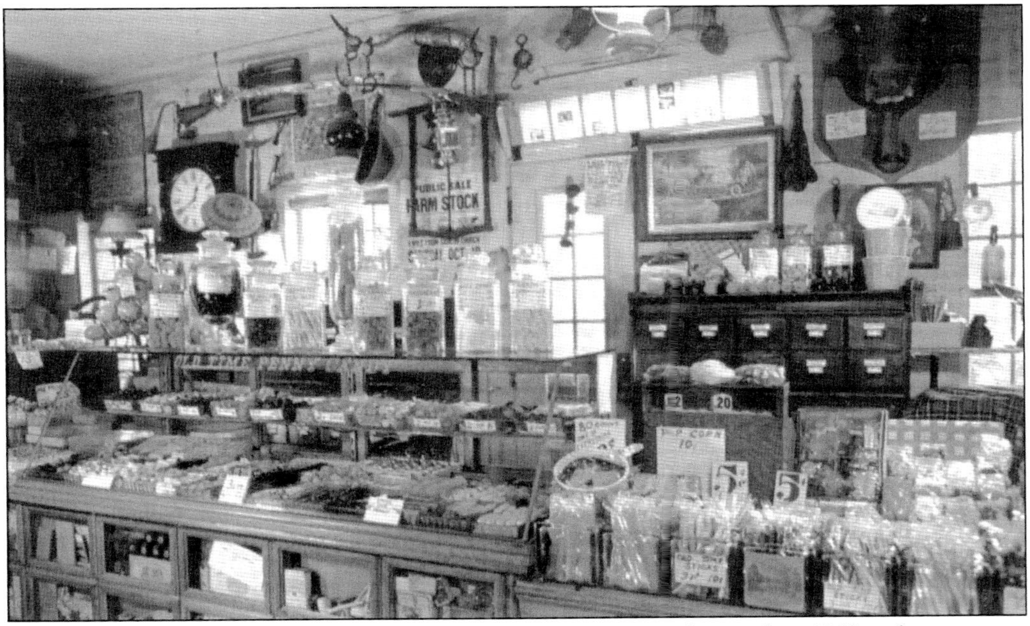


The penny candy counter at the Wayside Country Store was featured in 1955 as having over 90 types of candy for sale for a penny. The counter was at the back of the store. Lines of eager customers extended all the way out the door for 100 feet on Sundays; it took 10 clerks just to service this counter and pack Memory Bags, which sold for 25¢ in the striped candy bag that Leona Johnson lent Milton Swanson to reproduce and use.

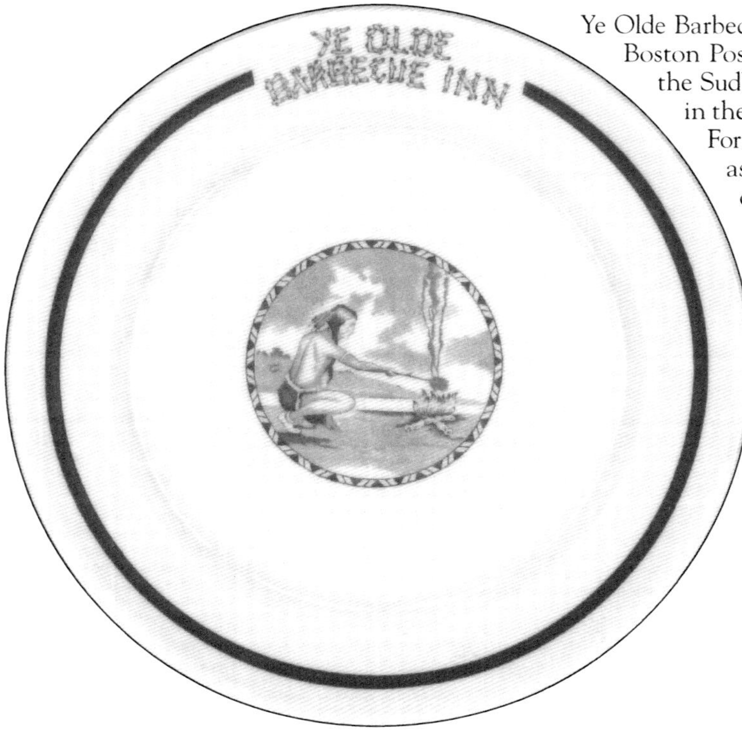


Ye Olde Barbeque Inn was located at 410 Boston Post Road in what had been the Sudbury Inn. As a young man in the 1920s, late town historian Forrest Bradshaw was employed as a night watchman/night clerk. When they went out of business, Bradshaw was paid with the inn's china service for 50 in lieu of cash. The china is white with a maroon stripe and is trademarked Shennago China, New Castle, Pennsylvania.

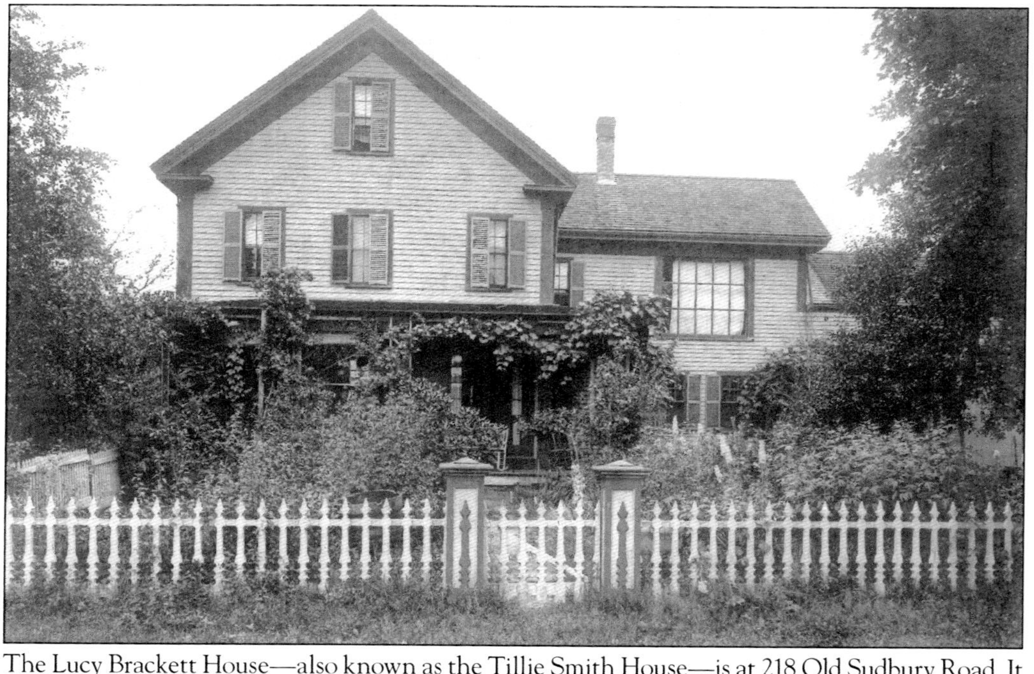

The Lucy Brackett House—also known as the Tillie Smith House—is at 218 Old Sudbury Road. It was built in the Greek Revival style in 1850. Brackett was a teacher at Sudbury School. Before her death, she gave donations to all the churches in town. The First Parish named a room after her, which had a working fireplace and was used for small meetings, to remember her for her thankfulness.

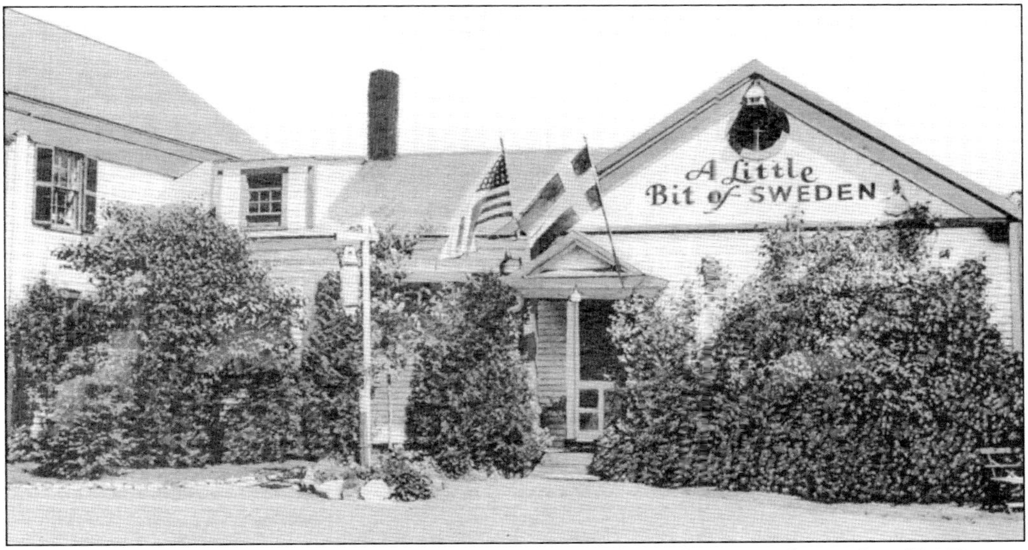


The Gvensk Kaffe Stuga, a Swedish coffeehouse in South Sudbury, was located at 394 Boston Post Road. Very popular in its day, it attracted customers from 50 miles around. Founded in 1928, it was run by Paul Ecke and his family. As the sign says, it really was "a little bit of Sweden." Swedish families who had arrived as immigrants around 1900 had moved up to the middle class by the 1940s and enjoyed a touch of their homeland with good Swedish food.

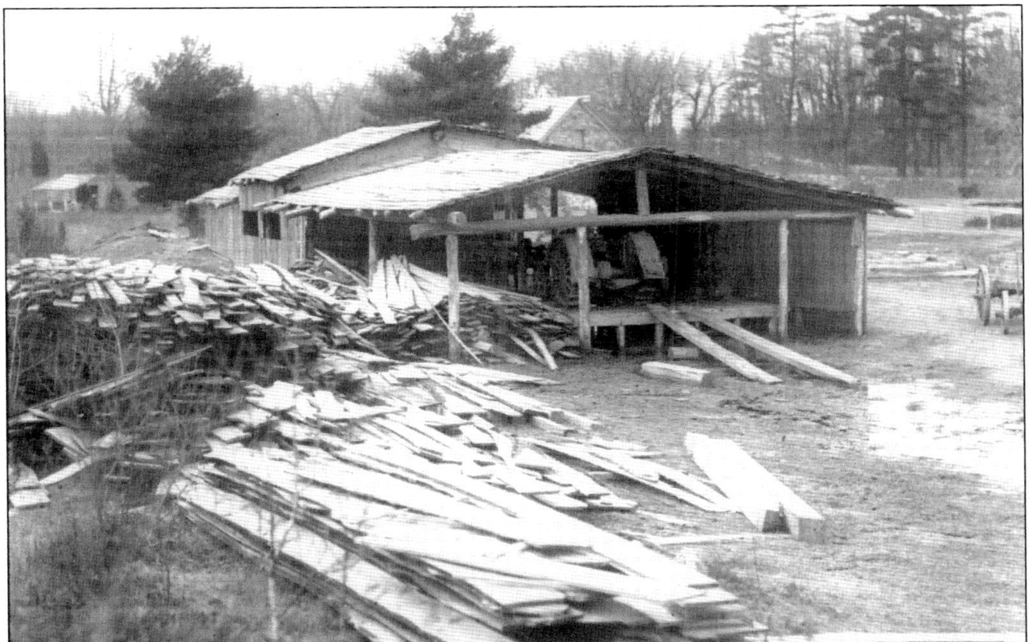

Henry Ford had a portable planing and sawmill in use from 1927 to 1929 on the Wayside Inn grounds, where workmen were building what would become the Wayside Inn Gristmill. In the center background, the mill's granite walls are up, with a roof. The interior of the gristmill is mostly chestnut, but includes pine as well. Later, the planing and sawmill was moved to the Dutton Road salvage yard and then down to Hager Pond in Marlborough after the 1938 hurricane.

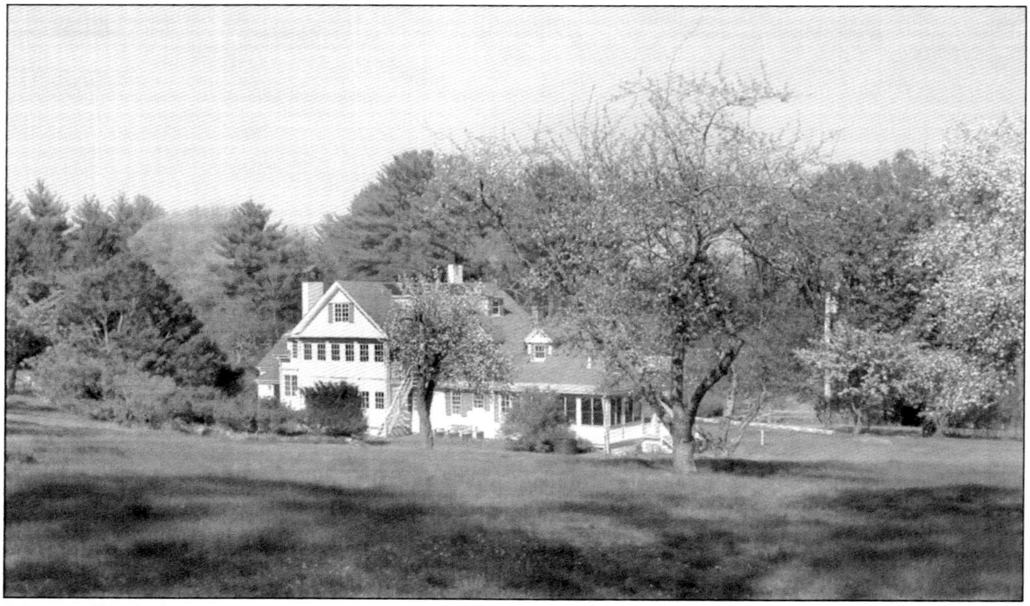

The Wolbach farm was comprised of 100 acres at 18 Wolbach Road. Dr. S. Burt Wolbach was the Shattuck professor of pathology at Harvard Medical School from 1922 to 1954, receiving many honors. The Wolbach family used it as a summer home until it was given to the Sudbury Valley Trustees (SVT) by his son John Wolbach. SVT, a nonprofit group that oversees and purchases land for preservation, took it over in 2004 and carefully restored the home, barn, and grounds.

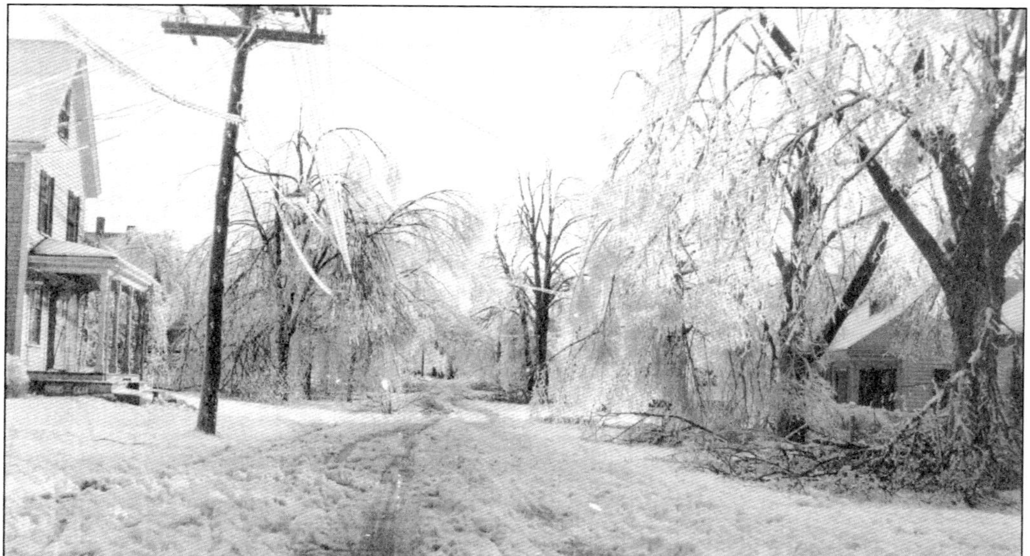

A record ice storm hit Sudbury and the Boston Post Road in 1915. This photograph was taken looking east from the corner of Concord Road. The house on the left is 354 Boston Post Road, which is now the Sudbury Music Center, and the house on the right is No. 357. The storm hit when horse and carriages were gradually losing out to automobiles and trucks. Previously, the snow had been rolled for the use of sleighs, but now with automobiles, plowing was necessary and was almost impossible in an ice storm with the equipment available at the time.

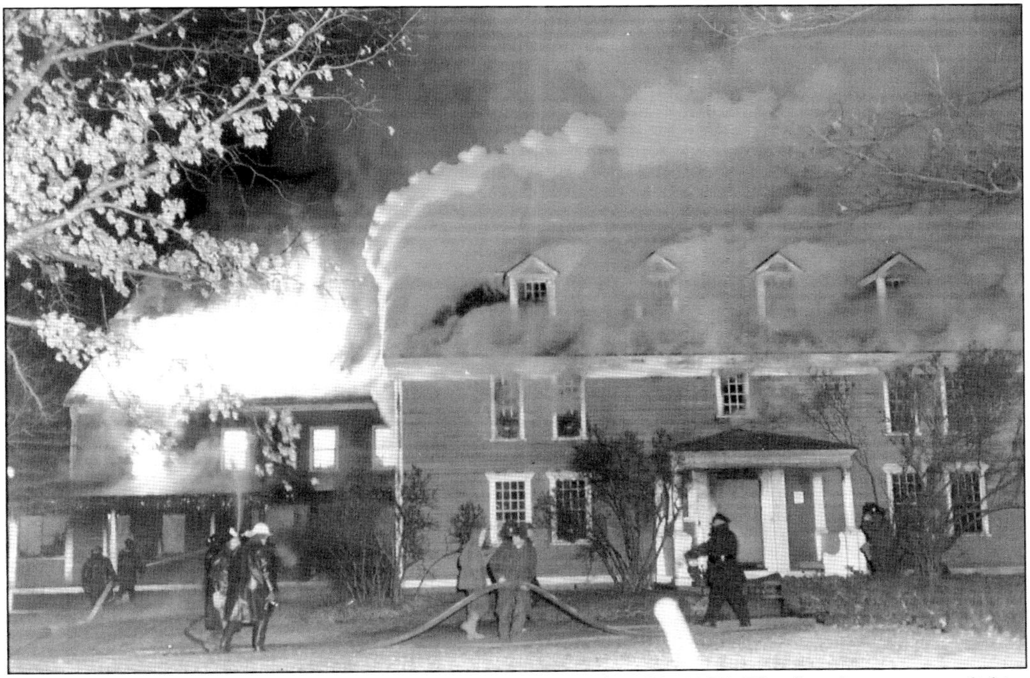

The Wayside Inn had a major fire at 2:00 a.m. on December 22, 1955. The fire department did its best but the inn sustained massive damage. The fire started in the back, progressed to the west wing, and then moved forward to the old part of the structure. The firemen had to cut through 18 inches of ice to get to the water from the inn's Josephine Pond. By 2:45 a.m., 11 pieces of equipment from four neighboring towns were helping to put out the fire.

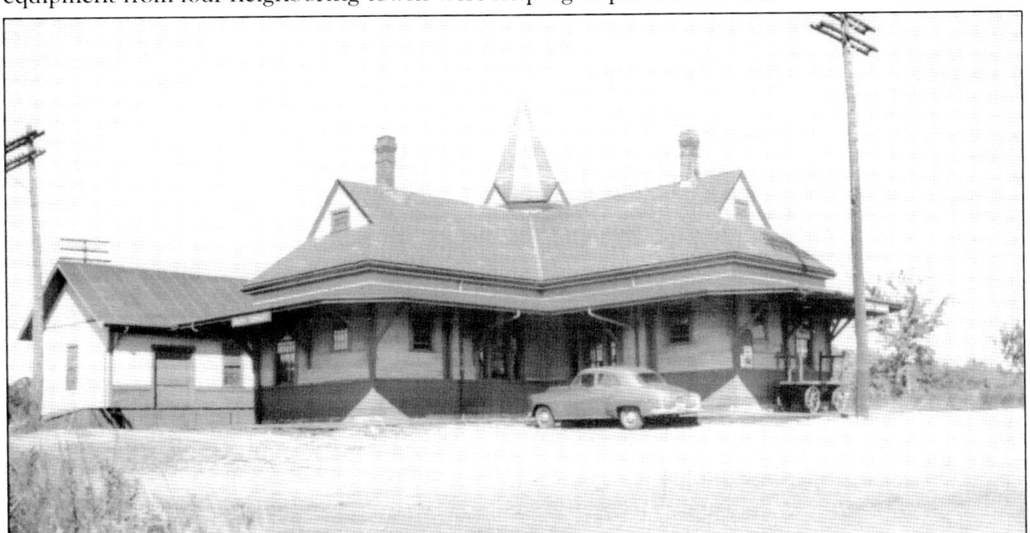

This is the South Sudbury railroad station, opposite what is now 28 Union Avenue. It is called Union Avenue because it is the union of two different railroads, which cross at the station. The east-west line was the B&M Central Massachusetts line and the north-south line was the Hartford, New Haven, Framingham, and Lowell branch of the B&M. The station was torn down in 1955, and a small waiting room was built nearby, which is now a livery service.

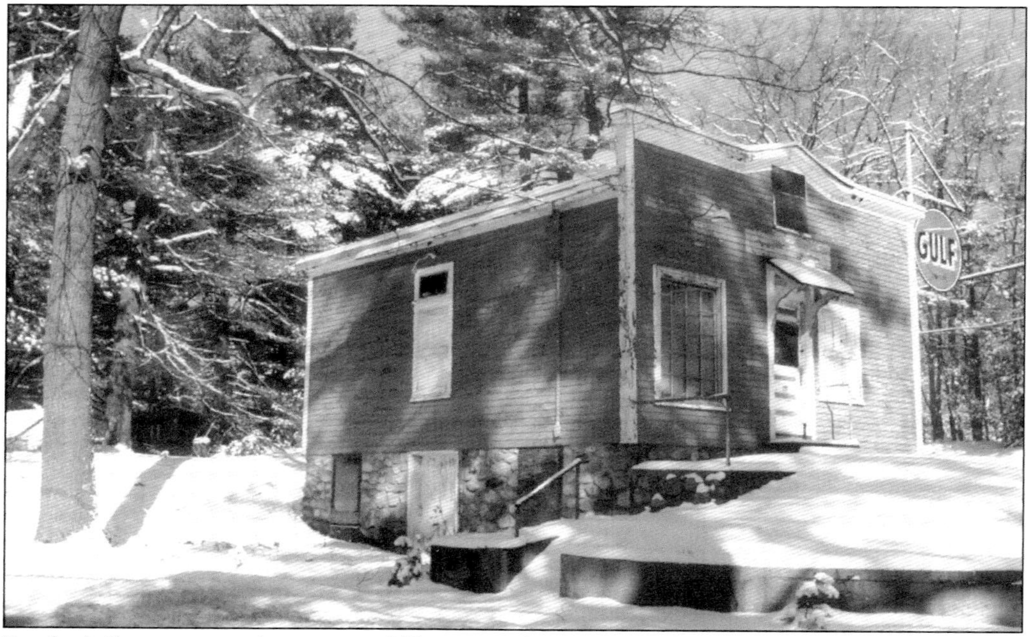


Bowker's Store was at the corner of Haynes and Pantry Roads. Some think it was the North Sudbury railroad station, but it was not; Everett W. Bowker and his wife tended store here for more than 40 years. It served the public as a general store, a gas station, and the North Sudbury Post Office. It closed sometime after 1961.

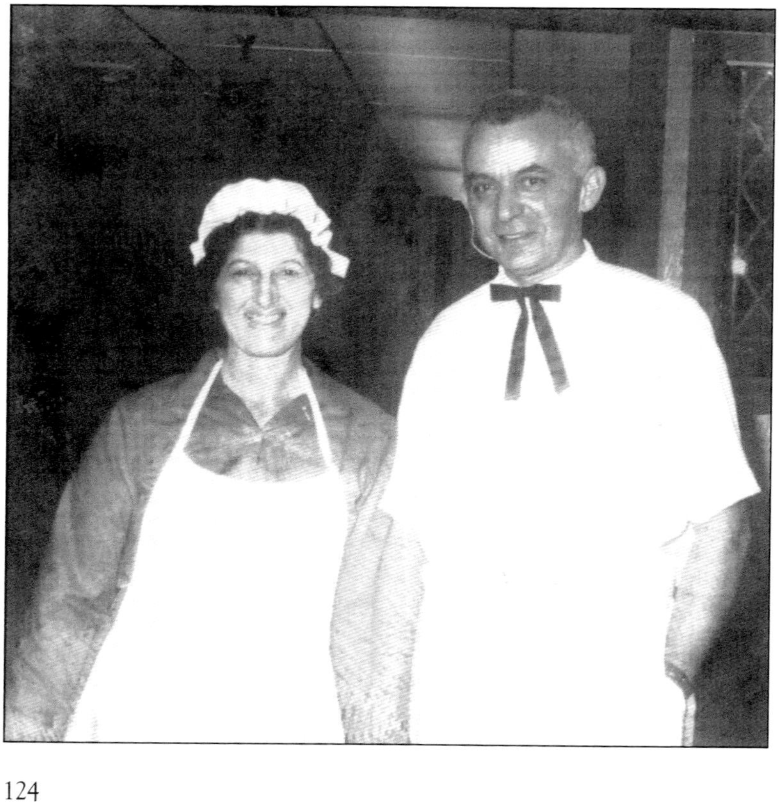

Ruth and Hank Greenblatt are dressed in their uniforms for the opening of their store, "Hello Deli."

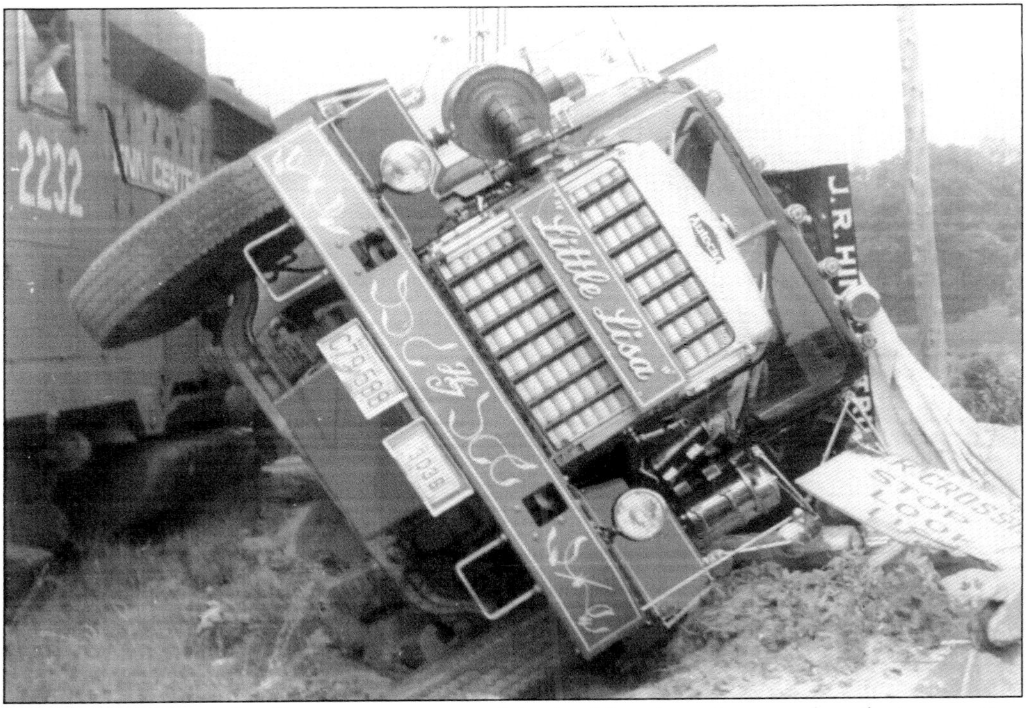


The new truck "Little Lisa" ran into a train, resulting in this unique photograph at the intersection of the B&M railroad line at 394 Boston Post Road in 1955. George Halloran used to be the gatekeeper for the crossing, which was extremely dangerous. The railroad provided a little white shack for him to sit in with a heater, and when a train came, he would crank down the gates to stop traffic. This accident happened after he was laid off without a replacement.

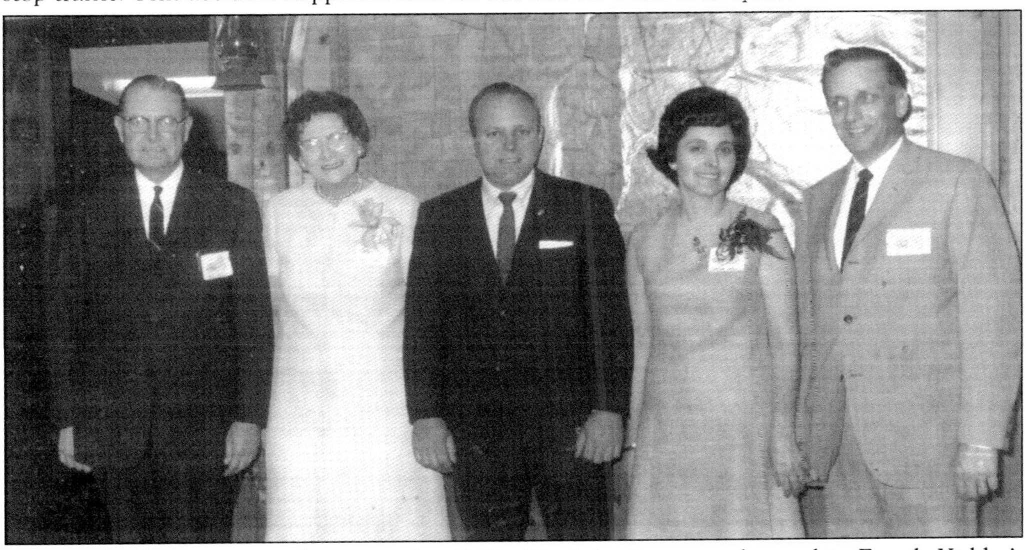

Hall Realty hosts an open house in the 1960s. Their business was located in Enoch Kidder's building at 361 Boston Post Road, next to the present-day Mill Village. The employees were, from left to right, Bob Ayers, Jessie Hall, Earl Midgely, and Lorraine and Bill Hall. The Halls still live in Sudbury.

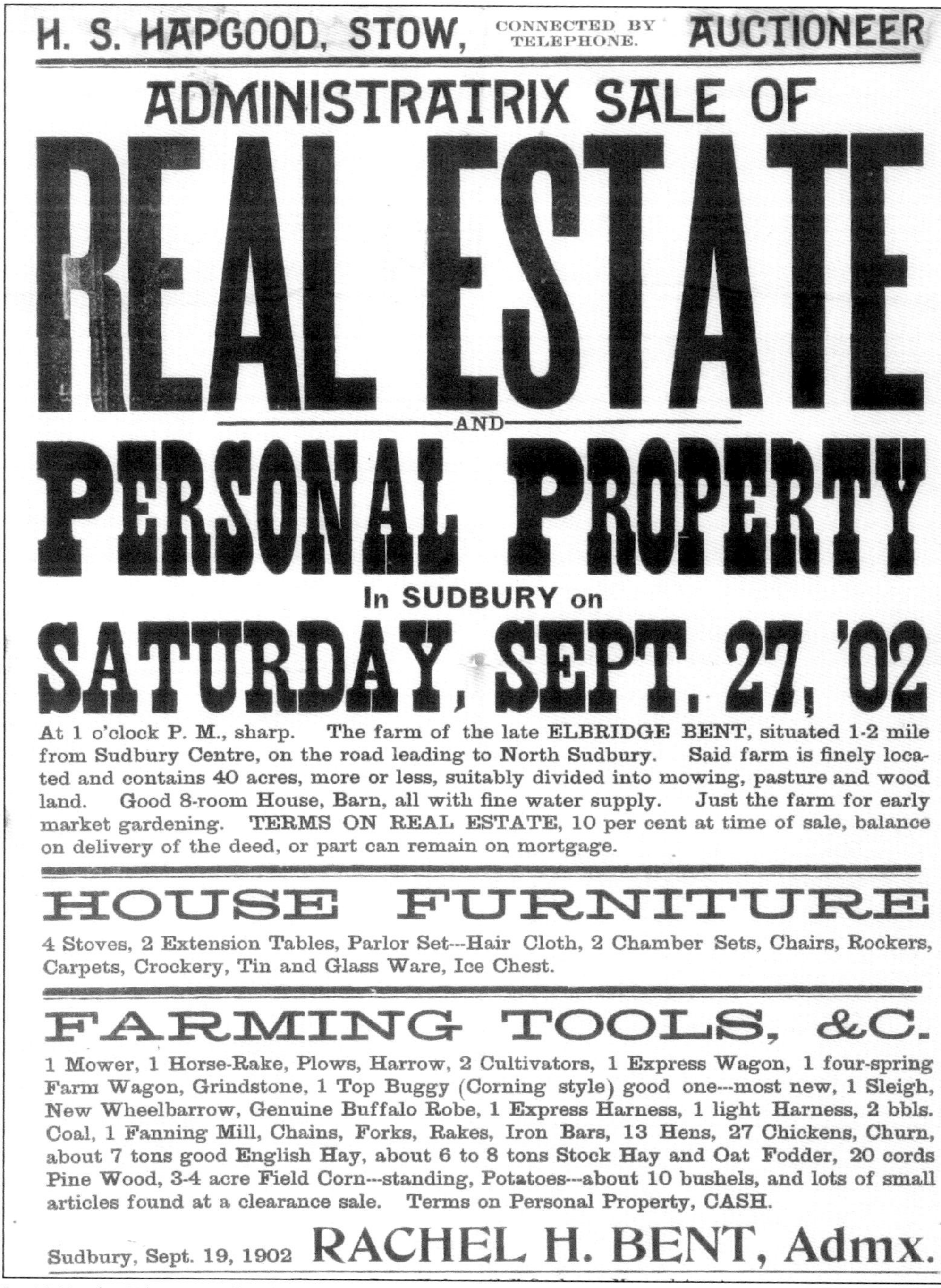

H. S. HAPGOOD, STOW, CONNECTED BY TELEPHONE. AUCTIONEER

ADMINISTRATRIX SALE OF

REAL ESTATE

AND

PERSONAL PROPERTY

In SUDBURY on

SATURDAY, SEPT. 27, '02

At 1 o'clock P. M., sharp. The farm of the late ELBRIDGE BENT, situated 1-2 mile from Sudbury Centre, on the road leading to North Sudbury. Said farm is finely located and contains 40 acres, more or less, suitably divided into mowing, pasture and wood land. Good 8-room House, Barn, all with fine water supply. Just the farm for early market gardening. TERMS ON REAL ESTATE, 10 per cent at time of sale, balance on delivery of the deed, or part can remain on mortgage.

HOUSE FURNITURE

4 Stoves, 2 Extension Tables, Parlor Set---Hair Cloth, 2 Chamber Sets, Chairs, Rockers, Carpets, Crockery, Tin and Glass Ware, Ice Chest.

FARMING TOOLS, &C.

1 Mower, 1 Horse-Rake, Plows, Harrow, 2 Cultivators, 1 Express Wagon, 1 four-spring Farm Wagon, Grindstone, 1 Top Buggy (Corning style) good one---most new, 1 Sleigh, New Wheelbarrow, Genuine Buffalo Robe, 1 Express Harness, 1 light Harness, 2 bbls. Coal, 1 Fanning Mill, Chains, Forks, Rakes, Iron Bars, 13 Hens, 27 Chickens, Churn, about 7 tons good English Hay, about 6 to 8 tons Stock Hay and Oat Fodder, 20 cords Pine Wood, 3-4 acre Field Corn---standing, Potatoes---about 10 bushels, and lots of small articles found at a clearance sale. Terms on Personal Property, CASH.

Sudbury, Sept. 19, 1902 RACHEL H. BENT, Admx.

In 1902, the Thomas Elbridge Bent estate sale was of great interest to the townspeople. His house was located at 531 Concord Road. Bent, who was born in 1812, had inherited it from his father. Rachel H. Bent was the administrator of Bent's estate and sold the property. After 108 years, in 2010, basketball player Shaquille O'Neal leased part of the original property, located behind the house, while he played for the Boston Celtics.

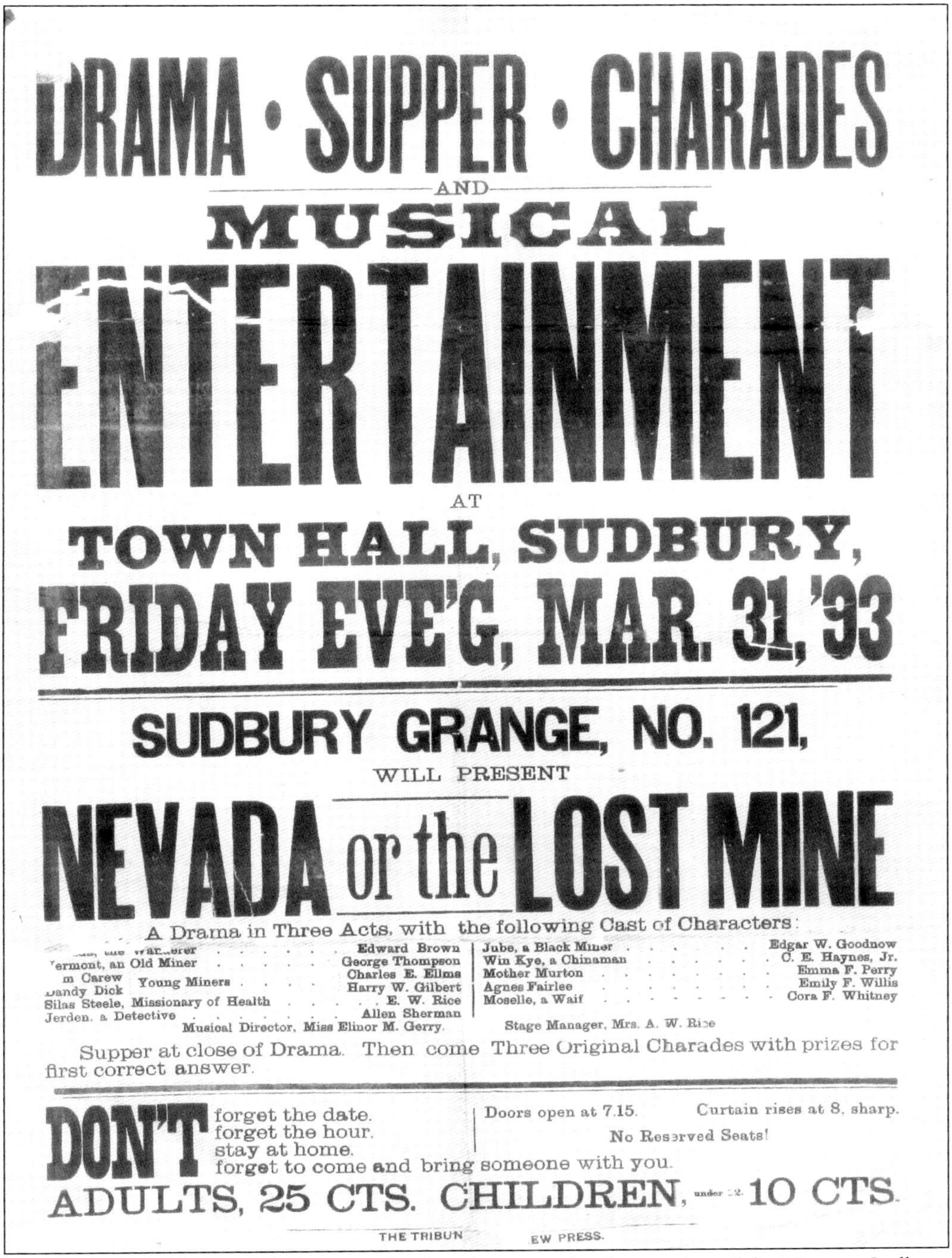

DRAMA · SUPPER · CHARADES

AND

MUSICAL

ENTERTAINMENT

AT

TOWN HALL, SUDBURY,

FRIDAY EVE'G, MAR. 31,'93

SUDBURY GRANGE, NO. 121,

WILL PRESENT

NEVADA or the LOST MINE

A Drama in Three Acts, with the following Cast of Characters:

..., the Wanderer . . . . . . . . Edward Brown
Vermont, an Old Miner . . . . . . . George Thompson
m Carew } Young Miners . . . . . Charles E. Ellms
Dandy Dick } . . . . . Harry W. Gilbert
Silas Steele, Missionary of Health . . . . . E. W. Rice
Jerden, a Detective . . . . . . . . Allen Sherman
Jube, a Black Miner . . . . . . . Edgar W. Goodnow
Win Kye, a Chinaman . . . . . . . C. E. Haynes, Jr.
Mother Murton . . . . . . . . Emma F. Perry
Agnes Fairlee . . . . . . . . Emily F. Willis
Moselle, a Waif . . . . . . . . Cora F. Whitney

Musical Director, Miss Elinor M. Gerry. Stage Manager, Mrs. A. W. Rice

Supper at close of Drama. Then come Three Original Charades with prizes for first correct answer.

DON'T forget the date.
forget the hour.
stay at home.
forget to come and bring someone with you.

Doors open at 7.15. Curtain rises at 8, sharp.

No Reserved Seats!

ADULTS, 25 CTS. CHILDREN, under 12, 10 CTS.

THE TRIBUN... EW PRESS.

In 1893, the town hall was the host site for this play put on by the member of the Grange. Sudbury was a farming community and the Grange was organized by farmers to be the voice of the farmers, cloaked in fraternal garb and ritual. Many of the people featured in these pages took part in this play, staying up until midnight and then rising with the roosters.

IMAGES of America

# LITCHFIELD PARK

I0806207

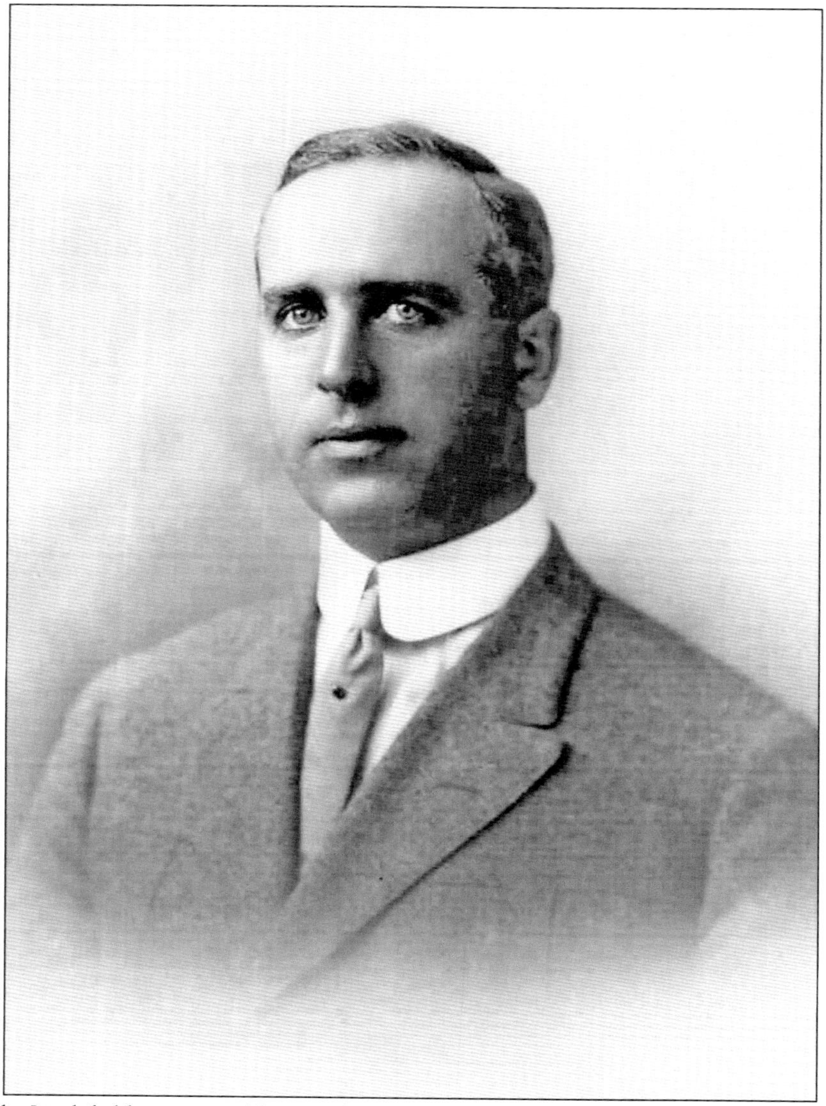

Paul Weeks Litchfield is pictured here in his 30s. He joined Goodyear Tire & Rubber Company in 1900 and during his career was awarded many patents for tires. In 1916, he came to Arizona to plant cotton that was required for the cord of his newest tire patent. With the invention of the pneumatic tire, farm equipment would soon be rolling on rubber. (Courtesy of Goodyear Tire & Rubber Company.)

**On the Cover:** Paul Litchfield sits on a tractor with pneumatic tires. This c. 1938 photograph shows the replacement of the old steel wheel with a new pneumatic rubber tire patented by Litchfield. (Courtesy of Goodyear Tire & Rubber Company.)

IMAGES
*of America*

# LITCHFIELD PARK

Celeste S. Crouch

ARCADIA
PUBLISHING

ISBN 978-1-4671-3044-8

Published by Arcadia Publishing
Charleston, South Carolina

Printed in the United States of America

Library of Congress Control Number: 2013933332

For all general information, please contact Arcadia Publishing:
Telephone 843-853-2070
Fax 843-853-0044
E-mail sales@arcadiapublishing.com
For customer service and orders:
Toll-Free 1-888-313-2665

Visit us on the Internet at www.arcadiapublishing.com

*To Paul Litchfield and the early pioneers from Goodyear Tire & Rubber Company, who had the vision to turn the barren desert into an oasis*

# Contents

# Acknowledgments

A special thank you to the many people who generously gave of their time to help with this book. Local family members of early Goodyear farm employees were very helpful in identifying people and places from past years.

Dr. Robert (Bob) McMillan, Carl Clarino, Belen Moreno, Linda Lamm, Margaret McMicken Bartol, Phyllis Figueroa, and the Wigwam Resort were very supportive contributors. Julia Sweeney, Sara Homan, Barbara Dienes, Tim Barrow, Michael Levine, Frances Martin, and Edna Pasqualetti were helpful with pictures and historical research. A special thanks to Michael Jordan for his photography and support.

Thank you to Meredeth Stucky and Judy Cook for their support and especially to Charlotte Cohen for her expertise and assistance in completing the final phases of the book. Special thanks to my husband, Jeff, and daughter, Sherry, for their assistance.

Thank you to the City of Litchfield Park, Arizona State University, Litchfield Park Historical Society, Luke Air Force Base History Department, SunCor, the Tom Doyle family, Steve Hoza, Libby Hilton Rouse, and local families who contributed pictures and historical information.

Unless otherwise noted, all images are property of the Goodyear Tire & Rubber Company and are from the Goodyear Collection stored at the University of Akron Archives in Akron, Ohio. All other photographs will be cited following the captions.

In an effort to continue Paul Litchfield's legacy, author royalties from the Litchfield Park book have been designated to the City of Litchfield Park for the restoration of the Litchfields' family home, called Rancho La Loma Homestead.

# INTRODUCTION

It is believed the Hohokam people reached the Salt River Valley around 700 AD. The Hohokam culture was rich and highly advanced. They masterminded an advanced system of irrigation, including many miles of canals. Some of their canals were still visible to the Spanish missionaries and explorers of the 16th and 17th centuries and formed the basis for the modern irrigation systems in Arizona. Some of the canals extended out from the west bank of the Agua Fria River towards present-day Litchfield Park.

Settlers came and went across this region, yet at the opening of the 20th century, no permanent settlement had been made on the land that includes Litchfield Park. The reason seemed to be the difficulty in irrigating the land, which was several miles from the source of water.

The first attempt to develop the land west of the Agua Fria River was by an organized group of settlers who were interested in obtaining cheap land. William G. Kriegbaum, a citrus grower from Riverside, California, first came to Arizona in 1908, looking for a climate suitable to grow citrus. He soon recruited another 21 settlers from California to come in 1910 to establish the Air Line Water Company and to file desert claims on the land.

Under Statute 377, passed by the US Congress in 1877, each person could claim 320 acres of desert land if he or she could supply water. Kriegbaum and his wife together claimed 640 acres, and each of the settlers from California laid claim to land. The challenge was to find a way of diverting water from the Agua Fria River, which was located miles to the east, for irrigation. Each group dug lateral canals to make water available to its tract. Water rights were established by the Air Line Water Company in 1910. As development increased, the water demand also increased, and several wells were dug to supplement the canals. The settlers started to clear the desert by dragging railroad ties, pulled by mules, over the land.

In 1911, Kriegbaum's son Lawrence arrived to assist his father in developing the area. They lived in a tent, and after clearing land, they built a small frame house. This was the first building on the present site of Litchfield Park. Soon after the house was completed, a tornado blew it away. They made adobe bricks and built a six-room adobe house. There were no roads, and the nearest store was Billy Moore's store on Buckeye Road, approximately six miles away. They received mail at this store in a mailbag that was delivered by stagecoach from Phoenix, 20 miles away. The Kriegbaums laid out roads that were scarcely more than trails. Buckeye Road was the only road into Phoenix. Transportation improved when the Arizona Eastern Railroad was built across the Agua Fria River from Phoenix. Eventually, around 5,000 acres of desert land was developed in the Litchfield Park area by the Kriegbaums and other settlers.

World War I and the German U-boats had cut off the supply of cotton from Egypt and other Mediterranean countries. The Goodyear Tire & Rubber Company needed this supply of cotton for its pneumatic tires. The supply of cotton in the Southeastern states was destroyed by an infestation of boll weevils. The US Department of Agriculture had succeeded in growing Pima cotton in the Southwestern states, where the climatic conditions were similar to those in Egypt.

This knowledge brought the Goodyear Tire & Rubber Company to the Salt River Valley to grow long staple cotton needed for its tires.

Paul Weeks Litchfield of the Goodyear Tire & Rubber Company came to this area in 1916 and helped to establish the Southwest Cotton Company, a new subsidiary to handle the cotton-growing project. He approached the Kriegbaums and other settlers to purchase their land for approximately $25 an acre. That year, Goodyear Tire & Rubber Company acquired 16,000 acres along the Agua Fria River (called Litchfield Ranch) and 8,000 acres in Chandler (called Goodyear Ranch). By 1921, the Southwest Cotton Company also purchased land in present-day Sun City (called Marinette Ranch), totaling 38,000 acres of property with 20,000 acres cultivated.

To establish the Litchfield Ranch, a small camp called Algodon (meaning "cotton") was set up one mile east of the present site of Litchfield Park. Temporary buildings were erected there until the Kriegbaums' adobe home was purchased and used for the Litchfield Ranch headquarters. In the fall of 1917, the company moved the Algodon camp to the present site of Litchfield Park, and new buildings were added to facilitate farming activities. This was the beginning of what is now Litchfield Park.

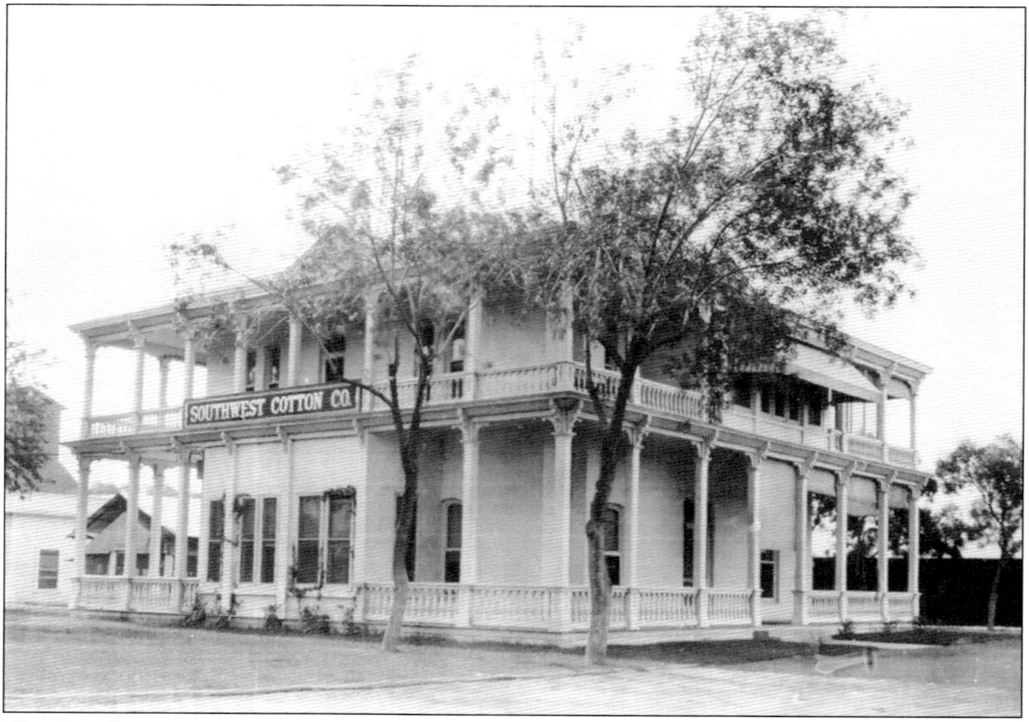


The Southwest Cotton Company, a subsidiary of the Goodyear Tire & Rubber Company, established a cotton-buying office in Phoenix on Seventh and Grant Streets to take advantage of the increase in cotton production in the area. The office was named Sarival after the first few letters of the Salt River Valley. This office was active in Phoenix until 1928, when the headquarters were moved to the Litchfield Ranch. (Courtesy of Michael Levine.)

# *One*

# Early Development of Farms

The Southwest Cotton Company had the gigantic task of preparing the land for its first cotton crop, which was started on Litchfield Ranch in January 1917. Approximately 3,500 acres of land that had not been cleared by the previous settlers were cleared and leveled. The land was further developed to include wells and irrigation canals.

In 1918, electric energy was obtained for pumping and lighting. The Southwest Cotton Company built its own lines from Phoenix, including 118 miles of transmission lines, which were eventually sold to the Central Arizona Power and Light Company. The company also built 42 miles of telephone lines.

The original work was supported in 1917 by mule trains. There was a real need to improve transportation. The company eventually constructed 158 miles of new roads through the desert and constructed a spur from the Arizona Eastern Railroad. The first train came into the Litchfield Ranch on July 31, 1920, and was used for freight service only.

By the fall of 1917, the ranch produced its first crop of 1,500 bales of cotton. Kenneth McMicken, a cousin of Paul Litchfield and an experienced farmer, was tasked with the study of cotton cultivation and development. In late 1917, McMicken traveled to Egypt to study long staple cotton, and upon his return in February 1918, he was named ranch foreman, implementing the Egyptian principles that were best adapted to the Southwest.

In the winter of 1917–1918, approximately 264,000 pounds of cotton were picked. A crop rotation plan was implemented after 1918, which included the planting of acres of alfalfa to revive the quality of the soil. The cotton harvest increased from less than one bale per acre in the first year to up to three bales per acre. Only one year later, approximately 6,734,000 pounds of cotton was produced.

By 1921, the Southwest Cotton Company handled 30 percent of Arizona's total cotton crop. However, cotton prices fell that year due to a recession, and cotton production was further challenged during the stock market crash of 1929. Several hundred acres held by the Southwest Cotton Company were leased during this time.

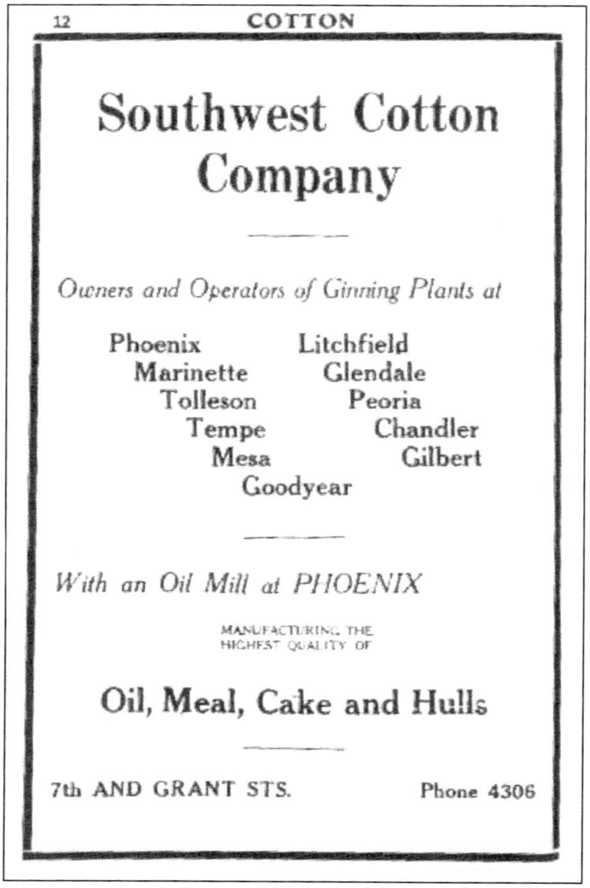
12 COTTON

# Southwest Cotton Company

*Owners and Operators of Ginning Plants at*

Phoenix, Litchfield, Marinette, Glendale, Tolleson, Peoria, Tempe, Chandler, Mesa, Gilbert, Goodyear

*With an Oil Mill at PHOENIX*

MANUFACTURING THE HIGHEST QUALITY OF

**Oil, Meal, Cake and Hulls**

7th AND GRANT STS. Phone 4306

This is an advertisement of the Southwest Cotton Company in the 1923 Phoenix telephone book. Originally, all of the ranches in the Southwest Cotton Company were served by a six-press cotton oil mill built in Phoenix between 1918 and 1919. By 1920, it was enlarged to a capacity of 124 tons of cotton seed a day, making it one of the largest in the Pacific coast area. (Courtesy of Michael Levine.)

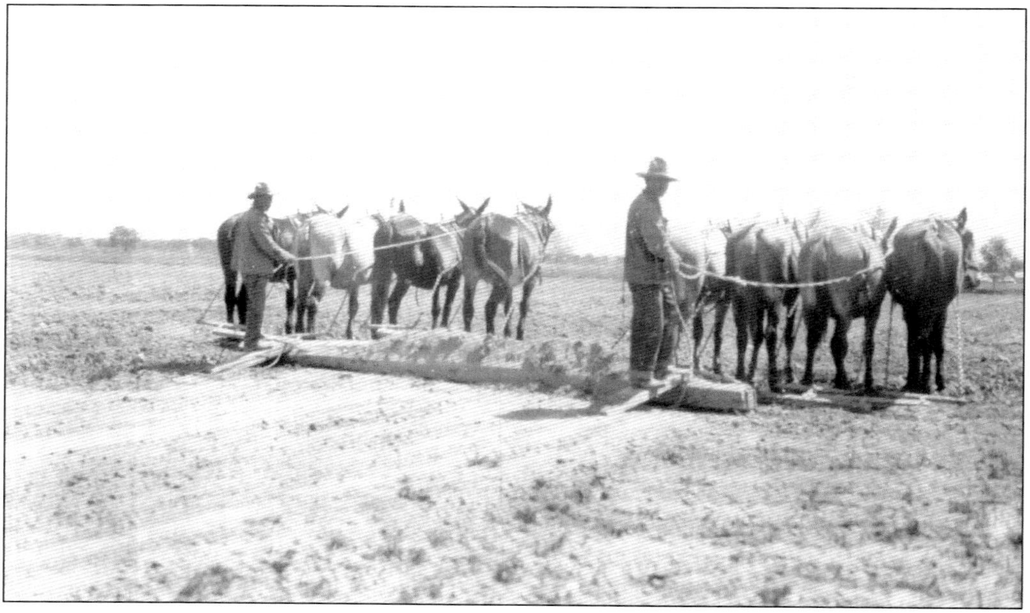

Clearing the land for the Litchfield Ranch was a tremendous task. Up to 2,500 men used 1,200 mules and brood mares to pull railroad ties. The brood mares were obtained from Jim Cassion, who lived east of the river on Buckeye Road. He raised mares for the Arizona Eastern Railroad, being built near his home. (Courtesy of the City of Litchfield Park.)

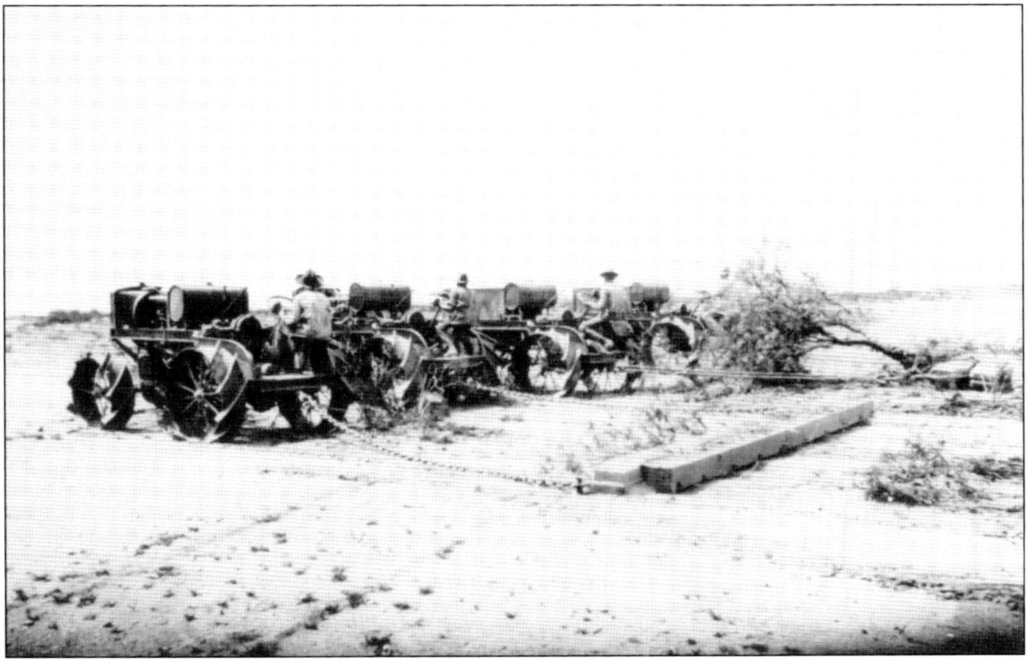

More than a dozen steel-wheeled tractors with gasoline engines were provided to clear the desert of cactus, sagebrush, mesquite, and other vegetation. The tractors were lined up in pairs with a 40-foot-long steel rail lashed so that it would drag on the ground, and over 6,000 acres were cleared in 1917. (Courtesy of the City of Litchfield Park.)

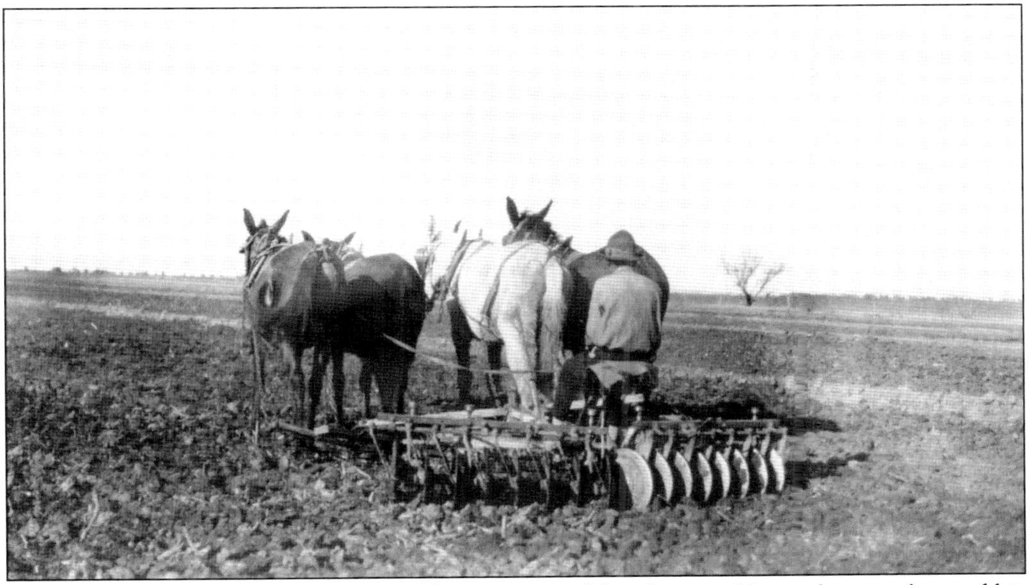

This was a familiar scene of the ground being prepared for planting. Here a farm worker and his team of mules pull a disc over the land to break up the soil in preparation for planting cotton. (Courtesy of the City of Litchfield Park.)

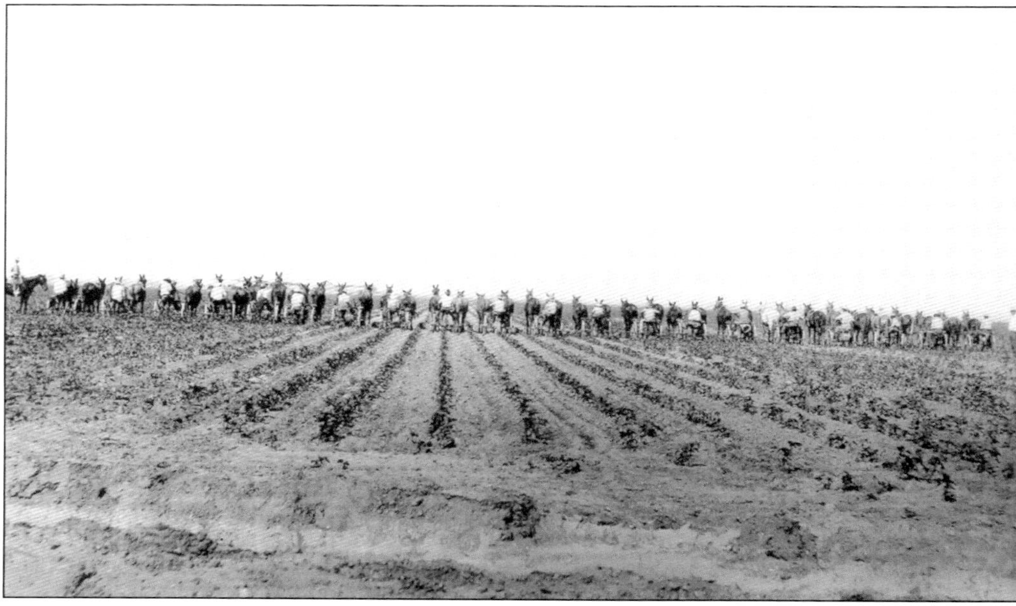

Mules and men made up a team that changed the desert forever. While there were 1,200 mules that worked from 1917 to 1919, by 1929, the same work was accomplished with only 200 mules and 35 tractors. Nationally during the period from 1935 to 1941, thousands of tractors were changed annually from steel rims to rubber, and the percentage of new tractors equipped with pneumatic tires increased from 14 percent to 96 percent. (Courtesy of Chandler Historical Society.)

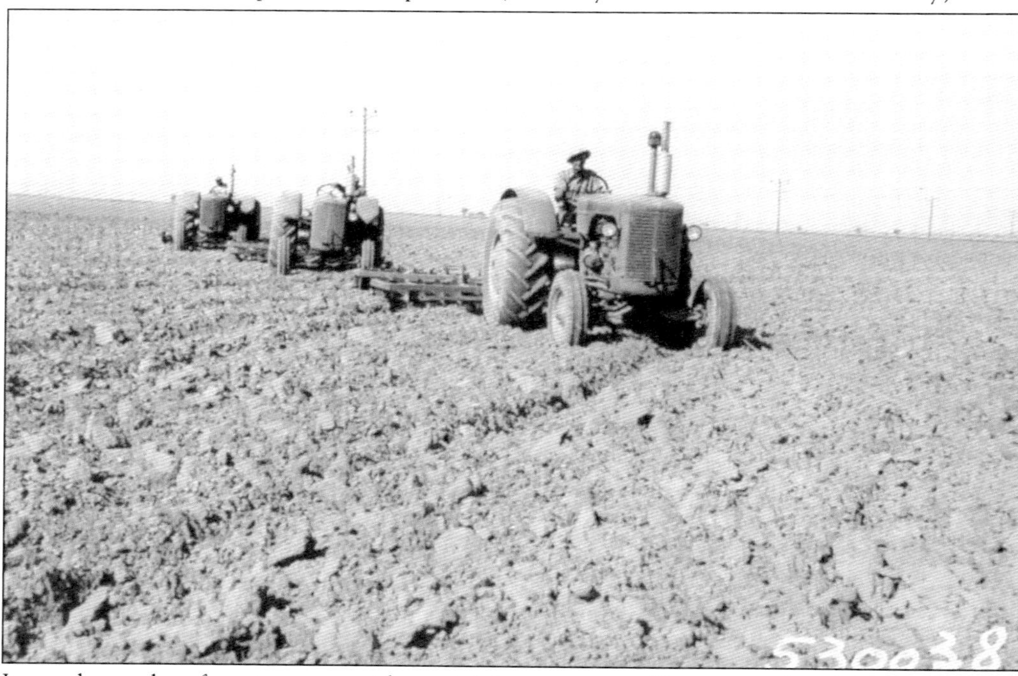


It was the modern farm tractor—with special, low-pressure rubber tires—that did more than any other single development to revolutionize and advance agricultural methods. (Courtesy of the City of Litchfield Park.)

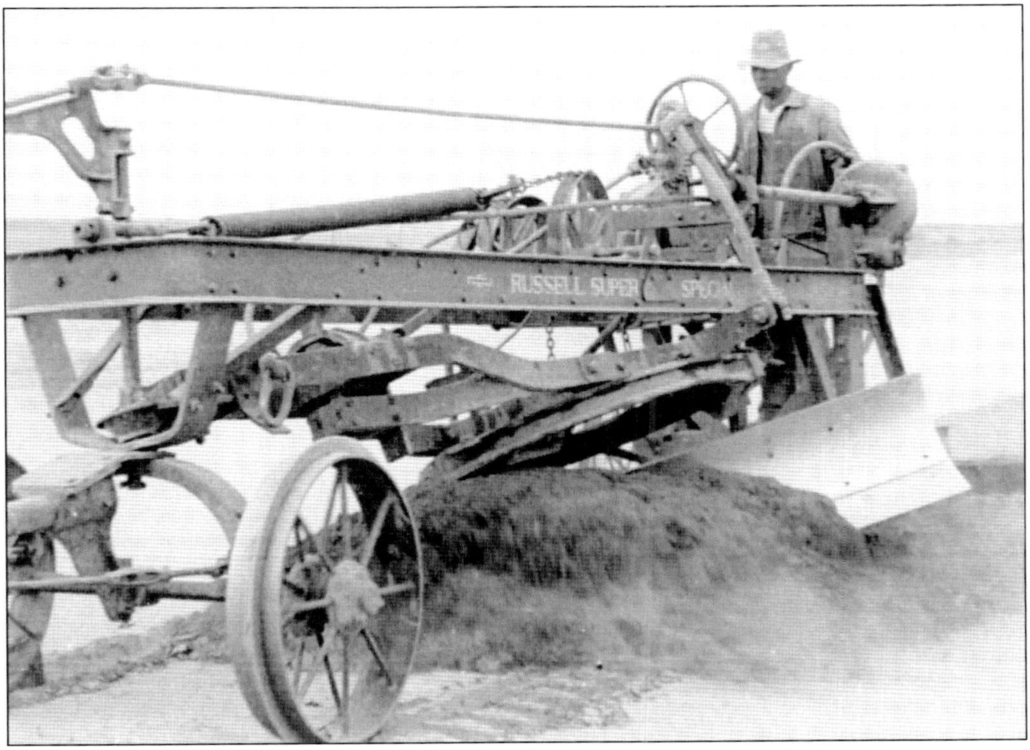


The Russell Super Special was an important piece of early farm equipment. This earth-moving equipment was used as a grader to clear and level the land for cultivation. It was also used to dig ditches and canals for irrigation. (Courtesy of the City of Litchfield Park.)

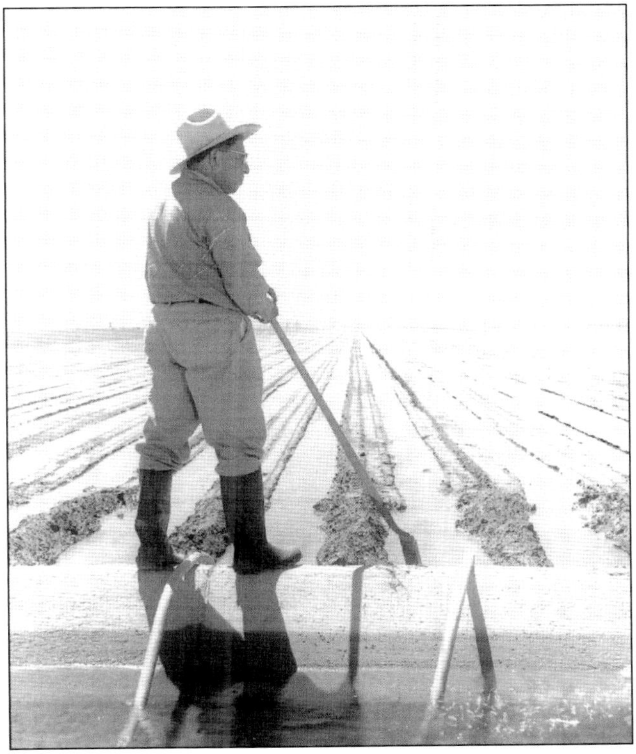

Irrigation supervisor Ramon Soto tends to the irrigation of the cotton fields. Irrigation water for the 11,000 acres was supplied by the Air Line Canal Company. The water supply was from the intake of the Agua Fria River and additional wells that had been drilled. The Southwest Cotton Company improved the canals by adding concrete sides and extending irrigation to the land being cultivated.

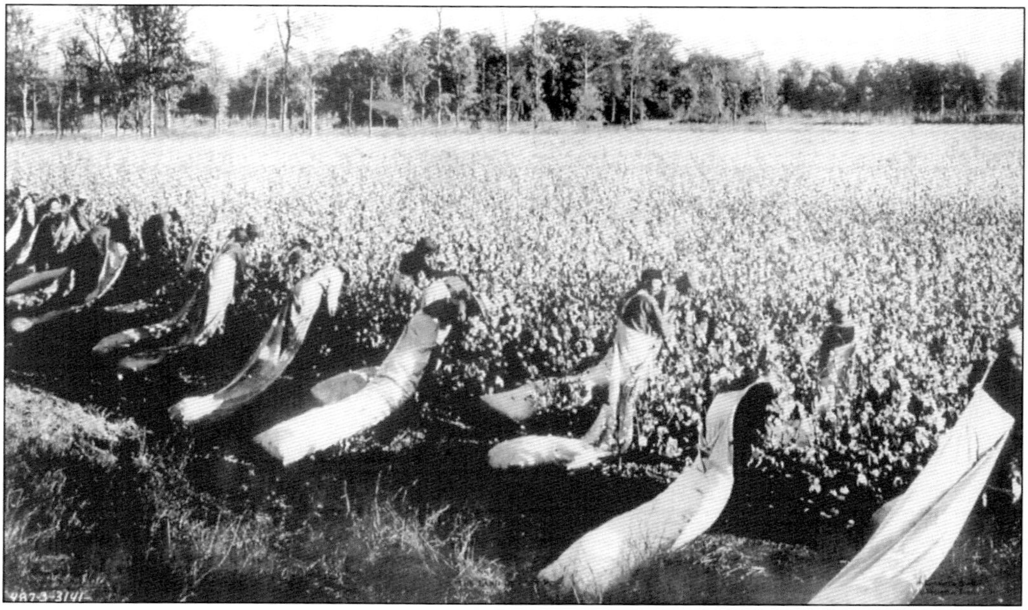

This was a typical scene in the cotton fields on the Litchfield Ranch. It took hundreds to gather cotton for the Southwest Cotton Company. The first laborers were migrant workers brought from Mexico in 1917 for six months under bond by permission of the immigration authority to clear the land. Many of them remained on the Litchfield Ranch and became citizens. As cotton production expanded, Mexican laborers were obtained through the Arizona Cotton Growers Association, also under the immigration authority. Laborers also included Native Americans, such as the Yaqui Indians from the village near Guadalupe and Scottsdale. Field workers to pick the cotton were brought in from many outside areas. Some were brought in from the drought-stricken districts of Texas. (Courtesy of the City of Litchfield Park.)

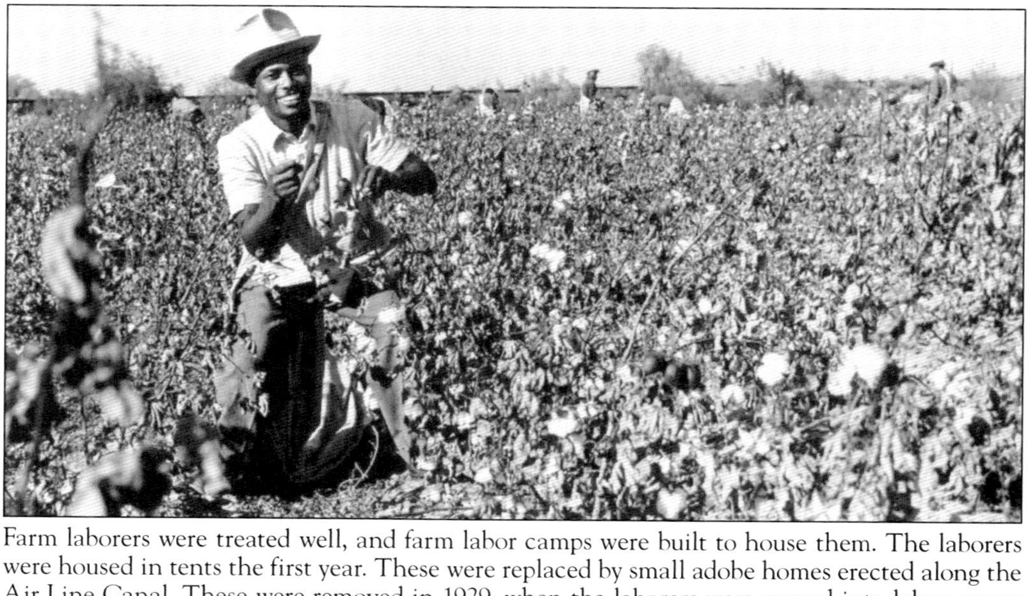

Farm laborers were treated well, and farm labor camps were built to house them. The laborers were housed in tents the first year. These were replaced by small adobe homes erected along the Air Line Canal. These were removed in 1929, when the laborers were moved into labor camps built outside of town. (Courtesy of the City of Litchfield Park.)

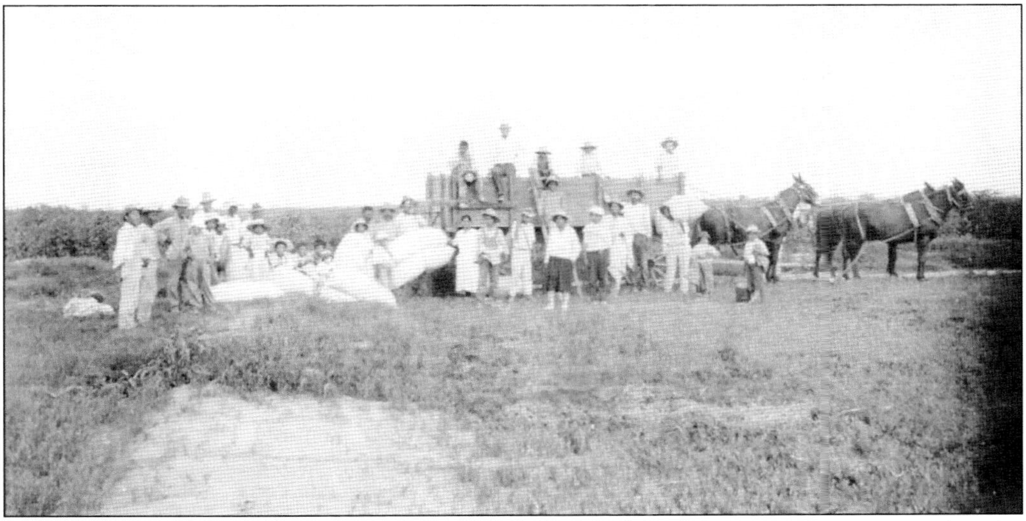

Laborers were paid by the pound for the cotton they picked. In this picture, one can see that the pickers included whole families. This was a popular scene in the early 1920s, before mechanical help was available to pick and process cotton. (Courtesy of the City of Litchfield Park.)

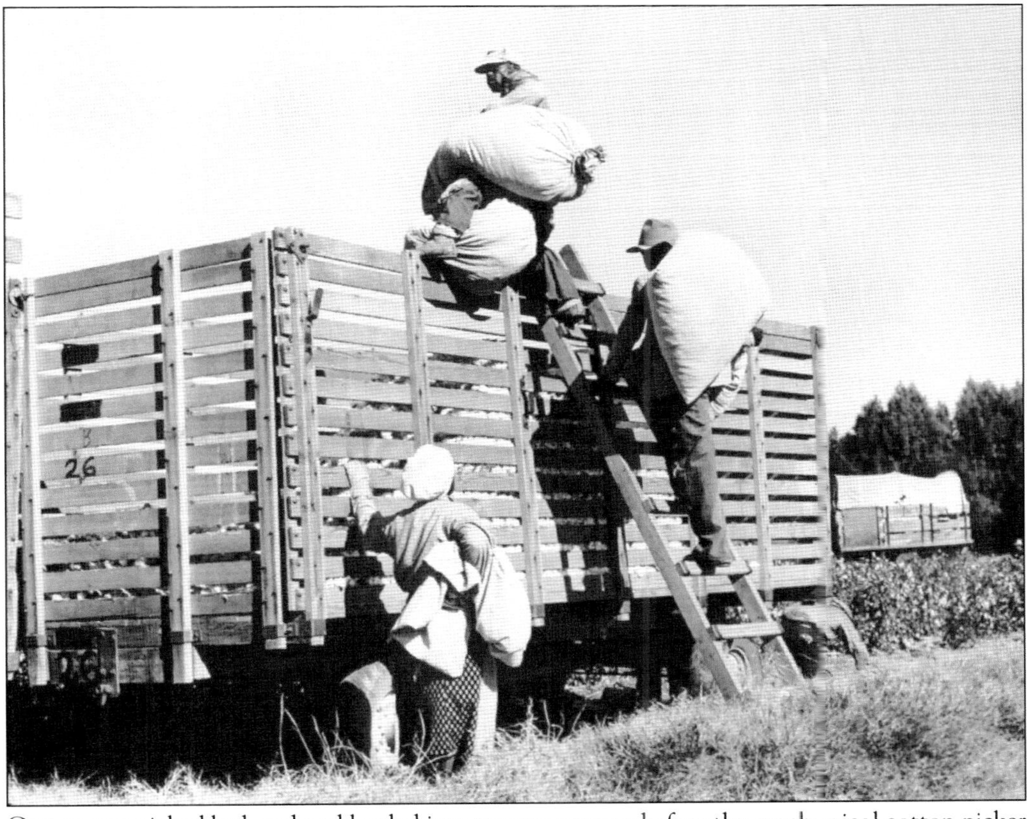

Cotton was picked by hand and loaded into storage wagons before the mechanical cotton picker was developed. Despite the limitations of hand labor, over six million pounds of cotton were picked in 1919. (Courtesy of the City of Litchfield Park.)

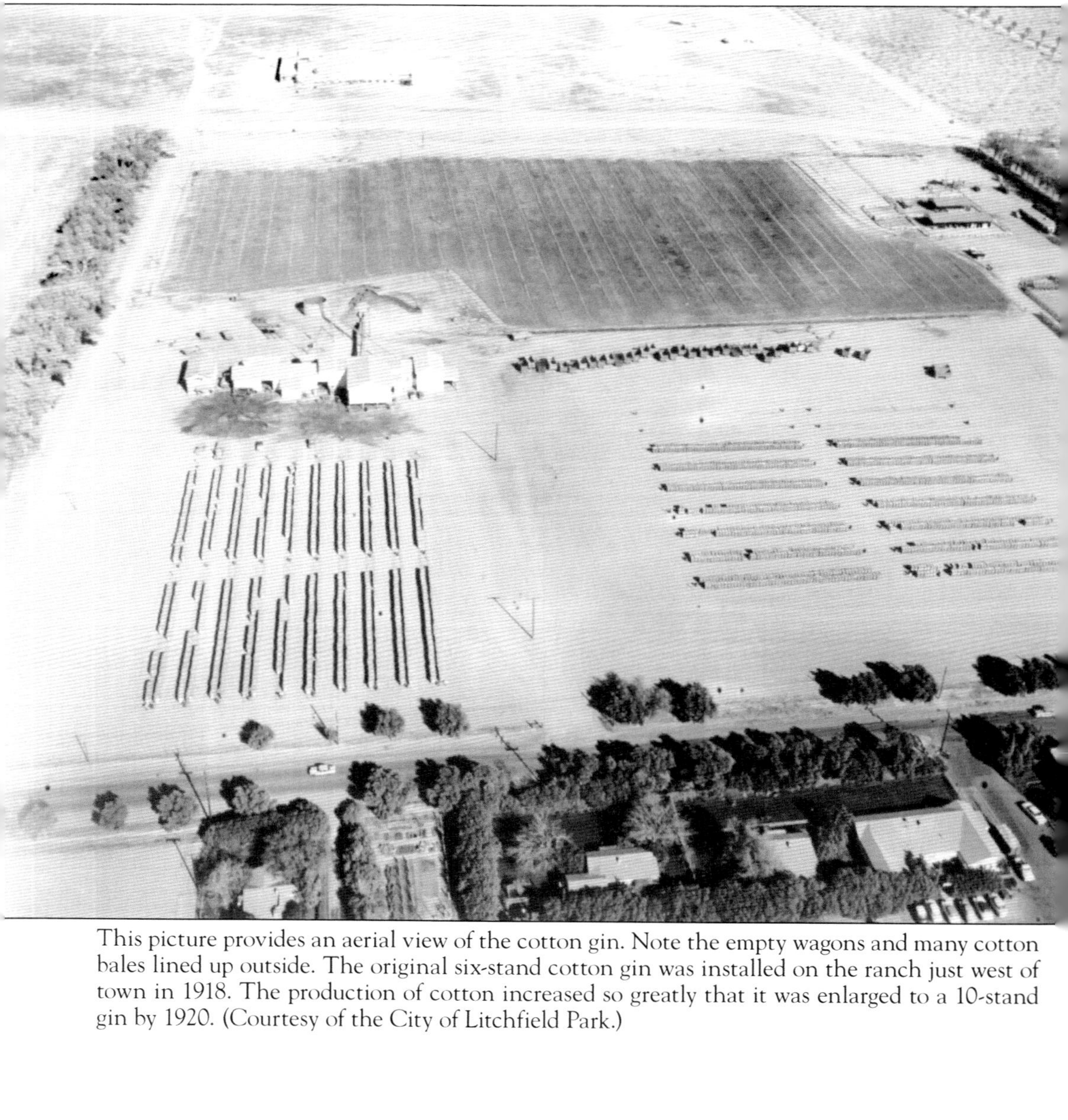

This picture provides an aerial view of the cotton gin. Note the empty wagons and many cotton bales lined up outside. The original six-stand cotton gin was installed on the ranch just west of town in 1918. The production of cotton increased so greatly that it was enlarged to a 10-stand gin by 1920. (Courtesy of the City of Litchfield Park.)

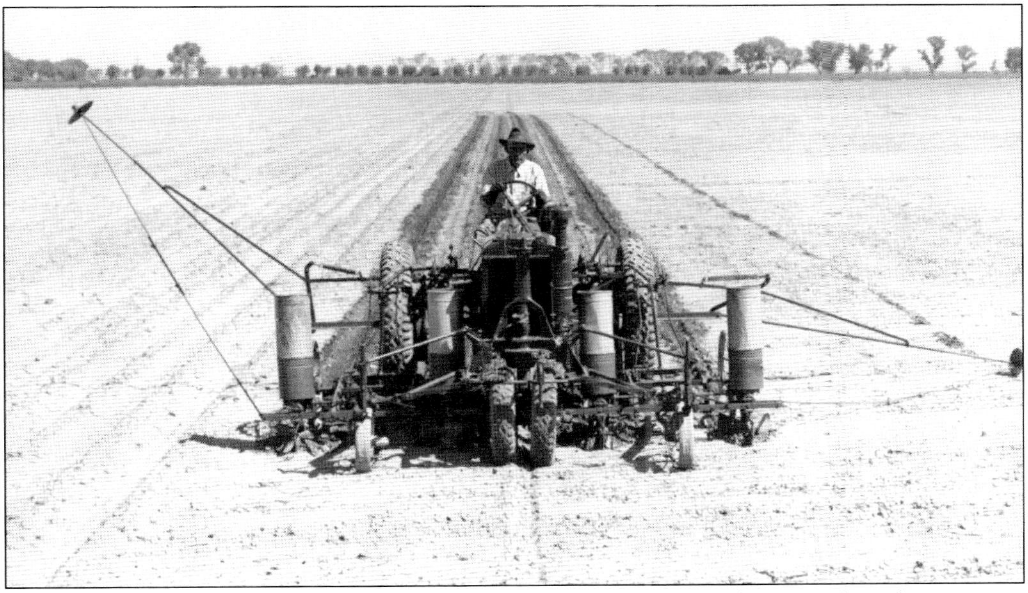

Cotton was the last major crop to be converted to mechanical farming. The picture here demonstrates one of the first mechanical cotton planters. (Courtesy of the City of Litchfield Park.)

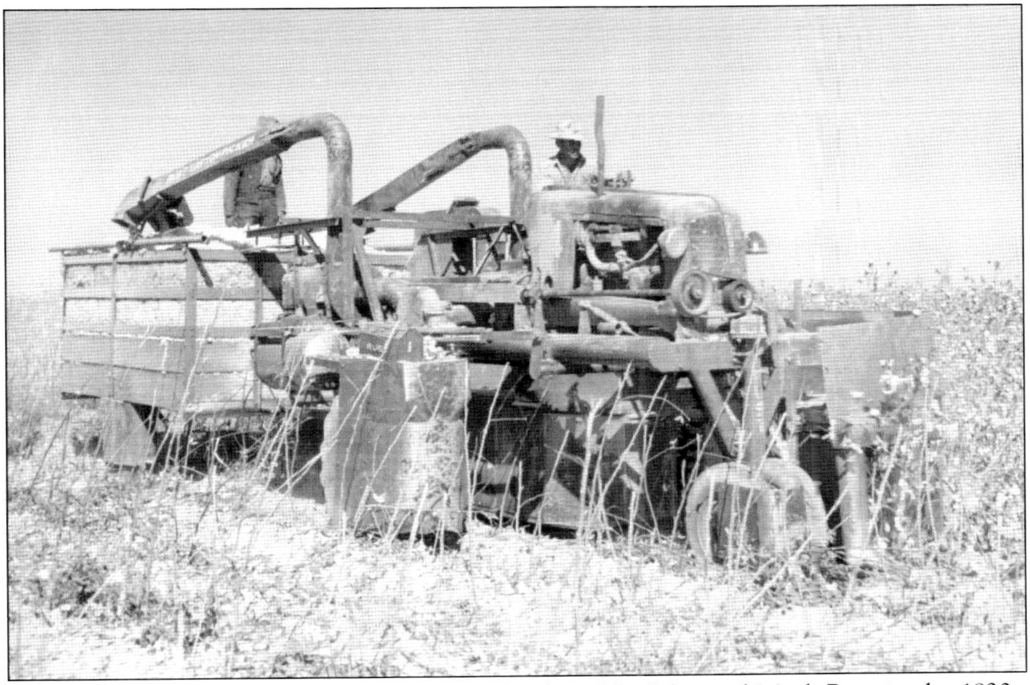

This picture shows the Rust Cotton Picker, developed by John and Mack Rust in the 1930s. John realized that moistened spindles would cause the cotton to stick to them like cotton sticks to a moistened hand. The fiber sticks to the spindled belt, carrying the seed cotton to a storage container as the machine moves through the field. This revolving-spindle cotton picker is still used today. The equipment replaced many men and mules used in the early days of planting cotton at the Litchfield Ranch. (Courtesy of the City of Litchfield Park.)

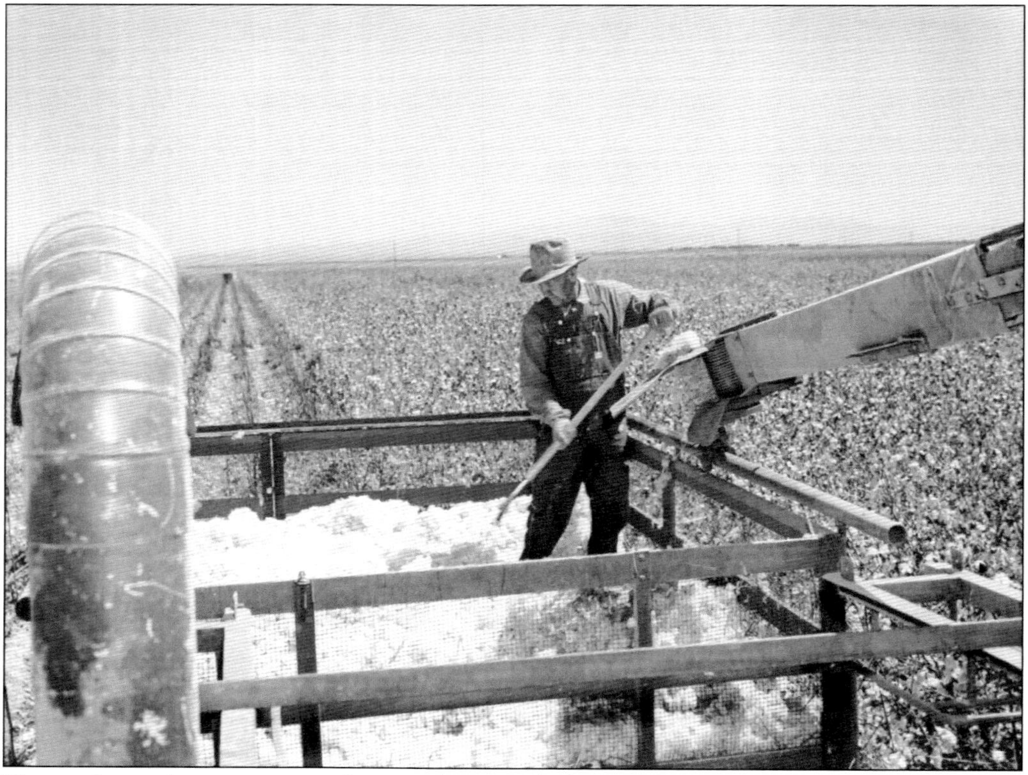

The mechanical equipment was faster, and man's job changed dramatically from picking cotton by hand to assisting the machine in the gathering process. The picture here demonstrates a laborer gathering cotton from the picking machine. (Courtesy of the City of Litchfield Park.)

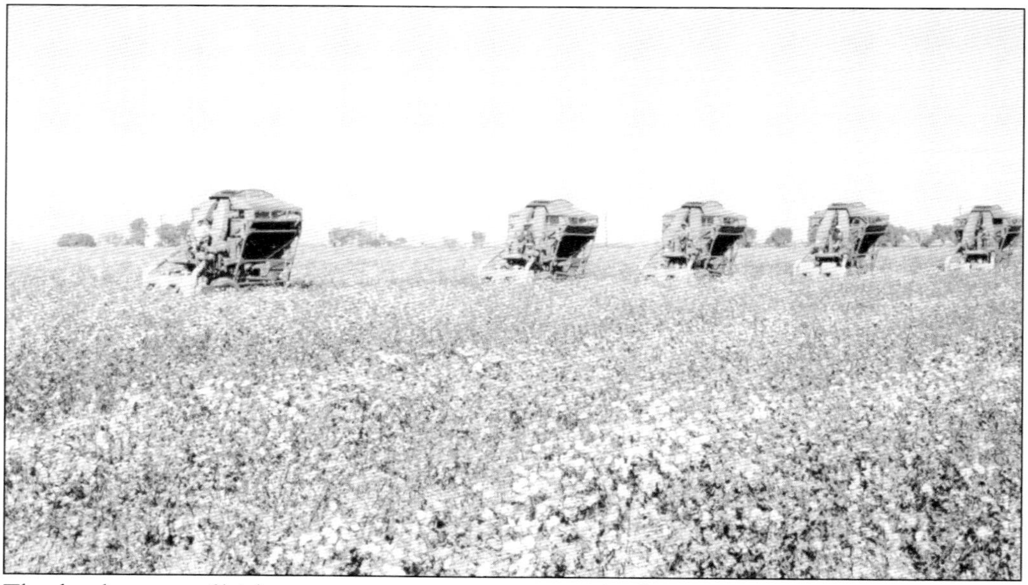

The development of higher-capacity equipment soon evolved into multi-machine harvesting and major increases in daily yields. (Courtesy of the City of Litchfield Park.)

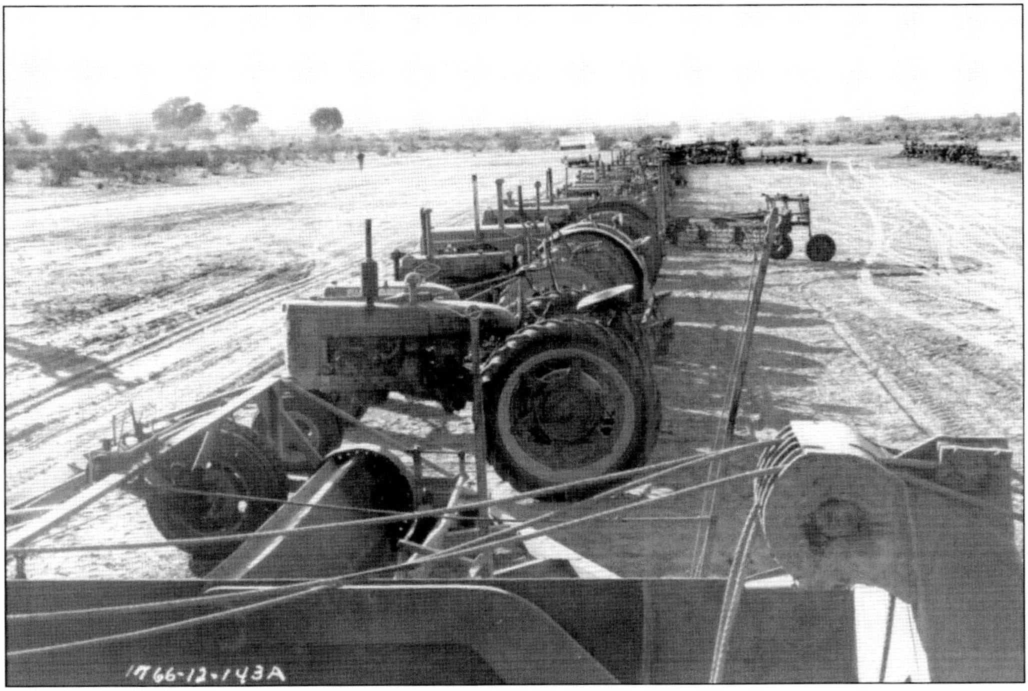


A lineup and display of tractors is seen here at the Southwest Cotton Company farm equipment storage yard, ready to roll into action. An assembly of 130 pieces of rubber-tired agricultural equipment was used on the Goodyear Farms, said to be the largest diversified rubber-tired farm in the country. Equipment from most of the nation's leading farming equipment manufacturers was used. (Courtesy of the City of Litchfield Park.)

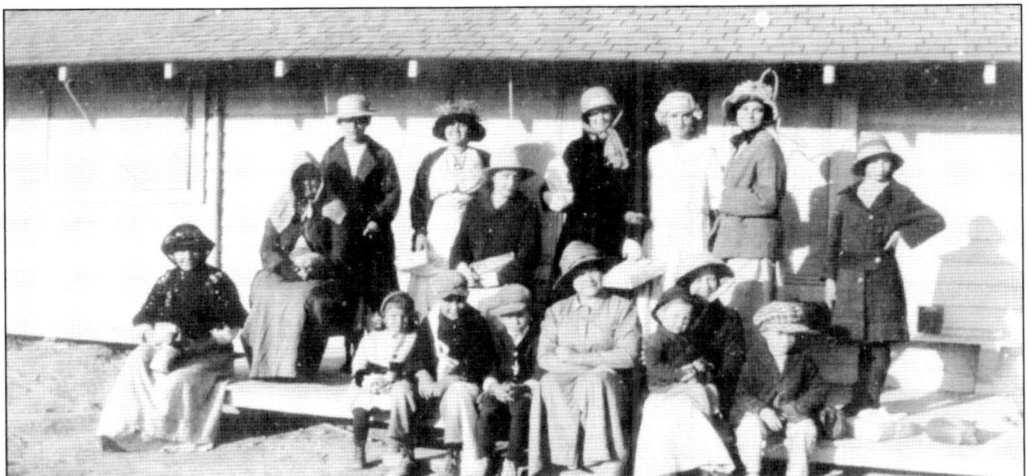

This rare picture is from 1918 and features the Women's Club of Litchfield Park. It was intent on helping with the post–World War I effort, as was popular for local citizens at that time. The club proposed to help by picking cotton. The story goes that this effort lasted only one day before the women gave up this noble act of good citizenship.

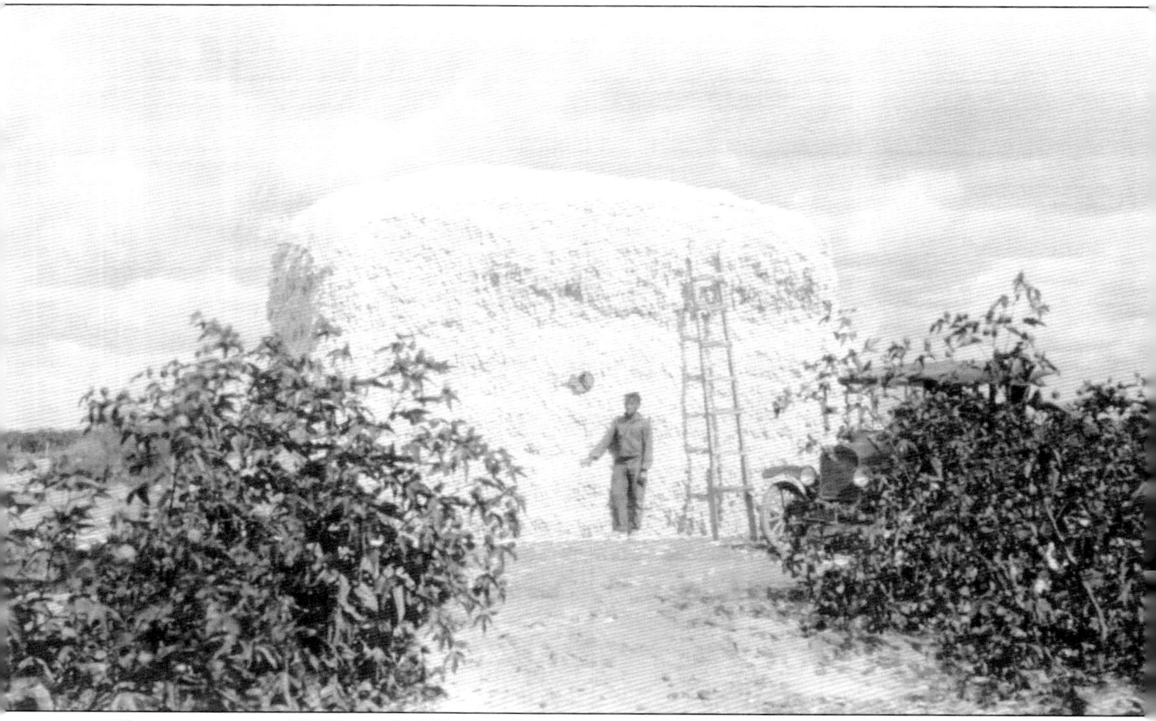

The mountain of "White Gold" would be used to supply the strong, heavy-duty cord needed for the new pneumatic tire designed by Paul Litchfield in 1903 and manufactured by the Goodyear Tire & Rubber Company. The heavy-duty tire needed a strong fabric that could be woven only from long staple cotton. Arizona proved to be an ideal climate for cotton production. (Courtesy of the City of Litchfield Park.)

# *Two*

# Early Development of Downtown

The present town site of Litchfield Park was laid out in 1918 by Paul Litchfield and Phoenix architect L.G. Knipe. Litchfield Avenue was developed to go north and south and Aqua Fria Street to go east and west. City blocks were zoned for business, residences, and recreation.

The permanent residences were north of the business zone, and the east side was reserved for a guest inn with spacious grounds. The land where the present golf course is located was reserved for recreation. The first permanent houses were frame buildings on the west side of Litchfield Avenue. Several stucco houses were built on the east side along with a circular street called Plaza Drive where the Wigwam is currently located.

The permanent town site included a complete water and sewerage system. In 1918, water mains were laid out to all parts of the town, and a 325,000-gallon reservoir was built at La Loma and completed in 1921. This water was used for domestic consumption.

In 1919, an organizational house was built for company visitors. This building soon became the Guest Inn, now known as the Wigwam Resort. It was built to provide accommodations for Goodyear executives when they came to visit and inspect the Litchfield farming operation.

There was only one road into Phoenix, and that was Buckeye Road. In 1918, the Agua Fria River bridge washed away in a flood. To get across, several travelers had to get a team of mules to pull them across the river. The downtown business section grew very slowly. The first business was originally a company store managed by William Burke. The store had groceries, general merchandise, and drugs. It was all destroyed by fire in 1918. It was rebuilt in 1920 as a larger store with postal service.

A hospital was built in 1918 because of the flu epidemic. This global Spanish influenza pandemic killed one in 10 Arizonians. The Goodyear Cemetery was started the same year as the influenza epidemic and is still active for descendants of Goodyear employees.

In 1919, the St. Thomas Aquinas Catholic Mission Church, the first church in Litchfield Park, was built for the farm workers.

The Litchfield School District No. 79 was formed on June 25, 1917, and the first school opened on October 9, 1917. This was a temporary building located in the back of a warehouse in the midst of the camp. The school was moved to a larger building on January 1, 1918. School bonds for $6,000 were voted in without opposition on August 1, 1918. Four one-room adobe buildings were built on the current school site. The land was donated by the Southwest Cotton Company.

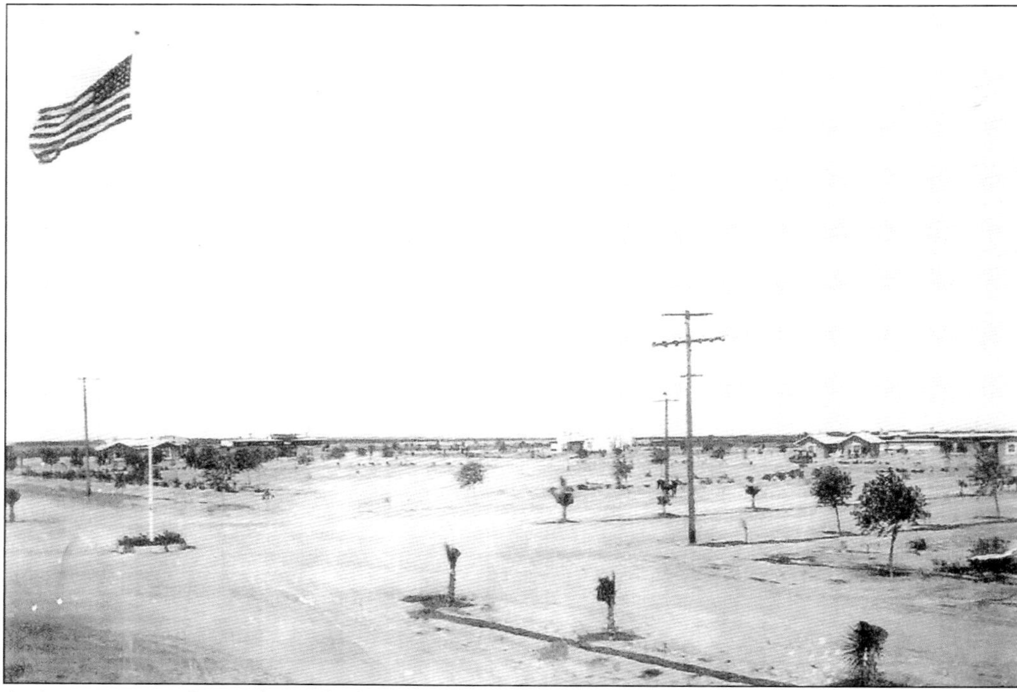

A classic picture shows the early downtown as it is known today. Landscaping for the entire town was started in 1918. Trees and shrubs were set out along the main street to provide shade and beauty. Later, citrus and palms were added, and they made a picturesque scene in later years. In 1919, sidewalks were laid and the main streets were graded with a border in the center to make provisions for flooding. The flag pole is still the center of town. The Wigwam can be seen in the background.

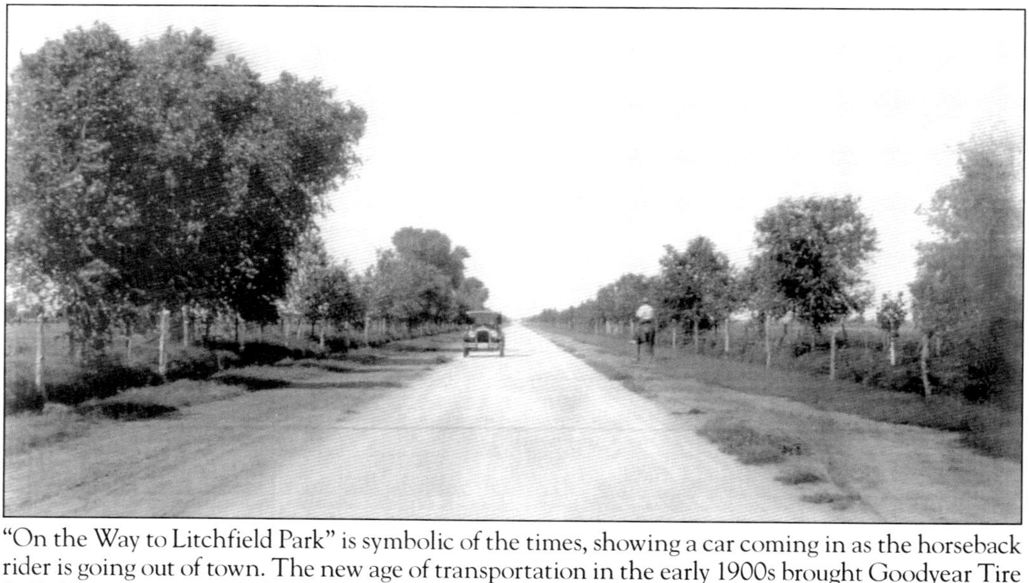

"On the Way to Litchfield Park" is symbolic of the times, showing a car coming in as the horseback rider is going out of town. The new age of transportation in the early 1900s brought Goodyear Tire & Rubber Company to this area, and Litchfield Park was created as it is known today. (Courtesy of the City of Litchfield Park.)

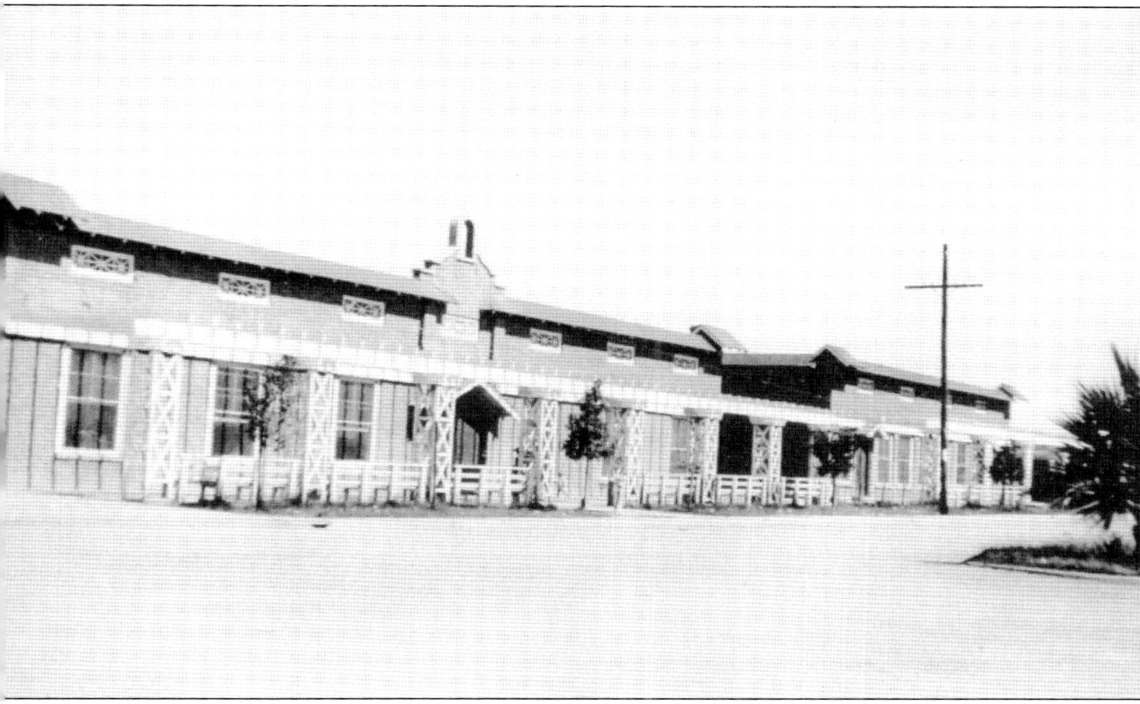

This is a picture of the downtown when it was originally built between 1918 and 1921, constructed of adobe brick. It housed the general store, a restaurant, a pool hall, and a barbershop. The local mail was brought to the general store by stagecoach from Phoenix and addressed to the people in care of the Southwest Cotton Company. (Courtesy of the City of Litchfield Park.)

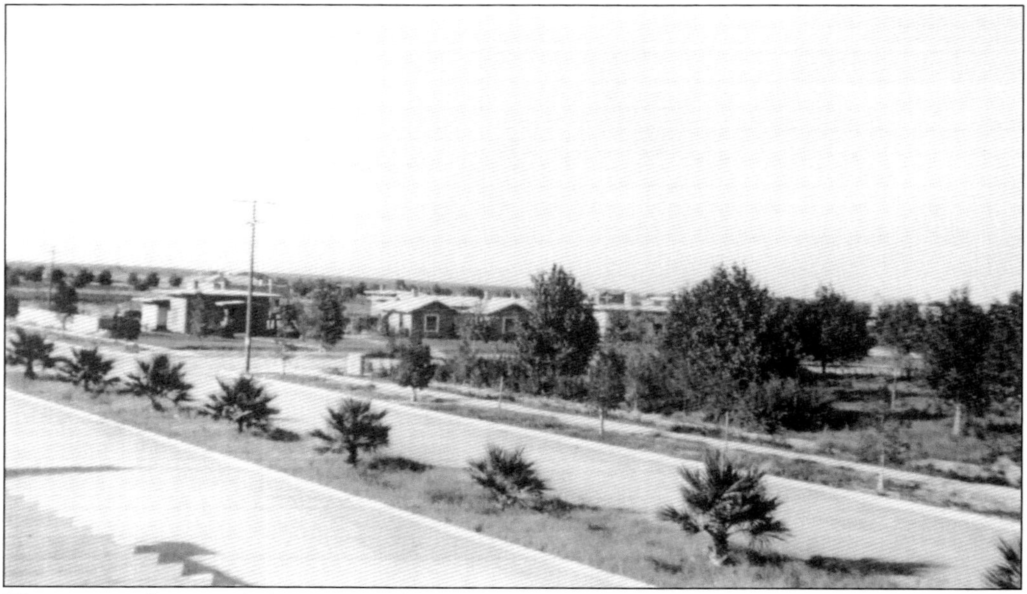

This picture shows early housing on the northeast corner of Litchfield Avenue, looking towards the organization house or current-day Wigwam. Several stucco houses were built in this area in a semicircular street later called Plaza Drive. (Courtesy of the City of Litchfield Park.)

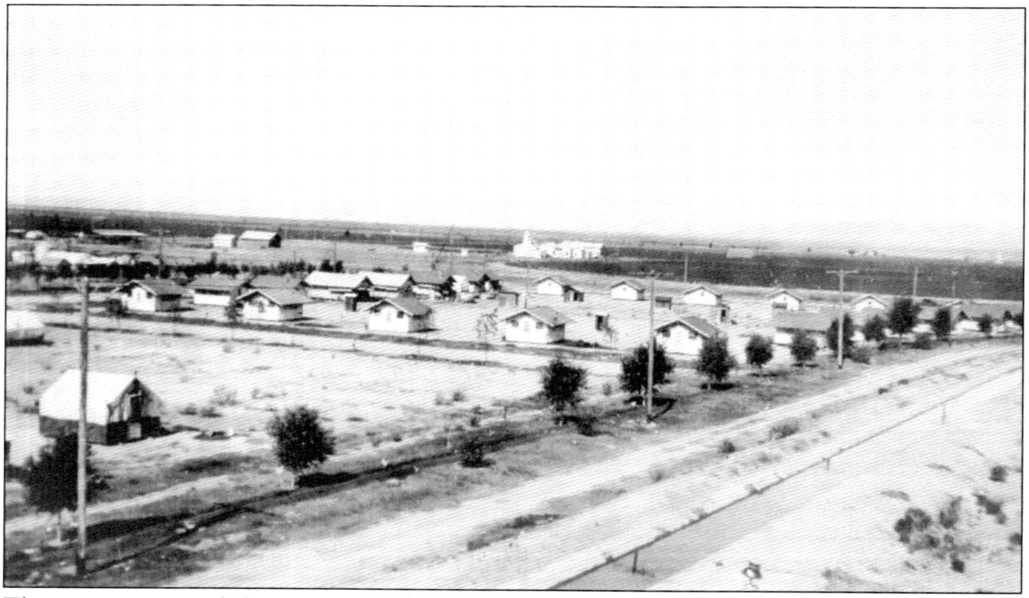

The temporary ranch housing west of downtown was built in 1917. The houses were 10 feet by 12 feet and 14 feet by 20 feet in size. Notice the canvas flap sides covering the screen windows. The cotton gin can be seen to the west. (Courtesy of the City of Litchfield Park.)

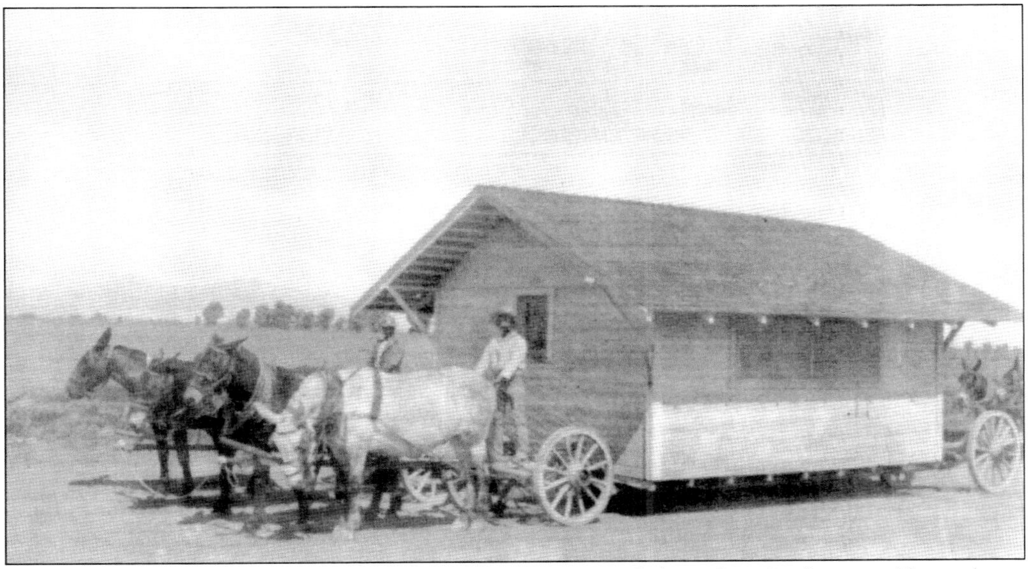

When the Goodyear Ranch (Chandler) and Marinette Ranch (now Sun City) were sold, employee housing owned by the Southwest Cotton Company was moved to the Litchfield Ranch by a team of mules and a specially designed wagon. (Courtesy of the City of Litchfield Park.)

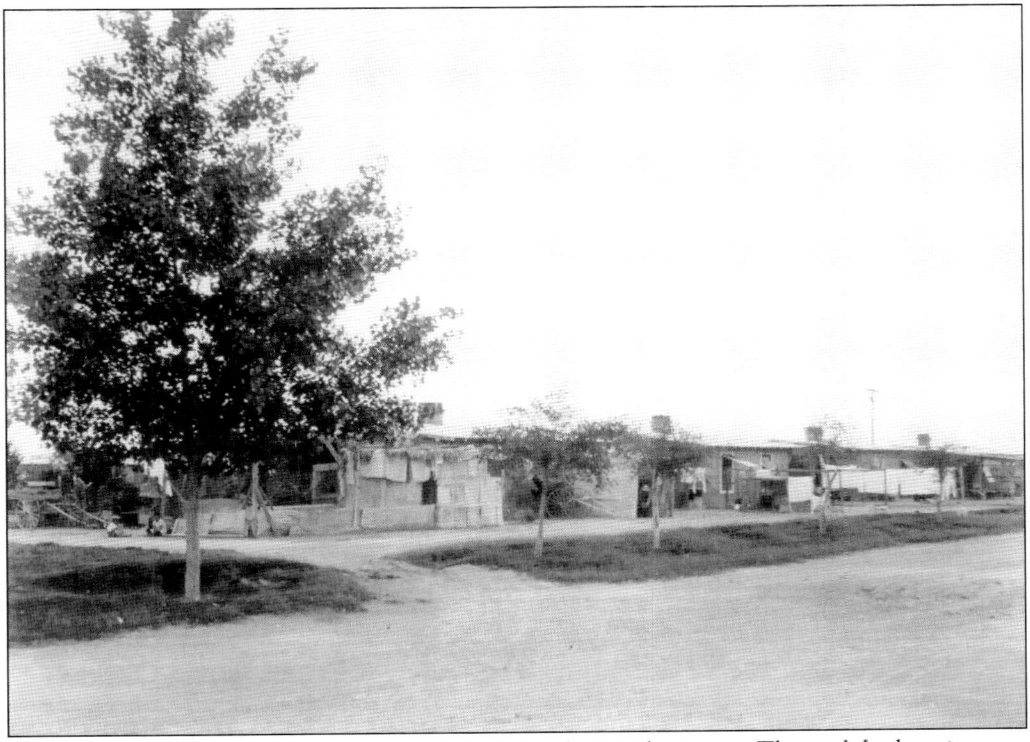

Mexican quarters on the ranch were temporary and started as tents. Then adobe housing was provided in several areas of the town site and along the Air Line Canal. The adobe houses built along the Air Line Canal were known as Bachelor Row. A Mexican primary school was added in 1920 in a small adobe building north of the canal. (Courtesy of Litchfield Park Historical Society.)

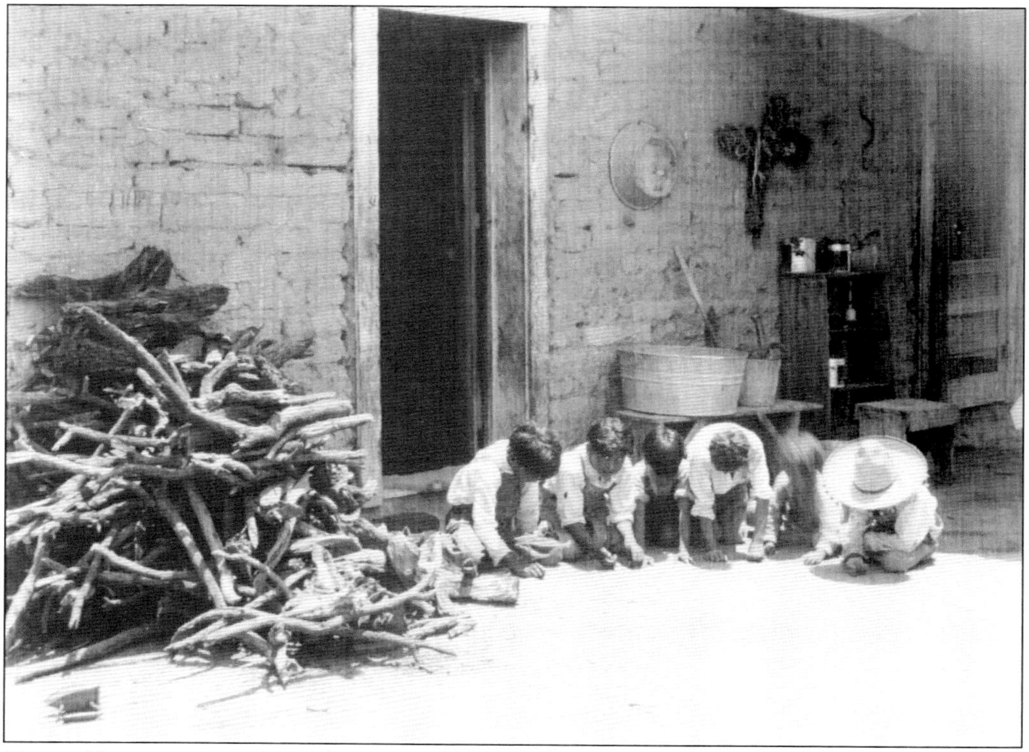

Pictured here are young boys playing marbles outside their adobe home. Spanish melodies could be heard coming from the homes of many of these families. In 1929, all of these houses were removed, and new labor camps were established outside the town. (Courtesy of Litchfield Park Historical Society.)

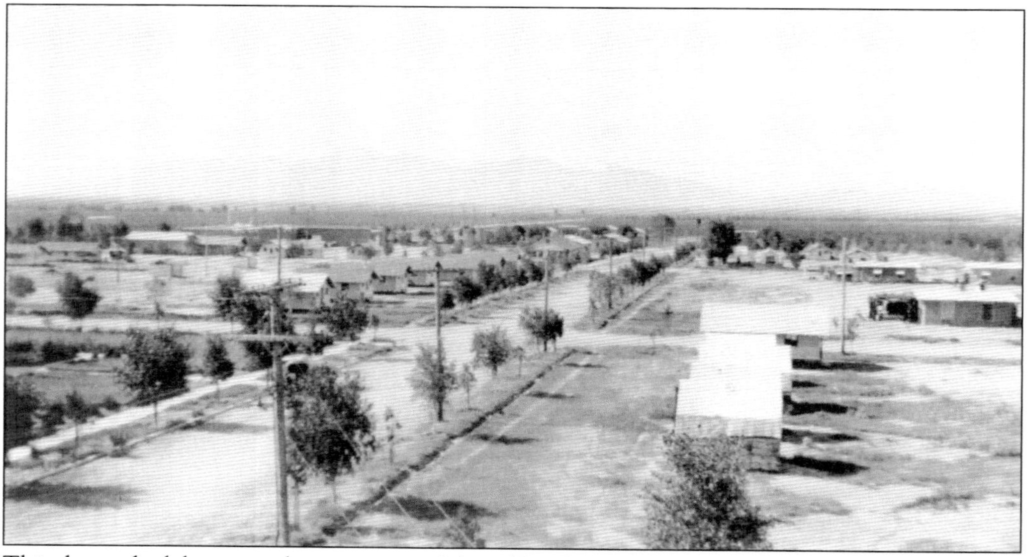

This shows the labor camp housing west of Agua Fria Street and north of the machine shops. Note the White Tank Mountains in the background. The housing on the right shows the canvas-flap roofs. (Courtesy of the City of Litchfield Park.)

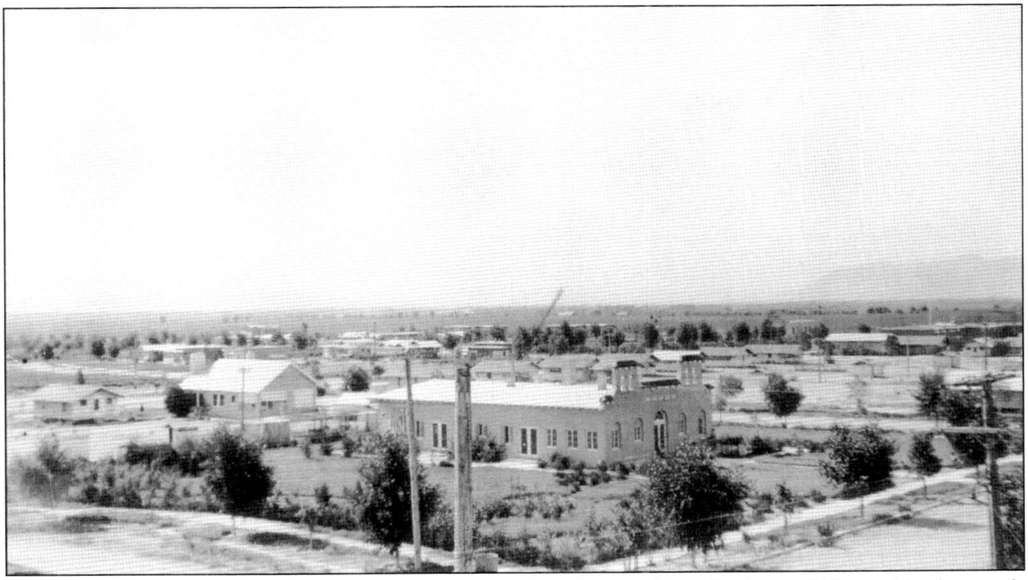

Following the 1918 Spanish flu epidemic, a permanent hospital was built in 1919 two blocks north of the downtown business section. For $1.50 a month, hospitalization insurance and service was provided by Goodyear to all employees who needed it. In the mid-1920s, Dr. Ralph Penn served the hospital. His home can be seen behind the hospital. He served until 1932, when the hospital closed as most people went into Phoenix for medical services due to improved transportation. Twenty-six babies were born in this hospital. In later years, the hospital was used as an annex by the Wigwam. (Courtesy of the City of Litchfield Park.)

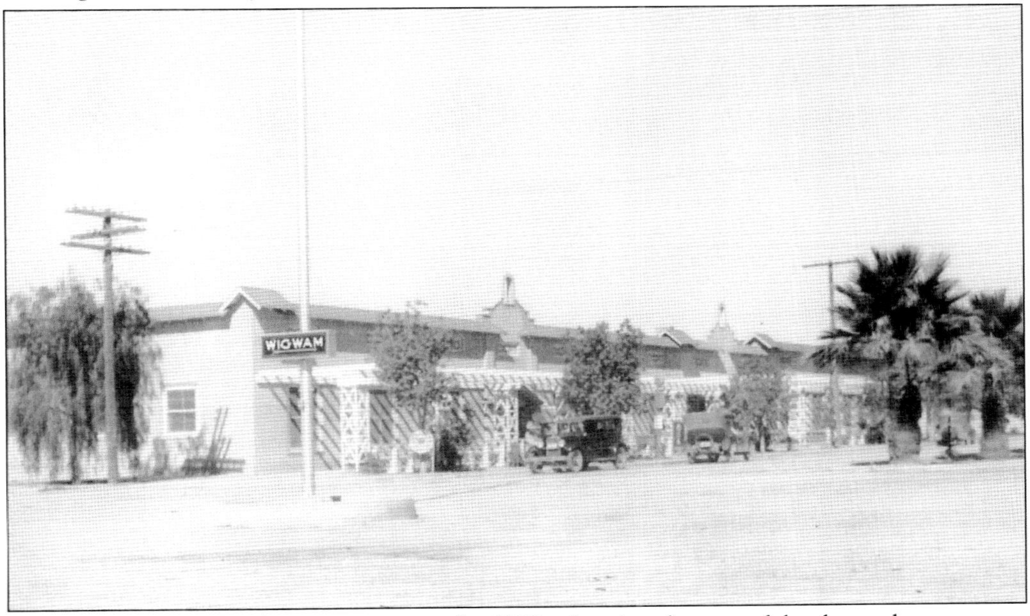


This is a picture of the downtown area in the 1930s, showing the cars of the day and a gas pump. The canopy and lattice work were added decor. The palm trees have continued to grow since they were planted in 1918. The landmark flagpole still stands in the center of town. The streets were not paved until 1935. (Courtesy of the City of Litchfield Park.)

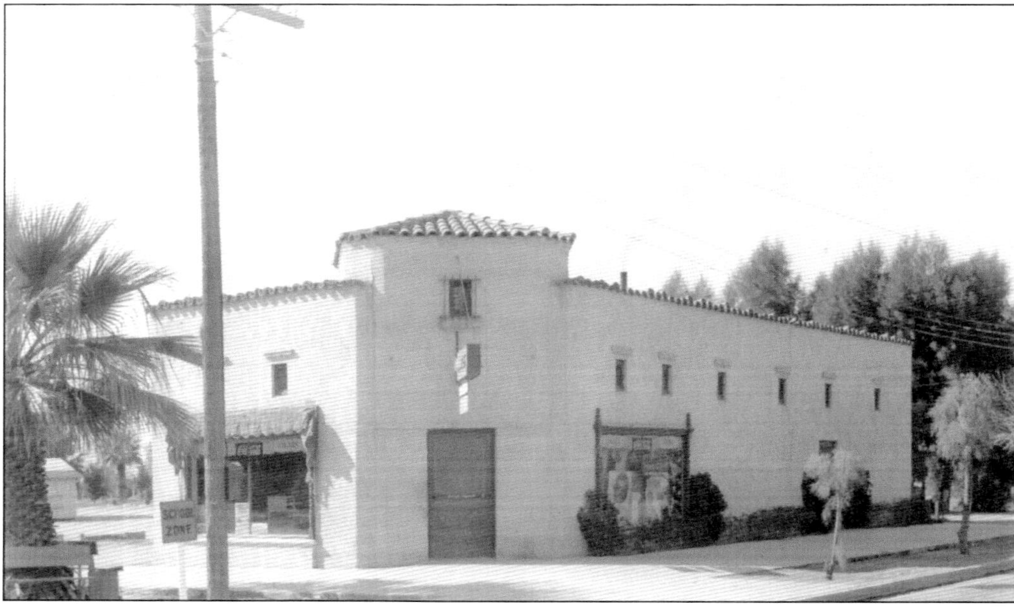

The Southwest Cotton Company added a drugstore in 1928–1929 on the northwest corner of the business block. The Apache Drug Company was owned by D.P. Kimball of Phoenix. In 1933, the post office was moved into the drugstore from the general store, and it was located there until 1945. In 1942, Joel F. Stone purchased the drugstore and remodeled it to include a modern fountain service. (Courtesy of the City of Litchfield Park.)

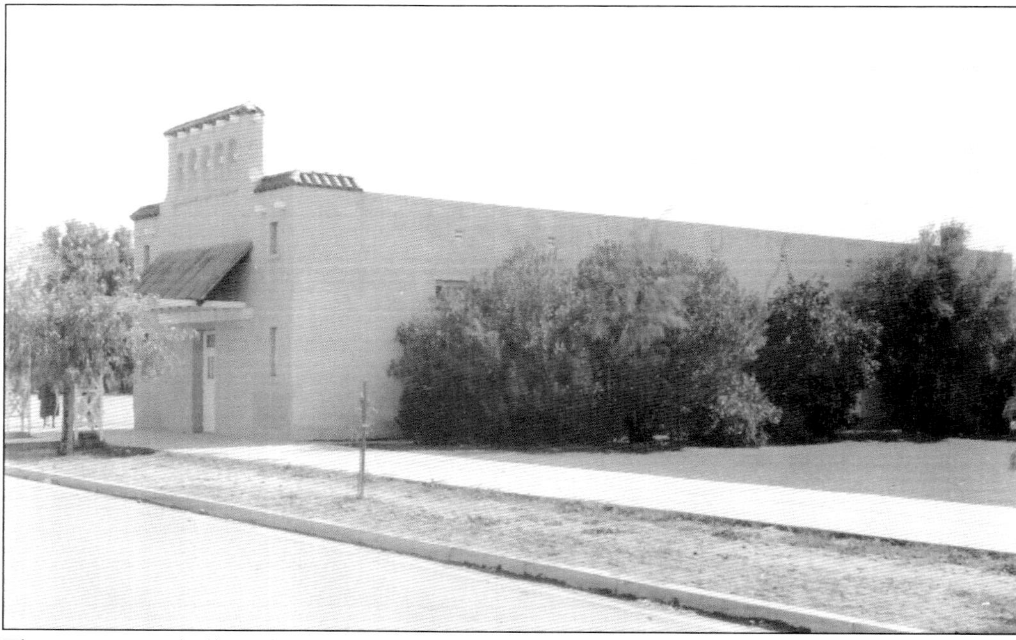

The community hall was located one half-block east of the general store on the south side of Agua Fria Street. Built in 1920, it was used for community meetings and banquets and as a music room by the Litchfield School. Movies were shown there until 1947, when the building was remodeled. The community hall was torn down in 1960. (Courtesy of the City of Litchfield Park.)

Frank Serrano was very instrumental in the early development of the town. After the general store fire in 1918, a new store opened in 1920 with Frank Serrano as manager. He became part owner of the store as the Southwest Cotton Company started a percentage lease program and abandoned the idea of ownership of the company store. Frank was also instrumental in getting the St. Thomas Aquinas Catholic Mission Church built. (Courtesy of Frances Martin.)

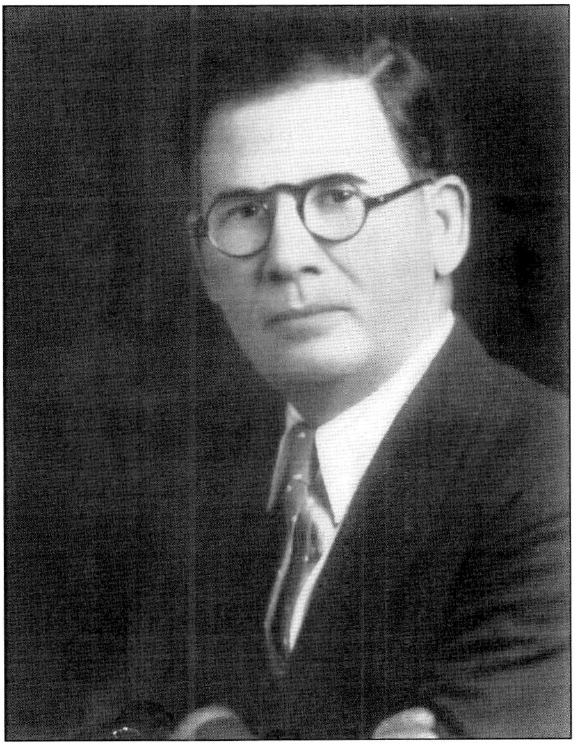

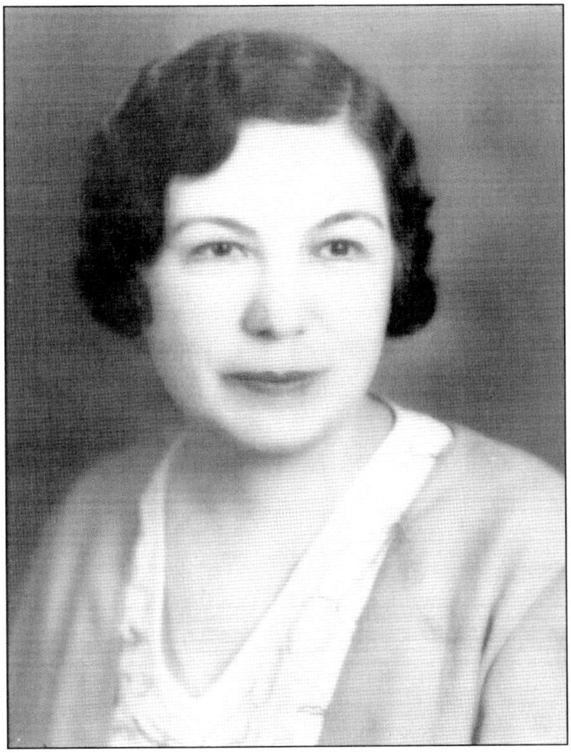

Sara Serrano was also a great asset to the development of the town. Sara assisted her husband, Frank, in managing the general store. A post office was added at the general store, and Sara became the postmistress. She retained that title until 1934. Sara and Frank Serrano held Catholic mass in their home before the St. Thomas Aquinas Catholic Mission Church was built and completed in 1921. They assisted Paul Litchfield in working with Bishop Daniel Gercke of the Diocese of Tucson to get the church dedicated. (Courtesy of Frances Martin.)

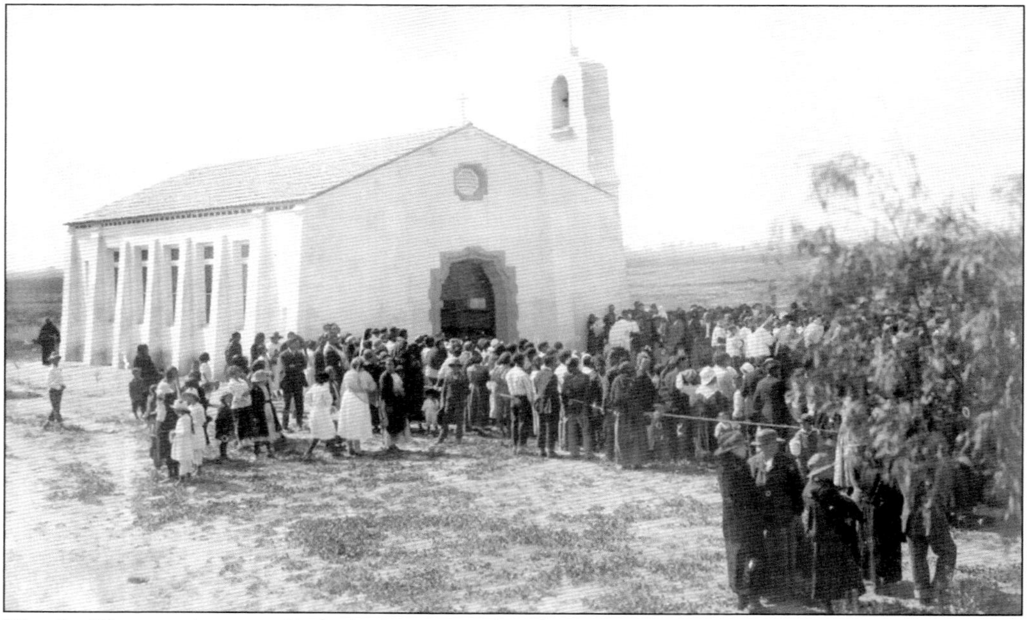

The St. Thomas Aquinas Catholic Mission Church was the first church in Litchfield Park. Paul Litchfield had it built in 1919 for the migrant farm workers. This picture was taken at the dedication of the church in 1921. The architectural design was changed from the original building, and this final design was completed in 1923. Litchfield sold the land to the Tucson Diocese for $1. Bishop Gercke named the church St. Thomas Aquinas in honor of Tom Doyle, a local cattle rancher who took the financial responsibility to have it built. (Courtesy of the Tom Doyle family.)

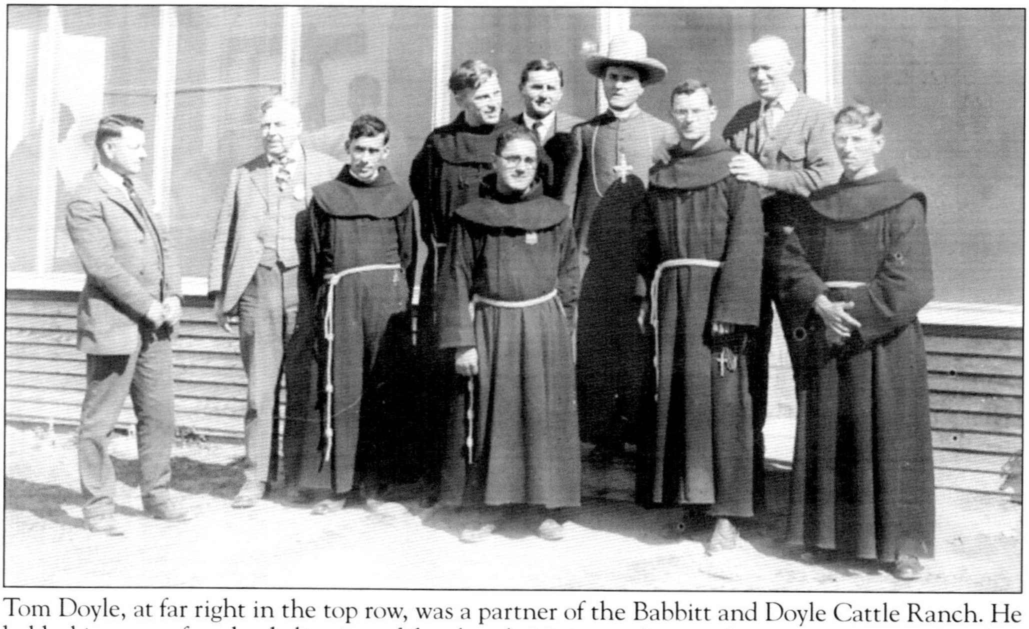

Tom Doyle, at far right in the top row, was a partner of the Babbitt and Doyle Cattle Ranch. He held a big party after the dedication of the church. He is seen here with visiting priests and Bishop Daniel J. Gercke of the Tucson Diocese wearing Doyle's cowboy hat. The first priest assigned to the mission church was Father Ambrose. (Courtesy of the Tom Doyle family.)

Jonathan Lambert Rayner founded the Litchfield School District on June 25, 1917. The first day of class was on October 9, 1917. Rayner lived on the Agua Fria River east of the town. He moved into this area from California. (Courtesy of Edna Pasqualetti.)

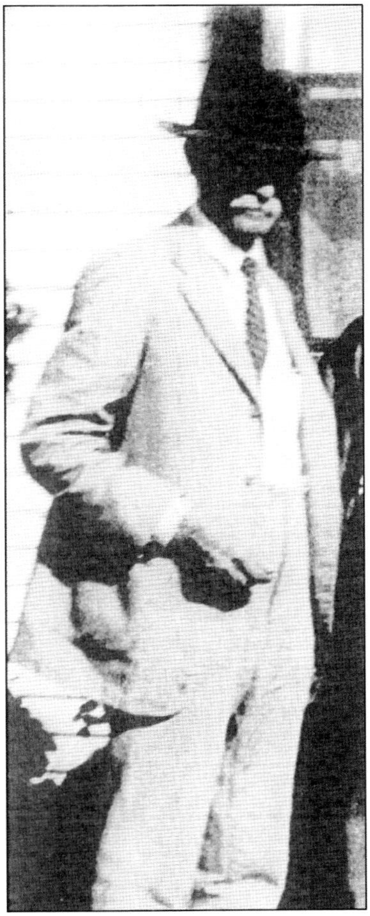

Mabel Padgett was the first teacher in the Litchfield School District. She is shown here with her eighth-grade class standing in front of a one-room adobe school building. In a letter to a friend in the summer of 1918, Padgett wrote, "the boys and I climbed through the wire fence out to the cotton field to begin staking out the building. Of course, we had to cut down some of the cotton stalks." The first adobe school building was constructed east of the downtown flag pole in 1918. There were four one-room adobe school buildings that are still on the campus today in a converted form. Mabel's husband, John, was a surveyor for Goodyear Farms and laid out the land in this area. In the 1920s, the Mexican Primary School was operated in the Mexican housing until the Mexican labor was moved to the labor camps on the ranch. An old company building was moved to the school site for the Mexican Primary School. The Mexican students were kept separate to facilitate the learning of the English language and other subjects in the Spanish language. (Courtesy of Litchfield Park Historical Society.)

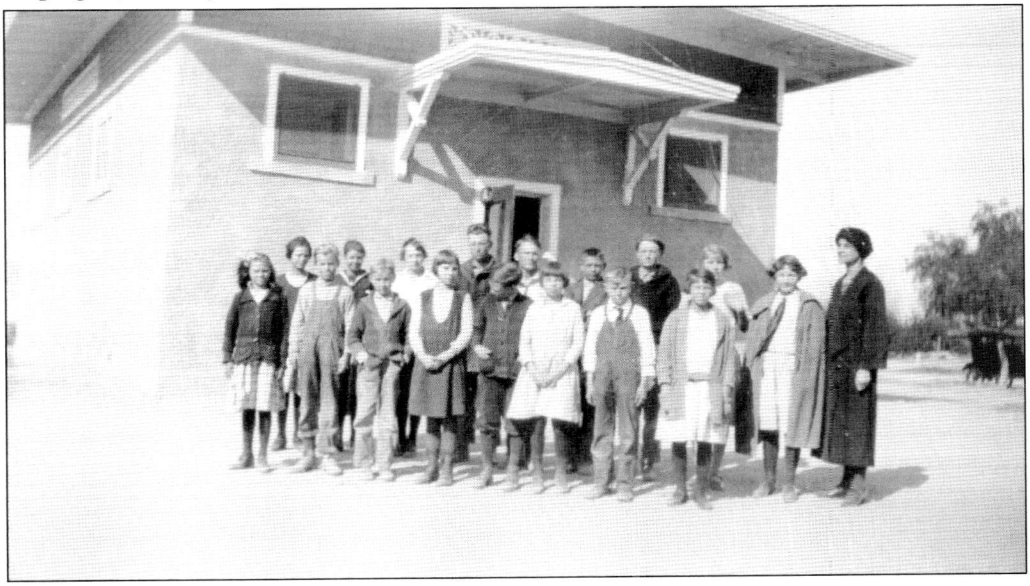

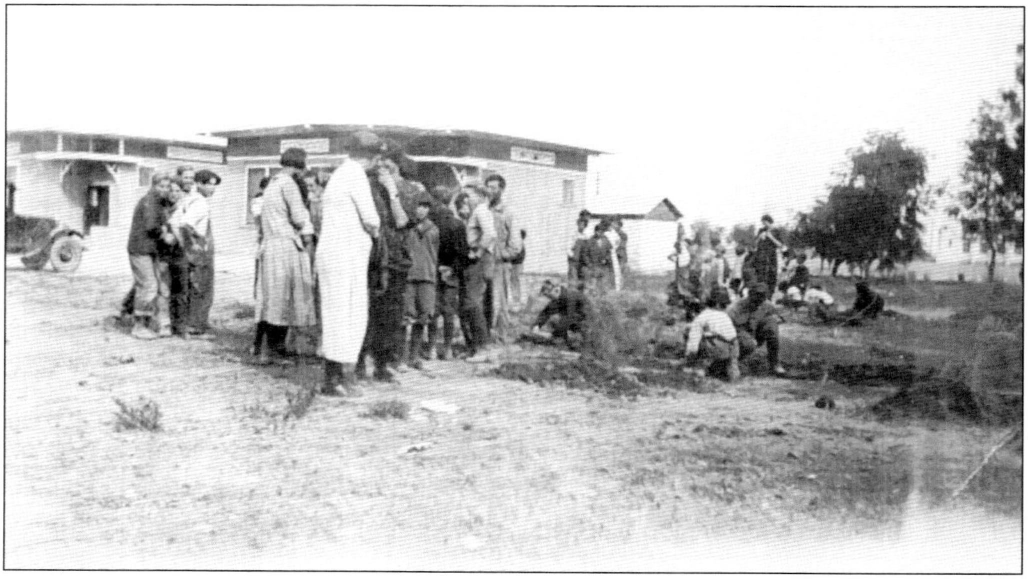

An outdoor scene here, from the early 1920s, shows the teacher and students in front of the Litchfield School one-room adobe buildings. Note the St. Thomas Aquinas Catholic Mission Church in the far right corner and the old car parked to the left as it helps to identify the date. (Courtesy of Edna Pasqualetti.)

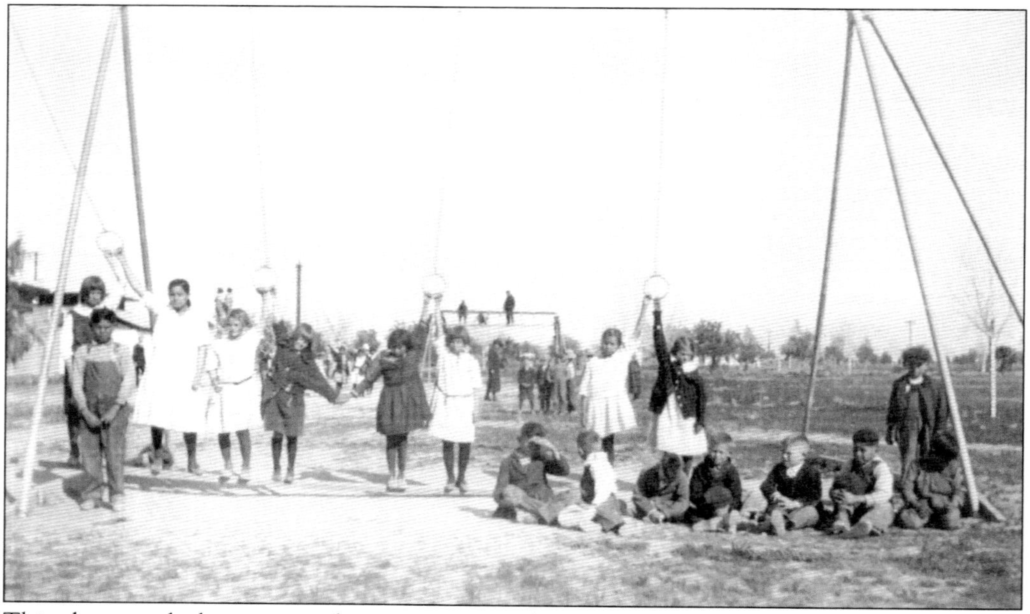

This photograph shows an outdoor swing set on the Litchfield School playground in 1925. This early playground equipment was taken down in recent years. (Courtesy of Edna Pasqualetti.)

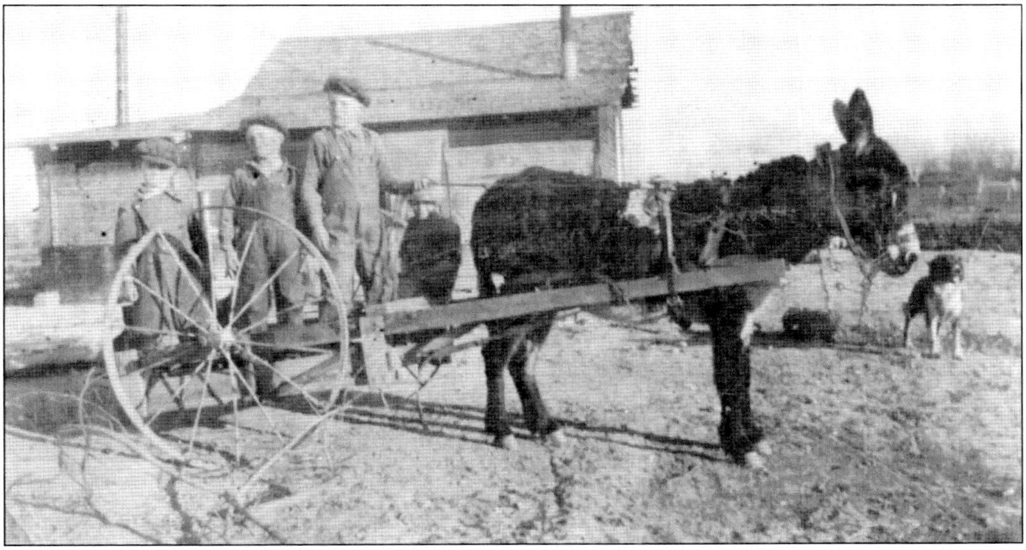

The Rayner family was transported to Litchfield School from their home on the Agua Fria River in this steel-wheeled cart pulled by a donkey. Pictured from left to right are Jack Bales, Jack Rayner, Earle Rayner, and Mabel Rayner. (Courtesy of Edna Pasqualetti.)

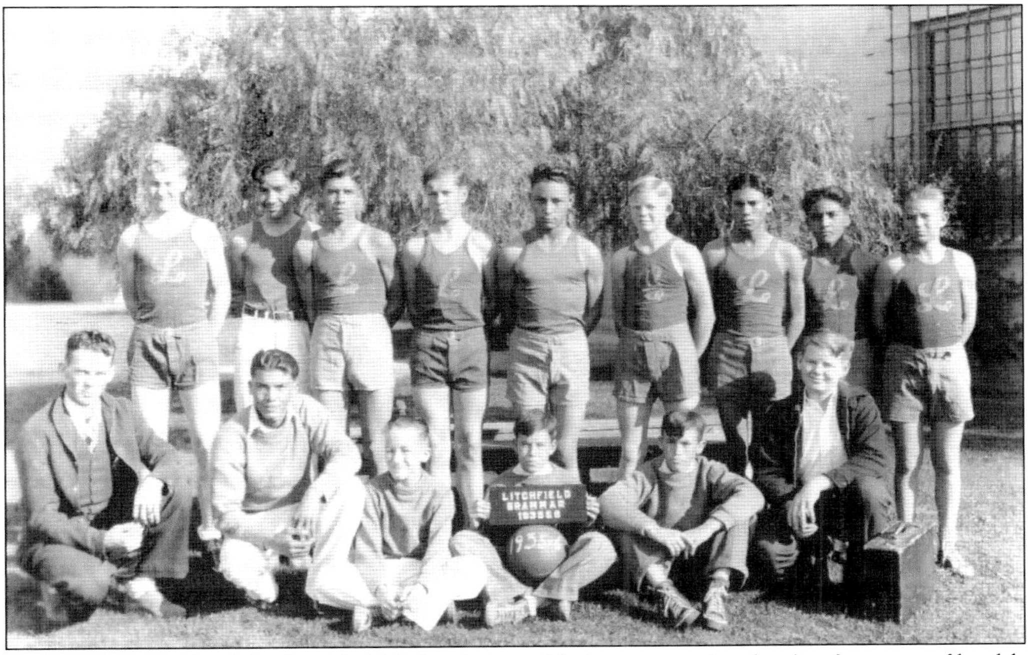


During the growth of the Litchfield School, the athletic program for the development of health and sportsmanship was not neglected. L.D. Shumway, superintendent of Litchfield Schools in 1928, had facilities for every sport. Pictured here is the 1935–1936 basketball team. From left to right are (first row) Coach Trimble, Fernando Castillo, Keith Shumway, Elwood Phillips, Ethridge Lays, and manager Howard Wood; (second row) Bill Zieske, Benaturo Pablos, Julio Martinez, Dan Cooper, Raymond Trehio, Jack Yarger, Frank Salizo, Louis Gailez, and unidentified. (Courtesy of Jack Yarger.)

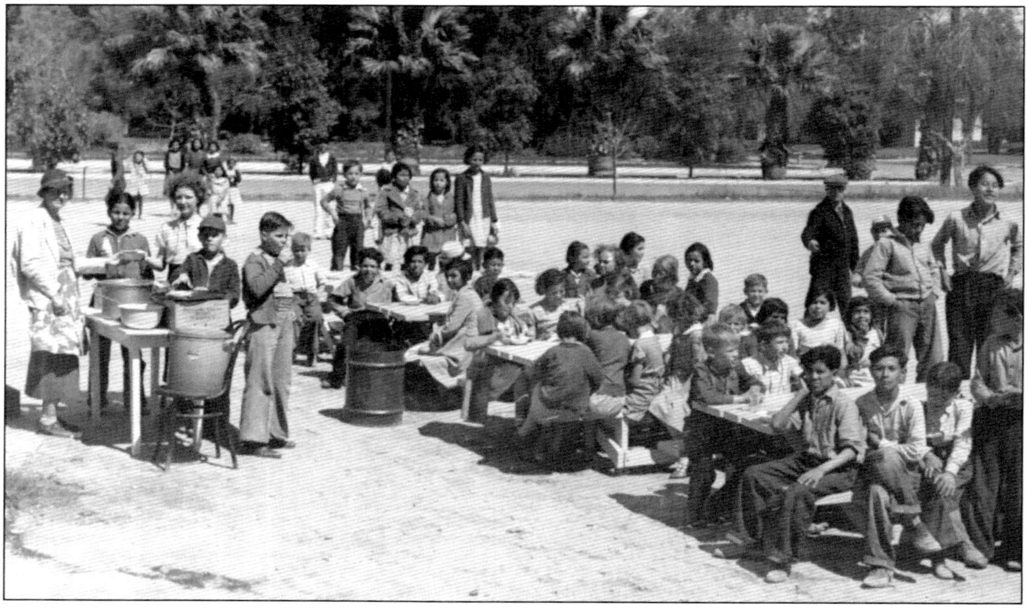

Litchfield School children are enjoying a picnic-style lunch outside in 1937. In 1940, an old cottage was renovated into a cafeteria that seated 60 people. By rotating classes, approximately 90 students were fed daily. In 1942, it had expanded to support about 200 students. The food was received from surplus commodities, the WPA thrift center, and the grocery store. Lunch cost 10¢, and milk was 1¢. (Courtesy of Litchfield Park Historical Society.)

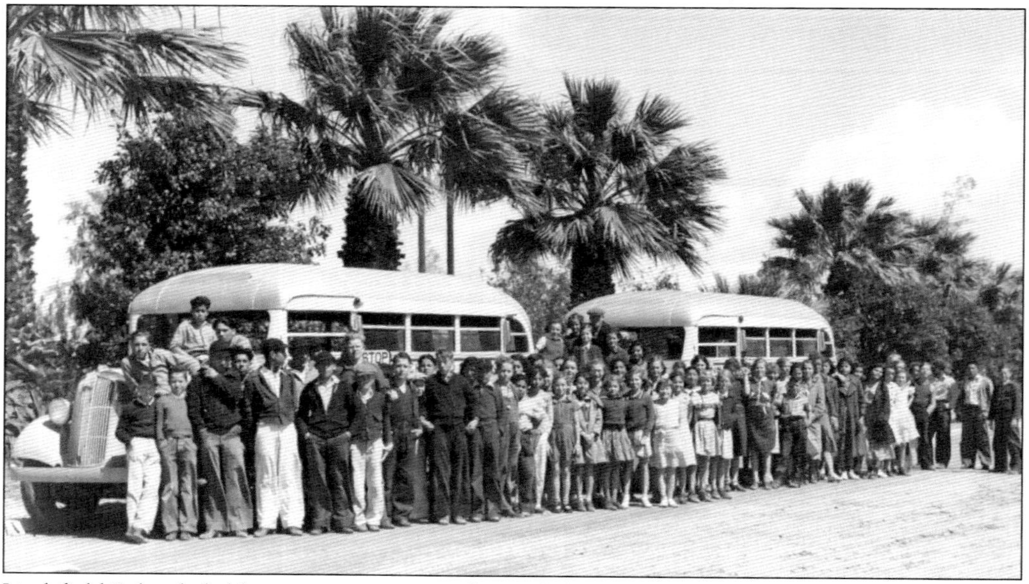

Litchfield School children are seen waiting for a ride home in the school buses in 1937. In the 20 years since the school opened, the buses are welcomed, since the first mode of transportation to school was either a cart pulled by a donkey or a horseback ride. Many students rode horseback, and a corral was maintained on the south side of the school to house the horses during the day. When school ended, the horses were saddled up for the students' transportation home. (Courtesy of Litchfield Park Historical Society.)

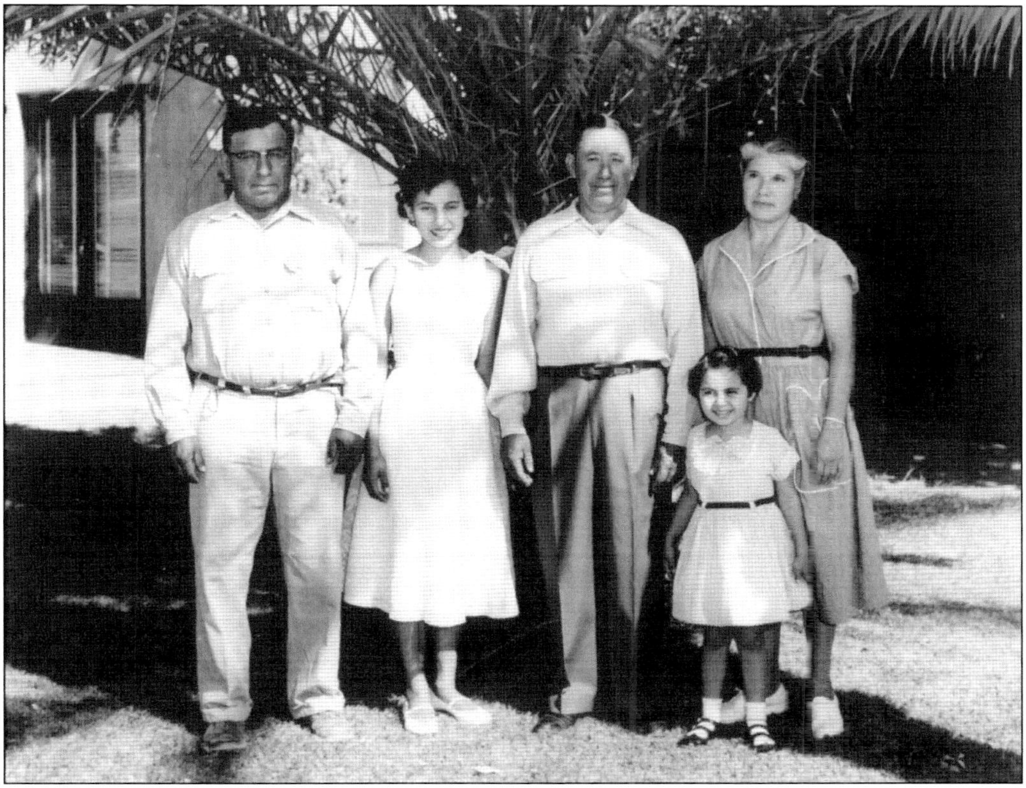

Pictured is Belen Soto as the valedictorian of the class of 1954 at Litchfield High School. From left to right are Belen's father Ramon Soto, Belen Soto, Trini Rodriguez, Brigida Rodriguez, and Brigidita Rodriguez. Ramon Soto was the superintendent of irrigation for Goodyear Farms. Belen was born on the Goodyear Farms Marinette Ranch and went to Litchfield Elementary and Litchfield High Schools. She was in one of the last classes of Litchfield High School before it moved to Agua Fria as a regional high school. (Courtesy of Belen Soto Moreno.)

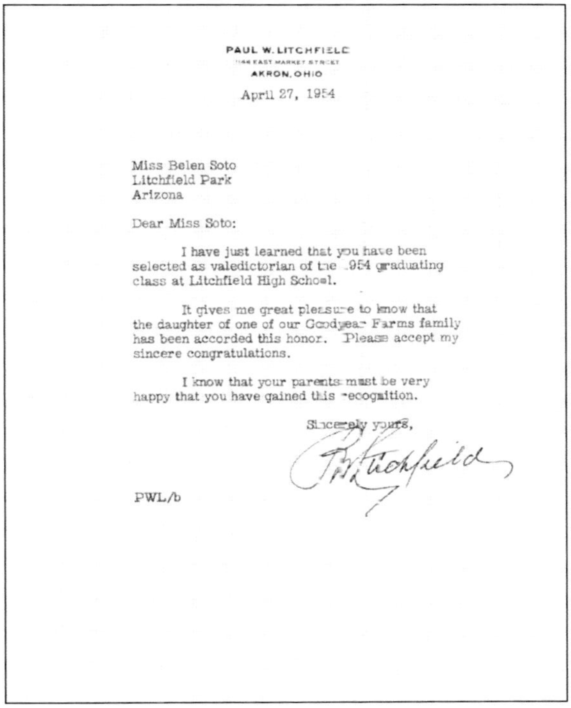

PAUL W. LITCHFIELD
1144 EAST MARKET STREET
AKRON, OHIO

April 27, 1954

Miss Belen Soto
Litchfield Park
Arizona

Dear Miss Soto:

I have just learned that you have been selected as valedictorian of the 1954 graduating class at Litchfield High School.

It gives me great pleasure to know that the daughter of one of our Goodyear Farms family has been accorded this honor. Please accept my sincere congratulations.

I know that your parents must be very happy that you have gained this recognition.

Sincerely yours,

P. W. Litchfield

PWL/b

Seen here is a letter of congratulations to Belen Soto from Paul Litchfield after being named valedictorian of the class of 1954 at Litchfield High School. (Courtesy of Belen Soto Moreno.)

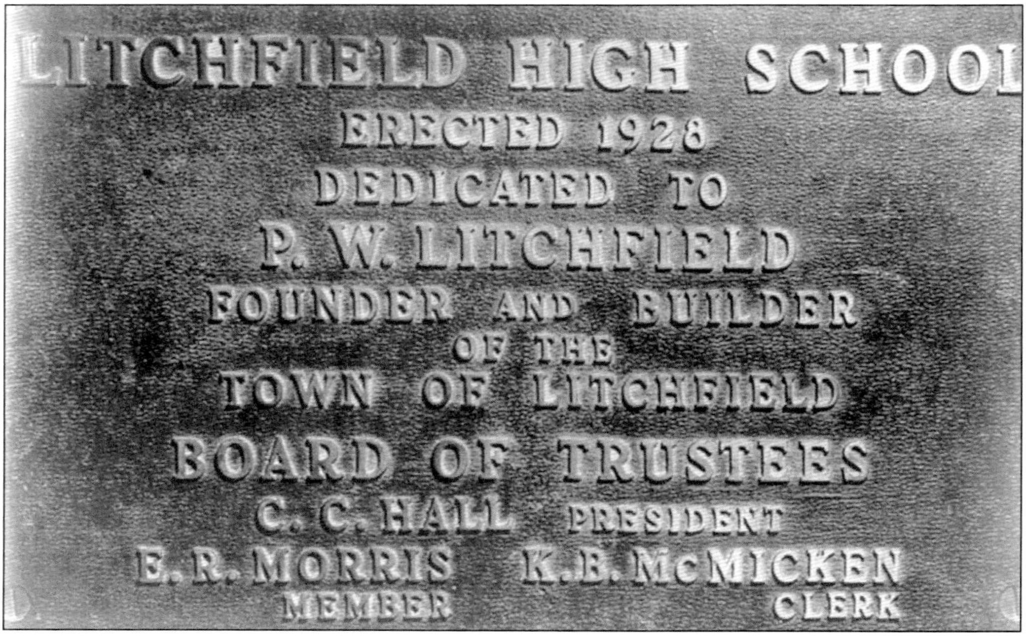


Litchfield High School was built and dedicated to Paul Litchfield in 1928. Boundaries were the same as the elementary school, only extended further north. The high school increased in size in 1941 because of World War II, when Luke Field opened and also the Goodyear Aircraft Company became operational. By 1944, there were 334 high school students. Litchfield High School was the first high school in this area and was active until 1956, when Agua Fria High School in Goodyear opened as a regional high school. The lyrics of the "Litchfield Park High School Fight Song" read: "Litchfield we're loyal to you, and we will give / our best to you, / In all our studies and plays we'll be boosters for / The Gold and the Blue, / And when our school days are o're and the / years are passing by, / We'll be glad we have the mem'ry of our dear Litchfield High." (Courtesy of the City of Litchfield Park.)

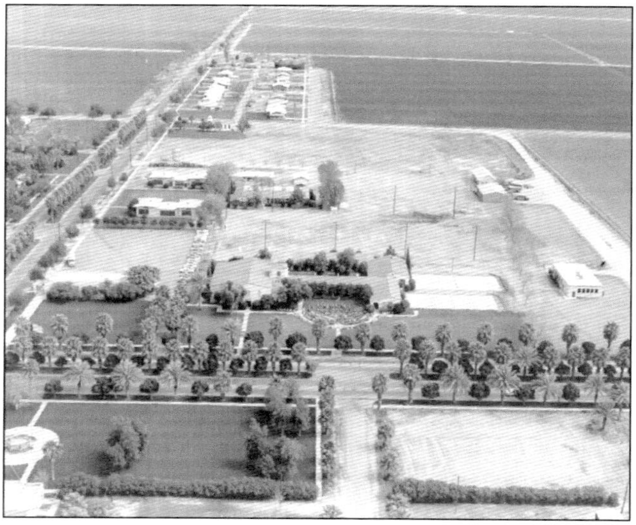

Seen here is an aerial view of the Litchfield schools looking east from Litchfield Avenue. A bond issue for $36,000 was passed in May 1928—$24,000 for the high school and $12,000 for the elementary school. A gymnasium was built to be used by both schools. In 1935, a $7,000 bond issue was voted in, and another elementary school building was completed in 1938 with assistance from the Works Progress Administration (WPA). The one-room adobe buildings have now been enclosed and a tech building and bus barn added to the campus. (Courtesy of the City of Litchfield Park.)

# *Three*

# Paul Litchfield Family and La Loma

Paul Weeks Litchfield, born in Boston, Massachusetts, on July 26, 1875, became dean of the American rubber industry and rose to chairman of the board of Goodyear Tire & Rubber Company.

In 1896, he graduated from MIT as a chemical engineer and started his career in a bicycle tire factory. In 1900, he joined Goodyear in Akron, Ohio. Goodyear was a startup company that was to become one of the world's largest manufacturers of tires and later the world's leader in rubber products. Litchfield played a leading role in the company's expansion worldwide. He was superintendent of production, development, and engineering and became factory manager by 1911.

In 1916, as a young executive in the company, he was the man behind the Goodyear Farms operations in Arizona. Under his guidance, the Arizona desert became productive, growing long staple cotton for Goodyear tires, and it later became a great experimental laboratory for testing farm equipment. In Litchfield Park, an important chapter was written in the story of American agriculture.

Litchfield was a world leader in rubber circles and was also very active in the developing world of aeronautics. He was made president of the Goodyear Zeppelin Corporation in 1926. Goodyear built the USS *Akron*, which was the largest airship in 1934. During World War II, Goodyear Aircraft Corporation ranked as the one of the 10 largest in the country.

By 1926, he was elected president of Goodyear, and by 1930, he was elected chairman of the board while still president. He was responsible for the design and development of the straight-side tire, the first belted-cord tire, the first pneumatic truck tires, and all-weather tread designs. He held many patents for various designs. This commentary lists a few of the accomplishments of Litchfield. He wrote three books, one being his autobiography, *The Industrial Voyage*.

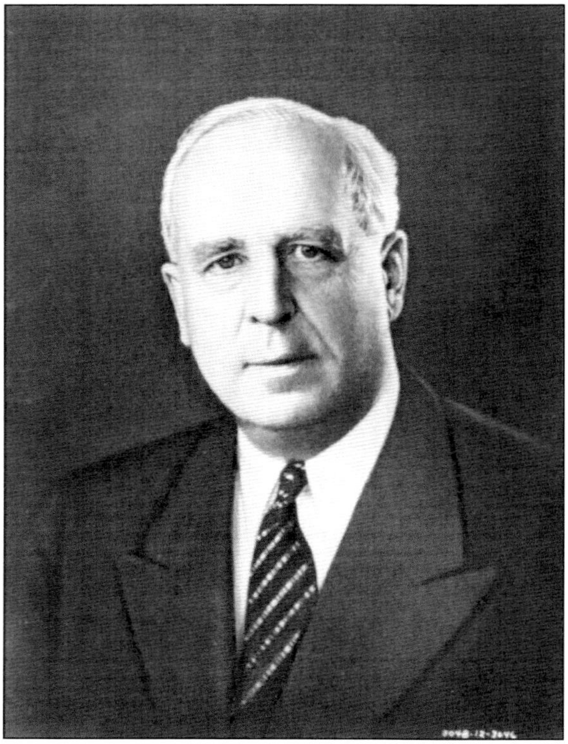

Paul Litchfield's contributions to industry and the betterment of mankind will stand through the ages. His life was a movement of his principles, vision, insight, and inspired leadership. His actions were constantly guided by his profound spiritual values. Under his brilliant guidance and excellent judgment, the Goodyear Corporation achieved and maintained a position of leadership that is internationally recognized. He was truly a citizen of the world and was one of the great industrial leaders of the 20th century. He was a teacher, a scientist, a philosopher, and a salesman. Combine all of these qualities for success in each of these fields and add a great organizational ability, and one can understand how he helped to build the Goodyear Tire & Rubber Company into the successful company it became.

Florence Pennington Brinton was born on November 30, 1880, in Ashland, Ohio. She was the youngest in a family of four girls. Florence was a fun-loving child and always an eager student. She graduated from Ashland High School with honors and attended Lake Erie College in Painesville, Ohio. She was working at a newspaper when she met Paul Litchfield in 1903. They were married on June 23, 1904, and settled in Akron, Ohio, where Paul was employed by the Goodyear Tire & Rubber Company. She kept step with her husband's progress at Goodyear and was the gentle, kind, and quiet strength behind his success. She was the ultimate hostess and was known to have a backbone of steel. She was a devoted wife and mother of two daughters, Katharine, born in 1905, and Edith, born in 1910. Florence devoted many hours to her favorite charities. She served the Red Cross during two world wars and was active in Akron's Garden Club and in her church. After Paul's death in 1959, she continued her interest and devotion to people in all walks of life. She was loved by all who knew her for her gentleness and sincerity. Florence died on June 6, 1972, at age 91.

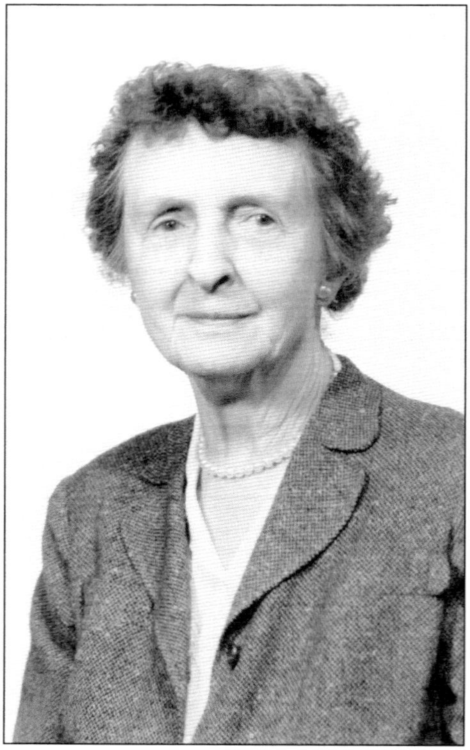

Seen here is a family picture taken in 1954 at the Litchfields' 50th wedding anniversary celebration. Paul and Florence are joined by their daughters Katharine (left) and Edith (right) in celebration at Anchorage, the Litchfield family home in Akron, Ohio.

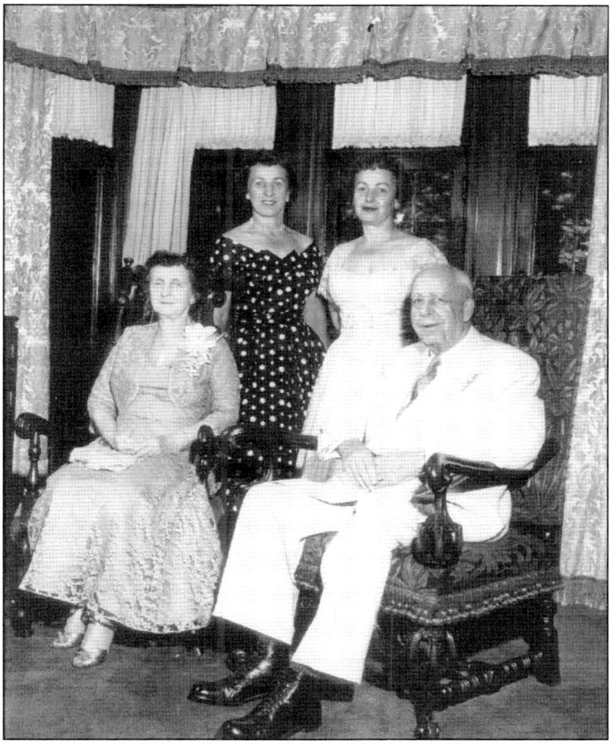

Paul and Florence Litchfield are seen relaxing at Anchorage, their family home in Akron, Ohio. They spent time between their two homes, Anchorage and La Loma in Arizona.

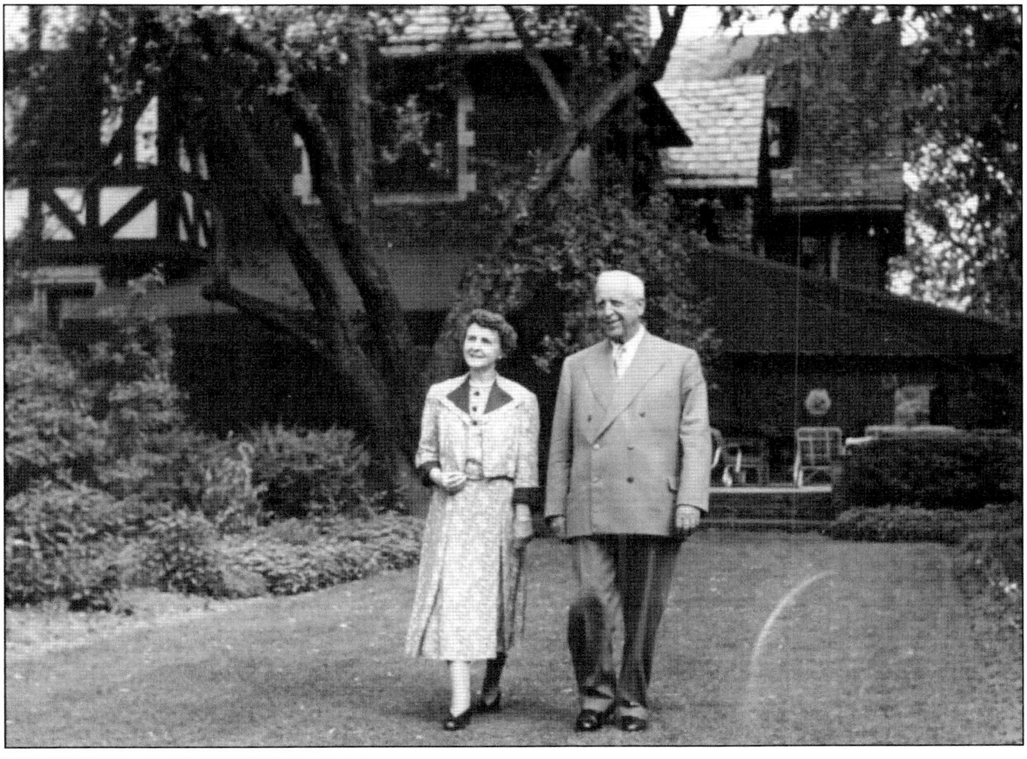

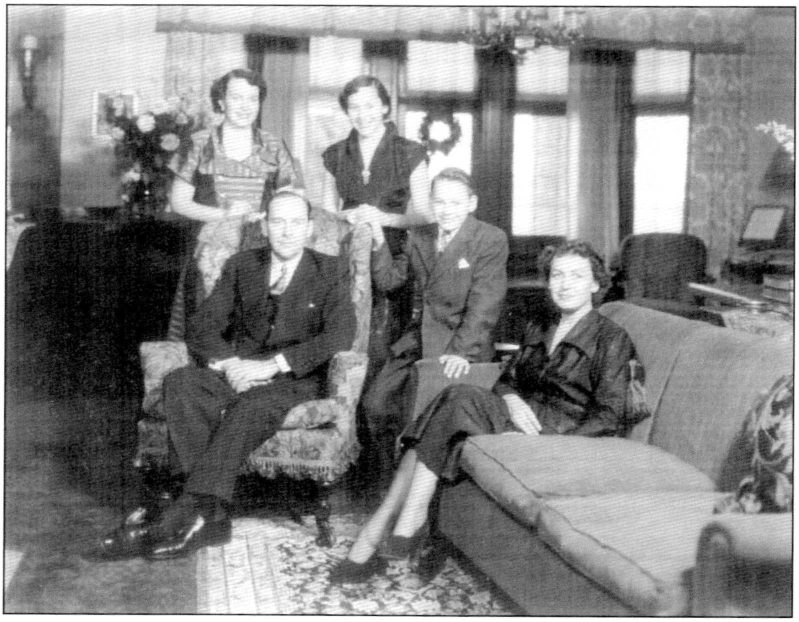

The family of Edith and Wallace Denny are seen here celebrating Christmas at Anchorage, the Litchfields' family home in Akron, Ohio, around 1948. Wally and Edith are seated with their family, standing from left to right, Julia, Pamela, and Peter. Wallace Denny was vice president of Goodyear in Canada.

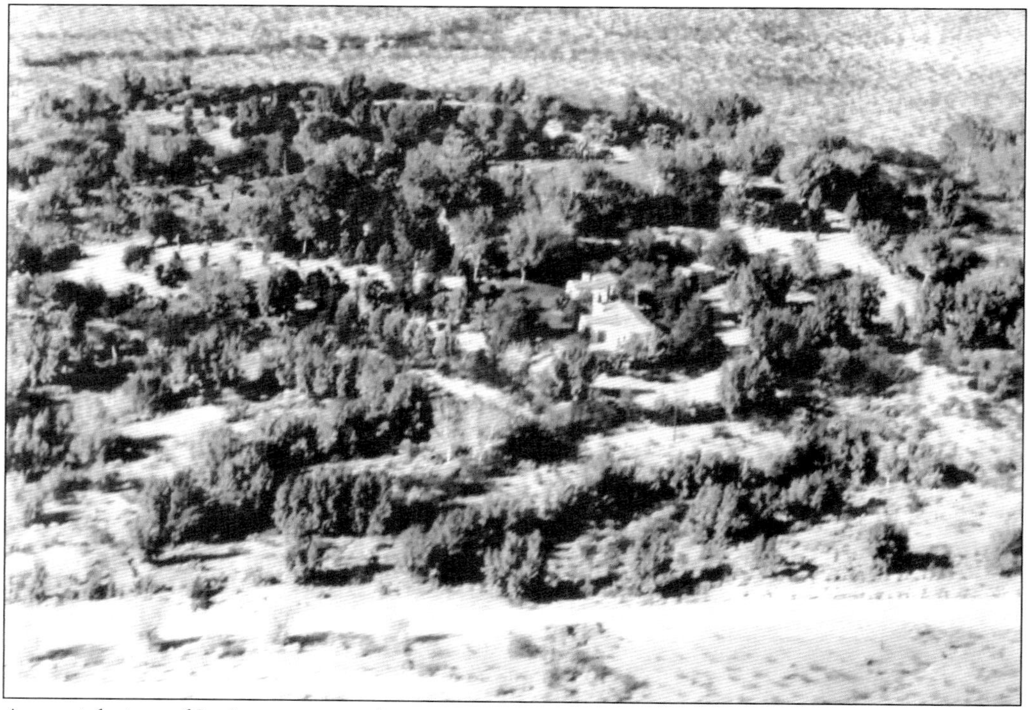

An aerial view of La Loma is seen here. La Loma is known as "the hill." La Loma is a hump in an otherwise level stretch of desert. It supposedly resulted from a gas bubble when the earth's surface was developed at this point in the valley. The site of Paul Litchfield's private estate, it is heavily planted with a wide variety of shrubs and trees. Dirt was hauled into the hill to create a higher hill than was created from the gas bubble in the earth's surface. (From an article by Allen C. Reed in *Arizona Highways*, April 1952.)

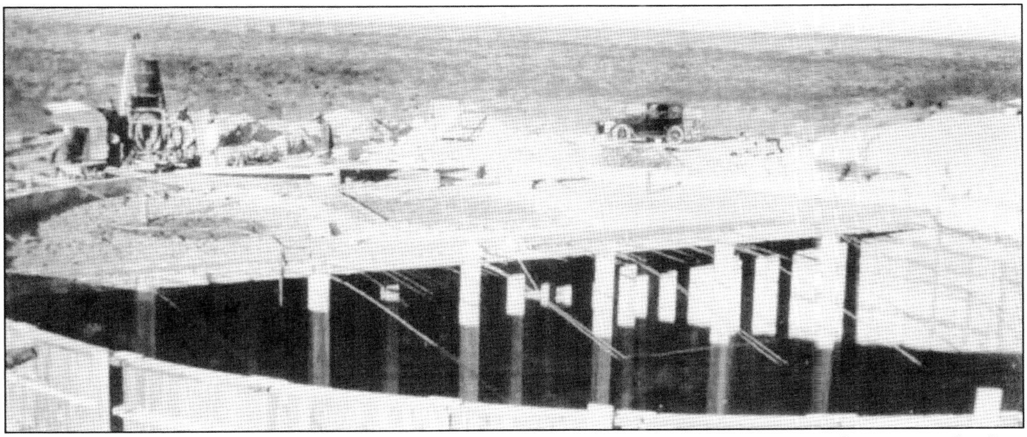

A reservoir was dug into the hill to provide water for the town. Terraces and contour ditches were laid out around the irregular topography of the hill so that water could be carried to every part of the property. On May 1, 1920, W.E. Gableman of Quinton, California and Code and Hill consulting engineers from Los Angeles supervised the building of La Loma's new water system. A 325,000-gallon reservoir was built north of the town at La Loma. Under the direction of Gableman, redwood piping was laid, and the reservoir supplied water for the domestic needs of Litchfield.

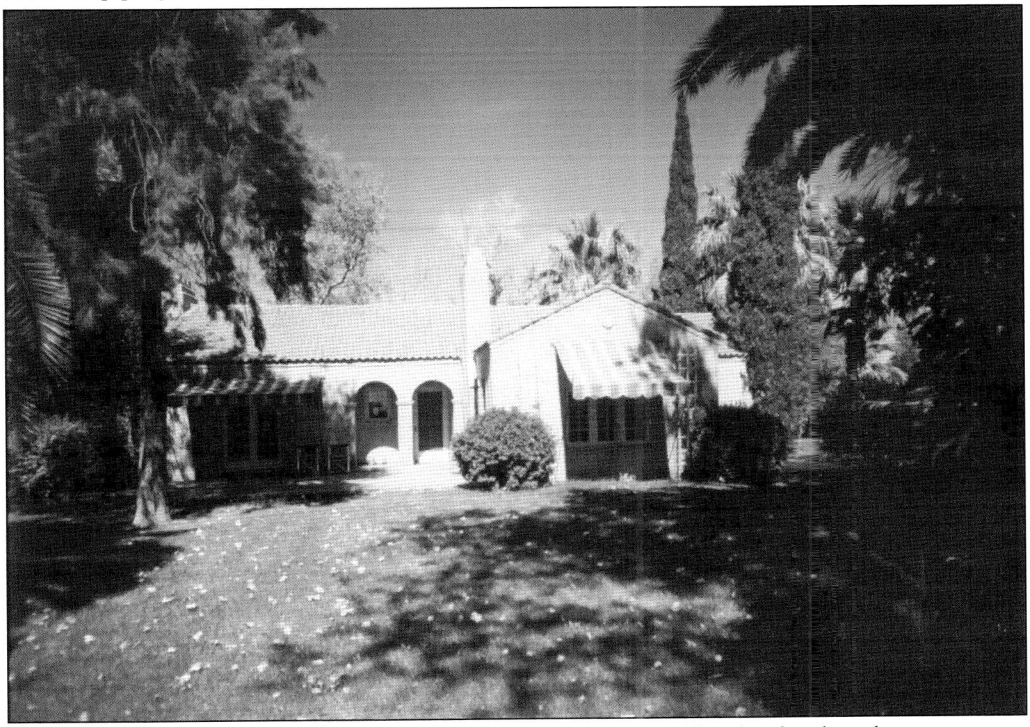

The La Loma property was purchased in 1921 by Paul Litchfield to be developed into a winter residence. It consists of 360 acres; 40 acres were planted in fruit trees, 40 acres landscaped, and 280 acres left as virgin desert. The hill rises 200 feet above the desert floor. The main house was built in 1925 and restored and enlarged by Edith and Wallace Denny by 1978. The other houses on the hill were known as cottages and were constructed between 1925 and 1932. The bandstand was built in 1932.

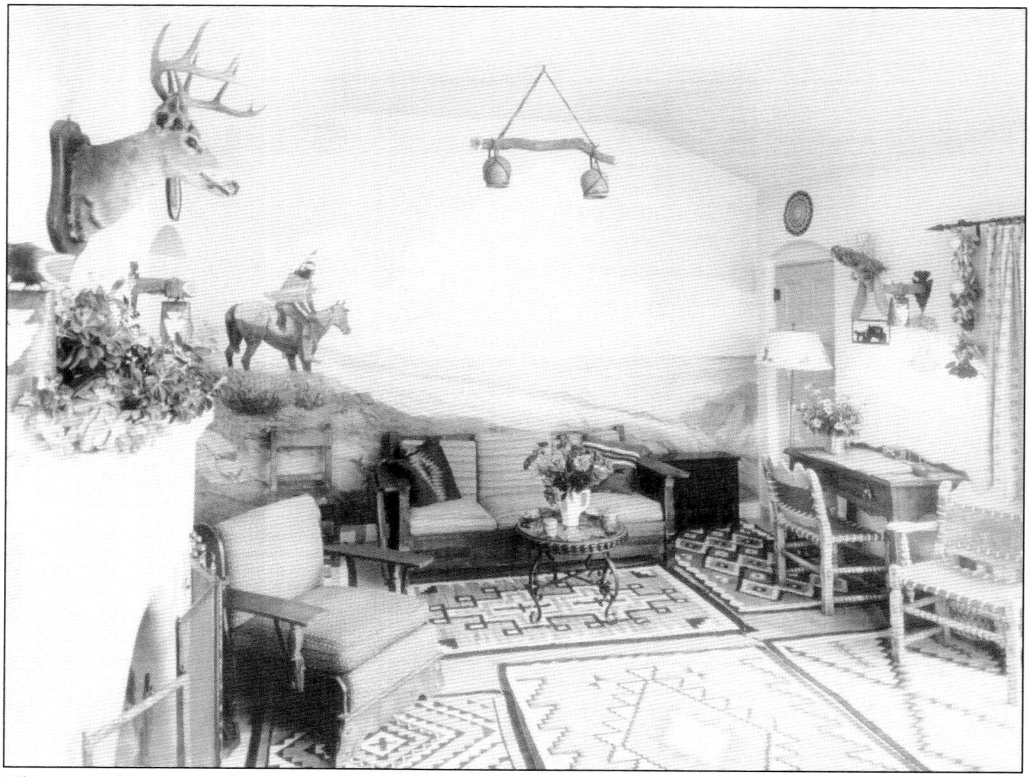

The main house was known as Florence Litchfield's house, as each member of the family had a designated property. The room pictured is the library or den in the main house. Paul Litchfield surprised Florence with the Indian scout wall mural when she returned from a trip. It was painted in 1935 by Farrington Elwell and his student R. Ellen Barr. The old Mission furniture was made of eucalyptus wood and was original to the house. The terra-cotta pot light fixtures were also used in the Wigwam and in The Church at Litchfield Park. The metal wall light fixture with the arrowhead design was made by Goodyear Farms employee Pedro Acuna. These metal light fixtures can also be seen in the Wigwam and The Church at Litchfield Park.

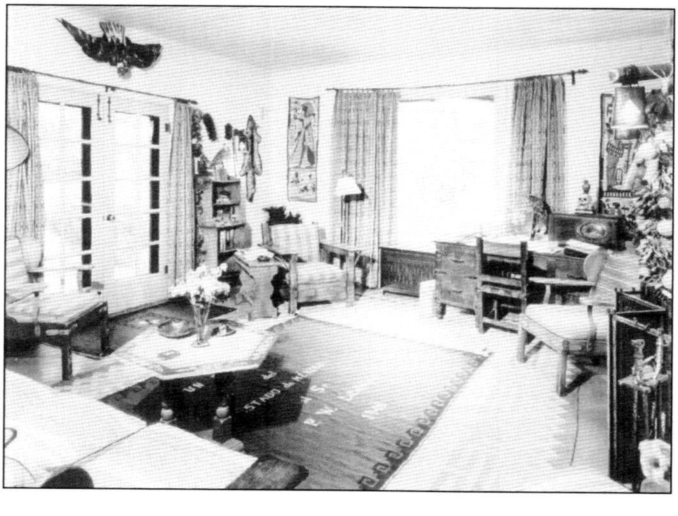

Pictured is Paul Litchfield's study or main office at La Loma. This was identified as Cottage No. 3 and was located just east of the main house. It was furnished with antique Mission-style furniture. The rug, dated 1946, was a gift to Paul from Mexico.

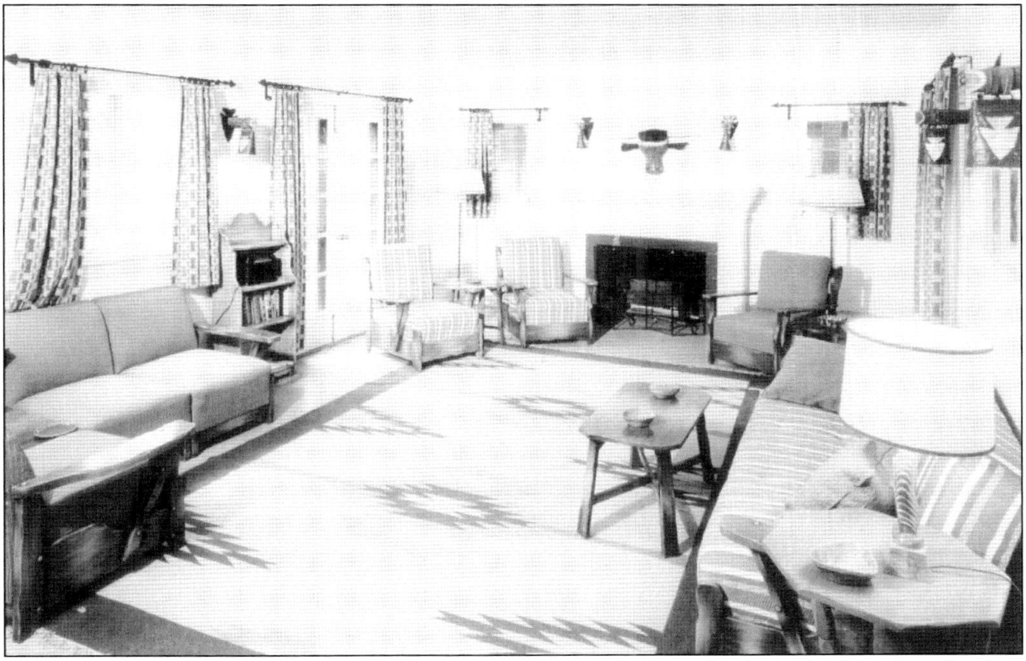

Pictured here is Cottage No. 4, designated as a guest cottage. It had two bedrooms, a bath, a small kitchen, and a dining room. It was located near the outdoor pool. It was also furnished with Mission-style furniture and Indian rugs.

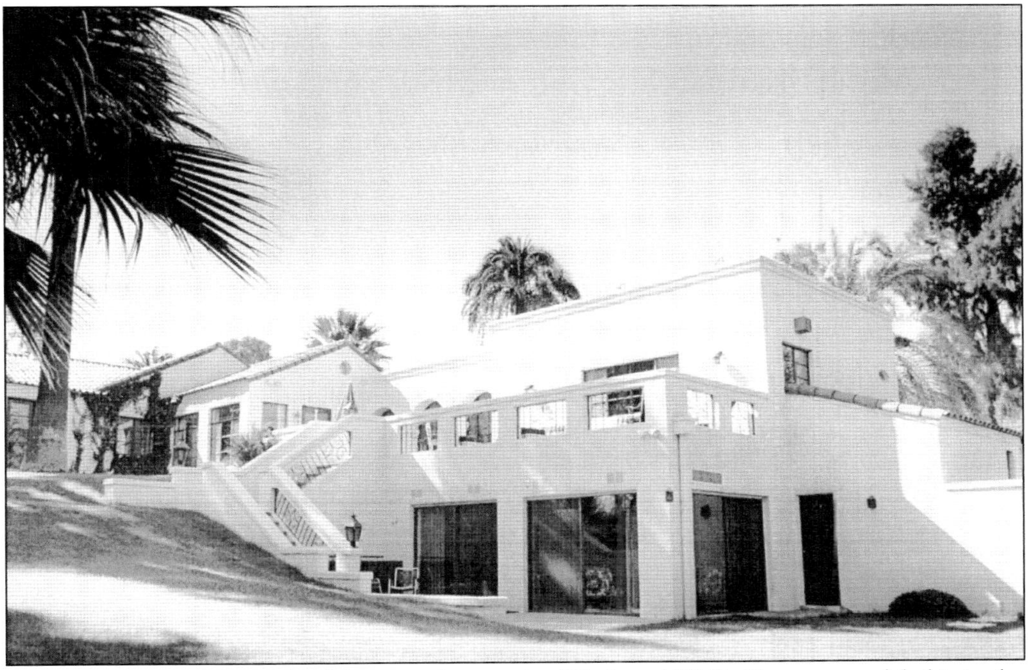

This is a picture of the back of the main house after Edith and Wally Denny remodeled it in the late 1970s. The outdoor pool was moved inside the basement of the house. Above the pool, Wally Denny added his office with a patio.

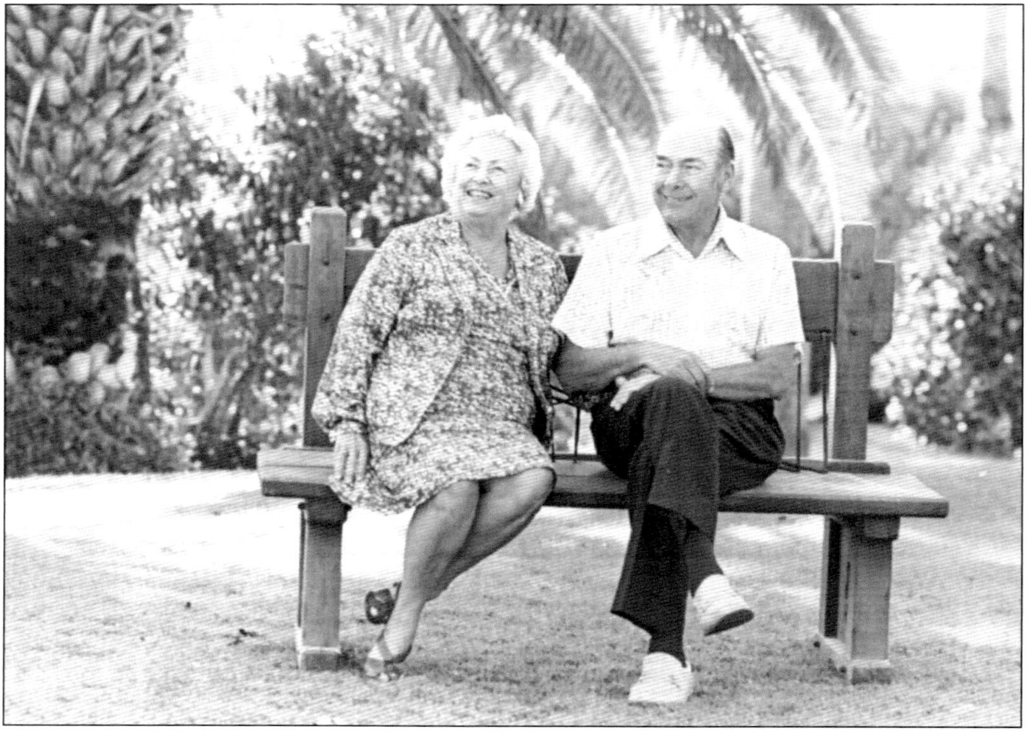

Edith and Wallace Denny enjoy the outdoors at La Loma. The Dennys retired to La Loma in 1978 after spending their working years in Canada. Wallace worked for Goodyear Tire & Rubber Company in Canada from 1938 to 1978. This special couple was married in 1930 and left their wedding reception in the *Pilgrim*, Goodyear's first blimp. Edith threw her wedding bouquet from the blimp. They had two daughters and a son. The Dennys celebrated their 70th wedding anniversary in October 2000.

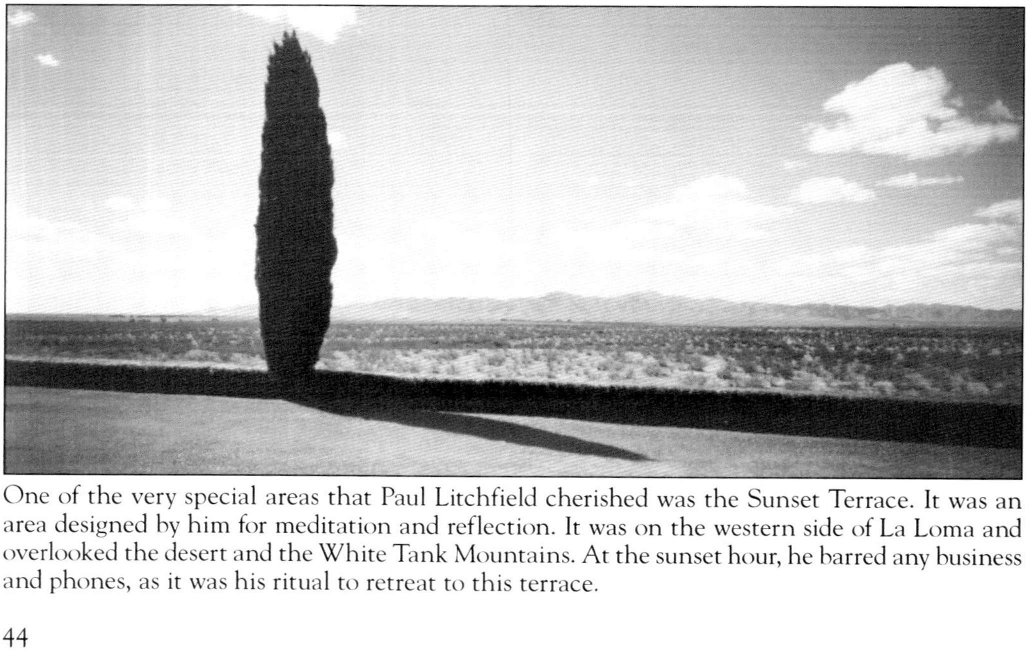

One of the very special areas that Paul Litchfield cherished was the Sunset Terrace. It was an area designed by him for meditation and reflection. It was on the western side of La Loma and overlooked the desert and the White Tank Mountains. At the sunset hour, he barred any business and phones, as it was his ritual to retreat to this terrace.

Seen here is a view of a cross in the desert, looking out from Sunset Terrace. Litchfield felt that the desert in Arizona and La Loma had a little different place in his life than any other. It reminded him of the high places listed in biblical times when people reached out over such a desert to commune with God. He found peace and serenity in the desert and loved the view from the hill.

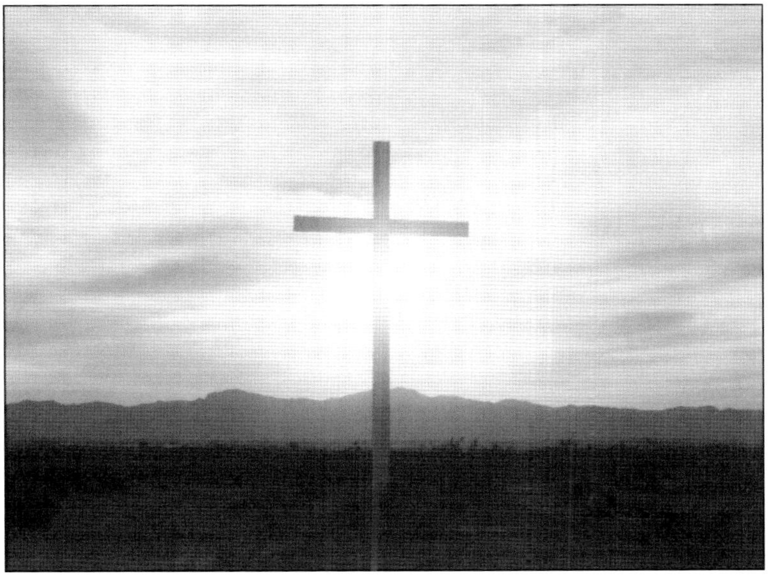

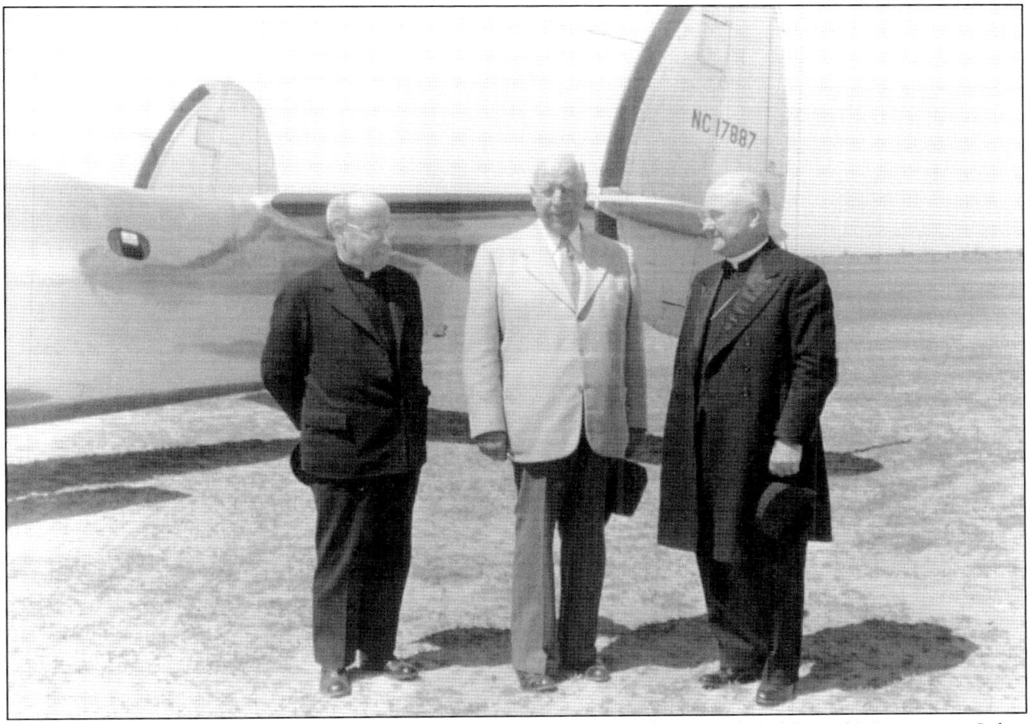


Pictured from right to left are Cardinal Francis Spellman, Paul W. Litchfield, and Monsignor John Nelson. Cardinal Spellman was a special guest of Litchfield's at La Loma. They met in New York when the Goodyear Tire & Rubber Company sponsored an award-winning national radio show called *The Greatest Story Ever Told*. Cardinal Spellman was the military vicar of the American Armed Forces and visited the military troops throughout the world. He visited Luke Air Force Base while at La Loma. He said Catholic mass in the St. Thomas Aquinas Catholic Mission Church when he visited in 1948.

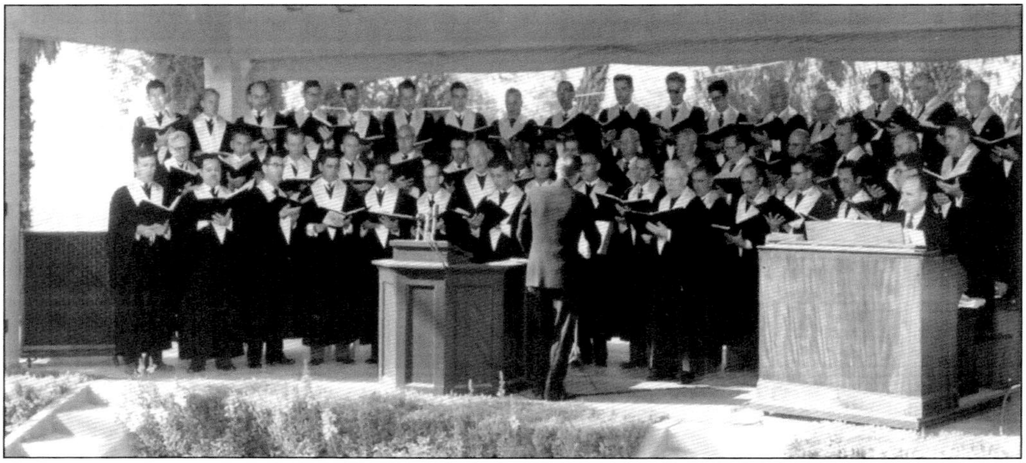

Pictured here is a men's chorus singing at the bandstand at La Loma. This was part of the Desert Devotionals held at La Loma starting in 1949. Inspiration for the devotional services had its start with the Goodyear-sponsored radio program *The Greatest Story Ever Told*, which had millions of listeners each Sunday and was widely acclaimed by persons from all faiths. The Church at Litchfield Park hosted the Desert Devotionals in March and April on Sunday afternoons. The purpose of the devotionals was to encourage closer interfaith fellowship among people of differing churches.

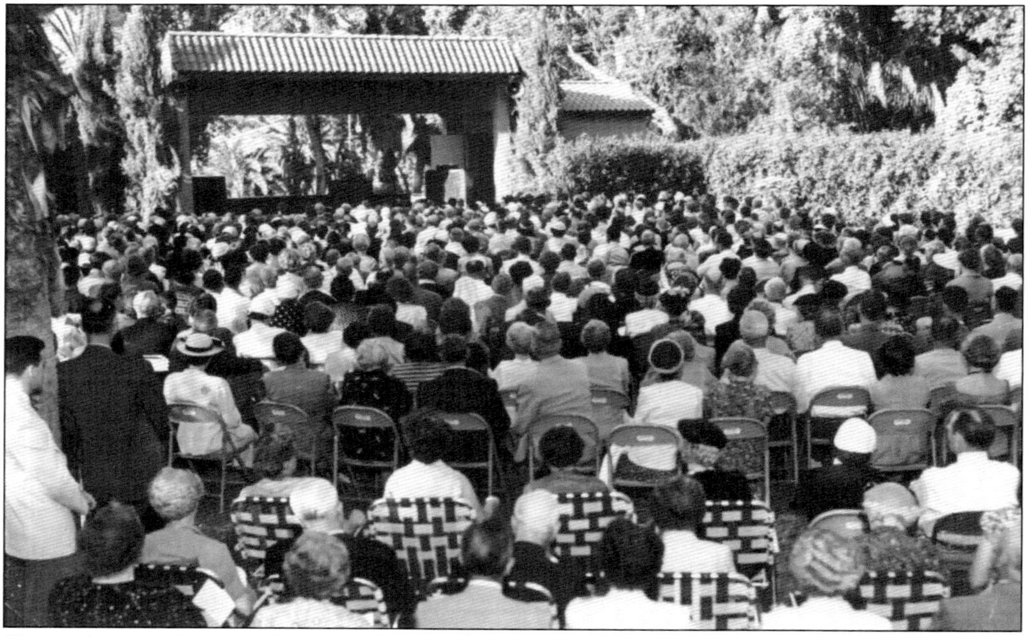

Shown here is the attendance at the popular Desert Devotionals held at La Loma on Sunday afternoons. Prominent church leaders and lay people from around the country were guest speakers. Singing and organ music were provided for each program. Popular choruses from universities and glee clubs were invited to Arizona. The favorable response led to the Arizona Council of Churches becoming a cosponsor of the program with The Church at Litchfield Park. The largest crowd that ever attended a Desert Devotional was in 1953, when the guest speaker was Pres. David O. McKay of the Church of Jesus Christ of Latter-day Saints from Salt Lake City, Utah. His visit brought 3,600 to La Loma for the Desert Devotional.

Arizona senator Barry Goldwater was a guest speaker at the March 26, 1956, Desert Devotional. Senator Goldwater was a captain while stationed at nearby Luke Air Force Base

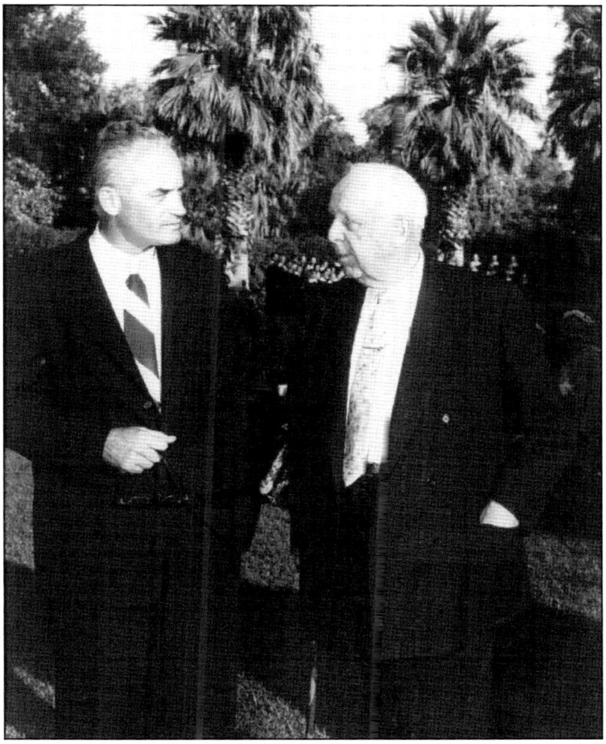

A Luke Air Force Base fly-over is seen at Sunset Point, an outdoor picnic area owned by Goodyear Farms for its employees. Sunset Point was located just north of La Loma and south of Luke Air Force Base. It was popular for parties and awards ceremonies for the Goodyear Farms employees. This photograph was taken in 1956, when the Luke jets entertained the winners of the Goodyear Soil Conservation Awards.

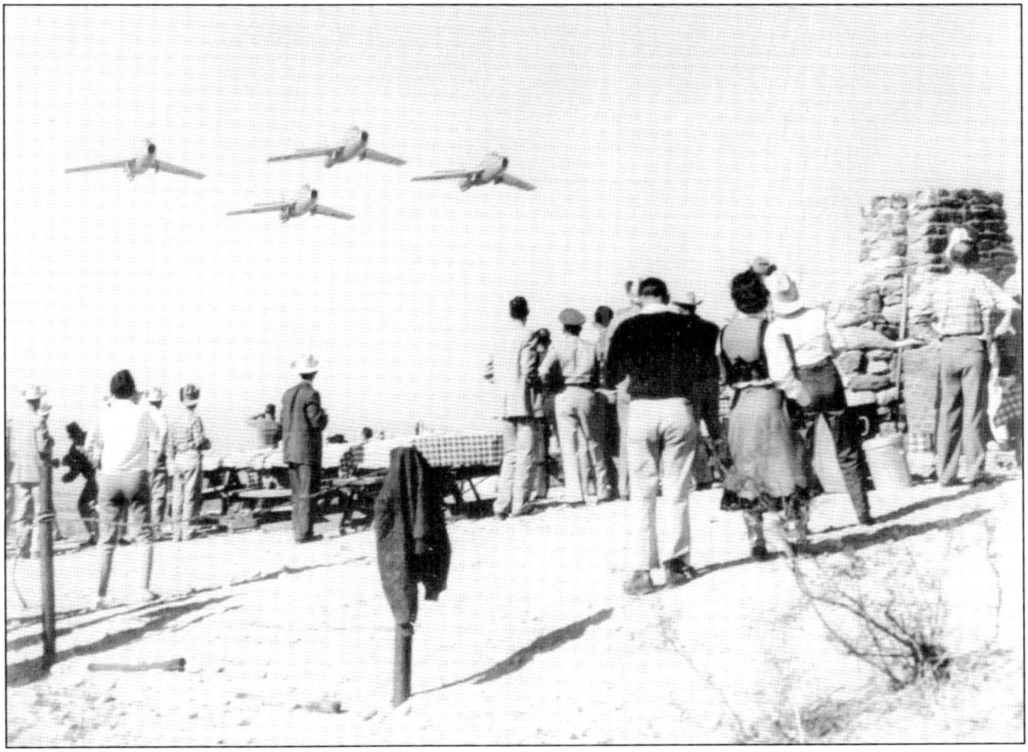

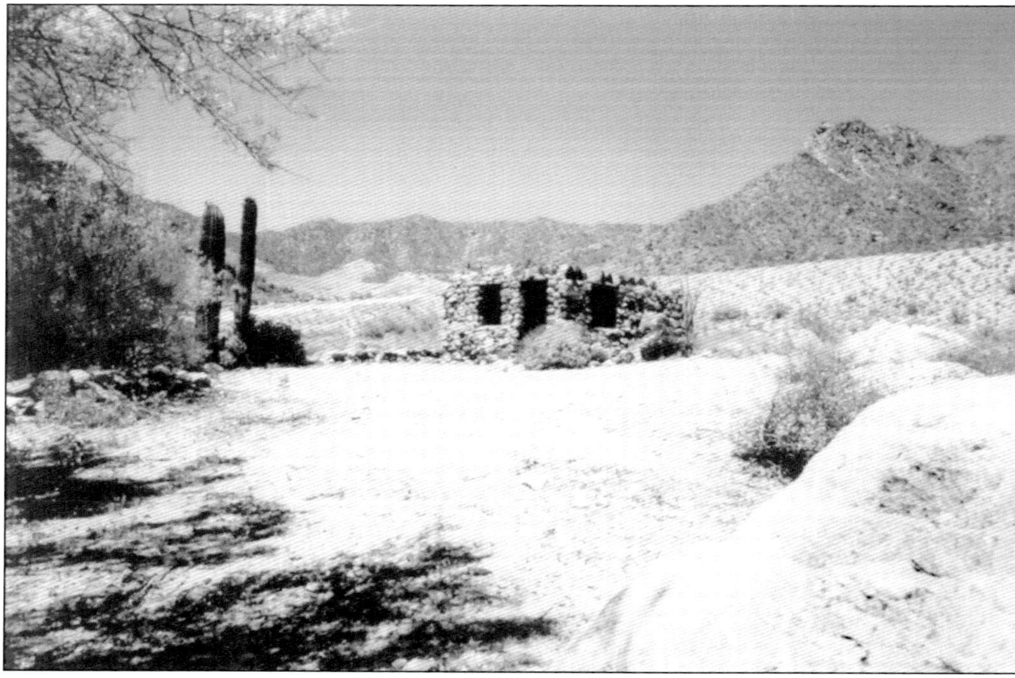

An exterior view of the Eagles Nest, built by Paul Litchfield in 1934 in the White Tank Mountains, is seen here.

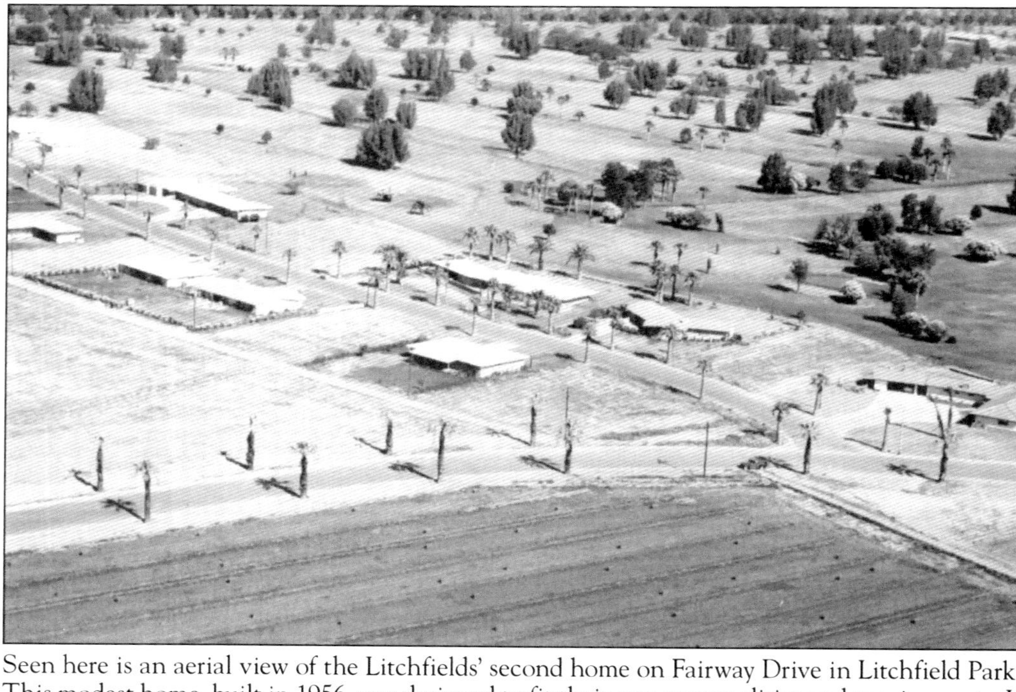

Seen here is an aerial view of the Litchfields' second home on Fairway Drive in Litchfield Park. This modest home, built in 1956, was designed to fit their own personalities and requirements. It was located adjacent to the Wigwam Country Club in a newly developed home area of Litchfield Park. (Courtesy of the City of Litchfield Park.)

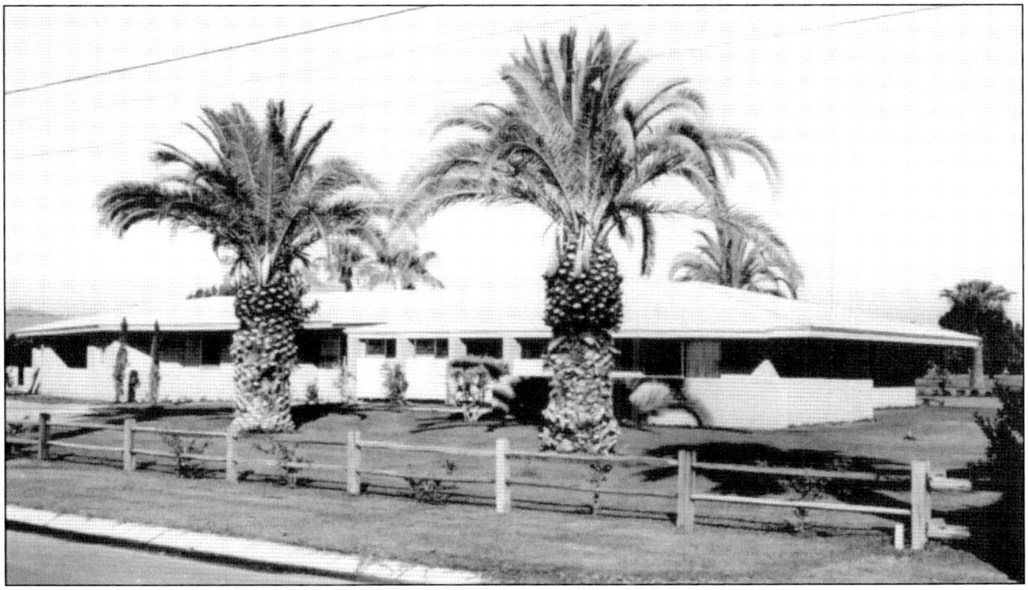

A front view of the Litchfields' home built on Fairway Drive is seen here. It was a comfortable home for their family and friends to enjoy the pleasant climate and surroundings of Litchfield Park. (Courtesy of the City of Litchfield Park.)

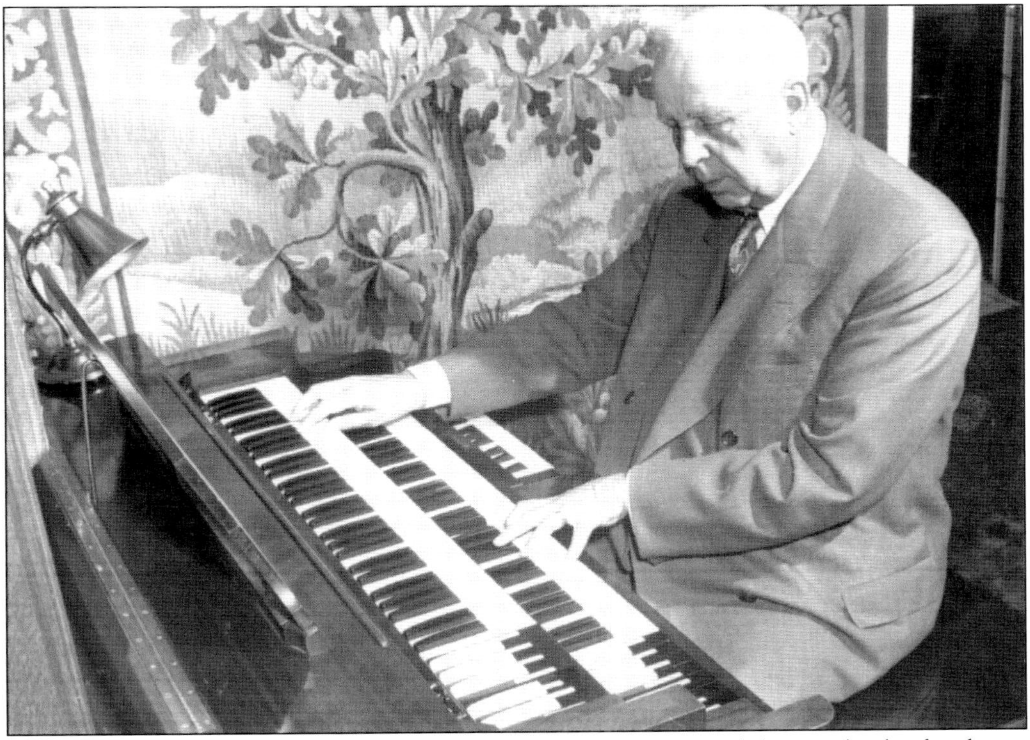

Paul Litchfield is seen playing the organ. This side of Litchfield was rarely known, but his family was inclined to be musicians. His daughter Edith was an accomplished pianist. Upon their retirement to La Loma, the Dennys were avid supporters of the Phoenix Symphony.

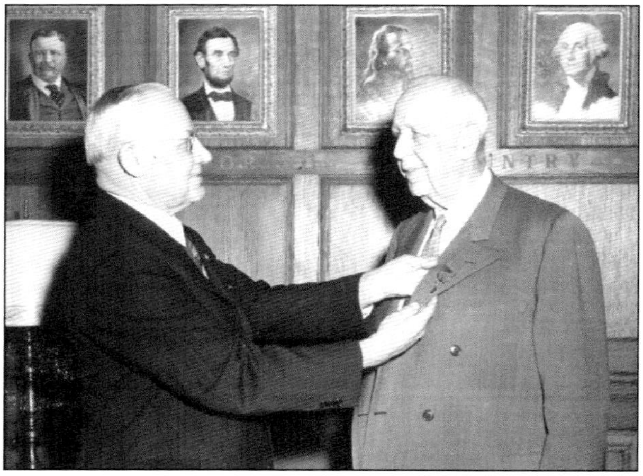

Paul W. Litchfield is seen receiving his 50-year membership pin in the Masons. The official title of the award was "50 Year Ohio Grand Council Masonic Medal," being presented by Earl V. Carter from Akron, Ohio. Mr. Litchfield referred to the pictures behind him as his personal board of directors.

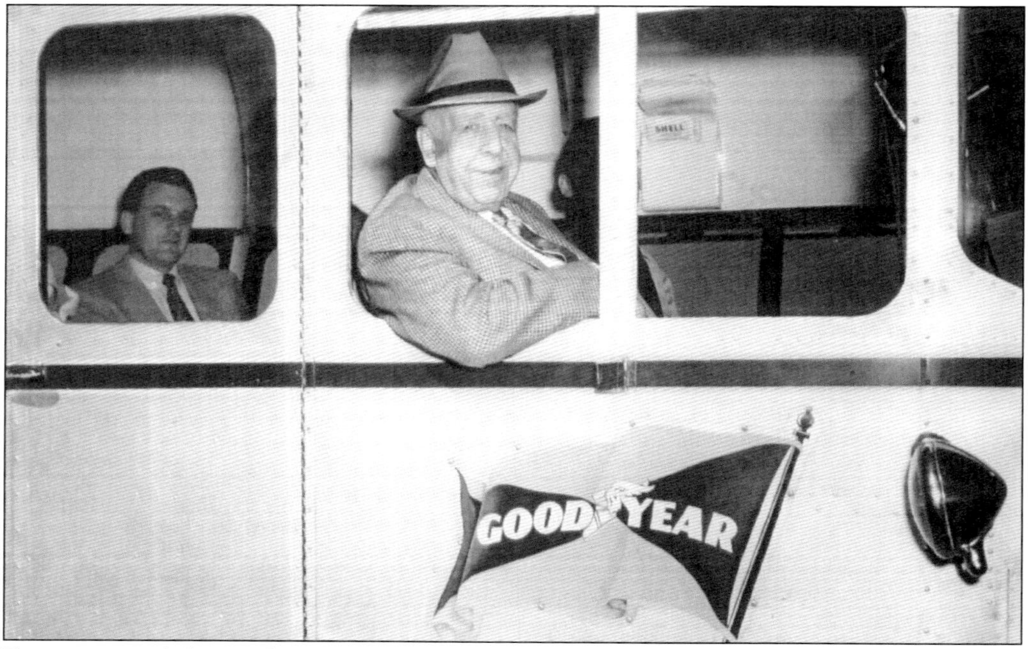


Few men reveal the attributes of true greatness and in their lifetime develop their capacities to the fullest, but such a man was Paul Weeks Litchfield. One of Litchfield's important human values was his respect for the worth and dignity of the individual, and he strived to bring out the best in people around him. He was very aware of the value of time. He made the most of his time, and his many accomplishments proved good use of it. He was associated with Goodyear for 58 years, and in that time, he contributed to the tire industry the inventions of the first straight-sided tire, the first cord tire, the first pneumatic truck tire, and many others. He played a major role in producing synthetic rubber. He was also very active in the field of aeronautics as a champion of both the airplane and dirigibles. He received numerous awards both domestic and foreign in recognition of his contributions to rubber, automotive, and aeronautical sciences. His world-wide reputation was made as one of the great industrial leaders of the 20th century. It has been said of Litchfield that he gave his strength to the weak, his sympathy to the poor, and his heart to God. He was constantly striving for perfection and always looking for ways to make improvements. Litchfield's death came on March 18, 1959. (From a memorial from Goodyear Corporation.)

# *Four*

# The Wigwam

In the winter of 1918, the Goodyear executives coming to visit from Akron, Ohio, had to travel most of a day to get to Litchfield Park by horse and buggy. It was so time-consuming that the Goodyear executives decided to build the Organization House. The original building served six people and had a fireplace room, three bedrooms, two baths, a combination living and dining room, a kitchen, and a terrace. It was dubbed the Wigwam by its regular occupants. The Organization House was opened to the public on Thanksgiving Day in 1929.

In 1929, it expanded to 13 rooms with accommodations for 24 guests. The Wigwam Resort assigned everyone a horse upon check-in and was originally considered a dude ranch. After a successful season, the resort extended to several wickiups (guest houses), and by 1939–1940, the Wigwam could accommodate 66 guests.

Trips on horseback were regularly planned for guests along with sightseeing tours in the Goodyear blimp *Resolute*. In 1930, a private landing field was built near the resort for the blimp. In 1946, a runway was also constructed for small planes. The resort was closed to the public during World War II, while guest rooms were leased to the military at Luke Air Force Base. After the war, the Wigwam added housing and could accommodate 120 guests. By 1949, two decades after it opened to the public, the Wigwam had progressed from a dusty dude ranch to a popular retreat that offered tennis courts and a swimming pool and had expanded kitchens to add restaurants and lounges.

Golf was introduced to the Wigwam in 1930, shortly after the resort opened to the public. Jacque Phillips, a gardener from Scotland, where golf originated, suggested golf to the Wigwam because of its success in Scotland. The first nine holes had oil added to the sand to keep it from blowing. The course was expanded to 18 holes by 1941, and it was redesigned by Robert Trent Jones in 1965.

In 1965, a second 18-hole golf course was designed by Robert Trent Jones, and the two 18-hole courses were named the Blue and Gold Courses in honor of Goodyear's company colors. In 1975, a third 18-hole west golf course was designed by Robert "Red" Lawrence and named the Red Course in his honor and also for Red Allen, the Wigwam golf pro of 41 years. With the completion of the Red Course, the Wigwam is now the only resort in Arizona with three 18-hole golf courses.

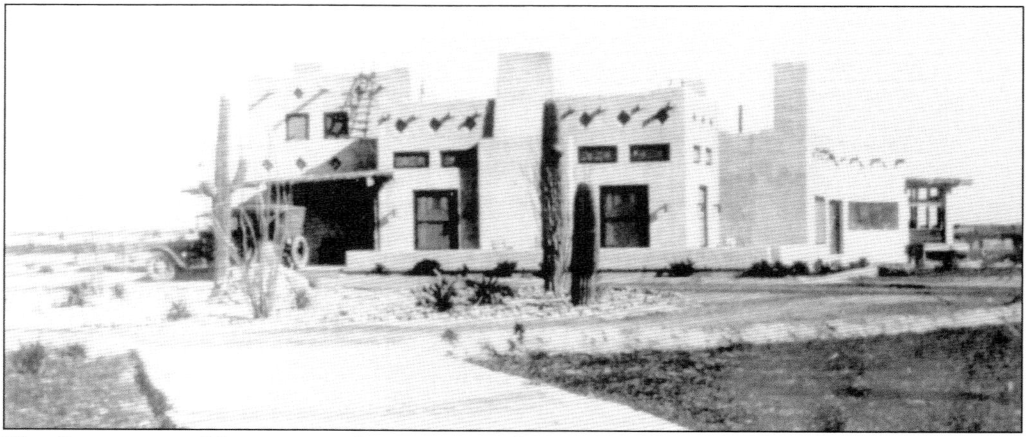

The Organization House is seen here as it was designed and built in 1918–1919. The Goodyear executives who came to check on the Southwest Cotton Company operation enjoyed their visits to Arizona and loved staying in their guest house. The decision was made to expand on the grounds and the house and use it for vacations. The Organization House turned out to be one of the most exciting spin-offs of the Goodyear cotton operation. In 1929, the house had been enlarged to accommodate 24 guests and was opened to the public as the Wigwam Resort. (Courtesy of Wigwam Resort.)

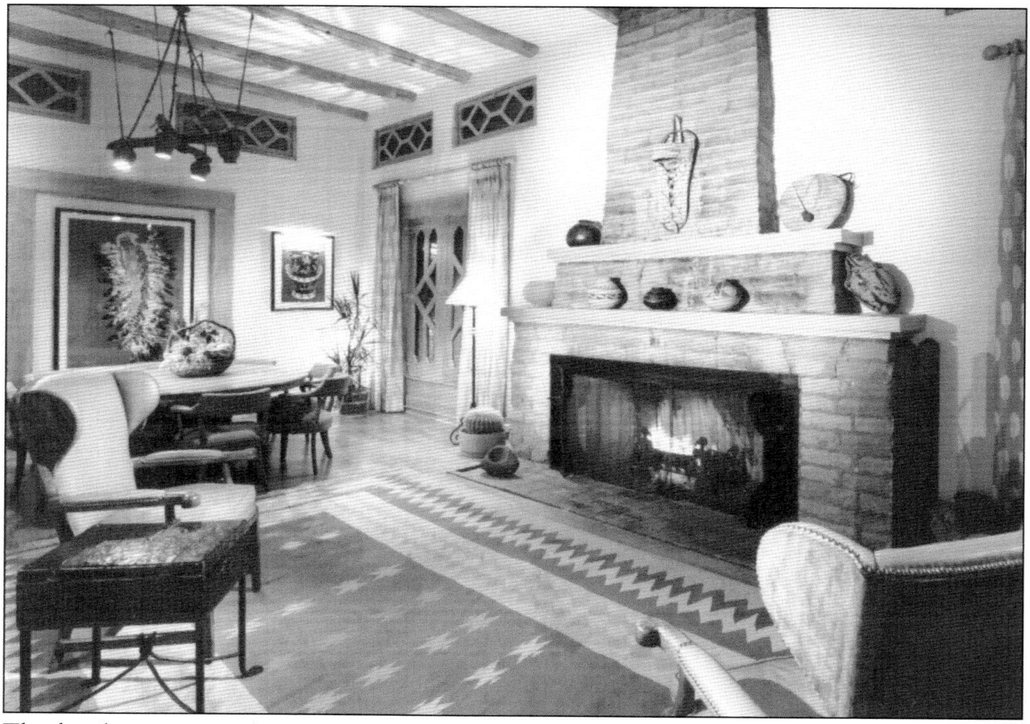

The fireplace room at the Wigwam is a famous and very historic room. It is original to the 1918 house and is made of adobe bricks. The Native American decor as shown here has been the consistent theme since 1918. The fireplace room is still very popular with Wigwam guests and is used for many social occasions as well as a quiet place to read a book from its small library. (Courtesy of Wigwam Resort.)

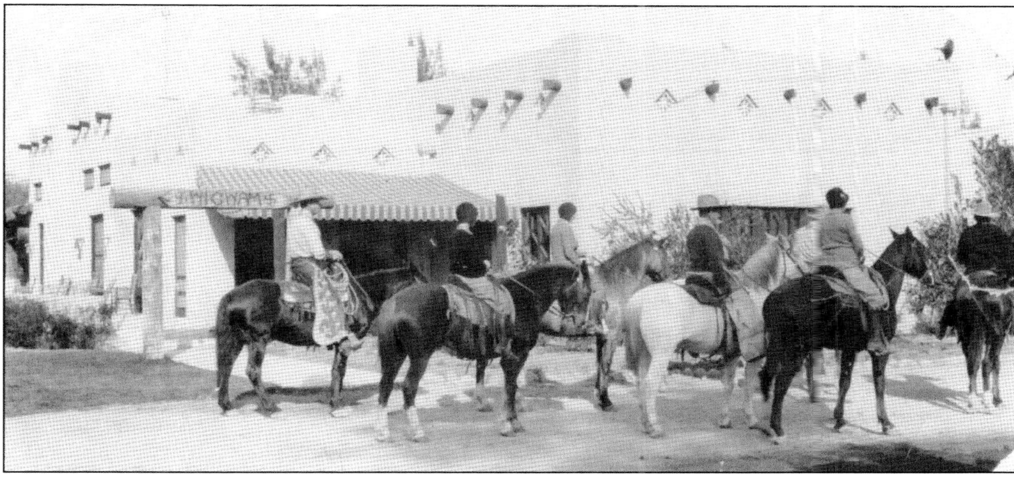

The Wigwam was opened to the public in 1929 as a dude ranch. It is said that each new guest was issued a horse and a towel. The Wigwam Stables housed the horses, and trail rides were to local areas and also to Sunset Point, an outdoor picnic and party area located just north of La Loma. (Courtesy of Wigwam Resort.)

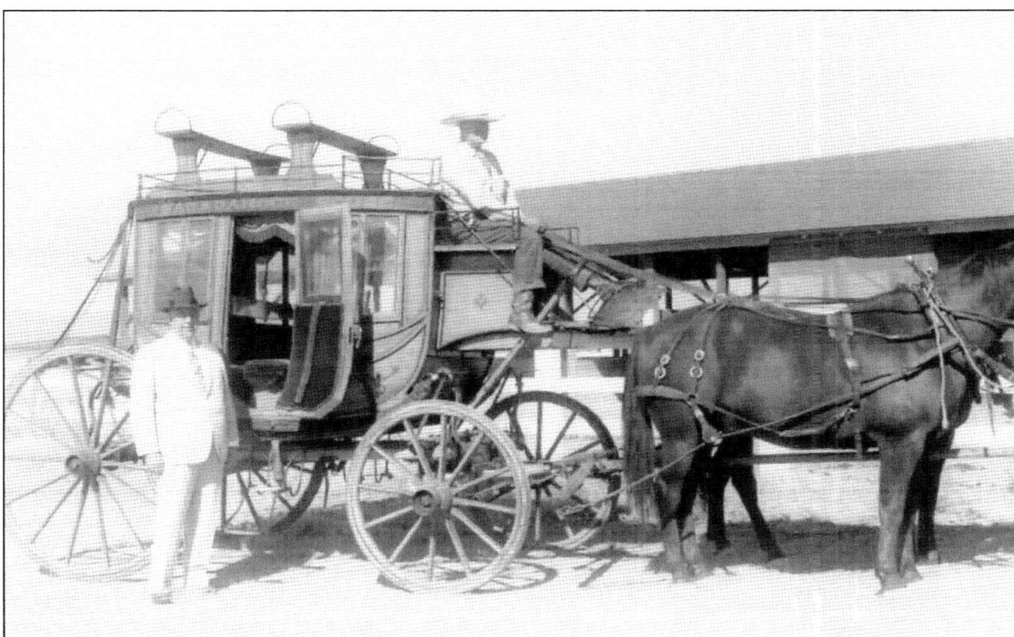

Paul Litchfield is standing beside the carriage he had shipped to Arizona in the 1930s from Boston. This carriage had belonged to his mother and it is said that his parents met sitting in this carriage. He had it shipped here for the Wigwam guests to enjoy. (Courtesy of Wigwam Resort.)

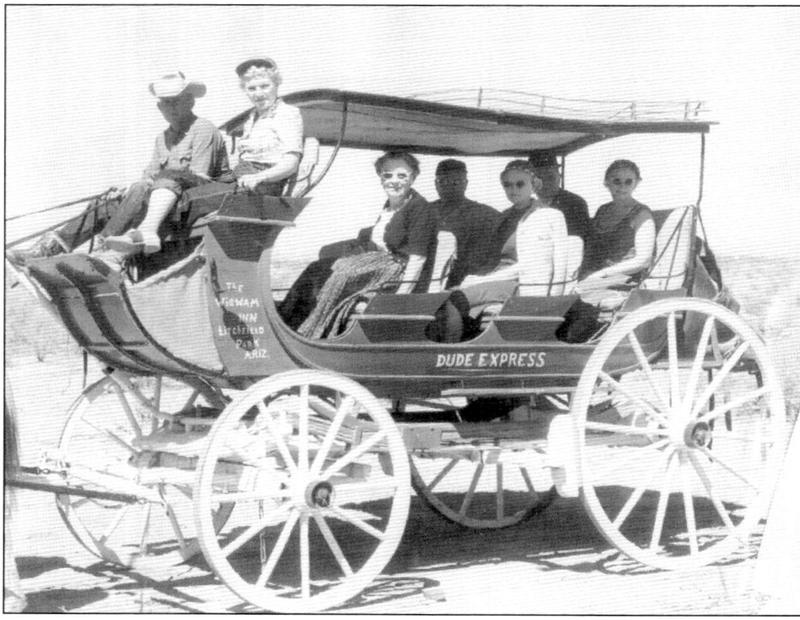


The Dude Express carriage was very popular at the Wigwam. It was available for guests to enjoy and was especially popular with families with children. Local tours were made available as a part of the dude ranch activities. (Courtesy of Wigwam Resort.)

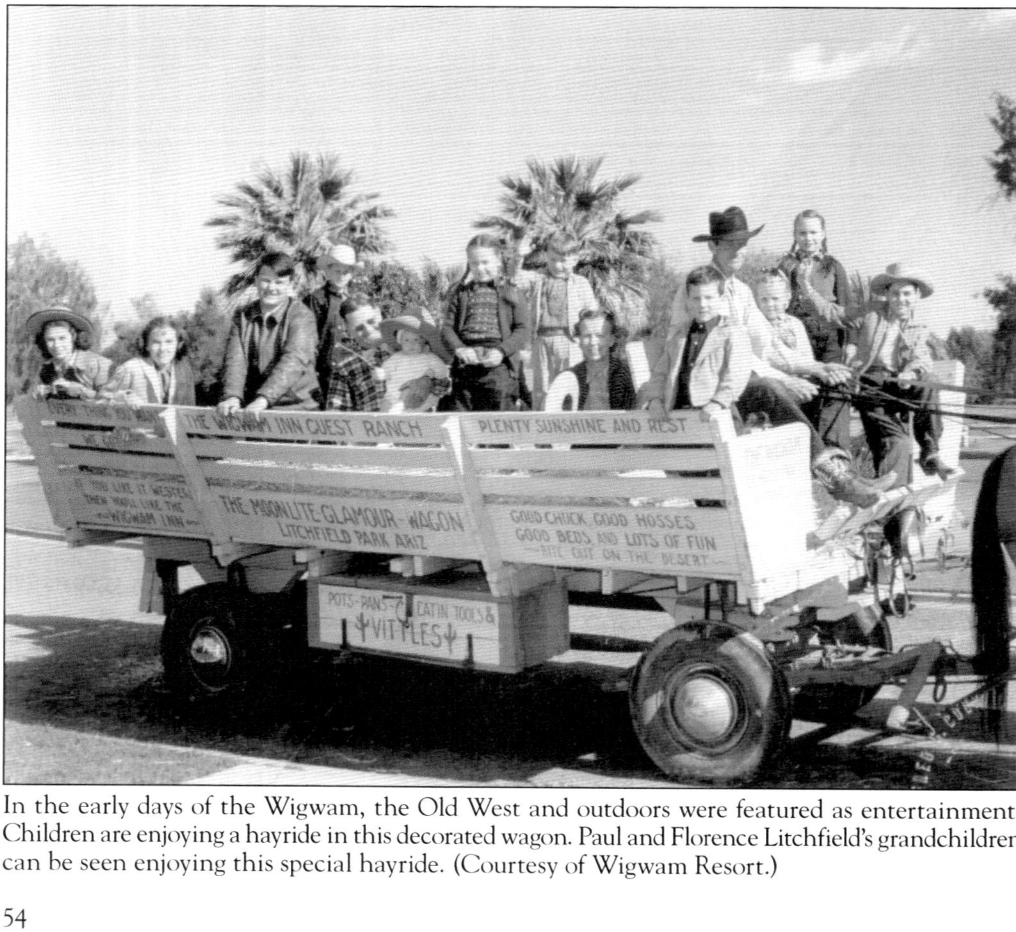


In the early days of the Wigwam, the Old West and outdoors were featured as entertainment. Children are enjoying a hayride in this decorated wagon. Paul and Florence Litchfield's grandchildren can be seen enjoying this special hayride. (Courtesy of Wigwam Resort.)

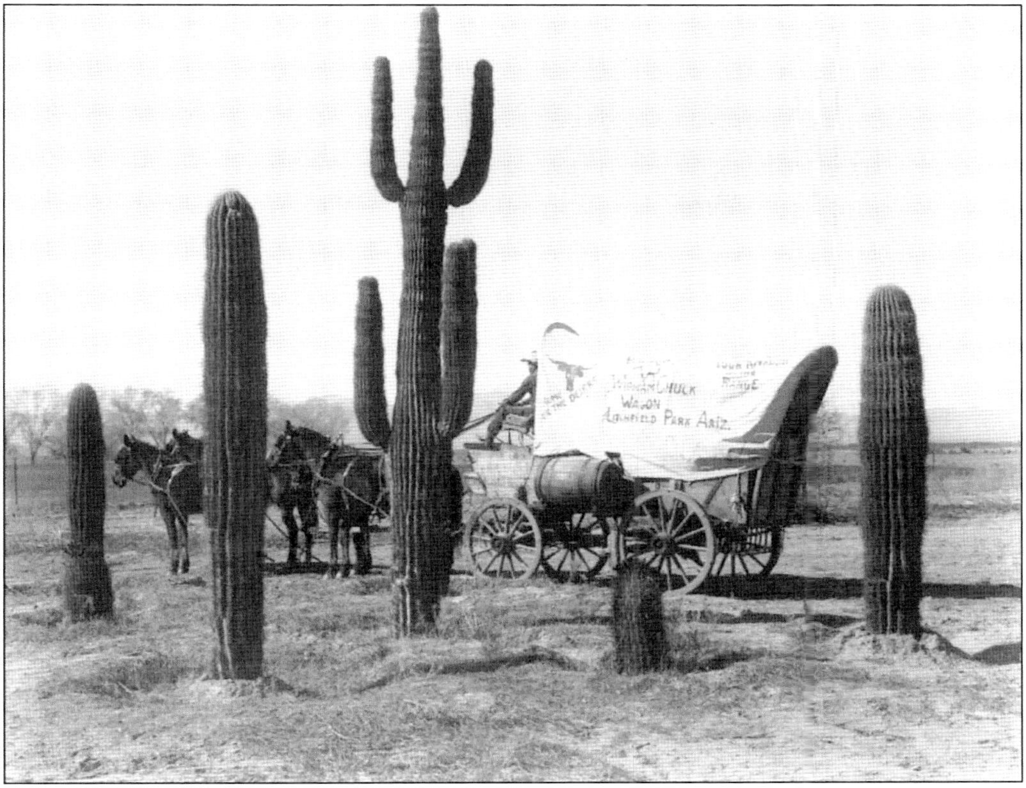


An old covered chuck wagon is seen going into the desert for a cookout. Note the barrel attached for water, and the wagon cover identifies it as a kitchen on the range. (Courtesy of Wigwam Resort.)

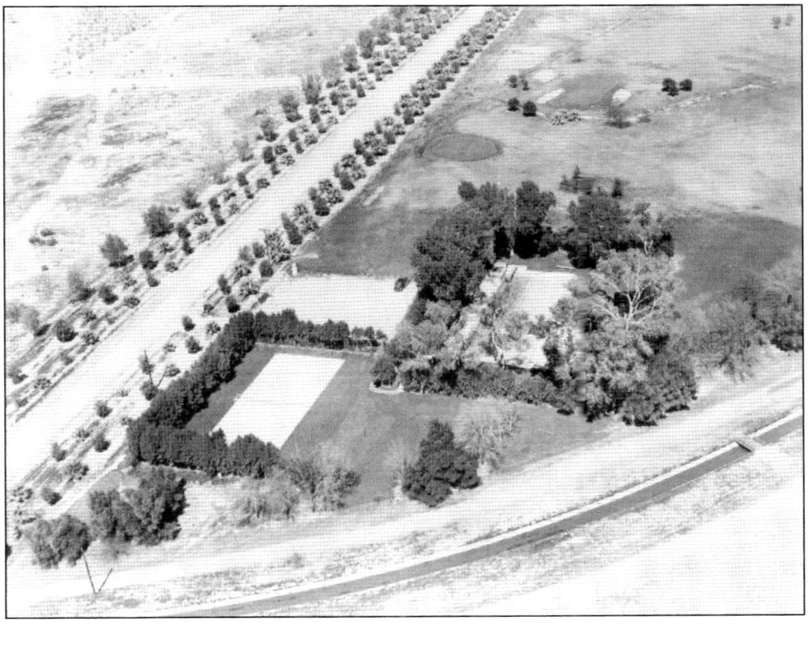

The original tennis court and pool were located east of Litchfield Avenue, where the current tennis courts are today. A golf clubhouse was built north of this area. (Courtesy of Wigwam Resort.)

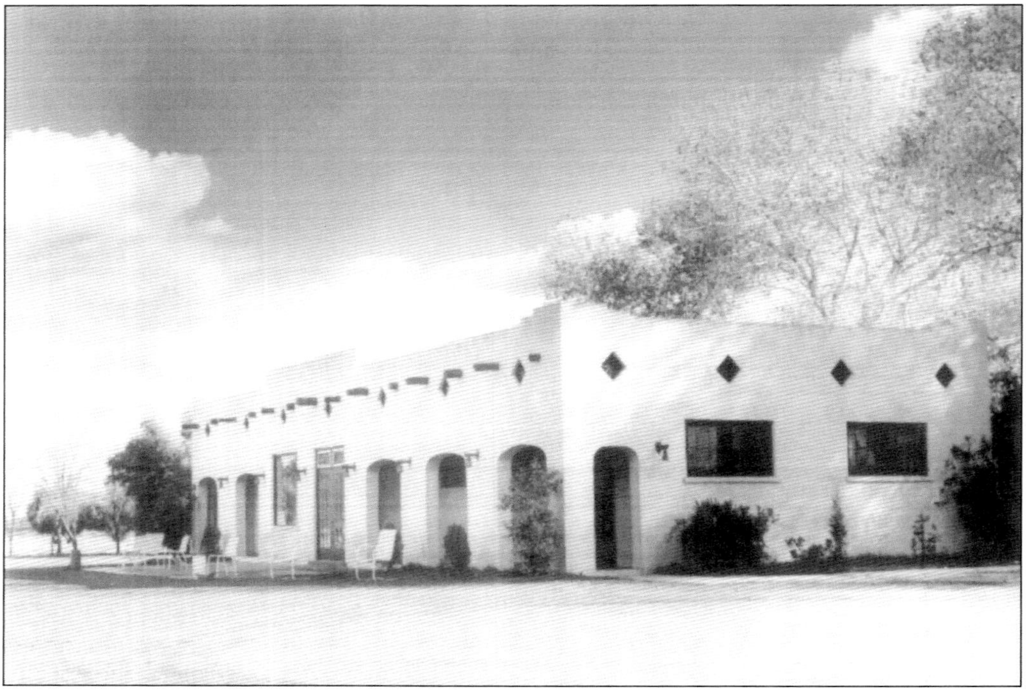

The Wigwam Golf Club memberships started in 1955, and its first president was Chris Fuller. The clubhouse, shown here, was destroyed by fire in July 1969 and rebuilt in 1971. (Courtesy of Wigwam Resort.)

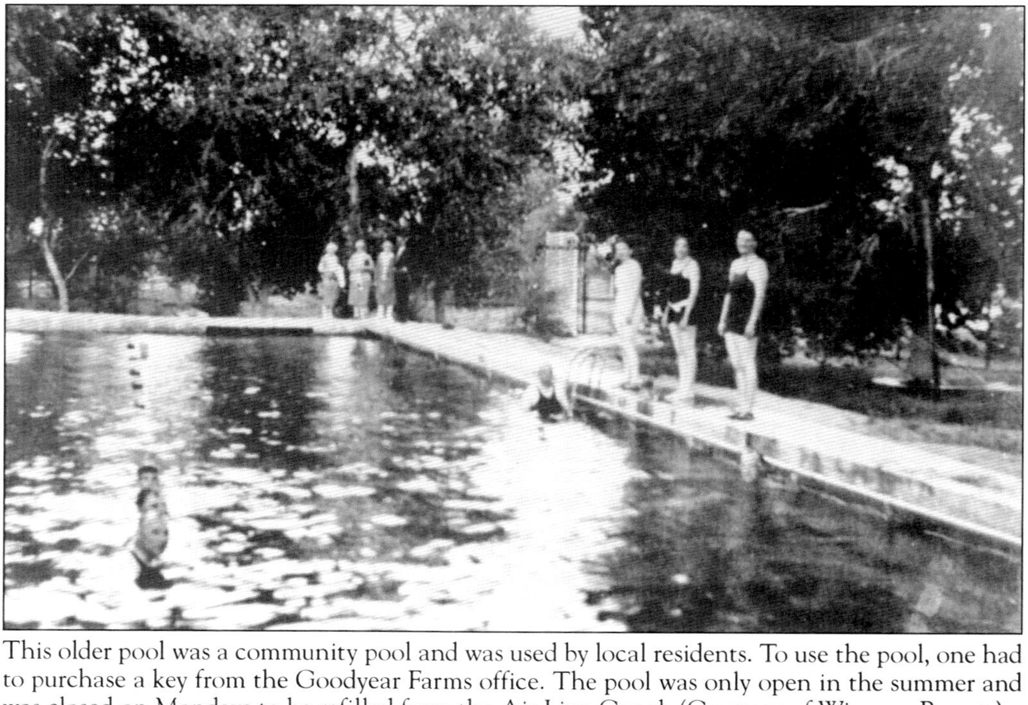

This older pool was a community pool and was used by local residents. To use the pool, one had to purchase a key from the Goodyear Farms office. The pool was only open in the summer and was closed on Mondays to be refilled from the Air Line Canal. (Courtesy of Wigwam Resort.)

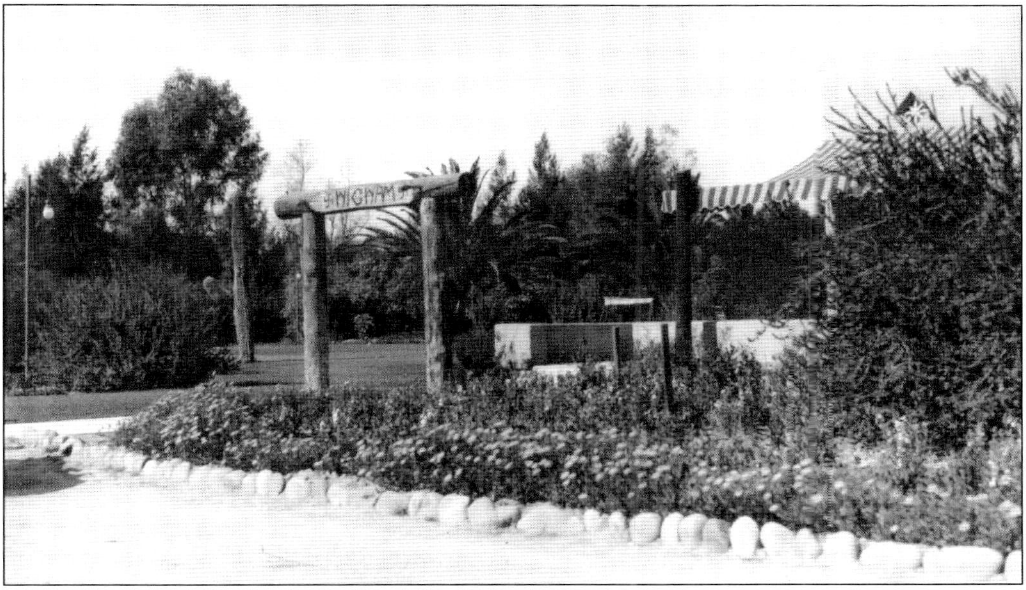


A very early picture of the front entrance to the Wigwam is seen here. It was presented as an early rustic and Western look. The current Wigwam owners have brought this same sign back to the front entrance for its historic value. (Courtesy of Wigwam Resort.)

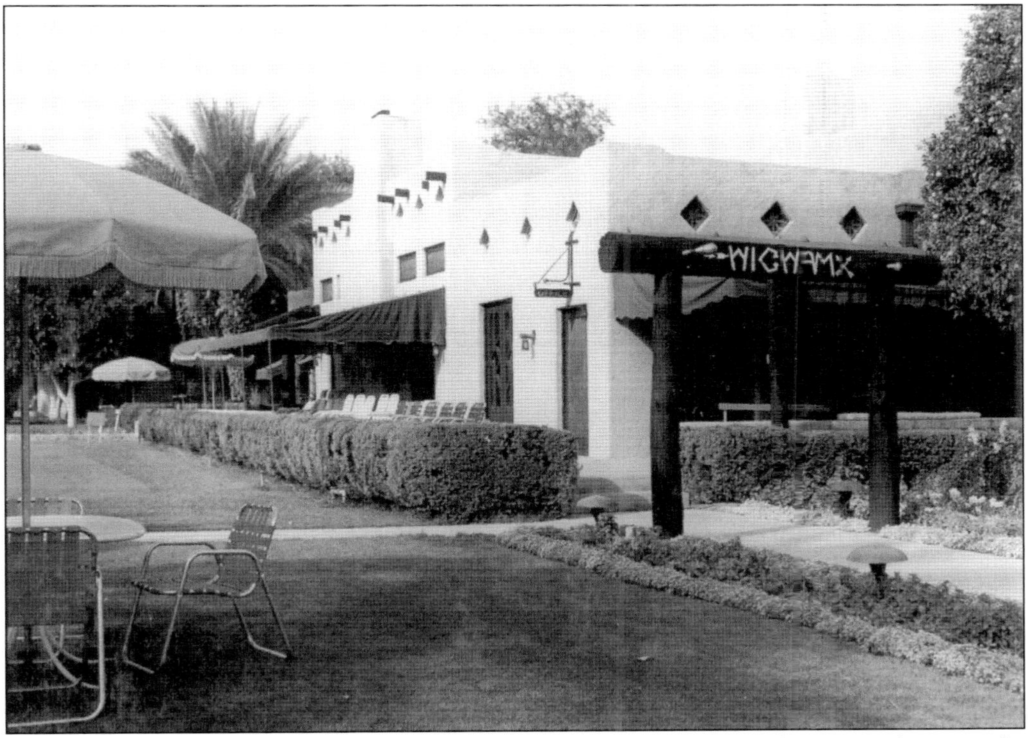


A putting green was added to the entrance area of the Wigwam. This was a fun area for guests as well as an area for competitive games while practicing their golf strokes. (Courtesy of Wigwam Resort.)

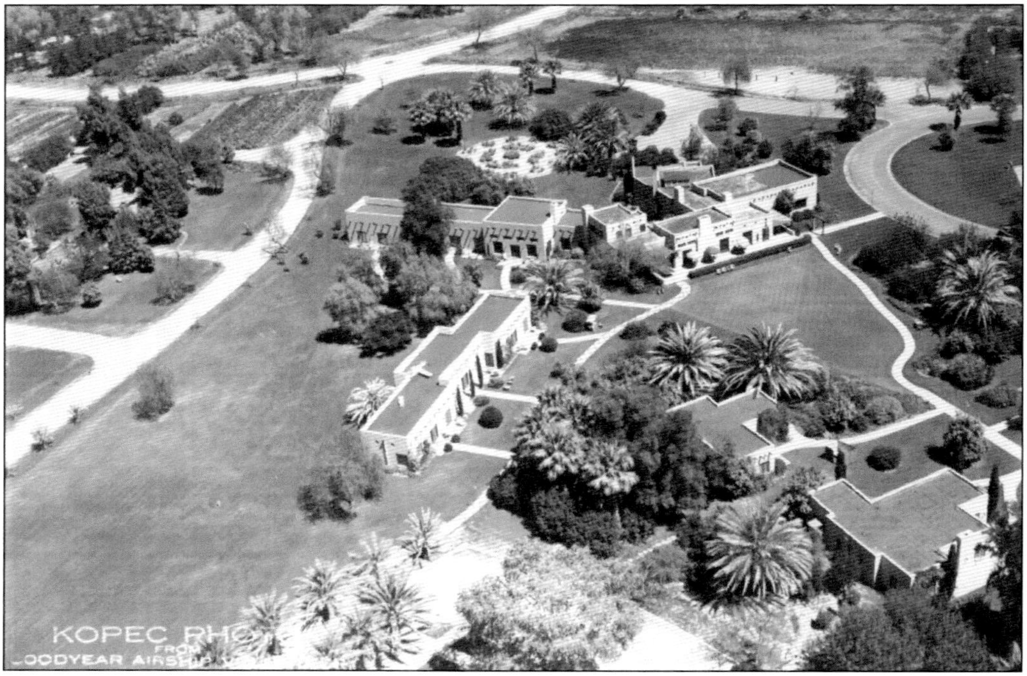


This aerial view of the Wigwam in the 1930s shows the new resort's growth since it opened in 1929. Executives were pleased with the success of the inn, and from this time on, the resort was developed as a luxury destination. The first nine-hole golf course opened in the second season, and golf soon became a popular pastime. The Wigwam closed in the summer months for many years and did not become a year-round resort until 1986. (Courtesy of Wigwam Resort.)

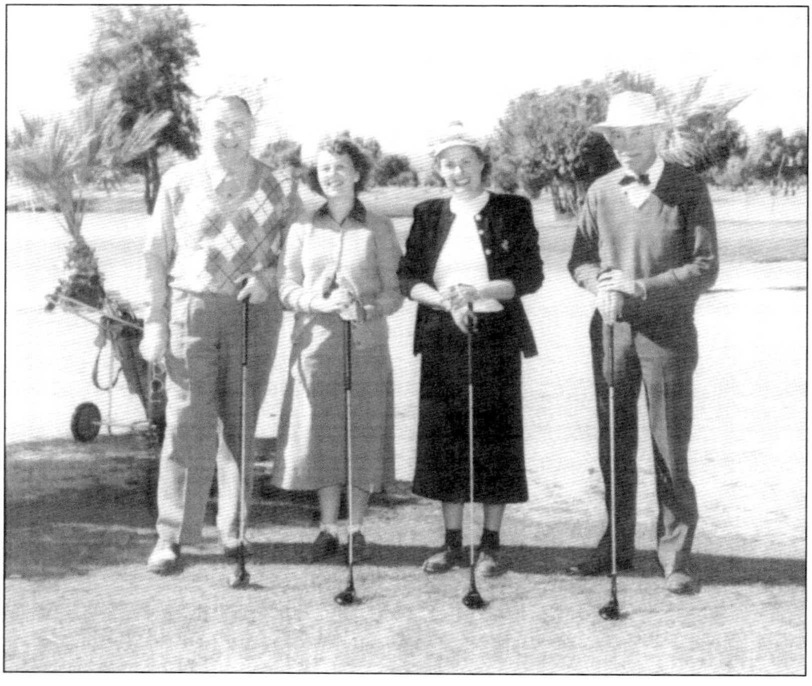

Golf is being enjoyed by Wigwam guests. It was a very social game, as shown here in the attire worn to play the game. Women enjoyed the game as well as the men. (Courtesy of Wigwam Resort.)

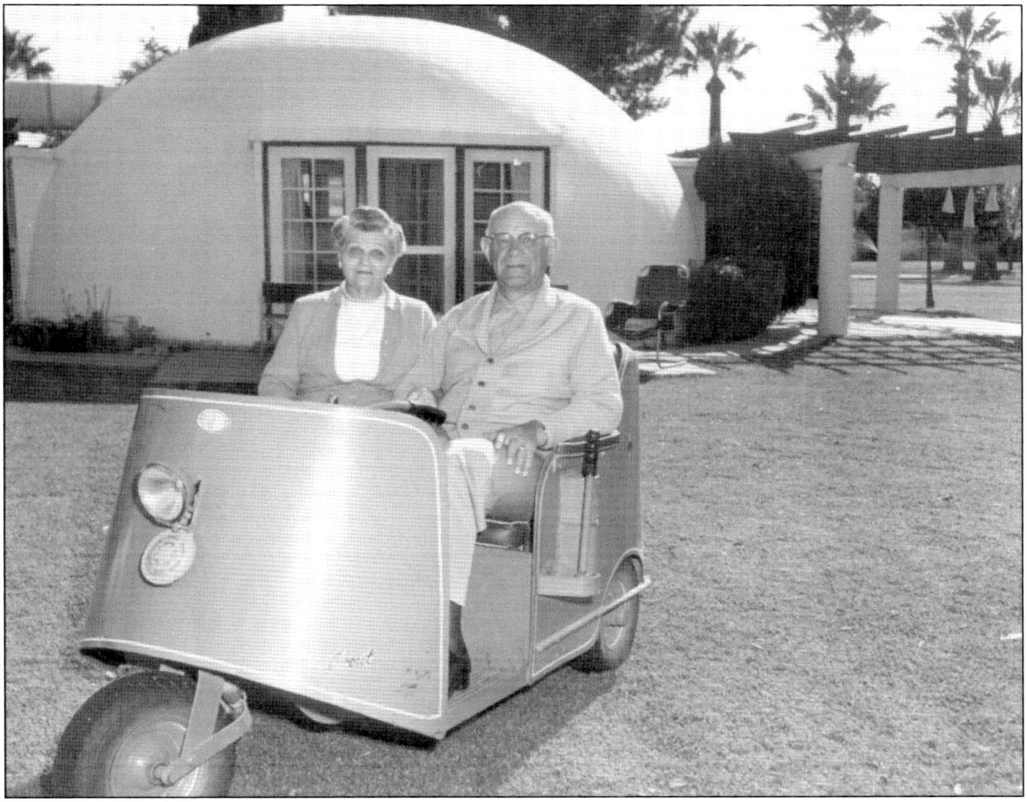

Bubble Houses were a popular sight on the Wigwam Golf Course during the late 1940s. These houses were made with a large rubber balloon and sprayed with gunite, which left a concrete shell. When the concrete dried, the balloon was deflated and removed. Wigwam guests also enjoyed the use of electric golf carts starting in the late 1950s. (Courtesy of Wigwam Resort.)

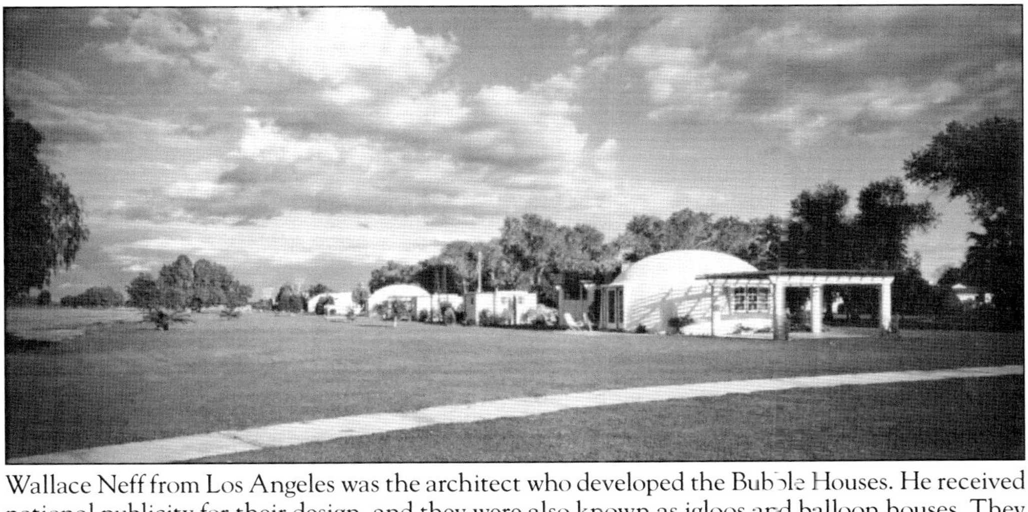

Wallace Neff from Los Angeles was the architect who developed the Bubble Houses. He received national publicity for their design, and they were also known as igloos and balloon houses. They were popular at the Wigwam from the late 1940s until the 1970s, when the concrete started to crack and they were removed. (Courtesy of Wigwam Resort.)

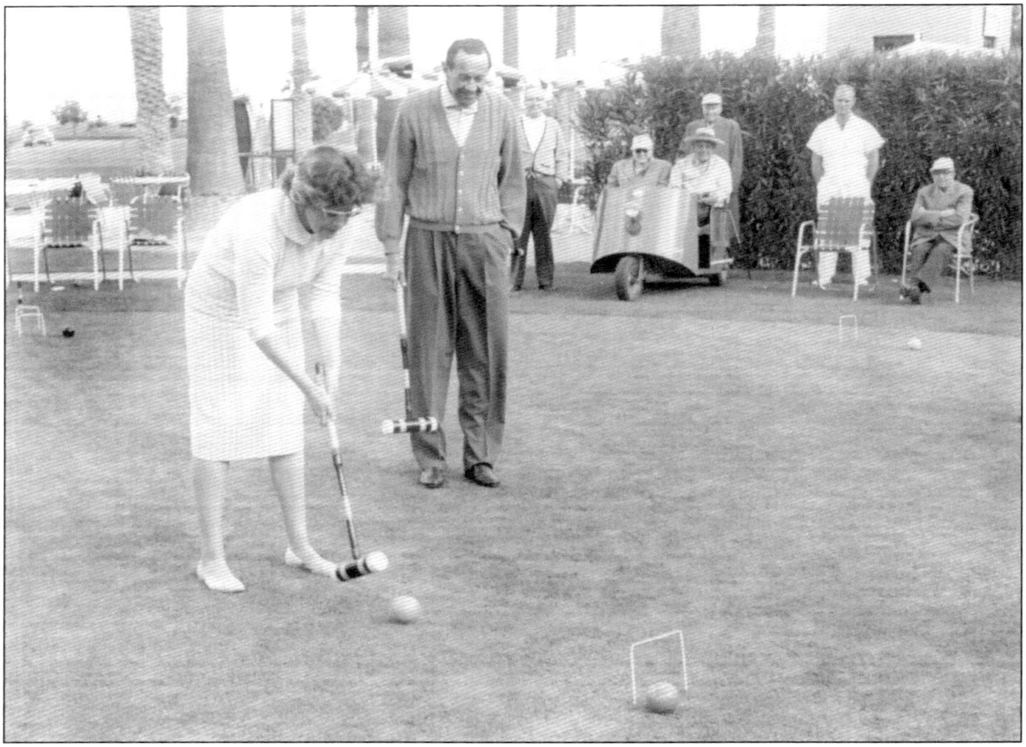
Guests of all ages enjoyed outdoor games such as croquet. (Courtesy of Wigwam Resort.)

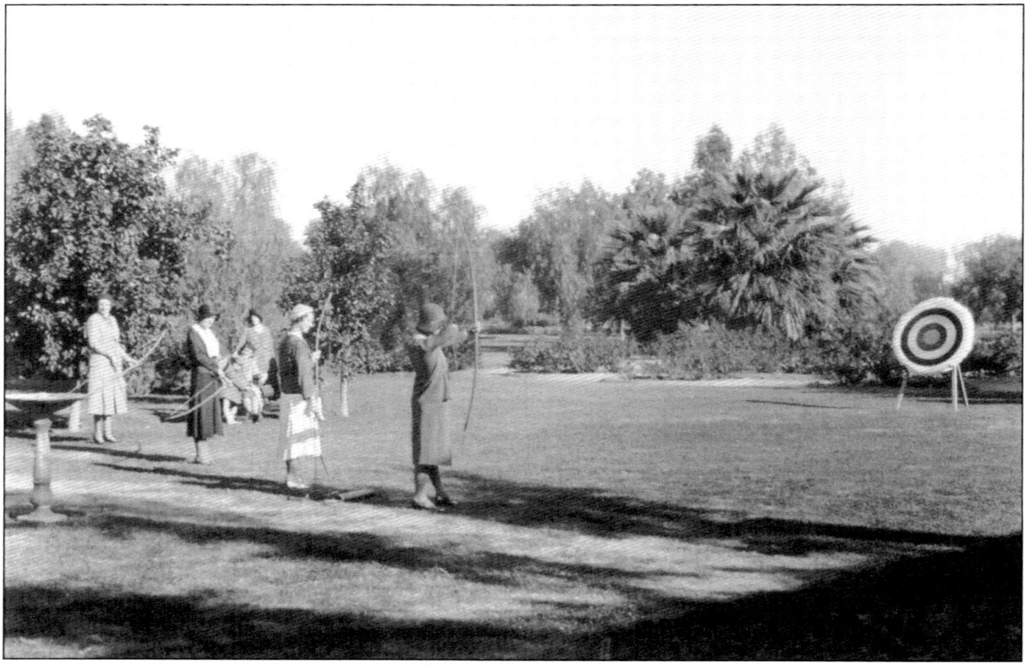
Archery was a fun outdoor sport that is not seen much in current-day resort activities. (Courtesy of Wigwam Resort.)

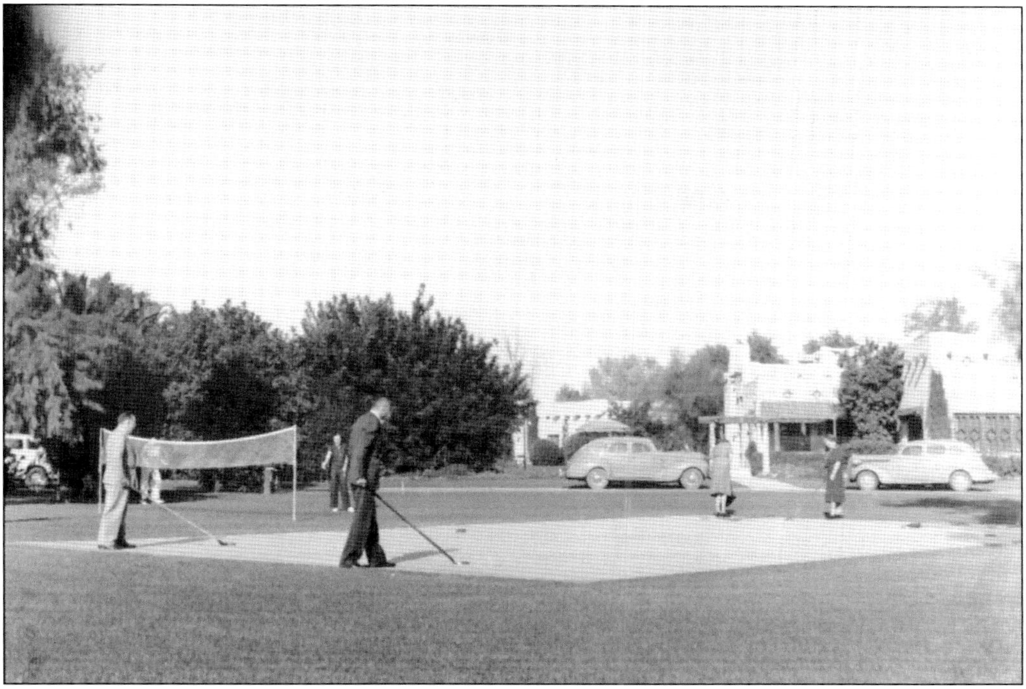

Shuffleboard was a popular outdoor sport, especially enjoyed by the older guests. (Courtesy of Wigwam Resort.)

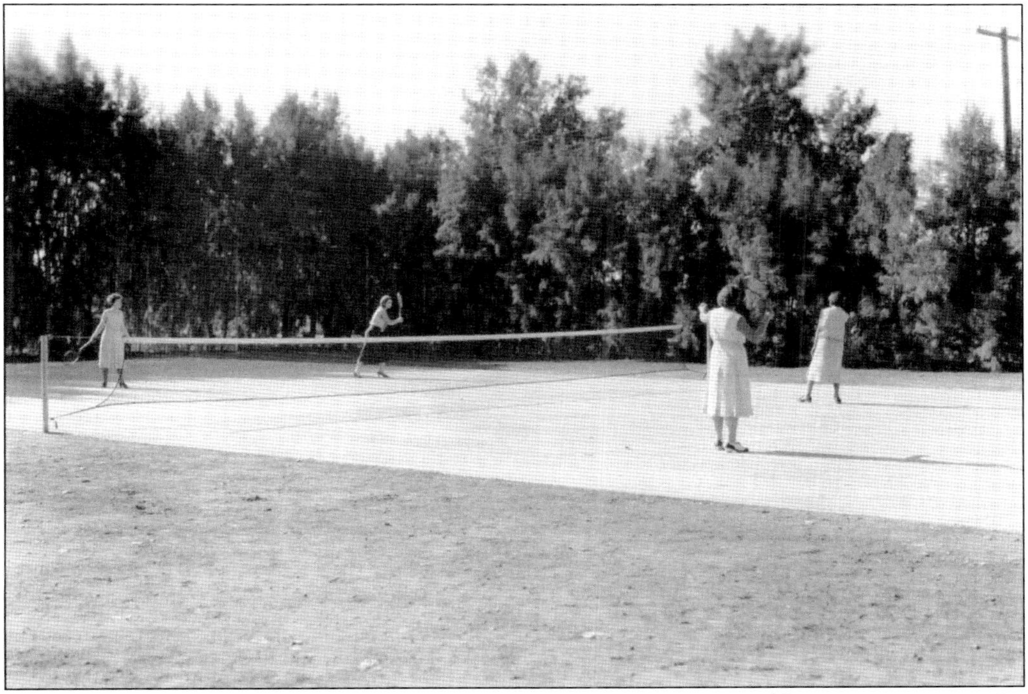

Tennis grew in popularity and is still an active outdoor sport enjoyed by many guests at the Wigwam. (Courtesy of Wigwam Resort.)

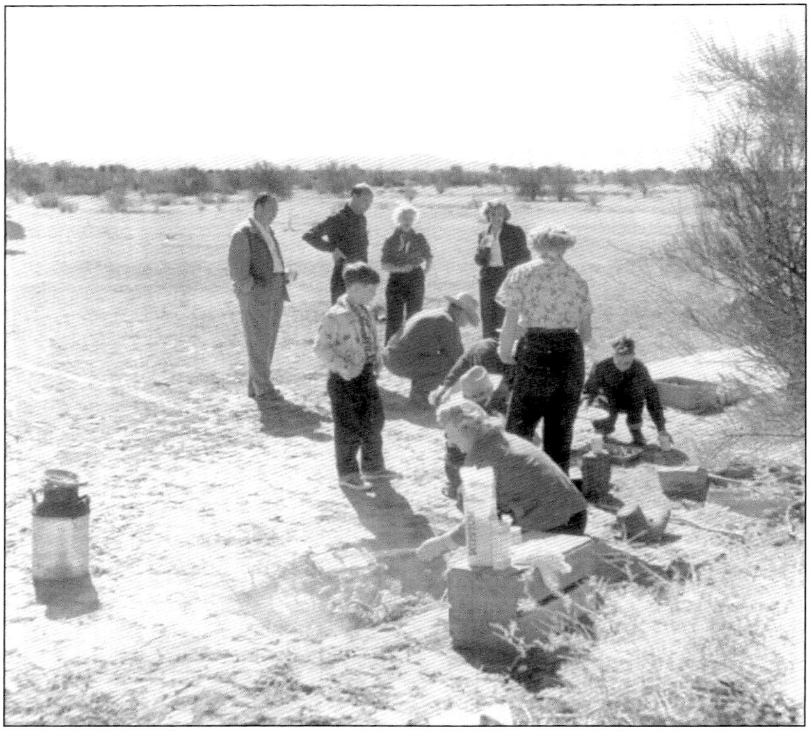

This old-fashioned fire pit is a reminder of the very early days of the Old West when food was cooked outside. This dates to the early Wigwam as guests enjoyed the outdoors. (Courtesy of Wigwam Resort.)

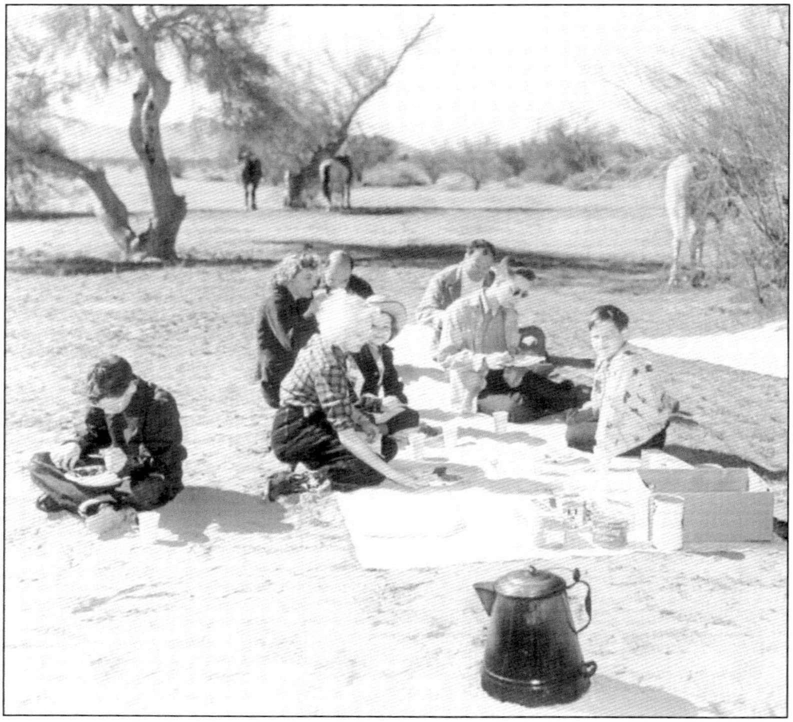

Wigwam guests enjoy the open spaces of the desert for an old-fashioned picnic. The sheet on the ground and the horses in the background provide a clue as to the entertainment during the early days of the Wigwam. (Courtesy of Wigwam Resort.)

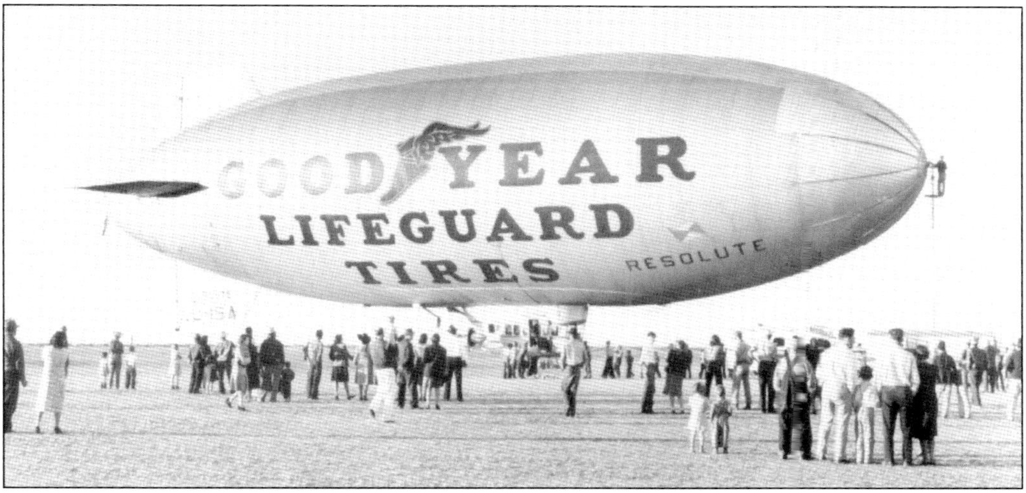


The Goodyear blimp *Resolute* was a common site at the Wigwam and the West Valley as it was used to transport guests on sightseeing tours of the Salt River Valley. In 1930, a private landing field was built for the blimp a short distance from the Wigwam, but it was not until 1946 that a runway for planes was provided. This improvement was an added convenience for guests wishing to land near the resort. (Courtesy of Wigwam Resort.)

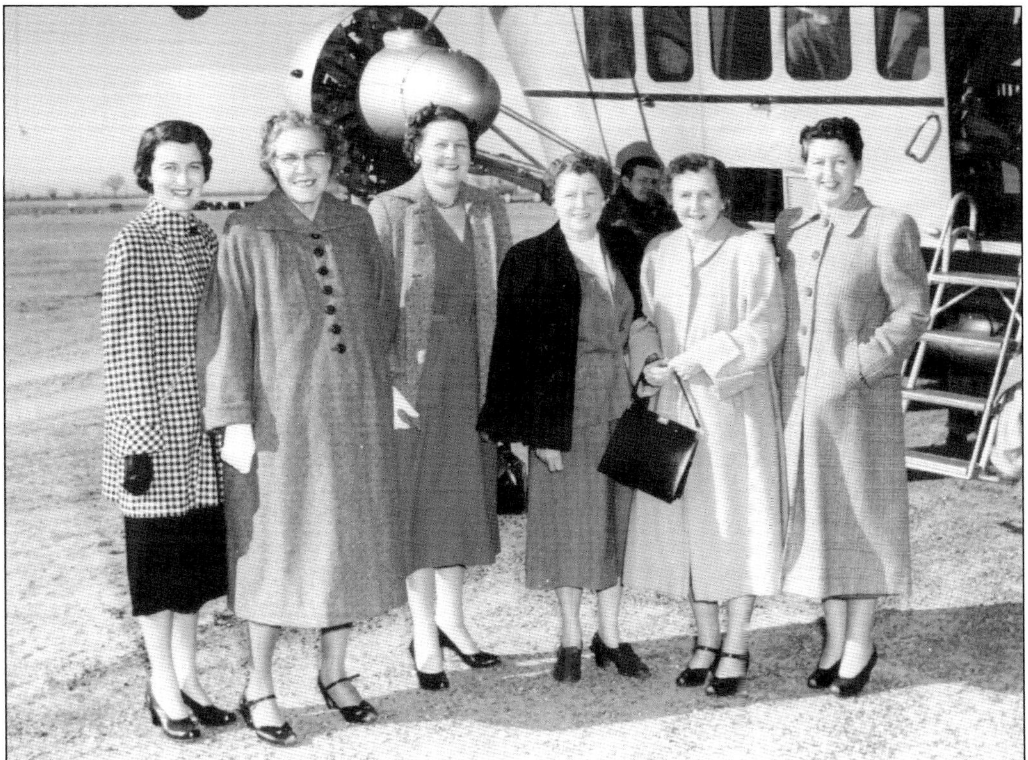

In the 1940s, wives of local executives enjoy a blimp ride at the Wigwam. They are, from left to right, Roberta Hilton, Leck Owens, Dora Kring, Ethel McMicken, Florence Litchfield, and Grace Humphrey. (Courtesy of Wigwam Resort.)

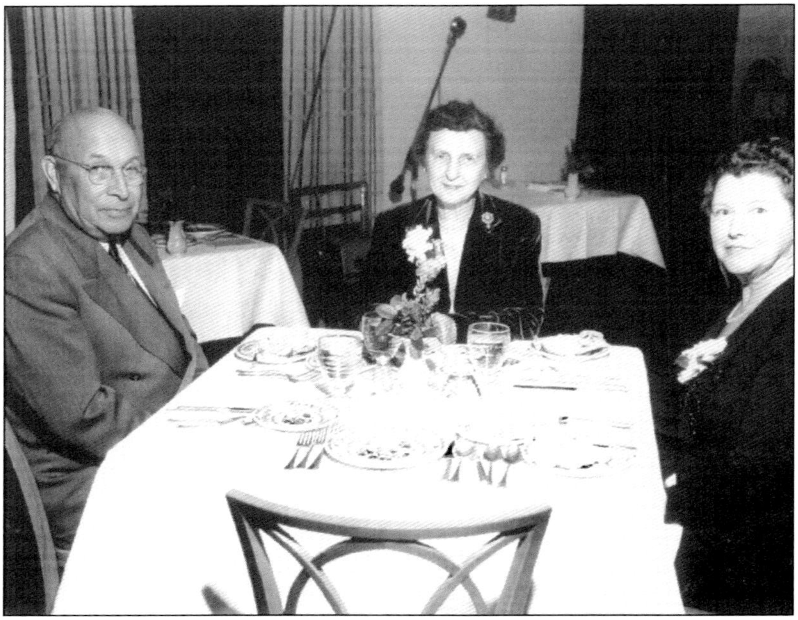

Enjoying an evening out at the Wigwam dining room are Kenneth McMicken, a cousin to Paul Litchfield; farm superintendent Florence Litchfield in the center; and Ethel McMicken to the right. (Courtesy of Wigwam Resort.)

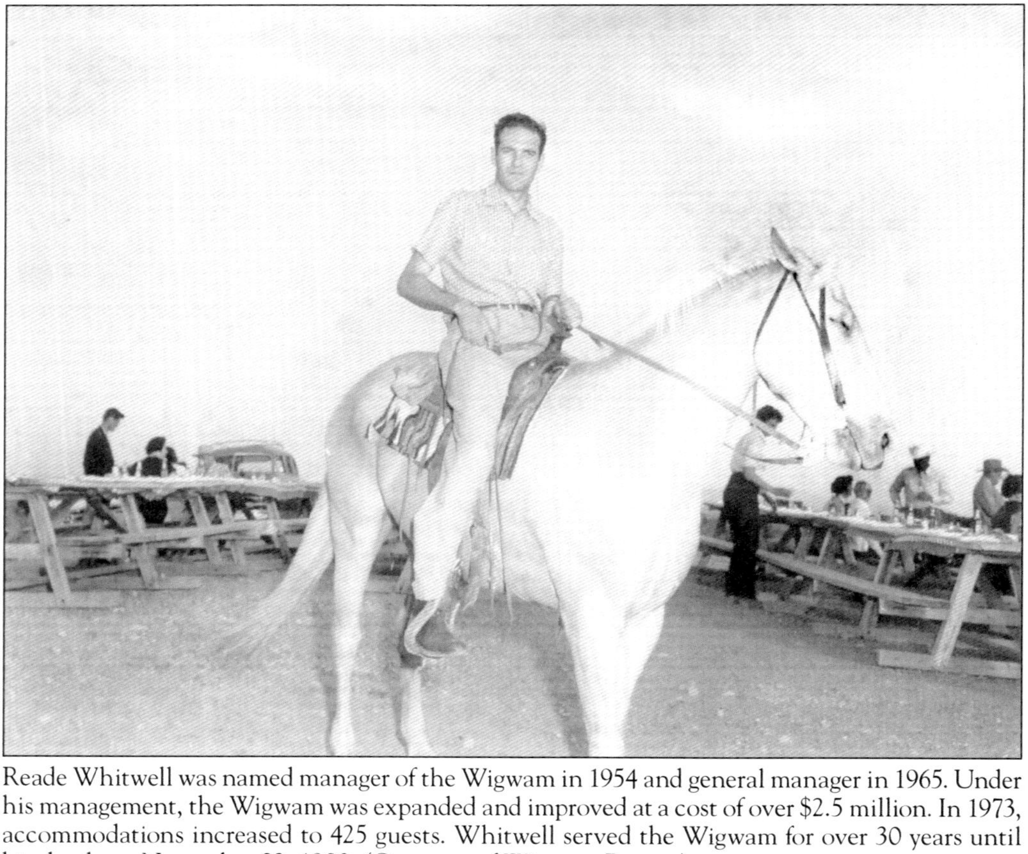

Reade Whitwell was named manager of the Wigwam in 1954 and general manager in 1965. Under his management, the Wigwam was expanded and improved at a cost of over $2.5 million. In 1973, accommodations increased to 425 guests. Whitwell served the Wigwam for over 30 years until his death on November 22, 1980. (Courtesy of Wigwam Resort.)

Millicent DeBelle Whitwell, wife of Reade, was a talented musician and made noteworthy contributions to the cultural development of the community. She was active in civic and theatrical projects in the area. She served as organist and choir director for The Church at Litchfield Park and provided piano and organ music for many public and private functions. She worked closely with the local schoolchildren and developed choirs and music programs. (Courtesy of Wigwam Resort.)

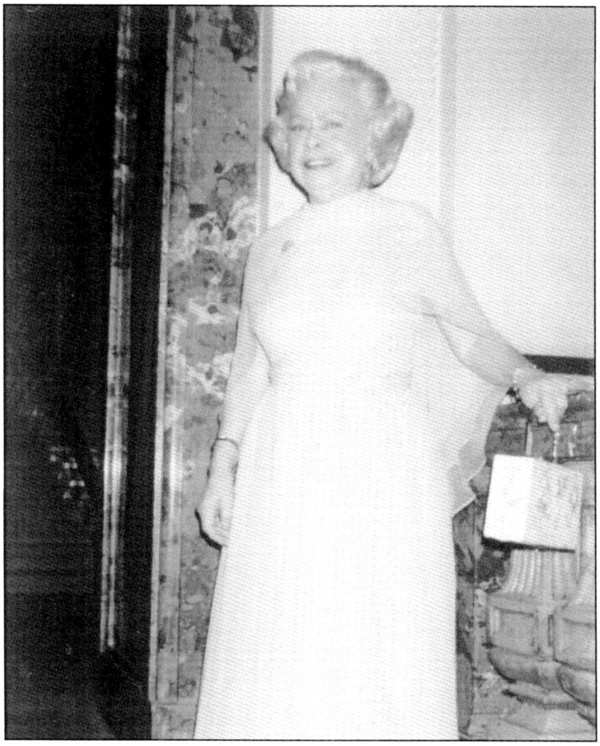

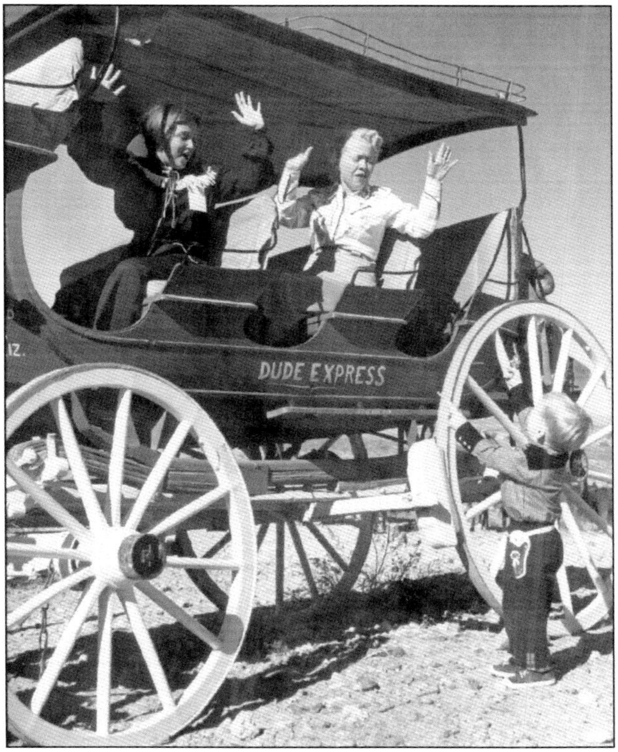


Millicent is seen enjoying a ride in the Dude Express carriage at the Wigwam until she is surprised by a young cowboy guest who has seen too many Western movies. This photograph relays her playful side and the fact that she enjoyed children. (Courtesy of Wigwam Resort.)

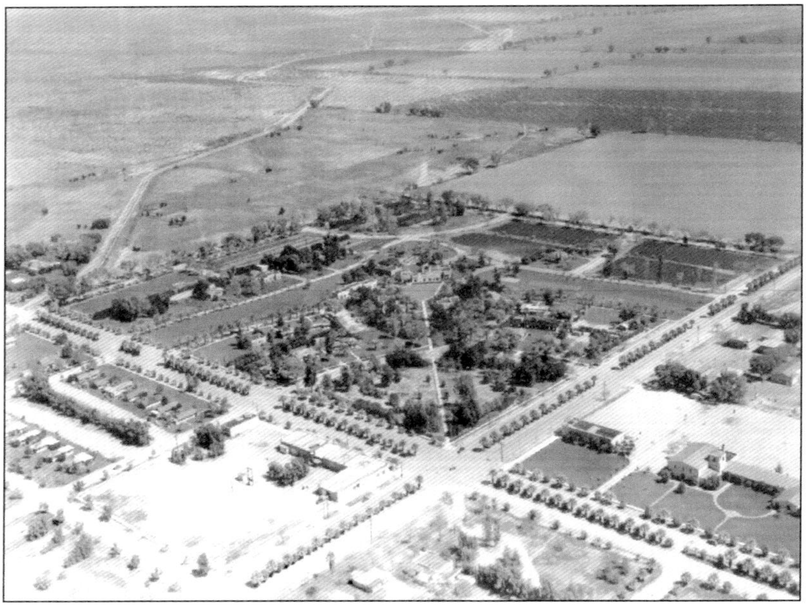

Seen here is an overview of Litchfield Park with a view of the Air Line Canal. The canal, a long flow that can be seen on the left, is moving the length of the property. This gives a view of the lifeline that provided water for the upkeep of the golf courses and still runs there today. (Courtesy of Wigwam Resort.)

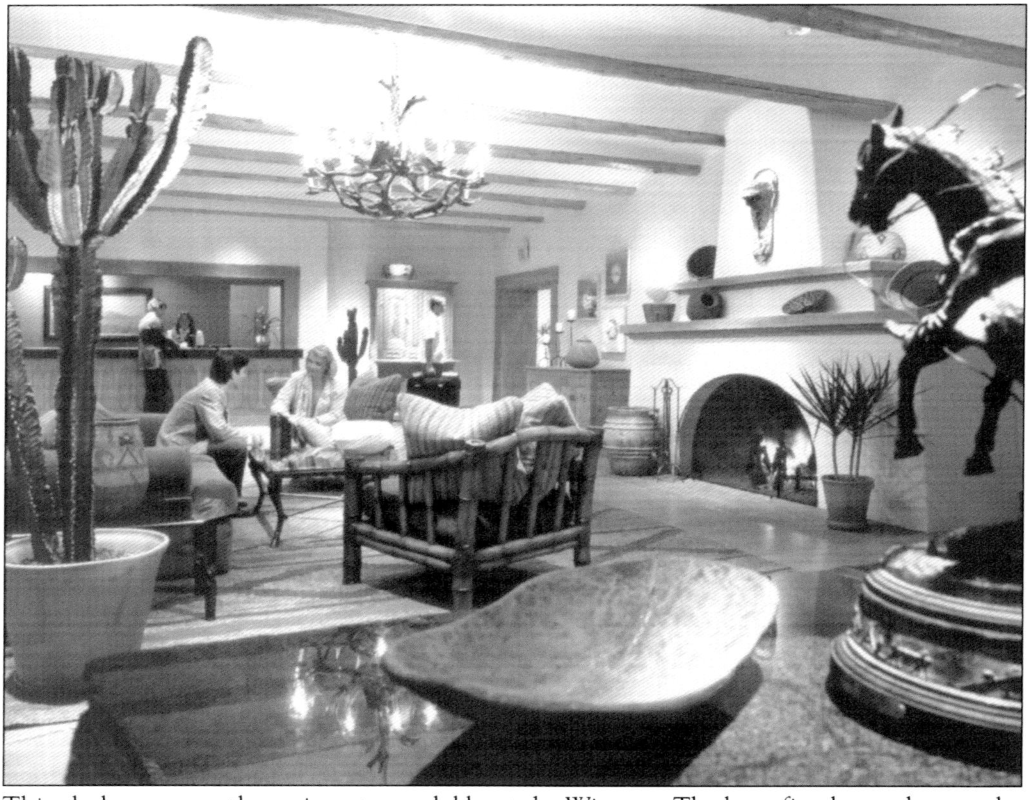

This plush room was the main entrance lobby at the Wigwam. The large fireplace enhances the numerous Western artworks and antiques. The ceiling beams are original, and so is the maple slat floor. (Courtesy of Wigwam Resort.)

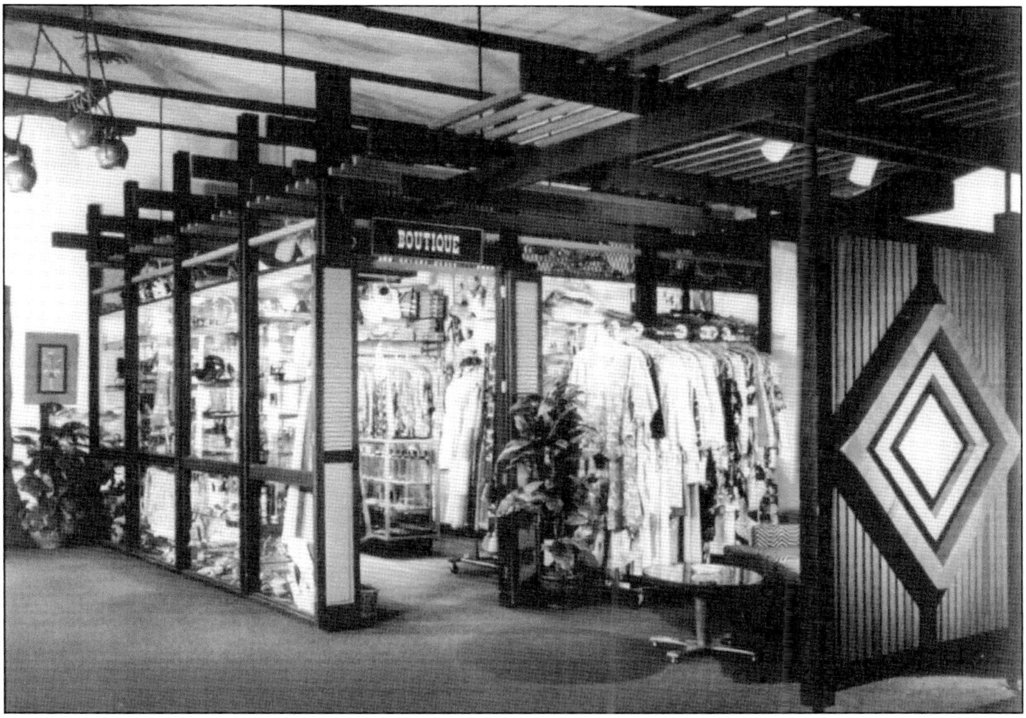


The boutique and gift shops were added in later years for the shopping convenience and pleasure of Wigwam guests and the local community. Notice the god's-eye or diamond-shaped decor on the wall, as it was symbolic of the Wigwam. (Courtesy of Wigwam Resort.)

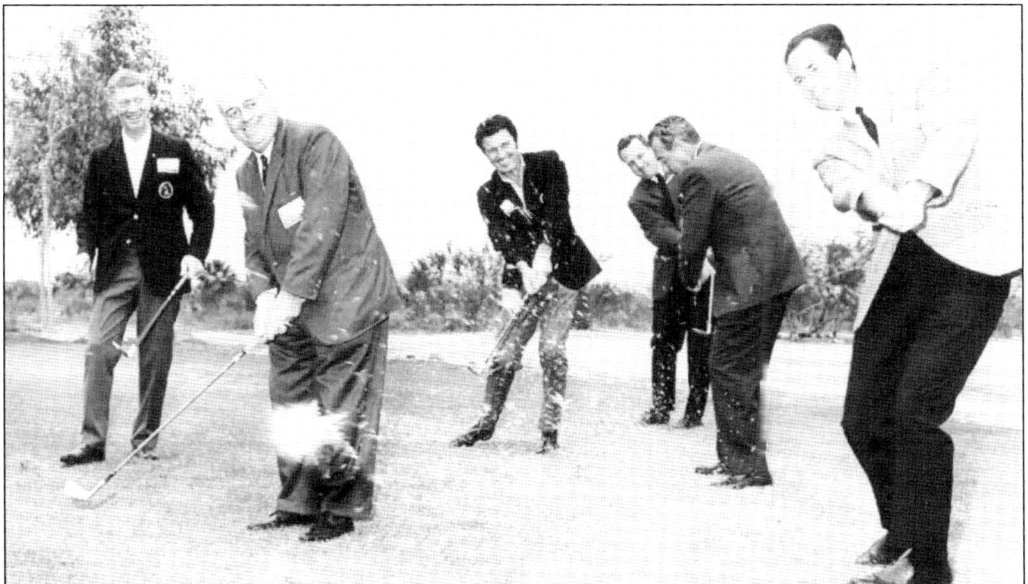

Noted golfers are trying out the new Wigwam golf course. Pictured from left to right are Red Allen and Robert Trent Jones along with professional golfers and local dignitaries trying out the new course designed by Robert Trent Jones. (Courtesy of Wigwam Resort.)

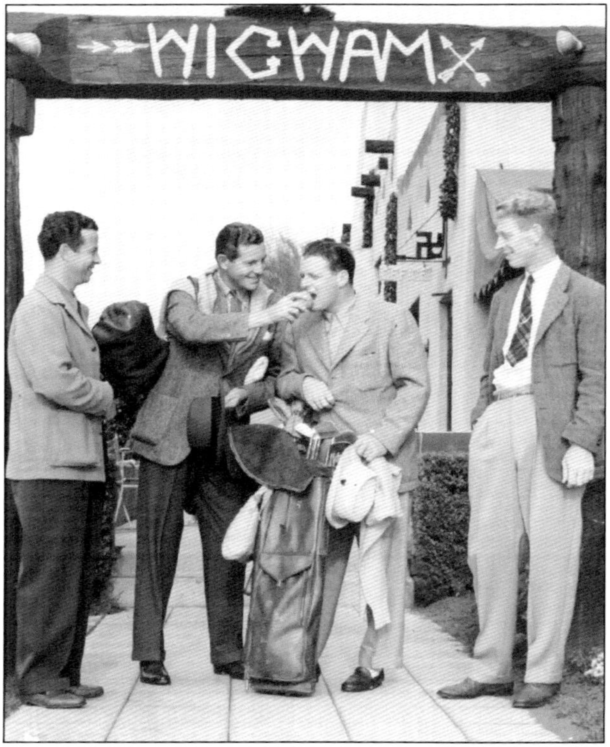


The first golf pro at the Wigwam was Johnny Turnac. In 1935, V.O. "Red" Allen succeeded Turnac, and he was the pro for the next 41 years. Red retired in 1976. Following Red as Wigwam pro were his son Doug and his grandson Craig. Pictured here, from left to right, are Wigwam manager Murray Stevenson, Horton Smith, prior Masters champion Jimmy Thompson, and Red Allen. (Courtesy of Wigwam Resort.)

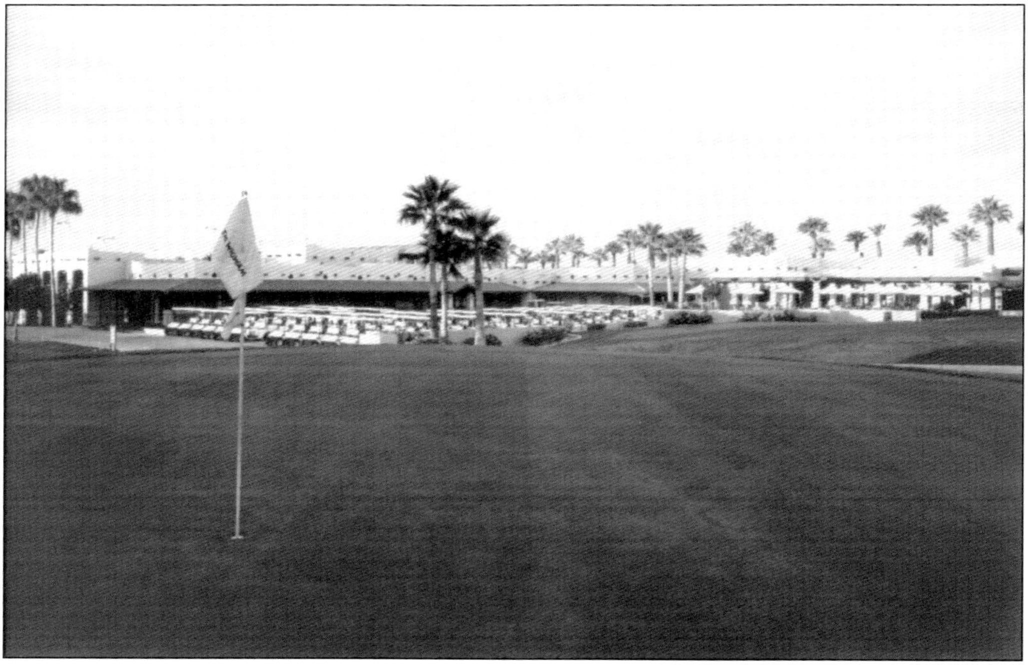

A more modern-day look shows the clubhouse and the Wigwam Resort with the many golf carts waiting for golfers. The Wigwam Resort and the three golf courses have grown into a premier vacation spot in the Southwest. (Courtesy of Wigwam Resort.)

# *Five*

# Diversified Farm Development

By the late 1930s, the Litchfield Ranch was well launched on a more diversified farm program, and it continued into the early and mid-1940s. Cotton production was reduced following the 1929 stock market crash. Much of Goodyear's land was leased or rented through 1935.

Practically all of the idle land was converted into pasture for grazing several thousand head of sheep and cattle. Citrus trees were planted, and as cotton prices rose, cotton was again planted. Pima cotton was practically abandoned, since Goodyear was turning to the use of rayon for tire production. Several new enterprises developed in the mid-1940s. A grain center for treating and cleaning grain was installed. Several grain elevators were erected for storage space. Chief crops included cotton, alfalfa, barley, wheat, and sorghum grains. The name of the Southwest Cotton Company was officially changed to Goodyear Farms in 1943.

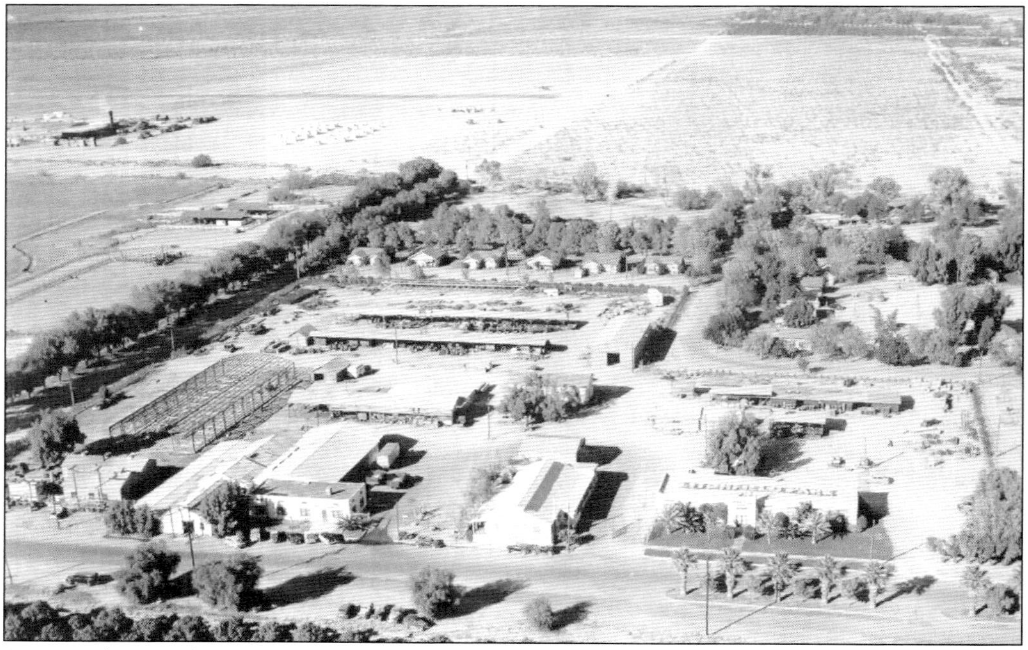

In 1948, the Goodyear Farms operation increased as shown in this aerial view of the activities. In the very back left, one can see the runway built for small planes, and just south of the runway is the mooring area for the Goodyear blimp. South of this, one can see the Wingfoot Homes being built and stored. Just south of this area is the Wigwam Stables and rodeo area. Across the tree-lined street is a farm equipment storage and maintenance area, and north of this, one can see employee housing. The Goodyear Farms headquarters building and other farm office buildings are seen in front. A large citrus orchard is seen across the street. (Courtesy of the City of Litchfield Park.)

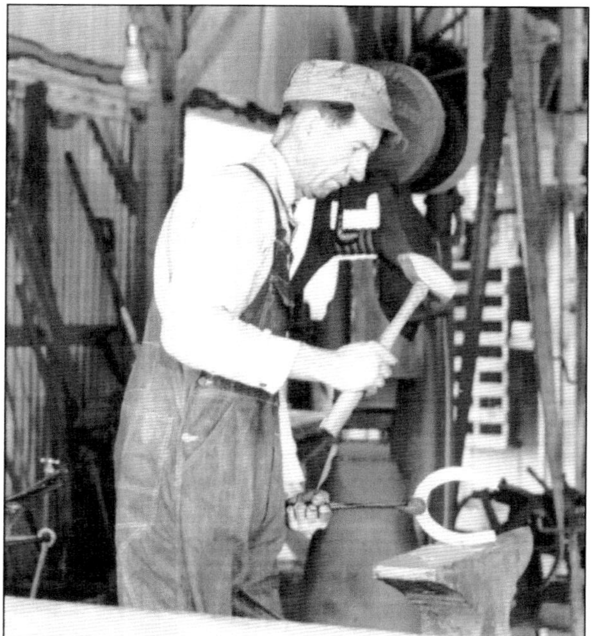

In the first years of activity, a small field office was placed just northwest of the downtown area. Buildings were erected for a warehouse, machine shop, carpenter shop, and blacksmith shop. Pictured here is a blacksmith in one of the early shops. (Courtesy of the City of Litchfield Park.)

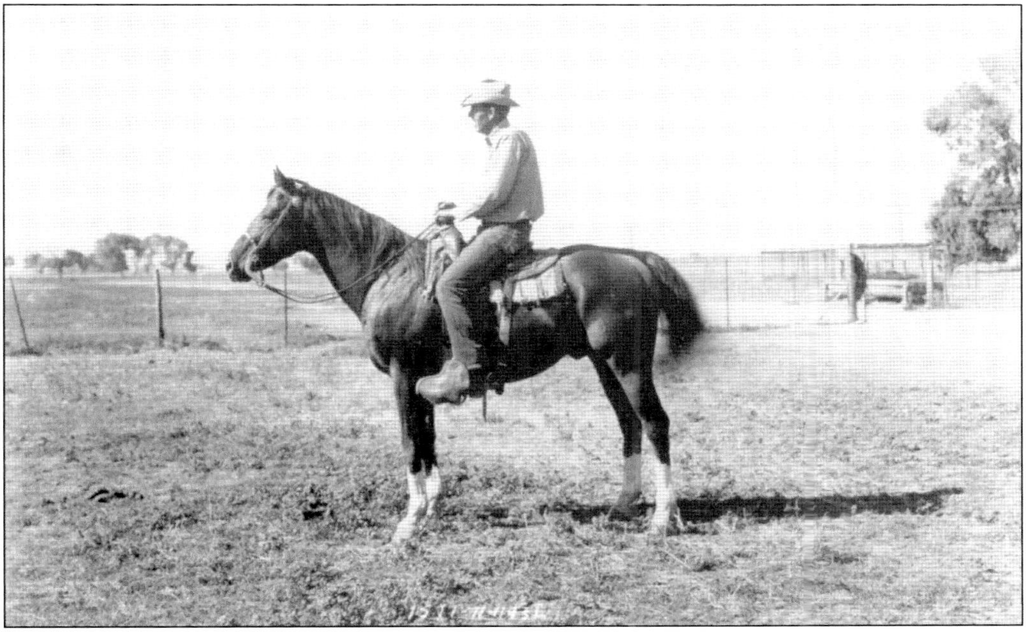

King of the Litchfield horse herd was Galus, a chestnut-colored stallion owned by the US Army and at the ranch on loan from the Army's Remount Branch. He was handpicked by ranch manager K.B. McMicken and the Army to be shipped to the ranch after experts had studied the Litchfield herd and the horse handlers. (Courtesy of the City of Litchfield Park.)

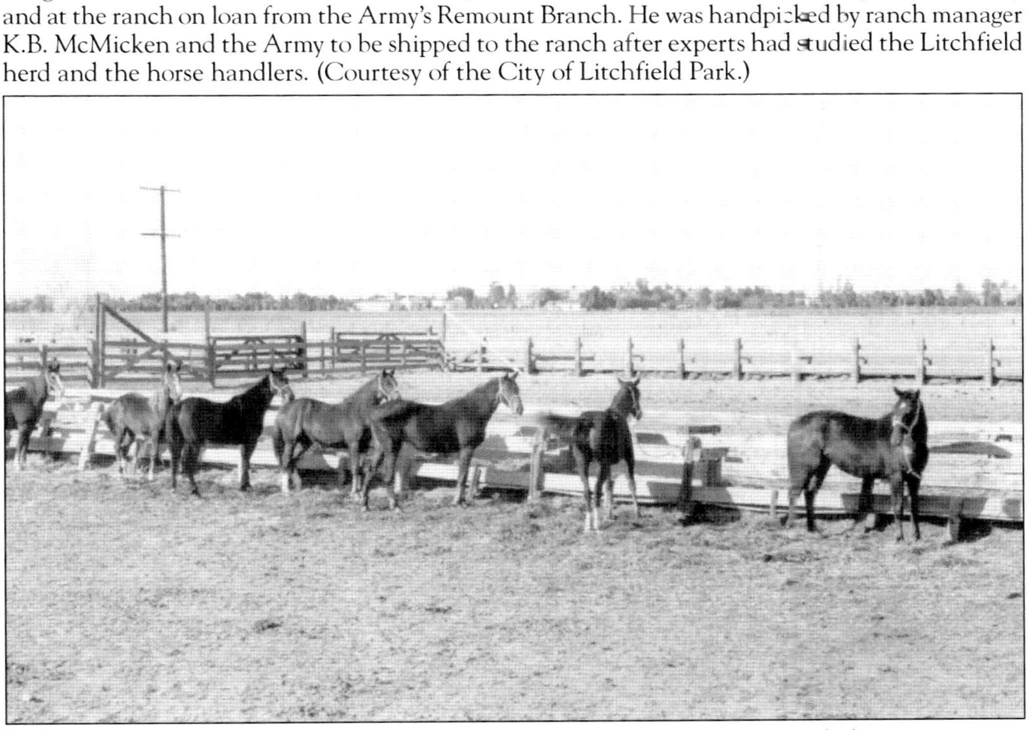

Horses always had their place in the ranch operations. When raising cattle became a major operation, their importance increased. The Wigwam opened in 1929 as a dude ranch, and there was a need for horses for guests. Cows, horses, and pleasure saddle-mount horses showed the diversified use of livestock at the Goodyear Ranch. (Courtesy of the City of Litchfield Park.)

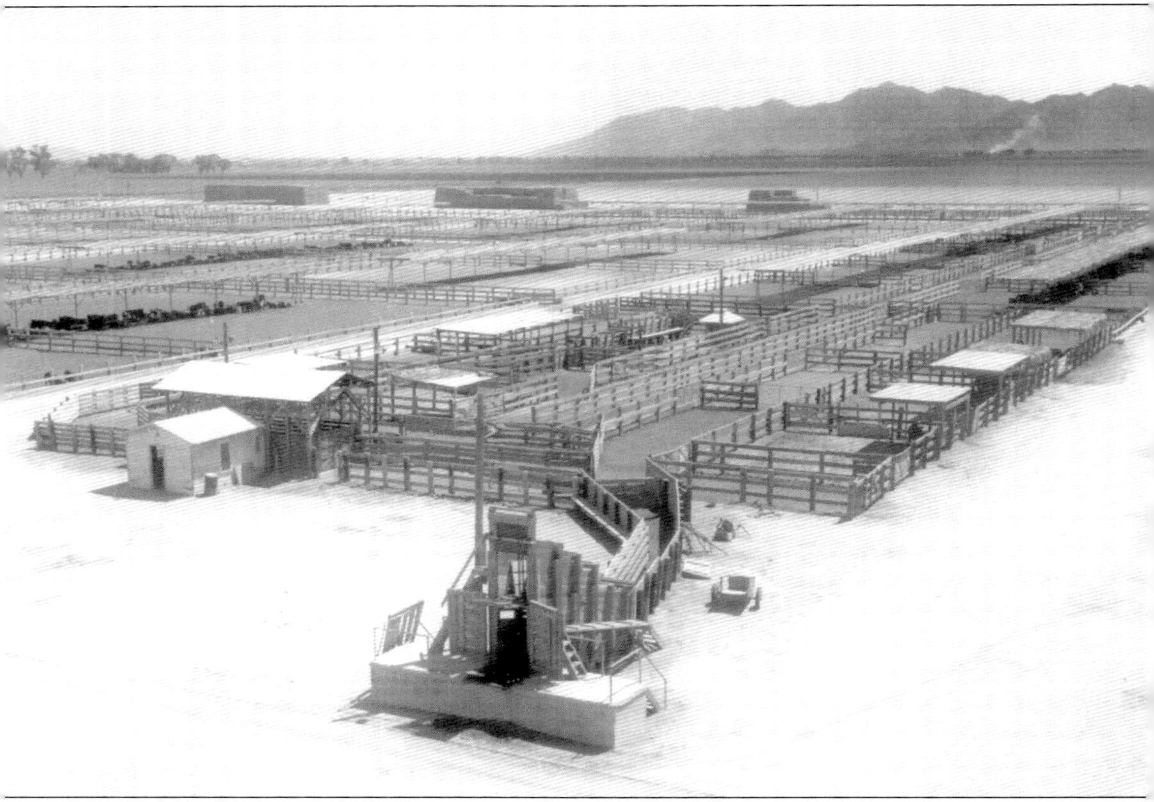

The cattle operation at Goodyear Farms, which started in 1950, grew into a very large operation under the management of James (Jim) Humphrey. He started contracting cattle to be brought in from farmers around the country. They were shipped by railroad, and a railroad spur, as seen in this picture, brought the cattle directly to the feedlot, where they were unloaded. The cattle pens held 100 to 200 cattle per pen, and if stretched end to end, the pens would extend six miles. When palm trees along Litchfield Road were trimmed, the palm fronds were used to cover the pens to keep the cattle cool. The pens were located on current-day Litchfield Road between Indian School Road and Thomas Road. Goodyear no longer owned cattle after it started contracting with farmers. (Courtesy of the City of Litchfield Park.)

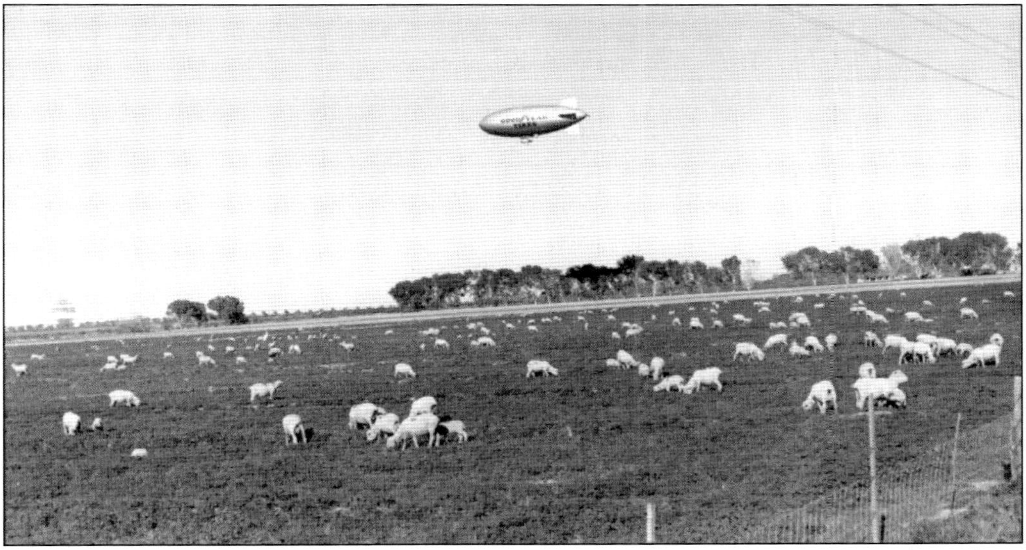

One of the largest area sheep operations was in Litchfield. The Espil family had very large sheep herds, and they were fed from food harvested by Goodyear Farms. They are being serenaded by the Goodyear blimp. (Courtesy of Wigwam Resort.)

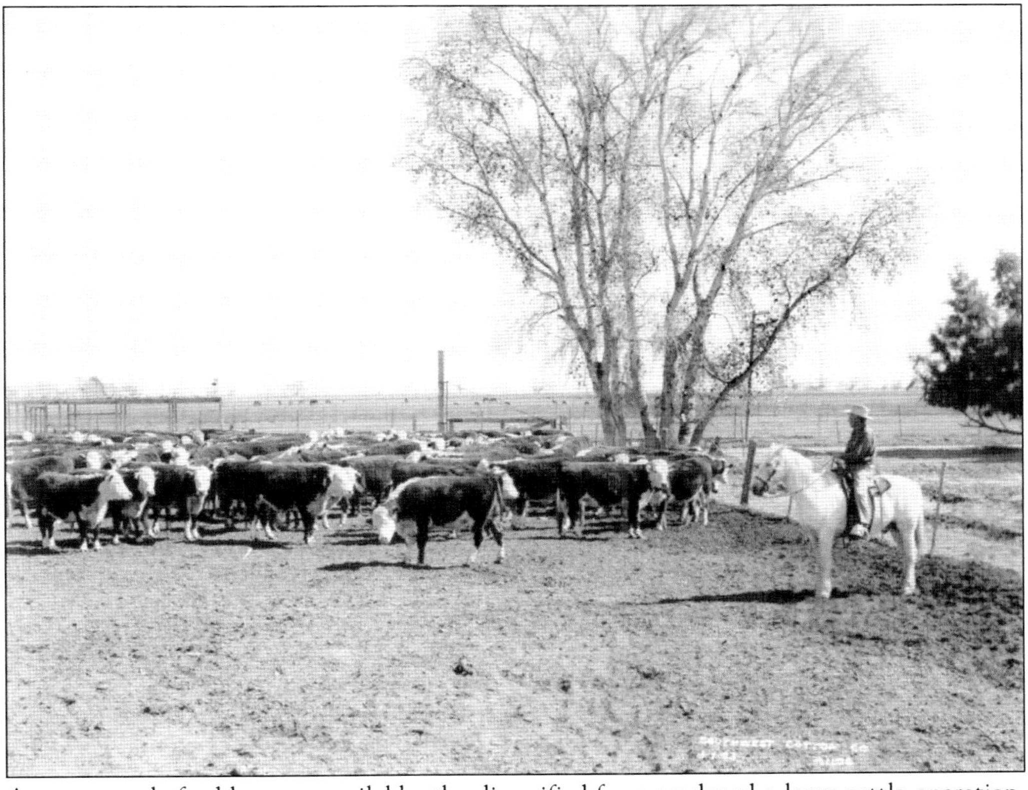

As more cattle feed became available, the diversified farm produced a large cattle operation. Shown here some of the cattle and a cowboy on horseback providing a new use for the cotton fields. (Courtesy of the City of Litchfield Park.)

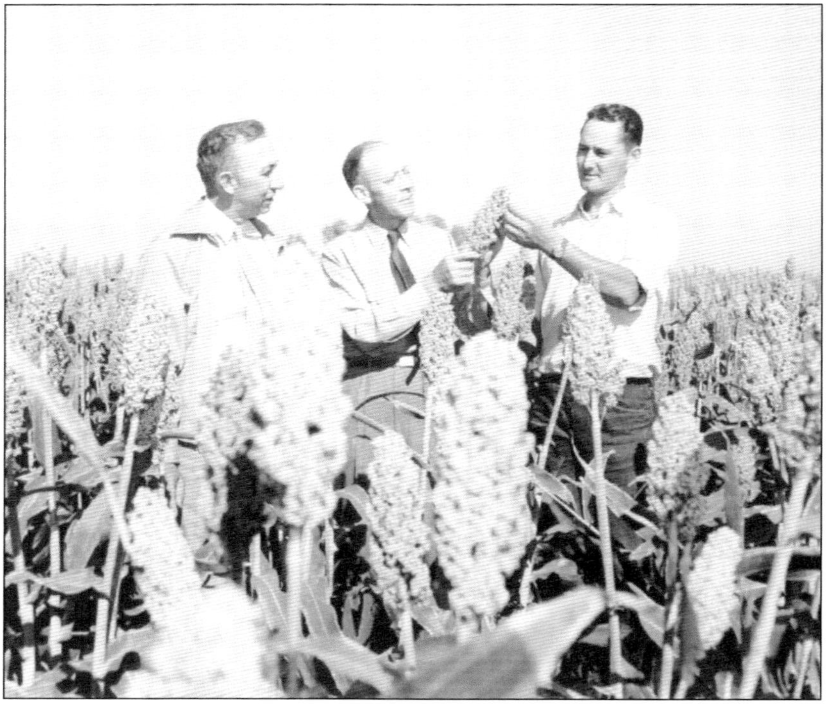

Sorghum was a scientific food for the cattle. The contracted cattle were brought in twice a year and fed for six months or 120 to 200 days. (Courtesy of the City of Litchfield Park.)

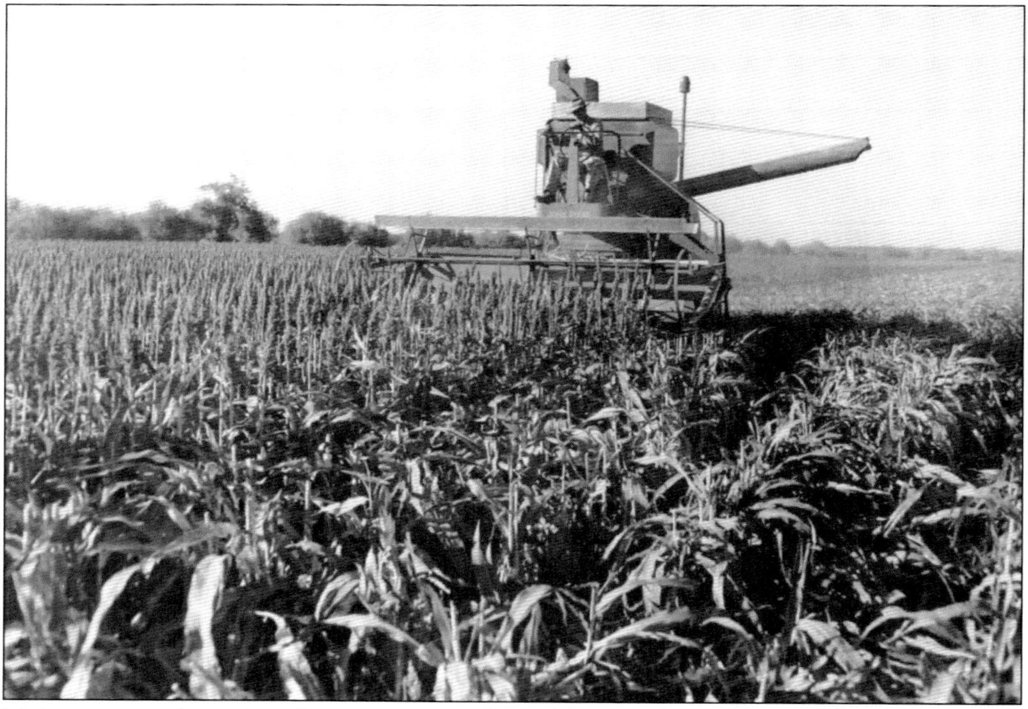

Maize was another scientific grain source planted by Goodyear Farms for the cattle. There were as many as 4,000 to 4,500 head of cattle at one time to be fed. (Courtesy of the City of Litchfield Park.)

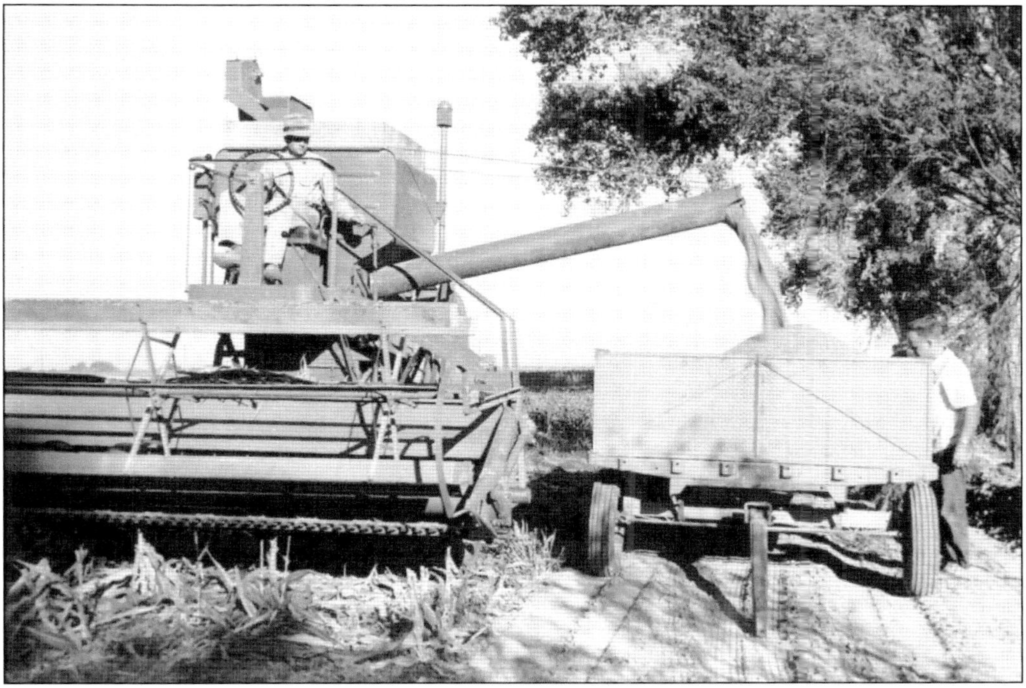

Grain is being processed for the feeding operation. Over a six-month time frame, up to 8,000 to 9,000 head of cattle were fed scientific food from Goodyear. The cattle came in at around 400 pounds, and when they reached 1,000 pounds, some were shipped off on the railroad to California for market. They were shipped at night to keep their best weight. Some were sold in Phoenix and Tolleson to Cudahy Meat Company. Marketing of the cattle was sometimes done by their owners. (Courtesy of the City of Litchfield Park.)

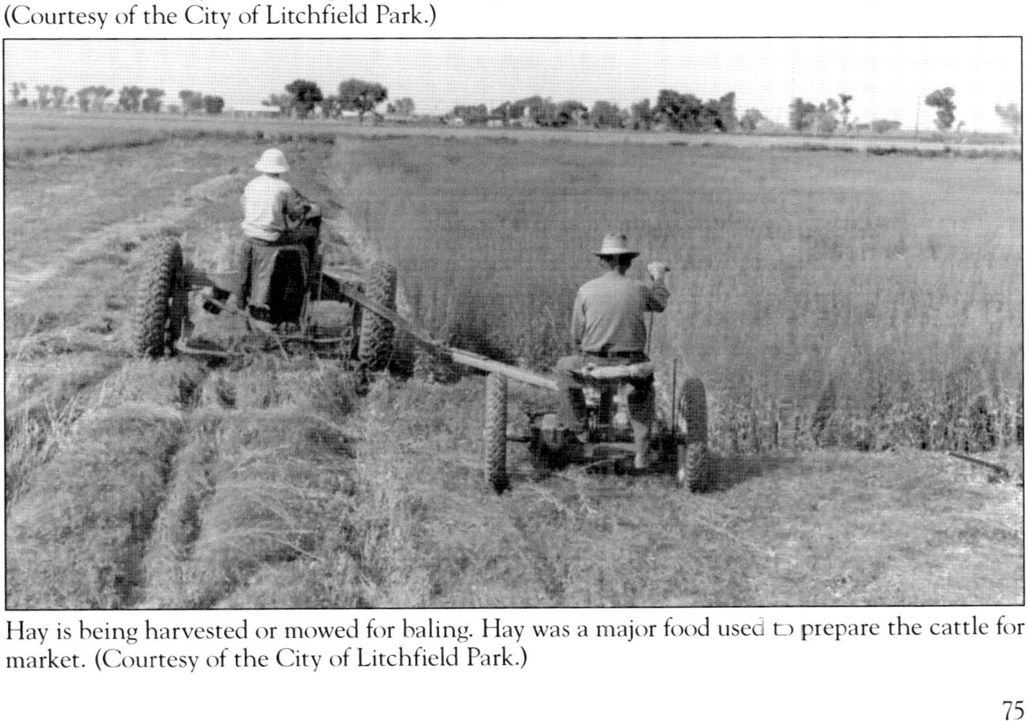

Hay is being harvested or mowed for baling. Hay was a major food used to prepare the cattle for market. (Courtesy of the City of Litchfield Park.)

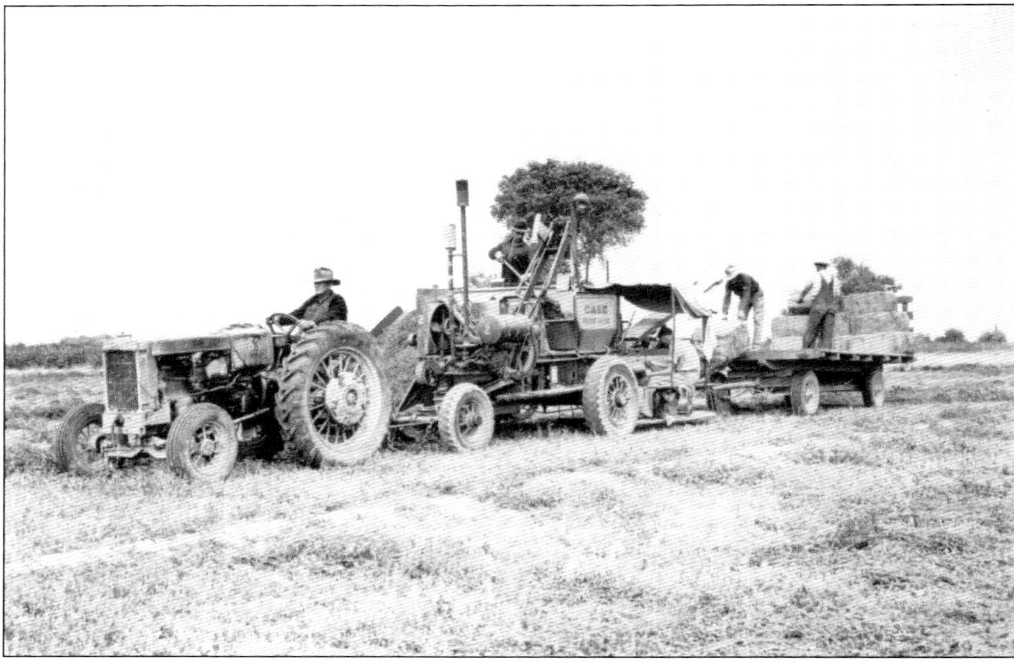

Hay bales are being processed in the fields of Goodyear Farms. Hay was a large part of the cattle-feeding operation. This equipment had the capacity to gather the hay and process it into bales right in the field. (Courtesy of the City of Litchfield Park.)

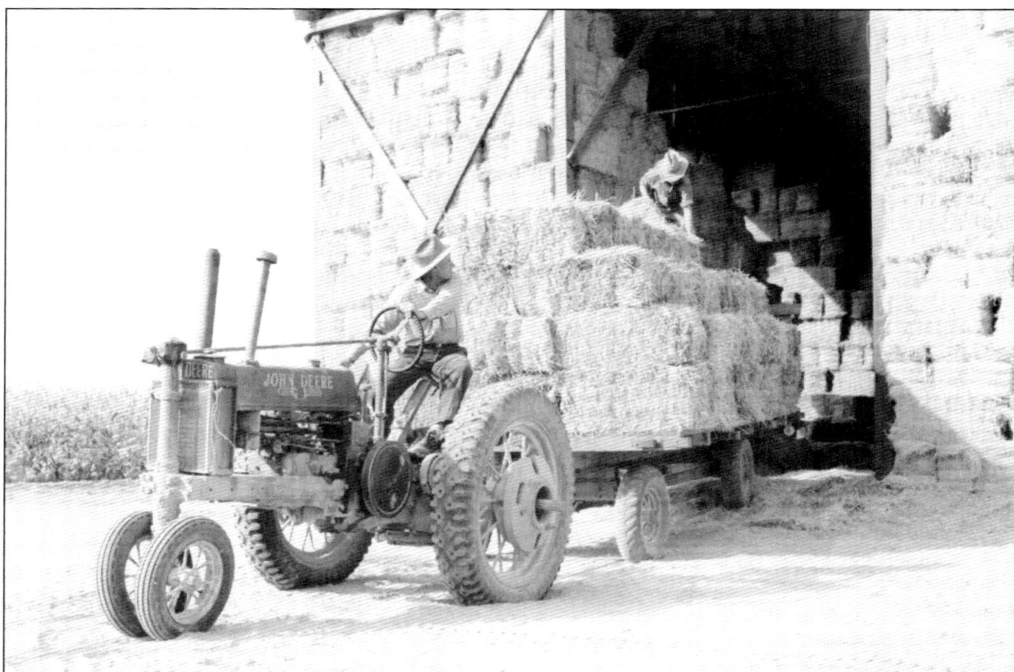


Bales of hay are hauled into barns for storage. The cattle operation was prepared by supplying many storage barns, as the cattle required so much food. (Courtesy of the City of Litchfield Park.)

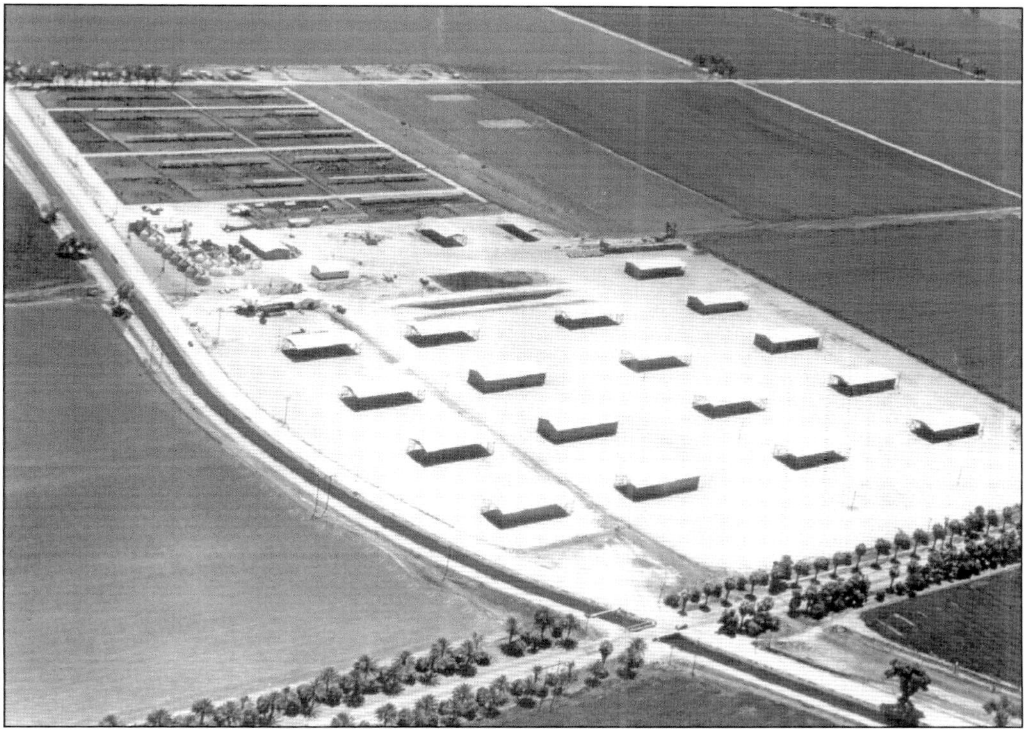

Barns used for storing the bales of hay can be seen in this aerial view. This shows storage for the extensive operation of feeding up to 8,000 to 9,000 head of cattle twice a year. (Courtesy of the City of Litchfield Park.)

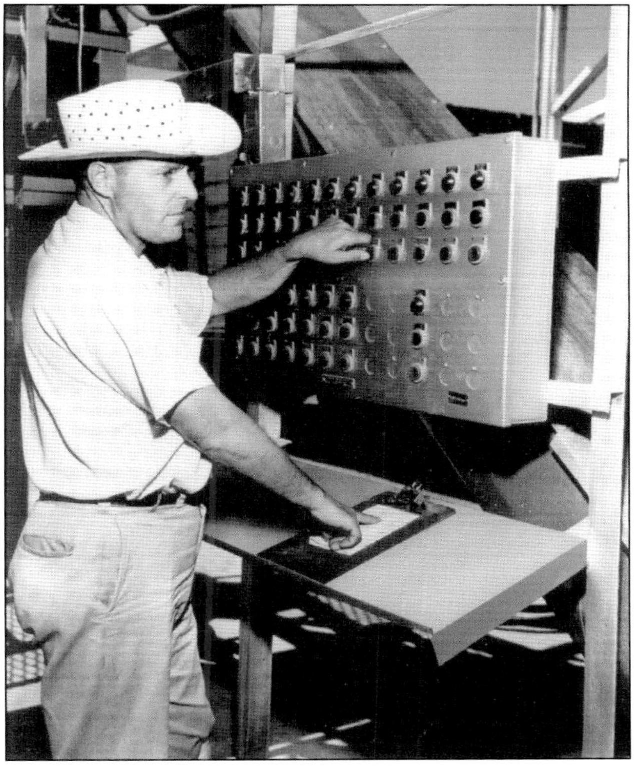

Jim Humphrey is shown here at the controls of the cattle-feeding operation. With this automatic feeding system, Humphrey could push a button and feed up to 600 cattle at one time. (Courtesy of the City of Litchfield Park.)

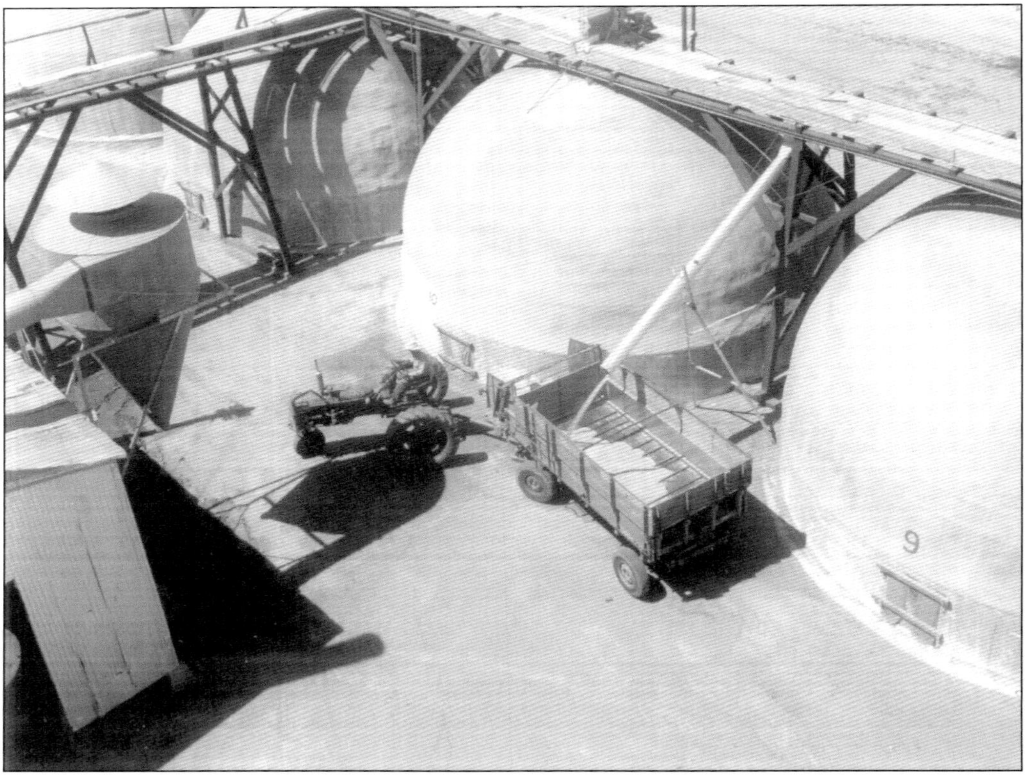

The scientific cattle food was stored in Bubble Houses. These igloo-shaped storage bins were made by inflating balloons and coating them with concrete. When the concrete set, the balloons were deflated and removed. (Courtesy of the City of Litchfield Park.)

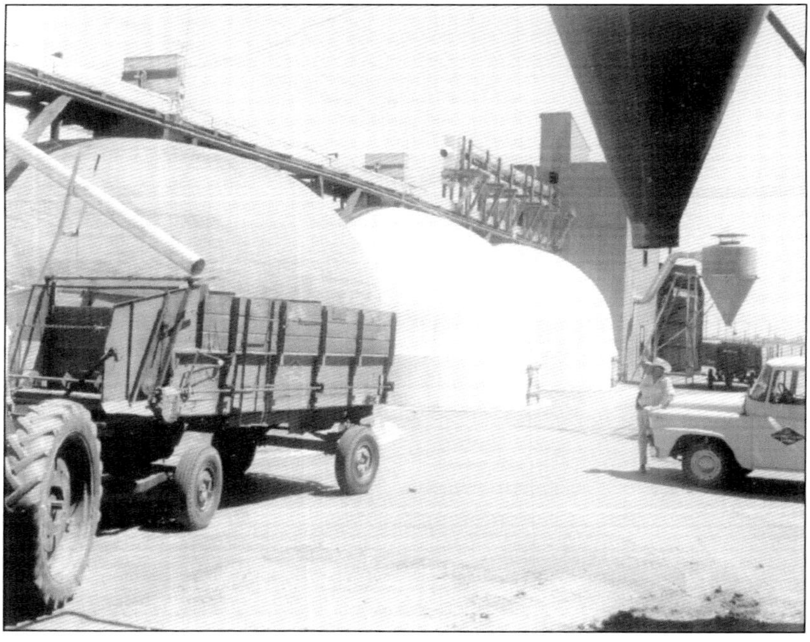

Seen here is another view of the Bubble House storage units used by Goodyear Farms. This amazing operation was created to feed up to 18,000 head of cattle per year. (Courtesy of the City of Litchfield Park.)

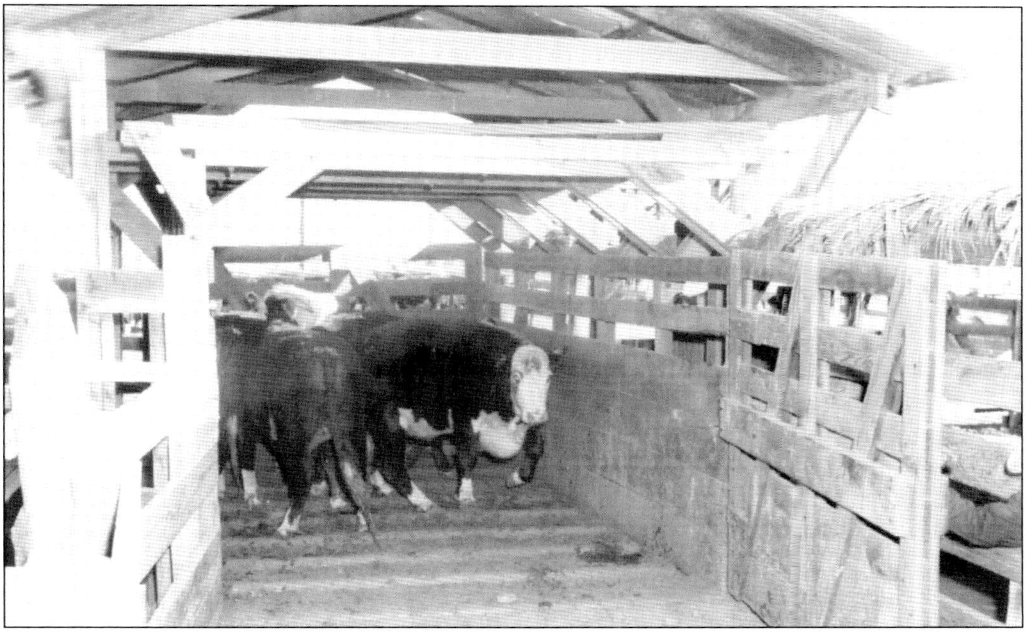

Cattle are shown here in the chute they were brought into the front of for dehorning and also to be inoculated. The cattle were well fed and well cared for once they were contracted by Goodyear Farms. (Both, courtesy of the City of Litchfield Park.)

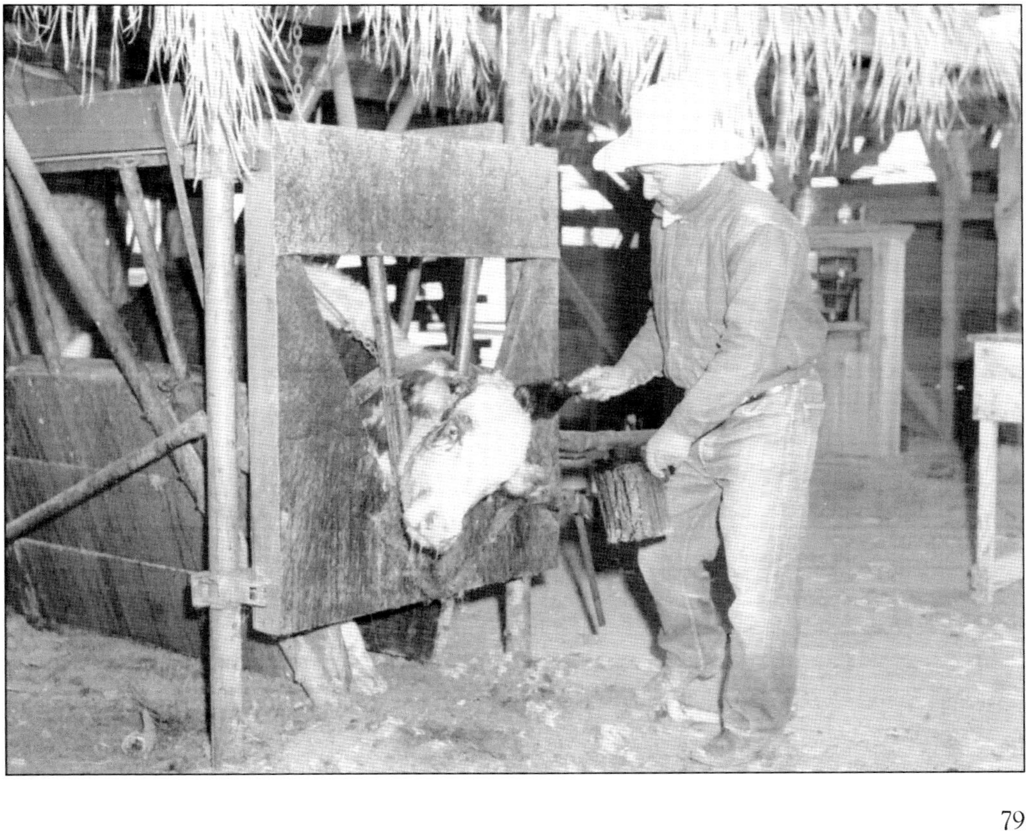

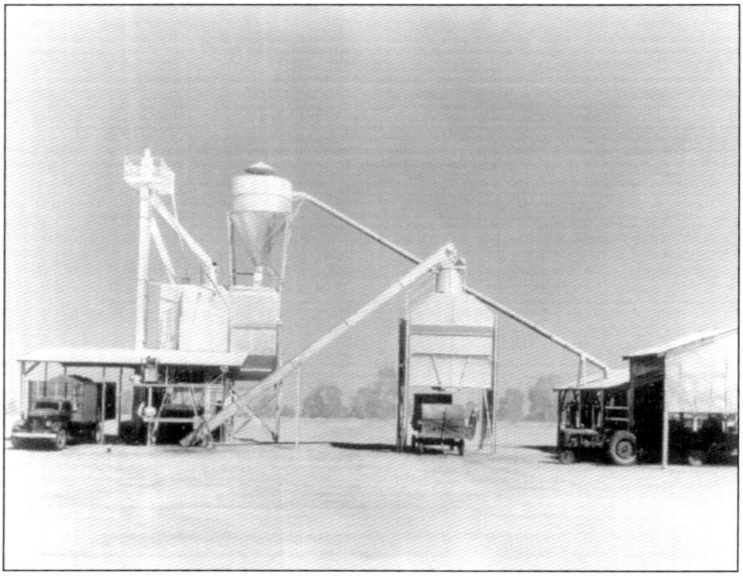

Pictured here is one of the feed mixing and distribution systems. At the feeding center, dry hay, grain, and cotton seed meal were received from a chute and mixed with alfalfa. Concrete troughs at the pens were filled automatically with this mixture as a tractor and wagon were piloted along the feeding alley. Water tanks were placed inside the pens to provide the cattle with fresh water. (Courtesy of the City of Litchfield Park.)

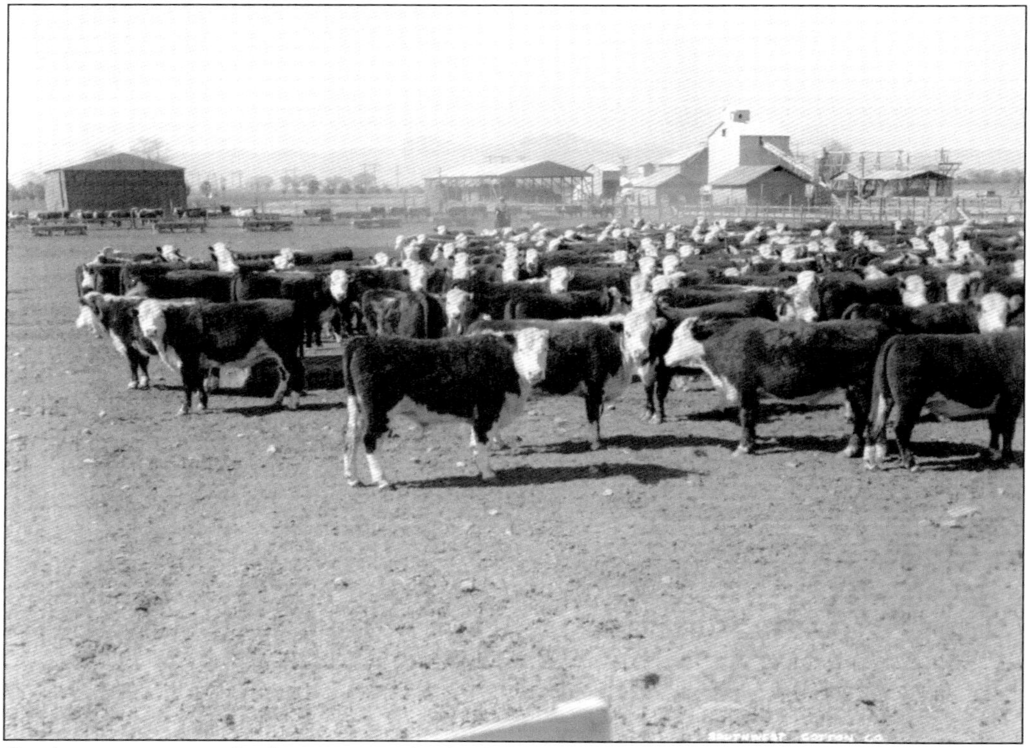

Cattle are seen outside their pens with the feed mill operation in the background. The cattle operation was closed down in 1964–1965. Ed Thomas, chief executive officer of Goodyear, was a guest at the Wigwam Resort once when the wind was blowing a strong odor from the feedlots. He ordered the feedlots closed in order to protect the Wigwam guests from the odor. This decision stopped not only the cattle operation but the grain operation as well. (Courtesy of the City of Litchfield Park.)

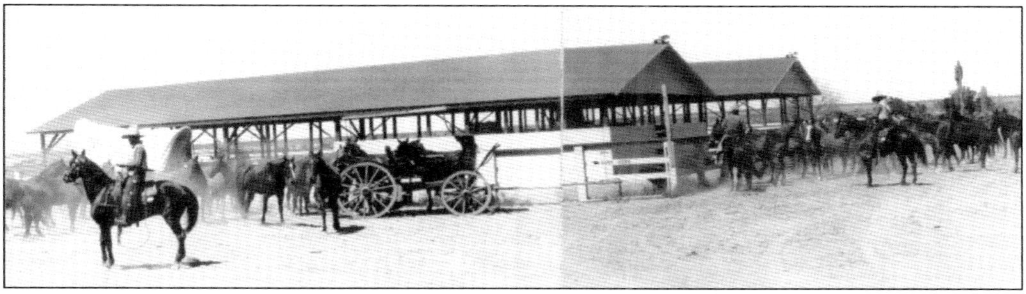

The Wigwam Corral was located on the northwest side of Litchfield Road across the street from the Goodyear Farms headquarters building. The corral was very popular, as it housed the horses used at the Wigwam to entertain guests. The horses used for riding and for wagon trips to Sunset Point were housed at the corral as well as horses used on the Litchfield Ranch. (Courtesy of the City of Litchfield Park.)

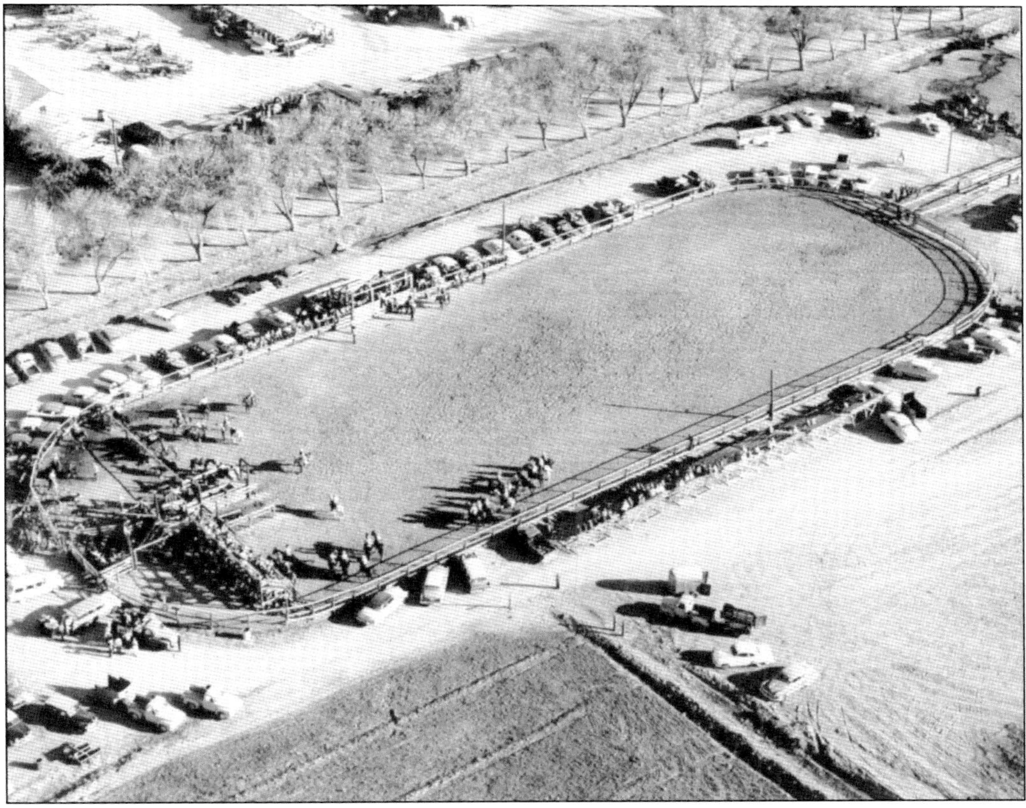

Wigwam Rodeo Arena was located just north of the Wigwam Corral and was very popular for entertainment as well as local competition. The Wigwam guests were entertained with rodeos to get a taste of the Old West. In the early days as a dude ranch, horses were a big part of the entertainment of the Wigwam. (Courtesy of the City of Litchfield Park.)

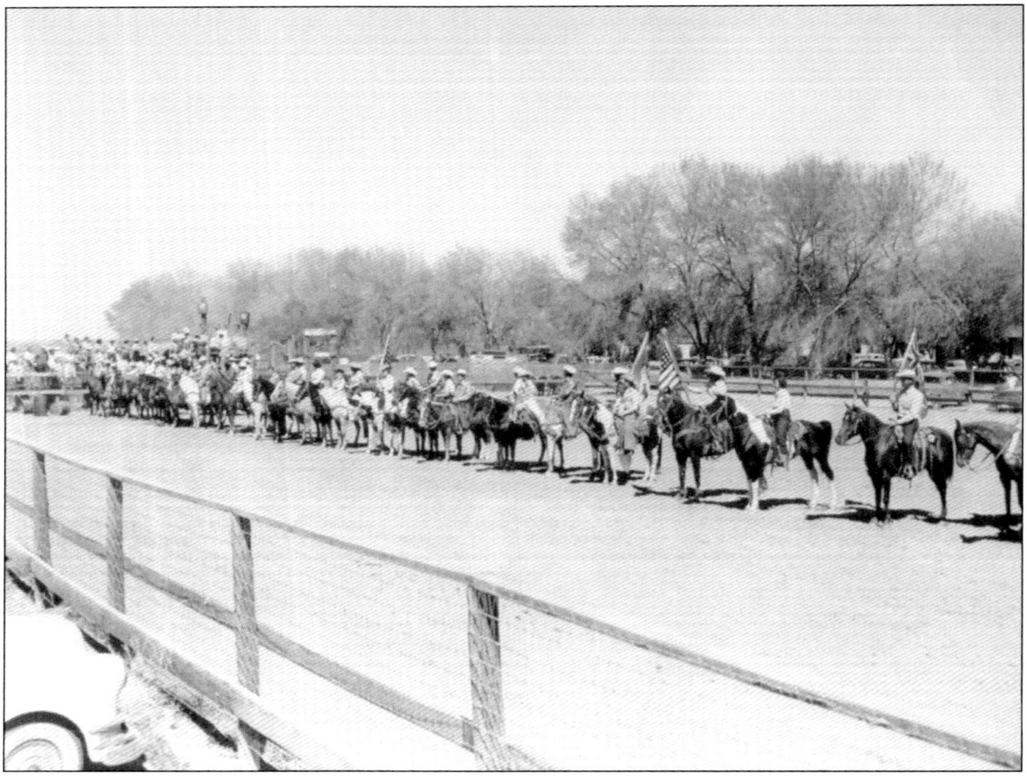

Rodeo participants are lined up for the opening ceremony of a competition sponsored as a fundraiser by local Boy Scout Troop 90. This event was held in 1955 and included Goodyear employees as well as local citizens as participants. (Courtesy of the City of Litchfield Park.)

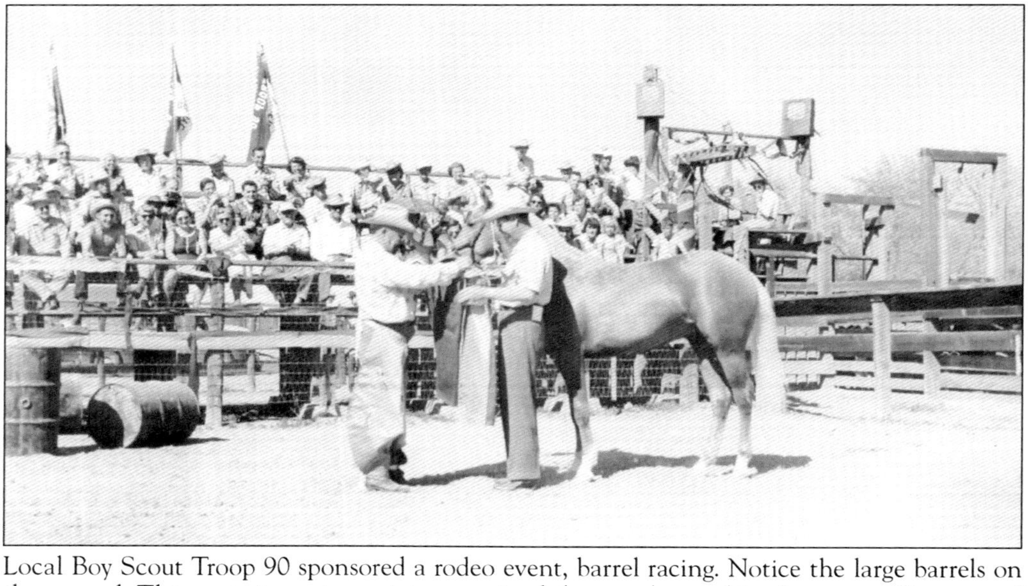

Local Boy Scout Troop 90 sponsored a rodeo event, barrel racing. Notice the large barrels on the ground. This participant is receiving a pair of chaps to be used in the event. (Courtesy of the City of Litchfield Park.)

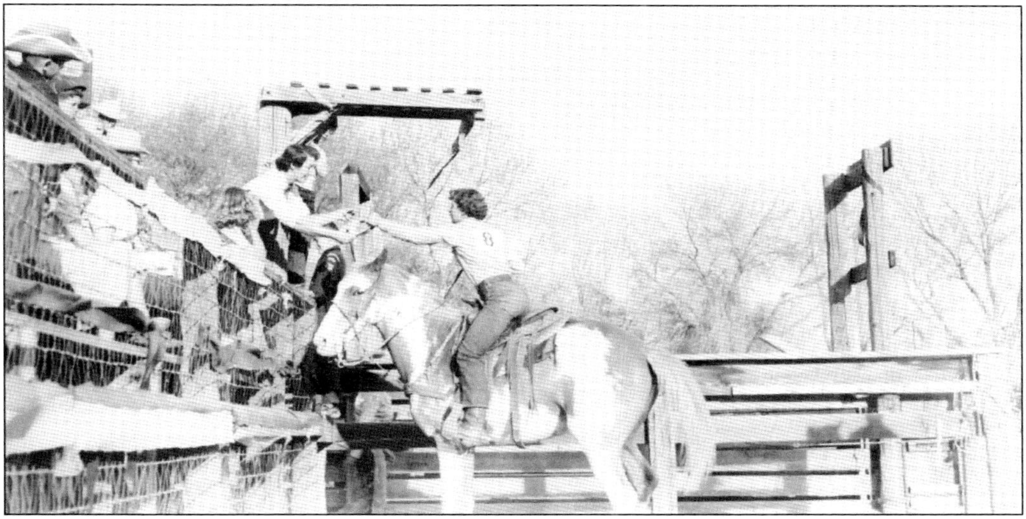
Women participated in the competitions. Pictured here is a winner of a barrel race receiving an award. (Courtesy of the City of Litchfield Park.)

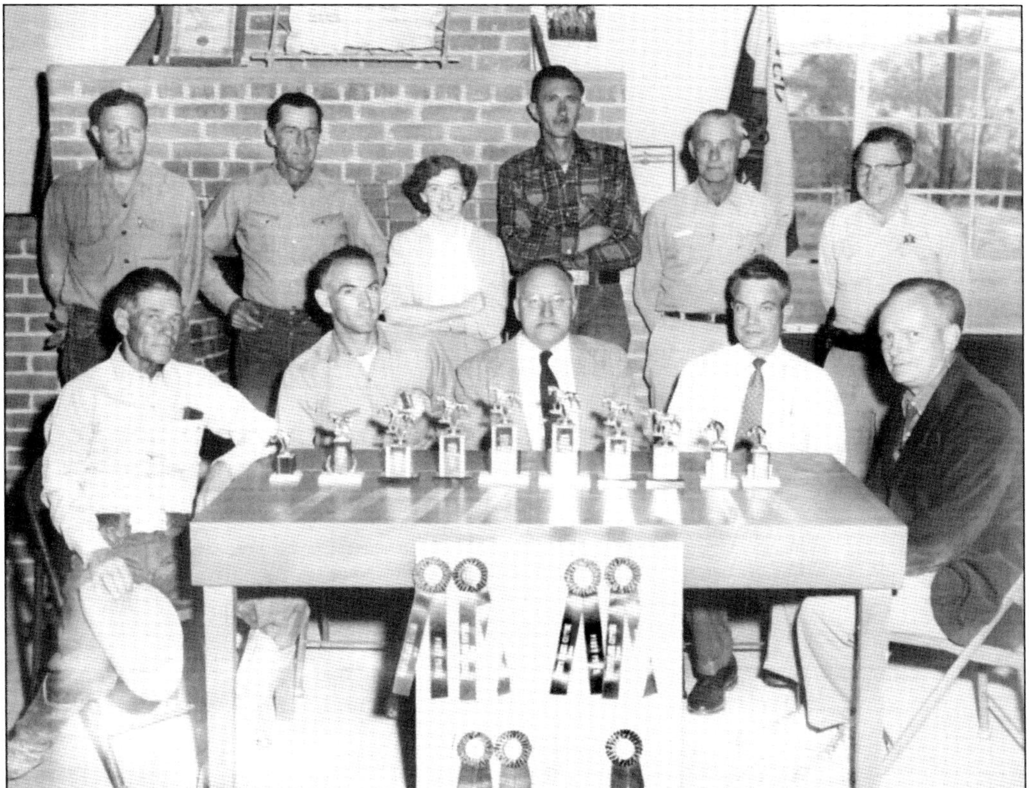
Pictured at the new Scout Lodge, dedicated in 1954, is the committee for the Boy Scout Troop 90 rodeo competition. On the table are the trophies and ribbons awarded to the winners. Seated in the center of the table is Pete Clarino, chairman of the event. (Courtesy of the City of Litchfield Park.)

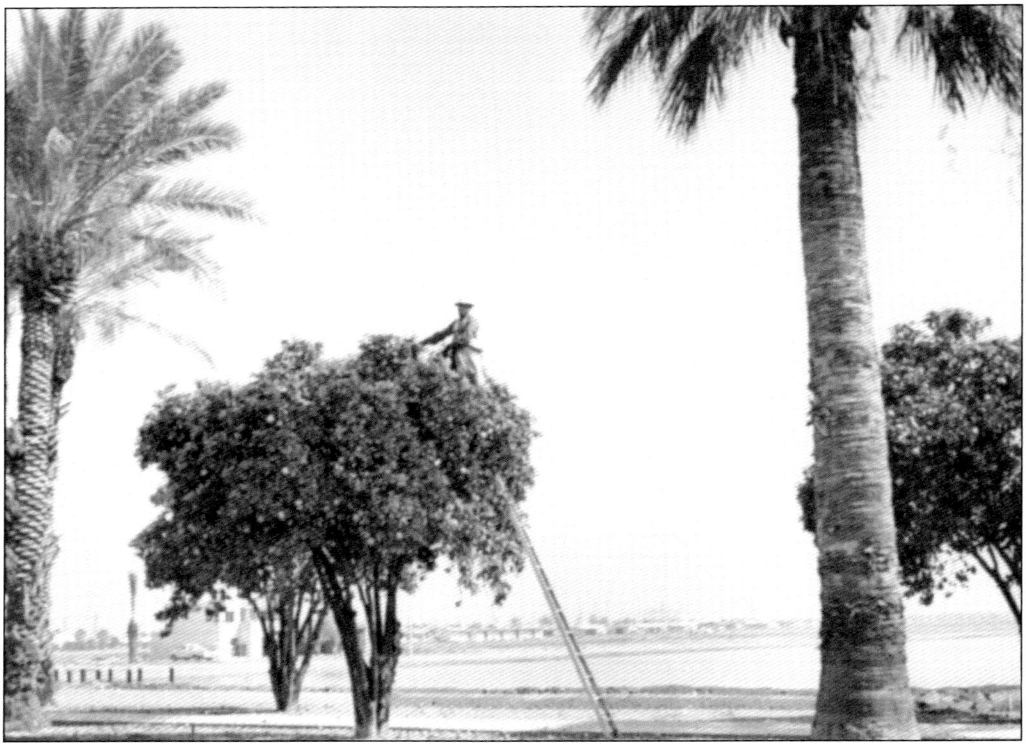

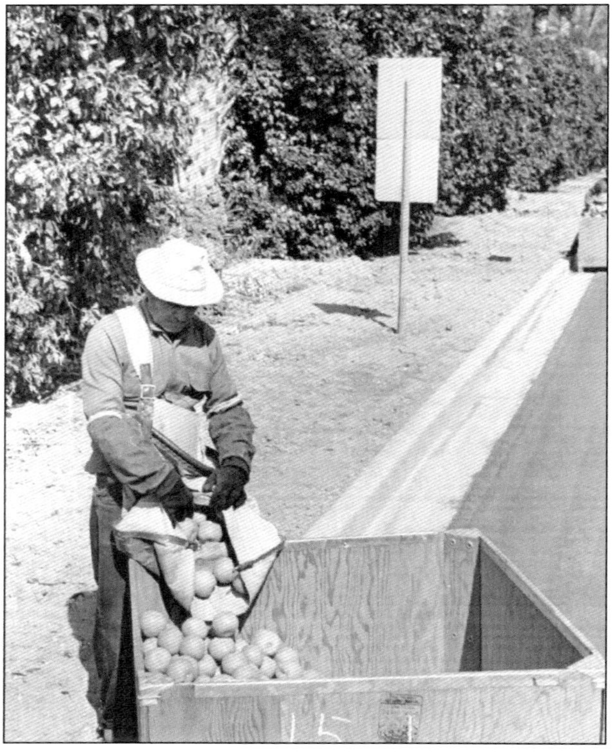

Citrus was a major part of Goodyear Farms. January is a popular time in Litchfield, when the oranges grown downtown are harvested. Many different companies have handled both the picking and processing over the years these trees have produced oranges. (Courtesy of the City of Litchfield Park.)

Oranges are gathered into large bins after being picked. The pickers are contracted by the city, and the Seville oranges are then sold privately to a company that makes them into marmalade. (Courtesy of the City of Litchfield Park.)

A classy lady is seen picking grapefruit. Grapefruit is locally grown, as are lemons, but oranges are the most marketable, as they are made into marmalade and other products. (Courtesy of the City of Litchfield Park.)

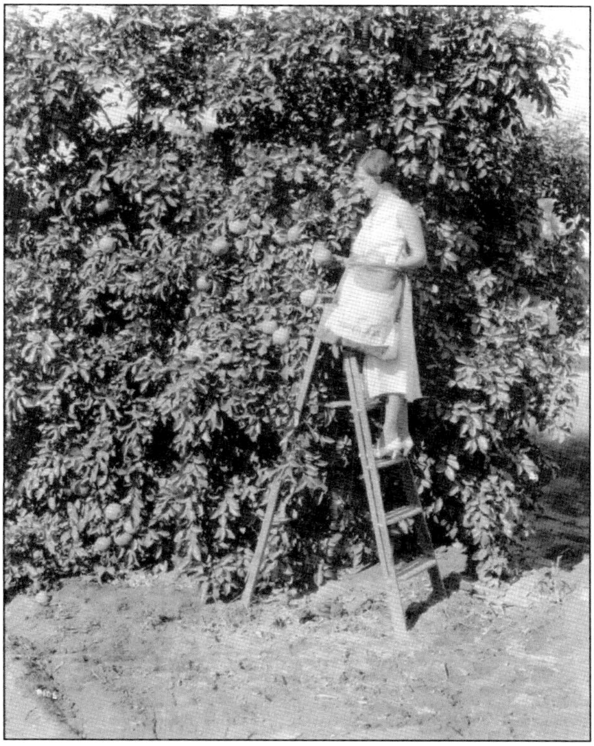

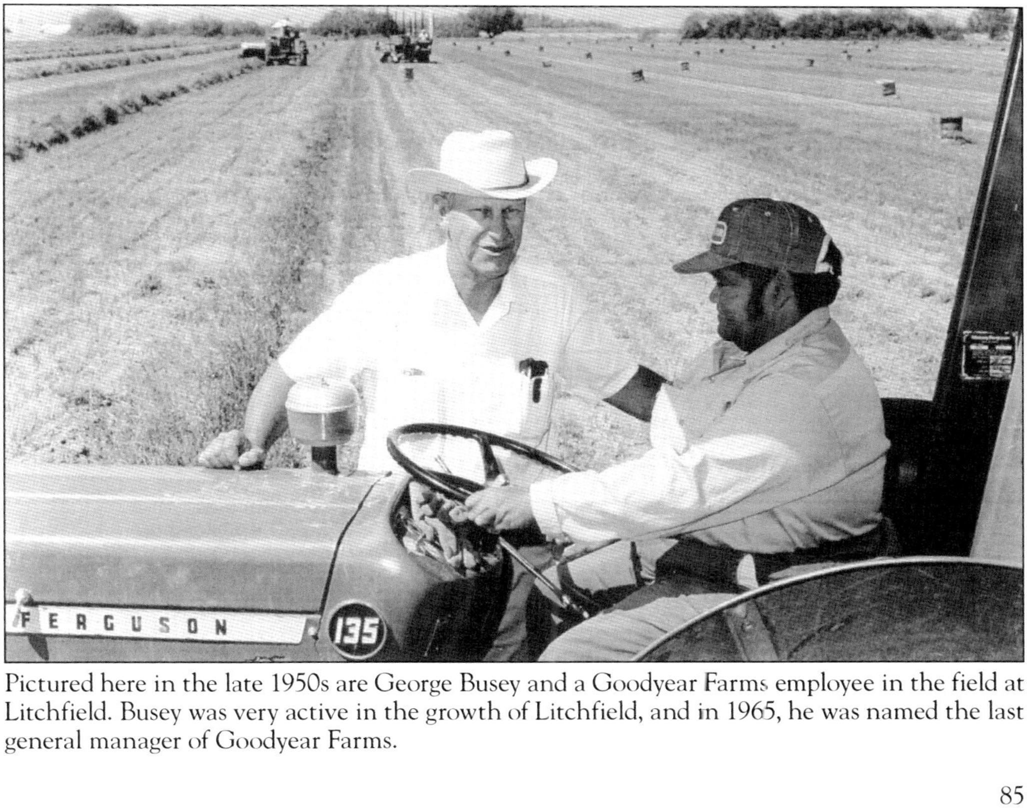


Pictured here in the late 1950s are George Busey and a Goodyear Farms employee in the field at Litchfield. Busey was very active in the growth of Litchfield, and in 1965, he was named the last general manager of Goodyear Farms.

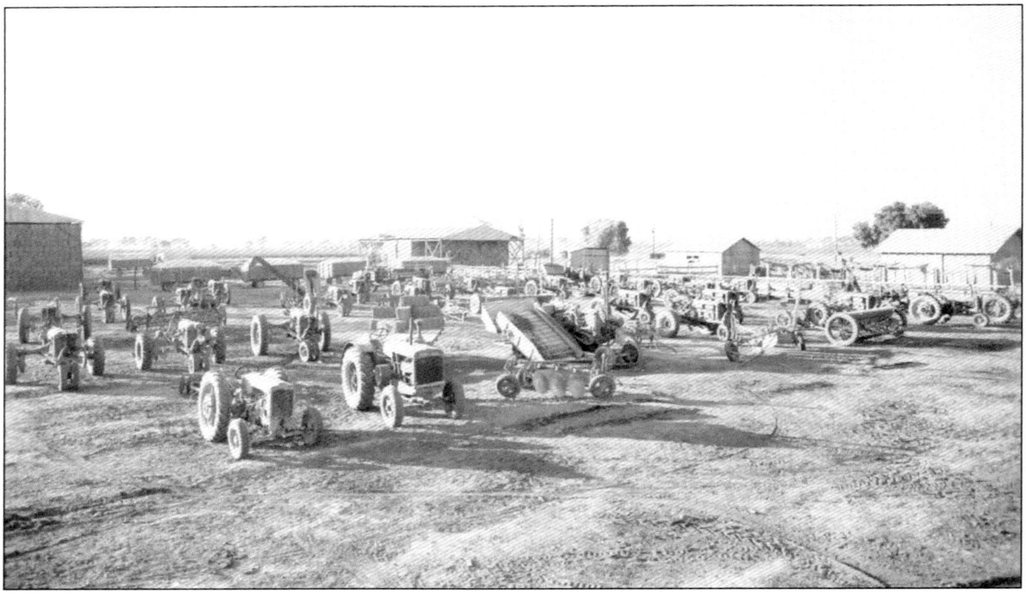

This array of farm equipment shows the variety of farming activities on Goodyear Farms. It was known to have one of the largest collections of equipment on any ranch.

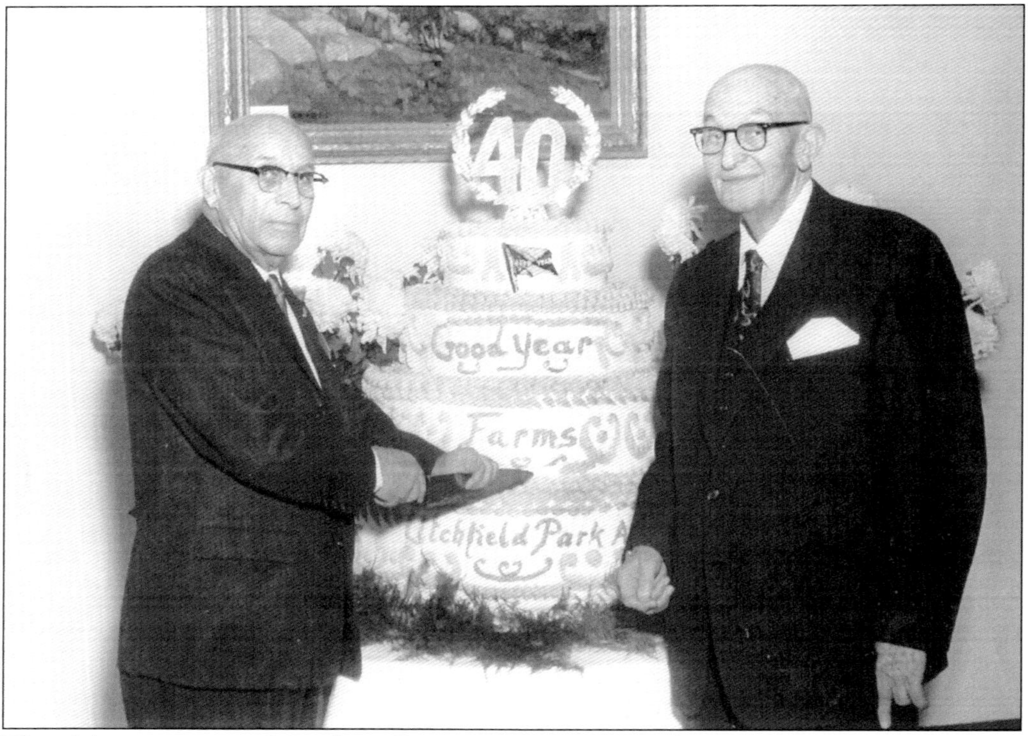


The 40th anniversary of Goodyear Farms was celebrated at the Wigwam with a special cake and a very special guest. Congressman Carl Hayden (1912–1969) was on hand to help Kenneth McMicken (left) cut the cake. Hayden (right) was Arizona's first congressman, and McMicken was the general manager of Goodyear Farms.

# Six

# Testing Tires and Farm Equipment

For several years, Litchfield Park was a center for tire testing activity. The Goodyear Test Fleet was sent to Litchfield Park, as Goodyear found Arizona climatic conditions to be an ideal outdoor laboratory for highway testing of automobile and truck tires. Dominant factors were the dry, abusive road surfaces and high temperatures. Summer high temperatures were ideal for testing tires, fabrics, compounds, balloon cloth, and other rubber products. Trucks were overloaded as much as 200 percent to bring strain on the tires. The speed was rapidly increased until the tires finally blew out. The findings were then sent to Goodyear in Akron. Development engineers had an excellent "Laboratory on Wheels" to make first studies of tire performance.

An important chapter has been written in the story of American agriculture right in Litchfield Park. Inspired by the genius of Paul Weeks Litchfield, who was behind the farm operation in Arizona, Goodyear Farms became a great experimental laboratory for testing rubber tires on farm equipment. Pneumatic tires were placed in actual field work on every type of farm equipment. This included road graders, side-delivery rakes, balers, cotton planters, plows, power weed sprayers, and furrowing machines.

Farmers from all around the world have their work made easier and more effective because of studies made and accomplishments achieved at Goodyear Farms.

Power farming after World War I brought a series of developments that increased the utility of the tractor and paved the way for complete farm mechanization. The tricycle-type tractor was introduced in 1924, and in 1932 came rubber tires and other farm equipment vehicles. By 1936, mules had disappeared from the Goodyear Farms scene. The years 1932 and 1933 brought a flurry of farm equipment experimentation to Goodyear Farms. The final battle between the steel-wheeled tractor and the rubber-tired tractor occurred in Litchfield Park. The modern farm tractor did more than any other piece of equipment to revolutionize agriculture methods. Compared to steel wheels, most field operations were 25 to 50 percent faster on rubber. The pneumatic tires increased the drawbar power of the tractor by 20 to 25 percent and saved up to 25 percent on fuel. Farm operators doubled their accomplishments with rubber-tired tractors compared to horses. Farm machinery was changed to pneumatic tires, and soon, all farm equipment vehicles were rolling on rubber. From 1935 to 1941, tractors using pneumatic tires increased from 14 to 96 percent.

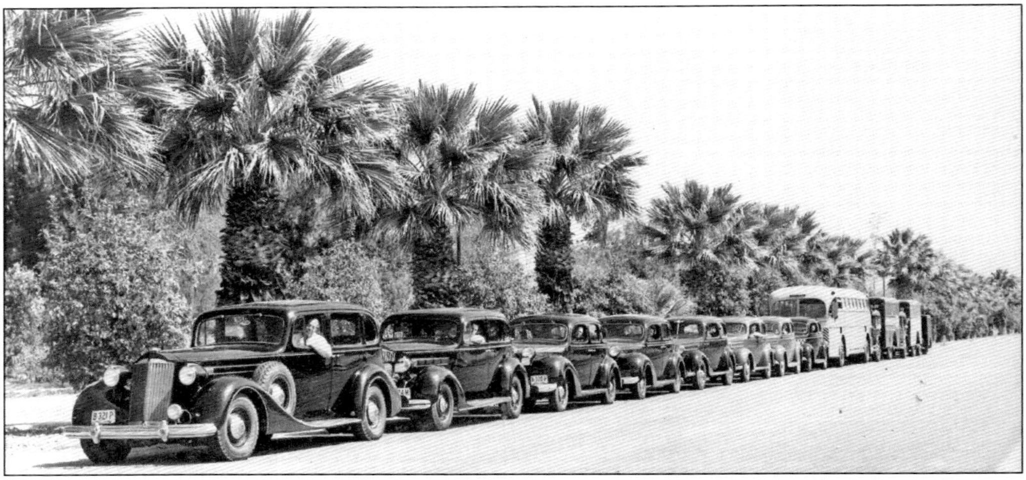

From 1931 to 1936, the Goodyear Tire & Rubber Company sent its testing fleet from Akron to Litchfield Park. It was sent here during the winter months and returned to Akron in the summer. In 1937, the entire test fleet was sent to Arizona and became a permanent resident. The test fleet consisted of passenger cars, trucks, and tractors that were maintained solely for test purposes.

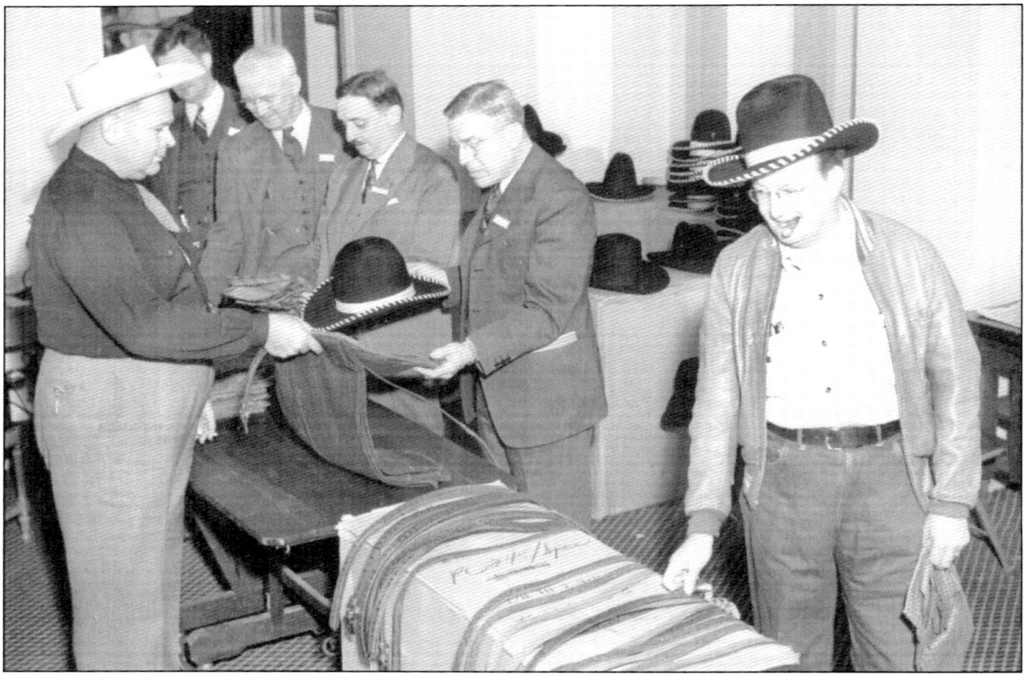

In 1943, Goodyear Farms hosted a Farm Forum at the Wigwam Resort. Many special people who worked in the farming profession were brought here to see the great strides that Goodyear had made in the use of rubber tires and to show the relationship of rubber products to the agricultural industry. The group invited included farm implement manufacturers and their technical staffs, farm magazine editors, and agricultural college professors. Several Goodyear Tire & Rubber Company officials, including the president and vice president, attended the forum along with agricultural technical staff from the University of Arizona who came to help in presenting the agricultural story of the Salt River Valley.

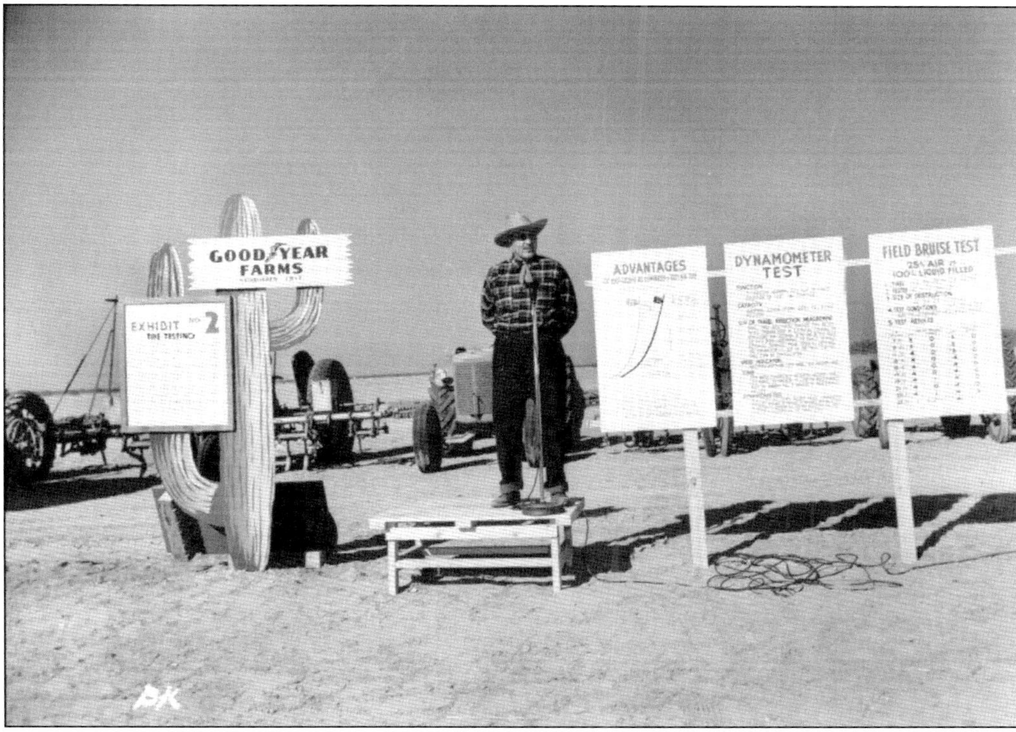


This exhibit was set up to show the guests at the 1943 Farm Forum the results of the dynamometer test. These exhibit areas were set up around the farm.

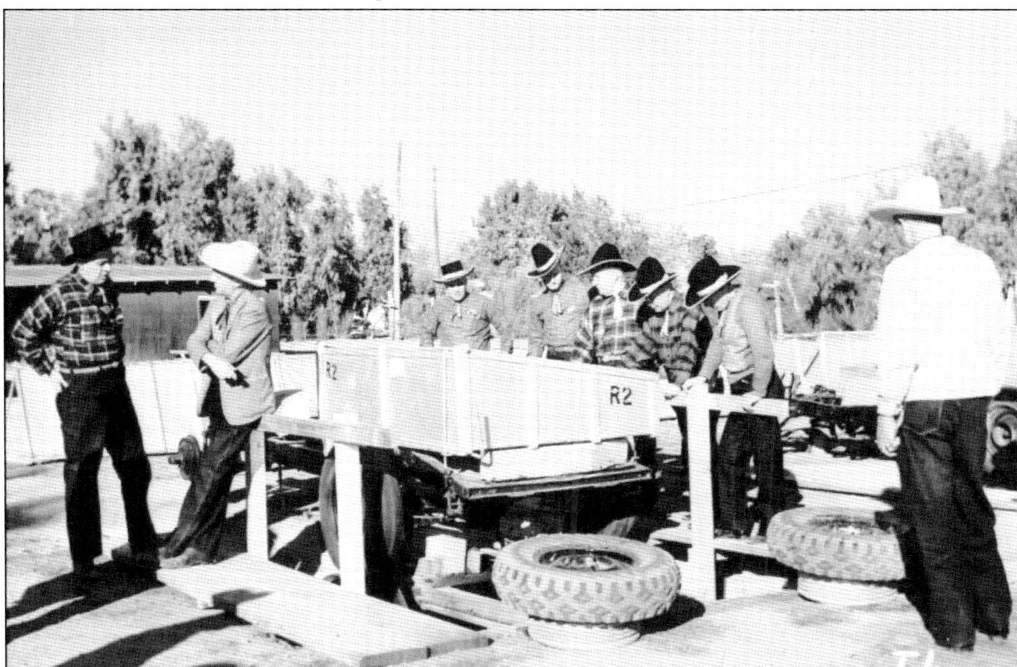


A group of Farm Forum guests examines the test areas.

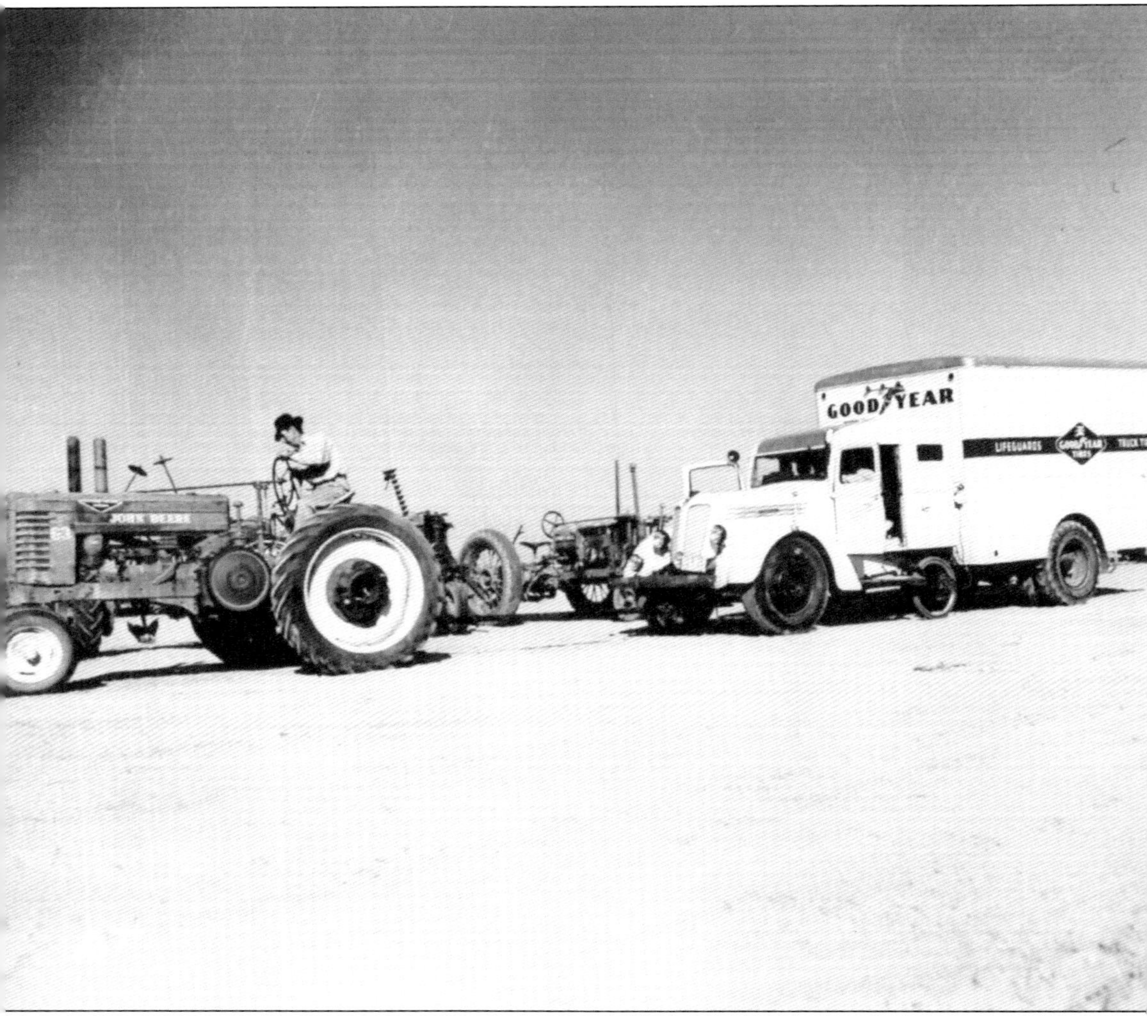


Many demonstration areas were set up to show the results of Goodyear's tire testing. One area showed the increased drawbar pull of tractor tires filled with a liquid called Solution 100 compared to those filled with air as indicated by the use of the dynamometer test. The center wheel of the dynamometer resembles a bicycle wheel and records the exact distance the equipment travels.

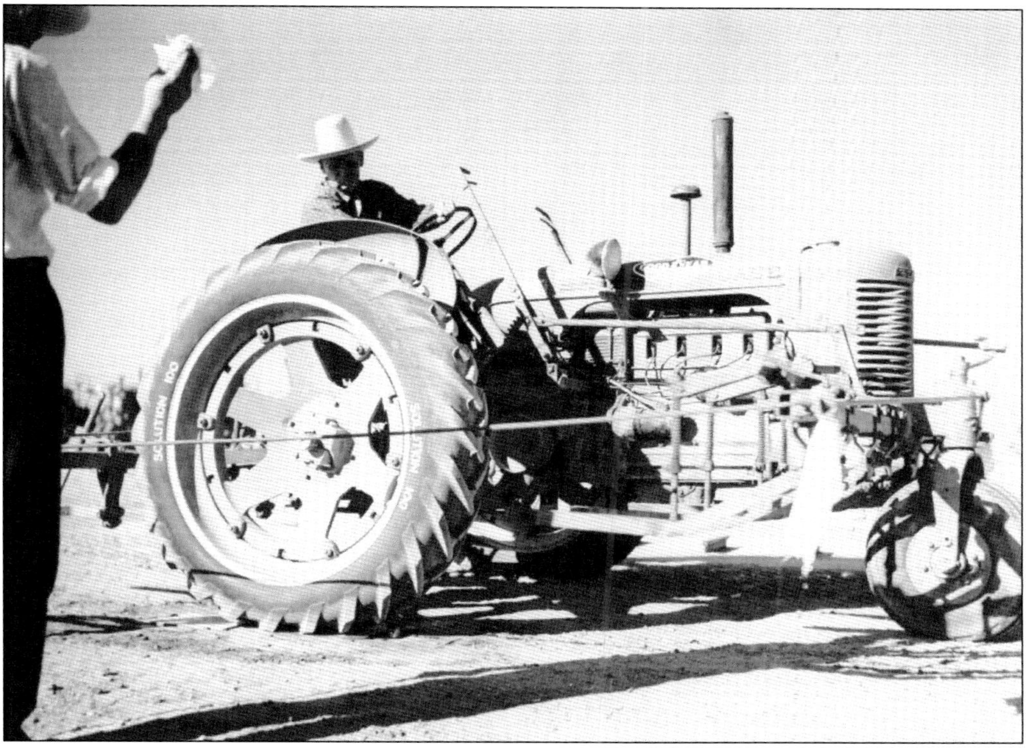


Solution 100's advantages over air-filled tractor tires are being demonstrated here. Note the tractor tire is about to run over a metal peg to show resistance to bruising of the tire filled with liquid. Tests revealed that liquid-filled tractor tires slipped less than those filled with air. Goodyear developed pumps and connections to add or remove water from tractor tires and special calcium chloride solutions to prevent freezing and add weight to the water.

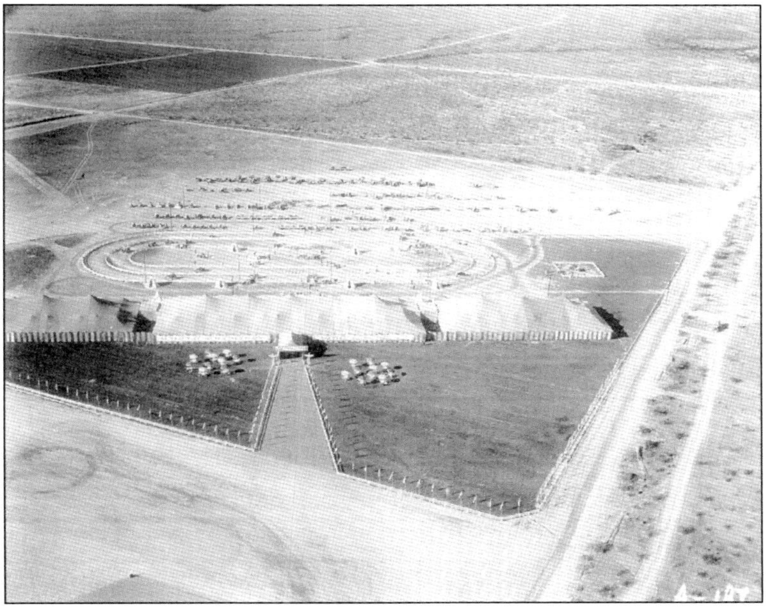

Case Farm Equipment Company had its 1960 world premier showing of its farm equipment in the West Valley. Some of its new equipment was on display, especially the rubber-tired tractors.

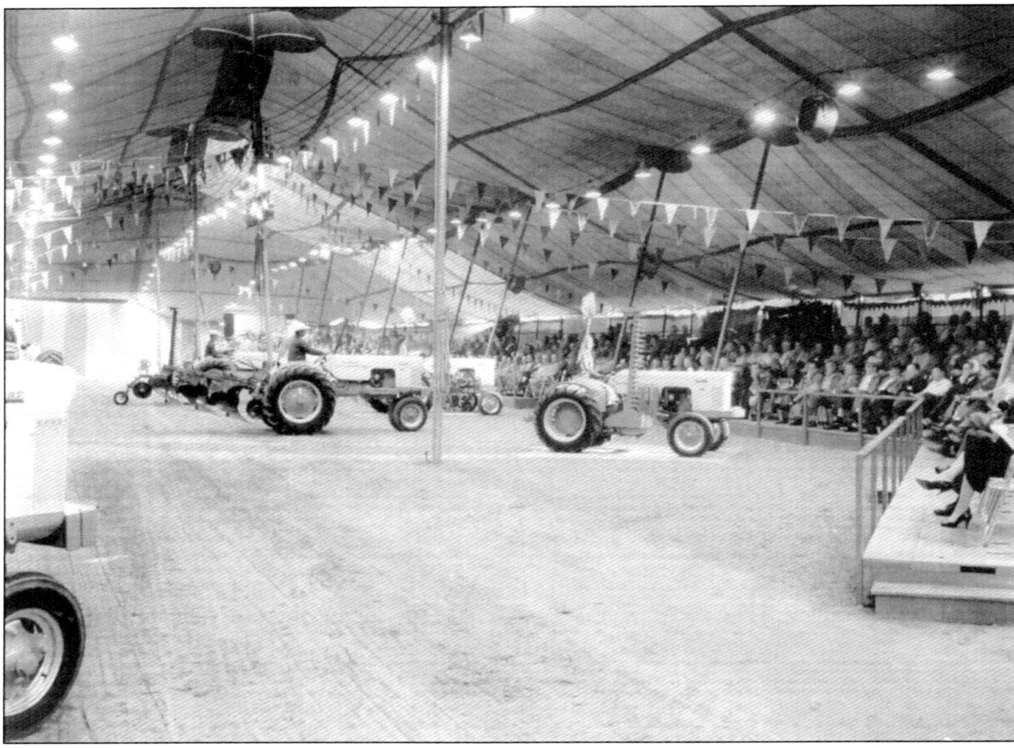

Major farm equipment companies sent their design engineers to Litchfield to learn and share in the great changes that were being made in the design of farm equipment and the use of rubber tires.

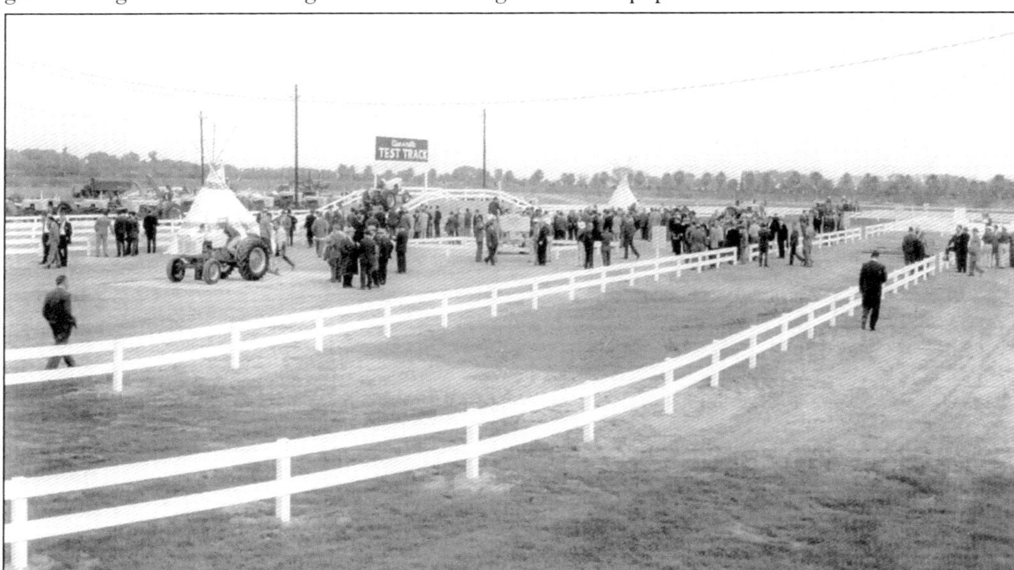


The Case Farm Equipment Company worked closely with Goodyear Farms in testing rubber tires. Case would add Goodyear's new rubber tires to its equipment for six months and then return them to Goodyear for inspection. Shown here is a test track and exhibit tent located in the west area of downtown.

## *Seven*

# Apprentice Farmers

In the fall of 1936, Paul Litchfield was chosen as one of the judges to select the outstanding farm youth within the Future Farmers of America. The young men in the competition left an impact on him. What did it take to make a star farmer? He was told they all wanted to be independent and own farms of their own, but only a few would fulfill their goal. Litchfield was touched by the needs of the young farmers.

The Litchfield Apprentice Farmer Program was started in 1937. The program was patterned after the Flying Squadron Program at Goodyear corporate offices. The Flying Squadron Program was for a select group of young men who were chosen to be trained in all aspects of the corporation and were ready to be assigned wherever they were needed with the industrial operation; the Apprentice Farmer Program would follow the same concept. The plan for the apprentice program was broad and flexible. The company furnished the land at a fair value, housing, training, and capital. The apprentices furnished the labor.

Goodyear set aside approximately 2,800 acres of developed irrigation land on the northwest corner of the ranch. All of the apprentice homes were built on Sarival Avenue. The young men were selected based on their health, character, knowledge, teamwork, and thrift. They came from California, New Mexico, Texas, Missouri, Illinois, Oklahoma, Utah, Nevada, Montana, and Arizona. These young farmers were paid employees of Goodyear Farms and moved to all operations of the ranch to learn agricultural production. They learned marketing, financing, and budgeting, working in teams and learning thrift. They were required to make a yearly budget and crop plans and account for their monetary needs in machinery, livestock, seed, and household expenditures. They formed a co-op called Adaman Farms Co-operation, and through this action they shared hay, grain storage facilities, shop buildings, machine sheds, scales, and corrals. The co-op also shared machinery and equipment. They all advanced toward farm ownership and equity in livestock and machinery. They had share-crop phases, cash leasing of land, and finally, purchase of their farms on a contract basis.

The first apprentices arrived in 1937. There were 35 in the program. As 22 went into World War II, 11 resigned, and a few became employees of Goodyear. In December 1943, seven who had completed the first cycle of the plan received a 15-year contract to purchase their 80-acre farms from Goodyear. The Apprentice Farmer Program ended in 1951.

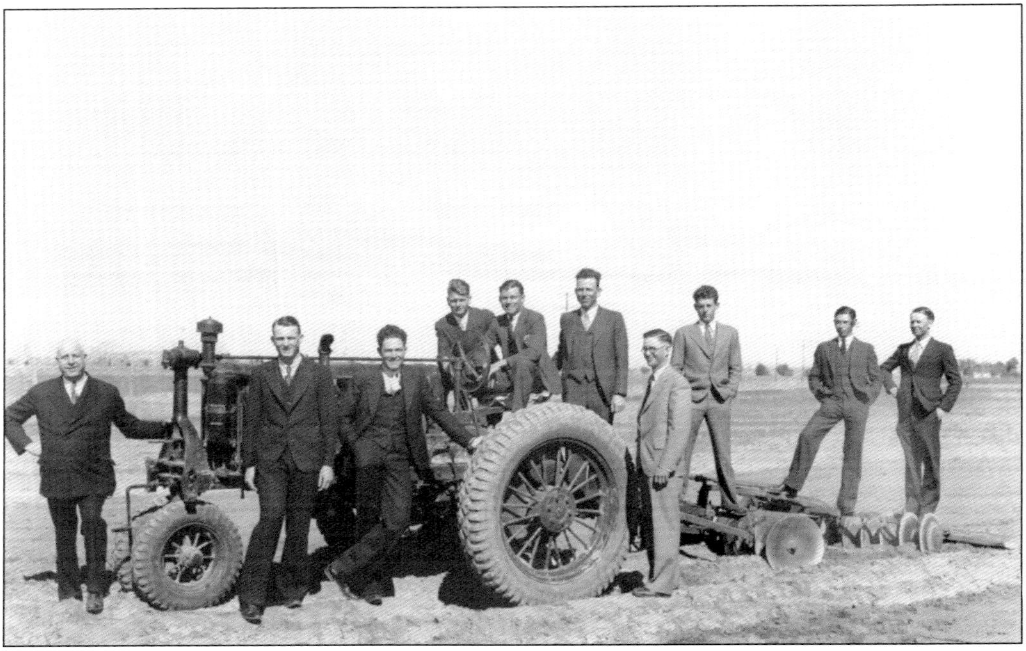

Paul Litchfield is seen with apprentice farmers and two instructors. Shown here as professionals, these seven young farmers are to use the concept of farming as they would business.

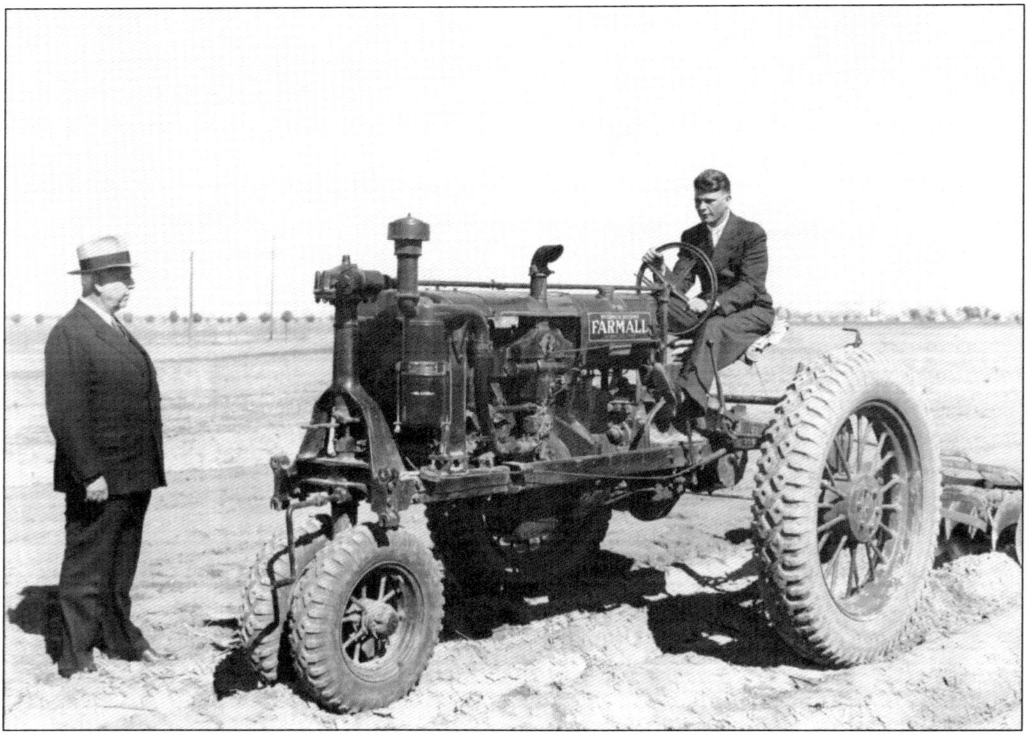


Paul Litchfield is seen here with apprentice farmer Martin Grove enjoying the tractor with the new pneumatic tire featuring the diamond tread designed by Litchfield.

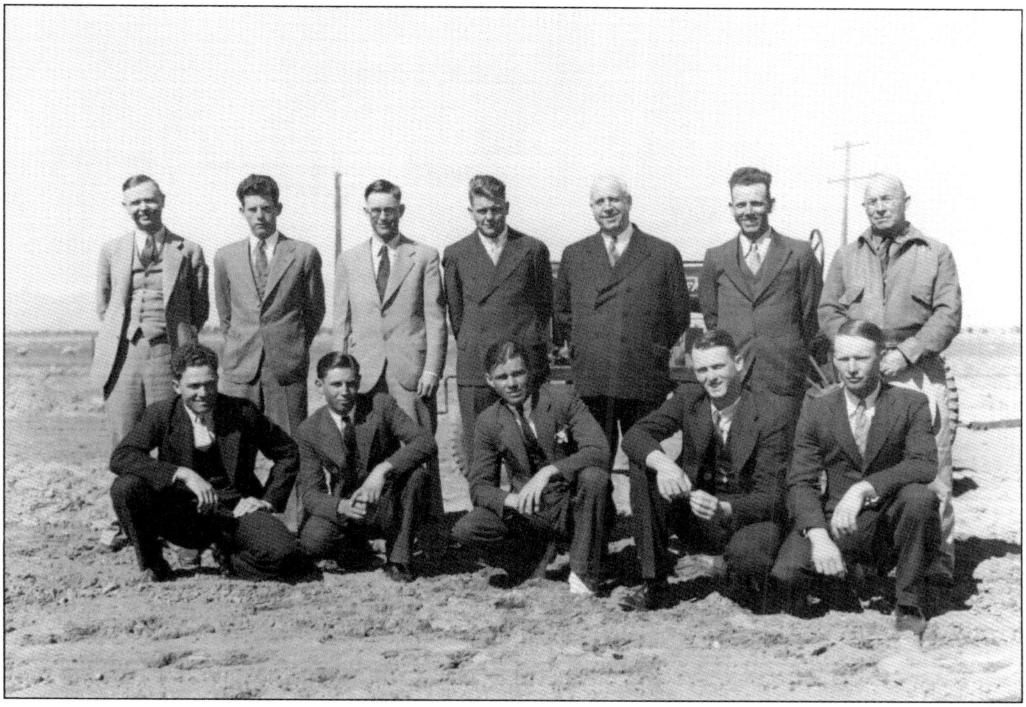

Apprentice farmers are shown here with local managers of Goodyear Farms operation. The ranch served as a training school in theoretical and practical farming for the three-year course. From left to right are (first row) Armon Curtis from Arizona; Juan Brashear from New Mexico; Royal Dorsett from California; Jack Rogers from New Mexico; and Charles Kimsey from Arizona; (second row) A.H. Zieske, resident manager; ? Gansberg from Nevada; Richard (Dick) Lyman from California; Martin Grove from Montana; Paul Litchfield; John Edge from New Mexico; and farm superintendent K.B. McMicken.

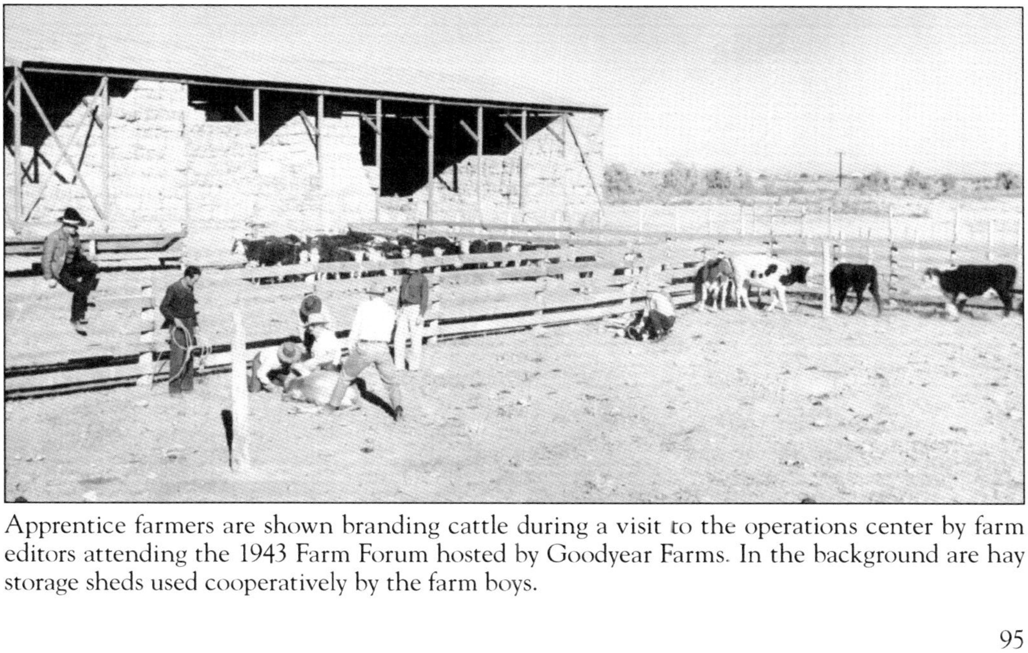

Apprentice farmers are shown branding cattle during a visit to the operations center by farm editors attending the 1943 Farm Forum hosted by Goodyear Farms. In the background are hay storage sheds used cooperatively by the farm boys.

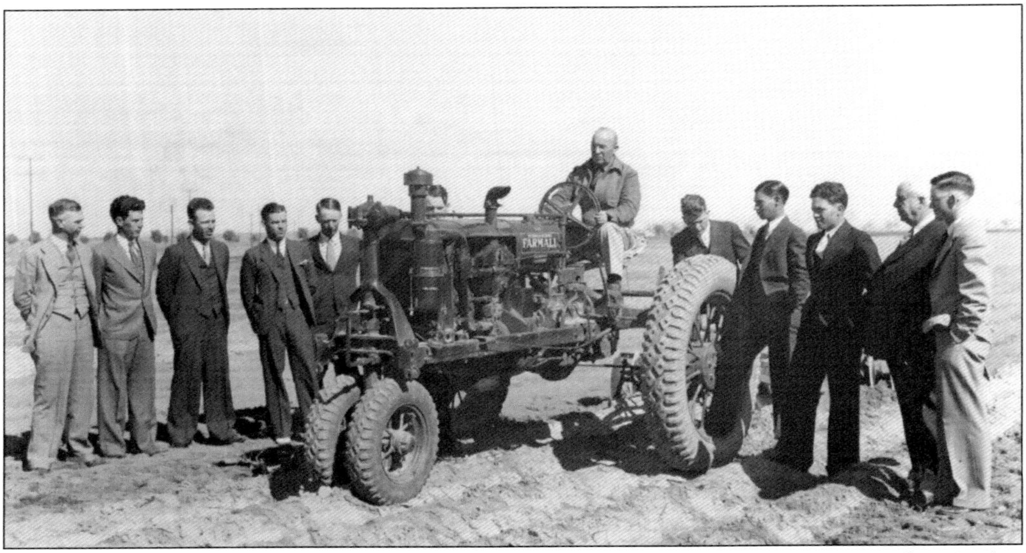

The apprentice farmers are pictured with their instructors and resident manager Arthur Zieske, Paul Litchfield, and farm superintendent Kenneth McMicken sitting on the tractor as they are checking out the pneumatic tires on the tractor.

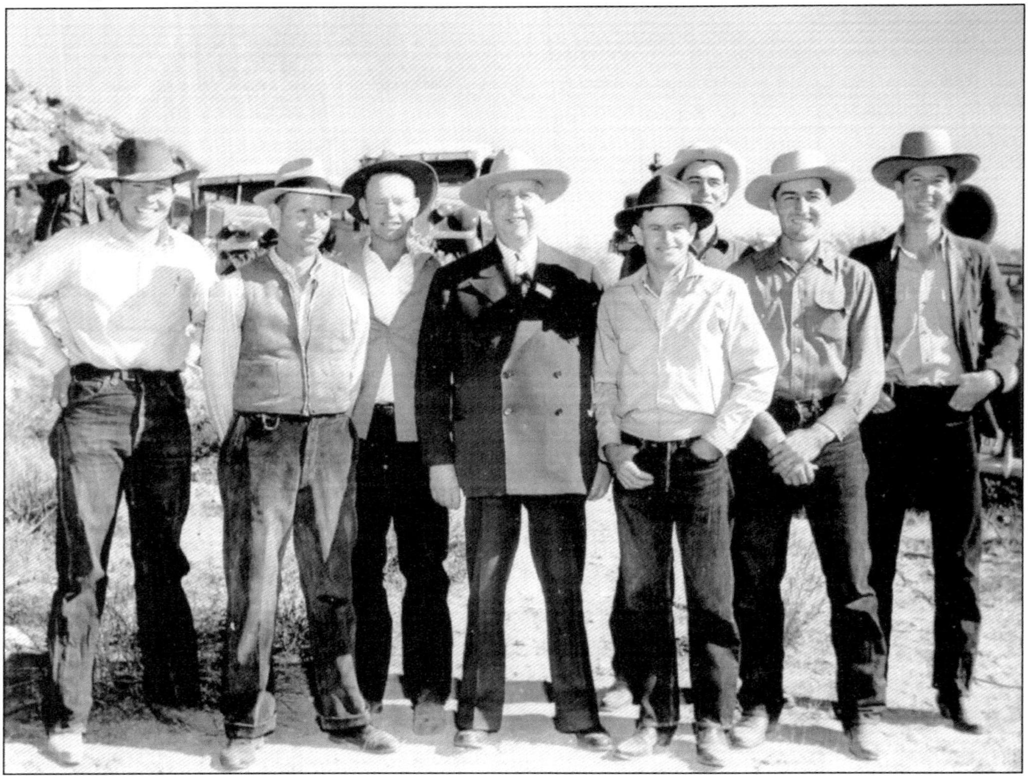

Seven new land owners who received their apprentice farmer land contract pose with Paul Litchfield. They are, from left to right, Armon Curtis, John Edge, Charles Kimsey, Litchfield, George Reismann, Ralph and Chester Hunt (brothers), and Hallam Hestand.

# *Eight*

# Community Development

Many changes took place in the Litchfield Park area in the 1940s and 1950s. The Goodyear Farms operation had gone through many different concepts since it began as a cotton farm in the early 1900s. The community was developing into a popular place to live and visit. World War II was a turning point, as it brought Luke Field into the area and an influx of new people and activities. The Wigwam Resort was closed to the public and housed the military during the early 1940s. The Goodyear Aircraft Corporation in Goodyear added many new people to the area. The Goodyear Aircraft Corporation employed around 7,500 in 1945. The new people moving into the West Valley changed the lifestyle, as the schools had to be enlarged; new retail services and a bank were added. New medical services and doctors were brought into the area.

For the first time, Goodyear allowed private citizens to own homes in Litchfield Park, as it had always been a company town and only had employee housing. The Wigwam Resort had grown in size and popularity, and its growth had a great impact on the community. By 1960, the area had changed so much that Goodyear Tire & Rubber Company made the decision to turn the farm land into villages. Goodyear Farms established a new subsidiary called the Litchfield Park Land and Development Company. Victor Gruen and Associates of Los Angeles was employed to make a study of the development potential and a program.

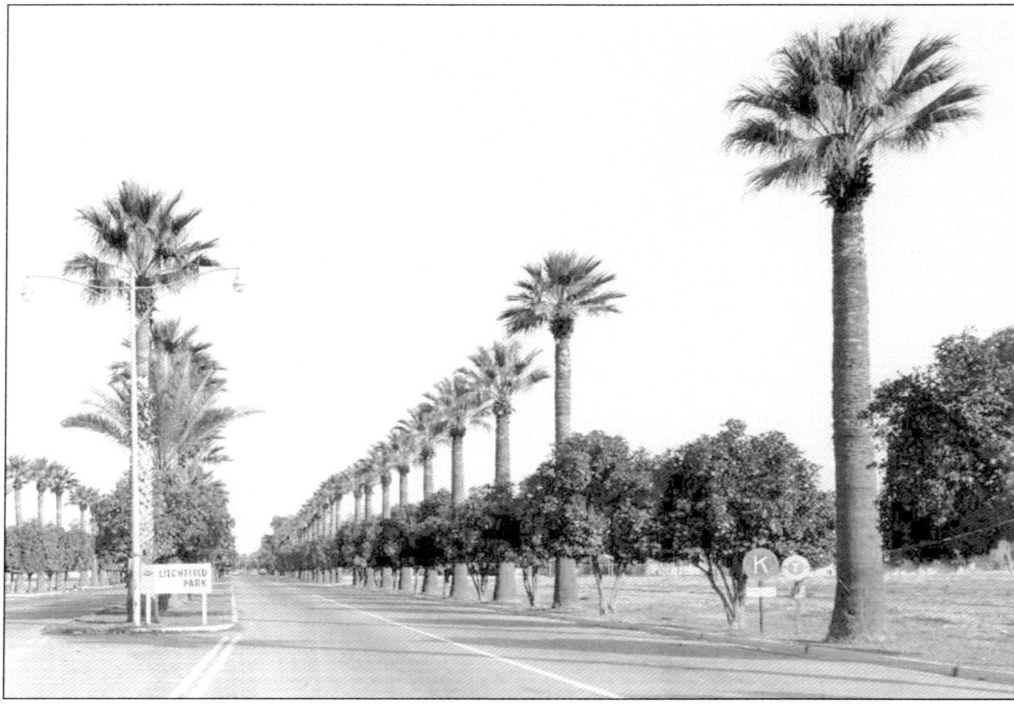


This photograph is looking into Litchfield Park from the south entrance on Old Litchfield Road in the late 1950s. On the left are the last of the Wingfoot homes built in the mid-1940s to alleviate the area housing shortage. The Kiwanis of Litchfield Park sign can be seen on the right. (Courtesy of the City of Litchfield Park.)

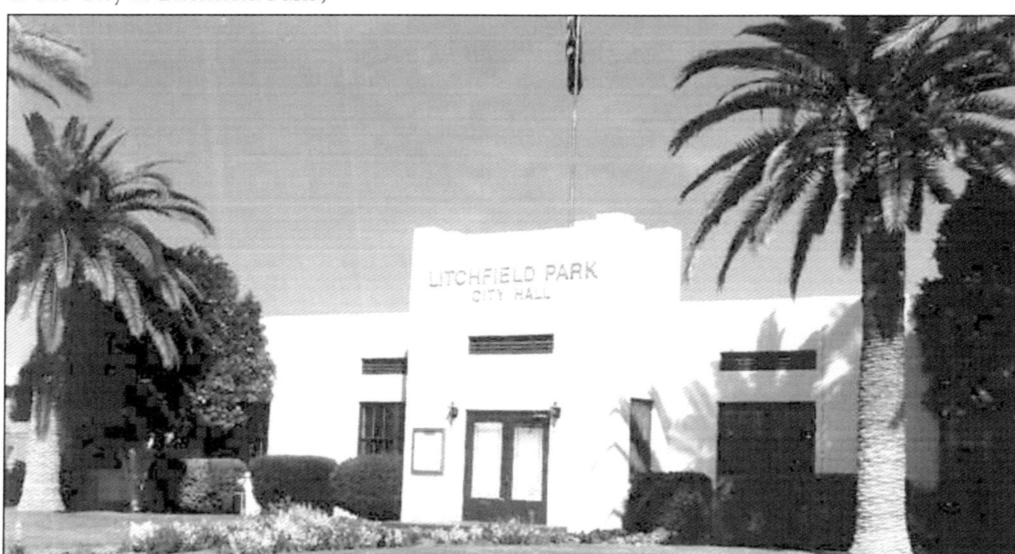


Litchfield Park was incorporated as a city in 1987, after the Goodyear Corporation sold this area in 1986 to SunCor, a subsidiary of the Pinnacle West Corporation of Phoenix. The headquarters building was purchased as the Litchfield Park City Hall on November 16, 1994. (Courtesy of the City of Litchfield Park.)

The headquarters building of the Southwest Cotton Company, built in 1938 of adobe bricks, was designed by architect Jan Furey Munz of Pasadena, California. John "Shorty" Hall is seen standing in front of the Southwest Cotton Company headquarters building on October 10, 1942, after receiving his 25-year service pin from Goodyear. The Southwest Cotton Company moved its headquarters from downtown Phoenix to a temporary building in 1928. (Courtesy of the City of Litchfield Park.)

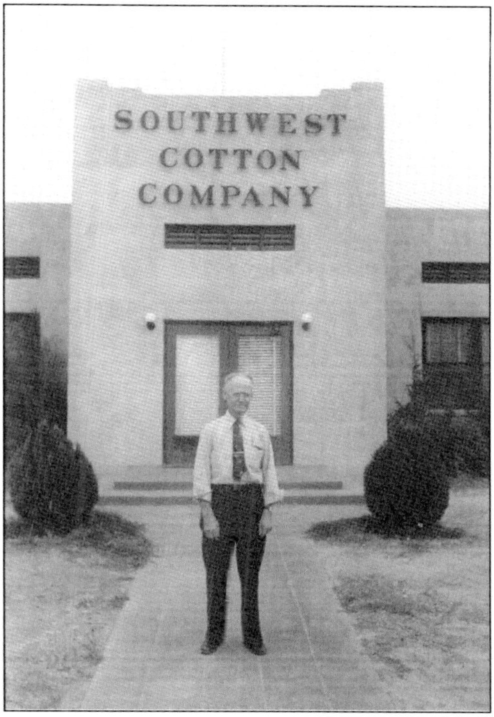


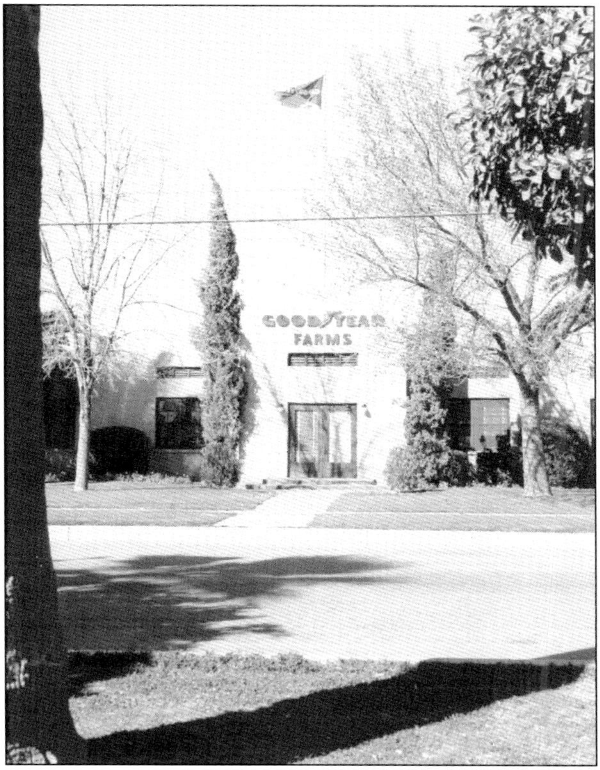


In 1943, Goodyear changed the name from the Southwest Cotton Company to Goodyear Farms. Cotton was no longer the primary crop, as the company had diversified into other crops. (Courtesy of the City of Litchfield Park.)

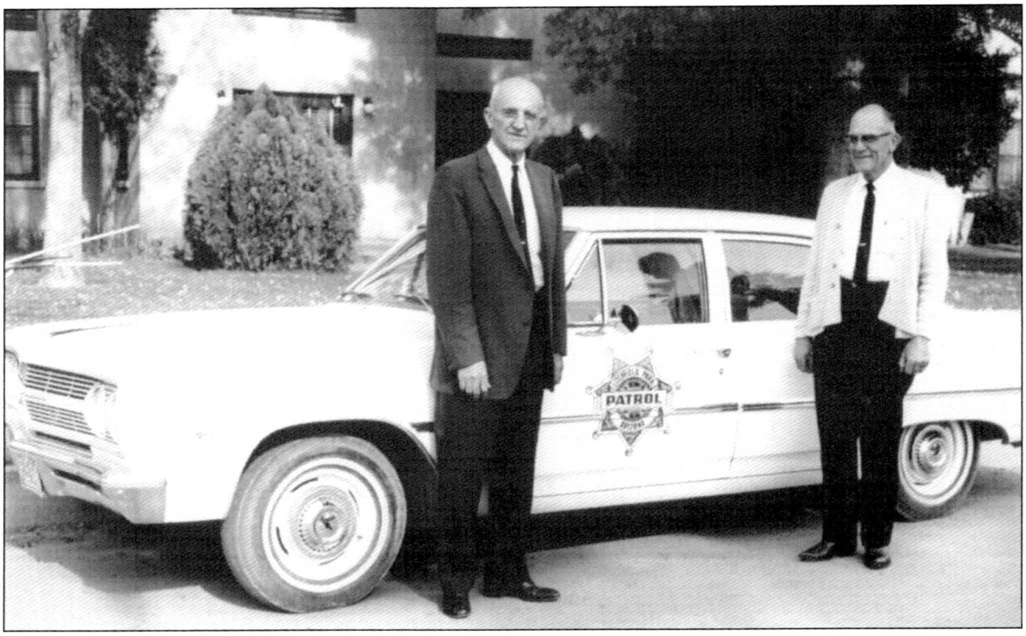


A Litchfield Park patrol car is shown here in the early 1960s. On the left is Newell Kring, and the security officer on the right is John King. Litchfield Park was not incorporated under Arizona state law, since it was a company town; the general manager of Goodyear Farms was responsible for its government. The operation of the town was divided into departments of law enforcement, with Goodyear setting regulations. It employed a watchman who was deputized and worked in cooperation with the sheriff of Maricopa County. If a county, state, or national law was violated, he had the authority to make an arrest. (Courtesy of the City of Litchfield Park.)

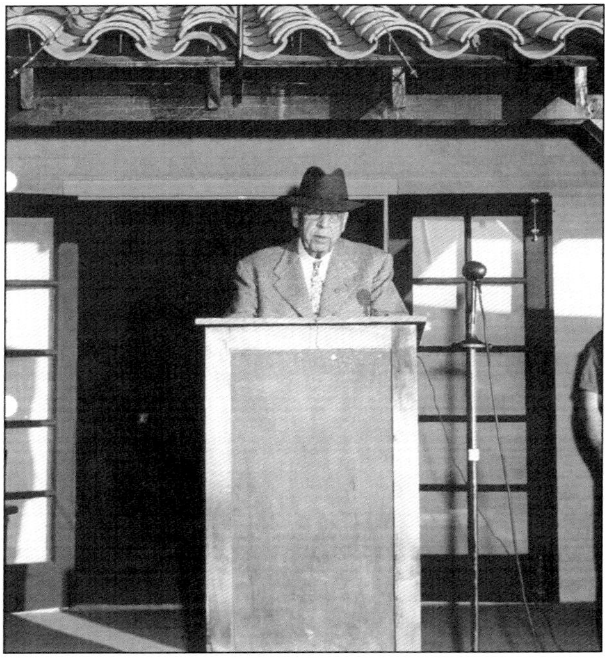

Seen here is the dedication of the Scout Lodge by Paul Litchfield on January 30, 1954. Litchfield had a very special interest in Scouting, even though he had no sons. It was his belief that world peace would be an easier goal if every country involved its young men in learning the values taught in Scouting. His involvement in Boy Scouting started in 1911. By 1914, he had begun to organize troops throughout the Goodyear Company for the employees. In 1936, he was elected as a representative to the National Council of Boy Scouts of America from the Akron, Ohio, area. In 1945, Litchfield was awarded the Silver Buffalo, the highest award presented by the Boy Scouts of America.

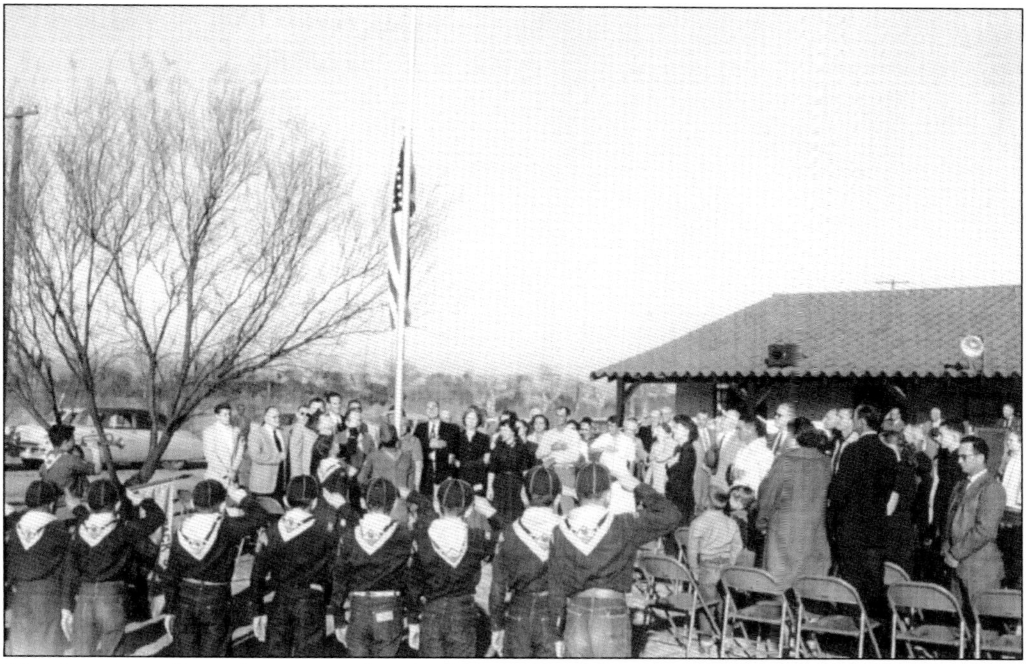

The American flag is being raised at the dedication of the Scout Lodge in Litchfield Park. Still active today, Boy Scout Troop 90 originated in 1929 and was a member of the Roosevelt Council in the White Tanks District.

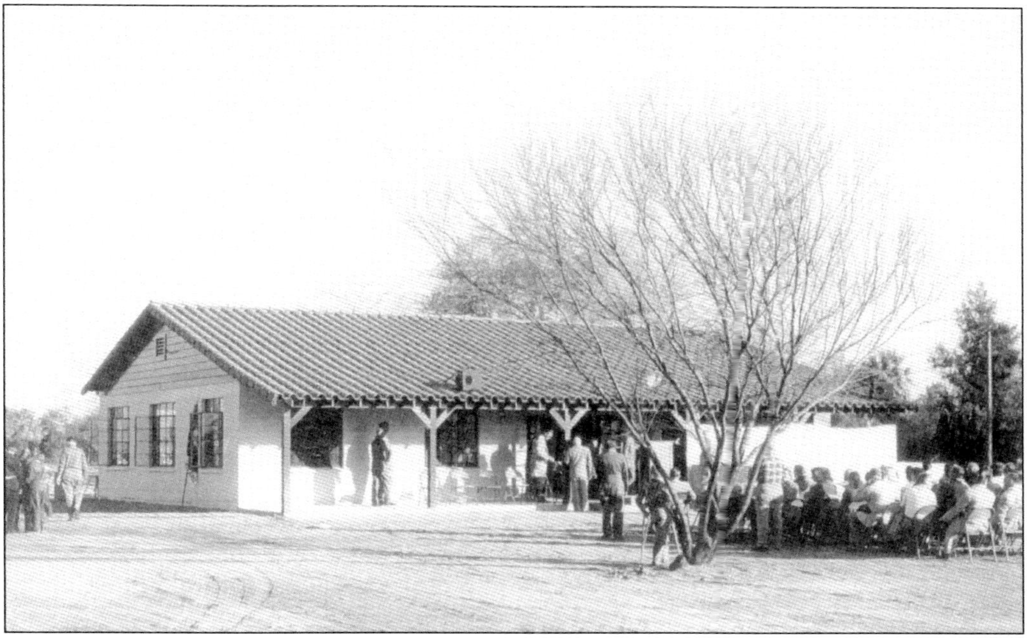

The new Scout Lodge was very special, as the Scouts had been meeting at the Wigwam Corral in the tack room where the saddles were kept. Today, the Scout Lodge is very popular and is used daily by both the Boy Scouts and the Girl Scouts. Scout Park was not established until later, after the Scout Lodge was dedicated.

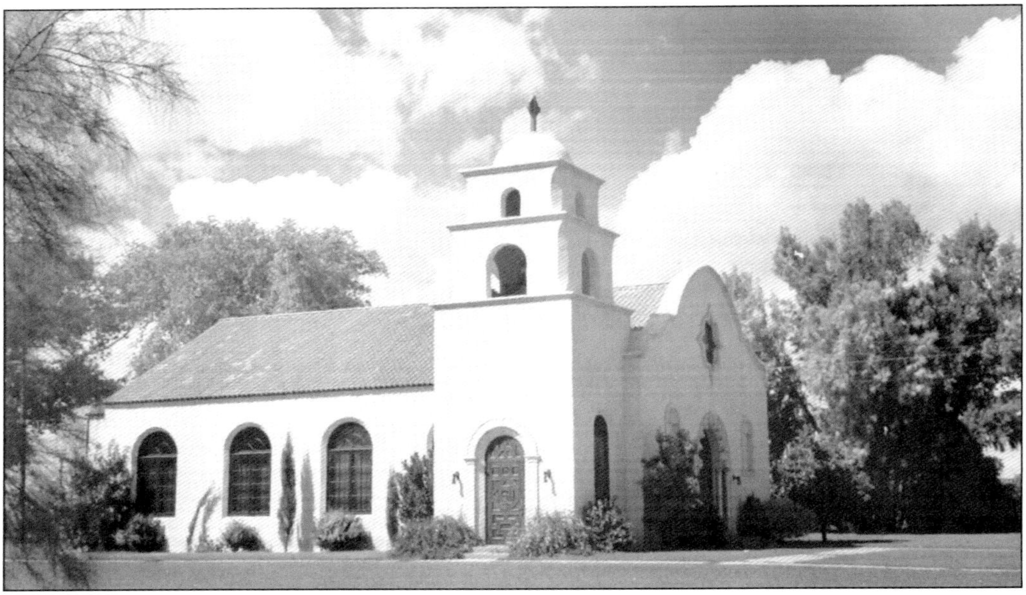

The Church at Litchfield Park, a nondenominational church, was built by Goodyear as a company-owned church. Paul Litchfield played a major role in the design of the church as well as getting funds allocated for the building. Ground was broken on September 10, 1939. The sanctuary in the Mission-style church seated 200. Litchfield brought the bell for the tower from San Diego. The cornerstone, set on November 6, 1939, contains a Bible, the church role, and copies of the constitution and by-laws. (Courtesy of Litchfield Park Historical Society.)

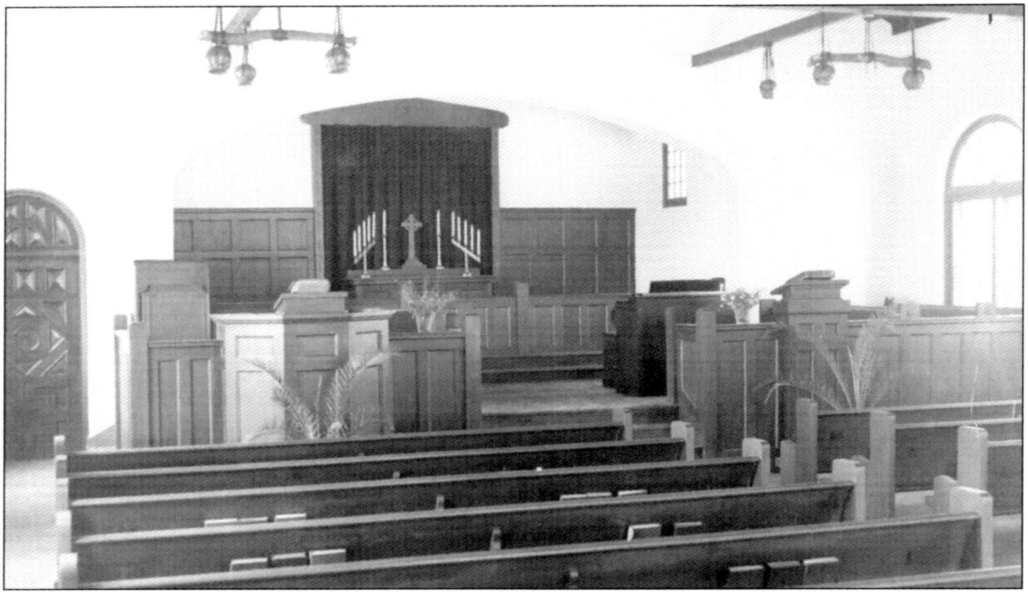

The interior of The Church at Litchfield Park is seen here. The church was built by engineers of the Southwest Cotton Company in 1939. It was deeded over to the congregation in 1971. Before The Church at Litchfield Park was completed, Arthur H. Zieske, Goodyear Farms general manager, had arranged for the nondenominational church services to be held in the community hall. (Courtesy of Litchfield Park Historical Society.)

Zieske came to Litchfield Park as resident manager of Goodyear's farming operations in 1933. He was very active in community development, and it was his leadership that pulled the Protestant faiths together to establish the nondenominational Church at Litchfield Park. He served as the first chairman of the church council. The Arthur H. Zieske Fellowship Hall at the church was named in his honor.

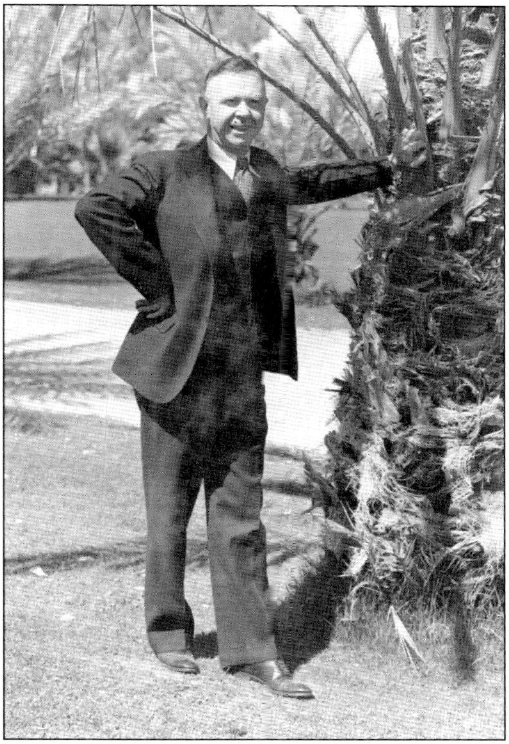

Seen here is an aerial view of The Church at Litchfield Park in the late 1940s. The Air Line Canal runs to the north of the church. The old hospital just west of the church was made into a Wigwam annex. It was still standing in 1975. Employee housing is across the street and north of the Wigwam area.

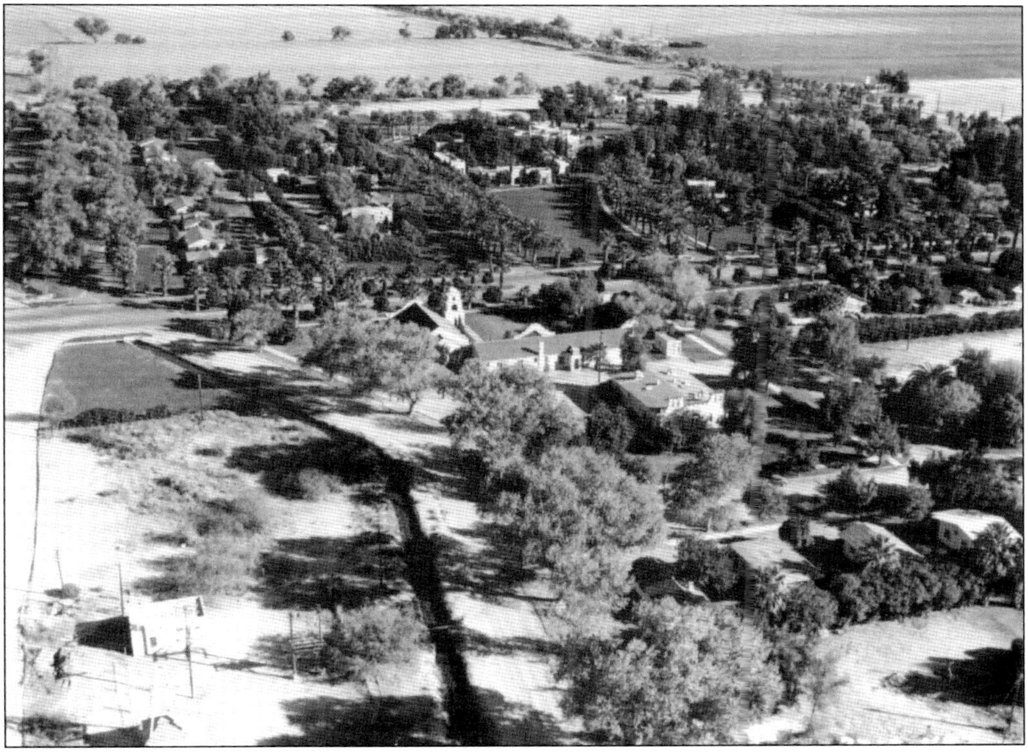

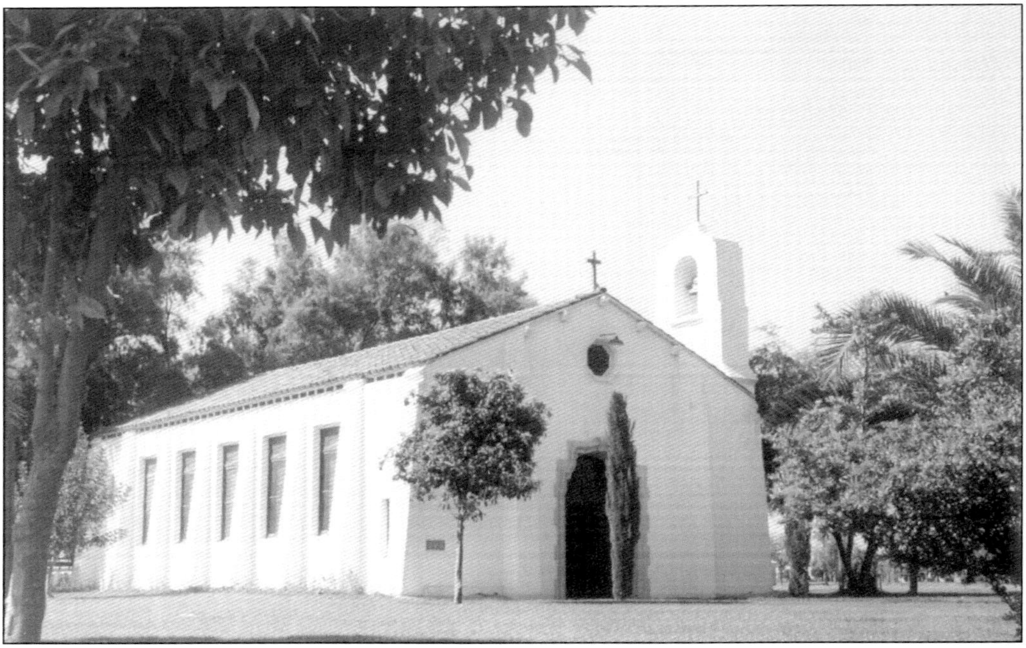

The St. Thomas Aquinas Catholic Mission Church was the first church in Litchfield Park. The church was built by Paul Litchfield in 1919 for migrant farm workers and only seated about 125 people. It was used by Wigwam guests and also local members. The Wigwam guests donated statues to the church. It was the only Catholic church in Litchfield Park until it was sold in 1973, and a much larger church that seated around 700 was built in the early 1980s across from the lake.

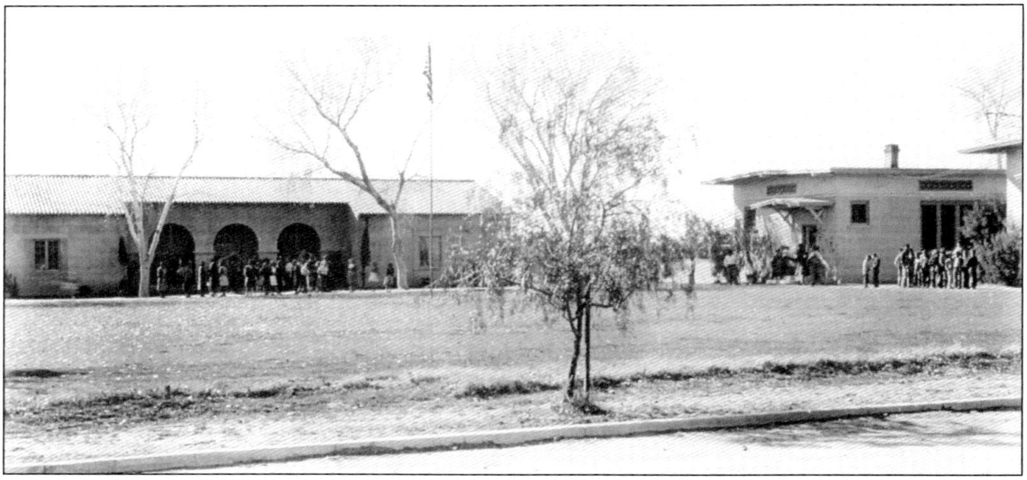

The Litchfield Elementary School went through many changes as the area grew in population. All four of the one-room adobe buildings were occupied by the third year the school was open. The main elementary school building was completed in 1938 with WPA assistance. The high school started in 1928, and grade school and high school students shared buildings. With the addition of more students moving into the area during World War II, another building project had to be launched. The Lanham Act, a federal act to assist war emergencies, provided the finances needed to obtain the additional space. The crowded conditions were eliminated by 1942. (Courtesy of the City of Litchfield Park.)

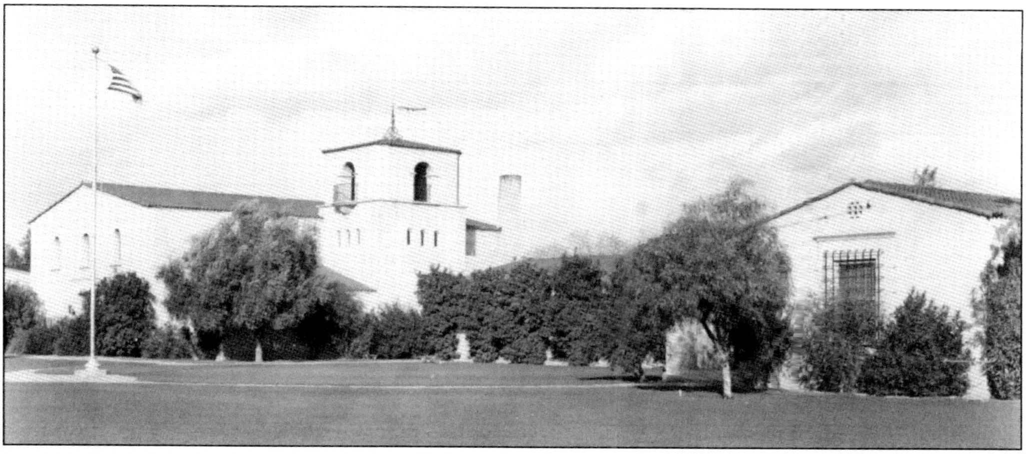

Litchfield High School was founded in 1928. A few classes were held in temporary buildings before the school was created. The only opportunity to attend high school before 1928 was Phoenix Union High School in Phoenix. (Courtesy of the City of Litchfield Park.)

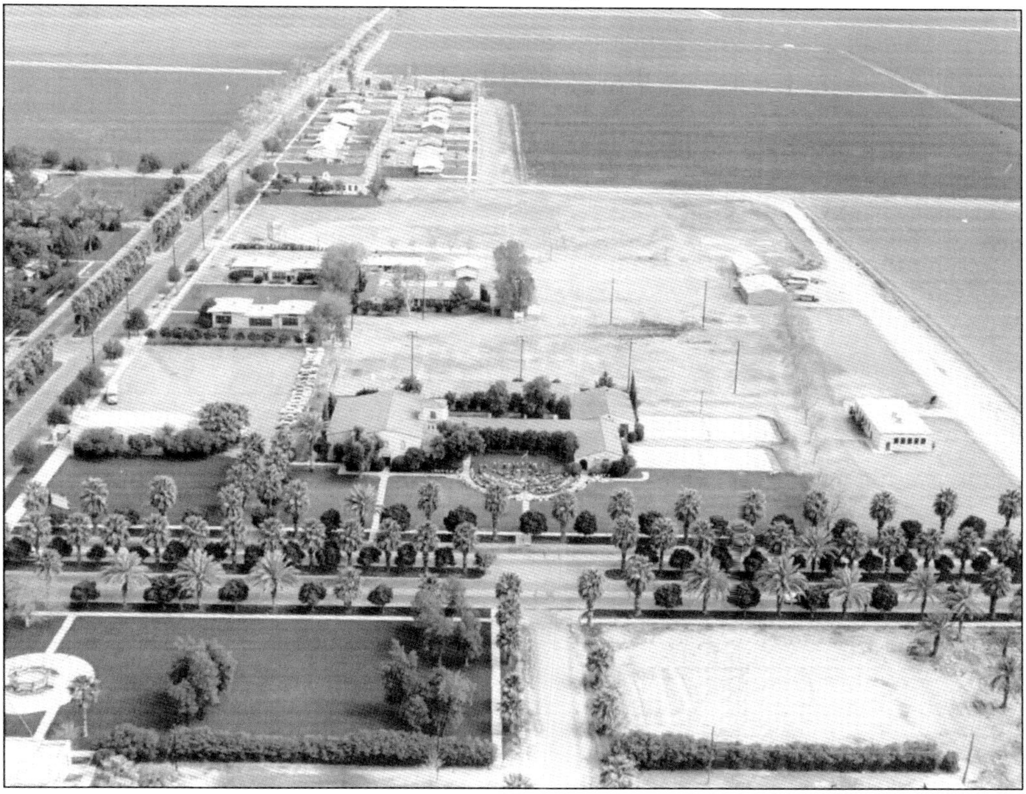

Seen here is an aerial view of Litchfield High School. L.D. Shumway became superintendent of Litchfield schools in 1928 and retained this position until 1947. During his administration, the school grew and became one of the outstanding schools of its size in the valley. He attributed the success to the high quality of his teaching staff. One of the notable graduates of Litchfield High School was Lattie F. Coor Jr., who was president of Arizona State University from 1990 to 2002. (Courtesy of the City of Litchfield Park.)

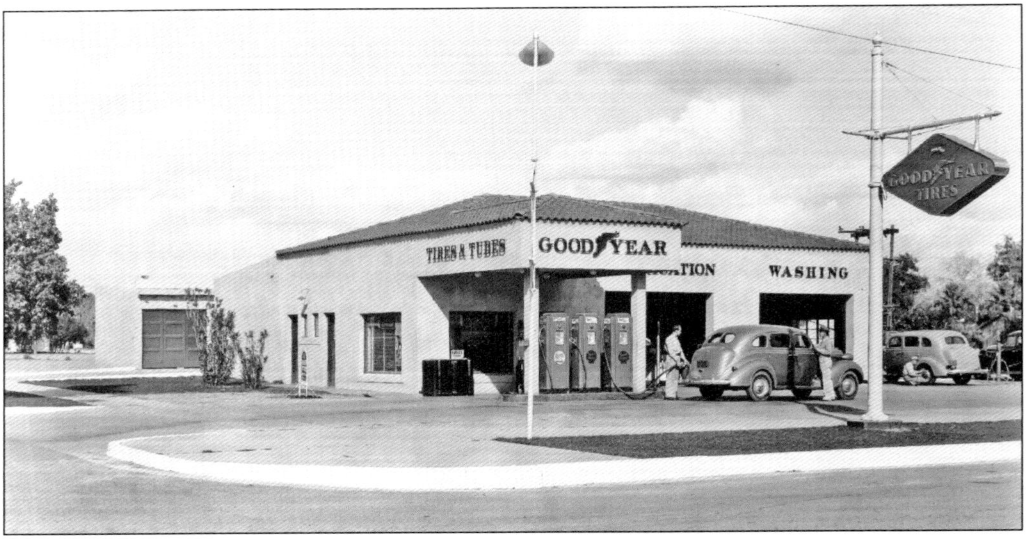

The Goodyear Auto Service Center was one of the many signs of change and growth in the area in the early 1940s. The increased population brought on by the involvement in the World War II activities at Luke Field and at the Goodyear Aircraft Corporation created many new businesses. (Courtesy of the City of Litchfield Park.)

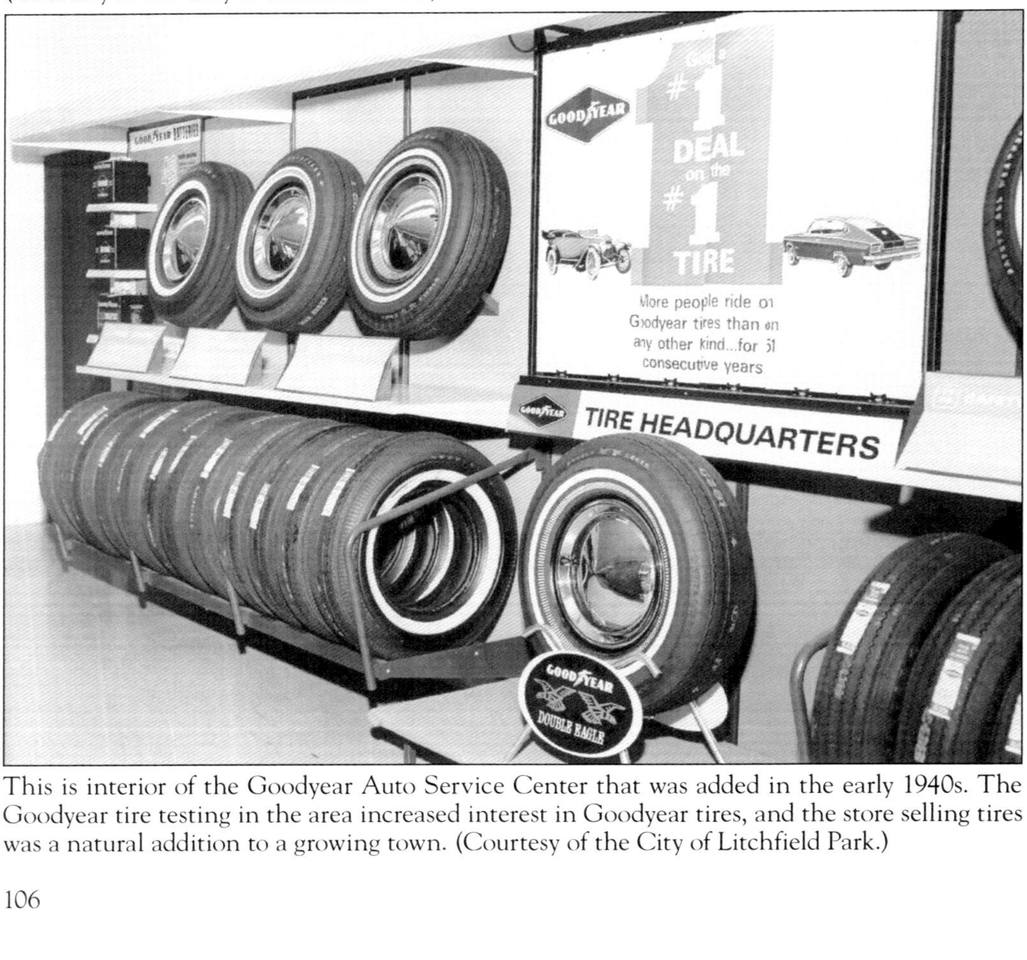

This is interior of the Goodyear Auto Service Center that was added in the early 1940s. The Goodyear tire testing in the area increased interest in Goodyear tires, and the store selling tires was a natural addition to a growing town. (Courtesy of the City of Litchfield Park.)

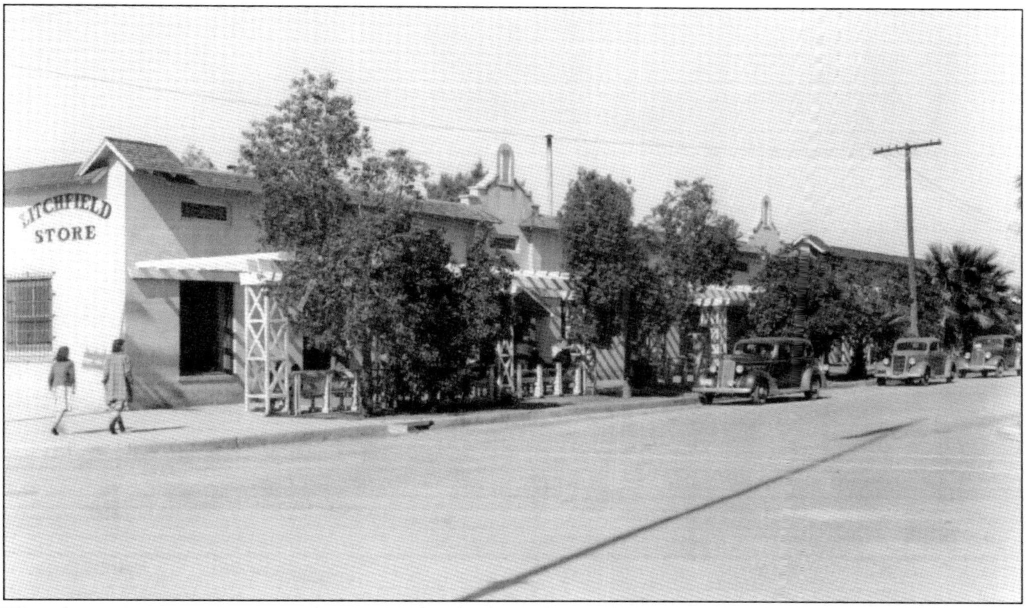


The downtown area is seen here as it looked in the early 1940s. This picture was taken prior to the 1943 fire downtown. The Litchfield Store was a general store as well as a grocery store and supplied almost every household need as well as clothing and hardware. Nadge Abraham purchased it in September 1933 and was the owner during the big fire. (Courtesy of the City of Litchfield Park.)

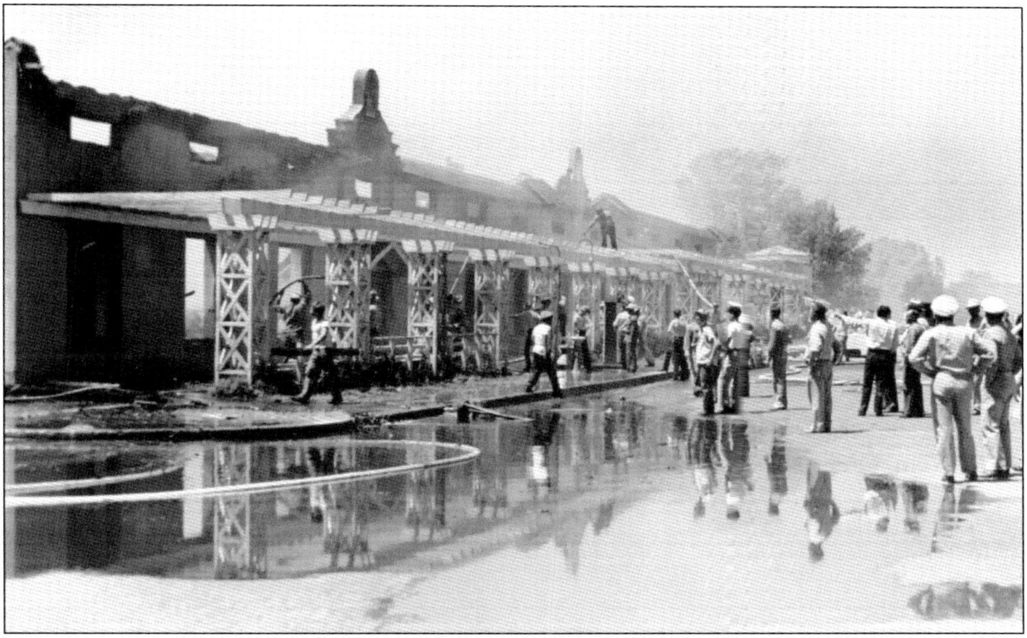

The downtown fire was in September 1943. After the fire, a modern grocery store was built instead of the old general merchandise store. A larger building providing room for a warehouse was constructed and extended west to the alley. A café was built to the north, and a banquet room was built in conjunction with the café. (Courtesy of the City of Litchfield Park.)

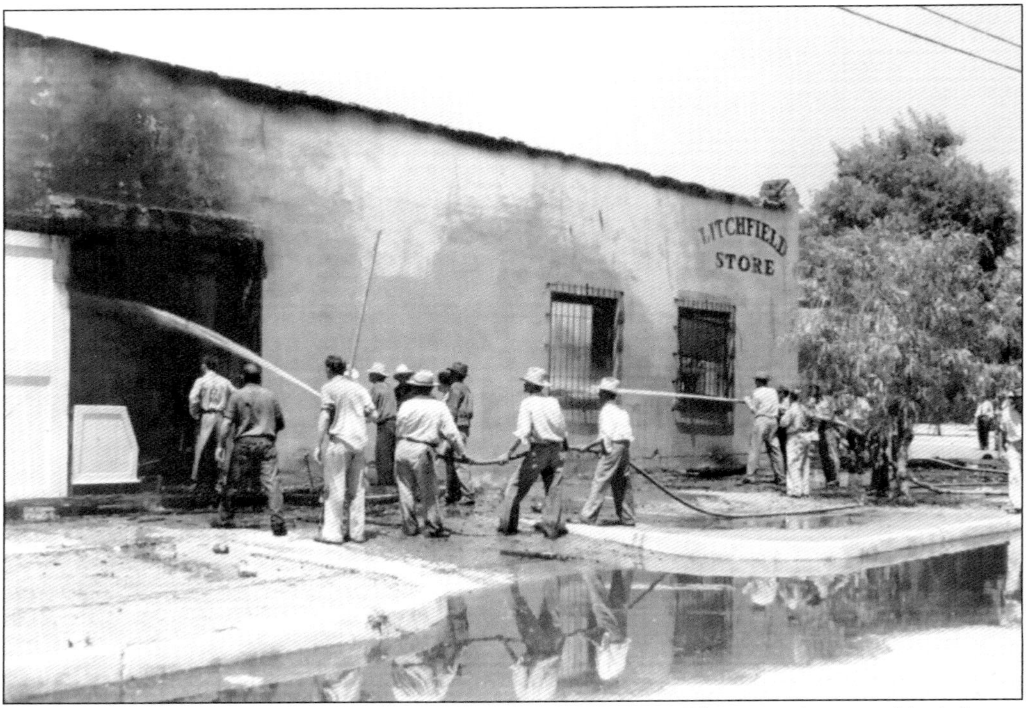


The intense fire did quite a bit of damage to the downtown area. The entire business block facing Litchfield Avenue was remodeled after the fire, and new shops and a medical office building were added. A space for a post office, which had outgrown the drugstore location, and a new Valley National Bank were added. Dr. R.K. Hilton, MD, and Dr. George McMillan, DDS, the town's first dentist, were brought into the medical offices, which adjoined the drugstore. (Courtesy of the City of Litchfield Park.)

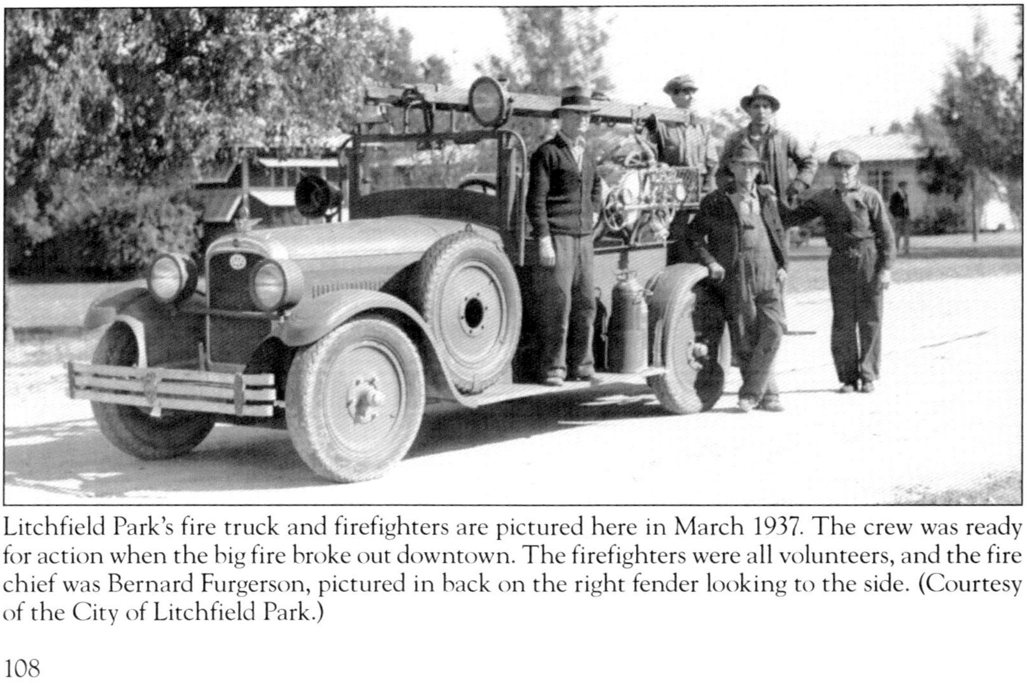

Litchfield Park's fire truck and firefighters are pictured here in March 1937. The crew was ready for action when the big fire broke out downtown. The firefighters were all volunteers, and the fire chief was Bernard Furgerson, pictured in back on the right fender looking to the side. (Courtesy of the City of Litchfield Park.)

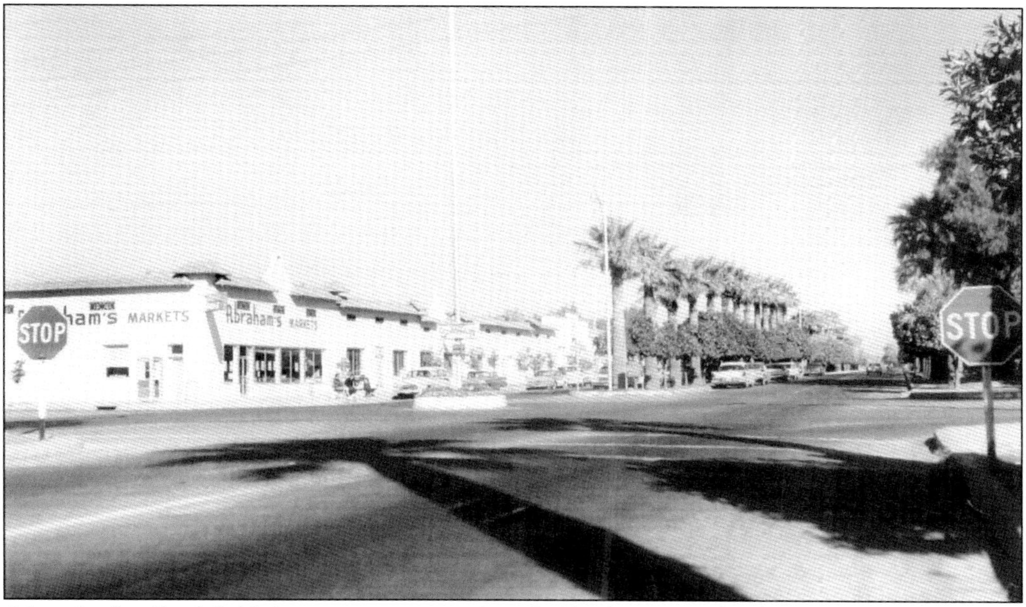


After the fire, Litchfield Avenue was renewed, with Abraham's Market facing the flagpole in the town center. The downtown area had a new and fresh look and was finished in stucco and red tiles. Later a building was placed on the north side of the business block for Litchfield Cleaners, a dry cleaning and pressing business. (Courtesy of the City of Litchfield Park.)

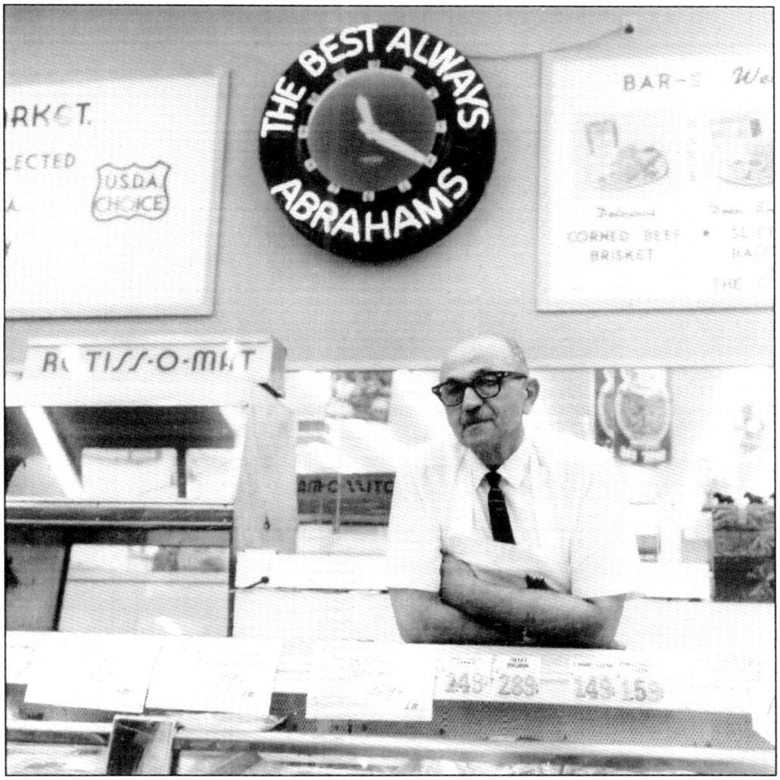


Nadge Abraham is seen at the meat counter in Abraham's Market. Abraham was returning from Phoenix and greeted by the sight of his market engulfed in flames. The community center was used for the market until it was rebuilt. Abraham continued the store's operation until April 1970, when he sold the business and retired. (Courtesy of the City of Litchfield Park.)

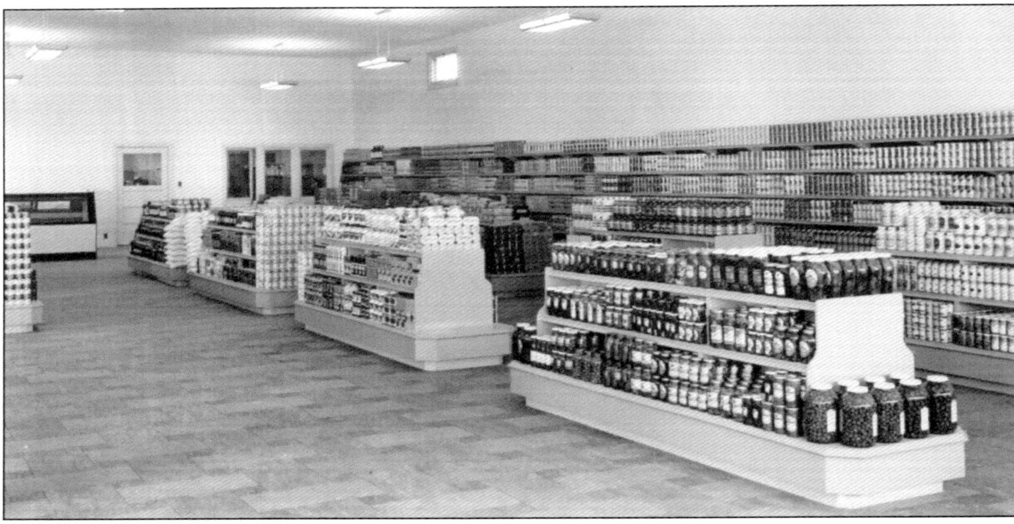

Seen here is an inside view of Abraham's Market after the fire, when it was only as a grocery store and no longer stocked hardware, clothing, and household items. (Courtesy of the City of Litchfield Park.)

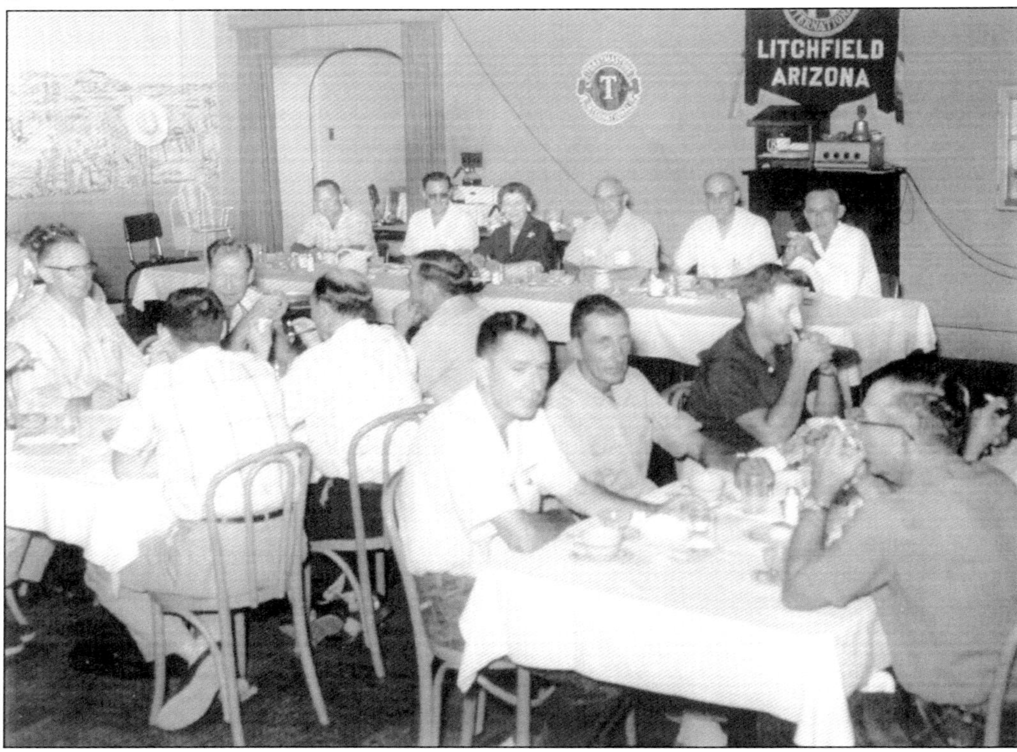


The Kiwanis Club of Litchfield Park is having a luncheon meeting in the Harmon's Café conference room in 1950. Harmon's Café was built north of Abraham's after the 1943 fire. The Litchfield Kiwanis Club was chartered on October 8, 1940, and the first president was K.B. McMicken, early manager of Goodyear Farms and a cousin to Paul Litchfield. The Litchfield Kiwanis Club is one of the oldest civic organizations in the West Valley. (Courtesy of the City of Litchfield Park.)

Dr. Robert K. Hilton arrived in Litchfield Park in June 1941 from Clarkdale, Arizona, in the Verde Valley where he had practiced for 12 years. He and his wife, Roberta, a registered nurse, served the residents of Litchfield Park and the surrounding area until his retirement in 1975. He was the fourth doctor to practice in Litchfield Park. Besides local residents and employees of Goodyear Farms and Goodyear Aircraft (later Goodyear Aerospace), he and Mrs. Hilton tended to the needs of Wigwam guests as needed. He made house calls at the Wigwam Hotel and the camps alike. A native of New Mexico, his fluency in Spanish made him a natural for caring for the Mexican workers, who might not be entirely comfortable expressing their medical concerns in English. Dr. Hilton lived to be 102 years old and died at his home on January 24, 2005. (Litchfield Park Historical Society.)

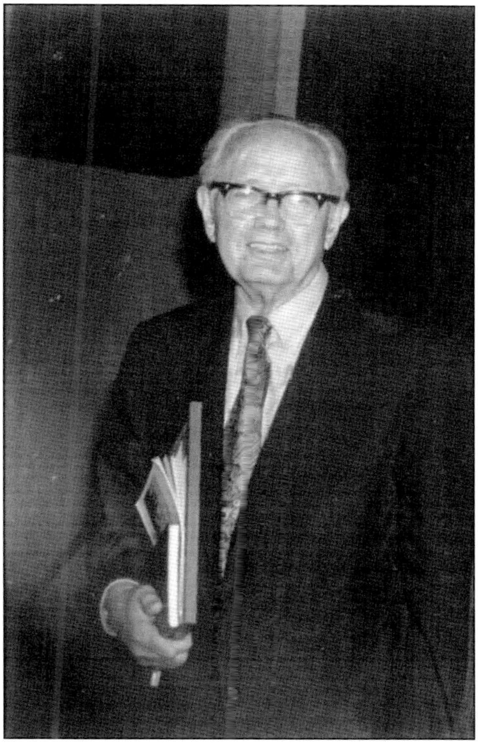

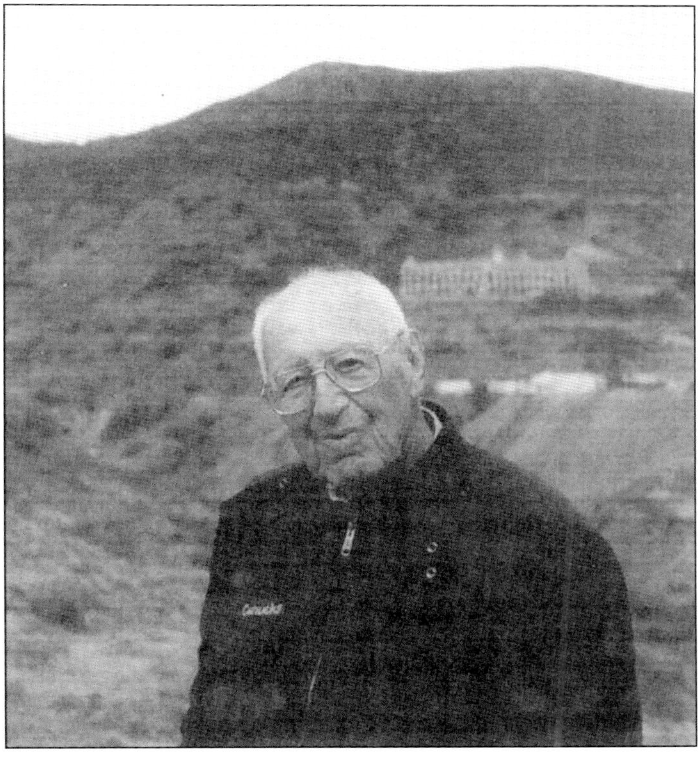

Dr. George H. McMillan was the first dentist in Litchfield Park and was enthusiastically welcomed by local residents. He practiced dentistry here until his retirement in 1978. He died in February 2001 at 95 years of age. Dr. McMillan came to Litchfield Park from Clarkdale, Arizona, at the prompting of his friend Dr. Robert Hilton. The two families lived next door to each other in the first two privately owned homes in Litchfield Park. Dr. McMillan was joined by his son Dr. Robert (Bob) McMillan as an associate in 1963. Dr. Bob retired in 2001 and is still active in the community. (Courtesy of Dr. Robert McMillan.)

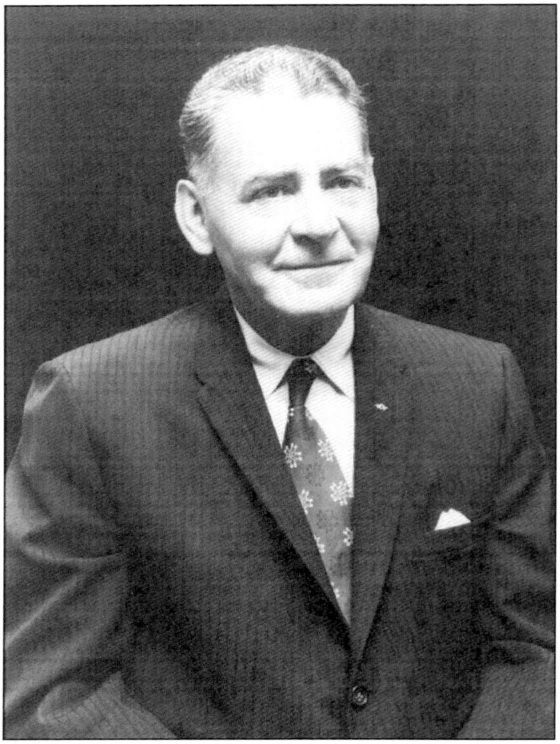

Charles A. Barrow, founder of Barrow Neurological Institute in Phoenix, first came to Litchfield Park in the late 1930s when he and his grandfather stayed at the Wigwam Resort. He later moved to Litchfield for the warm climate in Arizona in support of his wife, Judy, who had health problems. Dr. John Green, a famous neurosurgeon in Phoenix, cared for his wife. Death came to Judy in 1957. In 1962, ground was broken for the Barrow Neurological Institute proposed to St. Joseph's Hospital. The institute is now noted as one of the top 30 in the world. The Barrow family left Litchfield Park and moved to Phoenix in the late 1960s. Charles's son Tim Barrow, who grew up in Litchfield Park, became active in Phoenix. He was named chairman of the Arizona Statewide Home Appraisal Program in 1967 and also became the youngest majority whip and state speaker of the house in the United States in 1969–1970. In 1974, Tim Barrow was elected mayor of Phoenix. (Courtesy of Tim Barrow.)

Jacque Mercer, Miss America 1949, was born and raised in Litchfield Park. She was an ambitious, talented, and intelligent young person, in addition to her natural beauty. Jacque developed a résumé for success. She grew up in a rural setting and was a member of 4-H, where her many talents were nurtured, particularly her sense of design. She was valedictorian of her grade school; modeled throughout her high school years; performed as a lead in class plays; was a member of the National Honor Society; maintained honor roll status in high school and college; and was seriously interested in theater. Her degree from Arizona State University in 1954 is in fine arts. She majored in theater and costume design. In 1949, Jacque Mercer became Miss Phoenix, then Miss Arizona, and finally Miss America. She also won first place in the talent and swimsuit competitions. Jacque went on become a successful businesswoman and was the mother of two children. (Courtesy of Arizona State University.)

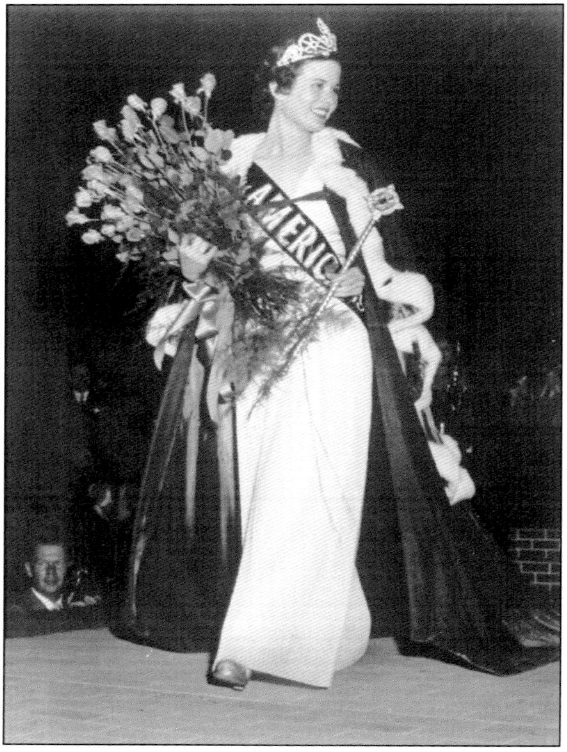

# *Nine*

# World War II

World War II brought a new lifestyle to Litchfield Park with the establishment of Luke Field Army Air Base and the Goodyear Aircraft Corporation. As these became operational, an influx of new people brought many changes to the area. There was a shortage of housing and services, and the schools were overcrowded. Luke Field was activated on April 21, 1941. This brought many changes to Litchfield and Goodyear. Along with the new challenges, it also brought improvements. Services in the area improved as the influx of several thousand military and civilians increased the population.

Litchfield changed from a quiet and reserved town to one of much activity. The Wigwam Resort was closed to the public from 1942 to 1945 and leased to the government to house the military personnel from Luke Field. Transportation improved with bus service from the Phoenix City Bus Company. The Central Arizona Power and Light Company added substations to supply additional power, and a new gas line supplied gas to each house, solving cooking and heating problems. The number of telephones increased from 33 to 613 during the war.

The Goodyear Aircraft Corporation in Goodyear made a real impact on this area, as it brought in up to 7,500 workers by January 1945. Again this created a housing shortage, and this gave Paul Litchfield the incentive to build Wingfoot Homes to help alleviate the problem. In 1943, a US Navy facility was installed to work in conjunction with the Goodyear Aircraft Corporation. Its function was to receive the planes modified by the Goodyear Aircraft Corporation and deliver them to the proper destination. In 1945, when the Goodyear Aircraft Corporation closed, the primary function of the naval air facility was to become a preservation and storage area for planes. By the close of 1947, one thousand planes had been stored there.

One of the interesting developments in this area was the new subsidiary started by the Goodyear Corporation known as Wingfoot Homes. It was organized in 1944, and the plant was located a half-mile northwest of Litchfield Park. The Wingfoot Homes were portable housing and had wings so they could be compacted for transport by truck or freight. A new area opened for the Wingfoot Homes in the southwest section of town west of Litchfield Avenue. The construction of the homes was discontinued in 1949.

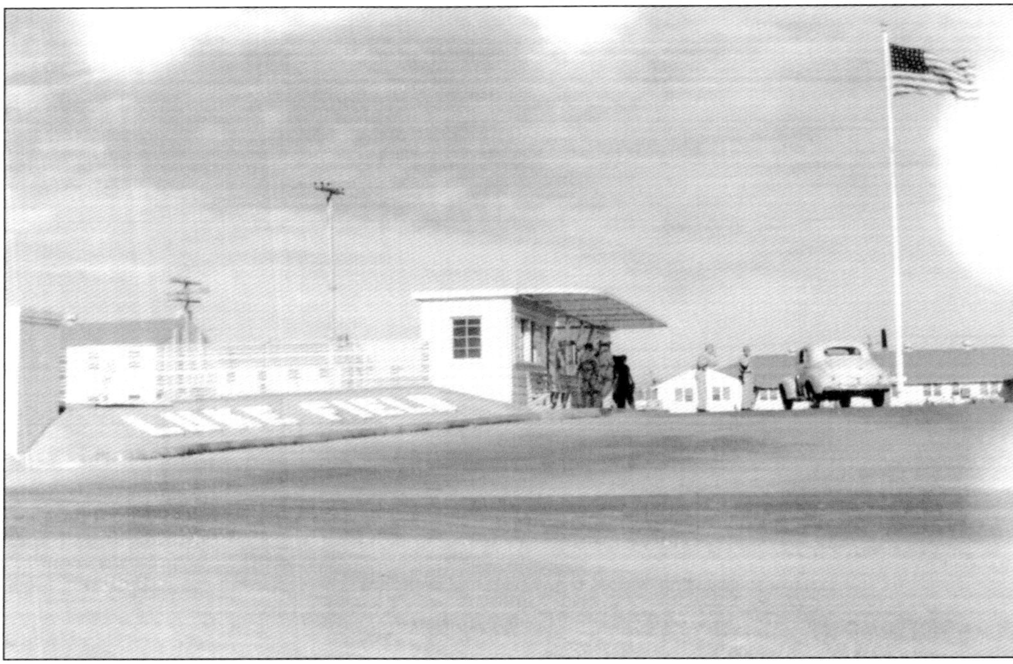


Luke Field was established on April 21, 1941. Forty-five cadets started advanced flight training on June 6, 1941. Luke Field was officially dedicated on September 29, 1941, in honor of 2nd Lt. Frank Luke Jr. on the 23rd anniversary of his death. (Courtesy of Luke Air Force Base History Department.)

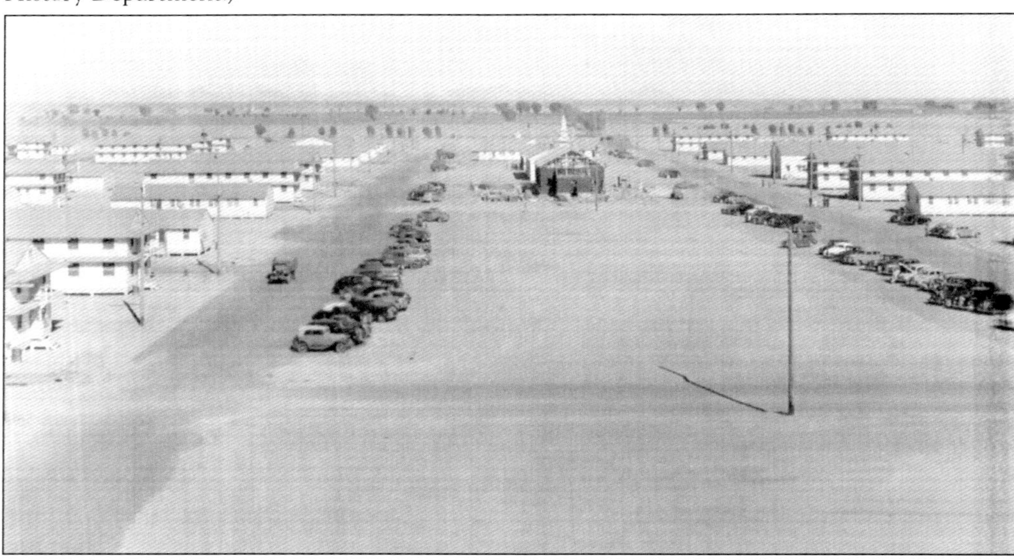

Luke Field neared completion as the nation entered into World War II. It was considered miraculous, as raw desert became a bustling air base in less than nine months. Its population peaked in 1942, and only 375 people remained at Luke when the base closed on November 30, 1946. It reactivated on February 1, 1951, as Luke Air Force Base, part of the Air Training Command under the reorganized US Air Force. Today it remains as the largest fighter training base in the world. (Courtesy of Luke Air Force Base History Department.)

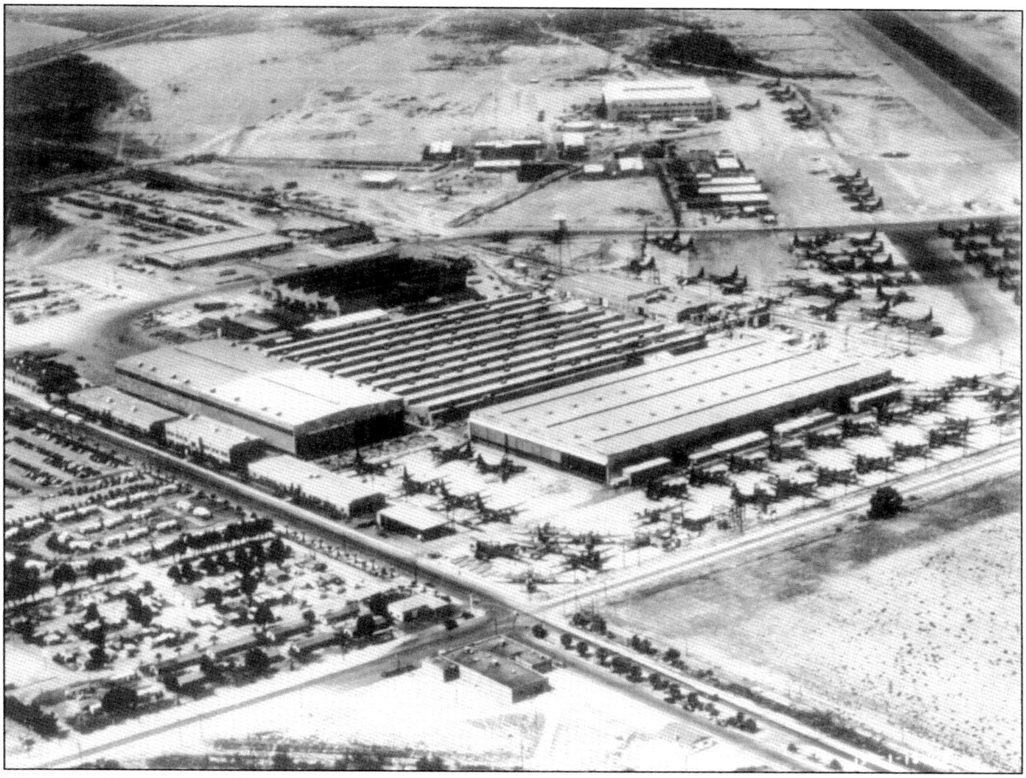

The Goodyear Aircraft Corporation in Goodyear was a very busy location during World War II. The construction of the aircraft corporation started in August 1941, and it was built in three units. The purpose was to establish an airplane parts factory, and it came soon after the building of Luke Field. Paul Litchfield looked for ways his company could assist the government in its defense program and was convinced that increased aircraft production was the most important factor.

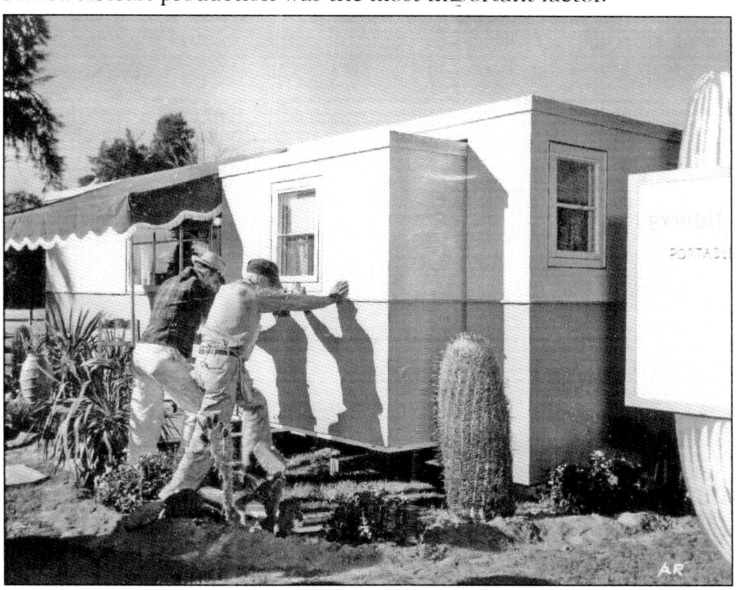

The war industries brought such an influx of workers that much housing had to be provided. Among the types of homes built were Paul Litchfield's Wingfoot Homes. These were prefabricated homes with unique moveable bays that would contract for travel or easy transport. The two men pictured here are pushing the sleeping bay in to make it easy to transport. These homes were built in the Litchfield Park area during the war.

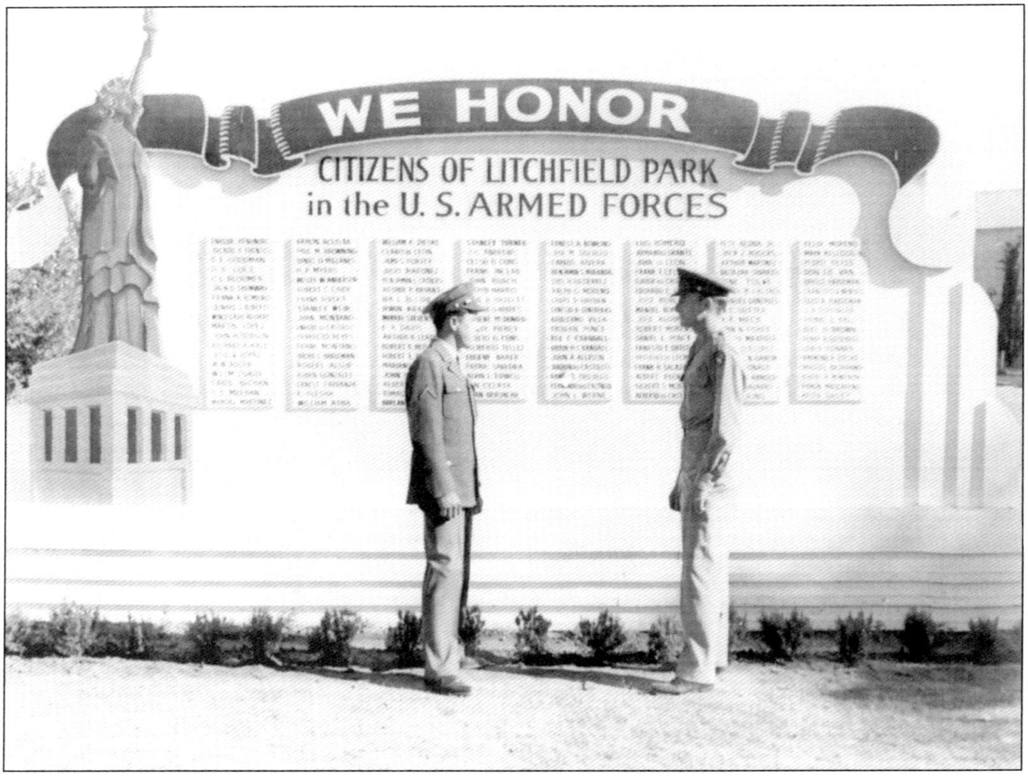


Goodyear Tire & Rubber Company was very loyal and proud of its employees and members of their families who served in World War II. The war was a real turning point for the West Valley. Luke Air Force Base, just north of La Loma on Litchfield Road, still serves as an economic and social asset for Litchfield Park and the area. Goodyear was very connected to the war effort. A memorial to the local men who served in World War II was established downtown in 1943. The memorial listed 188 names, with five killed in action.

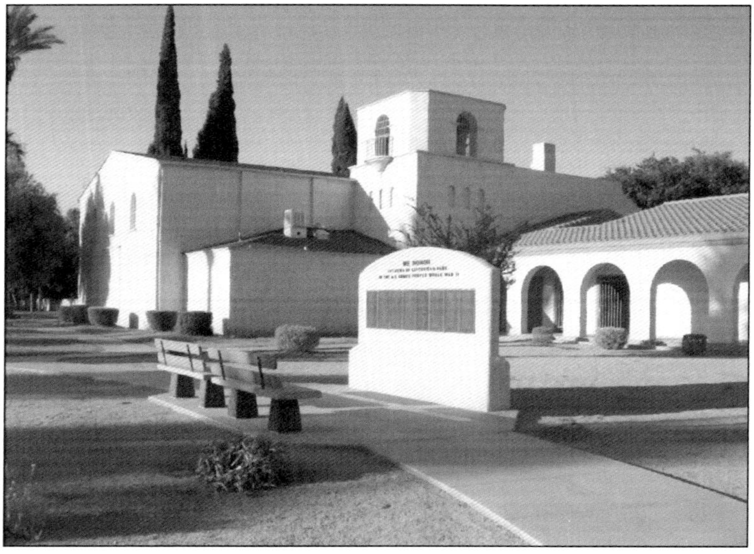

A new World War II memorial was dedicated in May 2007 to replace the memorial that was torn down in the 1960s because of deterioration. The Litchfield Park Historical Society placed this memorial under the flagpole at the old Litchfield High School on Litchfield Road. (Courtesy of Michael Jordan.)

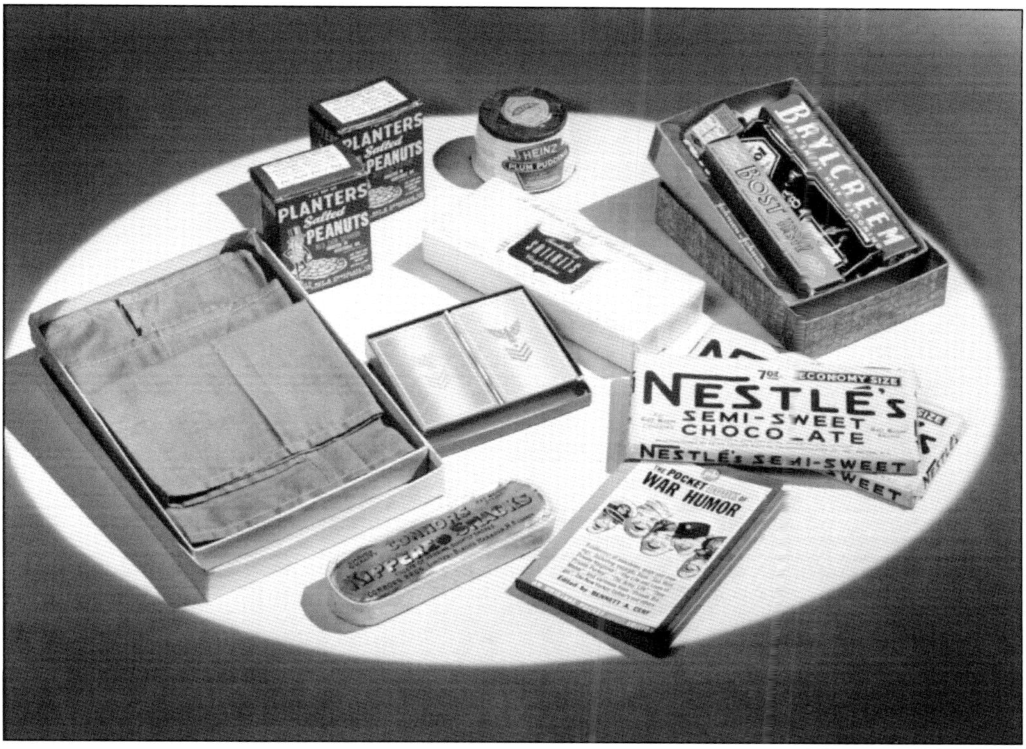


In 1943, Goodyear Tire & Rubber Company management approved a budget of $100,000 to send Christmas packages to all Goodyearites serving in the armed forces. Each person serving received a gift box and a return card to let Goodyear know he received the box. Many cards were received from grateful young men serving around the world in World War II.

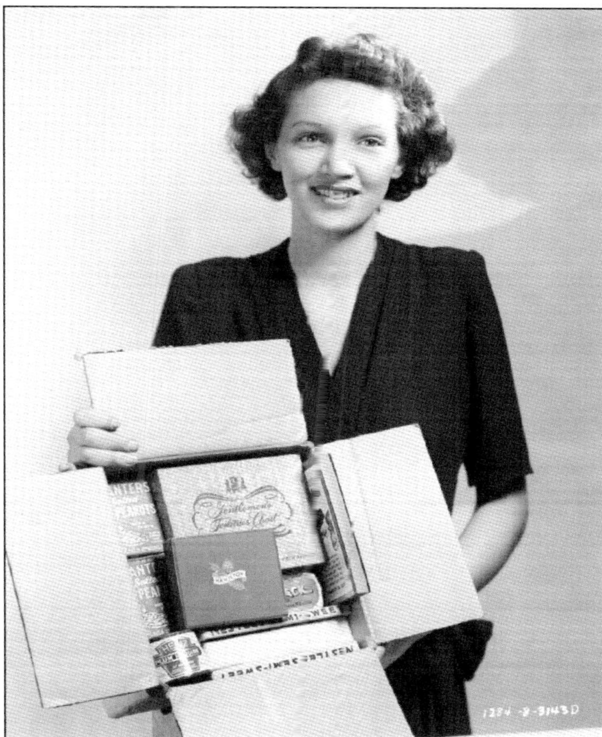

Goodyear's gift boxes were filled with special treats and snacks plus practical and usable items.

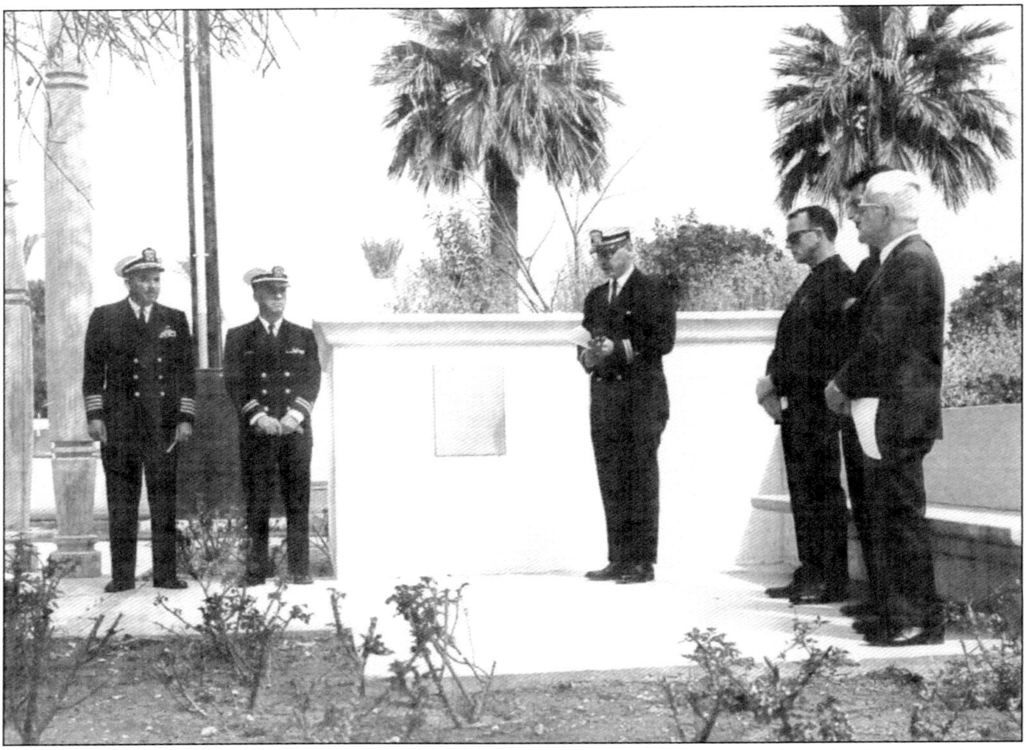

A memorial to naval air facility member John Daly McManus is located on the tree well just north of the Litchfield Library entrance. This memorial was donated by his parents, Capt. and Mrs. John W. McManus. (Courtesy of SunCor.)

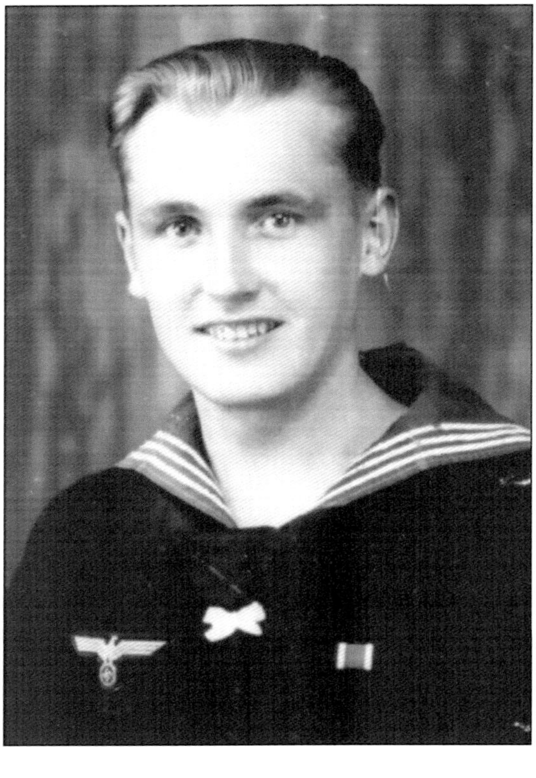

A little-known fact about World War II is the German POW camp located on the southwest corner of Olive Avenue and Cotton Lane, northwest of Luke Air Force Base. It was called Camp No. 6 (Outcamp Litchfield Park). This was one of many POW camps in Arizona. Germans and some Italians were made to work in the cotton fields when the Southwest Cotton Company was operational. Pictured here is Alfred Dietrich from Germany, who was a POW at Camp No. 6 during World War II. (Courtesy of Steve Hoza.)

# *Ten*

# Maturing Town

Litchfield Park went through many changes in the 50 years that this book represents. Paul Litchfield arrived here in 1916, and by 1966, the raw desert had been transformed into a thriving, active community. When the decision was made to change from a farming operation to a village concept, Goodyear hired a new planning and design team. The Litchfield Land and Development Company became a new subsidiary of Goodyear Farms. Victor Gruen and Associates of Los Angeles was employed to make a study of the potential development of the village concept. The Gruen company's master plan was to create 12 villages or communities patterned after Litchfield Park. The first village was identified as Tierra Verde Village.

By 1964, Goodyear had transferred 2,100 acres to the Litchfield Park Land and Development Company. The Litchfield Park Club was established with an Olympic-size swimming pool and tennis courts with facilities ready for use in the summer of 1966. The Litchfield Park Library offered service from the new medical building. Forty miles of pathways for bikes and golf carts were paved, and a six-acre lake was dug. Utility lines were placed underground, and custom homes were either completed or planned. The second village was planned to be developed in the area bound by Litchfield Road on the west, Dysart Road on the east, Thomas Road on the north, and McDowell Road on the south. The Tierra Verde Village was the only village that was completed, as the other villages were never built.

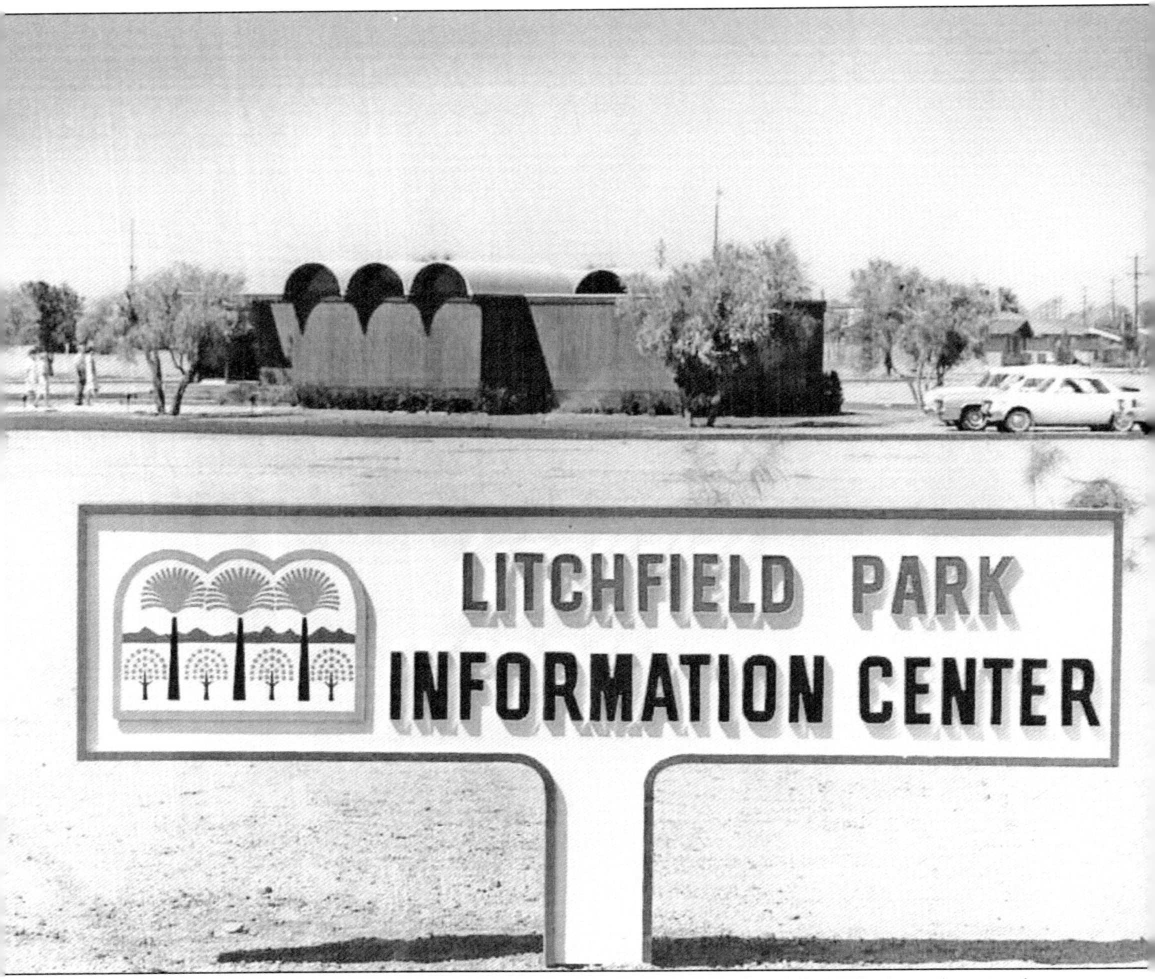

Litchfield Park Information Center's sign was a welcome to Litchfield Park and invited guests to learn more about the Tierra Verde Village and the other planned village communities. (Courtesy of SunCor.)

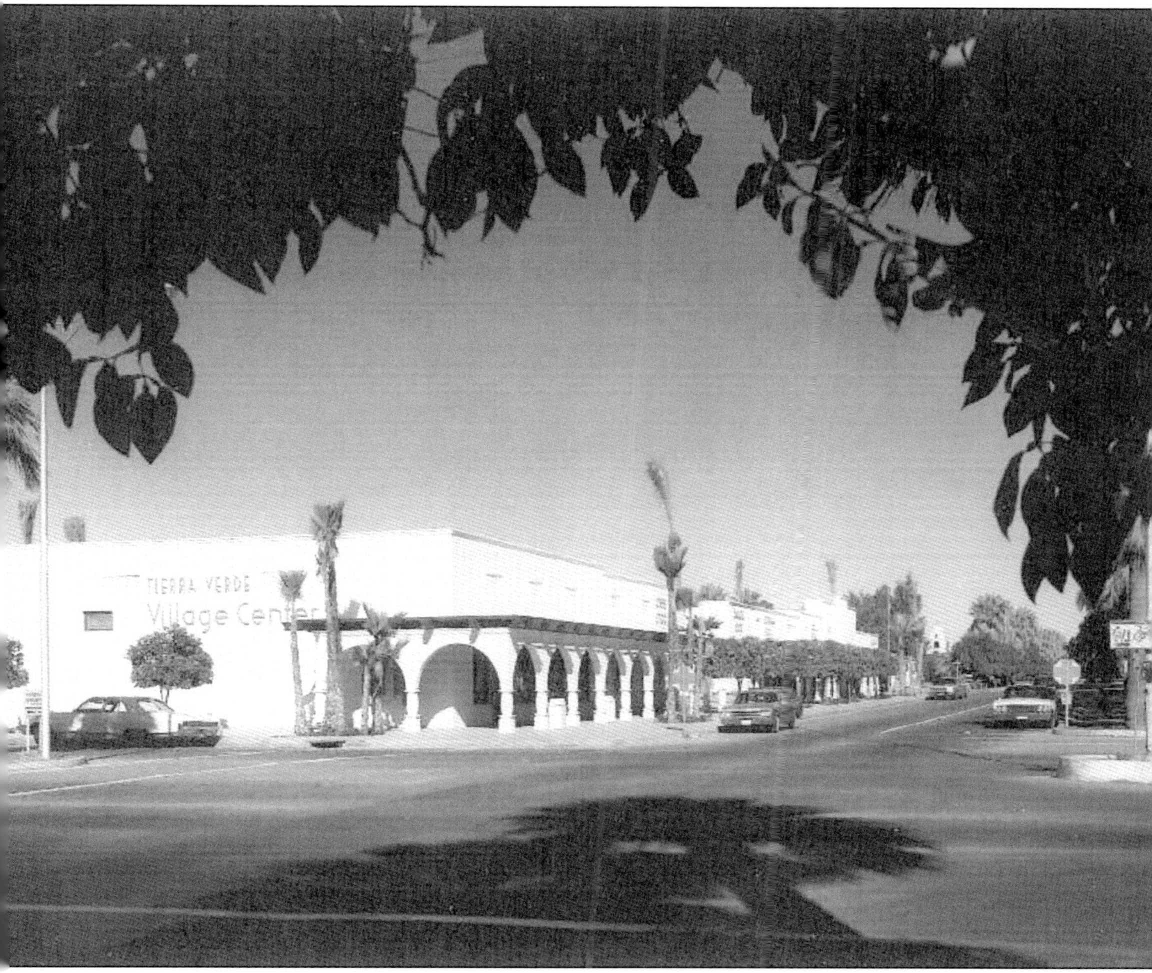


Pictured is downtown Litchfield Park after it became Tierra Verde Village. The arches that start to appear in the design are from architect Bennie Gonzales. Bennie was a renowned Southwest architect who was brought in to help with the new designs of the villages. Bennie's signature was arches, and they can still be seen in almost every building in town. They have become such a part of Litchfield Park that the city logo at one time featured an arch.

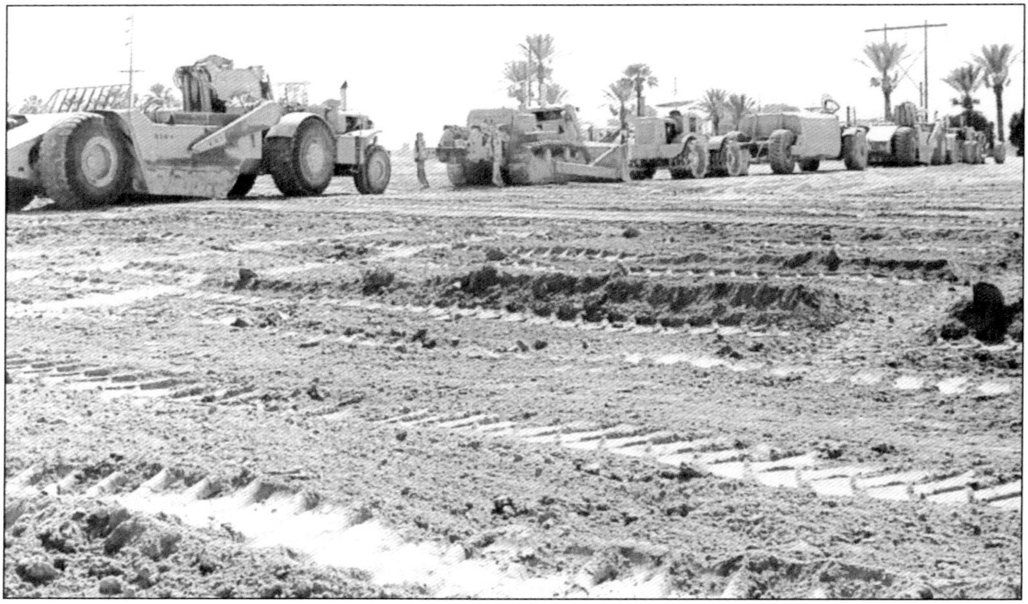

The dirt-moving equipment shown here was sent here to dig the lake. It was a big project to dig a six-acre lake. It is a very special asset to Litchfield, as it is used for personal recreation as well as by the city. Fishing derbies and boat races are planned events sponsored by the city. (Courtesy of SunCor.)

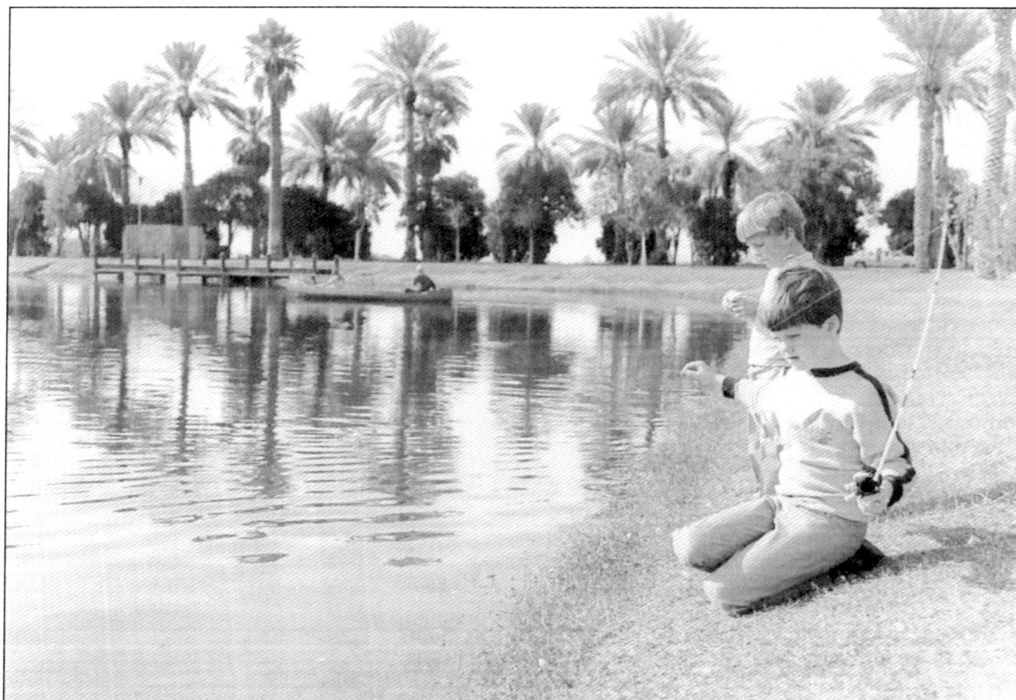

This picture of boys fishing at the lake makes a great memory of their childhood growing up in Litchfield Park. (Courtesy of SunCor.)

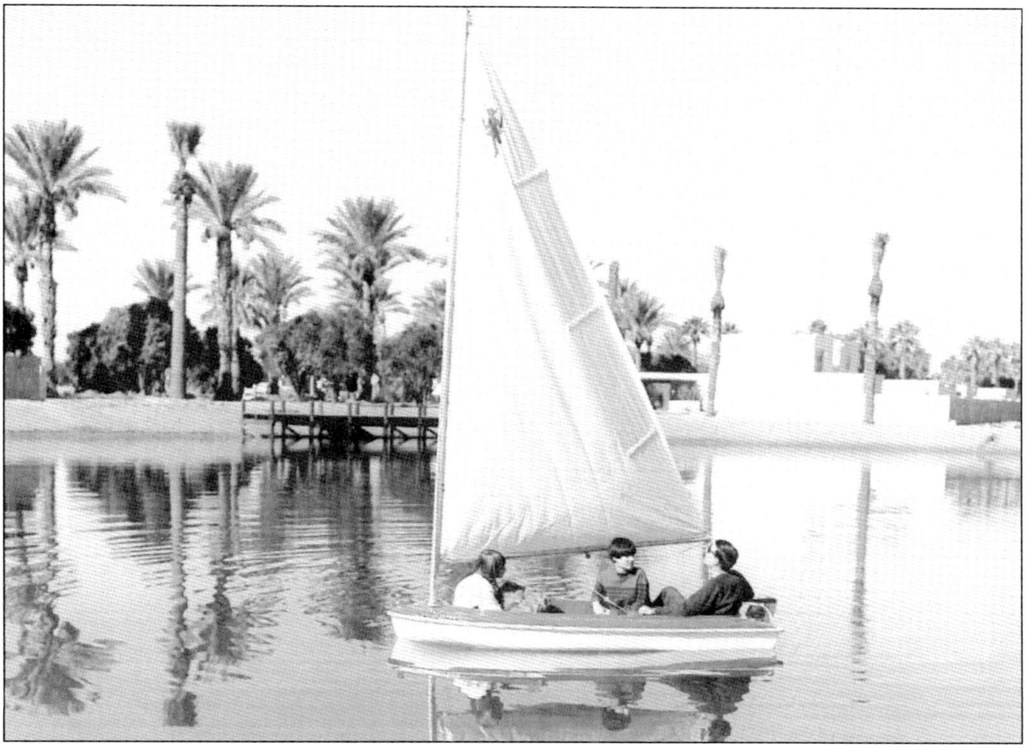

Sailing on the lake for pleasure and competition is a popular pastime. This beautiful lake in the middle of town not only adds beauty and pleasure but also makes for a memorable family outing. Pictured from left to right are Debbie Bailey (Nordenberg), Cindi Bailey, and Ron Fuller. (Courtesy of SunCor.)

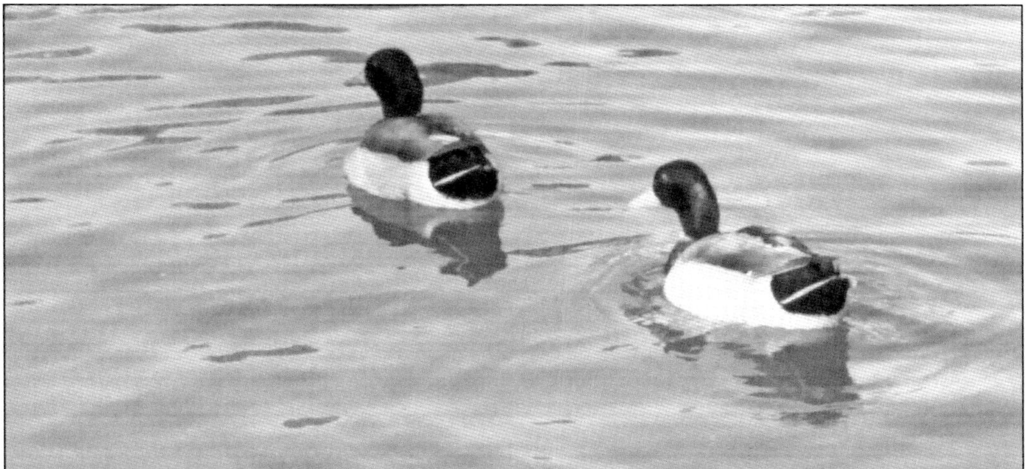

Ducks have been very popular at the Litchfield lake since it was dug in the 1960s. The first mallard duck was brought to the lake by Litchfield Park residents Joe and Tillie Cano in 1968. They brought Peppy from a farm in Glendale, and he became the first duck in the lake. Since that time, more that 15 different types of waterfowl stop over at the lake during their migrations. Several have become permanent residents along with the fish and turtles. Every kid in the area has been to the lake to feed the ducks.

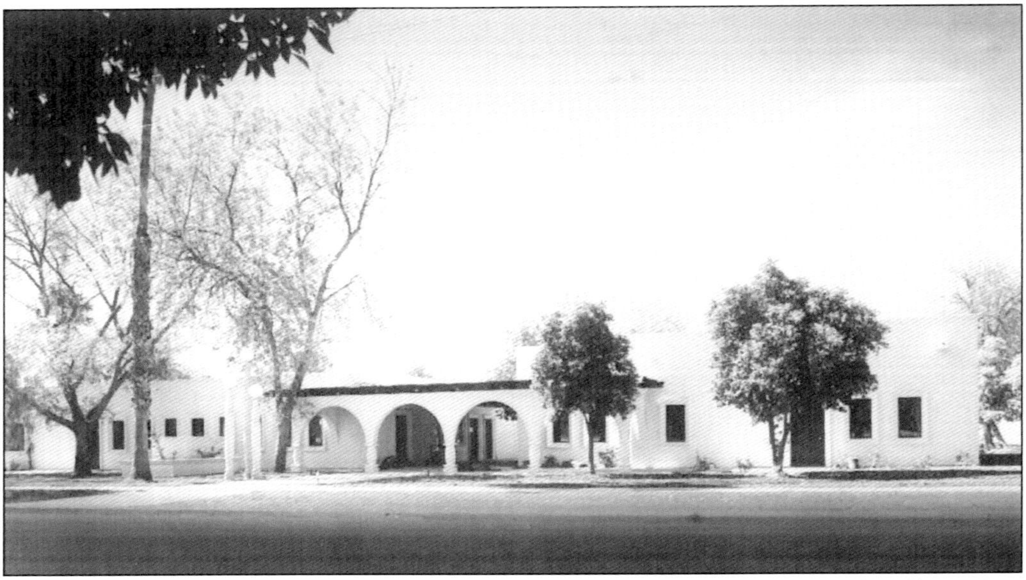

The downtown medical building was added in the 1960s as part of the Tierra Verde Village. Note the arches in the design, a common feature in all new buildings in Litchfield Park. (Courtesy of SunCor.)

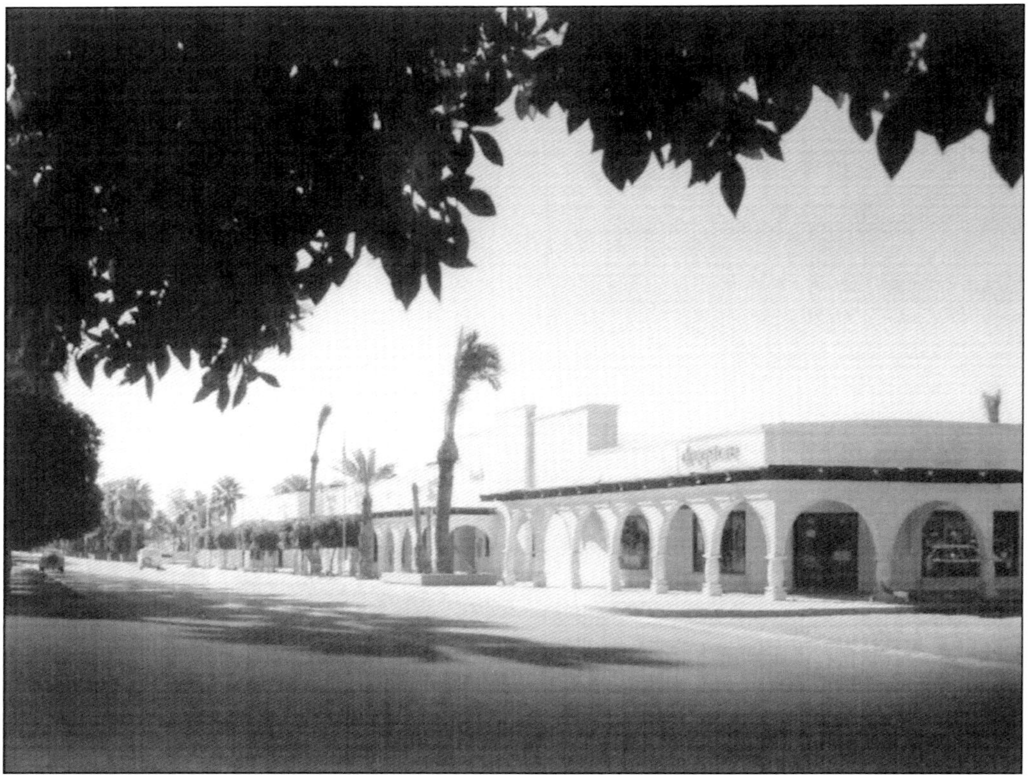

Seen here is a front view of the business section downtown after it had been remodeled to feature arches. It has grown into a small-town look. (Courtesy of SunCor,)

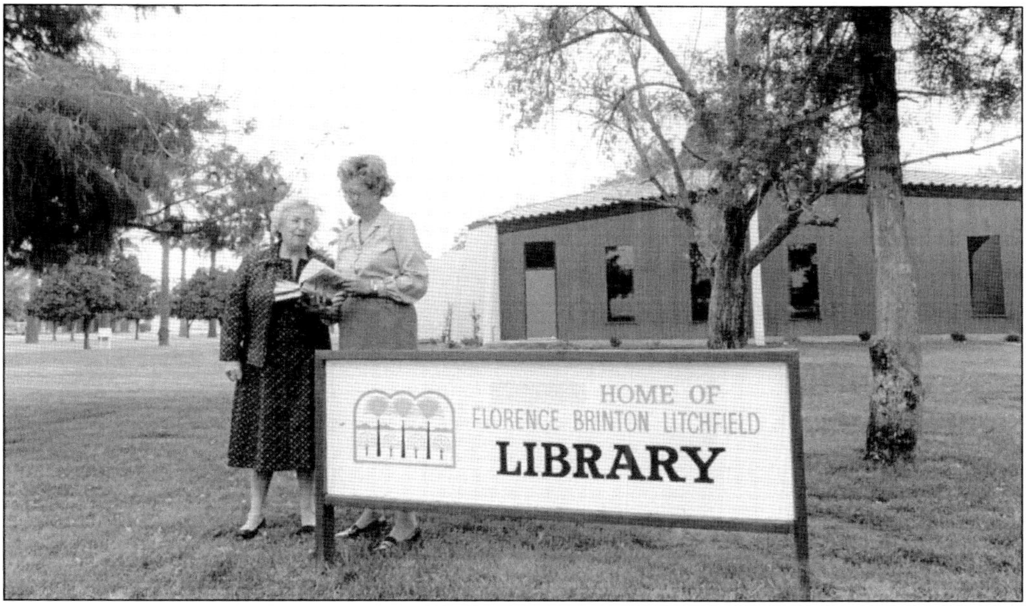


The Florence Brinton Litchfield Library was dedicated in 1979. Edith Denny, Florence and Paul Litchfield's daughter, initiated a successful fund drive to build the library. Denny donated the first $50,000, the Goodyear Tire & Rubber Company contributed, and the rest of the money was given by the Litchfield Library Association members and local citizens. Before the library was opened, the library was housed in a room in the medical building. (Courtesy of Michael Jordan.)

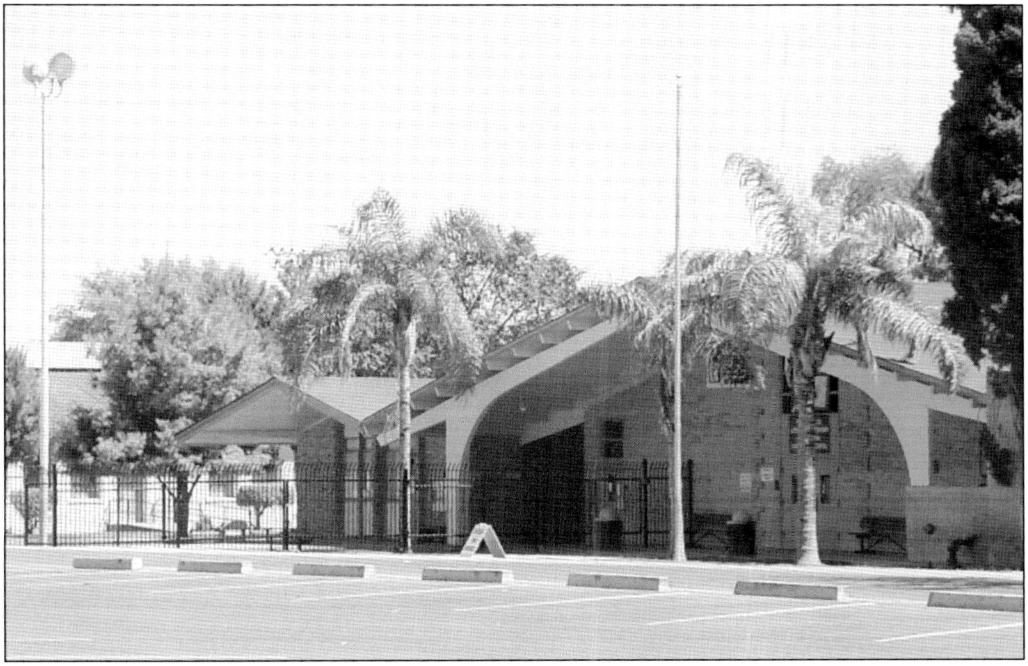

The Litchfield Elementary School shown here is very historic and holds many memories. The small building on the left is the office, and the large entrance to the right is the cafeteria and auditorium where many graduations and special events were held. (Courtesy of Michael Jordan.)

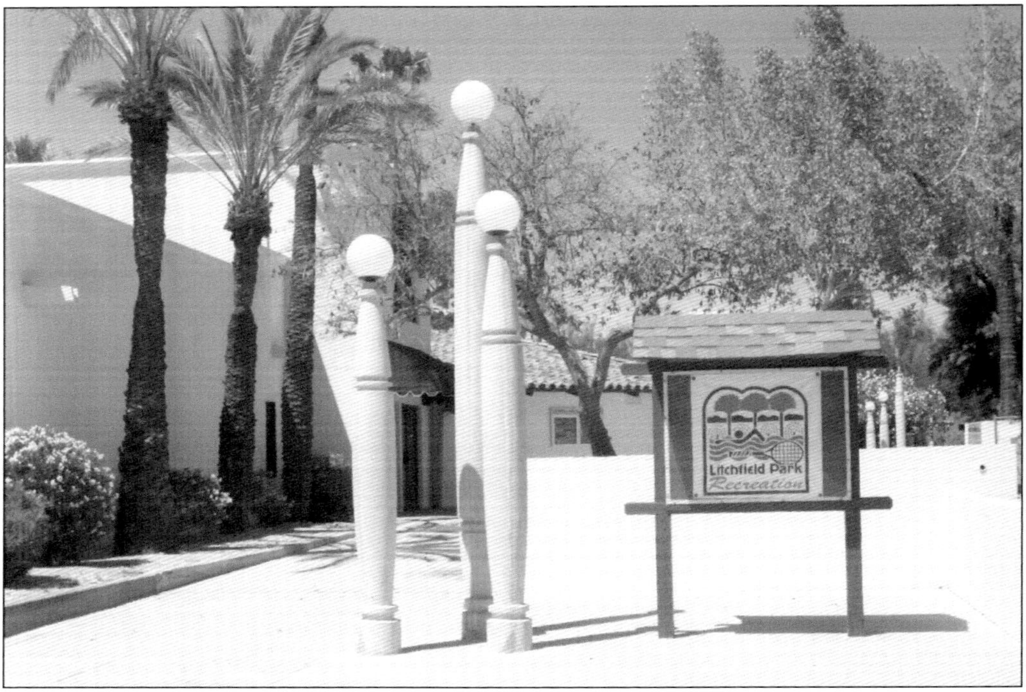


The recreation center has been a very active part of Litchfield Park with the swimming pool in which swim teams have competed. Notice the three light fixtures that are sized to represent a family. The dad, mom, and child are an idea of Bennie Gonzales, the architect hired by Goodyear to redesign the town. (Courtesy of Michael Jordan.)

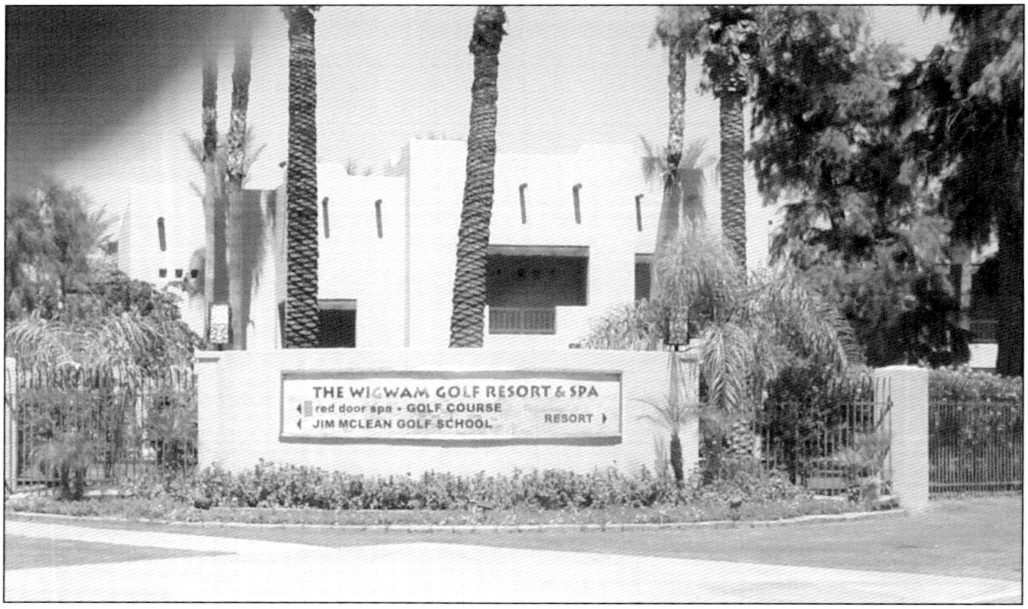


The Wigwam Resort continues to be very popular and is the center of downtown activity. Many new features have been added over the years, the Red Door Spa being one of the newest additions. (Courtesy of Michael Jordan.)

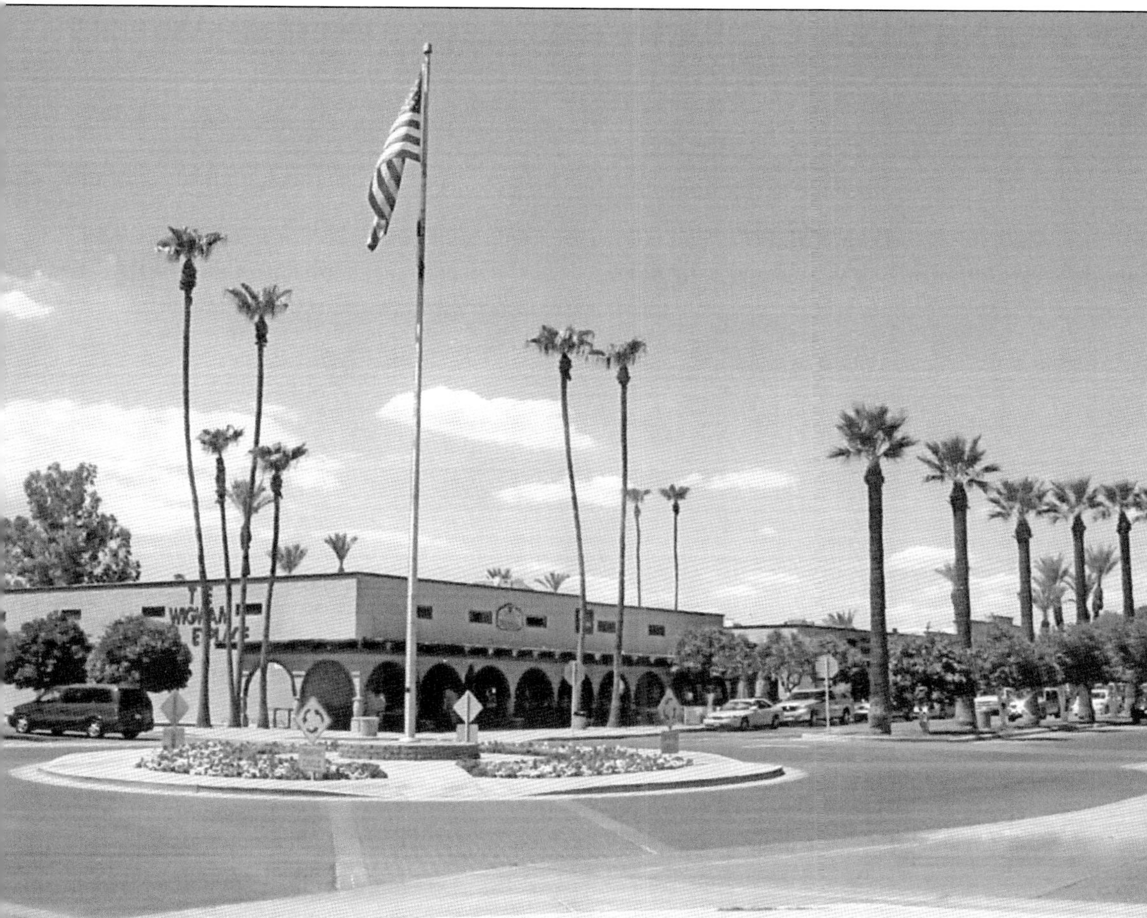

The center of Litchfield Park shows the growth and development as the community grew. The flagpole is still the center of downtown since 1918, when the town was founded and planned by Paul Litchfield.